UNITED NATIONS DEVELOPMENT PROGRAMME
ARAB FUND FOR ECONOMIC AND SOCIAL DEVELOPMENT
ARAB GULF PROGRAMME FOR UNITED NATIONS DEVELOPMENT ORGANIZATIONS

The Arab Human Development Report 2005

Towards the Rise of Women in the Arab World

Regional Bureau for Arab States

Available through:
United Nations Publications
Room DC2-853
New York, NY 10017
USA

Telephone: 212 963 8302 and 800 253 9646 (From the United States)
Email: Publications@un.org
Web: www.un.org/Publications
Web: www.undp.org/rbas

Cover Design:
Shady Mohamed Awad

Layout and Production: SYNTAX, Amman, Jordan

Printed at: National Press, Amman, Jordan

ISBN: 92-1-1261740-0

Printed in the Hashemite Kingdom of Jordan

Foreword by the Administrator, UNDP

This year's Arab Human Development Report marks the fourth, in a four-part series that has made a significant contribution to the debate on the development challenges facing the Arab world.

The pioneering first report, issued in 2002, identified three critical development "deficits" – in the acquisition of knowledge, in political freedoms, and in women's rights – that have held back human development throughout the Arab region despite considerable natural wealth and great potential for economic and social progress. The second and third reports focused on the deficits in knowledge and freedom, respectively.

This year's report presents a compelling argument as to why realising the full potential of Arab women is an indispensable prerequisite for development in all Arab states. It argues persuasively that the long hoped-for Arab "renaissance" cannot and will not be accomplished unless the obstacles preventing women from enjoying their human rights and contributing more fully to development are eliminated and replaced with greater access to the "tools" of development, including education and healthcare. By placing Arab women firmly in the centre of social, cultural, economic and political development in the entire region, the Report goes beyond arguing that half the population deserves half the participation. In fact, it asserts that irrespective of the numbers, Arab women have already accomplished great strides that are transforming the region's political economy and social demography. While lauding these achievements and making a strong case for facilitating this strong current of positive social transformation, the Report also analyses the remaining impediments, and suggests concrete steps towards their elimination.

The Arab Human Development Reports have succeeded beyond all expectations in triggering a lively debate about the challenges, opportunities, and exigencies that must be reckoned with if good governance, respect for human rights, and human development are to become defining characteristics of the modern Arab state. What started out as a daring experiment itself has served as a catalyst for other work and given rise to innovation and change throughout the region.

No reform – whether political or otherwise – can take place, let alone succeed, without an active exchange of ideas. Sometimes, this process takes place harmoniously, with a convergence of views that leads to consensus. Sometimes, the end result can be nothing more than an agreement to disagree. Given the contentious nature of the issues covered in the AHDRs, it should come as no surprise that their preparation has tended to fall into this latter category, with this year's report being no exception.

In this regard, it is necessary for me to reiterate the statement of my predecessor, Mark Malloch Brown, who wrote in last year's report, "the AHDRs are, deliberately, not formal UN or UNDP documents and do not reflect the official views of either organisation. Rather they have been intended to stimulate and inform a dynamic, new, public discourse across the Arab world and beyond… I feel it necessary to state that some of the views expressed by the authors are not shared by UNDP or the UN". All four AHDRs have been prepared by the authors with this shared understanding, reached with UNDP management when the series was launched in 2002.

The AHDRs – this year's included – articulate some views that UNDP does not share, and at times uses language that is unnecessarily divisive. Since 2002, UNDP has helped provide a platform for debate in the region and beyond. Unfortunately, the language used in part of this debate has not always been compatible with the cause of reform and understanding based on reasoned arguments.

The Arab world and the Middle East region have for years suffered from deep divisions, violence and conflict, also involving external actors. UNDP management believes the building of freedom and good governance, which is the stated aim of the AHDRs, requires moderation and arguments based on reason and respect for the views of the "other", all hallmarks of the golden age of Arab greatness, a time when the Arab and Muslim worlds were prosperous, strong and standard-setters for others. Progress in the Arab world in this age of global economic forces will also require much closer cooperation and economic integration, a process which can only take place if Arab countries, governments and civil societies can move closer together, despite their diversity. As cooperative processes in other parts of the world have shown, progress requires caution, a willingness to find compromises, as well as a firm long-term strategy for greater unity.

While we do not agree with all of the sentiments and judgements expressed in this report, we can be motivated all the more to reflect on the factors behind them. The sense of anger palpable in certain sections of this report is widely shared in the region and has been deepened by recent events and the extensive loss of innocent life.

By any measure, the AHDRs have attracted enormous interest and made a unique contribution to stimulating debate on how the Arab region can move forward in advancing the goals of good governance, equitable growth, and greater respect for human rights.

Many individuals have made this possible, but I would like to take this opportunity to stress the leadership role of one in particular: Dr. Rima Khalaf Hunaidi. Rima has guided the AHDR "experiment" from the very outset – without her leadership the four reports could not have been produced. Earlier this year, Rima retired from UNDP after leading UNDP's Regional Bureau for Arab States for almost six years. This fourth report was started while she was still directing the bureau. Rima continues to be a driving force in the debate on reform throughout the region and beyond. I wish her well in her new pursuits.

Kemal Derviş
Administrator, UNDP

Foreword by the Regional Director, UNDP Regional Bureau for Arab States

This fourth report in the Arab Human Development Report (AHDR) series completes the frank examination of some of the obstacles to Arab human development initiated by its predecessors. With the same independence that distinguished the previous reports, AHDR 2005 analyses the dynamics of women's advancement in the Arab world. Its focus is on all women in the Arab countries, without discrimination. It situates the problematic nature of the equality of their rights, capabilities and opportunities in the context of history, culture, religion, society and the political economy. It outlines a vision for the achievement of gender equality built on the assurance of full citizenship rights for all through the reform of Arab governance.

Like the others in the series, this report is Arab in inspiration, authorship and ownership. It does not originate in abstract formulas for change removed from the play of forces in the region. Its authors and advisers are anchored in a broad diversity of intellectual, philosophical and cultural currents in the Arab world. Each has a firm stake in the issues at hand and accepts the risks entailed in tackling a subject loaded with cultural, religious and social sensitivities. Each understands that, optimally, the wider reforms they seek would grow from a multi-level consensus centred on mutual understanding among all actors, respect for differences and recognition of common ground. All however encounter today the degeneration of the reform debate into exclusivist rhetorical firestorms with the work of ascendant conservative forces seeking to reduce political choices to stark absolutes.

An Arab intellectual who today brings "Western" ideas of gender equality into such polarised arenas faces outright dismissal. In this environment, one who advocates for homegrown democratic change to speed women's empowerment while Israel's occupation of Palestinian territory, its aggression against neighbouring countries and the military interventions of foreign powers continue, is seen as the pawn of a discredited model. With their arguments derailed by intervention from abroad, and stifled by reactionary forces at home, Arab moderates are increasingly embattled, frustrated and angry. And while anger, by its nature, is an invitation to dialogue, in a world of divides it is easily misunderstood as yet another form of intransigence. The accents of that anger reverberate through parts of this report, at times conveying a combative tone. To some, this may be dismaying; to others, it may simply be a genuine reflection of the authors' political, intellectual and moral ordeal. We continue to believe that providing the authors with a platform not available to them anywhere in the region makes accessible a body of salutary and instructive messages that the world needs to hear.

The situation of women in the Arab countries has been changing over time, often for the better. Arab women have made outstanding national and international contributions to the arts, sciences, politics and other fields of human endeavour, achieving results that equal, and often surpass, those of men. Yet many continue to struggle for fair treatment. Compared to their sisters elsewhere in the world, they enjoy the least political participation. Conservative authorities, discriminatory laws, chauvinist male peers and tradition-minded kinsfolk watchfully regulate their aspirations, activities and conduct. Employers limit their access to income and independence. In the majority of cases, poverty shackles the development and use of women's potential. High rates of illiteracy and the world's lowest rates of female labour participation are compounded to "create serious challenges". Though a growing number of individual women, supported by men, have succeeded in achieving greater equality in society and more reciprocity in their family and personal relationships, many remain victims of legalised discrimination, social subordination and enshrined male dominance. Unacceptably, physical and mental violence against women often destroys their personal health and security and even their right to life. Such abuse is by no means uniquely found in the Arab world but is part of a global problem.

The Report lays out a comprehensive set of priorities for accelerating the rise of women. In its human development perspective, women not only require access to the tools of development in order to help society to progress; as human beings, they are in themselves the agents of that development.

In that light, the Report stresses the need to eliminate the seeds of discrimination against women in Arab tradition and to promote ijtihad (interpretative scholarship) in religious matters to overcome cultural obstacles. It outlines changes in patterns of upbringing, education and media presentation that could revise social norms, erase harmful stereotypes and vitally transform relations between the sexes in a culture of equal treatment. It proposes a battery of legal reforms to guarantee women's political, civil and economic rights. They range from the full alignment of national legislation with the Convention on the Elimination of All Forms of Discrimination against Women (CEDAW) and with international labour treaties through time-bound quotas for women in political assemblies to the adoption of updated personal status codes. The Report also advocates measures to protect the civil and personal rights of all women in Arab countries including expatriate women. More broadly, it calls for the opening of the economic sphere to women to address income poverty and for investments in women's education, health and social safety nets to reverse the spread of human poverty. Taken together, its findings constitute an important framework for the development efforts of governments, civil society and regional and international organisations, including UNDP.

Not all will agree with everything the authors have to say, which encourages us to anticipate a lively debate around their analysis. Few however will deny that, ultimately, women's advancement in the Arab world is inseparable from society's progress towards democratic and empowering forms of governance that uphold the citizenship rights of all. If that conclusion in turn prompts vigorous discussion and thought on how these two interrelated goals might be achieved together, the authors will be more than amply rewarded for their efforts.

Our readers will find that we have, once again, been caught short in our coverage of world events in Part I which stops at the end of January 2006. Various delays in publishing this Report have, unfortunately prevented us from reviewing many seminal developments in the course of the year but I am confident we will be able to do them justice with the continuation of these Reports.

AHDR 2005 represents the work of many hands. I congratulate all who took part in its preparation, review and editing. Like others, I wish to single out my distinguished predecessor, Dr. Rima Khalaf Hunaidi, the inspired innovator behind the entire series, whose guidance is felt everywhere in this Report. I am very grateful to the core team, especially the lead authors, the veteran Dr. Nader Fergany and Dr. Islah Jad, for their tireless commitment and invaluable work. I also thank the distinguished Advisory Board for its vigilance and advice, which have kept the report anchored in its regional moorings. I am indebted to Kemal Derviş, Administrator of UNDP, for bravely supporting the publication of the concluding part of this unusual series, notwithstanding some differences of views and risks associated with the effort. I owe a particular note of appreciation to my colleagues in the Bureau's Regional Programme Division under the leadership of Nada Al-Nashif for their dedicated and unflagging support to this demanding endeavour. Finally, I salute our regional co-sponsors the Arab Gulf Programme for United Nations Development Organizations and the Arab Fund for Economic and Social Development for their prized partnership and collaboration. While the original concept of the series in four installments is now complete, I am pleased to confirm that more reports will follow.

Amat Al Alim Alsoswa
Assistant Secretary General and Assistant Administrator, Regional Director,
Regional Bureau for Arab States, United Nations Development Programme

Foreword by the Director General and Chairman, The Arab Fund for Economic and Social Development

Economic and social development cannot occur in isolation from human development, which is the lynchpin and goal of comprehensive development. The first three issues of the Arab Human Development Reports series espoused, affirmed and explored this concept in relation to different topics. It is only natural, therefore, that the fourth and final report in the series, dealing with the topic of Arab women, should analyse women's situation and role in development in the same comprehensive perspective.

In examining Arab women's issues and the obstacles to the improvement of their social and economic condition and rights, and in calling for a perfect social partnership, this report remains in a tradition of development literature which historically has stressed the importance of collective collaboration for development without discrimination on the basis of race or sex. The report thus takes its place among the intellectual and practical efforts exerted since the beginning of the Arab Renaissance early in the last century in the area of Arab women's issues and rights, efforts that continued through the work of noteworthy thinkers, scholars and reformers. From the third decade of the same century, these efforts were supplemented by those of women's movements which, by the end of the century, had been transformed into communal and political movements within Arab civil society that aimed at fashioning inclusive developmental visions and implementing their goals in the real world. Among these goals has been the realisation of the perfect partnership of Arab women in state and society.

This report illuminates the many different political, economic, social and legal dimensions relevant to Arab women, the developments, negative and positive, that have affected them and the difficulties that they have faced in playing their full role in economic development and in political and social modernisation. It also illustrates what the report's authors consider to be the political and intellectual trends and demands in the areas of rights and society at the various levels necessary to assure the rise of Arab women, their ability to perform their role and undertake their responsibilities as required, and their perfect partnership in Arab society. All this is of interest to development agencies in general and, in particular, to the Arab Fund for Economic and Social Development, which has been concerned to activate women's participation in development through both its orientations and policies and its programmes and projects. The Fund has also been anxious, via its support for the report, to ensure that the latter be honest and bold, both stylistically and substantively, in its illumination of Arab women's reality.

With a subject of such importance, complexity and sensitivity, certain gaps and minor shortcomings in the report's data are perhaps inevitable. Some contributions and analyses may be more detailed and extensive than strictly warranted, but this is only to be expected when the perspective is a broad based vision of human development with a varied scope, multiple points of intersection and widely branching issues. Points of consensus within the report's generalisations and conclusions may be numerous, and those on which there will be no consensus may be yet more so, but this, of course, naturally follows from presenting a multiplicity of outlooks. In any case, this report is the work of independent thinkers, researchers and specialists and bears no official stamp; the authors have been encouraged to participate in order to express, as far as possible, both the cultural and intellectual diversity of Arab society and its geographical distribution. Their participation also accords with the conviction of the sponsoring institutions that a project for Arab women reflecting the spirit of the Arab Renaissance must be inclusive, representative and open.

This report, its content, its methodology, its conclusions and its speculations, does not constitute the final word, just as it does not form the only project to take on the complex issues of the rise of Arab women. It is rather a supplementary attempt, characterised by a degree of boldness, to initiate an Arab dialogue around the issues and theses. It seeks to start a broad debate on how best to confront these complex issues and arrive at economic, communal and political solutions that will gain the widest possible support and contribute to the rise of Arab women.

We feel that a number of facts should be brought to the reader's attention. The most important of these are:

1. Arab women have in no way fallen short in performing their role over the various phases of the development of Arab society throughout history, despite certain limited attempts to marginalise that role. The great contributions of Arab women in the traditional economy and in family and social structures are those of fundamental and indispensable partners. No less important are their struggles to assert that partnership via political and emancipatory movements and civil society institutions, which have increased and grown in recent decades, realising important achievements which are today admired and respected all across Arab society.

2. Arab women have achieved much by way of enlarging their capabilities through their own efforts. They have registered outstanding progress in education, made their mark through their merits and skills in work and business, asserted their capacity to assume leadership positions, increased their participation in economic activity and pushed forward their role in national public affairs in all Arab countries. This must be the starting point for Arab development efforts and the basis for pursuing improved development indicators and progress in the deployment of women's capabilities. On this foundation, women will increase their participation in the job market and raise their contribution to economic activity on a basis of justice and equality between the sexes.

From another perspective, efforts towards political reform must work to ingrain the principles of good governance nationally and locally and to develop systems and legislation that accord with the principles of freedom, equality, and social justice. That is how social reform and economic reform can complement one another and thus form the two wings on which Arab development will fly towards the goals of the Arab renaissance project.

3. The rights of Arab women and the improvement of their condition are not a luxury or a subject for mere theorising, neither are they simply a call for reform. On the contrary, they have become today a fundamental component of the rights of humankind as confirmed by the Convention on the Elimination of All Forms of Discrimination against Women, while calls for the rights of women and demands for their economic and social betterment have become a global movement supported by international law. By the same token, work on behalf of these goals has become a communal movement supported by the forces of Arab civil society, in whose institutions Arab women have come to assume important positions and to the realisation of whose goals they contribute effectively.

This report, with all that may be said for it and against it, is now set before all Arab citizens, and it is to the Arab citizen, first and last, that it is addressed. I expect its publication to be a beginning and not an end. It provides an opportunity for a constructive civilisational dialogue that will do more to bring people together than to force them apart and more to gather them than to divide them, in the service of the rise of Arab women and of our nation. I would like to express my sincere thanks and appreciation to all who contributed to its preparation and publication and to the United Nations Development Programme for their good offices in providing for its follow-up and supervision. I offer my thanks as well to all participating institutions and parties.

"God is the guardian of success."

Abdel Latif Youseff El Hamed
Director General / Chairman of the Board of Directors
Arab Fund for Economic and Social Development

Foreword by HRH the President of the Arab Gulf Programme for United Nations Development Organizations (AGFUND)

Arab Women and the Mechanisms for the Desired Change

An observer of social developments in the Arab world will be aware of a number of positive changes caused by the publication of the Arab Human Development Report (AHDR) since its initial appearance in 2002 under the title *Creating Opportunities for Coming Generations*, as it has prompted both controversy over, and engagement with its authors' themes, findings and recommendations.

The AHDR series was prepared by leading specialists preoccupied with issues of concern to the Arab human being, and it raises and explores in depth issues of direct and profound import for development in its three dimensions: social, economic and political. For this reason, these reports are, in our estimation, among the most outstanding products of Arab development thought to emerge so far in the third millennium, with all that the opening years of this century have witnessed in the way of changes and transformations benefiting humanity.

The fourth edition of the AHDR takes on additional importance because it raises the issue of women's development as the critical issue in all Arab societies. Its objective presentation of the obstacles to Arab women's development is part of a sequence. Thus, in its third edition the Report investigated the dialectics of freedom in the Arab world, in the second it dealt with the topic of knowledge, and in the first it treated the creation of opportunities for coming generations.

Anticipating the debate that will surround this edition, we would like to state that we believe that the experts and the authors behind this effort have applied their knowledge to illuminate crucial aspects of the situation of Arab women, and especially the continuance of outmoded attitudes towards women, their status and role.

Such attitudes are, regrettably, linked to certain interpretations of religion, even though a careful study based on the facts will reveal that they have their origins in custom and tradition. Religion has no connection with any of the mistaken practices that are carried out against women. Our societies, however, give precedence to custom over true worship and provide foundations for assumptions that have no grounding either in the Holy Qur'an or in the authenticated practices and sayings of the Prophet (the Hadith).

Most of the sufferings of Arab women is attributable to the accumulation of such customs and traditions. It follows that the correction of outmoded assumptions and attitudes is a leading priority, one that demands, in the first place, cultural and societal measures to instil in coming generations a balanced vision of women and their role. This report, with its probing analyses, statistics and data, is a part of these required measures. For this reason, we shall continue to support its publication, in co-ordination with our partners in development.

We believe that Arab societies must shoulder their comprehensive and necessary responsibility to re-evaluate women's role and to protect their rights. In that respect, it should be noted that all Arab countries have signed the Convention on the Elimination of All Forms of Discrimination against Women. Yet we also consider that women themselves are those most capable of defending their rights and of bringing their issues to public attention. Indeed, were this not so, Arab women's problems might continue to be sidelined and buried for ages to come. Actual indicators, however, and the examples we see of Arab women's activism, incline us to optimism.

We have always believed that Arab women (as mothers, sisters, wives, daughters) are not less, in any way, than women in societies that have preceded us on the ladder of development. Arab women are creative innovators who display initiative when provided with the means. This is what has encouraged us to sponsor a developmental organisation specialised in women's issues, the Centre for Arab Women's Training and Research (CAWTAR), and to entrust its leadership, administration and planning to a group of outstanding women. The latter have shown what they can accomplish in realising the Centre's most important strategic goal of becoming a point of reference in the Arab world for women's issues. CAWTAR continues to train women cadres, to help overcome deficient images of women in society and to ensure that the voice and demands of women reach decision-making circles. There can be no future for a society that impedes half its population in the exercise of their potential, ignores their demands and marginalises their entitlements.

This same orientation is adopted at the Arab Open University and at the "Bank for the Poor", which target the poorest of the poor. Women have shown themselves to be extremely able in managing small and micro-loans to good effect and to be more reliable than men in honouring their commitments to lending institutions.

Without prejudice to the importance of new legislation, revised codes and statutes and evolving constitutions in guaranteeing women's rights, the laying of a foundation for enlightened thought must come first. After all, legislation, no matter how contemporary, developed and favourable to women's aspirations, cannot function in an intellectual and moral vacuum.

Rather, positive values in harmony with religion and authentic Arab tradition must first inform our view of women. These values must be nurtured, in the first place, through teaching and their integration into curricula from kindergarten to higher education. They must be popularised by a media committed to the issues and concerns of society. These mechanisms are important levers for desired changes in the cultural structure. Indeed, no change can be expected if we do not begin by developing the inner workings of our culture, which determines our rules and how we see ourselves.

May God grant success to all who work for the good of the Arab World.

طلال بن عبد العزيز

Talal Bin Abdul Aziz
President, The Arab Gulf Programme for
United Nations Development Organizations (AGFUND)

Report Team

Advisory Board
Rima Khalaf Hunaidi (Chair), Ahmed Kamal Aboulmagd, Haifa Abu Ghazaleh, Fowziyah Abu-Khalid, Nidal Al-Ashkar, Aziz Al-Azmeh, Khadija Ahmed Al-Haisami, Nasser Al-Kahtani / Jebrine Al-Jebrine (Arab Gulf Programme for United Nations Development Organizations), Farida Allaghi, Nabil Alnawwab / Fatima Sbaity (Economic and Social Commission for Western Asia), Soukaina Bouraoui, Mohamed Charfi, Hani Fahs, Ziad Fariz, Mohammed Fayek, Fahmy Howeidy, Taher H. Kanaan, Clovis Maksoud, Bader Malallah (Arab Fund for Economic and Social Development), Abdelouahab Rezig, Abdulaziz Sager, Leila Sharaf, Haifa Zangana.

Core Team
Nader Fergany (Co-Leader), Islah Jad (Co-Leader), Kamal Abdellatif, Ebtisam Al-Kitbi, Mohamed Nour Farahat, Haytham Manna, Naila Silini.

Contributing Authors
Kamal Abdellatif, Rula Abu-Duhou, Fowziyah Abu-Khalid, Lamis Abu Nahleh, Badria Abd Allah Al-Awadhi, Aziz Al-Azmeh, Ali Abdel Gadir Ali, Baqer Alnajjar, Madawi Al-Rasheed, Mustapha K. Al Sayyid, Mohammed Aref, Mohsen Awad, Munir Bashshur, Noha Bayoumi, Rachida Benmessaoud, Azmi Bishara, Mohamed Charfi, Hafidha Chekir, Khadija Cherif, Mouna Cherkaoui, Violette Daguerre, Abdelwahab El-Affendi, Hoda Elsadda, Ikbal El Ameer El Samalouti, Heba Raouf Ezzat, Mohamed Nour Farahat, Samir Farid, Mona Fayad, Hala Fouad, Abdelaziz Guessous, Hassina Hamzaoui, Nadia Hijab, Fahmi Howeidy, Islah Jad, Nadim Jarjoura, Nahawand Kadiri, Elham Kallab, Azza M. Karam, Fadia Kiwan, Eileen Kuttab, Maroun Lahham, Latifa Lakhdar, Mohammed Malki, Haytham Manna, Moncef Marzouki, Zineb Miadi, Emily Nasrallah, Naziha Rjiba, Nader Said, Rafif Sidaoui, Naila Silini, Mustapha Touaiti, Mohsen Tlili, Marie Rose Zalzal.

Readers Group
(Arabic)
Khalid Abdalla, Ghanim Alnajjar, Abdulkarim El-Eryani, Nawal Faouri, Samia Fessi, Najla Hamadeh, Maryam Sultan Lootah, Gamil A. Mattar, Hassan Nafaa, Hassan Rahmouni, Marie Rose Zalzal.

(English)
Leila Ahmed, Sakiko Fukuda-Parr, Ziad Hafez, Rami G. Khouri, Dina Rizk Khoury, Tufan Kolan, Omar Noman, Maureen O'Neil, William Orme, Marina Ottaway, Eugene L. Rogan, Mark Tessler, Richard J. Wilson.

UNDP RBAS / UNOPS
Amat Al Alim Ali Alsoswa, Nada Al-Nashif, Benjamin Craft, Melissa Esteva, Ghaith Fariz (Report Coordinator), Oscar Fernandez-Taranco, Jacqueline Ghazal, Sausan Ghosheh, Randa Jamal, Mary Jreidini, Azza M. Karam (Report Coordinator), Jeremy King, Madi Musa, David Morrison, Julia Niggebrugge, Winmin Nu, William Orme, Ghia Osseiran.

Editorial Team
Arabic Version: Fayiz Suyyagh
English Version: Zahir Jamal (Editor), Barbara Brewka (Associate Editor)

Implementation of the "Rise of Women" survey
• Middle East Marketing and Research Consultants (MEMRC) / Amman, Jordan (Coordination + Questionnaire Design & Unifying Data Files)
• Market Egypt / Cairo, Egypt
• Societé d'Etudes de Realisation de Consultants (SEREC) / Casablanca, Morocco.
• Statistics Lebanon Ltd. / Beirut, Lebanon.

Translation Team
Humphrey Davies (Coordinator), Susan Smith Abou-Sheika, Peter Daniel, Philip Gordon, Hala Halim, Jeff Hayes, Nancy Roberts, Paul Roochnik, Nehad Salem, Yasmine Pauline Salih, Mahmud Suqi, David Wilmsen, Patrick Werr.

Cover Design
Shady Mohamed Awad

Technical Consultant for Design and Printing
Hassan Shahin

Contents

LIST OF BOXES

PART ONE

PART TWO

LIST OF FIGURES

LIST OF TABLES

EXECUTIVE SUMMARY

Introduction

"Towards the Rise of Women in the Arab World" is the fourth issue in the UNDP-sponsored series of Arab Human Development Reports. It concludes a comprehensive analysis of development deficits affecting the region by examining shortfalls in women's empowerment.

The Report opens with a survey of development trends in the region during the period in review. Its analysis of its main theme starts by outlining some core concepts and defining issues that frame the human rights and human development dimensions of the rise of women in Arab countries. The Report next offers a situational analysis of the state of women in Arab societies, focusing on the acquisition and use of essential capabilities, and resulting levels of well being. Following an evaluation of the historical achievements and limitations of Arab women's movements, the central chapters probe the interaction between cultural, religious, socioeconomic, legal and political components of Arab societies that influence the status and prospects of women. The report concludes with a strategic vision offering broad guidelines for promoting the advancement of women in the region.

I. CHANGES IN HUMAN DEVELOPMENT SINCE THE LAUNCH OF AHDR 2004

As in the past, the Report begins by reviewing national, regional and international events believed to have influenced overall trends in Arab human development since the publication of the previous issue.

THE REFORM PROCESS AND ISLAMIC MOVEMENTS: RECONCILING FREEDOM AND FAITH

Widespread and thoroughgoing political reform, leading to a society of freedom and good governance, is the means of creating a free society, in the comprehensive sense, which in turn, would be equivalent to human development (Arab Human Development Report, 2004). For such a thoroughgoing reform process to start and succeed, three cardinal conditions will have to be met: all reform groups must respect the key freedoms (opinion, expression and association); accept the principle of participation to include all forces in society, particularly those that command a strong popular following; and respect the principles of universal human rights.

No political power can ignore the fact that religion, and especially Islam, is a crucial element in the cultural and spiritual make-up of the Arab people. However, the reopening of the door of independent jurisprudential thinking, its encouragement and affirmation, remain a basic demand if the creative marriage between freedom in its contemporary, comprehensive definition and the ultimate intent of Islamic law (Sharia) that is required for the society of freedom and good governance, is to be achieved. The Islamic currents that are solicitous of the renaissance of the Arab world must add to their agenda and responsibilities the assumption of a lead role with respect to this demand.

The Islamic currents constitute a wide spectrum, with wide internal variation. The great majority of Islamic currents in Arab countries represent widespread societal forces and have deep popular roots as a result of their practice over many years of social and political action among ordinary people. The mainstream currents have experienced important developments over the past five decades with regard to their stance on certain societal issues, such as respect for human rights and good governance or democracy, that will be crucial for the future. Such developments will make it impossible to characterise them, should they attain power, as theocratic. Similarly, most of these mainstream currents are witnessing a noticeable growth, among their relatively younger generations, of an enlightened leadership, at the moment that these younger generations are increasingly appearing at the top of their organisational hierarchy. In addition, there is growing activity from the grass-roots demanding greater internal democracy. However, these positive developments do not mean that the mainstream Islamic currents have succeeded in eliminating all concerns of other societal forces in Arab countries as to the negative impact they might have on freedom and good governance should they come to power, and this is especially so with regard to the issues of women and minorities.

Negative reactions on the part of hegemonic forces inside or outside the Arab world to the possible outcomes of reform that may not prove acceptable to them, remain one of the most important issues that could slow down the course of reform in Arab countries. One example was the rejection by certain Arab regimes and some global forces of the sweeping victory of the Islamic Resistance Movement (Hamas) in the Palestinian legislative election, agreed to have been free and fair. A similar response followed the success of the Muslim Brotherhood in Egypt's recent legislative election

THE GROWTH OF ACTIVISM IN CIVIL SOCIETY

Arab civil society organisations took a higher profile, thrusting themselves into the public space with increasing vigour and impact. Adopting firm positions through the independent press, on satellite television,

in public rallies and private meetings and on the Internet, they demonstrated close solidarity with political movements and, at times, the ability to take the lead in spurring political change. Egypt's "Kifaya! (Enough!)" Movement openly opposed the President's re-election and the transfer of power to his son, drawing support for an end to hereditary succession from all shades of the political spectrum, including the Muslim Brotherhood, the National Rally for Democratic Change and the National Alliance for Reform and Change. In Lebanon, groups clamouring for state and institutional reforms to give citizens more voice and representation joined the mainstream political scene and public debate in force. In Syria, different opposition groups united to issue the Damascus Declaration insisting that the ruling party adopt more thoroughgoing changes to the constitution, the conduct of presidential referenda and the alternation of political power. Throughout the period, civic action in the region was distinguished by a growing pluralism and enlarged Internet presence, testifying to a new assertiveness and sense of public mission in civil society.

GIVING THE LIE TO REFORM

Arab governments announced a host of reforms targeting freedom and good governance, most of which remained on the surface of their ambitious agendas. Some regimes tightly limited the scope of reforms they introduced while others continued to violate human and political rights while purporting to adopt enlightened changes. Observers noted that reforms often seemed empty gestures to cover up the continuation of an oppressive status quo.

A Wave of Mostly Flawed Elections

A wave of elections, many either hampered by adverse circumstances or flawed by irregularities, swept the region in this period. In the occupied Palestinian territory, elections judged to have been mostly free and fair despite tough conditions of occupation and severe external pressures produced a victory for Hamas that shook expectations. In Iraq, elections to the transitional National Assembly in January 2005 took place amid a severe breakdown of security and a terrorist campaign against candidates and voters. Nonetheless, subsequently almost 70 percent of Iraqi voters turned out for the country's December 2005 elections to the National Assembly, which were however marred by forgeries and stolen ballot boxes. Saudi Arabia saw municipal council elections held for the first time, a progressive step that was undermined by the exclusion of women and by restrictions on the proportion of council members chosen by election. In Egypt, Article 76 of the Constitution was amended to permit multi-candidate presidential elections. The amendment however arrived freighted with various restrictions such that it seemed but a formalised codification of the existing referendum system for choosing the president. Some licensed opposition parties boycotted the subsequent presidential election, which produced a landslide victory for the incumbent. Its notable aspect was that, according to official statistics, the participation rate amounted to only one fourth of those entitled to vote. Judges monitoring the parliamentary elections that followed afterwards reported irregularities favouring ruling party candidates in two major districts. Evidently, electoral reform in the region has some distance to cover before elections become a component of the society of freedom and good governance.

WORSENING HUMAN RIGHTS VIOLATIONS IN THE ARAB COUNTRIES

VIOLATIONS RESULTING FROM OCCUPATION AND ARMED DOMESTIC CONFLICTS

Violations of individual and collective human rights worsened during the period under review. Grievous abuses occurred under foreign occupation where women often bore the brunt of this decline amid deteriorating humanitarian conditions, the spread of lawlessness and rape, and hardships brought on by the separation of male breadwinners from their families during conflicts or long periods of detention. Armed domestic conflicts were another theatre of

serious human rights abuses, with women being especially vulnerable to rape and murder, not only under military assaults but also during flight and emigration. International human rights circles have condemned atrocities committed by government forces and their allies, as well as by rebel forces, as tantamount to war crimes and crimes against humanity. Somalia remained in the grip of armed conflict and lawlessness, which exacted a rising toll on civilian lives.

The Government of one Arab country launched a large military campaign to put down a rebellion led by the leader of an opposition organisation in a province. More generally, political conflicts have constituted still another locus of human rights violations. In this connection, three Arab governments have disclosed attempted coups, which have led to trials and harsh sentences.

VIOLATIONS OF PUBLIC LIBERTIES AND FREEDOMS OF OPINION AND EXPRESSION

Public freedoms in the region, especially those of opinion and expression, came under further pressure. In a peremptory move, one Gulf state stripped members of a clan of their nationality, later conceding to local and international pressure by reinstating some members and naturalising the rest. Another country not only held back on promised reforms for enhancing media freedoms; it actually stiffened freedom-restricting penalties for journalists. A third state similarly introduced draft laws curbing freedom of the press. The region remained a dangerous place for reporters. Indeed, among world regions, the Arab world sees the highest prevalence of murder or abduction of journalists and other media personnel in areas affected by armed conflict.

TARGETING REFORMERS AND HUMAN RIGHTS ACTIVISTS

In most Arab States, reformers and human rights advocates have become open targets of official repression. Such figures frequently risk prosecution and arrest, and sometimes assassination, while many Arab CSOs run

Violations of individual and collective human rights worsened during the period under review.

Public freedoms in the region, especially those of opinion and expression, came under further pressure.

*International and
regional conditions
arising from the
"war on terror" and
the occupations
of Palestine and
Iraq continued to
undermine human
development and
human rights in the
Arab world.*

a gauntlet of legal obstacles to their work. In three Gulf states, several applications for permission to form human rights organisations were simply frozen. The same trend was evident in a Mashreq country, which also saw numerous activists rounded up and detained and several civil society organisations closed down. A north African country continued to obstruct the work of civic bodies, independent professional associations, labour unions and human rights institutions. Among Arab States, the same north African country has gained notoriety for restricting freedom of expression in general and the use of the Internet in particular although, when it comes to cyberspace, a recent survey demonstrated that only three countries, Jordan, Qatar and the United Arab Emirates, permit relative freedom of Internet use. Another Gulf state subjected several civil society groups to official harassment, refusing to grant legal recognition to a number of them.

UNFRIENDLY INTERNATIONAL AND REGIONAL ENVIRONMENTS

International and regional conditions arising from the "war on terror" and the occupations of Palestine and Iraq continued to undermine human development and human rights in the Arab world. The Report warns that continued occupations and the failure to reform global governance in order to provide security and help achieve prosperity for all may push the region further towards extremism and violent protest.

THE ISSUE OF TERRORISM AND ITS CONSEQUENCES FOR FREEDOM IN THE ARAB WORLD

The war on terror

In the "war on terror", the Arab region in general and Islamic movements in particular have been stereotyped as breeding grounds for terrorism. This campaign has blurred the distinction between what may rightly be termed the terrorising of innocents on one hand, which the Report affirms is an unacceptable affront to the human conscience, and, on the other, legitimate resistance to foreign occupation, as

recognised by the Geneva Conventions and United Nations resolutions. Acts of terrorism have spread in a number of Arab countries killing and/or wounding thousands.

Mirroring global trends, under the pretext of combating terrorism, Arab governments have consolidated emergency laws and passed additional anti-terrorism legislation. Scores of those pursued by such governments have been killed, while thousands of citizens have been arrested on the basis of administrative decisions, some of whom have been subjected to torture and ill-treatment. Most Arab states refer terrorist cases to special tribunals such as military courts or national security courts, which usually fall far short of international standards for a fair trial.

The Occupation continues to frustrate human development

The Israeli occupation of Palestine continued to deny Arab people the most basic political, economic and social rights and to threaten the security and safety of the region as a whole.

The Report maintains that Israel's withdrawal from the Gaza Strip took place as part of a unilateral disengagement plan launched by the Israeli Prime Minister (Ariel Sharon) to relieve Israel of the security burdens entailed by the occupation and to enable it to avoid serious negotiations aimed at a settlement. At the same time, Israel has reserved the right to intervene militarily in Gaza whenever it sees fit and to maintain control over its air space, regional waters and most border crossings. These considerations led the Special Rapporteur of the UN Commission on Human Rights to conclude that Gaza remains occupied territory.

The Report details how Israel's construction of the "separation wall" has accelerated the systematic destruction of the Palestinian economy, with severe impacts on the health and livelihoods of Palestinians, thousands of whom have been separated from their agricultural lands. The wall and constant border closures have led to the extreme deterioration of living conditions throughout the Palestinian territories.

In Iraq, the rising human costs of occupation became clear in a context of growing lawlessness and internal conflict. With the election of a Permanent National Assembly and the formation of a new government in 2006, the great challenge for the incumbent authority remains the reform of the constitution. This is necessary in order to guarantee the territorial integrity of Iraq, the protection of human rights, the achievement of national reconciliation, and the elimination of anarchy and corruption, in a unified country free from foreign occupation and terrorism.

Evidence of the use of torture by both the occupying powers and the former Iraqi government continued to emerge. Material damage inflicted on Iraq under the occupation extends to its assets, including oil resources and a cultural heritage that belongs to humankind.

PROGRESS TOWARDS OVERCOMING DEFICITS IN HUMAN DEVELOPMENT

The increasing restriction of public freedoms and the perpetuation of oppressive systems of rule in Arab countries remained the main features of this period. Nonetheless, some positive steps towards widening the margins of freedom in the region were taken.

Egypt's National Council for Human Rights issued its first annual report (2004-2005) which highlighted some of the most serious human rights violations in the country and called for an end to the state of emergency. Jordan's National Centre for Human Rights also published its first annual report. Bahrain issued a decree requiring that democracy and human rights be taught in the State's schools and in the United Arab Emirates a human rights association was formed. Morocco's efforts to purge a long history of oppression moved forward when its Justice and Reconciliation Commission submitted its final report proposing legal, institutional and cultural reforms. The President of Algeria announced a similar initiative in national reconciliation in his country.

In addition, nine Arab States appointed women to prominent positions at the national, provincial and municipal levels in moves to increase women's empowerment.

II. TOWARDS THE RISE OF WOMEN IN THE ARAB WORLD: CONCEPTS AND PROBLEMATIC ISSUES

CONCEPTS

The Report considers that, as human beings, women and men have an innate and equal right to achieve a life of material and moral dignity, the ultimate goal of human development. It thus views the rise of women in the joint framework of human rights and human development. In terms of human rights, the advancement of women is to be achieved as part of society's advancement to freedom, in its most comprehensive definition. This definition includes not only civil and political rights, the mainstays of citizenship, but freedom from ignorance, disease, want, fear and all else that diminishes human dignity.

In terms of human development, the rise of women entails:

- Complete equality of opportunity between women and men in the acquisition and employment of human capabilities;
- Guaranteed rights of citizenship for all women on an equal footing with men;
- Acknowledgement of, and respect for differences between the sexes. Women are different from men, but that in no way implies they are deficient. Under no conditions is it acceptable to use gender differences to support theories of inequality between the sexes or any form of sexual discrimination.

Historically, various women's non-governmental organisations have focused on different objectives. Some have concentrated on promoting women's equal rights and the elimination of discrimination embedded in Arab laws, whether these concern personal status issues or social guarantees. Others have targeted charitable development activities, providing loans and income-generating projects for women or services in health, education and other sectors. Relatively few however, have focused on women's empowerment as the collective goal and undertaking of society as a whole.

The Report considers that, as human beings, women and men have an innate and equal right to achieve a life of material and moral dignity, the ultimate goal of human development.

THE QUESTION OF THE "INTERNAL" AND THE "EXTERNAL"

The spread of the concept of "women's empowerment" in the Arab region has excited the rancour of certain socio-political forces. They have tended to see it as "imposed" by the West and not emerging from either the realities or needs of Arab societies, which are based on the entrenched role of the family as society's basic building block. This has driven some to resist development plans that adopt the gender perspective and to resist the governments and the women's organisations which work in accordance with it.

An enforced anatomic separation between what is deemed local and what is deemed foreign is no longer possible in this age. What we call "foreign" culture actually thrives within Arab societies – particularly in terms of values and modes of behaviour – owing to the increasing globalisation of Arab societies. Nor is such a separation beneficial for the aspiration for progress in the Arab world— which is an authentic aspiration— and which has continued, since the beginning of the Arab Renaissance, to be positively influenced by the best human accomplishments of the prevailing Western civilisation.

To be more precise, there is a largely beneficial collaboration between the struggle for women's emancipation in Arab countries as a liberating dynamic in society, and women's movements around the world, including those in the West. The efforts of international organisations are particularly important here, especially the agreements, resolutions, mechanisms and international activities aimed at protecting women's rights and equal treatment.

However, the crassness of the call from outside for reform, sometimes imposed by force, has elicited a negative reaction among some segments of society. This reaction, directed against a dominant Western-imposed women's empowerment agenda, is considered by such segments to be a simultaneous violation of Arab culture and of national independence.

The Report maintains that the rise of women, in both intellectual and practical terms, remains an essential axis of the Arab project for a human renaissance. The advancement of women - viewed both as struggle against despotism on the inside and appropriation from the outside - is part of the construction of a renaissance that will bring about freedom, pride and vigour for all Arabs, men and women on an equal footing.

Despotic authority and the rise of women

Paradoxically, repressive regimes, for their own reasons, have encouraged women's rights in ways that might not have been possible if matters had been left to the natural progress of society, given its imposed and inherited constraints. The mechanisms of political oppression have even served at times to accelerate the rise of women. But the Report notes that this imperious, top-down style of "progress," however enlightened, inevitably encounters objections and resistance from the popular base. It argues that a shift to free and well-governed societies in Arab countries would be quite capable of realising those historic breakthroughs required for women to advance, while also attracting broad social support that will guarantee the movement popular strength and sustainability.

The undervaluation of women's participation in economic activity

Arab society does not acknowledge the true extent of women's participation in social and economic activities and in the production of the components of human well being, and it does not reward them adequately for such participation. Since most women work without pay for their families, their contributions are not recognised as economic activity.

This historical prejudice is reflected in the undervaluing of women's contributions to different types of human activity in general, and to economic activity in particular.

A proper evaluation of women's contribution to producing the elements of human welfare requires a creative theoretical foundation that goes beyond the national accounts' system, restricted as it is to market exchange and the cash valuation of goods and services. This can be done by using a broad definition of human welfare that is commensurate with the concept of human development. From a procedural perspective,

> Arab society does not acknowledge the true extent of women's participation in social and economic activities and in the production of the components of human well being, and it does not reward them adequately for such participation.

this will require diligence in developing research and statistical tools that aim to measure accurately women's contribution to the production of human welfare and the construction of human development. This is a field that remains open to research.

THE STATE OF WOMEN IN THE ARAB WORLD

The state of women in Arab countries results from, and contributes to a number of cultural, social, economic and political factors which interact to affect levels of human development. Some factors are problematic in nature and thus call for a close analysis of various components of Arab society.

The Report examines the situation of women in the region by tracing a basic axis of human development: the acquisition and utilisation of human capabilities and resulting levels of well being. It probes levels of health and education in particular. It also assesses experiences in the advancement of women by reviewing two factors crucial for the success of such a movement: the extent of Arab society's desire for such progress and the forms of social action adopted to pursue it.

ACQUIRING CAPABILITIES: THE DENIAL OF OPPORTUNITIES TO WOMEN

Health

Women in Arab countries, especially the least developed countries, suffer unacceptably high rates of risk of morbidity and mortality connected with pregnancy and reproductive functions. The maternal mortality rate in Arab countries averages 270 deaths per 100,000 live births. This rises to over 1,000 deaths in the poorest Arab countries (Mauritania and Somalia) and falls to levels such as 7 for every 100,000 births in Qatar.

Women lose a larger number of years to disease, and this appears to be unconnected to standards of living, risk factors, and deaths linked to pregnancy or childbirth, indicating that this relatively greater loss is attributable to general life styles that discriminate against women.

The Arab region remains one of those relatively least affected by HIV/AIDS at present. Despite this, women and girls are increasingly infected by the disease and now represent half the total number of people carrying the virus in the Arab world. Women are at greater risk of catching the virus and contracting the disease: the probability of infection among females from 15 to 24 years of age is double that of males in the same age group.

Education

Despite the tremendous spread of girls' education in Arab countries, women continue to suffer more than men do from a lack of opportunities to acquire knowledge. This occurs despite the fact that girls excel in knowledge pursuits, outstripping boys in competitive academic performance.

In terms of basic indicators, the Arab region has one of the highest rates of female illiteracy (as much as one half, compared to only one third among males). It also displays one of the lowest rates of enrolment at the various levels of education. This is in spite of the success of some Arab states, most notably those in the Gulf, in increasing the percentage of girl's enrolment and narrowing the gap between the sexes at the three levels of education.

The relatively greater denial of educational opportunities to girls contrasts with Arab public opinion. The Report's field study indicates that the majority of people believe that girls have a right to education on an equal footing with men.

Female enrolment in university education has risen, yet women are still concentrated in fields such as literature, the humanities and the social sciences where they constitute the majority. These are the subjects in least demand by employers. By contrast, enrolment rates for females in fields that lead to jobs, such as engineering and science, are noticeably lower. Again, this trend runs counter to Arab public opinion which favours letting women students choose their fields of specialisation.

International data indicate that girls in the Arab region perform better in school than boys.

Women in Arab countries, especially the least developed countries, suffer... high rates of risk of morbidity and mortality connected with pregnancy and reproductive functions.

Despite the tremendous spread of girls' education in Arab countries, women continue to suffer more than men do from a lack of opportunities to acquire knowledge.

Drop out rates for girls are lower than those for boys in all the countries for which data are available. Notwithstanding this, discrimination against women in Arab countries continues to limit their access to knowledge despite the mass of statistical and other evidence indicating that Arab girls are the better learners, especially on the first rungs of the educational ladder.

The share of girls among top scoring students in all Arab countries where data is available is over 50 percent. Since, on average, girls account for fewer than half those enrolled in education, this achievement underlines their academic ascendancy. Such achievement is all the more remarkable given the unhelpful societal and familial environment that some face arising from the myth that a girl is destined for the house and that education and work are basically male domains.

The Report thus stresses that Arab countries stand to reap extraordinary benefits from giving men and women equal opportunities to acquire and utilise knowledge for the advancement of society. What deprive the region of these gains are its harmful and discriminatory practices that hold back women.

THE USE OF HUMAN CAPABILITIES

ECONOMIC ACTIVITIES

Slow growth in the region predisposes economies towards low demand for female labour. In addition, the traditional view that the man is the breadwinner blocks the employment of women and contributes to an increase in women's unemployment relative to men. Women thus encounter significant obstacles outside family life that reduce their potential. Most limiting of these are the terms and conditions of work: women do not enjoy equality with men in job opportunities, conditions or wages let alone in promotion to decision-making positions.

Starting from a low base, between 1990 and 2003, the Arab region witnessed a greater increase in women's share in economic activity than all other regions of the world: the increase for Arab women was 19 per cent compared to

3 per cent for the world as a whole. Despite this, Arab women's economic participation remains the lowest in the world: not more than 33.3 per cent of women fifteen years and older in contrast to the world average of 55.6 per cent. Furthermore, their participation does not exceed 42 per cent that of men, again the lowest rate in the world compared to a global average of 69 per cent.

Except in low-income economies where women work primarily in agriculture under conditions of poverty, they tend to find jobs in the services sector, which in the Arab world is characterised by low productivity and low remuneration. Women thus commonly experience low returns on work.

The causes of Arab women's weak economic participation include but are not confined to the prevailing male culture where some employers prefer to employ men, the scarcity of jobs in general, employment and wage discrimination between the sexes, and high reproductive rates. Laws hindering women, including those designed for their "protection," such as personal status and labour legislation, also restrict women's freedom by requiring a father's or a husband's permission to work, travel or borrow from financial institutions. Additionally, women's job opportunities have been undercut by weak support services and structural adjustment programmes.

Dependency ratios in the Arab region remain the highest in the world, with each worker supporting more than two non-working people, compared to less than one in East Asia and the Pacific. The principal reason for this is the low rate of participation by women. The situation becomes even graver when this high level of family maintenance occurs in combination with an absence of pension plans and of a National Insurance network covering all worker cohorts.

With the increasing expansion of the informal sector, where worker coverage is low, family support becomes a tremendous burden for the small number of those working. The strains on women in providing care for children and the sick, elderly, disabled and handicapped without sufficient social support also continue to grow.

The causes of Arab women's weak economic participation include but are not confined to the prevailing male culture where some employers prefer to employ men, the scarcity of jobs in general, employment and wage discrimination between the sexes, and high reproductive rates.

The failure to use human capital, especially highly educated women, curbs economic development and squanders important energies and investments, which might otherwise contribute to greater economic development for all.

ARAB WOMEN IN THE POLITICAL SPHERE

In the Report's field survey, Arab public opinion clearly endorses the right of women to participate in political activity and to hold the highest executive positions. Yet these are areas from which women are often excluded.

In most Arab countries (with the exception of the Gulf States) women obtained the right to vote and be candidates in parliamentary elections in the fifties and sixties of the past century. Lebanon was the first Arab country to grant women these two rights, in 1952.

Later, the adoption of quota systems increased women's parliamentary participation in Jordan and Morocco. Despite these favourable changes, the proportion of women representatives in Arab parliaments remains the lowest in the world at under 10 percent.

Arab women have shared in executive power in some Arab countries since the middle of the last century. The first woman minister was appointed in Iraq in 1959, in Egypt in 1956 and in Algeria in 1962. The number of Arab countries that appoint women as ministers has increased in the last three years to the extent that women now participate in all governments except that of Saudi Arabia. Such appointments do not however reflect a general trend towards women's empowerment. Women in power are often selected from the ranks of the elite or appointed from the ruling party as window dressing for the ruling regimes.

OUTSTANDING ACHIEVEMENTS OF ARAB WOMEN

Certain Arab women have realised outstanding achievements in various fields, including those in which women do not receive training on an equal footing with men, such as athletics and the natural and precise sciences.

Literary creativity: Women writers have proved that they can write and are capable of equalling and, at times, surpassing their male colleagues.

Artistic creativity, with the cinema as an example: Arab women have played an outstanding role in the effective foundation of the cinema.

Social sciences: The works of pioneering feminists such as Nawal al-Sa'dawi and Fatima Mernissi evince a joy in the discovery of unknown "continents" in the history, heritage, beliefs and renaissance of the Arab world. Though such writers set up a sharp and divisive dualism based on male/female antagonism, the following generation transcended the issue and its writings reveal a more balanced scholarly tone without the loss of a feminist orientation.

Natural and exact sciences: Despite severe barriers to women's entry into scientific fields, a galaxy of Arab women has made stellar contributions to the natural and exact sciences. Indeed, when Arab women scientists and technicians have been given an opportunity to use their abilities at the international level, they have succeeded in producing exceptional results.

Athletics: In the last six Olympic Games (1984-2004), six women from the Arab world, five from the Maghreb and one from Syria, carried off one of the three top prizes in track and field events. Two-thirds of these are gold medal winners, a relatively high figure given that only a quarter of male Arab Olympic medallists won gold.

Business: The region's movement towards free market economies, together with growing advocacy for the empowerment of women in Arab countries, have combined to increase the contributions of women entrepreneurs in Arab economies and to augment their influence in private sector business organisations. It has given rise to their own business organisations, even in those Arab countries most conservative on women's issues.

LEVELS OF WELL BEING

No clear scientific indicator exists for the feminisation of poverty defined as lack of income. However, women apparently suffer higher levels of "human poverty" as measured

The number of Arab countries that appoint women as ministers has increased in the last three years to the extent that women now participate in all governments except one.

in terms of deprivation of the three dimensions of the human development index, namely, health, knowledge and income.

Specifically, women suffer from a noticeable impairment of personal liberty.

THE SPREAD OF POVERTY AND THE DISEMPOWERMENT OF WOMEN

The Report indicates that the spread of income poverty generally leads to women's disenfranchisement in the areas of parliamentary participation, professional and technical employment, and control of economic resources. Human poverty results in the wide disempowerment of women and the exclusion of women from upper-level legislative, administrative and organisational jobs as well as from the professional and technical arenas.

THE IMPAIRMENT OF PERSONAL LIBERTY

The forms of violence practised against Arab women confirm that Arab legislators and governments, together with Arab social movements, face a large task in achieving security and development in its comprehensive sense. The mere discussion of violence against women arouses strong resistance in some Arab countries.

The most important step to oppose violence in the Arab world is to fight against its concealment, to remove the cloak of silence surrounding it and to expose it wherever it occurs, whether in public or in private. Continued silence on the subject will incur a heavy cost for individuals, society, and even the state. It is equally important to place forms of violence that many women affected have come to accept as natural in the category of unacceptable behaviour.

Such forms of violence range from honour killings, in which a woman is killed on the pretext of protecting family honour, to domestic violence, which is found and condemned in many areas of the world. Additionally, the high incidence of female circumcision in some Arab countries leads to serious health complications for women.

Women living in difficult circumstances, especially those in areas of conflict or under occupation, suffer additional difficulties. Women living in desert and marginal regions and in informal settlements are often unaware of their rights and of the services available to them. Often, they do not possess the papers, such as birth certificates, that would permit them to receive such services. Many of them endure violence in some form.

Foreign female domestic workers in Arab countries are often victimised. Labour laws do not protect their work, they endure unspecified working hours, and they are denied freedom of movement and residence. Some female workers in this sector are also exposed to physical and mental violence from their employers, including sexual assault.

Fortunately, Arab public opinion as indicated by the Report's field survey overwhelmingly condemns violence against women of any form.

THE ARAB WOMEN'S MOVEMENT: STRUGGLES AND EXPERIENCES

The most influential factor in the history of the women's movement may have been its involvement in the struggle for liberation from imperialism before it embarked on the struggle for women's liberation within Arab societies.

The first generation of women's associations (formed at around the end of the nineteenth century) was focused on charitable work. They emerged amid the wealthy classes and their standard was carried by aristocratic women, or women from ruling families.

The colonial period impacted the women's movement by dislocating the structure of occupied Islamic countries. Traditional Arab economic, social, cultural and moral frameworks were shaken. It thus became necessary to marshal national sentiment and consciousness in order to conduct national struggles of liberation as the overriding priority. As a result, social development, and the rise of women as a part of it, remained hostage to the drive for national independence, falling much lower on the list of priorities.

The 1940s and 1950s were rich for the moulding of women's discourse. Political

The most influential factor in the history of the women's movement may have been its involvement in the struggle for liberation from imperialism before it embarked on the struggle for women's liberation within Arab societies.

parties started to form women's associations under their own banners, thereby bringing men into the women's movement. Thus, immediately following the Second World War, another set of women's associations emerged throughout the Arab world.

The Arab women's movement went through a host of transformations during the colonial period as a result of social changes. The Report cites the spread of education among females; the entry of many women into the higher professions as doctors, university faculty, engineers and lawyers; the accession by some women to positions of power in the leadership of political parties and governments; the development of a well rooted consciousness of the situation in which women were living; and an increase in societal sympathy for women's issues.

Governments attempted to bring women's associations together into "unions," in line with a common phenomenon in the Arab world, namely, the confinement of women within a framework monitored and directed by the male power structure. Some scholars describe this as the feminisation of the ruling discourse.

This trend coincided during the last three decades with another significant development, the rise of Islamic movements and the spreading influence of proselytisers urging a return to the Islam of the "venerable forebears" (Salafism). These movements held women responsible for the difficulties that society was undergoing. They based their attacks on the idea that equality in public life would, by its nature, reduce men's opportunities in the job market and that the man was the master of the family and the woman his dependant.

Starting with the 1975 UN Conference in Mexico and under the influence of international organisations working for the rise of women, new instances of the so-called "feminisation of the state" began to emerge.

A number of Arab regimes saw in the Islamic groups a means to weaken leftist and labour forces. This led to the growth of the Islamic revivalist movement, whose concerns extended to all spheres of public and private life and whose discourse attracted broad segments of youth, especially young women.

In response, a call emerged for the restriction of Islam to the realm of personal belief and spiritual value. Some groups were obliged to modify their stance, asking that the door to independent religious thinking (ijtihad) be opened on questions connected with women in the belief that enlightened readings of the regulatory Qur'anic verses would establish a new discourse on women nourished by the Islamic heritage. The second half of the 1970s saw the founding of women's organisations independent of official political organisations. Debate centred on the inadequacy of, and loopholes in, the Personal Status Code in terms of achieving equality, notwithstanding its pioneering nature compared with family legislation in many other Arab countries. Attention also concentrated on forms of violence inflicted upon women and on how this violence was reflected in their status in society.

The women's movement saw a qualitative upswing in the 1980s in the establishment and extension of associations. Politically active associations emerged, linked to parties. The eighties were also a crucial period in the transformation of the women's movements, especially in the Maghreb countries. It is no coincidence that the names of the new women's associations included words such as "democratic," "progressive," and "rights." Their independence and courage distinguished these movements as they trod a path strewn with obstacles, under siege from, and beset by the ruling regimes.

The new generation of women's associations is distinguished by its qualitative closeness to the topic of women and women's issues. It considers these as central questions no less important than those of democracy, development, and human rights.

The international discourse on women has been a significant influence on the Arab women's movement and a driving force in the latter's perseverance and reformulation of its goals. The new consciousness was reinforced at international conferences, chiefly those convened under the auspices of the United Nations. The new approach aimed to dislodge traditional views still clinging to the women's question. Thus, personal status laws were the most important priority among these goals,

The new generation of women's associations is distinguished by its qualitative closeness to the topic of women and women's issues. It considers these as central questions no less important than those of democracy, development, and human rights.

followed by the enactment of legislation guaranteeing the equality of women and men in political and economic life. Women's associations were also active in urging Arab governments to implement the international agreements that they had approved, especially the Convention on the Elimination of All Forms of Discrimination against Women (CEDAW).

The 1990s are considered to have been difficult years for Arab society, filled with contradictions, tribulations, and successive, bitter disappointments. The Report observes that it lies beyond the power and resources of the women's movements to affect such an entangled politico-social situation by themselves, which confirms that the fight for women's freedom is the fight of Arab societies as a whole.

EVALUATING ACHIEVEMENTS FOR WOMEN

The participation of women in national movements helped women to articulate their case and enhanced their legitimacy in society's eyes. Nevertheless, and despite some palpable gains by women, the postponement of the resolution of their social and political demands had regrettable consequences after independence (Algeria is an excellent example of this). For, in most cases, the new nationalist governments pretended to forget or ignored some or most of these demands, especially those related to the Personal Status Codes. In general, and with the exception of the modifications made to the personal status laws in Tunisia, unequal relations of power within the family survived.

The impact of women's movements in Arab countries has varied from one country to another. Their principal achievement may have been to increase awareness among women of the lesser status accorded to them and the need to work to change it. By concentrating public scrutiny on Personal Status Laws, the movement has impelled Arab states to take tangible steps to improve family law and legislation on marriage and divorce in general.
The Tunisian experience: Tunisia remains a model among the Arab states in terms of women's emancipation. Half a century

has passed since the issuing of its Personal Status Code, through which Tunisian law gave legal effect to the principle of women's equality with men. The changes to family law instituted by President Habib Bourguiba soon after independence sprang from a reformist movement that viewed the rise of women positively on the social, economic and political levels. Likewise, it is important to note that the laws of the Personal Status Code sprang from an initiative undertaken by two schools of Islamic jurisprudence, the Maliki and the Hanafi.

However, progressive changes in family laws have coincided with restrictions on the freedom of action of activist women and with state monopolisation and monitoring of the movement's discourse. This leaves only a limited field for women's initiatives and demands. The tendency to transform the rise of women into a political tool that may be used to enhance the image of the state abroad, even at the expense of women, has become very clear.

The Moroccan experience: The Moroccan women's movement has become acutely conscious that amendments to the legal code are the key to women's ownership of their own issues. Its struggle in that area was crowned by the new Family Code, issued in 2004.

Looking at experiences in other Arab countries, at the present time, Egyptian women have only managed to win the right, granted in 2000, to initiate divorce proceedings (khul'), after waiving certain financial rights entailed in other forms of divorce. They have also won the right to travel without their husbands' permission and to obtain Egyptian nationality for their children by a foreign husband.

Jordan has raised the legal age for marriage to eighteen years for both spouses and granted women the right to obtain a passport without their husbands' permission.

In Algeria, the Family Law still remains in force. However, there are positive signs in the difference between the form the latter took in 1984 and the modifications issued in 2005.

The Report concludes that re-evaluating the position of Arab women today is a sine qua non for a stronger civil society, one that demands a conviction that overrules pretexts for inaction that reject all forms of women's development

The impact of women's movements in Arab countries has varied from one country to another. Their principal achievement may have been to increase awareness among women of the lesser status accorded to them and the need to work to change it.

as part of the culture of "the Other".

THE SOCIETAL CONTEXT OF THE STATE OF WOMEN

CULTURE

The Report considers social patterns that contribute to shaping the position of women in Arab societies today. It focuses on three central sources of influence: religious heritage, popular culture and Arab intellectual, artistic and media production.

Religious heritage: gender bias in juristic interpretations

In Arab Islamic history, religious culture is not built on sacred texts of indisputable authority, but, rather, on differing interpretations of the content, substance, forms and views of multiple writings and sayings in the collective memory of society. It is also based on customs and traditions that have been consolidated to preserve a specific order for the family and society.

General principles of interpretation enable us to infer the broad outlines of a social system that responds to the objectives accepted by the Islamic community in order to live a life of interdependence and consensus, while recognising the equality of all human beings, males and females. On the other hand, juristic interpretations, crystallised in some schools of Islamic jurisprudence, contributed to the establishment of a number of norms approving the principle of discrimination between the sexes.

The strictness of legislation in Islamic jurisprudence conceals other matters that originate in Arab Islamic society itself, particularly since jurists deliberately read the canonical provisions through the lens of custom. They believed that any other kind of readings would disrupt the continuity of the social order in its reinforcement of social cohesion, which, in their view, was congruent with "the order of nature".

Men have always been given priority and preference in jurisprudential studies related to women. This predisposition entrenched itself as a result of reading the Qur'an with a bias in men's favour. Nonetheless, enlightened legal interpretations did exist.

Because the dynamics of transformation in contemporary Arab societies are different from those in Arab societies at the time when the schools of jurisprudence were established, earlier endeavours are no longer appropriate to either the nature or pace of current social transformations. Rather, it is a right to try to open the gates of interpretation anew and to seek further understanding of the spirit of the Qur'anic text in order to produce jurisprudential texts based on values of equality. Such texts will seek to embody a jurisprudence of women that goes beyond the linguistic and historical equation of what is feminine with what is natural (pregnancy, childbirth, breast feeding, upbringing and cooking). They will contribute to the promotion of feminine cultural values and transform them into a general attitude.

THE ARAB WOMAN IN POPULAR PROVERBS

Arab popular culture projects contradictory images of women, girls and wives at different stages of their lives. Proverbs dealing with women are repeated in most Arab social classes and generally provide clear examples of the perception of women as inferior, indicating that popular awareness is isolated from the fundamental transformations taking place in Arab societies. The proverbs create several myths about the conditions and state of women, which often conflict with women's actual circumstances.

Hundreds of popular proverbs project an attitude akin to that which led to the burying of girls alive. In order to justify their retrograde spirit, these proverbs use moral and other arguments expressed in the language of tales and myths. Some also rely on psychology. In their various forms, these proverbs serve to underline the inferior social and moral position of women in society. Some go even further, considering a woman to have only half a mind, half a creed, and half an inheritance, and to be worth only half a male. Their general drift is to limit women's biological and domestic life and denigrate their worth and independence.

The strictness of legislation in Islamic jurisprudence conceals other matters that originate in Arab Islamic society itself, particularly since jurists deliberately read the canonical provisions through the lens of custom.

Yet several popular traditions and texts render another image of woman, a woman who is intelligent, articulate and, indeed, something of an enchantress but in the positive sense of the word.

WOMEN IN CONTEMPORARY ARAB THOUGHT

TOWARDS THE EMERGENCE OF NEW SOURCES OF AUTHORITY

Contemporary Arab thinking on women and the theories supporting it are closely tied to the Arab Renaissance movement and its struggles against all forms of inherited traditional authority. At the outset of the social transformation that led to this renaissance towards the end of the nineteenth century, reform-minded political thinkers and intellectuals recognised that European societies had specific features that accounted for their strength and progress. An excellent representation of this particular moment is the reform project of Shaykh Rifa'a Rafi' al-Tahtawi.

First attempts to restrict gender-biased jurisprudence

Reformers such as Qasim Amin, Nazira Zayn al-Din, and later al-Tahir al-Haddad and others, were acutely aware of the necessity for change in the position of women. These thinkers did not believe that any significant contradictions existed between European society, the values and lifestyle emerging in contemporary Arab society and the principles of Islamic law. They also initiated a debate on the reinterpretation of certain Qur'anic verses, with the aim of unmasking biased interpretations. Their efforts stand out in Arab cultural history because they succeeded in opening wide a door for women at the centre of the solid wall of Arab society.

The participation of women in civil society organisations for legal and political action further helped to re-educate society to accept an active female presence. It contributed to replacing the traditional feminine stereotype with an image of women engaged in other activities that rested on much greater freedom

of action, production and creativity.

Today, the type of dissent expressed by women in the Arab world transcends what is expected of women in society and embraces a more comprehensive position in step with the major transformation taking place in Arab societies involving questions of renaissance, development and progress. Arab women have made the project of political and economic reform, and positive interaction with the human rights system, part of their direct objectives. This is also reflected in the increasing presence of women in the organisations of civil and political society.

Women and the media

The Report observes that the women's movement has benefited from new media forms such as the Internet, chat rooms, and television channels and their specialised programmes, all of which generate perspectives based on the power of dialogue. These media forms have facilitated a new discourse of liberation by enabling women to occupy public spaces that they could not have entered through the use of written material and newspapers alone. They have helped to promote gender awareness oriented towards social cohesion, equality and the principle of equity as the appropriate alternatives to discrimination between the sexes.

The broadcast media, notably satellite channels, and print media, are employing more women in some countries yet, a few exceptions notwithstanding, the ownership of political and hard news media remains a male bastion. Women play no role in planning media policy or making media decisions. The Report questions the extent to which the increased number of Arab women in the media positively influences the general orientation of programming and the popular image of women.

Women in the Arab novel

The Report illustrates that there are four main images of women to be found in women's novels - the woman deprived of her rights, the militant woman, the rebellious woman, and the 'multiple' woman. The term "multiple" refers to splitting and fragmentation, and highlights

The participation of women in civil society organisations for legal and political action further helped to re-educate society to accept an active female presence.

The Report questions the extent to which the increased number of Arab women in the media positively influences the general orientation of programming and the popular image of women.

multiple identities within one being. Most of these novels reflect the expansion of the image of Arab women into the space once occupied by uniform stereotypes which are inadequate vis-à-vis the social transformations which these works portend. In building new linguistic and aesthetic sensibilities, these writings support values capable of breaking down such stereotypes.

Arab novels also shed light on aspects of women's oppression as well as their role as accessories in perpetuating male dominance. The confusion and contradictions that many novels reveal point to conditions of cultural refraction that may be interpreted in the context of the global environment and the transitional historical stage through which Arab societies are passing, both of which frame the world of fiction.

The image of women in the cinema

Arab cinema plays an important role by raising public awareness of women's issues and the injustices that befall them from harsh traditions or unfair laws. Among the most important contributions of Arab cinema to challenging society's sexual hierarchy is its visual exposure of the mechanics of women's submission.

However, Arab cinema, like all arts, plays a dual role stemming from its commercial nature. On the one hand, using the power of moving images, it generalises values of sexual discrimination. And, at the same time, the new cinema emerging in more than one Arab country is sending messages that reflect the wishes of new generations of women seeking freedom and full selfhood as complete and independent human beings.

Other forms of cultural production

Television serials are especially influential in challenging or entrenching the traditional image of women, as are TV commercials that portray women through different images and settings. This is true not only of Arab television channels but of that vast network of channels that enter Arab homes and present Arab families with images and attitudes containing more disparities than similarities.

The Arab living room has become

a veritable battleground in the war of information. Like the wars over the interpretation of Islamic jurisprudence, the clash of popular proverbs and the struggles of Arab civil society to promote the values of freedom and equality, it is a conflict that confronts citizens with different and confusing choices. For example, most Arab satellite channels produce religious programmes aimed at spreading an Islamic culture. The scholars that are charged with issuing fatwas are careful to preserve the prevailing patriarchal system of Arab societies and make little effort to bring Islamic jurisprudence up to date. An increasing number of conservative channels are consolidating the image of women on the lower rungs of the gender hierarchy. At the same time, numerous channels that claim modernity in fact project a demeaning portrayal of women, seen mainly as physical bodies and mere commodities.

This Arab media operates in societies governed by strong central powers where the worlds of money, authority and the media intermingle in the shadow of fierce competition among media channels for a constrained advertising market. This makes the industry run after a large Arab public with significant purchasing power, in particular the Arab Gulf public, about whom it has preconceived ideas.

SOCIAL STRUCTURES

TRIBALISM AND PATRIARCHY

Arab tribal society understood very well the structural and functional importance of women to its existence. It viewed honour, respect and protection as a unity linking any one of its members with the whole and thus also the women with the whole. This made any interference with the status of women a matter touching the very heart of her kinfolk's security and standing.

Islam brought with it the concept of the umma (the Islamic community) as an expression of collective identity to replace that of the tribe. However, the Arab tribes, primarily the Bedouin but also the urban-rural tribes, preserved their authoritarian structures

The Arab living room has become a veritable battleground in the war of information. Like the wars over the interpretation of Islamic jurisprudence, the clash of popular proverbs and the struggles of Arab civil society to promote the values of freedom and equality, it is a conflict that confronts citizens with different and confusing choices.

unchanged.

Although Islam established the notion of individual responsibility for both men and women, and emphasised respect for both sexes and their rights, the socio-cultural and economic-political formation of the conquests imposed limits on these broad vistas that the new religion had opened for women.

The emergence of the modern authoritarian system played a large role in curtailing the growth of civil institutions. Though European capitalism brought with it new values relating to the state, politics and society, these did not originate in local conditions. Hence the cycle through which the foundations of a law-based state and an independent civil society resistant to oppression might have been established was never completed.

Initially, the all-encompassing Arab state contributed to a greater participation by women in the public sphere, professional fields and social services, as well as to the relative protection of motherhood and childhood. But in the end, bureaucratic rigidity, the expropriation of different social and civic initiatives and the system of the local dignitary (a man, of course) as the sole intermediary between authority and society held women's rights hostage to the nature and vicissitudes of power. The symbiotic relationship between state authority and patriarchy saw to it that these early achievements soon became opportunities for personal gain. The position of women thus continued to deteriorate with the retreat of citizenship rights and the return of organic patriarchal rights as the final means of self-defence of a society forbidden to engage in the various forms of civic activity.

Relations within the family have continued to be governed by the father's authority over his children and the husband's over his wife, under the sway of the patriarchal order. Changes to which this authoritarian family framework has since been subjected cannot be considered far-reaching. Nor have they appreciably affected the functional nature of the relationship between the sexes. While they have had an effect on some forms of discrimination between men and women, they have not effected a qualitative change in the nature of the relationships between them

except in limited circles. Male control at the economic, social, cultural, legal and political levels remains the abiding legacy of patriarchy.

The belief that women must be controlled remains, of course, subject to variation across different countries, social classes, standards of living and general consciousness. It shows itself particularly among the poor whose marginal position in society affords them less legal and social protection and leaves them exposed to the dominant patriarchal culture.

Yet despite lacking political freedoms, women have been able to manoeuvre under traditional social conditions to defend their rights by establishing charitable, medical or literary women's or family organisations. They have formed delegations to demand their rights, benefiting from the social space allowed them in some countries that nevertheless restrict their ideological space. Some resourceful women activists have taken advantage of this narrow latitude to establish civil society groups for women's rights, ironically creating social change out of the very structures that have restrained it.

In some societies, the qualitative accumulation of small victories by women has caused patriarchal hegemony to retreat, to varying degrees. And women often rise to the challenge of coping with harsh changes and have proven to be the protectors of social existence in exceptionally tough situations as is the case with women under siege and sanctions in Iraq, and under the multi-faceted violence afflicting Sudan, Lebanon, Iraq, and Palestine. In this sense, social structures have not prevented women, in different degrees and forms, from becoming active players in the historical transition that some Arab countries are undergoing.

THE FAMILY AND THE STATUS OF WOMEN

The family continues to be the first social institution that reproduces patriarchal relationships, values and pressures through gender discrimination. Such pressures on women increase in violence at times of crisis when a woman becomes subject to surveillance. The man's right of disposal over her body, his watch over it, his use of it, his concealment, denial and punishment of it all become more blatant. This violence in turn comes into play to intensify the feminisation of poverty, political misery, dependency, domination and alienation.

To date, personal status laws constitute the most emblematic and profound embodiment of this problem. Matrimony is the first and foremost form of the relationship between women and men whether in the conscious or unconscious mind, in religion or society, in terms of the permissible or prohibited and the sacred or the desecrated. These laws may well represent the most pronounced embodiment of the relationship between Arab patriarchy and the forbidden and the taboo. Key laws relating to gender discrimination find refuge in that relationship, allowing family laws to become the lair protecting culture, traditions and customs, religious as well as popular.

Elements of modernity have reached into Arab traditional culture, within and across countries. Nevertheless, large social sectors still remain closer to tradition than to innovation. A girl pays a heavy price for asserting her independence in milieus where individualisation in both the human rights and economic senses is weak.

Yet the Arab family is too complex to be summed up in one generalised and absolute characterisation; nor should society succumb to a negative stereotype of fatherhood. Such one-sided images lead individuals to surrender to authority figures and give credence to the notion that rebelling against authoritarianism or changing the status quo is impossible. Additionally, the assertion that women are repressed denies value to their lives, implying that these are wasted. Under the shadow of any harsh environment, a woman can yet take possession of her freedom by taking decisions that will give her unexpected happiness. This freedom is the source of the inspiration for change.

SOCIALISATION AND EDUCATION

School systems under authoritarian rule rarely give sufficient encouragement to initiative, discovery or the development of creative and critical faculties or personal aptitudes. Despite the inroads Arab women have made in political, social and economic fields, the gap between such progress and the stereotypical images of women in school curricula is enormous. Those images invariably confine a woman to the roles of mother, homemaker and housekeeper.

As a result, pedagogy specialists have demanded that some curricula be modified, and that new guidelines and concepts be formulated for content that rescues girls from the superficial setting to which they are still confined. They have also called on Arab women to participate in drawing up educational policies, a task from which they have been almost completely excluded. Female participation in the setting of school subjects was estimated at less than 8 per cent in a random sampling of Arab curricula.

LEGAL STRUCTURES

Many laws in the Arab countries discriminate against women. Constitutional provisions for the protection of women's rights exist in nearly all countries but are often flouted, contradicted by other legislation or not enforced. The Report illustrates a range of discriminatory provisions and practices that reveal the bias of the Arab legislator against women.

ATTITUDES TOWARDS THE CONVENTION ON THE ELIMINATION OF ALL FORMS OF DISCRIMINATION AGAINST WOMEN

Most Arab states have signed and ratified CEDAW and are thus bound by its provisions, reservations excepted. Those reservations entered by Arab states (and they are many) give cause for concern; they put in doubt the will to abide by the provisions of CEDAW. Particularly worrying are their reservations with regard to Article 2, which establishes the principle of equality of men and women: reservations to this crucial article effectively render the ratifications meaningless.

Arab states based their reservations to the provisions of the Convention on one of two grounds: that the articles concerned contradicted national legislation or that they

Arab states based their reservations to the provisions of the Convention on one of two grounds: that the articles concerned contradicted national legislation or that they conflicted with the provisions of Shari'a (Islamic Law).

conflicted with the provisions of Shari'a (Islamic Law). On occasion this reservation was intended generally so as to absolve the state of its commitment to any provision of the Convention that it considered conflicted with Shari'a. In certain cases, a state would provide no justification for its reservation.

In a number of Arab states, and at the urging of civil society and some national institutions, legislative reviews are under way to reconsider the state's stand on reservations. This positive move deserves to be encouraged, along with greater efforts to raise awareness of the Convention in public and legislative circles and law enforcement agencies.

CONSTITUTIONAL CONDITIONS

Equality in the law

Most Arab constitutions contain provisions affirming the principle of equality in general and the principle of equality between men and women in particular. Some contain specific provisions for equality of men and women in, for example, employment in public office, political rights, and rights and duties. Some also contain provisions stipulating the right to equal opportunity; affirming the state's obligation to preserve the family, to protect motherhood and children, and to guarantee a proper balance between women's duties towards their families and their work in society; and prohibiting the employment of women in certain types of industries or at specified times of day.

Much to their credit, Arab legislators, and constitutional lawmakers in particular, have respected the principle of gender differences and have made provision for regulating the effects of these differences legislatively. Unfortunately, in many areas of law, legislators have leaned so heavily towards the principle of gender differences that they have codified gender discrimination, thereby violating the principle of equality, which is sanctified in religious canons and rendered an international obligation under international treaties.

Women's political and public rights

National legislation in many Arab states contains provisions guaranteeing women's political rights and stipulating the principle of equality of men and women in the exercise of the right to participate in electoral processes and to stand for public office.

Nevertheless, despite these constitutional and legislative guarantees of women's right to political participation, the actual extent of this participation is still meagre.

The paltry representation of women in parliament in the Arab Mashriq (eastern Arab world) should impel states of this region to seriously consider emulating the example of the Arab Maghreb (North Africa), where most states have adopted quota systems to ensure a significant representation of women in their parliaments.

Parliamentary quota systems for women

Even when laws provide for gender equality in political participation, such formal equality has been of little aid to women in a cultural and social environment inimical to women's acquisition and free exercise of their political rights. Affirmative legislative intervention to allocate a quota of parliamentary seats for women would help society to make amends for its historical injustice against women. Such action would also make up for lost time in giving effect to the principle of equal opportunity enshrined in many Arab constitutions. The Report firmly supports such steps.

Incrimination and punishment

Negative discrimination between men and women can be found in the penal codes of some Arab states. For example, in some Arab penal codes, in the crime of adultery, men are held guilty only if the act takes place in the marital home. Women are guilty regardless of where the act takes place.

Arab legislators have made inroads towards eliminating gender bias in Arab penal codes, but their approach remains ad hoc and piecemeal. Attention must be given to developing a more intensive and comprehensive approach.

Personal status laws

Arab personal status laws, with regard to

Despite these constitutional and legislative guarantees of women's right to political participation, the actual extent of this participation is still meagre.

Muslims and non-Muslims alike, are witness to legally sanctioned gender bias. This stems from the fact that personal status statutes are primarily derived from theological interpretations and judgements. The latter originate in the remote past when gender discrimination permeated society and have acquired a sanctity and absoluteness in that confused area where the immutable tenets of religious creed interact with social history.

Nonetheless, evidence from the report's public opinion survey indicates that the Arab public is moving towards a more liberal perspective on personal status issues, such as asserting women's right to choose a spouse.

The lack of codification in some States

Arab personal status laws remain conservative and resistant to change because a number of Arab States are reluctant to develop a national personal status code. Instead, they leave matters entirely to the judiciary, which is heavily influenced by the conservative nature of classical Islamic jurisprudence (fiqh). Some Arab states, such as Egypt, Lebanon, Qatar and Bahrain lack a unified personal status code entirely, whereas others have unified personal status codes for Muslims.

Personal status regulations for non-Muslims are derived from the canons of their respective religious sects or denominations. For the most part, these regulations sharply curtail the right of both spouses to divorce and, in some cases, prohibit it altogether.

In general, personal status law in the Maghreb is more progressive and less discriminatory than that in the Mashriq.

Nationality

In general, in Arab legislation, native nationality is determined by paternal descent. If a father is a citizen of a particular Arab country, his children acquire his nationality automatically. The children of a female national only acquire their mother's nationality if the father's identity is unknown or if he is stateless.

Recently Arab lawmakers have been working to counter the inhumane consequences of Arab states' long-held refusal to grant nationality to the children of female citizens married to foreigners (Egypt, Algeria, Lebanon).

AWAY FROM OFFICIAL LAW

The social environment is a crucial factor in discrimination against women, regardless of what the law may say. Because of what is commonly considered appropriate or inappropriate behaviour for a dutiful, decent and virtuous wife, recourse by a woman to the courts to demand her rights, or those of her children, is widely frowned upon as a form of public indecency. As a result, many women refrain from pursuing their family rights through official legal processes. Instead, matrimonial disputes in many Arab societies are resolved either within the family or through the unofficial channels of tribal arbitration. As these mechanisms evolved in the context of a male-dominated culture and male-oriented values, their biased outcomes are often a foregone conclusion.

AWARENESS OF GENDER EQUALITY AMONG ARAB LEGAL PRACTITIONERS

Arab tribal culture, which sanctions discrimination against women, has strongly influenced juristic interpretations that establish the inferiority of women to men. Otherwise put, the male-dominated culture has been a crucial factor in shaping juristic judgements and endowing them with religious sanctity.

Some Arab legislators evince hostility towards gender equality, despite the provisions of their national constitutions and the international conventions to which their states are party. Frequently, the application of the principle of gender equality founders on the reservations of Arab judiciaries, a resistance fuelled by the growth of fundamentalist trends and their increasing impact on the legal consciousness of Arab judges. The depth of male chauvinism among members of the judiciary in some Arab states can be seen in their opposition to the appointment of female judges.

Discrimination by the legal community against women is also evident in the way judges

Arab personal status laws remain conservative and resistant to change because a number of Arab States are reluctant to develop a national personal status code. Instead, they leave matters entirely to the judiciary, which is heavily influenced by the conservative nature of classical Islamic jurisprudence (fiqh).

use their discretionary authority to deliver lighter or harsher sentences in cases where a woman is one of the litigants. Many interpreters of legislation echo this discriminatory tendency when faced with the principle of equality before the law. In contrast to such views there exists a body of enlightened Islamic jurisprudence that interprets such texts in their context and inclines to the espousal of the principle of gender equality. However, the first – conservative – school of thought still finds a sympathetic ear in practice and still appeals to the man on the street because of the support it receives from conservative clerics.

POLITICAL ECONOMY

The extent to which women in Arab countries are empowered is significantly influenced by the political economy of the region. The mode of production in Arab countries is dominated by rentier economies and levels of economic performance marked by weak economic growth.

The combination of these two characteristics results in weak production structures in the Arab economies and a paucity of means of expansion, laying the groundwork for the spread of unemployment and poverty. The overall result is a pattern of economic activity that has disastrous results for human economic empowerment, with other social circumstances multiplying the harshest results when it comes to women because of their economic weakness.

These unhealthy effects include rising rates of unemployment in Arab countries, particularly among graduates, and the inevitable and consequent increase in poverty and misdistribution of income and wealth, since the labour market is the most important economic resource for most people in the least-developed economies. Since this mix of factors means a narrow labour market throughout the Arab world and low rates of expansion through creation of new job opportunities, rates of unemployment of the less-skilled labour force in the Arab world are affected disproportionately. This in turn, results in reliance on foreign labour. Naturally, the weakest social groups, including women, suffer most.

A tight job market, slow job creation and the spread of women's education, along with society's irrational preference that men should take what jobs there are, have combined to increase the unemployment of women, especially educated women, even in Arab countries that import non-Arab workers.

The state also has withdrawn from economic and service activity and limited government employment, which had previously represented the preferred form of employment for women and a bastion of their rights. As a result, the region is witness to an abundance of qualified female human capital suffering from above average rates of unemployment.

Another factor that disempowers women economically is the bias in labour practices against women when they do work, particularly in the private sector, which has reduced women's relative earnings.

GOVERNMENT INSTITUTIONS AND THE LIBERATION OR MARGINALISATION OF ARAB WOMEN

Appointing a woman to a ministerial position has been a general rule in most Arab governments since at least the 1990s, and the practice has grown steadily since then. However, the nature of women's participation in government has generally been either symbolic (one or two female ministers in most cases), social (usually ministries of social affairs or ministries related to women), or conditional (the number of female ministers fluctuates with numerous changes of government).

Undeniably, women have achieved representation in Arab government bodies, whether as a result of internal or external pressure, or both. Nonetheless, such progress remains limited. Women in decision-making positions tend to be sidelined in a predominantly male-oriented executive culture. While women's membership in parliament has taken off, and while equality of the sexes appears as one of the principles of Arab constitutions, their empowerment remains relatively partial; and some states still fail to apply the principle of gender

A tight job market, slow job creation and the spread of women's education, along with society's irrational preference that men should take what jobs there are, have combined to increase the unemployment of women, especially educated women, even in Arab countries that import non-Arab workers.

equality to their election laws. Moreover, the number of parliamentary seats held by women does not necessarily mean that women are democratically represented; it may in fact reflect concessions to a group of women supported by the state against other women on the fringes of dominant political forces.

Arab political parties have come to espouse the general cause of women, but from that initial point they diverge. The political failures attending reform or change in the region have led to fierce controversies, resulting in sharp political divisions, the balkanisation of the party-political map in Arab countries, and the fragmentation of party positions on women. Nevertheless, some political parties have helped to push the issue of women to the forefront. Additionally, growing demands by Arab women's groups and the increasing response from governments for quotas to help women reach decision-making positions, have led to certain positive changes. Quotas have also helped women enter local government councils.

ARAB CIVIL SOCIETY AND THE ISSUE OF WOMEN

Many Arab laws specify that private social and women's associations are forbidden to involve themselves in policy or in political matters. This legal obstacle to the free expression of opinion implies that politics is removed from the activities of civil society and from private charitable and social work.

Despite the importance of these organisations and groups in providing services that segments of the female population need, doubts exist about their ability to change the prevailing gender-biased power relationship in Arab societies. Representation of women in such groups is usually restricted to the educated middle-class, which means the most deprived and needy women are often beyond their operational reach. The spread of this type of social organisation would not necessarily mean greater political or social representation for all segments of the female population. Many of them do not basically seek to organise women to defend their rights and interests; rather rights are defended in general since achieving

these rights is in the interest of all women.

DIFFERENT POLITICAL POSITIONS ON WOMEN

Political forces on the Arab scene do not oppose the rise of Arab women or their political and social participation; all accept the legal and political equality of women. The problem lies in these forces' implementation of their principles in party and political life.

ISLAMIST POSITIONS ON WOMEN

The position of the Salafite movements has always been clear, namely, that a woman's place is in the home and that her role is to care for the family. While these movements may have accepted women's right to vote by analogy with allegiance to the ruler, they adamantly reject their right to seek and hold public office "to avoid pitfalls" (saddan lil-dhara'i'). The Salafites are opposed to women being active in civil society, adopting a division of social labour that limits women's role to that of reproduction, motherhood, and child raising and warning against the mixing of the sexes. The most that can be expected from the Salafites is an acceptance of independent feminist activity in private charities.

On the other side of the arena, the Muslim Brotherhood adopts a principled position in support of women's political rights, accepting in this regard the independent interpretations of contemporary scholars such as al-Ghazali and al-Qaradawi, which are based on jurisprudence.

Ultimately, the challenge before the Islamists is how to develop an alternative Islamic vision of women that can co-exist with differing or opposing trends and advance women's position in discourse and practice, not as a result of, but as one of the conditions for building the Islamic society they desire.

EXTERNAL PRESSURES FOR THE EMPOWERMENT OF WOMEN IN ARAB COUNTRIES

The international agenda has witnessed fundamental changes since the beginning of the 1990s, with the increased importance of issues

Growing demands by Arab women's groups and the increasing response from governments for quotas to help women reach decision-making positions, have led to certain positive changes.

Political forces on the Arab scene do not oppose the rise of Arab women or their political and social participation; all accept the legal and political equality of women. The problem lies in these forces' implementation of their principles in party and political life.

such as human rights, women's and minority rights and democratic change. Demands for change in women's status globally pressured Arab countries to respond.

But for many Arab rulers, the issue of women's political rights became a type of democratic façade. Women offered an easily manipulated symbol for countries that wanted to escape political criticism of their undemocratic conditions at a time when human rights reports and reports on women's affairs were pressing for change.

The Report observes that the new wave of Western interest in advancing the position of women has led donors to support projects solely because a visible women's or feminist institution puts them forward; or to support any projects to strengthen the status of women that seem topical. Seldom are proper studies carried out to measure the effect of these projects on the status of Arab women in their society, in the family or in relation to the state. Western pressure and the ready accommodation of it in some Arab countries are particularly clear with respect to the representation of women in the political framework, such as parliament and the cabinet.

The Report goes on to cite a series of positive developments in the consciousness and situation of Arab women flowing from the acceleration of the global women's movement after the 1995 Beijing International Conference on Women.

A STRATEGIC VISION: TWO WINGS FOR THE RISE OF WOMEN

KEY FEATURES

The rise of Arab women must go beyond a merely symbolic makeover that permits a few distinguished Arab women to ascend to positions of leadership in State institutions. Rather, it must extend to the empowerment of the broad masses of Arab women in their entirety.

In human development terms, the rise of Arab women requires, first, that all Arab women be afforded full opportunities to acquire essential capabilities firstly and

essentially in health. As a primary requirement, all Arab girls and women must also be able to acquire knowledge on an equal footing with boys and men.

Second, full opportunities must be given to Arab women to participate as they see fit in all types of human activity outside the family on an equal footing with their male counterparts.

It is also essential that the appropriate social value be given to women's role in the family as an indispensable contribution to the establishment of a sound social structure capable of supporting a project for the renaissance of the Arab world. From that follows the pivotal importance of the reform of education in Arab countries in order to ensure that all girls are guaranteed opportunities to acquire knowledge and to utilise it, within and outside the family.

In line with the calls in previous Reports for comprehensive, rights-based societal reforms, the rise of Arab women entails:

- Total respect for the rights of citizenship of all Arab women.
- The protection of women's rights in the area of personal affairs and family relations.
- Guarantees of total respect for women's personal rights and freedoms and in particular their lifelong protection from physical and mental abuse.

The achievement of these rights requires extensive legal and institutional changes aimed at bringing national legislation in line with CEDAW.

The Report also calls for the temporary adoption of the principle of affirmative action in expanding the participation of Arab women to all fields of human activity according to the particular circumstances of each society. This will allow the dismantling of the centuries-old structures of discrimination against women.

The Report envisages these societal reforms as one wing of the bird symbolising the rise of women in the Arab world.

The second wing is the emergence of a widespread and effective movement of struggle in Arab civil society. This movement will involve Arab women and their male supporters in carefully targeted societal reform on the one hand, and, on the other, empower all Arab women to enjoy the fruits of changes that serve the rise of both women and the region as a whole.

THE FIRST WING: SOCIETAL REFORM FOR THE RISE OF WOMEN

This will address attitudinal shifts and the reform of cultural frameworks. In particular, it will modernise religious interpretation and jurisprudence through the widespread adoption of the enlightened readings of ijtihad. The latter must escape the thrall of existing religious institutions and personages to become the right and duty of every Muslim of learning, woman or man, who has the capacity to engage in the study of her or his religion.

Efforts to overcome attitudinal obstacles will extend to new syllabi and techniques in social education that promote equal treatment between the sexes. They will associate the media in educating the public to understand the significance of CEDAW. Efforts to overcome structural obstacles will include deep-seated political and legislative reforms in the areas indicated in this Report. The latter relate particularly to the functions of the judiciary at all levels, and all political, administrative, local, academic and other leadership functions.

In particular, a culture of equal treatment and respect for human rights should be encouraged among men in the judiciary and all those responsible for enforcing the rule of law.

The first wing will also address the issue of social justice, aiming to reduce the spread of income poverty by supporting economic growth, and achieving greater justice in income distribution. It will simultaneously seek to reverse the spread of human poverty, which refers to the denial to people of opportunities to acquire and effective exercise their essential capabilities. Among the most important mechanisms for the attainment of social justice is expenditure on education, health and social safety nets.

A final priority under this wing is to confront reductions in women's personal liberties. This calls for inculcating an understanding that violence against women in all forms is a degradation of their humanity. It extends to the enactment of laws that criminalise violence against women and the provision by states and civil society of safe sanctuaries for women victims of violence.

THE SECOND WING: A SOCIETAL MOVEMENT FIT TO BRING ABOUT THE RISE OF WOMEN

The Report maintains that the rise of women cannot be separated from a wide and effective movement in Arab civil society aimed at achieving human development for all. Such a movement will be the means by which Arab women may empower themselves and their male supporters. It will have two levels. The first is national and will involve all levels of society in every Arab country. The second is regional: it will be founded on trans-border networks for the co-ordination and support of regional efforts to achieve a comprehensive Arab movement for the rise of Arab women, benefiting from modern information and communications technology. The movement will give birth to active civil society organisations in the Arab world linked to politically neutral international and UN organisations working for women's advancement.

This movement will begin by focusing on two sets of priorities:

1. Eliminating women's legacy of deprivation in health and in knowledge through education

Health

This requires guaranteeing that all women enjoy good health, in the positive and comprehensive sense. Thus, the general trend to ensure positive health for all, which is an integral part of human development, extends automatically to the provision of special care for the needs of the weak in general and of women in particular. Implementation of the Report's recommendations for the elimination of poverty, and especially human poverty, are relevant here.

Ending the denial of education to girls and women

Ending once and for all the denial to girls and women of their human right to education over

To change attitudes, efforts should extend to the educational domain and to the media. To overcome structural obstacles requires political, legislative, judicial reforms and new forms of leadership.

a period of, say, ten years is an indispensable requirement. The movement will be called upon to embark on a serious programme, with official and civic dimensions, as well as regional and national ones, over a finite decade, which would ensure all girls and women a complete basic education. The goal will be to achieve, by 2015, the eradication of Arab female illiteracy, and to ensure that every Arab girl completes twelve years of basic schooling.

2. Eliminating stubborn obstacles to women's use of their capabilities as they see fit

Priorities in this focus area include:

- Accelerating the rate of economic growth to enable the creation of employment opportunities on a large scale. The significant increase in the price of oil over the last few years constitutes a revenue source that may enable Arab economies to develop and diversify their productive infrastructure.
- Resisting the cultural obstacles facing women's employment of their full capacities in all areas of human development as freely chosen by them.
- Guaranteeing in Arab constitutions, legislation and implementation mechanisms equality of employment opportunities for all regardless of gender.
- Guaranteeing women's enjoyment of appropriate working conditions consistent with human dignity, and when necessary, providing some aspects of positive discrimination, protective of their family roles, without making them pay for this preferential treatment, by decreasing their work privileges vis-à-vis men.
- Building the mechanisms of an efficient and modern labour market both at the regional and national level, equally open to both women and men.

CONCLUSION

This Report argues that the rise of women is in fact a prerequisite for an Arab renaissance, inseparably and causally linked to the fate of the Arab world and its achievement of human development.

Despite Arab women's equal rights under international law, their demonstrated talents and achievements in different spheres of human activity and their priceless contributions to their families and society, many are not encouraged to develop and use their capabilities on an equal footing with men. In public life, cultural, legal, social, economic and political factors impede women's equal access to education, health, job opportunities, citizenship rights and representation. In private life, traditional patterns of upbringing and discriminatory family and personal status laws perpetuate inequality and subordination. At a time when the Arab world needs to build and tap the capabilities of all its peoples, fully half its human potential is often stifled or neglected.

In the short run, time-bound affirmative action to expand women's participation in society and dismantle centuries-old discrimination is both legitimate and imperative. However, the comprehensive advancement of Arab women requires accelerating and expanding past achievements through a collective renaissance project: a historic transformation that encompasses all of Arab society and aims to secure the citizenship rights of all Arabs, women and men equally.

The authors hope that the transformation they call for will be carried out under their preferred future scenario by taking the path of a vibrant human renaissance (izdihar) based on a peaceful process of negotiation for redistributing power and building good governance. Guaranteeing Arab societies the key freedoms of opinion, expression and assembly will facilitate the emergence of a dynamic, effective civil society as the vanguard of such a peaceful process that will avoid the impending disaster whose dark clouds are gathering in more than one key Arab country at this time.

The authors hope that the desired transformation will be carried out by taking the path of a vibrant human renaissance based on a peaceful process of negotiation for redistributing power and building good governance.

Part I

CHANGES IN HUMAN DEVELOPMENT IN THE ARAB COUNTRIES SINCE THE LAUNCH OF AHDR 2004

CHANGES IN HUMAN DEVELOPMENT IN THE ARAB COUNTRIES SINCE THE LAUNCH OF AHDR 2004

Introduction

Part one of the fourth Arab Human Development Report (AHDR 2005) reviews and evaluates national, regional and international events that the Report team believes have had a significant impact on the overall progress of human development in the Arab world since the third Report in this series was issued.

The previous such review, in the third Report, went as far as mid-2004. The present review thus covers the period from that time up to the end of January 2006.

Part one focuses chiefly on reform in the Arab world, currently the most urgent issue in the region and one that was examined extensively in AHDR 2004.

The succession of Arab Human Development Reports has given rise to a broad debate on reform in the Arab world and deepened awareness of the issue. Today not many, in or out of power, dispute the need for reform; rather, discussion has shifted to its nature. The Arab regimes themselves, as well as certain world powers, have proposed reform initiatives although these differ in goals and content. At the same time, forces of change in the various Arab countries have escalated their demand for true reform that goes beyond window dressing to address the profound problems from which the Arab States suffer: political repression, marginalisation and absence of the basic components of good governance.

Prospects for human development in the Arab world and the opportunities required for its achievement are closely linked to the realisation of the reforms needed to establish governance built on respect for human rights and guarantees of freedom. This chapter

therefore begins with an overview of the activities of the two main actors in such reforms, namely, the forces of civil society and Arab governments, in order to assess what impact these activities have had on the progress of change. This is followed by a review of how changes in the regional and global environment have affected opportunities for the realisation of human development in the Arab countries. Part one concludes with a survey of some positive instances of progress in human rights and freedom and in women's empowerment. In relation to building a knowledge society in the region, it underlines the importance of ensuring that the design of educational reforms contributes to reinforcing, and not eroding, human freedom.

THE REFORM PROCESS AND ISLAMIC MOVEMENTS: RECONCILING FREEDOM AND FAITH

The third Arab Human Development Report (AHDR 2004) argued that the way to establish truly free societies in the region is through broad and deep political reform centred on good governance and the protection of individual and collective freedoms.

For such a thoroughgoing reform process to start and succeed, three cardinal conditions will have to be met. The first is virtually a prerequisite: all reform groups must respect the key freedoms of opinion, expression and association in civil society, broadly defined (i.e., including both civil and political society).

The second condition entails broad acceptance of the principle that participation is the essence of the democratic process. The political process should include all forces

Today not many, in or out of power, dispute the need for reform; rather, discussion has shifted to its nature.

All reform groups must respect the key freedoms of opinion, expression and association in civil society.

in society, particularly those that command a strong popular following. Not only does the exclusion of any important societal force contradict the essence of democracy but, as experience in the Arab region shows, it can also lead to bitter civil strife, unacceptable to all.

The third condition is that all reform actors should respect the principles of universal human rights. The legal and institutional workings of the reform process and of any eventual society of freedom and good governance must safeguard minority rights under majority rule. A democratically elected majority must not be permitted under the law or in practice to tyrannise other social groups in violation of the principles of freedom and good governance.

Perhaps the factor that most divides Arab reformists on one side from some Arab regimes and foreign reform initiatives on the other is the variation in assent to these three conditions among the latter.

The issues raised here are of special importance when considering the growing role of Islamic movements in the Arab political arena yet, unfortunately, these issues are sometimes treated superficially.

No serious political power in the Arab world can ignore the fact that religion, particularly Islam, is an essential wellspring of the cultural and spiritual life of the Arab people. Any force that ever engaged in Arab politics and that neglected that lesson ended up as either marginal or defunct, whatever temporary successes it enjoyed.

In discussing politics, it is useful to recall one of the most relevant conclusions of AHDR 2004 regarding freedom and governance: there is no essential contradiction between the establishment of the society of freedom and good governance on the one hand and the ultimate purposes of sharia (Islamic law) on the other. Creating such a society would, however, require giving Islamic scholarship the scope to establish rules for harmonising freedom in its comprehensive sense with these ultimate purposes. This process of reconciliation would entail setting aside outmoded juristic interpretations that predominated in times of decline, and sanctioned persecution and despotism.

Encouraging and promoting independent interpretative scholarship (ijtihad) is therefore a basic requirement for wedding the ultimate goals of freedom, comprehensively defined, to those of Islamic law today. It follows that Islamic movements genuinely concerned with the advance of the Arab world will place this requirement high on their agendas.

It is equally important to keep in mind that Islamic movements present a wide spectrum of positions marked by very strong diversity. True, there are violent extremist groups that have opted out of the circle of peaceful change, adopting brute force as their means without qualms about terrorising innocent people. They have placed themselves outside the Arab reformist camp, which rejects their extreme methods and does not count such groups among those trying to build the Arab society of freedom and good governance. Yet these are the groups on which some western media outlets and official circles base their stereotypes and generalisations about Islam, Muslims and terrorism, under the rubric of "jihadist Islam". This characterisation is absurdly superficial and far from true.

The overwhelming majority of Islamic movements in Arab countries represent societal forces with a large following and deep roots in the population arising from their social and political work in the midst of the people for many years. Some have actively opposed a repressive status quo, and have at times faced persecution and torture by ruling regimes and, in the case of the occupied Palestinian territory, by the occupying power. Groups with considerable followings include the Muslim Brotherhood movement in Egypt and Jordan, the Justice and Development Party in Morocco and the Islamic Resistance Movement (Hamas) in the occupied Palestinian territory.[1]

In the last five decades, the internal dynamics of these movements, their relationship

---

[1] Owen Bowcott. "The Guardian." (2003). http://www.guardian.co.uk/alqaida/story/0,12469,881096,00.html (Accessed 1 May, 2006).
"Human Rights Watch." (2005). http://hrw.org/reports/2005/egypt0505/2.htm (Accessed 1 May, 2006).
"Amnesty International." (2001). http://web.amnesty.org/report2001/webmepcountries/PALESTINIAN+AUTHORITY?OpenDocument (Accessed 1 May, 2006).

to mainstream society and their positions on vital societal issues, on human rights and on good governance and democracy have undergone significant, progressive changes. The examples of Jordan, Morocco and, in a different context Turkey, illustrate this trend. Should such groups come to power, their changing platforms and profiles are likely to make them seem quite removed from religious government. Indeed some would argue that the participation of these movements in governance might enhance their civil, rather than their religious character.

Many middle-ground movements are seeing a growing number of relatively younger and enlightened leaders moving closer to the top of the organisational pyramid. Meanwhile, at their grass-roots base, they are witnessing a rising tide of popular demands for more democracy in their ranks and practices.

Notwithstanding these positive trends, middle-ground movements have yet to dispel public fears that their ascent to power would negatively impact freedom and good governance. Their positions on key questions such as the rights of women, especially in personal status matters, and the civil and political rights of minority communities and cultures, particularly religious minorities, are still pending. It is thus important for these movements to enact and adopt interpretative scholarship (ijtihad) in order to establish complete harmony between the ultimate and overall objectives of sharia and those of the society of freedom and good governance.

This argument leads one to a group diametrically opposed to the "jihadist" Islamists, namely, those Muslim scholars striving hard to achieve the reconciliation between freedom, good governance and Islamic law that has just been discussed. Their efforts put them at the centre of the Arab reformist camp. They include a model of government, inspired by enlightened Islamic interpretation and based on popular will, that would assure respect for the civil and political rights of women and minority groups. AHDR 2004 sought to present the outcome of this course of political development. Unfortunately, the significance of this group and its interpretative scholarship is little understood, particularly abroad.

Beyond these issues, perhaps the most serious obstacle to the reform process in the Arab countries is the kind of reaction that follows when democratic change produces results that are not "acceptable" to dominant forces both within the Arab world and without.

An important example is the rejection by certain Arab regimes and some global forces of the sweeping victory won by the Islamic Resistance Movement (Hamas) in the recent Palestinian legislative election, one that was widely agreed to have been free and fair. A similar case is the response to the success of the Muslim Brotherhood movement in the recent legislative election in Egypt, particularly in the first round, which evinced a wider degree of freedom and fairness.

Rejecting the outcome of a free and fair expression of popular will frustrates the aspirations of the majority, courts disillusionment with democracy and thus strengthens the hands of extremists. None of this advances the principles of reform and democratic electoral change as adopted in AHDR 2004.

OPEN SEASON ON REFORM, BUT THE "ARAB SPRING" HAS YET TO BLOOM

Observers have lauded certain political and social developments and reactions in Arab countries following the publication of AHDR 2004. Seeing such developments as important prologues to an Arab reform movement, they have styled this moment rather romantically as the "Arab Spring".

Viewed, however, from the perspective of freedom and good governance as defined in the previous Report, it is difficult to describe recent events in the Arab arena as the kind of widespread, thoroughgoing reform for which that Report called. Indeed, to do so would be to grasp at straws. To Arab citizens, it seems that the thick autumnal mists preventing true change have yet to dissipate despite the increasing protest against inaction by many governments and the intensifying demands for radical reform around the Arab world.

Many middle-ground (religious) movements are seeing a growing number of relatively younger and enlightened leaders moving closer to the top of the organisational pyramid.

Rejecting the outcome of a free and fair expression of popular will frustrates the aspirations of the majority, courts disillusionment with democracy and thus strengthens the hands of extremists.

THE ACCELERATING STRUGGLES OF CIVIL SOCIETY[2]

Arab civil society organisations (CSOs) have recently achieved what can be accurately called a qualitative leap in the pace, scope and impact of their activities. These organisations have demonstrated stronger solidarity with political movements and, at times, the ability to assume leadership roles in pursuit of political change. Their transformation has included establishing their presence more forcefully in the public mind by expressing themselves freely and vigorously through the independent press, satellite television, seminars, public and private meetings and, most importantly, via the acquisition of modern information and communication technology (ICT). Organisations and individuals alike have striven to use ICT effectively in order to express independent views and communicate with others. Hence the general crisis has a silver lining: it has led to processes of sifting and renewal and to new civic initiatives and new forms of public thought and action.

This major transformation has manifested itself most clearly in Egypt, which has witnessed significant changes in the political arena and how people respond to them. For example, the final months of 2004 saw the establishment of the Egyptian "Movement for Change". This movement has become known by its slogan, "Kifaya! (Enough!)", a reference to its opposition to the re-election of the President or transferring power to his son. The Egyptian public has been responsive to the Movement's watchwords "Enough! No to extension! No to hereditary succession!" and Egyptian cities have witnessed repeated demonstrations in its support. It has attracted public figures representing all colours of the political spectrum and has received support from major political parties and professional unions and organisations.

Other opposition forces have followed the Movement's lead, among them the Muslim Brotherhood, which staged large-scale demonstrations. In confrontation with security forces one demonstrator was killed.

Groups calling for change and reform have emerged among university professors, lawyers, journalists, writers and artists, while other forms of alliance have grown up among opposition factions. The most important of these include the National Rally for Democratic Change and the National Alliance for Reform and Change.

In Lebanon, following the assassination of the former Prime Minister, Rafiq al-Hariri, a mass movement took place that spanned most of the political spectrum and included CSOs and political movements. What has transpired in Lebanon by way of direct yet peaceful confrontations in the streets among various political groups has thrust a large number of Lebanese into political and civic life. Irrespective of their varying political and confessional leverage, groups demanding the modernisation of State and social institutions in order to give citizens due voice and representation have become part of the country's daily struggle and public debate.

In Bahrain, political associations and civic organisations led a widespread movement calling for more rapid political reform and rejecting the constitutional amendments issued in 2002. In April 2005, over thirty political and civic organisations signed a statement rejecting an anti-terrorism bill. They described it as a major setback for public and personal freedoms and a threat to the gains in freedom of expression, opinion and social and political action achieved by the Bahraini people over the previous four years.

Egypt's Kifayah! movement has been echoed in other Arab countries. Examples include Irhalu! (Get Out!) in Yemen and Khalas! (It's Over!) in Libya.

At the same time, in Syria, a number of opposition groups, as well as leading figures in civil and cultural life, issued the Damascus Declaration. This agreed text united various forces demanding democratic changes after the ruling party's conference accepted only limited reforms and sidestepped issues such as the democratisation of the constitution, the abandonment of one-candidate presidential referenda and the establishment of the principle of the peaceful alternation of power.

Arab CSOs have demonstrated stronger solidarity with political movements and, at times, the ability to assume leadership roles in pursuit of political change.

In Syria, a number of opposition groups, as well as leading figures in civil and cultural life, issued the Damascus Declaration.

---

[2] The present Report adopts here the broad definition of civil society used in AHDR 3, which covers both civil and political society as traditionally defined.

In January 2005, a group of Islamists in Kuwait announced the formation of the Umma Party as the State's first publicly proclaimed political party. In so doing, it was attempting to affirm the right to form political parties, which, it argues, is guaranteed by the Kuwaiti constitution although banned by the Government.

In the Sudan, the national arena has been the scene of widespread activity by political and civil society organisations amid moves to implement the peace agreement and approve a new constitution guaranteeing public freedoms. Most formerly banned parties have resumed public activity, while CSOs have been active on several fronts. However, the Government continues to try to curb civic opposition by new means. There have been instances of government supporters attacking their opponents, as happened when pro-Government students set fire to buildings at Omdurman Ahlia University in order to prevent student union elections that the Government feared would result in an opposition victory.

In Jordan, professional unions led a protest campaign against a new bill on professional associations, which would require these groups to obtain prior permission from the Ministry of the Interior to hold public gatherings and meetings and restrict discussion at these events to "professional issues". According to union representatives, the law would close off an avenue of free expression and assembly to the more than 150,000 members of these organisations.

In Saudi Arabia, a number of Arab and international human rights organisations have demanded the release of prisoners who have served their terms.[3] Several such organisations approached King Abdullah, on his accession to the throne, asking him to form a committee to follow up on the conditions of political prisoners in the context of his own initiatives. On 8 August 2005, the King issued a special amnesty that included four reform pioneers.[4] In addition, he called for a number of Muslim clerics to be assigned to open up discussions with prisoners accused of fomenting or practising violence, with the aim of persuading them, through amicable dialogue, to renounce its use against their fellow citizens.

One of the most important features of this new civic activism – in addition to the formation of popular groups merging disparate political hues – is the growth of pluralism. This trend is reflected in attempts to form unions and associations parallel to those falling under official control. These attempts can be seen as protests against many unions' loss of independence or effectiveness as well as a reinforcement of the concept of plurality among unions and civic organisations.

Another significant development during this period has been the growth of web-linked regional CSO networks that reinforce civic solidarity and cooperation across the Arab world. Their different goals range from the preservation of civil, social, economic or environmental rights to the elimination of corruption. The Arab Regional Resource Centre on Violence against Women (AMAN) (http://www.amanjordan.org/english/index.htm) in Jordan, for example, provides links to several web sites devoted to news coverage and analysis. These networks promote common understanding of issues and help activist non-governmental organisations (NGOs) to bridge differences, pool resources and work together. Their Internet presence is strengthened by such sites as the Arab Network for Human Rights Information (http://www.hrinfo.net/en/), the International Bureau for Humanitarian NGOs (IBH) (http://www.ibh.fr), the Sada ("Echo") web site for the defence of rights and freedoms (http://perso.wanadoo.fr/taysiralony/), and the Euro-Mediterranean Human Rights Network (http://www.euromedrights.net/). Such organisations have begun to move beyond joint activities on the Arab level to the formation of joint Arab-international pressure groups.

In sum, a number of Arab CSOs have started to demonstrate a new vitality and self-confidence. The trend represents genuine progress towards considerably more effective civic action, which in turn constitutes one of the most salient conditions for democratic transformation in the Arab world.

In Saudi Arabia, a number of Arab and international human rights organisations have demanded the release of prisoners who have served their terms.

One of the most important features of this new civic activism...is the growth of pluralism.

---

[3] The Arab Commission for Human Rights published in March 2005 a partial list identifying 120 such prisoners.

[4] Matruk al-Falih, 'Abdullah al-Hamid, 'Ali al-Dumayni and 'Abd al-Rahman al-Lahim.

GIVING THE LIE TO REFORM

The claim to be implementing reform often appears little more than a veil concealing the perpetuation of the current structures of oppression.

Several Arab regimes have announced political reform programmes, yet many initiatives announced barely scratch the surface of a reform agenda that would bring about a serious shift towards a society of freedom and good governance. Some reform initiatives have been emptied of any genuine content by being packaged with restrictions and "rules" that steadily limit the freedoms that they supposedly introduce. In other cases, authorities apparently pursuing reform continue with flagrant violations of the rights of those who call for it. To some observers, the claim to be implementing reform often appears little more than a veil concealing the perpetuation of the current structures of oppression.

Luminary: Hanan Ashrawi

Hanan Ashrawi is a Palestinian diplomat, negotiator and professor. She earned her Bachelor of Arts degree in English literature from the American University of Beirut, followed by a Ph.D. in medieval literature from the University of Virginia in 1971. She has been a political activist in a variety of organisations, including the General Union of Palestinian Women/Lebanon Branch (1967-1972) and the Information Office covering the Palestinian Liberation Organisation (PLO) (1968-1970).

The Israeli occupation forces prevented her from returning to the West Bank from 1967 to 1973. After her return, she worked as professor of English literature at Bir Zeit University (1974-1995), where she later served as Dean of the Faculty of Arts between 1986 and 1990, becoming the first woman to occupy this position at the University.

Her brilliance made itself felt upon her appointment as Official Spokesperson of the Palestinian Delegation to the Middle East Peace Process in 1991. Her eloquence and capacity to dialogue with the West in order to shed light on the plight of the Palestinian people made her a distinguished media spokesperson.

She became Palestinian Minister of Higher Education and Research and won renown for opposing some of the PLO policies, particularly in negotiations, and for advocating democracy and good governance. She resigned from the Palestinian Authority to establish her own NGO, the Palestinian Initiative for the Promotion of Global Dialogue and Democracy, also known as MIFTAH, and has led MIFTAH as Secretary-General since 1998.

Ashrawi is one of the founders of the Third Way electoral list, which ran for the Palestinian legislative elections in January 2006. The group obtained 2.41 per cent of the votes and was represented in the Palestinian Legislative Council through two seats.

Islah Jad

A Wave Of Mostly Flawed Elections

AHDR 2004 outlined a model of freedom and good governance that calls for representatives in governing institutions to be chosen by the people. This basic principle, however, assumes free and impartial elections based on citizenship for all in a societal context that guarantees the freedom to make a well thought out choice among alternatives that the citizen has been able to test through free discussion in the public sphere. Any elections in the Arab world that fulfil these conditions are to be welcomed and celebrated.

Yet good governance, according to AHDR 2004, is not limited to holding elections even if these are entirely sound. It is known that democratic arrangements, and particularly elections, can co-exist with open breaches of the model of freedom and good governance and specifically with violations of freedom in the inclusive sense that the present Report adopts, especially where national liberation is concerned.

In the occupied Palestinian territory, elections, which were not the first of their kind, were held to choose the president of the Palestinian Authority. The elections, which were the subject of close international scrutiny, saw more than one candidate run and were considered for the most part to have been fair. However, the Israeli authorities put major obstacles in the way of individual campaigns, even physically assaulting the second most prominent candidate at a checkpoint and preventing him from taking his campaign to Jerusalem.[5]

The Palestinian legislative elections of January 2006 shook political expectations through their conduct and results. In spite of a lack of experience, the hard conditions imposed by the occupation, and enormous outside pressures, the elections were conducted efficiently and responsibly. The victory of the Islamic Resistance Movement (Hamas), the strongest force within the opposition, is clearly significant in demonstrating both the peaceful transfer of power and the capacity of a political, economic and social programme to accommodate a pluralistic vision.

---

[5] Dr. Mustafa Barghouthi was detained for over two hours in East Jerusalem on the last day of the presidential campaign. "The Electronic Intifada." (2005). http://www.electronicintifada.net/v2/article3485.shtml (Accessed 14 April, 2006).

In occupied Iraq, elections to the transitional National Assembly took place in January 2005. These elections, which concerned the legislative body that was assigned the task of drafting the country's constitution, occurred in the midst of a severe breakdown of security and a violent terrorist campaign directed against both candidates and voters.

Administering elections had not been on the occupation authority's original agenda. Rather, according to plans announced in mid-November 2003, representatives of the national council were to be selected by caucuses in each governorate whose members would be named by organising committees assigned by the occupation forces. But the strong reactions of Iraqi civic and religious forces, notably Ayatollah 'Ali Sistani, to this model and their insistence on elections for the national legislature caused the occupation authorities to change their plans in line with public demand.

After the elected Assembly prepared a draft constitution that was approved by a referendum on 15 October 2005, elections of a new national assembly took place on 15 December 2005. The elections were characterised by wide participation, with nearly 70 per cent of Iraqis voting. However, according to the head of the Independent Electoral High Commission, the elections were marred by some problems, including forgery and the theft of some ballot boxes (Al-Sharq al-Awsat, London, 16/12/2005).

In Saudi Arabia, municipal elections were held for the first time. These 2005 elections were marred, in the view of the present report by a damaging flaw: the exclusion of women. Add to this the fact that voters were allowed to choose only half the members of the municipal council, and it is clear that a long way remains before all Saudi citizens elect a national legislative assembly in its entirety. Despite this, the elections represented the first steps towards reform inasmuch as they stirred a national dialogue about popular participation.

In Lebanon, parliamentary elections took place in the spring of 2005 for the first time after the withdrawal of Syrian forces.

In Egypt, the ruling regime made much of the President's request that one article of the constitution (Article 76) be amended to allow for multi-candidate presidential elections. The proposal was touted as the beginning of political reform. However, the amended article emerged weighted down with an array of restrictions that may make it little more than a formalised codification of the existing referendum system for choosing the president.

The amendment was put to a popular referendum, which some opposition forces called to boycott, while an independent judicial commission formed by the Judges' Club concluded that the referendum was sullied by widespread forgery and manipulation (Box I-1). On the day of the referendum, demonstrators protesting peacefully were assaulted.

Egypt's presidential elections were held on 7 September 2005. Some licensed opposition parties boycotted them, while the heads of certain other licensed parties, many of them marginal, took part. The list of candidates thus included the ruling president and nine others. When the results were announced, they revealed a landslide victory for the ruling president, who obtained 88.5 per cent of the votes. His two most important rivals received less than 10 per cent. The most notable aspect of the election, however, is that, according to official statistics, the participation rate came to no more than one fourth of those entitled to vote. Few observers were surprised by the public's reluctance after decades of sapping the political vitality of society by obstructing key

In Saudi Arabia, municipal elections were held for the first time.

According to official statistics, the participation rate (in Egypt's presidential election) came to no more than one fourth of those entitled to vote.

BOX I-1

Judges' Club Commission Concludes: "The Will of the Electorate Misrepresented".

- Subcommittees observed low voter turnout. Many subcommittees had no voters whatsoever appear before them, while the average turnout before the remaining subcommittees was no more than 3 per cent[6] of those listed on their rosters.
- The chairmanships of 95 per cent of the subcommittees were assigned to

government employees who enjoyed no autonomy or immunity, and who were intimidated by members of the police force. Such subcommittees altogether escaped the oversight of the judiciary and became arenas for violations of the law and falsification of the facts relating to voter turnout and opinions.

Source: Judges' Club Commission report, in Arabic at:
"Al-araby." (2005). "Egypt's Conscience". http://www.al-araby.com/articles/966/050703-966-jrn01.htm (Accessed 3 April, 2006).

---

[6] According to official results of the referendum, the participation rate came to more than 50 per cent.

While Arab governments announced a spate of reforms, the situation of individual and collective human rights worsened during the period under review as violations continued to increase.

Women have endured a double portion of suffering under foreign occupation.

freedoms and imposing emergency laws and given the paucity of alternatives. Subsequently, parliamentary elections were held in three phases in November and December 2005, but they were marred by many flaws.

According to the monitoring judges, the results of these elections were adjusted to favour the ruling party candidates in at least two major districts. The details of the forgery were exposed in an article[7] published by Councillor Nuha al-Zayni, one of the observers monitoring the elections in Damanhur.[8]

Some judges monitoring the elections as well as numerous voters were subject to assaults. This led the judges to call for a full monitoring of all phases of the elections, the formation of an independent judicial police team and the protection of elections by the army, as provided for under Egyptian law.[9]

In districts where ruling party candidates were most likely to lose, especially in the second and third phases, it has been reported that the security forces prevented voters from reaching designated ballot stations, which led, in some instances, to violent clashes resulting in injuries and deaths.[10]

In places, the votes of the poor, especially women, were purchased through bribes, a phenomenon some called "Ballot Slavery".[11]

As far as promoting the number of women in Parliament is concerned, the ruling party had only six female candidates on its list of 444 candidates. In terms of political opposition, the Muslim Brotherhood made very significant progress; in the final results announced, the ruling party did not obtain the sweeping majority that it had previously enjoyed in Parliament (excluding the party's independent candidates).

SUMMARY

Reflecting on these developments, the latest wave of elections in a number of Arab countries may be cautiously welcomed. They may presage the authorities' endorsement of the right to popular choice, especially in those Arab countries where elections were once viewed as a kind of political heresy. Nevertheless, some observers believe that "managed elections"[12] simply represent the newest way of buttressing regimes loyal to the West (Milne, 2005). What is certain is that electoral reform has a long way to go before elections can become a component of the society of freedom and good governance. The creation of such a society still requires extensive, radical reform, particularly in legal and political structures, changes that go beyond the holding of elections.

WORSENING HUMAN RIGHTS VIOLATIONS IN THE ARAB COUNTRIES

While Arab governments announced a spate of reforms, the situation of individual and collective human rights worsened during the period under review as violations continued to increase.

VIOLATIONS RESULTING FROM OCCUPATION AND ARMED DOMESTIC CONFLICTS

The worst violations occurred in the context of foreign occupations, which are themselves grave violations of human rights.

Women have endured a double portion of suffering under foreign occupation on account of several factors. First, women are more vulnerable to deterioration in humanitarian conditions. Second, women shoulder a dual responsibility for their families when

---

[7] To read the full text of her testimony in Arabic see:
Nuha al-Zayni. (2005). http://admins.20at.com/masr/shhada-noha0zene1.htm (Accessed 10 March, 2006).

[8] Amira Howeidy. "Aljazeera." (2005). http://english.aljazeera.net/NR/exeres/A8A39240-04C7-4CE5-8164-7569EB6EA4A8.htm (Accessed 9 May, 2006).

[9] "Aljazeera." (2005). http://english.aljazeera.net/NR/exeres/D153BDBA-873B-4543-B273-396F53B17B0E.htm (Accessed 12 April, 2006).

[10] Daniel Williams. "Washington Post." (2005). http://www.washingtonpost.com/wp-dyn/content/article/2005/12/07/AR2005120702611.html (Accessed 1 June 2006).

[11] "Al Arabiya." (2005). http://www.alarabiya.net/Articles/2005/11/27/18990.htm (Accessed 26 May, 2006).

[12] i.e., elections whose results are tampered with.

breadwinners are absent as a result of arrests and acts of violence, and third, they suffer from the loss of security and the spread of rape, which often accompany chaos and the rule of force. For example, reports convey a wretched picture of the women of Iraq. The same is true of the occupied Palestinian territory, where women have faced new waves of homelessness as a result of the destruction of homes and have been forced to deliver babies at Israeli checkpoints while waiting to be allowed through.

In another context, tens of thousands of civilians have continued to fall victim to armed domestic conflicts. Before the Sudan celebrated the peace agreements, which it signed to end the longest armed conflict ever witnessed on the African continent, Darfur had overtaken southern Sudan as a seat of disturbance in the country. The new conflict has brought devastation, murder and ruin to the residents of the region. Both government forces and their allies on one side and the rebels on the other have been implicated in human rights violations described as tantamount to war crimes and crimes against humanity[13].

In Somalia, an agreement reached among most Somali factions with support from the Intergovernmental Authority on Development (IGAD), the establishment of a new National Council and the choice of a president of the republic have not yet brought an end to domestic warfare. Rather, the country has remained a victim of armed conflict and lawlessness.

The Government of one Arab country launched a large military campaign to put down a rebellion led by the leader of an opposition organisation in a province. In the course of this campaign, government troops employed excessive force, which provoked the rebellion to flare up again in a quest for retribution on behalf of those killed. The Minister of the Interior announced 525 fatalities among army and security forces and citizens in addition to 2,708 wounded but failed to indicate the number of victims among the movement's followers, estimated by various sources to be in the hundreds. In addition, large numbers of citizens were arrested.

Women have been subjected to brutal assaults in the context of armed domestic conflicts. Some of these have taken place during attacks and counter-attacks on their towns in Darfur and Somalia. The most conspicuous incidents, however, have taken place during flight and emigration, and many women have been raped and physically assaulted in migration centres and shelters.

Political conflicts have constituted still another locus of human rights violations. In this connection, three Arab governments have disclosed attempted coups, which have led to trials and harsh sentences. Although one ruler later pardoned those convicted, a noted personality in that country paid for her investigation of the trials with an eighteen-month prison term. She was released after serving six months of her sentence, following an Arab and international solidarity campaign on her behalf.

VIOLATIONS OF PUBLIC LIBERTIES AND FREEDOMS OF OPINION AND EXPRESSION

There has been growing pressure on public freedoms both domestically and internationally. In October 2004, setting a dangerous precedent, a Gulf State issued a decree that strips members of a local clan – a branch of a tribe that has historically resided in the state - of their nationality. The decision affected no fewer than 972 heads of households. It also included all members of their extended families – a total of 5,266 individuals – or the entire sub-tribe. This decision was followed by government measures to have these individuals dismissed from their jobs, to require them to forfeit the residences in which they had lived as citizens and to deprive them of all privileges associated with citizenship. These benefits included health care, education, electricity, water and the right to engage in commerce. In addition, tribe members were required, under various security measures, to regularise their situations as non-citizens. The authorities justified their decision by arguing that the tribe has its origins in another country, whose

Political conflicts have constituted still another locus of human rights violations.

There has been growing pressure on public freedoms both domestically and internationally.

---

[13] To read the Report of the International Commission of Inquiry on Darfur to the United Nations Secretary-General pursuant to UN Security Council resolution 1564 (2004) see: "Global Policy" (2005). http://www.globalpolicy.org/security/issues/sudan/2005/darfurcoi.pdf (Accessed 31 May, 2006).

citizenship they still retained. According to the Arab Commission for Human Rights, many wives among the tribe were obliged to ask for divorces in order to retain their citizenship[14]. In response to local and international pressures, the authorities eventually resolved the issue by re-granting citizenship to some members and naturalising the rest.

In another country legislative reforms aimed at eliminating legal provisions that strip journalists of their freedoms have been slow in coming. Rather than following through on the President's promise at the previous ruling Party conference to rescind freedom-limiting penalties aimed at the press, certain political reform bills have actually made such penalties harsher. An example is Article 48 of the Political Rights Organisation Act. It stiffens the punishment for anyone found guilty of publishing or broadcasting false reports on the elections or the referendum with the intention of influencing their outcome. The Article is thus an invitation to restrict freedom by prosecuting for real or perceived intentions.

According to the Arab Organisation for Human Rights, other countries have proposed draft laws that tighten restrictions on press freedoms. The region overall sees the highest prevalence of murder or abduction of journalists and other media personnel in areas affected by armed conflict[15]. The Arab Commission for Human Rights has published a partial list that includes the names of 72 journalists who have lost their lives in Iraq since 8 April, 2003 as well as those of nine others who are missing (al-'Azawi and Manna', in Arabic, 2005, 25). Numerous newspapers have been stopped, and journalists have been arrested in many Arab countries. Al-Jazeera has had its licenses revoked in several Arab countries, while some of its correspondents have been harassed and persecuted. In one instance, Ahmad Mansur, a leading journalist working for the channel, was assaulted in Cairo in November 2005.

Similarly, al-Manar has been forbidden to broadcast in some Western States, and eight staff of the Al Arabiyah channel have died in Iraq, three of them directly as a result of action by the occupation forces.

On 26 September 2005, the Spanish National Court issued prison sentences ranging from six to twenty-seven years against what has been called the Syrian-Spanish Cell. A three-judge panel of the National Court heard the case in a special court house under tight security. The evidence included testimony of 107 witnesses - more than half of them police officers. Eighty-two NGOs and professional unions and more than 1,300 international personalities consider these sentences to be unjust, rejecting the politicisation of the case in the context of the "war on terror". The Supreme Court has consented to hear an appeal[16].

The targeting of the Fourth Estate and modern means of communication has brought many in the region to see the need for alliances between the media and NGOs. There are new forms of resistance and activism that rely on interaction and cooperation between the two in order to create democratic consciousness, oppose corruption, and deepen and spread the concept of participation in responsibility and decision-making.

TARGETING REFORMERS AND HUMAN RIGHTS ACTIVISTS

In most Arab States, reformers and human rights advocates have become visible targets of oppression. They often face prosecution and arrest, and sometimes murder. Obstacles to their work continue to multiply. Such impediments take the form of laws that restrict freedom of expression and association. Most civic and union-related activities are legally banned. This is the situation in one Gulf state where scores of individuals were tried on charges of forming a religious organisation and

---

In most Arab States, reformers and human rights advocates have become visible targets of oppression.

Most civic and union-related activities are legally banned.

[14] The Arab Commission for Human Rights and the delegate of the Office of the United Nations High Commissioner for Human Rights were promised that any injustices in this file would be investigated. The file constituted a real test for the National Human Rights Commission, which made strenuous efforts to put an end to the tragedy. "The Office of the United Nations High Commissioner." (2005). http://www.unhcr.org/cgi-bin/texis/vtx/rsd/rsddocview.html?tbl=RSDCOI&id=441821a525&count=1 (Accessed 9 March, 2006).

[15] Reports from Reporters Without Borders and statements by the Federation of Arab Journalists concerning victims of armed conflicts (www.rsf.org).

[16] Peter Bergen. "Arab Commission for Human Rights." (2005). http://www.achr.nu/art63.htm (Accessed 16 March, 2006).
Al Goodman. "CNN."(2005). http://www.cnn.com/2005/WORLD/europe/09/26/spain.terror.trial/index.html (Accessed 26 September, 2005).

received harsh sentences before being pardoned by the ruler following unprecedented popular protests. In a number of Arab countries, several applications for permission to form human rights organisations were put on hold. On the other hand, the UAE consented to the establishment of a Human Rights Association at the start of 2006.

A Mashreq country has seen numerous reformers and human rights activists arrested or detained. One reformer died in mysterious circumstances, scores of citizens have been detained without trial, and a number of people with Islamic leanings have been arrested on their return to the country. The authorities have also closed down all civil society forums established during the last few years in what was known as the "Spring". In June 2005, officials arrested the board of directors of a civic Forum, the last such body remaining, after learning that a letter from the leader of the banned Muslim Brotherhood had been read at one of its meetings. Previously, the Government had sought to tighten its restrictions on the Forum by obstructing its activities and flooding its meetings with "plants" (individuals associated with government security branches and government supporters) in order to steer its discussions in a certain direction. The Forum is still forbidden to hold monthly meetings. The authorities have released five of those arrested during the "Spring", after they had served a fourth of their sentences. At the same time, they have refused to release a number of other detained reformers and a number of Kurdish and Islamist cadres whose release has been demanded by human rights organisations.

In a North African country, authorities have continued to put obstacles in the work of civic bodies and independent professional associations serving attorneys, journalists and university professors. The authorities also refuse to recognise independent labour unions and human rights organisations. Amnesty International reported that activities of the Arab Human Rights Institute ground to a halt as a result of the freeze on its funding under the country's anti-terrorism law and following the authorities' objection to a member of the Institute's board of directors. The Government moved to intercept the Institute's mail and to prevent the distribution of its publications. After a broad-based civil solidarity campaign in both the region and worldwide, the authorities stopped their harassment, eased their restrictions and allowed the Institute to receive funds as before.

As another country prepared to host the World Summit on the Information Society (WSIS) in 2005, international human rights organisations complained in an article published on the Amnesty International website ("Hollow words on Human Rights at UN Information Society Summit") that the "appalling record of the host country of WSIS in Phase II – has seen cyber-dissidents jailed, Internet sites censored, human rights organisations harassed and independent news agencies closed. It is stifling the very rights and freedoms of expression the Summit is intended to promote".

It is not, however, alone in this respect, according to a report entitled "The Internet in the Arab world: a new arena for oppression" issued by the Arab Network for Human Rights Information in June 2005 and based on a survey of eleven Arab countries. The Network survey found that relative freedom in Internet use is allowed in only three States: Jordan, Qatar and the UAE. Remaining States do their utmost to control circulation of Internet content and spend heavily on Internet surveillance, "not to mention their use of new methods…such as source control by means of electronic filtering programmes…In addition, some states exercise a monopoly over Internet service provision… [in addition to] fabricating cases and jailing those who cross undefined red lines on the basis of flimsy allegations".

In a Gulf state, civil society and human rights organisations have also been subjected to official pressures. One example was when the Centre for Human Rights was threatened with legal action after participating in meetings held by the United Nations High Commissioner for Human Rights in Geneva in May 2005. At the beginning of February 2006, two-year sentences were issued against twelve Centre activists following a demonstration at the Airport. On 4 June 2005, a female activist, was brought to trial on charges of offending the judiciary, a step that led local and international organisations to call for solidarity with her. The

In a number of Arab countries, several applications for permission to form human rights organisations were put on hold.

Government also refuses to recognise a large number of civic organisations resulting from public initiatives. These include the Journalists' Association, the Scholars Council, the National Committee for Martyrs and Victims of Torture, the Unemployment Committee, the Women's Petition Committee, the Union of Women, and the Social Partnership for Combating Violence against Women.

In North Africa, one country has witnessed an increase in the violent beating and ill treatment of reform advocates, including the editor of an opposition newspaper[17] and four female journalists[18], and similar phenomena were witnessed in another country in that sub-region[19].

Two journalists[20] were assassinated in Lebanon and an attempt was made on the life of a third, while another journalist was assassinated in Libya in mysterious circumstances and the head of an organisation active in Darfur was detained.

RESTRICTING THE RIGHTS TO PEACEFUL ASSEMBLY AND TO ORGANISE

Limits on the public's exercise of the right to peaceful assembly have steadily increased. One Mashreq country rejected 70 per cent of all applications for permission to organise peaceful marches during 2004, according to its National Centre for Human Rights. Another country broke up peaceful marches calling for reform and arrested hundreds of demonstrators. A third forcibly dispersed a symbolic vigil in commemoration of the Universal Declaration of Human Rights and arrested some of those who took part in it. The decision to ban demonstrations in yet a fourth country has remained in effect.

The tragedy that occurred when a strike in an Arab capital by asylum-seeking Sudanese on 30 December 2005 was mishandled, as a result of which 25 people lost their lives, has shown that civil society can act not only on domestic issues but on inter-Arab ones as well. A non-governmental gathering assembled in solidarity with the victims and to initiate legal recourse.

In a Gulf country, authorities hindered demonstrations seeking reform. A Political Organisations Act was passed that political and human rights organisations consider restrictive of freedoms and in violation of international charters and covenants, spurring six of the country's most prominent political organisations to close their offices voluntarily for three days in July 2005.

In a Maghreb country, authorities used force to disperse demonstrations staged to criticise the Government's invitation to Israeli Premier, Ariel Sharon, to attend the World Summit on the Information Society in that country. (The suppression of these demonstrations was not condemned in Western circles.) An attorney remains in detention for having written an article on the subject. In another protest, prisoners from an opposition party, who have been detained for more than a decade and a half under harsh conditions, went on prolonged hunger strikes.

In the area of the right to organise, the Political Parties Committee in one country licensed two new parties but rejected applications from three others, according to their National Council on Human Rights. In the Arab Maghreb, another country also refused to license new parties (Arab Commission for Human Rights in Arabic, 2005), and the Government of yet another denied receiving an application to establish the Green Party, thereby hindering its formation.

UNFRIENDLY INTERNATIONAL AND REGIONAL ENVIRONMENTS

Global developments since the events of 9/11/2001 have led to mindsets and patterns of conduct that have not helped to advance the essential components of freedom and good governance. Indeed, some related developments

Limits on the public's exercise of the right to peaceful assembly have steadily increased

Global developments since the events of Nine-Eleven have led to mindsets and patterns of conduct that have not helped to advance the essential components of freedom and good governance.

---

[17] On 1 November 2004, the executive editor-in-chief of an opposition newspaper was assaulted. The incident was covered by all of the newspapers as well as in reports and statements issued by human rights organisations, the journalists' union and the National Council for Human Rights.

[18] Four female journalists were assaulted on 25 May 2005.

[19] Communist Party chief was the victim of a severe attack on 12 October 2004, while two women political activists were subjected to a similar assault.

[20] Journalist Samir Qasir, a noted political commentator for al-Nahar newspaper, was assassinated on 2 June 2005 in a car explosion, and Gibran Tueni, Chairman of the Board of al-Nahar, was assassinated on 12 December 2005.

may have actively obstructed that important cause. They include the emergence, outside the United Nations framework, of parallel structures in international affairs that rest on temporary alliances focused on a single tragedy and time rather than on the universal rule of law and justice. They extend to the signing of bilateral agreements that could inhibit the work of the International Criminal Court and to the creation of alliances that could limit the scope of international treaties concerned with development and the environment. This conduct has tarnished the image of the superpower by allowing discrimination, double standards and the precedence of vested interest over justice. It also represents an ideological misappropriation of human rights to justify impediments to development, including pre-emptive war and solutions to combat terrorism concentrating exclusively on security.

Successive events on the international and regional levels indicate the increased unfriendliness of the international environment to change in the direction of freedom and good governance as conceived in the Arab Human Development Reports, particularly AHDR 2004, and, most notably, as that concept relates to national liberation.

A UNITED STATES LAW TO DETER ANTI-SEMITISM

Prominent among such international and regional events was the passing of the Global Anti-Semitism Review Act of October 2004 sponsored by the current United States Administration. Following its passage, the latter began monitoring, through a specialised office established within the Department of State, what it classifies as "anti-Semitism" throughout the world.

There is no dispute that targeting the adherents of a specific religion or inciting harm against them is reprehensible and should be fought by all means. Yet from the perspective of the present Report, it would have been preferable had a measure of this kind covered harassment or incitement against all religions and all ethnic groups, anywhere in the world.

What is of concern here is the 10th finding of Section 2 of the Act: "Anti-Semitism has at times taken the form of vilification of Zionism, the Jewish national movement, and incitement against Israel". This could result in treating any criticism of Israel's practices in the occupied Palestinian territory or any condemnation of its discriminatory practices against Israeli citizens of Arab origin as acts falling under this law. Some Israeli academics share this position, noting that "[T]he accusation of anti-Semitism has become a powerful tool for silencing opposition to Israel's oppressive policies" (Kimmerling, 2003).

Such provisions of the Act could result in Israel imposing its views on all aspects related to the conflict, which would impede negotiations towards a permanent, just and peaceful resolution of the Arab Israeli conflict.

THE ISSUE OF TERRORISM AND ITS CONSEQUENCES FOR FREEDOM IN THE ARAB WORLD

The escalation of terrorist operations in Arab countries and the arbitrary nature of the "war on terror" and its collateral effects have severely impacted the lives and freedoms of Arabs. Devastating internal violence has continued in a number of Arab countries, bringing to mind the disturbing beginnings of the "impending disaster" against which AHDR 2004 warns.

Terrorism and some actions to confront it have aggravated the human rights and development dilemma in the region. The attacks on civilians of any nationality are abhorrent and to be condemned. Acts of terrorism have continued in Arab countries, including Algeria, Bahrain, Jordan, Kuwait, Lebanon, Saudi Arabia, Syria and Yemen. In Iraq, such acts must be distinguished from acts of legitimate resistance. During the period covered by the present Report, such acts spread for the first time to Mauritania and Qatar and resumed in Egypt[21] after having been in abeyance there

Terrorism and some actions to confront it have aggravated the human rights and development dilemma in the region.

---

[21] Egypt witnessed a series of terrorist acts during the period covered by the present Report. The first, on 8 October 2004, involved simultaneous attacks in three different areas of the Sinai Peninsula. Five Egyptians and 34 foreign tourists, most of them Israelis, were killed in the attacks. The second took place on 7 April 2005 in the Azhar neighbourhood of Cairo, killing three people. The third took place on 30 April 2005 in two simultaneous incidents in central Cairo.

*Thousands of
citizens have been
arrested merely
on administrative
decisions, some of
whom have been
subjected to various
forms of torture and ill
treatment.*

*Whereas violence
is the first choice of
terrorists, it is the last
option for resistance.*

*Counter-violence on
the streets and the
emergence of brutal
factions in reaction
to the violence of
occupation lead
common people to
lock themselves up in
the past.*

since the end of 1997. Thousands have been killed or wounded by such acts of terrorism.

Citing terrorist threats, governments have consolidated emergency laws[22] and passed additional anti-terrorism legislation. Scores of those being pursued by such governments have been killed, while thousands of citizens have been arrested merely on administrative decisions, some of whom have been subjected to various forms of torture and ill treatment. Thousands of others remain in detention even after being acquitted of the charges against them or completing their prison terms, as in Egypt (National Council on Human Rights, in Arabic, 2005). Dozens of suspects have been hauled before emergency courts that often fail to meet the requirements of justice and fairness.

Sources have revealed that some Arab governments have been involved in interrogations and torture connected with United States-led investigations of individuals suspected of terrorist activity via an "archipelago" of clandestine detention centres overseen by the United States Central Intelligence Agency (Amnesty International, in Arabic, 2005a).

The war on terror

Amid the "war on terror", following the events of September 11, 2001, the Arab region in general and its Islamic movements in particular have been roundly labelled as breeding grounds for terrorism. This war has blurred the distinction between what may rightly be termed the terrorising of innocents on one hand, which is an affront to the human conscience and morally unacceptable, and, on the other, the legitimate resistance to foreign occupation and exclusionary regimes as sanctioned by the Geneva Conventions and resolutions of the United Nations. Whereas violence is the first choice of terrorists, it is the last option for resistance, which usually does not resort to it until it has exhausted all other options through the media, diplomacy, demonstrations and, ultimately, civil disobedience.

It is worth recalling at this point the definition of terrorism taken up by the United Nations General Assembly at its sixtieth session as "criminal acts intended or calculated to provoke a state terror in the general public [or] a group of persons". According to the relevant resolution, such acts are "unjustifiable, whatever the considerations of a political, philosophical, ideological, racial, ethnic, religious or other nature that may be invoked to justify them" (A/RES/60/43).

Occupation authorities have tended to brand any resistance to their actions as terrorist activity. Efforts by some States to link their own pursuits to the United States-led war on terror have further obscured the definition of terror, posing the additional risk that this war may be hijacked by foreign interests. The [former] Israeli Prime Minister, Ariel Sharon, seized upon the war on terrorism and the vague American definition of "terrorism with a global reach" that has been both expedient and convenient in his efforts to suppress the Palestinians (Brzezinski, 2004, 32). This ambiguity in the definition of terror, which accommodates the special agendas of occupation powers, has eroded chances that such a war might actually eradicate terror.

The collateral effects of the "war on terror" could severely damage prospects for human development in the Arab world. Counter-violence on the streets and the emergence of brutal factions in reaction to the violence of occupation lead common people to lock themselves up in the past and immerse themselves in social conservatism. The results for Arab women, particularly under occupation, are grave.

Anti-terrorism laws in the Arab countries

Under the influence of the anti-terror campaign, new laws have been passed or existing laws amended so as to criminalise acts not previously viewed as such, strengthen the penalties for acts described as terrorist, relax the restrictions imposed on prosecution procedures and reduce the guarantees given to suspects.

---

[22] The provisional government in Iraq imposed a state of emergency in November 2004 and renewed it in March 2005. States of emergency have also continued in effect in Algeria, Egypt, Syrian and the Sudan.

In Bahrain, for example, there has been heated discussion within the Foreign Affairs, Defence and National Security Committee of the House of Representatives of a draft anti-terrorism bill that some Committee members believe conflicts with the Government's reform agenda and with ratification of the two covenants of the International Bill of Human Rights. This is particularly so with regard to the bill's stiffened penalties, adoption of the death penalty, and restriction of freedoms, especially freedom of thought. The latter may lead to treating every dissenter as a terrorist. The bill criminalises criticism of the constitution or demands for its amendment, even from members of the House of Representatives and even though such criticisms or demands fall squarely within their constitutional powers.[23]

At the same time, the campaign on terrorism has led to disregard for the enforcement of certain laws. Thus, although Algeria has introduced into its penal code a text that explicitly outlaws the torture of detainees, in some instances it has taken no action to enforce this prohibition nor has it investigated allegations of torture.[24]

Extraordinary courts

Most Arab States refer terrorism cases to special judiciaries, such as military tribunals, State security courts, and court-martials. Such courts are believed to lack proper standards for ensuring just trials, usually contenting themselves with initial investigations in the course of which confessions are sometimes extracted under torture while suspects who appear before them are deprived of the right to prepare a defence. The verdicts handed down by such courts are not subject to review.[25]

Illegal procedures

In addition to passing or drafting legislation that conflicts with laws that lay out the fundamental principles governing criminal trials,[26] which are highly stringent to begin with, governments in the Arab world often adopt administrative steps that do the same. For example, procedures imposed in the course of international cooperation in combating terrorism are frequently in violation of international law and, in some cases, of domestic law as well. Such violations are manifested in greater lenience towards police action such as night raids, torture and the extraction of testimony by force, incarceration in illegal prisons where torture is carried out, wiretapping without the permission of a court, indefinite detention without recognised charge, examination of suspects' bank accounts and extrajudicial executions.

Deteriorating conditions for women

Despite some progress in improving the situation of women, terrorism and the campaign against it have contributed to an overall collapse of security and acute setbacks in the pursuit of democracy of which women have been the primary victims. This is particularly evident in areas of armed conflict and, most notably, in Iraq. Instances of abusive treatment of women prisoners by some United States troops in Iraq and, in particular, in Abu Ghraib prison, are cases in point.

The absurd war on thought and belief

Following the war on terrorist organisations, chiefly Al-Qa'ida, in the course of which human rights violations have occurred, the most recent policy orientation in the campaign has been to attack what the United States Administration refers to as "aggressive ideologies".[27] Observers

Terrorism, and the campaign against it, have contributed to an overall collapse of security and acute setbacks in the pursuit of democracy of which women have been the primary victims.

---

[23] Bahraini newspaper al-Wasat, 25 April, 2005.

[24] "The United Nations Special Rapporteur on Torture indicated that Algerian authorities had denied, without investigation, the claims of torture which had been brought before them. Moreover, the Special Rapporteur was unable to visit Algeria despite his long-standing request to do so" (Amnesty International Annual Report, 2005a, 123).

[25] Such extraordinary courts can issue death sentences.

[26] The importance of the fundamental principles governing criminal trials lies in the fact that they regulate the means by which society defends itself against crises. At the same time, such means, even if technical in nature, are nevertheless related to the matter of human rights, and their success depends on their consistency with the legal and social system of the country concerned.

[27] President George Bush's speech before the United Nations General Assembly, 14 September 2005.

have found it difficult to distinguish between attacking beliefs thus designated and opposing freedom of thought and belief itself, a basic human right. Nonetheless, discussion has begun in more than one Arab country of how ideas and beliefs might fuel terror and of the need to impose restrictions on them. This at a time when, if Arab states have anything to complain about in this regard, it is likely an excess of restrictions rather than a dearth of them. This is not to deny that beliefs may serve as a motivation for committing terrorist acts, and that they may be used to incite others to commit crimes. However, it is unreasonable to maintain that ideas can be confronted by warlike means; rather, they must be confronted by other ideas that are not hostile or antagonistic towards others. Moreover, the act of fomenting crime is subject to criminal law no matter what its ostensible motives happen to be.

Indeed, waging war on beliefs and ideas held by individuals who do not belong to terrorist organisations and who are unconnected with any violent practice could be described as an act of absurdity and an attack on human rights.

Combating terrorism and respecting human rights

Combating terrorism is not inconsistent with respect for human rights. On the contrary, it is an integral part of such respect, for the right to life and personal security is matched by an obligation on the part of the State to ensure citizens' well-being and their security. Consequently, and in exceptional circumstances, the State may, in order to preserve the security

of society, place restrictions on individual freedom to the extent that is necessary and beneficial. The Berlin Declaration contains the standards to which the State must adhere in waging war on terrorism.[28]

The elimination of terrorism calls for a political decision that abides by the entitlements to human rights and justice in resolving international disputes within the framework of international law. Similarly, it calls for the adoption of a plan for human development in its comprehensive sense and a commitment to observe the rule of law and truth (within the limits set by the Berlin Declaration). In addition, it requires that Arab societies undertake a critical, honest and enlightened review of their heritage. After all, human rights will not be established unless human beings, whatever their background, are viewed as the pivotal and central value, unless the values of dialogue are supported and reinforced, and unless there is acceptance of a pluralistic society.

THE PALESTINIAN CAUSE

Gaza: disengagement does not end occupation

The end to colonisation and settlement in the Gaza Strip and the withdrawal of Israeli troops on 12 September 2005 were a rare exception to the deteriorating situation faced by the Palestinian people. Yet the withdrawal, rather than signifying a breakthrough in efforts to reach a settlement, was fraught with bad intentions. The latter were revealed by Dov Weissglas, senior diplomatic adviser to the Israeli Prime Minister, when he disclosed that the real reason for the withdrawal was to halt the peace process and impede the creation of the State of Palestine (Box I-2).

The withdrawal took place as part of the unilateral disengagement plan launched by the Israeli Prime Minister to relieve Israel of the security burdens entailed by the occupation and, evidently, to enable it to avoid involvement in serious negotiations aimed at a settlement. At the same time, Israel has reserved the right to intervene militarily in Gaza and to maintain

---

BOX I-2

The Gaza Withdrawal Is the Formaldehyde to Freeze the Peace Process

In an interview with Ha'aretz, Dov Weisglass states:

"The disengagement (from Gaza) is actually formaldehyde. It supplies the amount of formaldehyde that's necessary so that there will not be a political process with the Palestinians".

"The significance (of the withdrawal from Gaza) is the freezing of the political process. And when you freeze that process you prevent the establishment of a Palestinian state and you prevent a discussion about the refugees, the borders and Jerusalem. Effectively, this whole package that is called the Palestinian State, with all that it entails, has been removed from our agenda indefinitely".

Source: Shavit, 2004.

---

[28] The Berlin Declaration, which addresses the theme of human rights in the context of the war on terror, was issued on 29 August 2004 by the International Commission of Jurists.

control over its air space and regional waters. Israeli forces amass around the area in order to control almost all the crossings and thus also commercial activities, custom tariffs and people's mobility. These considerations led the Special Rapporteur of the Commission on Human Rights to consider that Gaza is still under occupation (Box I-3).

Perhaps the most important redeeming feature of this withdrawal is that it demonstrates that Israel's desire to withdraw from Gaza is due to the courageous perseverance of the Palestinian resistance.

Even as citizens rejoiced in the Israeli withdrawal, fears that the occupation of the West Bank would continue and expand, began to grow. After all, the Gaza territories make up only 5.8 per cent of the territories occupied since 1967, which means that more than 94 per cent of these territories remain occupied. The number of settlers in the Gaza Strip came to 8,475 (that is, only 2 per cent of the total number of settlers); in contrast, Israel increased the number of Jewish settlers on the West Bank by 12,800 during 2004 alone. In addition, it confiscated more Palestinian lands, including for the expansion of the Ma'aleh Adomim settlement (around Jerusalem) by 2,700 square kilometres. There are, in addition, growing signals from Israel that it intends to annex this settlement to Jerusalem.[29]

According to reports by Palestinian human rights organisations, the implementation of the unilateral disengagement plan was accompanied and followed by gross violations in the occupied Palestinian territory, many of which were serious enough to qualify as war crimes under international humanitarian law. In addition to their daily incursions into Palestinian cities and towns, raids on residences and arrest of their occupants, the occupation forces continued to open fire on civilians, bulldoze and raze houses, attack property, and confiscate land needed for the Annexation Wall on West Bank land. Occupation forces are working on the Wall around occupied Jerusalem at a rapid pace in order to isolate it from its geographical surroundings on the West Bank. Meanwhile, the expansion of

settlement projects on the West Bank and the tightening of restrictions on movement across checkpoints continue (Palestinian Centre for Human Rights, in Arabic, 2005).

Israel continued to launch rocket and missile attacks against Palestinians in the Gaza sector after its withdrawal, often allegedly in response to attacks. In addition to its usual practices, it has found a new means of intimidating and frightening people: the sonic boom of Israeli jets systematically and frequently breaking the sound barrier. Palestinian and Israeli human rights organisations have condemned these practices for creating fear and panic among civilians, especially children, and for contributing to aborted pregnancies (more than 70 cases) (Al-Sharq al-Awsat, 11/11/2005, 10).

The occupation continues to frustrate human development

Israel's occupation of the Palestinian territories and its concomitant measures continue to destroy the potential for liberation, autonomy and development, tearing away at the fabric of Palestinian society itself. Such measures have, in fact, lead to civilian injuries and loss of life on both sides.

Abuse of personal freedoms and the freedom of movement

Israel's military siege of the Palestinian territories has continued through the use of mobile and permanent military barriers, which has led to the dismemberment of the West Bank into more than 240 districts isolated from one another. In addition to the permanent checkpoints, totalling more than 605 in April

The implementation of the unilateral disengagement plan was accompanied and followed by gross violations in the occupied Palestinian territory.

---

[29] "Palestine Monitor." (2006). http://www.palestinemonitor.org/nueva_web/facts_sheets/settlers_disengagement_violations.htm (Accessed 7 May, 2006).

2005, Israel has begun to use mobile ones, numbering 374 in June 2005. Their random use was considered by the Special Rapporteur of the Commission on Human Rights to be a violation of human dignity in addition to being a violation of the Palestinians' freedom of movement.[30]

The occupation forces have also impeded residents' mobility in other ways. These include preventing Palestinians from using many roads reserved for the use of the Jewish settlers, a measure reminiscent of racial segregation, and requiring Palestinians to obtain special permits to access connecting roads.

"[T]here are still over 8,000 prisoners in Israeli jails. Of this number, some 120 are women. Over 300 children under the age of 18 are in Israeli detention centres. Forty per cent of them have been sentenced to imprisonment and 60 per cent are in pre-trial detention.... Allegations of torture and inhuman treatment of detainees and prisoners continue. Such

treatment includes beatings, shackling in painful positions, kicking, prolonged blindfolding, denial of access to medical care, exposure to extreme temperatures and inadequate provision of food and water" (Dugard, 2005, 14).

Escalation of settler violence against Palestinian civilians

The reporting period witnessed escalating violence by Jewish settlers against Palestinian civilians. Schoolchildren have been beaten and terrorised by settlers on the way to school. Settlers have destroyed crops, stolen sheep and goats, and intentionally poisoned fields and land in the Tutwani region (Dugard, 2005, 11, 16).

Amnesty International confirmed that toxic chemicals were spread in fields in Hebron in the West Bank, causing damage to farm animals and land pollution. Kate Allen, a spokesperson for Amnesty International, stated that "These poisoning incidents appear to be part of a deliberate attack on the livelihoods of Palestinian farmers". The organisation indicated that Israel has not attempted to remove these chemicals safely or to investigate the poisoning (BBC, 25 April 2005).

Arab victims are not eligible for the same compensation and rehabilitation from 'terrorist' attacks as Jewish victims; Israeli law for the compensation of terror victims and their survivors does not provide for rights of victims of terror if the perpetrators are Jewish, since the latter are not considered "hostile to the State of Israel's existence".[32] On the 6th of August 2005, an Israeli soldier shot a group of Arab Israeli civilians boarding a bus, killing 4 and wounding 15 others. Despite the extent of the atrocity and its targeting of civilians and in spite of its condemnation by many, including Israeli officials, as a terrorist act, Israel's Defence Ministry Court ruled that the victims cannot be considered "victims of terror because the perpetrator was Jewish" (The Guardian, "Jewish gunman was no terrorist, Israel rules", 1 September 2005).

BOX I-4

Life at a Checkpoint, Israeli Eyewitnesses

"The loss of time that the Israelis deprive three and a half million people of each day has widespread significance: in impairing their ability to make a living, in economic, family and cultural activity, in leisure time, in studies and artistic creation, and in limiting the scope of each person's life" (p. 15).

"Huwarra (6 September): A soldier said that every ninth adult male trying to cross the checkpoint should be detained. (19 September): Every man whose name is 'Mohammad' was detained, and this is a large population" (p. 17).

"Shavei Shomron (from the Beit Iba reports): It was clear that what was being carried out here was collective punishment" (p. 18).

"The 'Stop All Life' Procedure- This is another form of delaying, that the army calls 'stop all life'. Its name indicates its nature: a total freeze on movement that lasts for hours at a time. A population

of hundreds and perhaps thousands of people, among them the elderly, the ill, pregnant women, infants, and nursing mothers, are prevented from moving freely and are ordered to stop the course of their lives" (p. 24).

"Beit Furik (14 July): Hundreds of people were waiting to cross, exiting Nablus. But the checkpoint was closed – 'Stop All Life' was in place. On the other side lay a man connected to an IV [intravenous drip]; he had passed out after several hours in the sun. Evacuating him from the area was impossible. In the area where detainees are held, dozens of women had gathered in a closely crowded group. One was standing and changing a baby's diaper; a second held a boy of about five who was wearing hospital pyjamas. The boy seemed unconscious or sleeping heavily, and his mother shouted that he's very sick" (p. 25).

Source: Machsomwatch[31] 2004, in Arabic, 15-24.

---

[30] (Dugard) 2005:3. Available at: "United Nations Information System on the Question of Palestine." (2005). http://domino.un.org/unispal.nsf/eed216406b50bf6485256ce10072f63702bf82d785fe854a85257088004c374c!/OpenDocument (Accessed 24 March, 2006).

[31] Machsomwatch, is an Israeli humanitarian organisation founded in February 2001.

[32] "Institute for Counter-Terrorism." (2005). http://www.ict.org.il/editorials/editorialdet.cfm?editorialid=3 (Accessed 30 March, 2006). Jon Elmer. "The New Standard." (2005). http://newstandardnews.net/content/index.cfm/items/2300 (Accessed 30 March, 2006).

On the other hand, Israel has continued to violate the Palestinians' right to a clean environment through the discharge of sewage from Jewish settlements onto Palestinian land. This constitutes a serious hazard for the Palestinian environment, since many settlements in the West Bank have no form of treatment of industrial or domestic wastewater (Dugard, 2005, 16).

The Wall appropriates land and impedes development

Work continues apace on building the Wall, which the International Court of Justice has judged to be illegal, requiring the cessation of its construction and compensation for the damage that it has caused.

The construction of the Wall has had dangerous consequences for Palestinians living nearby. The structure has separated thousands of Palestinians from their agricultural lands, while Israel has refused to grant most Palestinians access to their plots. For those who were granted permission, it became clear that the gates did not open at the times specified (Dugard, 2005, 2). Approximately 50,000 Palestinians are caught in the "seam zone" between the Wall and the Green Line. "Israeli settlers or any person of Jewish descent from anywhere in the world can move freely in and out and around the Seam Zone, while Palestinians living or working between the Wall and the Green Line must apply for permits to continue living in their homes or to access their means of livelihood" (Human Rights Watch, 2005).

The Wall will lead to serious health hazards for Palestinians, according to a statement issued by the Médecins du Monde, the Palestinian Red Crescent Society, and Physicians for Human Rights-Israel. It will prevent approximately 10,000 Palestinians who suffer from chronic diseases and more than 100,000 pregnant women from obtaining necessary health care. It will also prevent more than 130,000 Palestinians from obtaining vaccinations. In addition, one third of Palestinian villages will be unable to reach health care systems (BBC, 15 February 2005).

With the building of the Wall, Jerusalem has been forcibly separated from the rest of the West Bank, making it more difficult to negotiate over, or implement, relevant United Nations resolutions. In addition, it hinders Muslims and Christians from reaching places of worship located in the city. Moreover, the structure's implications in terms of permanency and the divisions of the West Bank undermine hopes of achieving an autonomous, sovereign Palestinian State and of implementing United Nations resolutions in this connection.

Meanwhile, the Palestinian economy is being systematically destroyed and rendered dependent on the Israeli economy. Moreover, this process is being accompanied by measures leading to geographical fragmentation, the imposition of geopolitical facts on the ground and a forceful campaign to undermine Palestinian institutions' capacity to take any serious steps towards achieving human development.

The deterioration of living standards

The economic situation and standards of living remain poor. Data reveal that poverty rates are on the rise. Various estimates indicate that the overall poverty rate is more than 50 per cent and that it reaches 80 per cent in some areas (such as southern Gaza). Between the years 2000 and 2005, families' average monthly income declined from approximately $445 to $333 (that is, by one fourth). More than 53 per cent of families suffered during this period from an acute decline in income.

In response, families took a number of different measures to adjust to, and compensate for, shortfalls, with women playing a critical role in these economies and in bearing their consequences. Data collected during the last year (up to March 2005) indicate that 58 per cent of families reduced their spending, while 16 per cent resorted to raising livestock and engaging in domestic agriculture, the responsibility for which is borne primarily by women (Palestinian Central Bureau of Statistics, press release, August 2005). Other data indicate that

With the building of the Wall, Jerusalem has been forcibly separated from the rest of the West Bank, making it more difficult to negotiate over, or implement, relevant United Nations resolutions.

More than 53 per cent of families suffered during this period from an acute decline in income.. with women playing a critical role in making economies and bearing their consequences.

BOX I-5

Disfigurement of the "Kingdom of Heaven"

Jerusalem is an historical city of great beauty. The wall has done much to disfigure the city. Those responsible for planning and constructing the wall in Jerusalem have done so with complete disregard for the environment. All this has been done in order to transform Jerusalem into a Jewish city.

Source: Dugard, 2005:13

in order to support their families, more than 50 per cent of the women were obliged to sell the jewellery that represented their savings (Bir Zeit University, in Arabic, 2002 and 2004).

Unemployment rates varied between 32 per cent at the beginning of 2005 and approximately 27 per cent in the autumn of the same year.[33] Youth, particularly in the Gaza Strip, were the hardest hit; data show that 47.5 per cent of young men between the ages of 20 and 24 years in the Gaza Strip are unemployed, compared to 27.7 per cent in the West Bank for the same age group. Young women (between 20 and 24 years of age) are the worst affected of all groups, with the unemployment rate for this group reaching 48.4 per cent compared to 31.6 per cent for young men (Palestinian Central Bureau of Statistics, press release, in Arabic, July 2005).

In the area of health, vaccination rates have begun to decline in many areas and have slumped to 66 per cent for mumps, measles and German measles. Approximately 5 per cent of children are underweight, while approximately 10 per cent of children suffer from stunting (UNDP, 2005).

The beginnings of Palestinian reform

Palestinian reform continued to register progress with the holding of the second presidential elections on 20 January 2005, local elections in a large number of locations as well as the 2006 parliamentary elections. These elections revealed growing support for religious forces.

Responding to Palestinian public opinion and pressures from societal forces, NGOs and international parties, the Palestinian Authority has implemented a number of reforms in the State's security apparatus and other State institutions. Nevertheless, most Palestinians continue to view an end to insecurity and the establishment of the rule of law as among their most important priorities. In this vein, a survey conducted in 2005 by the Development Studies Programme of Bir Zeit University revealed that 54 per cent of respondents considered these issues priorities. Manifestations of the security breakdown include the spread of firearms and

their illegitimate use and an unprecedented rise in rates of domestic violence and murders of women.[34] In the same connection, steps have been taken to restructure Palestinian governmental institutions: a number of government institutions and ministries have been merged or abolished, while new institutions have been created in order to meet societal needs. Among these is the Palestinian Ministry of Women's Affairs, whose establishment is viewed as a significant victory for the women's movement. Even so, current events confirm that an improvement in the conditions of Palestinian women will require a total commitment to gender-sensitive national policies that contribute to comprehensive national renewal and to ending the Israeli occupation.

EXPOSING THE EFFECTS OF THE OCCUPATION OF IRAQ

The political process in Iraq witnessed important developments in 2005 as indicated earlier in this Chapter. These included legislative elections and the ratification of a new constitution, both of which represented positive developments not practised by Iraqis in the past with such vigour.

Under an initiative by the League of Arab States, Cairo saw the holding of a meeting from 19 to 21 November 2005 attended by representatives of the different political factions and forces in preparation for a national reconciliation conference in Baghdad at the start of January 2006. While condemning terrorist actions, participants agreed that resistance is a legitimate right of all people, and demanded a timetable for the end of foreign presence.

Following the election of a Permanent Iraqi National Assembly and the anticipated formation of a new government in 2006, the new authority will face considerable challenges. These include the implementation of the constitutional amendments that guarantee the unity of Iraq and the inviolability of its territory, anchoring human rights in law and practice, bringing about national reconciliation and eradicating chaos and corruption in a united

An improvement in the conditions of Palestinian women will require a total commitment to gender-sensitive national policies, comprehensive national renewal and ending the Israeli occupation.

---

[33] The average comes to 21.2 per cent according to the stringent definition of unemployment used by the International Labour Organisation.

[34] "Women's Center for Legal Aid and Counseling." (2005). http://www.wclac.org/ (Accessed May 10, 2006).

Iraq free of both foreign occupation forces and terrorist activities.

This latest political process, however, has coincided with setbacks in reconstructing the Iraqi State and its institutions in the context of continuing occupation and amid risks of the country's fragmentation as sectarianism becomes entrenched. The outcome of the process over the last year remains a reflection of the continuing occupation and its serious ramifications.

The human cost of the occupation: use of prohibited weapons and torture

In November 2005, Italy's official television channel broadcast a film indicating that the United States Army had used white phosphorous bombs that harmed civilians in the city of Fallujah. These bombs burn the skin and are banned from use against civilians (reported by the BBC, 8 November 2005).

More evidence is coming out confirming the use of torture under the occupation. In October 2005, some human rights organisations lodged complaints with the United Nations Commission on Human Rights against the United States Administration for committing serious offences against human rights in "tens" of prisons similar to the infamous Abu Ghraib prison (Inter Press Service, 26 October 2005).

Elements within the Government of Iraq had their share in torturing Iraqis. In November 2005, the American troops found a "secret torture centre" in the basement of the Ministry of Interior building in one of Baghdad's suburbs (New York Times, 16 November 2005). This led Iyad Allawi, the first Prime Minister of Iraq under the occupation, to complain that human rights offences are worse now than under the previous regime (The Observer, 27 November 2005).

Despite the shock caused by an estimate published in the British journal, The Lancet, in November 2004 (Burnham, in Arabic, 2004) to the effect that approximately 100,000 civilians had been killed since the beginning of the occupation of Iraq, civilian casualties did not

diminish. In fact, Coalition forces expanded their military operations in several Iraqi cities, at times destroying civilian structures and storming hospitals and houses of worship, in stated pursuit of "rebels and terrorists", persisting in arresting thousands. Coalition soldiers were implicated in war crimes, such as killing, wounding and torturing detainees, while the Coalition Authority's investigations into these crimes and their lenient sentences on their perpetrators left a climate of impunity or even tacit encouragement. Towards the end of 2005, the President of the United States estimated the number of Iraqis killed at 30,000, which is close to the number estimated by Iraq Body Count, which put the number of civilians killed in Iraq between 27,000 and 31,000 victims.

The Iraqi people's tragedy was worsened by the involvement of certain local militias, terrorist organisations and criminal gangs in crimes against civilians, such as murder, kidnapping and sabotage, which victimised thousands of people and threatened to ignite sectarian conflict (Amnesty International, in Arabic, 2005b).

Festering corruption

In July 2005, the British press published a report by the Bahrain office of a reputable American auditing firm[35] prepared for the International Advisory and Monitoring Board that had been established in October 2003 (The Guardian, 7 July 2005). It revealed instances of gross financial mismanagement on the part of the Coalition Provisional Authority and the Iraqi interim government. The report confirmed that both parties had wasted or misappropriated funds belonging to the Iraqi people. These funds had been earmarked for rebuilding the country that had been destroyed by the occupying Coalition troops. In the eight months during which Paul Bremer was the civil administrator of Iraq, it estimated that nearly $9 billion, most of which belonged to the Iraqi people, "disappeared".[36] (When Bremer left Iraq on 28 June 2004, the Coalition

More evidence is coming out confirming the use of torture under the occupation (of Iraq).

---

[35] KPMG

[36] "Fox News." (2004). http://www.foxnews.com/story/0,2933,129489,00.html (Accessed 18 July, 2006).

"CNN News." (2005). http://edition.cnn.com/2005/WORLD/meast/01/30/iraq.audit/ (Accessed 18 July, 2006).

"The Times." (2005). http://www.ftimes.com/main.asp?SectionID=1&SubSectionID=1&ArticleID=25316&TM=74844.16 (Accessed 18 July, 2006).

Provisional Authority had spent $20 billion of Iraq's money[37] compared with little more than $300 million of the money of the Government of the United States).[38] Auditors discovered that the occupation authority had not kept accounts for the hundreds of millions of dollars that it had kept in cash in its coffers. Some $8.8 billion, which had been transferred to the Iraqi interim government, are unaccounted for. Further, it appears that the failure to monitor the way in which Iraq's income is disposed of has continued since Bremer's departure (Harriman, 2005).

It is thus not surprising that the field survey of around 2,000 Iraqis carried out by the United States Department of State in 2005 reports that "most Iraqis say that corruption is worse now than before" (Government of the United States, Department of State, Office of Research, 2005).

The evidence of financial mismanagement and corruption on the part of the occupation authorities calls for the exposure of the facts and circumstances surrounding the misappropriation of Iraq's oil wealth. These facts are documented in a book by the Iraqi former Minister of Petroleum, 'Isam Chalabi, entitled, A Reading in Iraq's Oil Industry and Oil Policy. The study covers the destruction of installations and the theft of documents, machines and equipment during and after the occupation. Even two years after "liberation," Iraq's oil industry had not been able to restore production to its pre-war levels. Indeed, for the first time in its history, Iraq has been turned into a net importer of oil products at a cost of $3 billion a year ('Arif, in Arabic, 2005a).

A recent assessment by a London-based group concluded that Iraq stands to lose between $74 billion and $194 billion over the lifetime of production-sharing contracts signed with international oil companies. These estimates assume an oil price of $40 a barrel, based on only 12 of the 60 – at least – oil fields. In addition to relinquishing control of Iraq's oil industry to international companies, the contracts imply annual per capita losses of revenue over their 30-year lifetime that are estimated to be higher than Iraq's present per capita gross domestic product (Platform et al., 2005).

The occupation's destruction of Iraq's wealth goes beyond oil. It affects a spiritual treasure of importance to humanity: the relics of early civilisation in Iraq. Eleanor Robson, from the Oriental Institute at the University of Oxford, has compared the pillaging to "the Mongol sacking of Baghdad in 1258".[39] The Looting of the Iraq Museum, Baghdad, which contains contributions by a number of the most prominent archaeologists in Iraq, cites information on the recovery of 7,000 out of some 15,000 pieces that were stolen from the Baghdad museum during the first days of the occupation. Not one of these pieces has yet been returned to Iraq, while the fate of the museum's collection of Sumerian seals, which is estimated to contain approximately 6,000 items, some dating back to the dawn of writing and recordkeeping, is still shrouded in mystery. To this must be added the widespread damage to or destruction of important archaeological sites resulting from the occupation forces' construction of military bases and airports near them ('Arif, 2005b).

The total cost of the invasion and occupation of Iraq

The estimated economic cost of the invasion and occupation of Iraq, including direct financial costs (estimated by a recent study at around $255 billion, of which $40 billion is borne by the Coalition Members), and the loss of oil revenues and asset destruction, totals nearly half a trillion dollars ($500 billion). This cost is expected to double by 2015 (American Enterprise Institute-Brookings Joint Center for Regulatory Studies, 2005).

Iraqis want to see the end of the occupation

One of the leaders of the occupying coalition in Iraq ascertained the Iraqi public's strong desire to see the occupation end. A survey covering the entire country, funded by the British

---

[37] "Global Policy." (2004). http://www.globalpolicy.org/security/issues/iraq/dfi/2004/06fuelingsuspicion.pdf (Accessed 28 April, 2006).

[38] "The Guardian." (2005). http://www.guardian.co.uk/Iraq/Story/0,2763,1522983,00.html (Accessed 10 April, 2006).

[39] "The Guardian." (2003). http://www.guardian.co.uk/Iraq/Story/0,,979734,00.html (Accessed 28 April, 2006).

Ministry of Defence and leaked to the Sunday Telegraph, showed that more than 99 per cent of Iraqis do not feel that the presence of the Coalition forces is contributing to the security of their nation. Nearly half the respondents sympathised with the fierce attacks against the Coalition forces (The Guardian, 23 October 2005).

At the end of 2005, the military command of the United States forces in Iraq acknowledged for the first time that, to cope with wide public rejection of the occupation, it had paid Iraqi newspapers to carry positive news about United States efforts in the country (Washington Post, 3 December 2005).

SUMMARY

This section has illustrated how the international and regional environments have weakened human development in the Arab region, notably through the occupation of Palestine and Iraq and the "war on terror". In many cases, the basic rights and freedoms of Arab citizens, extending from the right to life through civil and political rights to economic and social rights, have continued to be violated. This is the situation today. Looking ahead, this negative environment could damage the prospects of a renaissance in the Arab world by impeding reform and obstructing opportunities for peaceful and just solutions to the occupation of Arab lands and the restriction of Arab freedoms and rights. A continued impasse over these matters may push the region further towards extremism and violent protest in the absence of a fair system of governance at the global level that can protect security and help achieve human prosperity for all.

PROGRESS TOWARDS OVERCOMING DEFICITS IN HUMAN DEVELOPMENT

BROADENING THE SCOPE OF FREEDOM

As the foregoing sections illustrate, the overall trend during this period has been that of steady erosion of freedom in support of the existing structure of authoritarian rule. It is, nevertheless, possible to trace some positive developments relevant to the broadening of freedom in the Arab countries.

Reinforcing and protecting a culture of human rights

In Egypt, the National Council for Human Rights issued its first annual report (2004-2005). The fact that the report dealt with some of the most serious aspects of human rights violations in the country and demanded an end to the state of emergency came as a gratifying surprise in human rights circles. It remains for the authorities to take effective measures on the basis of such reports to protect human rights and to punish those who violate them (Al-'Awwa, in Arabic, 2005).

In Jordan, the National Centre for Human Rights issued its first annual report.

Egypt and Tunisia ratified the Arab Charter on Human Rights Charter, and Syria became a signatory to the Convention against Torture and other Cruel, Inhuman or Degrading Treatment or Punishment.

Training courses in human rights were held for clergy and the police in Egypt.

In Bahrain, a decree was issued requiring that democracy and human rights be taught in the State's schools.

The United Nations Centre for Human Rights for Western Asia and the Arab Region is being established in Qatar.

A human rights association has been formed in the UAE.

The new authorities in Mauritania organised, for the first time, a civil assembly that brought together most opposition political parties. The meeting discussed the major challenges currently facing the country and outlined the features that participants wanted to see in its next, intermediate stage of development. The authorities also permitted several NGOs and centres for development research to begin operating.

Purging a long legacy of oppression in Morocco

Arguably, the most important recent deliberations in Morocco, in terms of political history, were the hearings organised by the

The military command of the United States forces in Iraq acknowledged for the first time that, to cope with wide public rejection of the occupation, it had paid Iraqi newspapers to carry positive news about United States efforts in the country.

The fact that the (Egyptian) report dealt with some of the most serious aspects of human rights violations in the country and demanded an end to the state of emergency came as a gratifying surprise.

Justice and Reconciliation Commission in 2005. The hearings fall within the agenda of the Commission, which seeks to provide new generations with knowledge and facts about the disturbing events that took place in Morocco between independence and the end of 1999. This work is part of the process of transitional justice in a Morocco that seeks reconciliation with itself. This goal is to be achieved by purging the legacy of a past laden with injustice.

Some sessions were scheduled to present the cases of victims affiliated with various opposition movements (nationalist and leftist), who were exposed to different forms of oppression in prisons and other places where crimes against human rights were committed.

The members of the Commission collected over 20,000 files and decided to hear 200 live testimonies, broadcasting them on Moroccan television and radio stations. The Commission has submitted its final report, which includes the results and summary of its findings together with recommendations for legal, cultural and institutional reforms necessary to overcome a history of oppression and prevent its recurrence.

Searching for national reconciliation in Algeria

The President of Algeria adopted an initiative to transcend the legacy of alienation and enmity resulting from the 1990s through the Charter for Peace and National Reconciliation, which was widely accepted through a national referendum.

Limited move towards democracy in the UAE

The President of the UAE declared a move towards democratic reform whereby half the members of the Federal National Council, which consists of 40 members, will be elected by 4,000 social elites to be appointed by the rulers of the seven Emirates.

Jordan expands popular participation

In Jordan, a commission established by the king and comprising members of various political affiliations prepared a National Agenda for political, social and economic reforms. Its recommendations included serious amendments to legislation governing

elections and parties that would deepen political development and expand popular participation. The biggest challenge is whether the Government will implement such far-reaching reforms.

KNOWLEDGE ACQUISITION IN PERSPECTIVE

The acquisition of knowledge is generally viewed by ruling regimes and foreign donors not as a means by which to overcome the erosion of freedom but rather as a politically neutral area and, therefore, open to broad application. However, the supposed political neutrality of knowledge acquisition is an illusion, while education, in particular, can be an effective instrument for reproducing or supporting structures of domination whether from within or without.

There have been successive attempts to modify Arab educational curricula and approaches, some designed to fulfil the requirements of externally initiated reform projects, which may not necessarily serve the interests of renewal in the Arab world. Specifically, Arabic educational curricula often come under external pressures that aim to "develop" them so as to incorporate values exalting human rights, the role of women, democracy and tolerance. From the perspective of the present Report, such changes must be carried out on several levels that work not only to introduce such universal values but also to modernise curricula in line with the information revolution and rapid communication among the peoples and States of the world. It should be kept in mind that targeting curricula that include "Islamic" values can backfire by aggravating extremism and internal resistance to change.

EMPOWERMENT OF WOMEN

The empowerment of women, the core theme of the present Report, is the human development deficit that Arab States have laboured to address, albeit inadequately. Efforts to address this issue have often been limited to cosmetic empowerment in the sense of enabling notable women to occupy leadership positions in the structure of the existing regime without extending empowerment to the broad base of women, a process that automatically entails the empowerment of all citizens.

At the same time, however, it is possible to cite positive trends in the area of women's empowerment. For example:

- In Kuwait, decades of struggle by women and their supporters were crowned by the decision of the National People's Assembly in May 2005 to pass a law that grants women the right to vote and to be nominated for public office in both general and local elections. This was followed by a government decree appointing a woman as Minister of Planning, the first appointment of a woman to a ministerial post in the country's history.

- In Egypt, a woman was appointed for the first time as president of a petroleum company; eleven women were appointed to the upper house of parliament, the Consultative Council; and the minimum age at which a girl may marry was raised to eighteen years. Also, in a cabinet reshuffle at the end of 2005, the Ministry of Manpower and Immigration was given to a woman for the first time.

- In Jordan, a cabinet reshuffle in April 2005 involved the appointment of four women to ministerial posts; however, this trend was reversed when a new government was formed in November 2005, and the number of women in it went down to one.

- In Lebanon, a woman was appointed as a minister for the first time in 2005. Six women won in the legislative elections.

- In the UAE, a reshuffle brought a woman into the Cabinet for the first time and the number rose to two when the Cabinet was formed.

- In Tunisia, a woman was appointed as a provincial governor for the first time .

- In Qatar, a woman became secretary general of the municipal council.

- In Syria, a woman was appointed to the Baath Party's national command.

- In Saudi Arabia, the legal condition requiring a woman to secure the approval of a "guardian" in order to obtain an identity card was abolished. In addition, two Saudi women won membership on a council representing journalists; three women won elections to the board of directors of the National Human Rights Association; women took part in elections for Riyadh's Chamber of Commerce and Industry, with two of them gaining seats on its board; and a delegation of 40 Saudi women was sent on an official business visit to the United Kingdom. King Abdullah also met with a delegation of professional women who presented him with their demands.

- In Bahrain, the requirement for Bahraini women to secure their husbands' approval before obtaining a passport was abolished, and women were allowed to work as traffic police.

- In Algeria, a woman was appointed chancellor of the University of Boumerdes.

- Libya ratified the agreement establishing the Arab Women's Organisation.

CONCLUSION

During the period covered by the present Report, the Arab world continued to suffer developmental labour pains whose outcome is difficult to predict. Certain reforms were achieved in the dissemination of knowledge and the empowerment of women. With few exceptions, no Arab country is now without a parliament or a cabinet or a local council in whose assigned tasks at least one woman participates in an able manner. Similarly, many Arab countries have started to look anew at how to improve their educational systems.

Progress towards political reform, on the other hand, continues to be erratic and the gap between reality and the aspirations of the vital forces in the Arab countries continues to widen as a result of both the slowness of reform and the invigoration of civil society. The latter, having broken through the barrier of fear that has held it in check for too long, is now formulating its demands for reform more clearly and with greater daring. Most of those ballots that have been held, despite being a step forward by comparison with earlier practices, remain far from the free and fair elections for which civil society has been agitating. Only timid and limited steps have been taken towards the programmes of political reform announced by

With few exceptions, no Arab country is now without a parliament or a cabinet or a local council in whose assigned tasks at least one woman participates in an able manner.

numerous regimes. Civil and political freedoms continue to be abused unimpeded and the right to political participation, though it may have broadened slightly, remains restricted in the face of legal and other limits to its practical exercise.

Reformers and human rights activists remain targets of repressive measures that endanger not only their well-being but also often their very lives as they seek to obtain freedoms and rights.

Notwithstanding the growing number of external initiatives for reform in the Arab world, the negative influence of an unfriendly global environment has grown. Terrorism and the collateral impact of the war against it continue to threaten not only the Arab citizen's right to freedom and growth but also her or his right to life. Foreign occupations, and especially the Israeli occupation of the occupied Palestinian territory, continue to deny Arab people the most basic political, economic and social rights and threaten the security and safety of the region as a whole.

For these reasons, the progress of development has remained haphazard, without impetus, organisation or a clear forward direction: the Arab world is left in a situation not far from that of the "impending disaster" of which the third AHDR (2004) warned.

Despite the gravity of developments in the region, aspirations for the rebirth and flourishing of a vibrant Arab world, as expressed in that Report, have not diminished. Indeed, it is in the hope of strengthening progress towards that goal that this fourth Report is published.

THE CONTENTS OF PART TWO OF THE REPORT

The major part of the present Report consists of a study of the third deficit identified by the first AHDR (2002): the disempowerment of women in the region. The analysis culminates in a strategic vision for overcoming this deficit through the advancement of women in the Arab world.

Chapter 1 lays down the conceptual foundations of the Report, which are anchored in the central perspective on freedom and human rights of the Arab Human Development

Report series. Starting from the premise that equality between men and women is the only gender relationship consistent with human dignity, the discussion then focuses on problematic issues associated with the current status of women in the region.

The chapter confirms that the status of Arab women results from the complex interaction of rooted cultural, social, economic and political factors. Some of these are systemic in nature and require a wide and deep analysis of many components of Arab societies in keeping with the systematic approach taken in these Reports. The Report thus elaborates the contemporary context of women in the Arab world as a prelude to developing a strategic vision for their rise.

The raison d'être of the Report is to examine the current situation of women in Arab countries within the framework of human development. It therefore focuses particularly on how Arab women fare in terms of being able to acquire and utilise capabilities essential to all human beings. It also considers the level of human welfare associated with women in the Arab world. In doing so, it probes whether men and women enjoy basic human rights equally. Furthermore, since women's empowerment rests largely on the will and efforts of society as a whole, chapters 2 to 5 review struggles and experiences in the advancement of Arab women in order to evaluate the nature and strength of such efforts.

Following this diagnosis, the Report next looks at how the societal context in Arab countries influences the situation of women. This situational analysis concentrates on cultural and traditional structures, especially religion and specifically Islam, as well as social and political structures (chapters 6 to 9).

Drawing together the threads of its diagnosis and analysis, the Report concludes, in chapter 10, with a strategic vision for the advancement of women in the Arab world. It stresses that, in moral and material terms, the rise of Arab women is an indispensable component of any free, knowledge-based and well-governed society. Indeed, it is both a necessary condition for, and the most meaningful proof of, the achievement of human development in the region in line with the comprehensive vision of this series.

The progress of development has remained haphazard, without impetus, organisation or a clear forward direction.

In moral and material terms, the rise of women is an indispensable component of any free, knowledge-based and well-governed society.

Part II

Towards The Rise Of Women In The Arab World

Frame Of Reference

CONCEPTS AND PROBLEMATIC ISSUES

CONCEPTS, THE HISTORICAL COURSE OF DISCRIMINATION AGAINST WOMEN, AND COUNTERMEASURES

CONCEPTS

THE RISE[1] OF WOMEN[2]

The rise of women in the Arab world is to be achieved as part of society's advancement towards freedom as advocated by the third Arab Human Development Report (2004). Arab countries can achieve this goal by eradicating all infringements on human dignity and specifically by guaranteeing full citizenship and the enjoyment of all human rights for all women on an equal footing with men.

The definition of freedom adopted here is not limited to civil and political freedoms – the pillars of citizenship. It extends to freedom from all that infringes on human dignity, including ignorance, illness, poverty and fear. This comprehensive notion of freedom follows the definition proposed in the third Arab Human Development Report on the one hand as well as the entire international human rights law on the other.

Enjoyment of human rights

It follows that the ultimate objective of the rise of women in the Arab region and the first organising principle behind it is for women – all women – in the Arab world to enjoy all components of human rights equally with men.

In the context of human development, "the rise of Arab women" entails liberating women from the legal and institutional constraints that tie their hands and assign them an inferior social status. It also means giving them the tools to advance through the development of their capabilities. This is to be accomplished by guaranteeing women and men equal opportunities to acquire and utilise capabilities essential for all human beings. This refers, in particular, to the acquisition of health (in its positive and comprehensive sense) and to the lifelong acquisition of knowledge, starting with complete equality in this respect between girls and boys.

Guarantee of equality of opportunity

It also entails guaranteeing complete equality of opportunity for the effective employment of such capabilities in all spheres of human activity – productive, social and political – so as ultimately to close the gap between the sexes in terms of their enjoyment of both the material and moral components of human welfare.

Complete equality of opportunity, based on respect for the right to freedom in its comprehensive sense, is thus the second organising principle in promoting "the rise of Arab women".

The main appeal in this Report, therefore, is not solely for justice for all women in Arab countries, though this must be achieved. It is for justice for all in those countries, both men and women. This leads to the subject of the rights of citizenship.

The rise of women in the Arab world is part of society's advancement towards freedom.

The ultimate objective ... is for women – all women – in the Arab world to enjoy all components of human rights equally with men.

---

[1] The first Arab Human Development Report (2002) used the terminology "women's empowerment," clearly an Arabisation of an English term. Perhaps a better term in the Arabic language is "the rise of woman" in contrast to "the empowerment of woman" to connote woman's struggle for her rights through the building of her capacity and its effective use in a conducive societal framework. These are all important elements of the Report's concluding strategic vision.

[2] "Women" in this context is a noun describing gender; hence, the reference is to ALL women in Arab countries without discrimination whatsoever.

Guarantee of full citizenship rights[3] for women

AHDR 2004 concluded with a comprehensive definition of freedom, which couples individual freedom with justice and is synonymous, on the one hand, with human development, and, on the other, with the entire human rights system as contained in the International Bill of Human Rights Law. This definition ties the maintenance of freedom to the establishment of good governance, thus ensuring complete rights of citizenship for all Arab citizens.

Since, however, citizenship rights are not fully respected in Arab countries, particularly in the case of women, human development requires first the respect of citizenship rights for all, and in particular for women on an equal footing with men. No infringement of women's human dignity or their effective citizenship rights can be justified on the grounds of gender. In this context, it should be noted that temporary affirmative action to facilitate women's attainment of the decision-making positions from which they have long been excluded is not equivalent to discrimination in rights of citizenship.

Therefore, the guarantee of full citizenship rights for all Arab citizens, particularly women, is the third organising principle in understanding "the rise of Arab women".

EQUALITY WITH RESPECT FOR DIFFERENCE

Women are certainly different from men, but that does not in any way imply they are deficient.

Bio-physiological differences, which are not deficiencies and may at times be advantages (Fergany, in Arabic, 2006), together with certain socio-historical differences, have been primarily responsible for the unjust treatment of women. At times, however, such differences may also be to a woman's advantage (as when she invokes her right under labour law to maternity leave, a right granted in view of the importance to society of her reproductive role).

The exploitation of differences between the procreative functions of the sexes and the resulting burdens for women gave men an advantage by endowing them with a freedom of movement that helped them to entrench themselves in society and to dominate it. They also provided men with the opportunity to establish the symbolic world (i.e., knowledge system) in keeping with their dominance. On the other hand, women's relative immobility, owing to their being occupied with the nurture of children, partly accounted for their weak participation in both the symbolic world and public activity in general. At the same time, however, that relative immobility gave women a better understanding and reading of the symbolism linked to the physical and emotional states associated with survival and health, and especially those of children (Nadeau, 1996, 50-60).

Equality between men and women does not mean denying differences. Differences may have emanated from biology, but they have been consolidated and exaggerated by inherited culture to the benefit of men. Respecting such differences in their proper context, without exaggeration or understatement, is necessary for achieving equality between the sexes. Exaggerating differences leads to further discrimination against women and deprives them of their rights. Understating such differences can result in cosmetic equality and also deny women their rights. This Report therefore affirms the principle of difference between the sexes without implying discrimination or the comprehensive superiority of one sex over the other. Additionally, it argues that making the most of this difference, and ensuring human dignity, can be a strong basis for human advancement. Consequently, the Report supports complete equality of citizenship for all citizens, i.e. for all men and women, while respecting the difference between the sexes in all forms of social organisation without detriment to women's rights so as to ensure the human dignity of all members of society and to empower them collectively to acquire and use essential capabilities efficiently. It follows that this will involve all of society, on equal terms, in a serious effort to achieve human development in the Arab countries.

This position is consistent with the adoption

Human development requires first the respect of citizenship rights for all, and in particular for women on an equal footing with men.

Equality between men and women does not mean denying differences to ensure the human dignity of all members of society.

---

[3] Meaning complete equality in rights and duties among all citizens.

BOX 1-1

Inequality between the Sexes through History

Since ancient times, the basic, primary relationship between man and woman has been one of mutual co-operation, with both working to enable the survival of the species, banish violence and maintain affection and compassion. These are values that not only persist, regardless of changing lifestyles, but that are also central to the prevention of extinction and the capacity to create and renew. The age of metals saw a new pattern of relationship between man and woman, for this period was linked to urbanisation, men's work, and the exclusion of woman's mental and physical labour from the public space. Muscle power and, subsequently, military skills predominated. The difference between the sexes in nature and role was turned into sex-based discrimination in rights and duties.

However, patriarchal society was unable to exclude the female in symbolic fields, where she was found in the form of the Goddess of Fertility and Beauty, for her presence was well established in myth, ancient belief and politics. The myth of Osiris, where Isis is the mother goddess, goddess of the earth and mistress of nature, acts out the image of a strong female presence in situations of human and physical production, an image that would later cross the Mediterranean without modification.

Women also played a leading role in the history of our region. The role of Egyptian queens in society, in authority, in government, in family structures, in marriage and in divorce reflects the importance of their role during the pharaonic period. In Mesopotamia, women had high social and religious status, reflected in statues of motherhood and fertility, and especially those of Ishtar, goddess of love, fertility and life. Women were linked to the moon, which was associated with sexual life and fertility. Even though the division of labour in Babylonian society was more patriarchal, the latter also guaranteed women rights relating to the ownership of property, work, divorce, and more.

When women were enslaved, they responded in many ways, some active. Strong women who reached positions of power shattered the preconceived images by unsettling the symbolic and ideological foundations of man's authority. Alternatively, women diverted themselves into roles behind the scenes in which they supported rulers, leaders and scholars.

The French Revolution broke the vicious circle of patriarchal logic. Although many Enlightenment thinkers could not set aside the heavy historical legacy, they put the central existential question on the table once again by asking, "Is discrimination against women the result of culture or nature?" Distinguished personalities such as Condorcet and La Cluse had the courage to respond, in the Encyclopaedia, that there is nothing in nature that allows discrimination; it is a consequence of social existence, and there is therefore no justification for making one sex the raison d'être of the other.

This revolutionary break freed woman as an individual and allowed the question of her rights to be raised in a new form. Women entered public life by force, as citizens, albeit without the rights of citizenship. Yet their role went beyond that of simple rebellion to become pivotal during major events of the Revolution (for example, those of 5 and 6 October 1789). Women stood up on podiums and in parliament, organised themselves in clubs and drew up petitions. This transformation succeeded in frightening even the most revolutionary men. Olympe de Gouges, author of the Declaration of the Rights of Woman and of the Female Citizen paid at the guillotine the ultimate price for her transgression against the spirit of the age.

Humanity's battle against the logic of discrimination began with the introduction of the positive concept of human rights, a framework that did not derive from a divine ruling denying women the status of individuals. But it would take humanity two hundred years to achieve the first international text demanding the abolition of all forms of discrimination against women. However, it took only about a century for this concept to enter the Arab world. This started the process by which the European experience became the inspiration for the rediscovery of the early Islamic belief in equality between the sexes. That early belief is manifested in the writings of Qasim Amin, Mohammad Abdu and an elite of enlightened Islamic thinkers who considered opposition to discrimination a return to the genuine essence of Islam. In what is now known as the Arab Renaissance, Mansur Fahmi and Salama Musa, meanwhile, argued for a break with the past as a pre-requisite to reshaping the relationship between the sexes on the basis of equality.

Source: Haytham Manna, background paper for the Report.

by the AHDR series, and especially AHDR 2004, of the human rights system in its fullest form as contained in the International Bill of Rights. Of particular relevance here is the Convention on the Elimination of All Forms of Discrimination against Women (CEDAW) (Box 1-3 and annex III).

THE RISE OF ARAB WOMEN AND HUMAN DEVELOPMENT IN THE ARAB WORLD ARE INSEPARABLY AND CAUSALLY LINKED!

Since the publication of the first AHDR 2002, this series has established the definitive

BOX 1-2

Qasim Amin: The Advancement of Women Is a Step towards Civilisation

As a whole, the progress of nations is contingent upon many diverse factors, among the most important of which is the progress of women. Conversely, the decline of nations is the product of many diverse factors, among the most important of which is the decline in the status of women. The inferior status of women in our country is one of the most formidable obstacles to the promotion of our own welfare.

Source: Amin, in Arabic, 1899, 132-133.

correlation, almost a causal one, between human development and the rise of women in the Arab World[4]. The causal correlation between the two logical concepts indicates that the validity of one entails the validity of the other.

---

[4] This position has been controversial among some observers and maybe among the Arab population at large (AHDR 2003, Box "what Arabs think of the Three Deficits" page19).

Excerpts from the Convention on the Elimination of All Forms of Discrimination against Women

Annex III provides the full text of the Convention.

Adopted by the General Assembly in its resolution 34/180 of 18 December 1979. Entered into force on 3 September 1981.

Article 1

"...the term 'discrimination against women' shall mean any distinction, exclusion or restriction made on the basis of sex which has the effect or purpose of impairing or nullifying the recognition, enjoyment or exercise by women, irrespective of their marital status, on a basis of equality of men and women, of human rights and fundamental freedoms in the political, economic, social, cultural, civil or any other field".

Article 2

"States parties condemn discrimination against women in all it forms, agree to pursue by all appropriate means and without delay a policy of eliminating discrimination against women and, to this end, undertake:

(a) To embody the principle of the equality of men and women in their national constitutions or other appropriate legislation...

(c) To establish legal protection of the rights of women on an equal basis with men and to ensure through competent national tribunals and other public institutions the effective protection of women against any act of discrimination".

Article 5

"States parties shall take all appropriate measures

(a) To modify the social and cultural patterns of conduct of men and women, with a view to achieving the elimination of prejudices and customary and all other practices which are based on the idea of inferiority or the superiority of either of the sexes or on stereotyped roles for men and women".

The AHDR series contends that "human development" means that human beings, by virtue simply of being human, are entitled to respect for their intrinsic human dignity and have an innate right to a life of material and moral dignity. This entails equal opportunities to acquire human capabilities and utilise them effectively to achieve the highest possible level of well-being for all. It follows that all forms of discrimination among humans are rejected regardless of the criteria of discrimination.

This definition also underlines that the achievement of human development in the Arab world follows necessarily from the rise of Arab women. In other words, the rise of women is a necessary, but not necessarily sufficient, condition for the realisation of human development. It must be accompanied by extirpating all forms of deprivation among all members of the society of freedom, including the denial of opportunities for the acquisition and effective utilisation of human capabilities.

Luminary: Nazik al-Mala'ika

Iraqi poet Nazik al-Mala'ika is regarded as the pioneer of modern poetry in the Arab nation and one of the first Arab poets to write stress-based verse. She is also considered a pioneer in the field of the critical theory of modern verse.

Al-Mala'ika was born in Baghdad in 1923. Her father was known for his interest in jurisprudence and logic and for his love of literature and poetry, while her mother, Salma 'Abd al-Razzaq, was herself a poet. In this fertile climate, Al-Mala'ika's poetic talent blossomed while she was still a young school girl. It comes as no surprise that her poem, "Cholera," regarded as the beginning of the departure from the columnar-arrangement tradition of Arabic poetry and a first triumph in the establishment of free verse, was published as early as 1945.

The poet graduated from the Fine Arts Institute in 1949. In 1950, she travelled to the United States, where she studied Latin and comparative literature at Princeton University. The study of French that she also undertook there, along with her mastery of English, enabled her to make translations of literature in these languages into Arabic. In

1959, she returned to Iraq to immerse herself once more in her literary preoccupations with poetry and criticism. Her experience of living overseas and reading widely in the most modern schools of world literature (including Chinese, German, Indian, Italian and Russian as well as American, French and English) left her culturally open to different human civilisations and endowed her with a diverse poetic vision and sensitivity. This clearly acted to deepen the innovativeness of her poetry and her prosodic theory. Al-Mala'ika lived in Iraq, working in its universities, including the University of Basra, without interrupting her poetic output until 1960.

At the start of the 1960s, with her move to Lebanon, the poet entered a new phase of her life, Beirut being, throughout that period and until the mid-1970s, the living heart of Arabic culture. Al-Mala'ika now started publishing works of poetry and criticism. These works were extraordinary in the way in which they confronted and clashed with poetic and critical assumptions that had remained contentedly comatose until challenged by her and certain other Iraqis of her generation, such as, in first place, Badr al-Shakir al-Sayyab, and

also Buland al-Haydari, 'Abd al-Wahhab al-Bayyati and Lami'a 'Amara.

Nazik al-Mala'ika published numerous collections of verse and critical studies though many of her poems are not included in these and remain scattered throughout the pages of innumerable Iraqi and other Arab literary magazines and journals. Her poetic output includes the following anthologies: 'Ashiqat al-Layl (Lover of the Night), 1947; Shazaya wa-Ramad (Splinters and Ashes), 1949; Qarar al-Mawja (The Bottom of the Wave), 1957; Shajarat al-Qamar (The Moon Tree), 1968; Ma'sat al-Hayat wa-Ughniyat al-Insan, Malhama Shi'riyya (The Tragedy of Life and the Song of Humankind, an Epic Poem), 1970; Yughayyir Alwanahu al-Bahr (The Sea Changes its Colours), 1977; and Lil-Salat wal-Thawra (For Prayer and the Revolution), 1978.

Her works of criticism include Qadaya al-Shi'r al-Mu'asir (Issues in Contemporary Poetry), 1962; Al-Sawma'a wal-Shurfa al-Hamra' (The Monk's Cell and the Red Box), 1965; and Sikulujiyyat al-Shi'r (The Psychology of Poetry), 1993.

Fowziyah Abu-Khalid

Source: "Azzaman." (2004). http://www.azzaman.com/azzaman/articles/2004/09/09-26/698.htm (Accessed 12 April, 2006).

The causal relationship between the rise of Arab women and human development in the Arab world will, therefore, be fulfilled only so long as it encompasses the human development of all citizens of the region.

MEANS OF COMBATING DISCRIMINATION AGAINST WOMEN: THE EVOLUTION OF CONCEPTS OF "WOMEN AND DEVELOPMENT"

The Global Level

Development programmes and policies relating to women have passed through many stages, reflecting changes in the economic development policies in the world generally. For example, from the 1950s to the 1970s, the prevailing thinking was that "modernisation"– usually equated with industrialisation and mechanisation – would improve living standards and life in developing countries for all sectors of society, including women. This period was characterised by the prevalence of a "charity-based" orientation towards women, centred on supporting women's reproductive role and on issues such as education and public health for women. The same period also witnessed the beginning of the shift from a charitable to a developmental orientation.

The United Nations Decade for Women: Equality, Development and Peace (1976–1985), launched at the first United Nations World Conference on Women in Mexico in 1975, was a major spur to the advancement of thinking with respect to women and development. The trend during this decade was towards women in development (WID), which acknowledged a difference between men's and women's realities and their experience in development. This, in turn, was reflected in the formulation of new strategies to improve the situation of women in developing countries, focusing on the productive rather than the reproductive side of their lives.

In this context, international donor agencies began implementing income-generating programmes for women, teaching them various skills and trades or enrolling them in cooperative production and marketing projects, as well as

developing technology to lighten the burdens of women's work. Attention was also given to seeking the equal participation of women in education and employment and to promoting a view of women as independent producers and not merely as adjuncts of their husbands. The previous approach to women was criticized for focusing on the productive side of women's lives while disregarding their reproductive roles, which were viewed as "private" issues outside the scope of revenue generating developmental projects (Rathegeber, 1990).

With the second Decade for Women, which began with the United Nations Third World Conference on Women in Nairobi in 1985, the prevailing perspective changed to "gender and development".

The gender-and-development perspective stems from a comprehensive vision of the socio-economic and political structure that seeks to understand the mechanisms of role distribution between men and women and the responsibilities and expectations of each. It therefore analyses the nature of women's contribution to the larger work environment inside and outside the home, including non-commodity production, and rejects the public/private work divide that has been used in general to downplay the significance of women's labour for the maintenance of the family and home.

The gender-and-development perspective also attributes an important role to the State in the liberation of women, especially in respect of providing social services that enable women to play their various reproductive, socio-reproductive and political roles. However, this perspective also emphasises that women are basic agents in bringing about change and not passive recipients of the assistance offered by development. It thus gives special importance to the need for women to organise themselves to become effective forces for political change (Rathegeber, 1990).

Critical evaluation of the application of "women-and-development" concepts in the Arab region

The development approaches described above have received attention within the Arab region. Between the 1950s and 1970s, members of

Women are basic agents in bringing about change and not passive recipients of the assistance offered by development.

The gender-and-development perspective also attributes an important role to the State in the liberation of women.

national elites motivated by the drive for modernisation came to power and concentrated on central planning, industrialisation and the more efficient employment of human resources. Regimes of this type, in Algeria, Egypt, Iraq, Syria and Tunisia, expanded health services and education to reach women in various social sectors and were concerned about enrolling women in general production. During this period, many Arab women gained important entitlements such as free general education. Their participation in the job market expanded, especially in the public sector, and they obtained health and social insurance. This period also witnessed new legislation, which granted women rights such as the rights to work, to education and to health in addition to certain political rights, such as the right to vote and to run for election to parliament. Women were also appointed as ministers, and "model" women in various practical and scientific fields were honoured by the State as a way for the latter to show its support for new roles for women in the public sphere.

Despite these important State accomplishments, often termed "developmentalist" or "State feminist," such policies were criticised by some as top-down gifts prepared without the participation of their supposed beneficiaries. The latter, however, were the same parties that were capable of protecting and developing them. Critics also contended that, at the same time as the State was granting women such recognition in the name of modernisation, it was working to destroy their unions and independent associations and either co-opt women within its executive framework or marginalise them. Women thus were left no space to criticize the problems and lapses of modernisation itself (Kandiyoti, 1991; Molyneux, 1991; Hatem, 1994a, 2000). Countries were also criticized for their reluctance to introduce radical changes to the law in general and especially to those laws relating to the internal organisation of family relations, thus preserving the view of a woman as a man's dependant.

As a result of the spread of economic restructuring and the allocation of a larger role to market forces and the private sector in the late 1970s, the State's role in national

development operations declined, as did that of the public sector, the largest employer of women. There was, however, no corresponding growth in the capacity of the private sector to absorb the increasing female workforce. With the withdrawal of the State from numerous productive and service areas, NGOs expanded significantly and were encouraged to fill the gap, especially with regard to the provision of social services and economic assistance.

The 1985 United Nations conference on women in Nairobi and the follow-up international conferences in the series were important points in the introduction of women-and-development concepts to the Arab region. They greatly assisted in exposing Arab NGOs and Arab governments to the issue of women development.

Though a large number of Arab CSOs continued with their charity-based approach to work, many others, especially among the new NGOs that began to appear in the mid-1980s, adopted the gender-and-development approach. This led to a substantial crop of papers, research projects and approaches analysing the situation of women from a gender perspective. These outcomes helped in raising awareness of the various types of discrimination against women and in pressuring governments to adopt policies fairer to women and to work to bridge gender gaps.

The spread of the women-and-development concept in the Arab region aroused the anger of certain socio-political powers. The latter felt that the concept was "imposed" by the West and did not arise from the reality or the needs of Arab women, which were assumed to centre on strengthening the role of the family as opposed to the individual as society's basic building block (Huwaydi, in Arabic, 1998). This reaction led some to resist gender-sensitive development plans and the State and women's organisations that adopted this perspective.

A number of development organisations have adopted the concept of "women's empowerment" as a general compass for policies and activities in women's development. As with many concepts relating to women's development, that of "empowerment" has caused controversy in women's and developmental circles. Some feel that the concept of empowerment is incapable of achieving the desired change because it focuses only on the empowerment of individuals. It neglects collective empowerment, which aims to change the social, economic and political infrastructure that generates oppression and discrimination not only against women but against the majority of the poor and the marginalised as well (Agarwal, 1994; Kabeer, 2003; Radtke and Stam, 1994; Rowlands, 1998).

The concept of empowerment was translated literally by many of the NGOs working for women's development. Some concentrated on empowering women to demand equal rights and the abolition of the discrimination in Arab laws, whether with regard to naturalisation rights, personal status or social security. Others focused on offering loans and establishing income-generating projects or providing services in the health, education or other sectors. Despite the importance of these interventions in assisting some women and individuals, the path to the collective empowerment of women has yet to be taken, as chapters 2 and 3 seek to illustrate.

PROBLEMATIC ISSUES IN THE RISE OF WOMEN

THE QUESTION OF THE "INTERNAL" AND THE "EXTERNAL"

It cannot be overemphasised that the cause of women is a global issue and not one that pertains only to the Arab world. Indeed, the successes and experiences of women's movements around the world have expanded the horizons of Arab women's organisations, provided windows of opportunity for their members and sustained their faith in the possibility of proactive change. Such change will nonetheless come about only if the interlocking impediments that prevent it from taking place are dismantled.

Likewise, an enforced separation between what is deemed local and what is deemed foreign is no longer possible in this age. What is called "foreign" culture actually thrives within Arab communities – particularly in terms of values and styles of behaviour – owing to the

BOX 1-4

Excerpts from United Nations Security Council Resolution 1325 (2000)

1. Urges Member States to ensure increased representation of women at all decision-making levels in national, regional and international institutions and mechanisms for the prevention, management, and resolution of conflict;
......

10. Calls on all parties to armed conflict to take special measures to protect women and girls from gender-based violence, particularly rape and other forms of sexual abuse, and all other forms of violence in situations of armed conflict".

Full text of the resolution is provided in annex III.

increasing globalisation of Arab communities. Nor is such a separation beneficial, for there can be no doubt that the aspiration for progress in the Arab world – which is an authentic aspiration – has been positively influenced since the beginning of the Arab renaissance by the best human accomplishments of Western civilisation.

Specifically, there is collaboration, largely beneficial, between the struggle for women's emancipation in the Arab countries as a liberating orientation in Arab society and women's movements around the world, including in the West. The efforts of international organisations are of special importance in this respect especially with regard to the agreements, resolutions, mechanisms and international activities aimed at protecting women's rights and equal treatment.

These positive advances, however, do not alter the fact that the empowerment of women in Arab countries has lately intersected with the political objectives of dominant world powers in the region that are reflected in externally initiated reform initiatives. These initiatives focus on empowering women, possibly as a type of reform tolerable to despotic regimes as an alternative to abolishing the structures of oppression. This may explain the relatively better progress made in women's empowerment compared to the faltering pace of political reform, through an increase in the number of high-profile women appointed to leading State positions. Despite this, however, women's share of such leadership positions still fails to reflect fully the reality of their effective presence in all domains.

Some feel that the concept of empowerment is incapable of achieving the desired change because it focuses only on the empowerment of individuals.

The cause of women is a global issue and not one that pertains only to the Arab world.

The violation of national sovereignty by external forces casts a shadow on the rise of women

In modern Arab history, the suffering of Arabs resulting from violations of their sovereignty by external forces has led to the even greater subjugation of women. Failure to confront the region's enemies is among the factors that have spawned a renewed emphasis on male-centred notions of honour and glory arising from an overwhelming feeling of humiliation.

This painful emotion is, on the one hand, denied and, on the other, transcended in hopes of saving the wounded male ego by grasping at illusory sources of personal power on the level of the self and its historical identity. These compensating assertions of power express themselves in the oppression of social groups, such as women, who are thought to be weak or deficient.

This problem appeared in a new light when the present American Administration designated the reform of Arab social structures as part of its "war on terror". Here the report refuses to accept the confusion of the criminal terrorisation of innocent people, which is unreservedly condemned, with legitimate resistance to foreign occupation and racism, which is justified in international human rights law.

While the "liberation" of Arab women has assumed a high position on the reform agenda of certain foreign powers, the eradication of totalitarian structures and authoritarianism has not received similar priority. The threat of foreign intervention in the Arab region, by coercion or by force of arms, also continues to be legitimised as a way to implement plans by dominant forces in the world power structure.

The nature of the American project for the Arab woman is revealed in its clearest form in the attempt to formulate a "guiding model" for Arab women on Iraqi soil (Box 1-5). This model aims to restructure the social fabric of that country as though the Iraqi woman had emerged with the invasion and occupation. It ignores her long patriotic struggle, first against British occupation, then under the previous despotic regime, and finally against the present American-British occupation.

Such ambiguous efforts have led many Arabs to stigmatise the endeavour to liberate women as a task taken from the agenda of Western imperialism and to demean those who call for it as creatures of the West. Moreover, foreign calls for reform, even if by force if necessary, have also created a backlash against Arab models for the rise of women, which have been bracketed with outside initiatives considered to encroach on Arab culture and sovereignty. All of this has harmed the cause of the rise of women in Arab countries and those who support it.

This does not mean, however, that the social struggle for women's development should be abandoned. Indeed, that reaction would leave the space open for externally imposed reform plans and strengthen them. It is unfortunate, though, that the rejection of foreign-inspired initiatives should negatively impact on genuine calls for the rise of women that are firmly grounded in national and humane frameworks.

BOX 1-5

Haifa Zangana: Iraqi Women and the Discourse of the American Occupation

In the months just before the start of the war on Iraq, a number of Iraqi and Iraqi-American women's organisations were founded, with two objectives. The first of these was tactical, namely, to provide a moral justification for the war following the increase in popular opposition in America and elsewhere. The second was strategic and had the goal of using the success of the women's agenda in Iraq as a model that could be replicated throughout the Arab and Islamic countries to sanctify United States political, military and economic activities. Thus the women members of the organisations in question undertook intense and enthusiastic activities of unprecedented scope in support of the United States in the stages leading up to the war and also, afterwards, in furtherance of the American discourse.

In line with American discourse on Iraq and the region, the programmes of these women's organisations and the statements of their members, whether inside or outside Iraq, are devoid of certain terms that are deeply rooted in Iraqi society and, indeed, throughout almost all societies in the world. These are the terms that denote concepts of nationalism, national sovereignty and independence. These matters are entirely missing, together with any call to put an end to the occupation. It may be that such terms are excluded because they express the principles that grant any occupied people the legal and moral right to resist.

This is why Iraqi women's organisations of this type have failed – despite their extensive material resources and the support of the American Administration and Iraq's temporary governments – to achieve any practical success in Iraqi women's circles and have been unable to win the Iraqi women's vote. Nor have they been able to expand. On the contrary, they have remained more or less limited to the names on the first list of founders. The reason for this is that they quite simply do not represent the Iraqi woman and have no relation to her priorities, her realities or her aspirations. Their programmes remain merely one more point of implementation for the American project in Iraq.

Source: Zangana, 2005.

Rather, the response to such imperious schemes and to those who use them as pretexts to delay or prevent Arab women from achieving their rights is to integrate the rise of women, in thought and practice, as a solid pillar of a comprehensive Arab renaissance project. This will be the most effective way to combat both despotism at home and interference from abroad, through a collective rebirth that would secure the dignity and inviolability of all Arabs, women and men alike.

An Arab renaissance integrates the rise of women, in thought and practice, as a solid pillar.

BOX 1-6

Arab Public Opinion in Four Arab Countries Bespeaks Strong Support for the Rise of Arab Women

The methodology of the Arab Human Development Report has been based on field-based research surveys on the topic of each particular Report with the aim of enriching the database on the subject at hand by adding epistemological insights that cannot be obtained from the standard sources of data and information.

For this edition, the Report team supervised the design and implementation of a public opinion survey on a number of issues relating to the rise of Arab women in four Arab countries (Egypt, Jordan, Lebanon and Morocco) whose diversity of geographical location and societal structures was expected to lead to diversity in the positions of the public on those issues; together these countries form more than one third of the population of the Arab region (36.5 per cent). The survey was conducted in each participating country on a representative sample of each society comprising around 1,000 people divided equally between men and women over 18 years of age. The national surveys were conducted by establishments in the countries involved independently of the Report team (Annex II).

Some of the results of the field survey are presented in the form of boxes inserted in the chapters of this Report under the title "Public Opinion on Aspects of the Rise of Arab Women, Four Arab Countries, 2005". Each box contains two charts. The one on the right summarises the results of the survey regarding the issue under study in the four countries taken together, while the chart on the left presents the results for each individual country with regard to one of the most critical of the responses to the question .

The most important result from the survey is that the Arab public, represented in the samples from the four participating Arab countries, aspires to a much greater degree of equality between men and women. This conclusion would, however, vary according to the extent of equality from one country to another and depending on the strength of traditional societal structures within the country.

Public Opinion on Aspects of the Rise of Arab Women, Four Arab Countries, 2005

Does gender equality relate to the total concept of freedom?

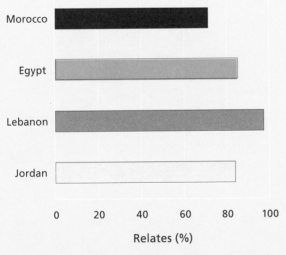

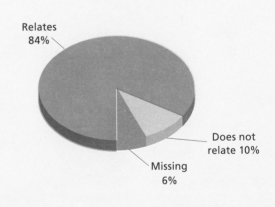

It is not surprising that the results of these surveys point to aspirations towards a level of gender equality higher than that found today and certainly higher than that which will result if societal structures that hamper the rise of Arab women continue unchanged. However, these results must also be understood in the light of the well-known distinction – recognized as being potentially great – between attitudes and actual behaviour on the one hand and the limited abilities of regimes in the Arab countries to give expression to the popular will on the other.

Accordingly, the survey results indicate a popular endorsement of the support expressed in the chapters of this Report for the rise of women and presented explicitly in its Strategic Vision (Chapter 10).

The survey results presented in the Public Opinion boxes at times support the Report's analysis but more often constitute a dialectical engagement with the contents of its analytical sections and their strategic and futuristic orientation, which culminates in Chapter 10.

Despotic authority and the rise of women

Ideally, a shift towards a society of freedom and good governance according to the concept outlined at the start of this chapter, would bring about the rise of Arab women as part of a comprehensive effort to realise human development in the Arab world.

Historical experience reveals, however, that the opposite was not always the case. In other words, the relationship between the nature of ruling authority and the advancement of women has always been complicated if only because of the complex nature of the surrounding social context.

On the one hand, repressive regimes have contributed to important achievements in favour of women's rights that might not been achieved if matters had been left to the natural progress of society, given its imposed constraints. At the head of such achievements is the exponential expansion in girls' education within a conservative environment; here it is possible to say that the various authorities, despotic as they may be, have been ahead of society. However, this sort of progress is not limited to this one achievement, which is common to nearly all Arab regimes. Important achievements, pioneering by any standard, have been realised in Arab countries under regimes that lack components of the society of freedom and good governance.

The most famous example here is Tunisia, which can boast of pioneering achievements in women's rights through the decrees of a leader who enjoyed historical and national legitimacy even though his rule failed to maintain freedom and democracy.

There are numerous other examples. Women have achieved significant progress under the previous despotic rule in Iraq. In Egypt and other countries, achievements in the rise of women have been registered under the sponsorship of the highest levels of authority, albeit represented in the person of a First Lady and without enjoying any mass support. Examples of this include the endorsement in Egypt in 2000 of a woman's right to initiate divorce (*khul'*), which caused feverish debate within the community as a whole as well as in the parliament prior to its endorsement. It may

even be said that the mechanisms of political oppression have served at times to accelerate the rise of women, but this imperious, top-down style of "progress", however enlightened, is bound to encounter objections and resistance from the popular base.

More recently, the question of the role of ruling authorities has intersected with the external/internal question referred to earlier. Under regimes that basically derive their legitimacy from foreign support, achievements in women's rights have been encouraged, possibly in order to appease dominant global powers who call for reform, including women's empowerment, in Arab countries. The latter area appears to be the type of reform least damaging for current regimes, especially if they do not follow it through to its logical conclusion, which would entail empowering all citizens, especially the broad mass of women. This explains why one may see a women's summit in Arab countries but never a summit to protect freedoms or human rights both of which remain hard to achieve under the current ruling structures in the region.

While repressive authorities occasionally support the rise of women, on the other side of the coin, they also sometimes fall back on conservative social forces, whose rights to organisation and expression they deny but which they do not mind exploiting, in order to wash their hands of such demands. The most important example of this is the abstention of some governments from ratifying CEDAW or their registration, on ratification, of reservations to some of its most important articles on the pretext of representing the positions of conservative social forces in their constituencies.

For reasons discussed, the position of this Report is that the move towards good governance and the society of freedom in Arab countries can be crucial in realising required historic achievements for the rise of women but that steps taken must also receive wide support in society to ensure their sustainability and popular adoption. In such an ideal situation, government decisions would, on the one hand, reflect the popular will transparently and, on the other, create an atmosphere of freedom and good governance in general. This would establish the

The relationship between the nature of ruling authority and the advancement of women has always been complicated.

While repressive authorities occasionally support the rise of women, on the other side of the coin, they also sometimes fall back on conservative social forces.

The transition towards good governance and the society of freedom in Arab countries can be crucial the rise of women.

bases of equality among all citizens in such a way as to ensure the stability of the rights of women in particular as an authentic component of the society of freedom and good governance.

The undervaluation of women's participation in economic activity

As in many developing societies, Arab society does not acknowledge the true extent of women's participation in social and economic activities and in the production of the components of human well-being, and it does not reward women adequately for such participation.

Since most women work, without pay, for their families, their contributions are not recognised as economic activity. This historical prejudice is reflected in the undervaluing of women's contributions to different types of human activity in general and to economic activity in particular. It is widely believed, for example, that the contribution of women to economic life in Arab countries is weak. The theoretical basis for statistics on women's participation in economic activity is the national accounts system, which in turn derives from the neo classical theory of modernism that defines human production in terms of goods and services exchanged in the market and their cash value.

A number of caveats need to be made with regard to this theoretical basis, especially from the perspective of women's participation in human welfare.

First, the criteria for transactions in the market and their cash valuation restrict human welfare to a narrow definition that development literature has long gone beyond and that has no place within the human development perspective.

Second, most goods and services produced by women fall into the category of unpaid work within the family. This national accounts-based starting point excludes from the beginning the production of all those elements of human welfare that women provide within the family because these are not exchanged in the market and are not evaluated in cash. It may be asked, however, whether the affairs of any individual, or of any society, can go well or, to be more specific, whether any creativity or production

in the restricted sense, can thrive without these contributions.

Third, standard statistical processes, especially those in developing countries, suffer from several defects that are exacerbated when the contribution of women to the economy is involved. This shortcoming is not, however, the source of the contemptuous view of women and their participation in society still prevalent in developing countries.

The result is that independent standard statistics gravely underestimate women's participation in economic activity. Even tightening definitions and improving the quality of statistical operations lead nonetheless to massive variances in estimating the extent of women's participation in the economy.

If available statistics underestimate women's participation in economic activity, imagine how much more they fail to grasp the value of their contributions, direct and indirect, to human welfare, which cannot be achieved without women's participation in human society – and that with a multiplier effect that adds to the contribution of men. Of course, this does not mean that women's capacities should be limited to household work. Rather, it means that women's contributions, as with any human contributions to the collective welfare, whether inside or outside the home, should be recognised as having a value beyond narrow monetary terms. Moreover, how a woman chooses to use her capabilities should be a decision taken freely only by her.

In short, traditional methods of measuring the employment of women's capabilities, especially in economic terms, entail a severe injustice in respect of their actual contribution, which must be rated highly, if not in financial terms, then in terms of human values.

The evidence for this comes from alternative measures such as time-use research, which tries to capture the enormous contribution of women to the production of the elements of human welfare, contributions that at times come close to outweighing those of men, especially in developing societies. Most of these activities, such as fetching water and gathering fuel for cooking, light and heating, are overlooked by statistics that follow the logic of national accounts systems and their statistical tools.

As in many developing societies, Arab society does not acknowledge the true extent of women's participation in social and economic activities.

Traditional methods of measuring the employment of women's capabilities, especially in economic terms, entail a severe injustice.

In Morocco for example, women's economic participation during 1997-1998 reached 71.4 per cent in the countryside, 34.6 per cent in towns and cities and 50.6 per cent at the national level. These percentages clearly exceed the traditional estimate (Morocco, Department of Statistics, in French, 1998).

On the other hand, if one uses the advanced criteria for human well-being broadly accepted in the field of human development, then no monetary evaluation of women's contribution to human welfare in Arab countries, no matter how high, will do justice to them or their potential to help build an Arab human renaissance.

A proper evaluation of women's contribution to producing the elements of human welfare requires a creative theoretical foundation that goes beyond the national accounts system, restricted as it is to market exchange and the cash valuation of goods and services. This can be done by moving to use a broad definition of human welfare that is appropriate to the concept of human development. In practical terms, this calls for the development of research and statistical tools that aim to measure accurately women's contribution to human welfare and human development. This is a field that is wide open to thought and research.

SUMMARY

This chapter has set out the conceptual framework of the present Report by revisiting the central concepts underpinning the series of Arab Human Development Reports, specifically those relating to freedoms, human rights, equality between men and women, and human dignity. Certain problematic issues related to the current situation of women in the Arab region have also been considered.

The contents of this chapter, especially of its second half, indicate that the situation of women in the Arab countries is the outcome of the interaction of many cultural, social, economic and political elements, which articulate in a complex manner. Some of these elements are problematically embedded in Arab societies and call for a wide, in-depth analysis of several components of these societies in order to diagnose the situation of women. Such an analysis should be followed by an attempt to interpret this situation objectively as a basis for crafting a strategic vision for the rise of Arab women in the Arab world.

THE STATE OF WOMEN IN
THE ARAB WORLD

CHAPTER TWO

THE ACQUISITION OF HUMAN CAPABILITIES

Introduction

In Arab countries, women have far fewer opportunities than men do to acquire essential capabilities and to utilise them effectively on a broad front. They are also more widely deprived than men of their civil and human rights. In human development terms, such deprivation is seen as the main characteristic of "the marginalisation of women". Women's opportunities to develop and utilise their capabilities differ greatly both within each Arab country as well as among them. However, available globally comparable statistics may not be sufficient to enable a comprehensive overview of these discrepancies.

BOX 2-1

Fowziyah Abu-Khalid: Images of Arab Women in the Mirror of Reality

Is there a sculpture however pregnant with countless possibilities and dreams that resembles her image? Is there a portrait, even one fashioned of flesh, blood and love, capable of reflecting the ephemeral world present in her features? Is there not enough darkness to cast into relief the image of the Arab woman, or is there not enough light to capture it in the first place? Where is her true likeness to be found?

In literature, images of Arab women are either those of victims or rebels, figures engaged in struggling against their respective conditions or torn between resignation, accommodation and defiance. In political discourse, images of women are similarly opposed. Women are either thrust aside from, or embroiled in, formulating the premises and corollaries of that discourse. Often, they themselves are divided over its assorted theoretical propositions about their identity, which variously portray them as conformist, non-conformist or indifferent. Sometimes, women are little more than female mannequins upon which the discourse tests its fancy. Such subjective discourse may conceal or emphasise features that reflect not so much the view that women or society have of women but rather the view which the authors believe that women or society should hold. Thus, the image of Arab women has been fabricated in the moulds of Western and enlightened Islamist liberation rhetoric alike, in the moulds of insular religious rhetoric and those of conciliatory or invented discourses, and in the innumerable imitative and derivative moulds to be found in the prevailing official discussion.

Even as the image of Arab women has been popularised in such simplistic forms in Arab literature and political rhetoric, the mirror of reality displays that image in all its rich variety and profusion.

Yet who sees the women of southern Saudi Arabia, their slender frames in flowing gowns bent over their tilling, their heads concealed by palm-frond hats, not to hide from prying eyes but because the sun forever tries to match the brilliant dawn that radiates from their hands, which spread across the land from the Sarawat mountains down to the Tihama Plains, which scatter artemisia, kadi and wheat, which mix their henna and massage their cracked heels in the seasonal rains?

Who sees those Algerian women no less proud and beautiful than Djamila Bouhared, reweaving the dismal darkness into new dreams, as though fearless of the looming spectres of failure and undaunted by the disaster-ridden pageants of the past?

Who sees the schoolgirls of al-Sham, outwitting their austere regime of khaki smocks and military marches as they tiptoe lightly out of doors in their apricot candy skirts, woven of the hearts of aloes with their reddish-orange pulp, like tendrils of jasmine silently threading their way out from behind walls and doors and trailing their fragrance through the alleys, with the daring of innocents, heedless of curfews and the barbed wire girdling the Golan Heights?

Who sees the ageing women on the pavements of the nation, their fragile spines gnawed away inch by inch, while they remain mute, loath to suffer the humiliation of complaining to anyone but God? With their hand-worked crafts, "women's" products and made-in-China wares, they are spread across the length and breadth of Arab streets, yet invisible to official eyes except the municipal officers who extract the fruit of their toil.

And who sees, in the breadth of Egypt, the woman dropped like a seed into the depth of the earth, kneading, baking, nursing and protecting the fields with her seven lives? She emerges with a body shaped not like a cotton flower or ear of wheat but like a question mark. In one guise, she digs her fingernails into her own flesh as though beset by [the disease] bilharzia; in another, she impersonates the brides of the Nile, who will change the fate of Egypt's daughters in ways no less confrontational.

Source: Abu-Khalid, in Arabic, background paper for the Report.

OBSTACLES TO THE ACQUISITION OF BASIC HUMAN CAPABILITIES

CHALLENGES TO HEALTH

The maternal mortality rate in Arab countries averages 270 deaths per 100,000 live births.

This section considers health according to the definition of the World Health Organisation (WHO), in its positive, comprehensive sense of complete physical and mental well-being.

How women fare on indicators of reproductive health

Women in Arab countries, especially the least developed countries, endure unacceptably high rates of risk of morbidity and mortality connected with pregnancy and reproductive functions (Figure 2-1).

The maternal mortality rate in Arab countries averages 270 deaths per 100,000 live births. This rises to over 1,000 deaths in the poorest Arab countries (Mauritania and Somalia) and falls to levels such as 7 for every 100,000 births in Qatar. The rate of births attended by trained personnel exceeds 80 per cent in most Arab countries, which indicates improved health coverage; however, it remains weak in less developed countries such as Mauritania, Somalia and Yemen. In Yemen, for example, only one quarter of births are attended by trained personnel. The level of effective supervision of pregnancy, which requires four medical visits, varies among countries and is not necessarily tied to income levels, since, for instance, it is higher in Lebanon than in Qatar.

Figure 2-1

Maternal mortality ratio (per 100,000 live births), 2000, and percentage of births attended by skilled personnel, latest year available during the period 1993-2003

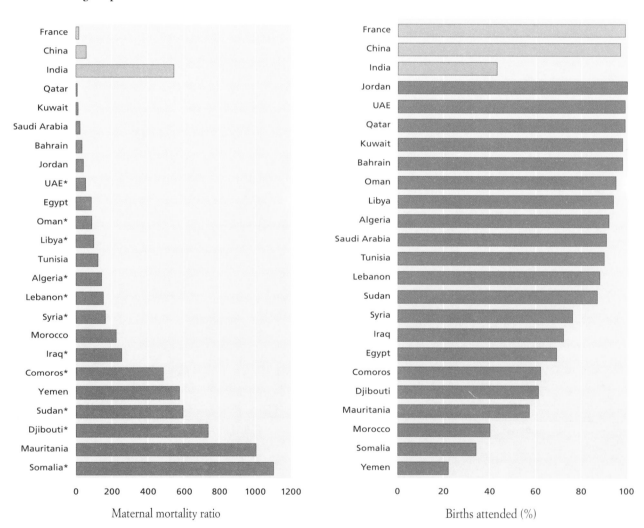

* Estimate derived by regression and similar methods.

Source: World Health Organisation, 2005.

Pregnancy supervision and continuing care for the new-born are in accordance with the Millennium Development Goals (MDGs), which encompass the improvement of puerperal (childbed) health and the reduction of infant mortality rates.

The average fertility rate in the Arab region remains high despite its decline to 3.81 live births for the period 2000-2005, down from 4.13 for the period 1995-2000. This is high compared to the rest of the developing world, where the rate does not exceed 2.9 live births (World Health Organisation, 2005). Fertility rates are especially high in the less developed Arab countries, such as Yemen, that do not have a health apparatus capable of providing necessary health care to mothers and infants. It is also worth noting the problematic consequences of unwanted pregnancies among married women in the Arab world. These lead not only to abortions, which are unsafe, but also to physical and emotional pressures on mothers and their children.

Likewise, the sterility problems and miscarriages from which Arab women suffer are ignored, a matter that seriously harms their mental and social well-being. Failure to bear children leads some women to resort to dangerous treatments (electric cauterization, dilation and curettage, and inflation of the fallopian tubes) that expose them to serious health hazards. It also contributes to social pressures and high rates of divorce (UNIFEM, in Arabic, 2004, 54).

Years of life lost to disease

"Years of life lost to disease" has become a critical global health (in its comprehensive sense) indicator in a given society.[1] On average, women lose a relatively greater number of years of life to disease than do men (Figure 2-2). This falls harder on women in wealthier Arab countries.

Since Arab women generally enjoy high levels of health care during pregnancy and childbirth, especially in the wealthier Arab countries (figure 2-1), the larger number of years they lose to disease is attributable to general differences in lifestyle that do not necessarily

Figure 2-2

Expectation of lost healthy years at birth (years), females as a percentage of males, Arab and comparator countries, 2002

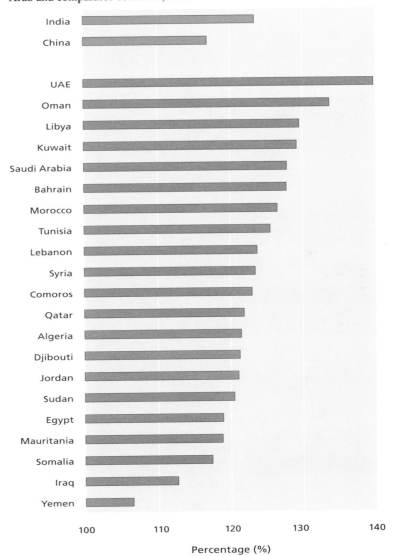

Source: World Health Organisation, 2004.

[1] On the other hand, the "life expectancy at birth" indicator points to the reduction of death rates in a society and thus how long an individual can expect to live. The importance of "years of life lost to disease" is thus its ability to indicate how many years on average an individual spends in illness.

depend on the wealth of the country. Rather, the higher rate of sickness among women has to do with deep-seated discrimination based on gender, on which the material wealth of the society has little impact.

Special health problems

Obesity and diabetes

The Arab region is witnessing a continuing transformation in its way of life as urban lifestyles move into the villages and desert. This transformation has led to a decline in the rate of bacterial, viral and parasitical diseases along with an increase in chronic diseases such as cancer, hypertension, diabetes and heart disease.

The spread of late-onset diabetes in the Arab world is worrying. The most important risk factor in the appearance of late-onset diabetes is obesity, which WHO considers (with AIDS) to be the epidemic of the age, with more than one billion adults suffering from overweight and at least 300 million of those suffering from obesity (World Health Organisation, 2003).

WHO measures levels of obesity and overweight on the basis of the increase of body mass.[2] It is clear that obesity and overweight constitute a widespread problem in richer countries both in the Arab region as well as in the rest of the world. Nevertheless, what is important to note here is that more women than men suffer from the problem in all the Arab countries where statistics were available, as opposed to comparator countries, where, apparently, on average, more men are overweight than women (Figure 2-3).

The problem of obesity and overweight has worsened as societies have moved towards urban lifestyles and as the need for physical exertion has diminished, coupled with a paucity of sports facilities, especially in crowded schools in rural areas. It has been compounded as corporations promote foodstuffs excessively rich in sugar, fats and salt – foodstuffs that, given cultural predispositions, facilitate the emergence of extremely serious health hazards, especially among children and women. Cultural and social factors may play a role in that they fail to encourage women and girls to engage in sports, partly reflecting the ingrained notion that the female body is deficient.

Acquired immune deficiency syndrome (AIDS) virus

The Arab region remains one of those currently least affected by the AIDS virus.[3] Despite this, Arab women and girls are becoming infected by it in increasing numbers and now represent half the total number of people carrying the virus in the region. Women are now at greater risk of catching the virus and contracting the disease: the probability of infection among females from 15 to 24 years of age is double that of males in the same age group (Joint United Nations Programme on HIV/AIDS, in Arabic, 2004, 5). Among the main causes of heightened risk are: the low level of empowerment of Arab

Figure 2-3

Rates of obesity and overweight (population 15+ years) by gender, Arab and comparator countries, 2005

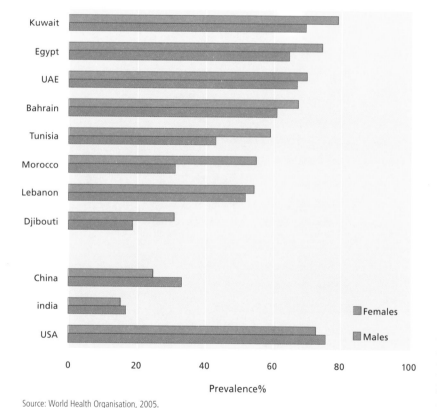

Source: World Health Organisation, 2005.

---

[2] The body mass index (BMI) relates weight (in kilograms) to height (in metres). A person is considered overweight if the index is higher than 25 and obese if the index is higher than 30.

[3] The number of people who tested positive for the human immunodeficiency virus (HIV) in the Arab region was estimated to be about 540,000 in 2004.

women; the poor quality of health services provided to them; poor monitoring and testing services; and the dearth of information on methods of protection against the AIDS virus in the prevailing culture of silence surrounding issues of sexual and reproductive health.

Many girls and women in Arab countries know little about their bodies, their sexual and reproductive health and the AIDS virus. High rates of illiteracy and the low rate of school attendance among females in some Arab countries compound the problem. A study carried out in 32 countries showed that the rate of awareness of facts about the AIDS virus was five times higher among women who had received some education beyond the basic level than among women who were illiterate (UNICEF, in Arabic, 2004, 31).

In addition, women in many parts of the Arab world are not economically independent, which increases their reliance on men and makes them more exposed to sexual subjugation and physical violence. This in turn limits their ability to protect themselves from the AIDS virus, especially since a large number of sexually active men do not use condoms, thus exposing their wives to the danger of infection. Estimates indicate that the vast majority of women in the Arab region infected by the virus contracted it from their husbands (Joint United Nations Programme on HIV/ AIDS, in Arabic, 2004, 39-40).

Practices such as female genital mutilation (female circumcision) increase the probability of female infection. This may result from the use of unsterilised tools during circumcision or from being exposed to tearing or injury during sexual intercourse, which leads to bleeding and increases the capacity for transmitting the virus. The problem is now manifesting itself in its ugliest form in Darfur in western Sudan, where many circumcised women have been raped during the conflict, leading to a sharp rise in the incidence of AIDS among the women there.

Factors adding to the suffering of women with AIDS are the discrimination, exclusion, and marginalisation to which they are exposed in their societies.

ACQUIRING KNOWLEDGE THROUGH EDUCATION

The quantitative spread

Despite the tremendous spread of girls' education in Arab countries in the last five decades (AHDR 2002 and 2003), Arab women remain poorly prepared to participate effectively and fruitfully in public life by acquiring knowledge through education. This is most clearly manifested in the extent to which girls and women are still deprived of education and knowledge, especially those forms of knowledge that bring high social returns. As shown in Figures 2-4 to 2-6, the Arab region

The vast majority of women in the Arab region infected by the AIDS virus contracted it from their husbands.

Arab women remain poorly prepared to participate effectively and fruitfully in public life by acquiring knowledge through education.

BOX 2-3

The Cairo Declaration of Religious Leaders in the Arab States in Response to the HIV/AIDS Epidemic, 13 December 2004

We, the assembled Muslim and Christian religious leaders . . . have agreed upon the following:

- Being aware of the value of every human being and conscious of God's glorification of all human beings irrespective of their situation, background or medical condition, we declare that we bear a major responsibility and duty to move rapidly in the face of the imminent danger of the HIV/AIDS epidemic.
- Illness is one of God's tests; anyone may be afflicted by it according to God's choice. Patients are our brothers and sisters, and we stand by them seeking God's healing for each one of them.
- We advocate the rights of women to protect themselves from exposure to HIV/AIDS and to take advantage of the relevant medical and educational services.

- People living with HIV/AIDS and their families deserve care, support, treatment, and education, whether or not they are responsible for their illness. We call on our religious institutions to provide them with spiritual and psychological aid and, in cooperation with other institutions, to assure them economic assistance. We also encourage them not to lose faith in God's mercy, and aspire to a rewarding and productive life to the last, embracing fate with courage and faith.
- We emphasise the necessity to abolish and reject all forms of discrimination, exclusion, marginalisation and stigmatisation of people living with HIV/AIDS and we insist on the necessity for them to enjoy their basic freedoms and human rights to the full.

Source: "Family Health International." (2006). http://www.fhi.org/NR/rdonlyres/ezq22beaksmsi57uhzlr5azfnhyup4oyyycluyhzvouua3cg7vmppsy3dkldicxz3hgnfllxkggtmh/CairoReligiousLeadersDec larationEnglish.pdf (Accessed 18 April, 2006).

Figure 2-4

Female literacy rate as a percentage of male literacy rate (age 15+ years), world regions, 2003

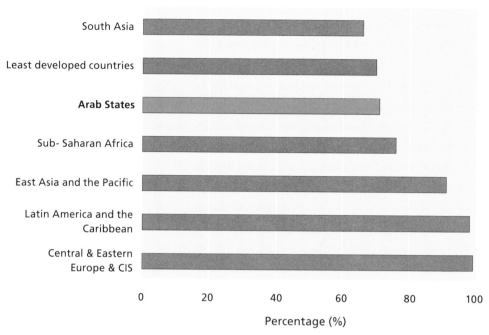

Source: UNDP, 2005.

has one of the world's lowest rates of female education, i.e., one of the highest rates of illiteracy (one half of females are illiterate compared to only one third of males), and of enrolment opportunities at the various levels of education, especially that of higher education.

The relatively higher deprivation of girls in terms of educational opportunities at all levels extends across all Arab countries, with female access to education remaining below that of males (three quarters of females versus four fifths of males) though the situation may vary from one to another (Figure 2-5). The enrolment rate of girls in several Arab oil-producing countries and in Jordan, Lebanon, the occupied Palestinian territory and Tunisia is higher than that of boys. The highest relative rate of deprivation of education occurs in the less developed Arab countries, such as Djibouti and Yemen, and in those with the largest populations, such as Egypt, Morocco and Sudan.

This relatively greater denial of educational opportunities to girls runs counter to Arab public opinion as indicated in the field survey, which unanimously affirms women's right to education on an equal footing with men.

Enrolment at various educational levels, by gender

Despite the success of Arab countries, especially Gulf Cooperation Council countries, in increasing the rate of female educational enrolment, which has narrowed the gaps between the sexes at all three educational levels, a number of Arab countries continue to exhibit large discrepancies throughout the education system.

Pre-school education

Statistics show a major deficiency in pre-school education in Arab countries. The Arab child on average is provided with 0.4 years of pre-schooling compared to 1.6 years in Latin America and the Caribbean, 1.8 years in Central and Eastern Europe and 2.2 years in North America and Western Europe (UNESCO, 2005, 1). In general, the enrolment rate in pre-school education in the Arab region is less than 20 per cent and reaches its lowest levels in Algeria, Djibouti, Oman, Saudi Arabia and Yemen, where it is less than 5 per cent. Kuwait, Lebanon and the United Arab Emirates are considered the most successful countries in that the pre-school enrolment rate has reached

Figure 2-5

Combined gross enrolment rate, all levels of education, female as a percentage of male, Arab countries, 2002/2003

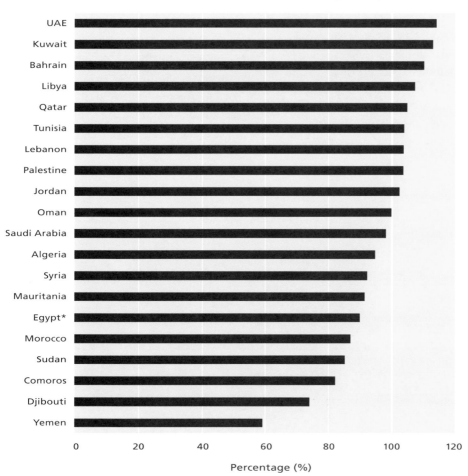

* Data for the year 2000/2001 (from: UNDP, 2003).
Source: UNDP, 2005.

Figure 2-6

Gross enrolment rate in tertiary education, females as a percentage of males, world regions, 2002/2003

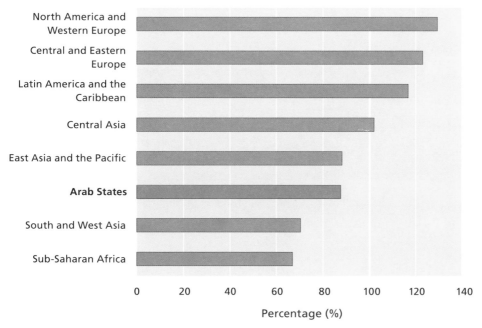

Source: UNESCO web site (http://stats.uis.unesco.org/ReportFolders/reportfolders.aspx, Table M)

70 per cent. Likewise, the rate is less than the average in developing countries (42 per cent compared to 47 per cent in 1995) (AHDR 2002, 52). Also, in general, most countries of the region fail to give the necessary priority to this level of education. For the most part, reliance is placed on for-profit private institutions or women's organisations, indicating a belief that the support of small children is considered basically a women's issue and not a public priority.

Primary education

The enrolment rate in primary education fluctuates greatly from one Arab country to another. It has reached 95 per cent in Syria and Tunisia but is less than 50 per cent in Djibouti and Sudan (Figure 2-7). Despite this, most Arab countries have taken great strides in reducing the educational gap between the two sexes at the primary level: the enrolment rate of girls is at least 90 per cent that of boys in all Arab States except the Comoros, Morocco and Yemen.

Figure 2-7

Girls' net enrolment rate in primary education (%) and girls' rate as a percentage of boys', Arab countries, 2002/2003

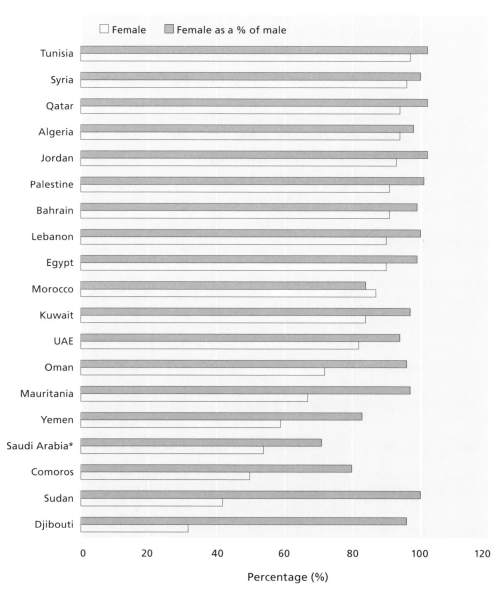

* National surveys in Saudi Arabia indicate that female enrolment at the elementary level is 95 per cent. However, this has yet to be entered in the international database used to monitor enrolment.

Source: UNDP, 2005.

Secondary education: academic and vocational

In general, the rate of female enrolment is lower in secondary education than in primary education. Fewer than 80 per cent of girls attend secondary school in all Arab countries except for four: Bahrain, Jordan, the occupied Palestinian territory and Qatar. Female enrolment is less than 20 per cent in Djibouti and Mauritania (Figure 2-8). As for the gender gap, nine Arab countries have been able to close it entirely, but it remains wide in Yemen, where female enrolment in secondary education is only 46 per cent that of male enrolment, and in Djibouti, where it is only 69 per cent.

Despite the focus on the web of customs and traditions normally cited to explain the social composition of secondary education, a number of experiments have demonstrated that the adoption by governments of serious policies to decrease the gap in this area bears fruit. In the occupied Palestinian territory, for example, the rate of girls in applied skills training rose to 45.1 per cent in 1999 from 38.9 per cent in 1995. The increase was due to the expansion of the number of classes open to girls near their homes and in their villages, with the number of first-level educational branches for girls rising to 160 in 1999 from 33 in 1995. One study indicated that, especially among the poor, economic reasons were considered to be the most important factor limiting girls' potential to complete their post-basic school education and that the factors preventing males from completing their education differ from those hampering females.

The factors preventing males from completing their education differ from those hampering females.

Figure 2-8

Girls' net enrolment rate in secondary education (%) and girls' enrolment as a percentage of boys', Arab countries, 2002/2003

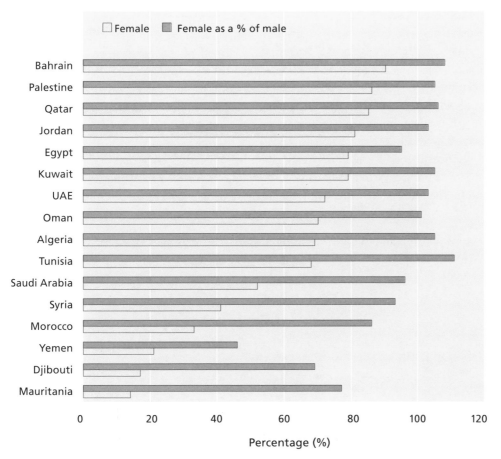

Source: UNDP, 2005.

It is clear from table 2-1 that family economic problems impact more negatively on female than on male education. Likewise, families perceive educating girls to be less important than schooling boys. It is the need to work that has the largest effect on the withdrawal of boys from school.

Discrepancies in the gender dimension of education become wider in vocational and technical education, where the rate of female enrolment is less than half that of male enrolment (UNESCO, 2002). In the occupied Palestinian territory, for example, in spite of an increase in the average enrolment rate of females to 23.8 per cent of all students in 1999 from 18.8 per cent in 1995, males still constitute nearly 77 per cent of this sector (Abu 'Awwad, in Arabic, 2003, 41). Similarly, this type of education generally tends to confirm the prevailing traditional division of the sexes in society, as girls generally move towards service-oriented professions, such as secretarial work, nursing or work as beauticians, whereas boys gravitate towards industrial, agricultural or vocational education.[4]

Some studies on how extra-curricular education (technical training, physical education, music and professional training) can confirm inequality between the two sexes have found that, in general, the participation of female students in physical education is neglected, especially in coeducational schools. The wearing of school uniforms is enforced more strictly for female students than for male students. The rate at which girls participate in extra-curricular school activities is lower than that of boys. Likewise, boys reject participation in home economics or sewing classes (Abu Nahla, in Arabic, 1996; Shukhshayr, in Arabic, 2000).

Higher education

Most data show that equality between the two sexes in higher education has been achieved in twelve Arab countries (Algeria, Bahrain, Jordan, Kuwait, Lebanon, Libya, occupied Palestinian territory, Oman, Qatar, UAE, Saudi Arabia and Tunisia). The number of women registered in higher education is greater than that of men in Kuwait, Qatar and the UAE. However, a large number of men are enrolled overseas, and most countries provide enrolment data only for local institutions. In light of this lack of reported data, it is likely that a hitherto improperly estimated gap between the sexes in higher education will be uncovered (UNESCO, 2002, 48).

In general, the enrolment of Arab women in higher education varies, being highest in Libya and the UAE, where the enrolment rate for girls is more than 50 per cent. Similarly, in Lebanon, the rate of female enrolment reached 48 per cent in 2002/2003. Female enrolment rates were lowest in the Comoros, Djibouti, Mauritania, the Sudan and Yemen where they did not exceed 10 per cent.

Despite the increase in female enrolment in university education, women are still concentrated in specialisations such as literature, the humanities and the social sciences, where

Discrepancies in the gender dimension of education become wider in vocational and technical education.

TABLE 2-1

Reasons for dropping out after basic education in the occupied Palestinian territory, by gender (%)

Gender	Reason			Total
	Desire to work	Family perspective on education	Family economic status	
Male	60	12	28	100
Female	37	30	33	100

Source: Abu Nahla, in Arabic, 1996, 117.

[4] Governments have a large role to play in changing views towards skills education. An example is the role played by the Palestinian Ministry of Education in opening up to girls new fields of vocational education that had long been closed to them. In 1998, industrial education was opened to girls though this was confined to computer maintenance. Agriculture was also opened up to them although this was limited to plant production at the expense of animal husbandry. Likewise, students were encouraged to enrol in commercial education, where girls constituted a majority: girls accounted for 85 per cent of enrolment in 1995, but later this rate fell back to 60 per cent as more boys enrolled (Nida' Abu 'Awwad, 2003:42).

Figure 2-9

Girls' gross enrolment rate in tertiary education (%) and girls' enrolment as a percentage of boys', Arab countries, 2002/2003

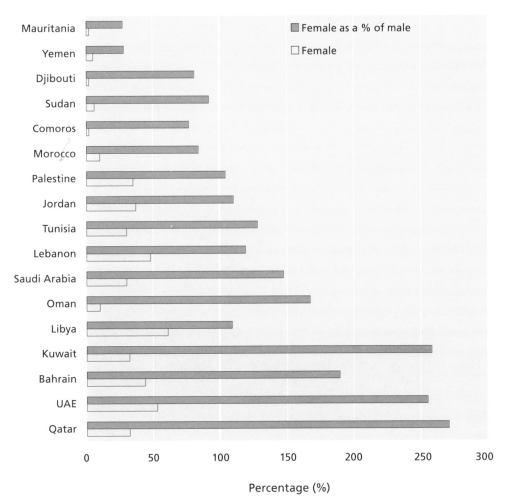

Source: UNDP, 2005.

Women are still concentrated in specialisations... which are not in high demand in the job market.

they constitute the majority, which are not in high demand in the job market. Enrolment rates for females are noticeably lower in the fields of engineering and industry, as table 2-2 shows.

This trend is due also to women's orientation towards jobs that permit part-time work and that do not contravene the traditional view of their reproductive role or the division of work in the house and the raising of a family. Examples are education and part-time jobs as civil servants. In addition, some universities discriminate against women in their acceptance criteria. At the University of Kuwait, for example, males are accepted in the engineering and petroleum studies on the basis of a grade point average of 67.9,

while female students must achieve an average of 83.5 to be accepted for the same fields of study. Even so, the region has witnessed a shift as more girls have moved towards scientific and high-tech fields. Discrepancies still exist, however, in terms of the areas of focus towards which girls are oriented within individual scientific fields. For example, most women who study engineering specialise in architecture or chemical engineering, whereas men lean towards mechanical or electrical engineering. In medicine, men gravitate towards surgery and other specialist areas whereas women take up gynaecology, paediatrics and dentistry.

Even so, the region has witnessed a shift as more girls have moved towards scientific and high-tech fields.

TABLE 2-2

Percentage of female students in selected specialisations in Arab universities, 2002/2003

Country	Humanities and literature	Business, law, social sciences	Science	Engineering, industry and construction
Bahrain	83	60	71	24
Djibouti	52	52	18	25
Jordan	37	37	51	30
Lebanon	56	56	42	21
Mauritania	23	23	14	-
Morocco	45	45	34	22
Palestine	34	34	49	35
Qatar	65	65	72	16
Saudi Arabia	30	30	41	1

Source: http://gmr.uis.unesco.org/ (14/2/2006 assembled from various tables).

The rate of illiteracy in the Arab world is higher than the world average and higher even than the average for developing nations.

Girls in the Arab region perform better in school than boys.

Illiteracy still high among women

The Arab world has certainly witnessed a tremendous expansion in female education, outpacing other regions, with the discrepancies between the region and other parts of the world decreasing. The success in increasing female enrolment in schools, however, does not mean success in eradicating female illiteracy overall. At a time when some countries at medium levels of human development such as Jordan and the occupied Palestinian territory have succeeded in raising the rate of adult (fifteen years and older) education of women to 85 per cent, the rate remains below 50 per cent in six Arab countries: the Comoros, Egypt, Mauritania, Morocco, the Sudan and Yemen. The rate of illiteracy in the Arab world is higher than the world average and higher even than the average for developing nations. Arab countries are entering the twenty-first century weighed down by the burden of about 60 million illiterate adults, i.e., 40 per cent of all adults, most of them impoverished and rural women (AHDR 2002, 51). The results of the public opinion survey confirmed the right of girls to any level of education and to the free choice of specialisation (Box 2-4).

Only a minority (not exceeding ten per cent) did not support the right of girls to choose the specialisation that they prefer. Among these respondents, the specialisations that some thought ought to be restricted to males included the military sciences (most Moroccan respondents), engineering (more than 15 per cent of respondents to this question in Egypt, Jordan and Lebanon) and medicine.

Girls are the better learners

International data indicate that girls in the Arab region perform better in school than boys. Dropout rates for girls are lower than those for boys in all the countries for which data are available with the exception of the UAE. The probability of a girl completing fifth grade exceeds 90 per cent in Algeria, Jordan, Oman, Saudi Arabia, Tunisia and the UAE. Similarly, the percentage of girls repeating a year is lower than that of boys in the countries of the region for which data are available[5] with the exception of the Sudan (UNESCO Institute for Statistics, 2002, 42-43).

All the same, discrimination against women in the Arab countries continues to limit their access to knowledge despite the mass of

[5] Algeria, Bahrain, Djibouti, Egypt, UAE, Iraq, Jordan, Kuwait, Lebanon, Morocco, Occupied Palestinian Territory, Oman, Saudi Arabia, Sudan and Tunisia.

BOX 2-4

Public Opinion on Aspects of the Rise of Arab Women, Four Arab Countries, 2005

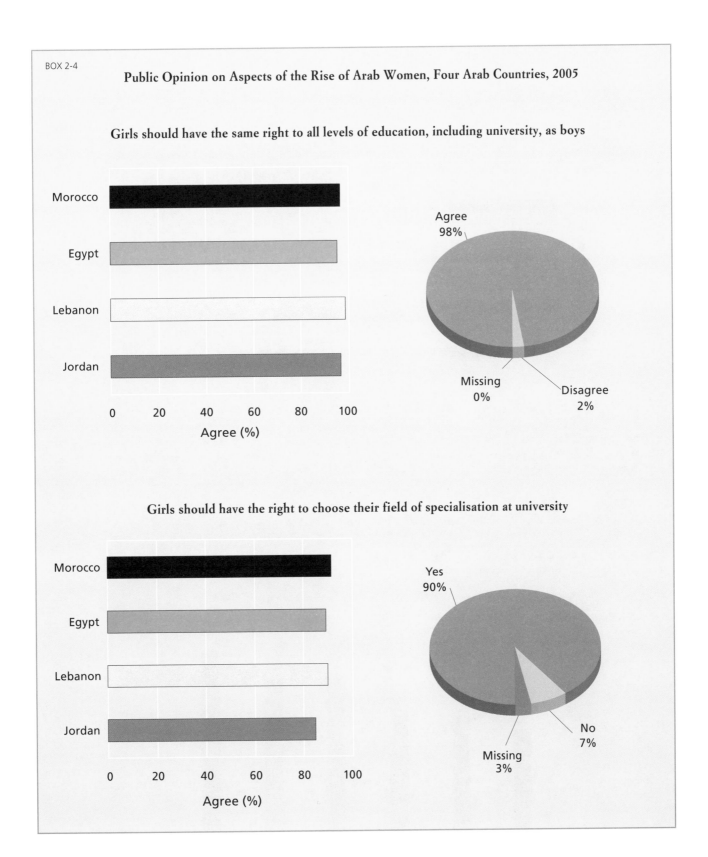

Girls should have the same right to all levels of education, including university, as boys

Girls should have the right to choose their field of specialisation at university

statistical and other evidence indicating that Arab girls are the better learners, especially on the first rungs of the educational ladder. This is illustrated in the following two boxes.

In Egypt in mid-2005, for example, the annual scene of girls securing the highest places in the national secondary school final examination – the great obstacle on the educational ladder for the wider public in Arab countries – was repeated. Despite

BOX 2-5

Girls Perform Better in Basic Education in Bahrain

The results of field studies provide ample evidence supporting the better performance of girls. In Bahrain, among the 20 students who received top scores in each of two tests, in Arabic and mathematics, 12 were girls. Of the 20 schools whose students achieved the highest average scores, 19 were girls' schools. Among the 20 lowest-scoring students, there was only one girl. The results of the analysis show that girls scored higher than boys, especially in the Arabic language.

Average scores in Arabic and mathematics (out of 100), by number of grades repeated and by gender, Bahrain, 1999

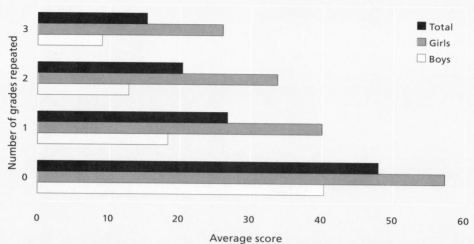

A low performance rate is associated with the repetition of grades, with the number of grades repeated by a pupil increasing as performance worsens. (The symbol "0" indicates the pupil has not repeated any grade). Girls maintain their excellence in all cases.

Source: Bahrain, Ministry of Education, Centre for Pedagogical Research and Development and Almishkat, in Arabic, 1999.

BOX 2-6

The Superior Performance of Girls in Primary Education in Kuwait

The results of an education-indicators project undertaken by the Kuwait Society for the Advancement of Arab Children show the overwhelming superiority of girls' academic scores in every subject covered by the study.

Girls' average scores in primary education subjects compared to those of boys, Kuwait, 2000

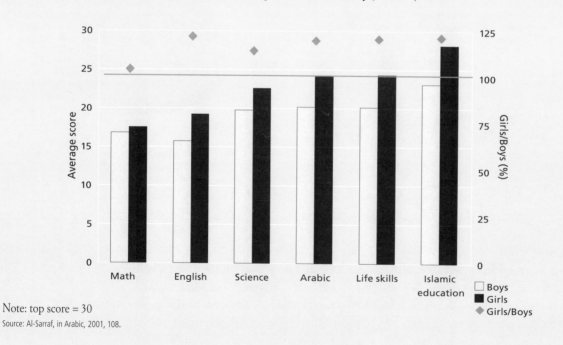

Note: top score = 30

Source: Al-Sarraf, in Arabic, 2001, 108.

the misconception that the humanities befit women most, a girl captured the number one place in both humanities and sciences. Among the top ten places, girls took 11 out of 12[6] in humanities and 7 out of 15 in sciences. The outstanding success of girls in the secondary school examination was not limited to Egypt (Figure 2-10). They also swept the board in humanities in the occupied Palestinian territory and the UAE.

Girls' share among top scorers in all Arab countries where data are available is over 50 per cent. The fact that, on average, girls make up less than half the total enrolment in education serves to confirm their higher level of academic achievement. Noticeable, too, is the higher level of academic achievement of girls in a wide variety of circumstances, in rich and poor Arab countries alike and under the most obstructive of military occupations, underscoring the intrinsic, non-circumstantial nature of their success.

The higher relative enrolment of girls in the humanities is largely due to the fields of employment open to women given current social beliefs. The jobs available tend to be linked to humanities subjects studied at the secondary level, which in turn direct girls' choices between the arts and science.

The higher level of achievement of girls extends to all levels of education, including higher education. It is important to emphasise that girls achieve their academic successes in spite of obstructive social and family environments, which envelop many of them in the fallacy that a woman's destiny is the home while learning and careers are basically the domain of men. The logical outcome here is a vindication of the distinctive qualities of girls that enable them to be proficient and, indeed, excel in the acquisition of knowledge against the odds.

In a more positive light, equality between men and women in the acquisition and use of knowledge would deliver tremendous gains, benefits that would elevate Arab society in all branches of human endeavour. At present, however, this rich harvest is something that harmful discriminatory traditions and practices prevent the region from reaping.

In reality, justice requires that the best performers be rewarded so that they and others

Despite the misconception that the humanities befit women most, girls captured the number one place in both humanities and sciences.

Figure 2-10

Percentage of girls among eminent secondary school graduates, five Arab countries, 2003-2005

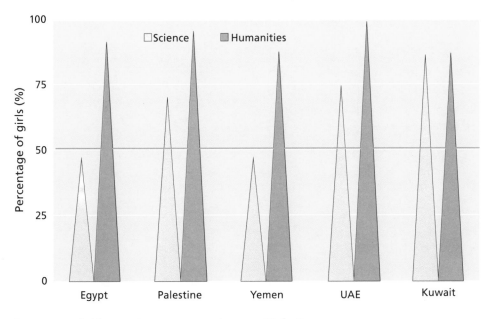

Source: compiled from various governmental sources, Nader Fergany.

Girls achieve their academic successes in spite of obstructive social and family environments.

---

[6] More than one person may be listed in each place in the case of a tie.

The release of Arab girls' and womens' capabilities...would be the freshest sign of spring in the blossoming of the Arab world.

may be encouraged, not merely that equality among the whole be imposed. If justice were done, the rewards that Arab countries would garner from the rise of women through a project for human renaissance are almost beyond reckoning.

The release of Arab girls and women's captive energies in the fields of knowledge and creativity through the creation of a familial and societal environment that rewards high achievement regardless of gender, would be the freshest sign of spring in the blossoming (izdihar) of the Arab world.

CHAPTER THREE

THE USE OF HUMAN CAPABILITIES

Introduction

No society can develop or prosper without women playing a pivotal role in its formation. This role is not restricted to their biological function as progenitors of, and caregivers for, the young, functions in which women have assumed a central responsibility since humans first emerged. Women have helped in shaping societies through all types of human activity from the earliest times – even before the advent of sedentary life. Yet a mixture of political, economic, social and cultural factors (the last being the rise of male hegemony) entrenched a distinction between the public and private spheres that assigns prominence to men. This distinction remains the basis of the criteria of societal worth, with the result that women have been largely sequestered in the private, familial sphere. Nevertheless, society does not accord even this vital role the importance that it merits, while society as a whole is deprived of the general good that would result from women's effective participation in production and in the public life of society.

ECONOMIC ACTIVITIES

Statistics on women's rates of participation in economic activities in the Arab region show these to be lower than in any other part of the world (figure 3-1). It should be noted, however, that these figures are reproduced with the caveat that they greatly underestimate women's true participation (chapter 1).

A mixture of political, economic, social and cultural factors entrenched a distinction between the public and private spheres that assigns prominence to men.

Figure 3-1

Female (age 15+ years) economic activity rate (%) and female activity rate as a percentage of male activity rate, world regions, 2003

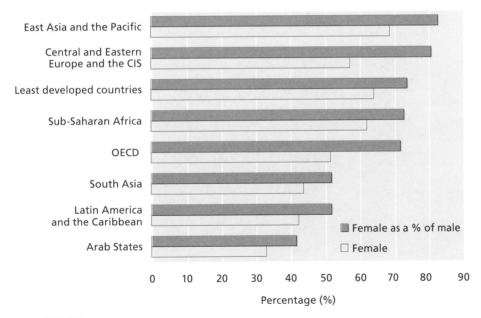

Source: UNDP, 2005.

Women have been largely sequestered in the private, familial sphere.

First, slow growth in the region predisposes economies towards low demand for female labour. In addition, the traditional view that men are the breadwinners further obstructs the employment of women and contributes to an increase in women's (blatant) unemployment relative to men. In the Arab countries, experience shows that in times of economic recession, women are the first fired while in times of economic expansion they are the last hired. This is illustrated by the decline in the number of working women during the first half of the 1990s, a period of slow growth, especially in the private sector, in Egypt while the number of male employment increased in the same period (Fergany, 1998).

Available statistics, despite their weakness,

also indicate a relatively higher level of women's unemployment than that of men even though many Arab women are willing to work (figure 3-2).

Given women's superior achievements in education, this trend goes against the grain of pure economic efficiency in that the sex with the greater potential for learning, and thus a greater potential to boost production, is less likely to be employed.

It is important to note that Arab public opinion, according to the field surveys mentioned earlier, runs counter to dominant discriminatory practices in Arab labour markets, clearly favouring women's right to equal opportunities to work, equal conditions and equal remuneration (Box 3-1).

Figure 3-2

Female unemployment rate as a percentage of male unemployment rate, Arab countries and world regions, most recent year available

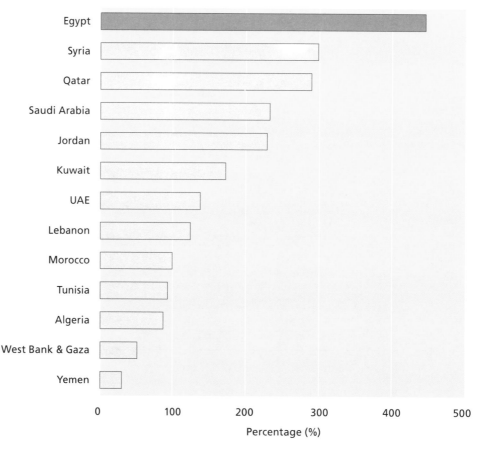

Source: World Bank, 2004.

BOX 3-1

Public Opinion on Aspects of the Rise of Arab Women, Four Arab Countries, 2005

Women should have an equal right to work

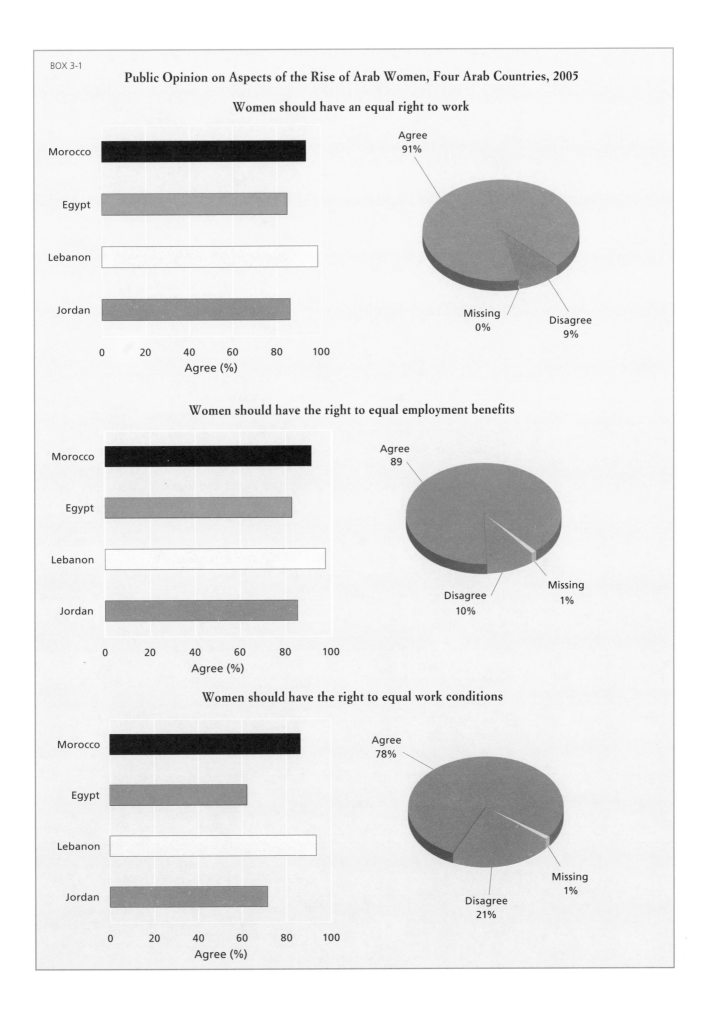

CHARACTERISTICS OF WOMEN'S PARTICIPATION IN ECONOMIC ACTIVITIES: SELECTED ISSUES

Despite their large, if unappreciated,[1] share in engendering human welfare and their activities in other spheres of human endeavour outside family life, women encounter many difficulties and obstacles that reduce their potential. Most important of all are the terms and conditions of work: women do not enjoy equality with men in work conditions, or in return on work, to say nothing of equality of opportunity for promotion to the top of the decision-making ladder in public or private enterprises.

THE EVOLUTION OF WOMEN'S PARTICIPATION IN THE ECONOMY AND THE LABOUR MARKET IN ARAB COUNTRIES

Starting from a low base, between 1990 and 2003, the Arab region witnessed a greater increase in women's share in economic activity than all other regions of the world: the increase for Arab women was 19 per cent as compared to 3 per cent for the world as a whole. Despite this, Arab women's economic participation remains the lowest in the world: not more than 33.3 per cent of women fifteen years and older compared to the world average of 55.6 per cent. The percentage of women participating in the economy in East Asia and the Pacific is a high 68.9 per cent. Moreover, Arab women's participation does not exceed 42 per cent that of men, again the lowest rate in the world, while that in East Asia and the Pacific is 83 per cent and in sub-Saharan Africa, 73 per cent. The world average is 69 per cent.

The highest rate of participation among Arab States is in Mauritania (63.1 per cent), followed by Qatar (42.6 per cent, a high proportion of which is comprised of foreign women workers) and then Morocco (at 41.9 per cent). In five other Arab countries, – Jordan, Libya, the occupied Palestinian territory, Oman and Saudi Arabia – it is still below 30 per cent even though the proportion increased by more than 50 per cent between 1990 and 2003 in Jordan, Oman and Saudi Arabia. The largest gap between women's and men's economic activities occurs in the occupied Palestinian territory, where women's participation reaches no more than 14 per cent of that of men; this is followed by Oman (27 per cent) and Saudi Arabia (29 per cent).

DISTRIBUTION OF THE FEMALE LABOUR FORCE IN PRIMARY ECONOMIC SECTORS

International databases do not provide solid ground for sufficient study of the sectoral distribution of women's work in Arab countries. Figure 3-3, which shows the data available from UNDP for 2005, is restricted to five Arab countries and highlights only three sectors: agriculture, industry and services.

From the graph, it is clear that the majority of the Arab labour force is engaged in the service sector. It is important to note that the service sector in the Arab countries is low in productivity and remuneration since it consists of a high proportion of public-sector and low-paying informal services.

There is a higher concentration of women in the services sector with the attendant implications just mentioned. The exception is in those economies where services are not the dominant sector (in Yemen, for example, agriculture predominates). Here the female labour force is concentrated in the primary sector, where productivity and remuneration are even lower than in services, usually at the expense of the other two sectors.

WOMEN'S OCCUPATIONAL STATUS

The highest percentage of women employed in those Arab countries for which figures are available (Egypt, Morocco, occupied Palestinian territory, Oman and Qatar) work

Women encounter many difficulties and obstacles that reduce their potential.

Arab women's economic participation remains the lowest in the world: not more than 33.3 per cent compared to the world average of 55.6 per cent.

---

[1] The official statistics cover only one area of women's work, namely, formal employment. Other types of work such as informal employment, the production of the necessities for daily survival, unpaid childcare and volunteer work are entirely excluded. Despite attempts to develop more accurate measurements of women's employment by applying the concept of "use of time", this method has been applied only in Morocco, the occupied Palestinian territory and Oman. It is thus necessary to use conventional means for measuring women's economic participation in order to make comparisons between the Arab region and other regions of the world, and among Arab countries themselves.

Figure 3-3

Labour force participation, by sector of economic activity and by gender, five Arab countries, 1995-2002

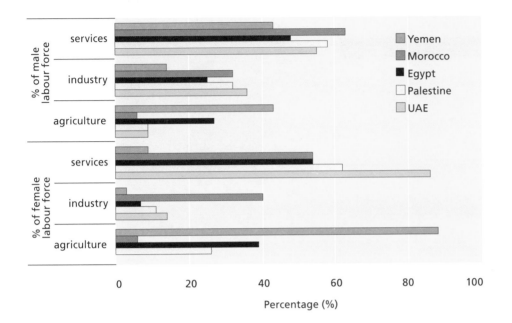

Figures for men and women working as salaried employees do not diverge much, but there is a great disparity in the nature of work for non-salaried workers.

Source: UNDP, 2005.

either as salaried employees or labourers. The figures for these categories, as percentages of women active in the labour market, are 68 per cent in Egypt; 55 per cent in the occupied Palestinian territory; and as high as 88 per cent in Oman and 100 per cent in Qatar. The figure is less than half in Morocco (34 per cent).

Figures for men and women working as salaried employees do not diverge much, but there is a great disparity in the nature of work for non-salaried workers. Most men working as non-salaried employees are either self-employed or are employed by others, while the greatest number of women in this category work as "family workers", that is, they work in the private sphere, most of them in unpaid work. The figure for such women in Egypt is 20 per cent; in Morocco, 52 per cent; and in the occupied Palestinian territory, 33 per cent. In those same countries, the percentage for men in the same category is 8 per cent, 22 per cent, and

7 per cent, respectively. This gap, which may seem at first glance to favour women, is actually a burden added to their daily responsibilities.

Among the Arab States, Saudi Arabia has the highest level of women in administrative positions (31 per cent).[2] In Iraq, the figure is 15 per cent; in the occupied Palestinian territory, 12 per cent; in Bahrain, 10 per cent; in Oman, 9 per cent; and in the UAE, 8 per cent. The lowest number of women in administration is in Yemen, where the number is 4 per cent.[3]

It is noteworthy that public opinion, as expressed through the AHDR survey, broadly supported women's ownership of assets and economic projects as well as their management of the latter. However, the degree of support for women project managers was slightly lower (Box 3-2).

Public opinion ... broadly supported women's ownership and management of assets and economic projects.

---

[2] This figure includes lawmakers, government administrators, senior administrators, directors of companies, and work supervisors. The degree of this discrimination may be attributed to the traditional separation between the sexes in administration and in government services such as the education sector.

[3] "United Nations Statistics Division." (2005). http://unstats.un.org/unsd/demographic/products/indwm/ww2005/tab5f.htm (Accessed 6 March, 2006).

BOX 3-2

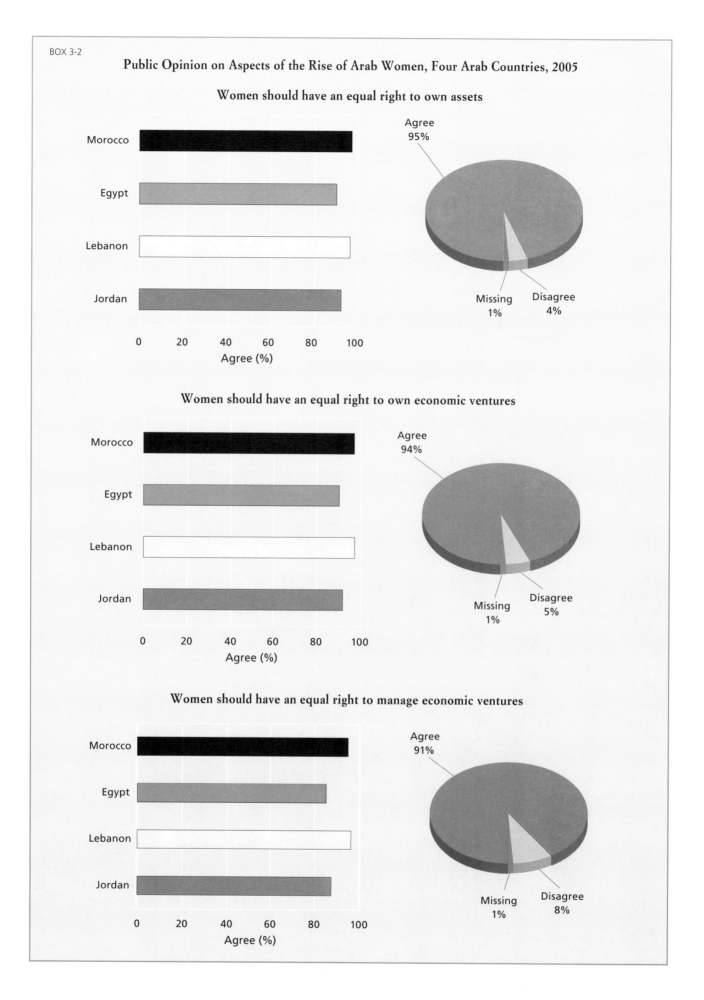

Public Opinion on Aspects of the Rise of Arab Women, Four Arab Countries, 2005

Women should have an equal right to own assets

Morocco
Egypt
Lebanon
Jordan

0   20   40   60   80   100
Agree (%)

Agree
95%

Missing
1%

Disagree
4%

Women should have an equal right to own economic ventures

Morocco
Egypt
Lebanon
Jordan

0   20   40   60   80   100
Agree (%)

Agree
94%

Missing
1%

Disagree
5%

Women should have an equal right to manage economic ventures

Morocco
Egypt
Lebanon
Jordan

0   20   40   60   80   100
Agree (%)

Agree
91%

Missing
1%

Disagree
8%

CAUSES OF ARAB WOMEN'S WEAK ECONOMIC PARTICIPATION

Many considerations help to explain the low participation of women in economic life and the high unemployment rates among their ranks, some of them related to demand for women's labour and others related to its supply.

The prevailing male culture

The prevailing masculine culture and values see women as dependants of men. As a result, men take priority both in access to work and the enjoyment of its returns. This tendency ignores the role of women in contributing to family income or in supporting entire families, a phenomenon that is on the rise in all societies, including Arab societies. It also overlooks the fact that, in reality, women exhibit no less responsibility and self-sacrifice in raising families than do men.

At the same time, some employers prefer to employ men in the belief that they are less expensive, using paid maternity leave as a pretext not to employ women as though such leave were a privilege for women and not a right of the new-born child and a service to society. Even though many Arab States extol family values in their public discourse, they leave it to employers rather than to the State to bear the cost of women's reproductive role in the replication of society, an approach that reduces job opportunities for women.

Scarcity of jobs

Slow economic development does not provide the jobs needed to absorb increases in the labour force, whether in the number of men or women. Nevertheless, the low number of jobs available has a greater impact on women. Figure 3-2 shows that the female unemployment rate was greater than the rate for men in two thirds of the Arab countries for which figures are available and that it was more than twice as high in half these countries.

The challenge of providing employment for women will increase in the coming years, especially in light of reports showing that the rate of increase in the female work force will exceed that for the work force as a whole.

The rate of growth in the work force in Arab countries has been estimated at 3.5 per cent per year for the period from 2000 to 2010, while that of the female work force has been estimated at 5 per cent (World Bank, 2003, 4).

Employment and wage discrimination between the sexes

Discrimination in employment and wages plays a part in restricting women's participation in economic life. Men's wages exceed those of women in various positions, especially in the private sector. This wage discrimination in the private sector propels women to work in the public sector for the equal pay and work conditions that it offers even as the public sector continues to contract in most Arab countries under structural adjustment policies.

The wage gap between men and women increases as their level of education decreases. In Jordan, for example, women university graduates earn 71 per cent of the amount earned by males in the same cohort; this drops to 50 per cent among those who have completed basic education only, while illiterate women earn less than 33 per cent of male wages (Moghadam, 2005). Women's suffering increases as their level of education drops, the latter usually being associated with poverty.

High reproductive rates

Women's labour participation rate, reproduction rate, average age of first marriage and level of education, as well as the percentage of the population who marry between the ages of 15 and 19, are linked factors. Similarly, women's participation in economic activity is the factor that most influences reproduction levels. In the Arab States, the lowest rate of women's participation in the labour market occurs in the occupied Palestinian territory, one of the States with the highest birth rate and the State with the highest rate of early marriage (15-19). Meanwhile, States such as Tunisia present the opposite pattern, with low recorded rates of early marriage, low fertility rates (2.1 compared to 4.2 for the Arab region) and a high rate of economic participation (32 per cent). (Fayad, background paper for the Report).

Men take priority both in access to work and the enjoyment of its returns.

Discrimination in employment and wages plays a part in restricting women's participation in economic life.

Laws hindering women, including those designed for their "protection"

Laws concerning labour and personal status are considered to be among the most daunting obstacles to Arab women's participation in economic life. Some personal status and labour legislation restricts women's freedom by requiring a father's or husband's permission to work, travel or borrow from financial institutions. Other labour laws close a number of fields of work to women in the name of "protecting" them (see Chapter 8). Hence "protection" is transformed into discrimination and restricts women's participation in economic activity (Abu Harithiyyeh and Qawwas, 1997).

Weak support services

Weak transportation and child care infrastructure act to discourage women from going out to work, as does the lack of social support for children or the aged, the burden of whose care falls on women. Numerous other factors also affect opportunities for women to find work, among them the disconnect between education and the needs of the labour market, the paucity of continuing training in further skills required by women seeking work and women's poor access to credit.

Impact of structural adjustment programmes

Throughout the eighties and nineties a number of Arab States adopted structural reform programmes to liberalise trade, privatise, strengthen the private sector and increase production efficiency in order to establish internal and external equilibrium and promote economic development. Views differ over the effect that these policies have had on women, their employment and their participation in economic activity. While contraction of the public sector has led to a reduction in formal job opportunities for women, some see these policies as affording women wider job and economic opportunities in the informal sector. Although this sector has grown, it does not, by its nature, provide women with any legal protections or guarantees of work.

ARAB WOMEN'S WEAK ECONOMIC PARTICIPATION LEADS TO LOW LEVELS OF INCOME

Dependency ratios in the Arab region remain the highest in the world, with each worker supporting more than two non-working people compared to less than one in East Asia and the Pacific. The principal reason for this is the low rate of participation by women. With real wages facing stagnation and increased rates of unemployment, it is extremely difficult for the small number of workers to provide a reasonable living for their families.

The situation becomes even graver when this high level of dependency occurs in combination with an absence of pension plans and of national safety nets covering all worker cohorts. A recent study shows that pension plans in Arab States do not cover workers in the private or agricultural sectors. While coverage in Libya, where the great majority work in the public sector, reaches 70 per cent, in Morocco, which has a large agricultural sector, it is only 20 per cent of the work force (Robalino, 2005). With the increasing expansion of the informal sector, where worker coverage is low, family support becomes a tremendous burden for the small number of those working, as does the burden on women in providing care for children and the sick, elderly, disabled and handicapped in the absence of sufficient social support. It is thus impossible to realise individual levels of advancement, much less general human welfare, without the participation of Arab women in the labour force.

The failure to use human capital, especially highly educated women, curbs economic development and squanders important energies and investments, which might otherwise contribute to achieving economic development for all. The low employment rates for women and the restriction of their return on their labour are at odds with the simplest principles of equality, which is a fundamental component of citizenship and of human rights. They undermine the foundations of economic development, militate against the requirements of human development and impede the rise of Arab women, the subject of this Report.

Laws concerning labour and personal status are among the most daunting obstacles to Arab women's participation in economic life.

The failure to use human capital, especially highly educated women, curbs economic development and squanders important energies and investments.

Young People's Opinions on Women's Issues in the Arab Region

In November 2005, the UNDP Regional Bureau for Arab States hosted a consultative session on Arab women's issues with young Arab people[4] as well as an electronic conference with youth leaders from Arab countries.

Participants agreed that culture, education, economics and political participation all had a great impact on the role of women in Arab society while also providing indicators of the situation of women in the region. The young people believed that religion, and especially Islam, played a large role in most thinking about women's rights, roles and responsibilities and stressed the need to respect religious opinions, while acknowledging that such opinions and interpretations of women's issues varied.

On education, there was agreement that academic curricula needed to be rethought, especially where the portrayal of women was concerned. At the same time, participants called for the teaching of sexual culture as a basic academic subject, especially given that Islam, according to the young people, was a religion of openness that encouraged rather than proscribed the broadening of knowledge.

The session also discussed the phenomenon of violence against girls in schools, which is on the increase, and the paucity of laws protecting girls and young women from such violence. The young participants commented on the rise in school dropout rates and found the rise in the illiteracy rate among young women a worrisome trend with negative implications for human development in the region.

The decline in the numbers of women involved in political decision-making processes prompted the participants to support affirmative action as a necessary policy response, including the allocation of quotas for women in legislative bodies. Noting that the patriarchal system throughout the region was one of the factors accounting for gender inequality in political participation, they called on the Arab media to play a more effective role in communicating the positive impact of women in leadership positions, as illustrated by success stories in different countries.

The young people remarked positively on the increase in women holding leading economic positions in the region, including in the most conservative Arab States. They noted that for these women, such positions also entailed the responsibility to show initiative in helping to expand the Arab market and create more jobs. They felt strongly that it was important to introduce the idea of shared social responsibility in the Arab economic sector. The sessions also discussed youth unemployment, especially as it affects girls and young women, and asked Arab governments to broaden their efforts to include the young men and women of their generation. All agreed that proficiency with twenty-first-century information technology is one of the many skills of young people today that could help to strengthen development generally.

ARAB WOMEN IN THE POLITICAL SPHERE

This section begins by illustrating that public opinion in those Arab countries where the Report's survey (see annex II) was conducted is generally positive about women entering the political sphere and occupying senior executive positions in government. Such approval extends up to the highest office of the State, particularly in Lebanon and Morocco although it diminishes with the importance of the position. (Box 3-4).

Women obtained the right to vote in and stand for parliamentary elections in most Arab countries (those of the Gulf States excepted) during the 1950s and 1960s, Lebanon being the first to grant women these two rights (in 1952).

The beginning of the third millennium saw some improvement for women in the Gulf. In 2003 in Oman and Qatar, they were granted the right to vote and to stand for parliamentary office for the first time. After forty years of struggle, Kuwaiti women gained complete political rights in 2005 (Annex IV, Table 23 and Figure 3-4).

The adoption of quota systems increased women's parliamentary participation in Jordan and Morocco. Despite these favourable changes, the proportion of women representatives in Arab parliaments remains the lowest in the world (Figure 3-5).

After forty years of struggle, Kuwaiti women gained complete political rights in 2005.

Women obtained the right to vote in and stand for parliamentary elections in most Arab countries during the 1950s and 1960s.

Despite favourable changes, the proportion of women representatives in Arab parliaments remains the lowest in the world.

---

[4] See annex V for list of participants.

BOX 3-4

Public Opinion on Aspects of the Rise of Arab Women, Four Arab Countries, 2005

Women should have an equal right to political action

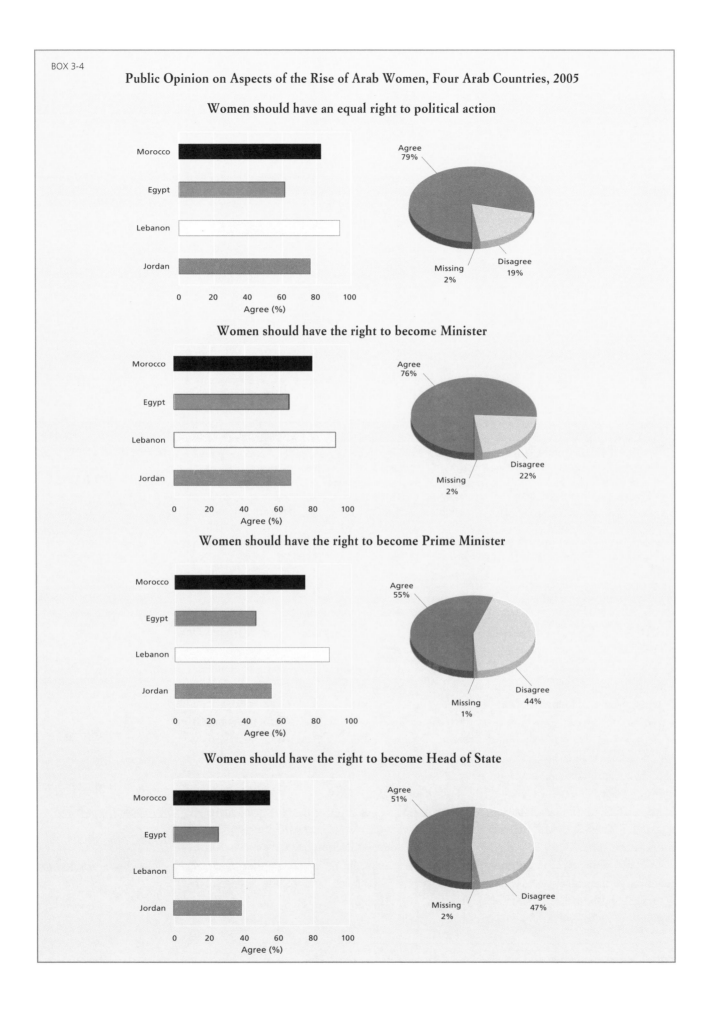

Women should have the right to become Minister

Women should have the right to become Prime Minister

Women should have the right to become Head of State

Figure 3-4

Year in which women were granted the unrestricted right to vote and the right to stand for election, by Arab country

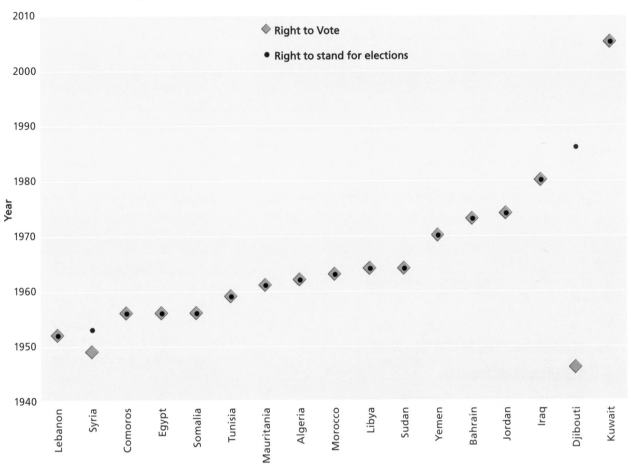

Source: "Inter-Parliamentary Unit." (2005). www.ipu.org wmn-e/suffrage.htm (Accessed 29 March 2006).

Figure 3-5

Share of women in parliament, by world region

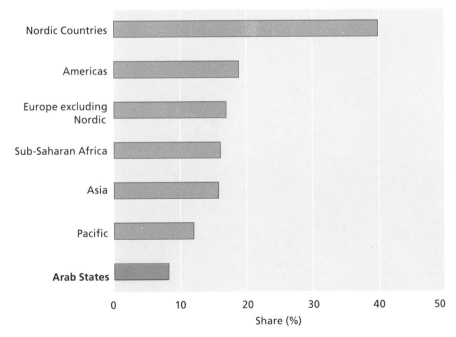

Source: www.ipu.org\wmn-e\world.htm, 15 October 2005.

Arab women have yet to receive ministries directly relating to functions of sovereignty, such as defence, interior or foreign affairs.

The Arab countries clearly differ in the extent of empowerment of women in parliament (Figure 3-6).

The highest level of Arab women's parliamentary participation in early 2006 is in Iraq (25.5 per cent) followed by Tunisia, where women were elected to 22.8 per cent of the seats in 2004. Sudan and Syria, with 66 and 30 representatives, respectively, or 14.7 and 12 per cent, follow. After that come Djibouti, Morocco and Somalia (with 10.8, 10.8 and 8 per cent, respectively). The lowest percentages are in Bahrain (zero), Yemen (0.3 per cent)

and Egypt (2 per cent). There are no elected legislative councils in Saudi Arabia or the UAE and parliamentary elections have yet to be held in Qatar.

Arab women parliamentarians have sometimes assumed significant positions in their assemblies, rising to vice speaker of the assemblies of Algeria, Egypt, Morocco and Tunisia. Not one, however, has risen to the position of speaker.

Some Arab States have established higher councils alongside elected assemblies, membership of which is entirely or partly by appointment. Generally, the executive, which makes appointments to these councils, names a relatively larger proportion of women to them to compensate for their lack of success in parliamentary elections.

Arab women have had a share in executive power in some Arab countries since the middle of the last century. The first woman minister was appointed in Iraq in 1959, in Egypt in 1956 and in Algeria in 1962. The number of Arab countries that appoint women as ministers has increased in the last three years to the extent that women now participate in all governments except that of Saudi Arabia. Given that no set quotas exist for women in any of the Arab countries, the number of those who attain ministerial rank varies from one period to another and from one government to another. By the same token, the number of women in the various ministries does not necessarily reflect the general status of the empowerment of women. In general, however, more women are thus employed in republics (such as Egypt, Iraq, Syria and Tunisia) than in monarchies (such as Jordan, Morocco and the Gulf States), albeit the latter have recently started to appoint women to ministerial posts.

In the first stage of their participation in government, women were usually given portfolios concerned with women, children or social development. While Arab women have yet to receive ministries directly relating to functions of sovereignty, such as defence, interior or foreign affairs, they have begun to occupy leading ministries such as planning, industry, trade, communications and mass media. Likewise, women have not attained the office of prime minister or deputy prime

Figure 3-6

Seats in parliament (lower or single house) held by women (% of total), Arab countries, 29 March 2006

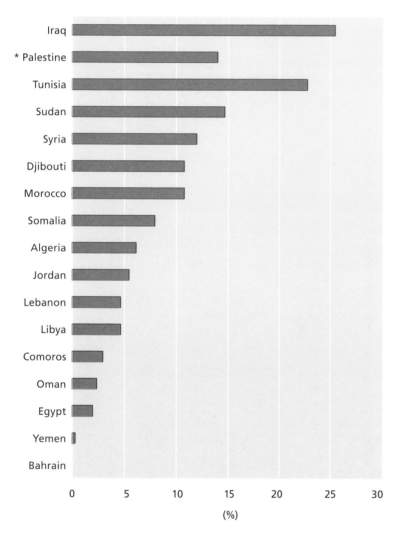

(%)

Source: www.ipu.org\wmn-e\classif.htm, 29 March 2006.

* http://www.elections.ps/pics/Statistic_reg_voters_2-ar.jpg

minister except in Jordan, where a woman became deputy prime minister in 1999.

Other data indicate that women are taking important positions in local administrations (four in Egypt, two in Lebanon), and they participate in local councils in the Comoros, Jordan, Mauritania, the occupied Palestinian territory and the Sudan. On the other hand, there is noticeable difficulty in nominating or electing women to executive positions at local administrative levels, with the result that women are almost entirely absent from these in most Arab countries. The number of women in the judiciary has reached 50 per cent in Morocco, 22.5 per cent in Tunisia, 11 per cent in Syria and 5 per cent in Lebanon. A woman has become a judge of the Supreme Constitutional Court in Egypt, and 76 women have attained judgeships in the Sudan, 53 in Yemen and 14 in Jordan. What is more, women participate in the administration of NGOs at a rate of 45 per cent in Lebanon, 42 per cent in the occupied Palestinian territory and 18 per cent in Egypt (UNIFEM, in Arabic, 2004).

Despite their disparate functions in government positions, women's performance, on average, has been at least as distinguished as that of men. Outstanding women parliamentarians and ministers have emerged as role models for women in the Arab world. In the Report's public opinion survey, two thirds of respondents considered the performance of women to be as good as, or better than, that of men (Annex II).

PARTICIPATION WITHOUT DIVERSITY

Women's assumption of high State positions does not necessarily mean women's political empowerment. In such a situation, women, like men, are not able to wield effective political influence in the absence of freedom and political plurality in the region.

Women in power are usually chosen from the ranks of the elite or they are appointed from the ruling party as window dressing for the ruling regimes, especially those that are autocratic, or in response to external pressure, as in Iraq and some of the Gulf States. For this reason, the increased participation of some women in the political realm does not prevent

Despite their disparate functions in government positions, women's performance, on average, has been at least as distinguished as that of men.

Women's assumption of high State positions does not necessarily mean women's political empowerment.

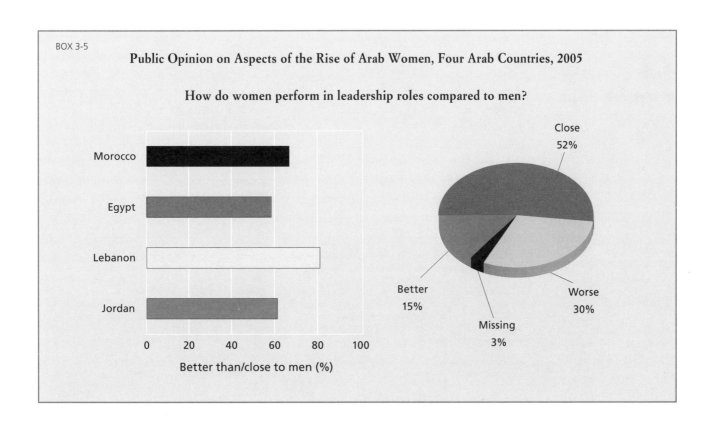

BOX 3-5

Public Opinion on Aspects of the Rise of Arab Women, Four Arab Countries, 2005

How do women perform in leadership roles compared to men?

the continued oppression of others, among them especially women active in Islamist movements or women in rights organisations calling for democratic reform.[5]

It should also be noted that women's political participation at high levels takes place in countries with one-party systems that usually restrict executive power and authority to a small cadre of supporters and where the prevailing value is that of loyalty rather than efficiency. Generally women's programmes in such countries, as elsewhere, conform to those of the mother party.

In rentier economies, known for widespread patronage,[6] bribery, corruption and favouritism, women are either excluded from politics by law or are marginalised by their lack of back-door influence of the sort available to men. In such cases, women rely completely on making common cause with the authorities or the ruling party and on forming close relationships with them through friends and acquaintances.

WOMEN AND THE ARAB STATE: COOPERATION OR CONFLICT

Arab women are faced by a worrisome dilemma over the nature of their relations with the State: should they realise their objectives by attaching themselves to government institutions or by working outside of them in the framework of civil society organizations?[7] Some Arab studies show that there is no significant difference between authoritarian and liberal regimes in matters relating to the rise of women (Hatem, 1994b, 661-676). Their increasing representation in authoritarian regimes, accompanied by marginalisation in politics in general, invalidates women's participation and separates women in power from any popular

base that they may have. This has a negative impact on women's empowerment through greater political participation. Work outside of government institutions exposes women activists to repression, especially when these activists link women's social rights to a lack of rights and civil and political freedoms in general.

WOMEN IN ARAB POLITICAL PARTIES

At the start, it must be said that the freedom to form political parties is not guaranteed in Arab countries. Some countries, such as the Gulf countries and Libya, ban their formation altogether; others permit them under their constitutions but restrict their establishment or their operation by law and in practice (AHDR 2004).

Women's ties to Arab political parties have varied over time and in line with the respective political structure of each Arab country. Many of the movements resisting colonization succeeded in attracting and mobilising large numbers of women throughout the twentieth century (for example, in Algeria, southern Lebanon, the occupied Palestinian territory and Tunisia). After independence, however, the political parties neither made sustained efforts to widen their bases among women nor sought to create comprehensive programmes for their advancement. Parties and movements that justified the rights "given" to women on the grounds of their participation alongside men in the struggle for liberation broke faith with their positions on women's rights because they had not based them on the concept of equality as a value springing from the rights of women as full individuals or as full citizens (Bishara, background paper for the Report).

Nationalist and Communist parties were

---

[5] Women Islamists in certain Arab countries are subject to raids on their homes at night with the consequent intimidation of their children. Some have been taken hostage in order to exert pressure on their relatives. Sometimes arrest, torture and sexual assault are involved. Likewise, some governments have the wives of political prisoners dismissed from their jobs as collective family punishment and to force them into divorce. Similarly, in Tunisia, the decree known as decree 108 (recently repealed), prohibiting the hijab (women's headscarf), led to an oppressive campaign against veiled women in public institutions, in the streets, on public transport and in hospitals. It included violence against the women, the tearing of their clothing and their removal to security centres. Some of them have been banned from taking public examinations for the same reason (Rjiba, background paper for the Report). Persecution extends not only to Islamist women but also to female activists working in the groups defending them and anyone else who may provide these groups with aid.

[6] Relations founded upon dependency (or quasi-feudal clans such as are found in the Levant) and through which the individual demonstrates his loyalty to those politicians who have the ability to dispense services and favours to a person or a group (for more information, see Waterbury, 1977).

[7] To follow this debate, see Yeatmann, 1990; Kuttab, in Arabic, 1996; Karam, 1998; and Goetz, 1997 and 2003.

interested in mobilising women as proof of their progressive ideas. Nevertheless, many Arab political parties, whether progressive or conservative, were keen to create separate and confining bodies for women, mostly under the administration of a woman. Such organisations constituted a domain specifically for women within the larger party. Although some believed that this would facilitate the gradual entry of women into the general political domain, the continued application of the principle limited their role in the party and, as a result, in society. When women did participate in party life, they usually did so at the grass-roots level of the party and in the context of the family (Fayad, in Arabic, 1998); they rarely reached the leadership, with the exception of Algeria, where a woman leads the Labour Party.[8]

While extolling its accomplishments on behalf of women when compared to the other Arab ruling parties, Tunisia's ruling Democratic Constitutional Rally has only 20.1 per cent female membership, which represents no more than 2.6 per cent of the leaders of branches of the party. Moreover, there are no women heading the Coordinating Committees that exist in the governorates, and there is only one woman among the eight members of the Political Bureau and one assistant general secretary charged with women's affairs.[9]

In Yemen, the percentage of women in leadership positions among all the parties is no more than 2 per cent. Among these, the General People's Conference (the ruling party) can claim first place (Abu Asbah, in Arabic, 2004, from Cherif, background paper for the Report), with women supposedly comprising 15 per cent of the leadership.

The same phenomenon may be observed in Egypt, where women play only a symbolic role in the party leadership apparatus. There are only two women in the upper echelon of the Wafd party out of a membership of 40, representing 5 per cent. Similarly, there are only three in the general secretariat of the Tagammu' party out of a total of 64, accounting for 4.6 per cent of the members. Only two women are on the central committee of the Nasserist Party, making up 7.2 per cent (Egyptian Centre for Human Rights, in Arabic, 2005).

WOMEN IN THE ISLAMIC MOVEMENTS

The situation varies somewhat regarding women's representation in Islamic parties. These parties have recently made the organisation of women a goal. For example, with respect to Hezbullah in Lebanon, women join the party's "women's bodies," which constitute its women's cadre, and they participate in most party social, educational, cultural and media institutions. They also play an effective role in the resistance. They are, however, still absent from the main councils of the party, such as the Decision Council, the Political Council, the Executive Council and the Central Council (Qusayr, in Arabic, 2004). In the occupied Palestinian territory, the picture is different: in the National Islamic Liberation Party, the proportion of women at the leadership level is 27 per cent and in the Political Bureau (the party's highest body), 15 per cent (with two members out of eleven) (Jad, 2004a). In Morocco, the official spokesperson for Sheikh Abd Al-Salam Yasin[10] and the Justice and Charity Movement, which can boast 20 per cent women leaders, is a woman.

The above indicators may point to the empowerment of women in the Islamic movements. Nonetheless, these movements contain within themselves contradictions of a different sort. Some of them occasionally wage war against the demands of secular women's movements for changes in laws and policies that marginalise women, as when the Islamic Bloc in the Kuwaiti parliament opposed granting women the rights to vote and stand for election.

Many Arab political parties, whether progressive or conservative, were keen to create separate and confining bodies for women.

Islamic parties. have recently made the organisation of women a goal.

---

[8] Louisa Hannoun leads this Trotskyite opposition party. Nominated in April 2003 in the presidential elections, she became only the second woman in the Arab world to compete with a man in a presidential race, the first being Palestinian Samiha Khalil, who ran against the late President Yasser Arafat in 1996.

[9] Web page of the Democratic Constitutional Rally Party, www.rcd.tn.

[10] Nadiya Yasin, daughter of Sheikh 'Abd al-Salam Yasin, leader of the Justice and Charity Movement in Morocco. Ms. Yasin is preparing to take over from her father as the leader of the movement and is working to modernise the image of Islamist women in Morocco (see Yassine, in French, 2005, and Dahbi, in French, 2004).

WOMEN, RESTRICTIONS AND PARTY POLITICS

That women's participation in politics remains weak is connected with the cultural legacy and the discriminatory patriarchal system prevalent in the Arab countries, as in many other countries in the world, which do not acknowledge that women are capable of assuming responsibility, including political responsibility.

The state of politics in the Arab countries and the nature of the parties themselves also explain women's lack of participation in party politics. The political process does not provide much security and immunity for those involved in it (UNIFEM, in Arabic, 2004, 267-268). This has produced, especially among youth, a lack of trust in the integrity and transparency of politics and an aversion to joining parties.

As for the parties, a number of them have retreated from the adoption of broad-based political programmes in favour of an increased linkage of such programmes to the person of the party leader. In addition, a tribe will sometimes be decked out in the garments of a political party, as in Yemen. In such cases, the influence of tribal elders and the exclusion of women not affiliated with the tribe will be plainly evident in the party and hence in political work (al-Samiri, in Arabic, 2001, 59-60).

Many studies also point to the role of election laws in limiting women's participation in politics. For instance, Sabbagh finds that in Yemen, the number of women candidates in parliamentary elections declined from 24 in 1993 to 11 in 2003, with a single woman candidate winning in that election (Sabbagh, 2004). The author interprets this decline as arising from the change in the law that required candidates to obtain the endorsement of 300 people from their electoral districts. This posed problems for all candidates, but especially for women, who traditionally encounter difficulties in mobility. On the other hand, however, the increase in the women's vote from 18 per cent in 1993 to 27 per cent in 1997 and to 42 per cent in 2003 means that women in Yemen are showing an increasing interest in the electoral process.

The situation in Jordan is different, with the adoption of laws facilitating the participation of women by abolishing election cards and permitting the use of identity cards. (The old system placed women and youth under the authority of the eldest male member of the household, subjecting them to a form of moral pressure.) Likewise, mobility is less of an issue, since voting occurs in the place of residence rather than the place of registration, which has also encouraged women's participation (Sabbagh, 2004). Some people, however, believe that the law, which is based on the principle of one person/one vote, will work to the disadvantage of women in that it will "return the elections to the old framework of clan and family, which is well known to favour male over female candidates" (Naffa', in Arabic, 1998). The same is true of Lebanon, where the clan/family/sect-based election law was the greatest obstacle to women's candidacies (Maqdisi, in Arabic, 2000, 81), since women are rarely permitted to represent specific groups when seats are apportioned.

With financing playing an increasingly important role in Arab elections, the lack of it is also a major obstacle to Arab women's candidacies, given women's limited means and economic dependence. In Lebanon, for example, in order to stand for election, a candidate must pay 10 million lira (about USD 7,000) over and above the costs of a media campaign. The same situation confronts Palestinian women, who "have limited financial resources owing to traditional standards that accord preference to men in employment" (Kawar, 2001, 20).

Poverty and illiteracy are also important factors severely obstructing women's participation in politics. Candidates often vie with one another to buy the votes of the poor, frequently paying men and clan chiefs to marshal their womenfolk's vote as a bloc or to take advantage of illiterate or needy women to mobilise support for a particular candidate. This puts women under much greater family and tribal pressure than men.

Some point to women's reluctance to employ men's coercive methods, especially smear campaigns impugning candidates' morals. Moreover, with the spread of the violence that now characterises elections in many Arab countries, candidates may be forcibly prevented from reaching the polls by supporters of their rivals. In Algeria, Egypt Jordan and Yemen, candidates have received death threats (UNIFEM, in Arabic, 2004, 280). In the occupied Palestinian territory, some women candidates in local council elections were physically beaten by their families, who opposed their standing for election or favoured a male candidate.

WOMEN'S PERFORMANCE AND CREATIVITY IN HUMAN ENDEAVOURS

Arab women's intellectual energy has been released in the last three decades with the expansion of universities and other educational institutions in most Arab countries and with the unprecedented engagement of women in higher education. Nevertheless, in the ranks of scientists and researchers, a discrepancy in favour of men remains although the reverse is true in the social sciences, education, and literature (UN and ESCWA, in Arabic, 2003, 6).

Noticeably, Arab women engage far more in intellectual, literary and media pursuits, especially the theatre, than in scientific, sporting and artistic endeavours. Historically, women's participation in theatrical creativity came late in relation to their involvement in other forms of artistic expression, with fewer women playwrights and fewer plays. This may be attributable to the meagre State funding for the written or visual arts or it may be attributable to the targeting by some fundamentalist movements of the performing arts in general, whether theatre or cinema. Moreover, there is a general paucity of writing for the theatre in the Arab world compared to other forms of artistic expression.

Arab women embarked on the craft of writing in general at the beginning of the twentieth century when Egypt and Lebanon both became bastions of women's journalism.

Towards the end of the twentieth century, the number of women writers in the Mashreq (the eastern Arab world) had reached 475; in Egypt, there were 167 women writers and in the occupied Palestinian territory and Syria, 81 each (Supreme Council for Culture and Nur Foundation, in Arabic, 2002). The number of Arab women creative artists is on the rise,

albeit slowly, with the exception of Iraq, where there is a decline in public access to women's creative products. The quality, style and different modes of expression employed by Arab women writers evince an increasing professionalism as they strive to capture and present a social reality of ever greater complexity.

Arab women's participation in athletics is modest; even worse, it is decreasing as a result both of the paucity of sports facilities in schools and universities and the opposition to women's involvement in activities of this sort by some hard-line fundamentalist forces. Lately, certain sports designed for women have appeared, especially in the Gulf States. However, this type of sport, even if it is itself good for the physical development of Arab girls, does nothing to change the stereotypical image of women and men, which blocks women's equal access to sports as a profession.

OUTSTANDING ACHIEVEMENTS OF ARAB WOMEN

Despite the unfavourable, or at least unencouraging, societal climate for women, reflected in the general trends described in the previous section, Arab history, both ancient and modern, records the achievements of numerous female luminaries who have scaled the heights of human endeavour in different spheres. This Report celebrates a small sample of these leading lights in boxes scattered throughout the various chapters. In addition, brief sketches of women's distinguished contributions to various activities in the Arab world are presented below.

The first generation

Among the most important women pioneers of the first generation was Huda Sha'rawi, who set off something close to a social revolution in Egypt and other Arab countries. She was the founder and patron of the Egyptian Feminist Union, which collaborated with women's unions across the Arab world and abroad. In Lebanon, Ibtihaj Qaddura became a celebrated social worker, driven by her awareness of society's need for solidarity and collaboration in the face of its diverse and multifarious

Arab women's intellectual energy has been released in the last three decades with the expansion of universities and other educational institutions.

Arab history, both ancient and modern, records the achievements of numerous female luminaries who have scaled the heights of human endeavour.

Figure 3-7

Percentage of Arab women researchers, by specialisation

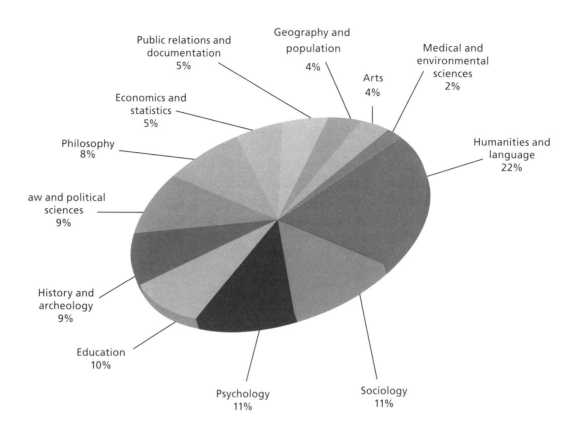

Public relations and documentation
5%

Geography and population
4%

Medical and environmental sciences
2%

Arts
4%

Economics and statistics
5%

Philosophy
8%

Humanities and language
22%

aw and political sciences
9%

History and archeology
9%

Education
10%

Psychology
11%

Sociology
11%

Source: Bayyumi, Hatit and Ghandur, in Arabic, 1999.

problems. Her example inspired other women to such an extent that another pioneer of her day, 'Anbara Salam al-Khalidi, said of her, "Ibtihaj is the history of the contemporary women's renaissance in this country...with her work, a major institution has arisen in Lebanon, and the eyes of women all over the Arab world have turned to her". Others said of her, "Hers was the first voice to be raised in our eastern Arab region on behalf of the political rights of women". She was not alone in the arena, however; she had daring, collaborative colleagues who also believed passionately in the importance of social work.

Space does not permit the mention of more than a few of the outstanding women of the first renaissance who made important contributions in various fields. Julia Tu'ma Dimashqiyya founded "Al-Mar'a al-Jadida"

(The New Woman) magazine, one of the 24 journals published by women in the early years of the last century. Anas Baz and Saniyya Habbub were pioneers of Lebanese medicine at a time when the university refused to accept women students in the College of Medicine. Rose El Youssef – pioneer of the stage and one of the earliest actresses, who went on to found the journal "Rose El-Youssef" and what, to this day, remains one of the most important press houses in Egypt – was a woman unique in her time. It was she who uttered the famous words, "I made this woman myself". One could also salute numerous female writers and educators who left their mark on Arab society, such as Widad al-Maqdisi Qurtas and 'Anabara Salam in Lebanon and Mary 'Ajami in the Syrian Arab Republic.

Women's writing, however, came of age

only with Mayy Ziyada, "Miss Mayy", who wrote of herself, "I was born in one country, my father in another, my mother in another, and I live in a fourth...The phantoms of my self move from country to country –so to which of these countries do I belong, and which of them should I defend?"

Mayy, who lived out and wrote this uncertainty, belongs to all Arab countries. She wrote a number of books, her works were translated into several languages, and she took her place alongside the great literary figures of her time as an equal and a partner. By inaugurating the "Tuesday Seminar", her celebrated literary salon, she brought about a literary revolution. She created a free arena to which poets and writers raced, bringing with them their works, and where they competed in reading, debating and contributing to the enrichment of a golden age unique in the annals of literary history. It could not have been otherwise, when the period numbered

among its pioneers writers and poets such as Ahmad Shawqi, Lutfi al-Sayyid, Khalil Mutran, al-Shalabi al-Shumayyil, Taha Husayn, Jurji Zaydan, 'Abbas Mahmud al-'Aqqad, Ya'qub Sarruf and others. The only woman among those who frequented the salon was the writer Malak Hifni Nasif, known as "Bahithat al-Badiya" (Searcher of the Desert) (Nasrallah, background paper for the Report).

Literary creativity

Many a woman's pen was prominent in literature and expressed itself with daring and beauty. The originality of some works took critics and readers by surprise, so much so that it was no longer possible to ask any of them, "Who does your writing for you?"

Women writers proved that they could write and were well capable of taking their place alongside their male peers and, indeed, of surpassing them. Among the figures who shone in the 1960s and who are still at work

Many a woman's pen was prominent in literature and expressed itself with daring and beauty.

Luminary: Fadwa Tuqan (1917-2003), from her autobiography

When I was six, I went to the government girls' school in Nablus and when I was eleven, they made me put on the veil and forced me to stay at home. My brother, the late poet Ibrahim Tuqan, discovered my inborn talent for poetry and took charge of me. He was my teacher, who taught me to write poetry. Ibrahim formed me and was my literary creator.

In the eyes of my cousins, I was the false note, the sheep that insisted on straying from the flock, and throughout my childhood and adolescence I remained the target of the "executioner's sword" that I mentioned in my first verse collection, published in 1952. That sword, or whip, continued to whistle over my head throughout my adolescence, in the name of tradition and ridiculous moral standards. However, the pressures exerted on me were no more than a venting of the malice and fury caused by my choosing the path of poetry, which I embarked on, and to which I devoted my life with a strange and mystical fervour. My cousins wore foreign clothes and spoke English, French and Turkish, and ate with a knife and fork, and fell in love, yet despite all this they kept me under a microscope because of my aspirations, my desire to realise myself through poetry and my devotion to culture and knowledge. They represented the schizophrenia of the Arab, one half of whom is for progress and keeping pace with the rhythms of modern life while the other half is fossilised and paralysed, haunted by the egotism ingrained in the soul of the Arab male with all that that implies about the oriental approach to the treatment of women.

In such a climate, I was incapable of the vigorous interaction with life required of the poet. My only world, in that terrible reality with its emotional void, was the world of books, and I absorbed myself in studying and writing, while my femininity howled like a wounded animal in its cage.

The subjects of my verse have become diverse, fluctuating among the pulls of the self, of contemplation, of humankind, and of the nation. After the first Nakba (Catastrophe), the social transformation that usually takes place following a war started to work itself through in my city of Nablus. The veil was abandoned and with that the modern woman advanced, new horizons of higher education and economic independence opening before her, while I myself escaped from the "magic bottle" of the harem to a life that I could touch with my fingers just as it touched me. My poetry started to become more mature and my experiments bolder. After the 1967 war, I dedicated my verse to resistance of the Israeli occupation and my encounters with the public at poetry readings, which were eventually banned by the occupation forces, became more frequent. Moshe Dayan, the former Israeli defence minister, made the famous statement that "every poem Fadwa Tuqan writes creates another ten Palestinian resistance fighters".

In 1978, I won the prize for authors and poets of the Mediterranean region awarded by the Italian Cultural Committee in Palermo.

Source: Campbell, 1996.

Women writers proved that they could write and were well capable of taking their place alongside their male peers and, indeed, of surpassing them.

today are the novelists Layla al-Ba'labakki and Layla 'Asiran and, later, Hanan al-Shaykh, Huda Barakat and Mayy Minassa from Lebanon, then Salwa Baker and Radwa Ashour from Egypt, and Colette Khoury from Syria. In Kuwait, Layla al-'Uthman's pen won renown and almost got her thrown in prison. In Iraq, Nazik al-Mala'ika was in the vanguard of modern poetry along with Lami'a 'Abbas 'Amara, while Dayzi al-Amir became known for her stories (Nasrallah, background paper for the Report).

Creativity in the arts, with a focus on the cinema

Arab women were as prominent in the founding of the cinema as they had been in the liberation of society and political awareness that Egypt witnessed at the start of the twentieth century. Cinema came into being in 1896 and in that same year, the Arab world, and Egypt above all, welcomed this new art form, which spread rapidly. Its creative content was eventually translated into an independent, self-standing, Egyptian and Arab visual art form whose cultural and artistic outlines women helped to define as producers, actresses and directors.

The Arab-Egyptian cinema was born thanks in no small measure to the efforts of women, who subsequently became vital forces in the films that they chose to make. These films reflected their readings of reality from a vantage point that let them survey the many facets of society, culture, education and popular awareness. The medium also enabled them to express the self, the spirit and the feelings of living beings. Although the Arab region at the time was suffused with puritanical religious teachings and mired in a conservative traditional culture and oppressive social climate that deprived women of many of their rights, women were nevertheless able to perceive a way out of the dark –provided that certain basic human conditions were

The Arab-Egyptian cinema was born thanks in no small measure to the efforts of women, who subsequently became vital forces in the films that they chose to make.

Luminary: Dr. Salma Jayyusi

Salma Khadra Jayyusi is an Arab-American writer, poet, literary critic and scholar. She grew up in Acre and Jerusalem and, as a native Palestinian, was one of the early innovators in the contemporary Arab poetic movement that first emerged after the Nakbah. She was one of the first Arab female poets to be mentioned in the Lebanese "Literary Magazine", her poetic accomplishments culminating in the publication of various collections of poetry, including Return from the Dreamy Fountain in 1960.

Jayyusi earned her bachelor of arts degree in Arabic and English literature from the American University of Beirut in 1945, after which she obtained her Ph.D. in Arabic literature from the School of Oriental and African Arts (SOAS) in London.

Soon after obtaining her doctorate, in 1970, she began her career as a professor, teaching first at the University of Khartoum (1970-1973) and then at the Universities of Algiers and Constantine between 1973 and 1975.

In 1975, the University of Utah invited her to be a visiting Professor of Arabic literature, after which she remained in the United States, teaching at various academic institutions, including the Universities of Utah, Washington and Texas.

While in the United States, she founded the Project of Translation from Arabic (PROTA) with the objective of translating Arabic literature into English and other languages in an effort to bridge cultural gaps. The PROTA mission was "the dissemination of Arabic culture and literature abroad". In less than a decade, PROTA initiated and supervised the publication of a body of translated works, extensively contributing to the repertoire of sources in English, particularly on Arab literature. At the end of the 1980s, Jayyusi launched another branch in PROTA for the translation of Arab cultural studies in addition to literary works, which came to be known as the East-West Nexus.

PROTA has consequently been able to publish a large number of books, including both anthologies and individual works. Prominent PROTA-translated anthologies edited by Jayyusi include The Literature of Modern Arabia and Anthology of Modern Palestinian Literature. In total, Jayussi completed more than forty works, including nine anthologies of Arabic literature. She also edited several books, including The Legacy of Muslim Spain and the folk romance, The Adventures of Sayf Ibn Dhi Yazan, as part of the East-West Nexus. Jayussi has also published two books on Jerusalem; the first in collaboration with Thomas Thompson and entitled Jerusalem in Ancient History and Tradition, and the second, My Jerusalem: Essays, Reminiscences, and Poems, in collaboration with Zafar Ishaq Ansari.

Jayyusi is currently working on an anthology of Palestinian literature and, with Roger Allen, on an anthology of contemporary Arabic theatre.

Source: "University of Arizona." (1994). http://fp.arizona.edu/mesassoc/Bulletin/allen.htm (Accessed 17 March, 2006).
"Khalil Sakakini Cultural Centre." http://www.sakakini.org/literature/literature.htm (Accessed 17 March, 2006).

Luminary: Umm Kulthum (May 1904-January 1975)

Known to millions in the Arab world as "Umm Kulthum, Star of the East," she gave her public, with her beautiful voice, exquisite performances, and fetching renditions of their best loved words and music, half a century of dedicated, brilliant artistry.

Her journey from simple peasant woman in a village to Star of the East was full of struggle, inspired by the pursuit of excellence that lasted to the end of her life. In the midst of wars and conflicts and before kings and commoners, Umm Kulthum sang to the glory and nobility of them all, moving the hearts of the Arabs in the East and the West for decades.

It is said of Umm Kulthum that the Arabs agreed on nothing so much as they did on her voice. Raised in song, it became the symbol of Arab identity, for she took great care in choosing what she sang, accepting only the words of the great poets, ancient or modern. The songs of Umm Kulthum nourished Arab nationalism with their ability to unify Arab passions and express authentic Arab feelings through song, music and performance.

Umm Kulthum was known for her strong personality and the high respect with which she treated both herself and her art. She was respected as much by kings and leaders as she was by ordinary people and was loved everywhere. Her artistic and social status was unique and one that no other oriental singer had achieved previously.

When Egypt suffered the defeat of 1967, Umm Kulthum decided to form an organisation for national solidarity and held concerts outside Egypt in support of the war effort.

She was awarded many prizes and decorations during her long journeys in the service of her art. In 1955, she received the National Order of the Cedar and the Order of Merit, First Class, from Lebanon. In 1968, she won the State Prize of Appreciation in Egypt. She was also given Jordan's Order of the Renaissance, the Mesopotamian Medal of Iraq, the Syrian Order of Merit and Pakistan's Star of Merit and obtained the Greater Order of the Republic from Tunisia in 1968 and the Moroccan Order of Excellence.

Umm Kulthum's songs still resound in the hearts of many and continue to top the musical charts in the Arab world today.

Source: "Almashriq." http://almashriq.hiof.no/egypt/700/780/umKoulthoum (Accessed 9 March, 2006).

met. So long as a woman could become aware of herself as a human being capable of being educated and acquiring knowledge and so long as she was able, as an artist or actor, to have her say in society, education and culture, she had options. The Arab woman thus began to leave the narrow orbit that male society had created for her, guided by a political, social and cultural movement in which women such as Huda Sha'rawi occupied a conspicuous position.

With the arrival in Cairo, from the end of

The Arab woman began to leave the narrow orbit that male society had created for her.

Luminary: Fairuz (November 1935 -)

The outstanding singer Fairuz (real name Nihad Haddad) was born in Jabal al-Arz, Lebanon, Fairuz joined the Conservatoire, where the director of the time, Wadi' Sabra, refused to accept tuition fees from her.

The Fulayfal brothers helped her to become a member of the Radio Liban chorus. She sang with them for two months, and was then chosen as a soloist, having been singled out by the composer Halim al-Rumi, who gave her her professional name (he offered her a choice between Fairuz and Sharazad, and she decided on the former). In 1951, Halim Al-Rumi decided to present Fairuz to the Rahbani brothers, Asi and Mansur, who were preparing a musical project of a highly unusual sort, namely the revival of traditional Lebanese music through the use of modern orchestration.

In 1956, Fairuz and the Rahbanis began their appearances at the Baalbek Festival. As they grew more famous, their shows went on tours around the world and Fairuz ceased to sing exclusively for the Rahbani brothers, collaborating with a number of composers such as Muhammad Abd al-Wahhab and Filimon Wehbeh while at the same time presenting anew the songs of Sayyid Darwish, including "Zuruni Kull Sana Marra" and others. Fairuz also took lead roles in several successful musicals and films, among them "Lulu, Bayya' al-Khawatim, Ayyam Fakhr al-Din, al-Mahatta, Jisr al-Qamar, and Mays al-Rim". At the end of the 1970s, Fairuz and Asi separated, but Fairuz continued to sing the songs of her son Ziad.

Fairuz refused to leave Beirut during the Lebanese civil war and started singing again as soon as it was over. The new stage in Fairuz's career found expression through her collaboration with her son Ziad Rahbani, whose new approach marvellously fuses Eastern and Western music. Fairuz's first album with Ziad was called "Keefak Inta" and was followed by other successful works, of which the latest is "Wa-la Keef" (2001). In 2005, Fairuz was awarded an honorary doctorate in voice by the American University in Beirut.

Sources: "Fairouz." (2006).http://www.fairouz.com/fairouz/tribute/fb.html (Accessed 24 March, 2006).

"Fairuzonline." (2006). http://www.fairuzonline.com/alegend.htm (Accessed 24 March, 2006).

the nineteenth century, of Arab women such as Asya Daghir, Mari Kiwini (Marie Queenie), 'Aziza Amir and others active in music and song, Arab cinema embarked on its long and difficult course towards the creation of a new artistic product. This circle of women gave birth to stories, screenplays and numerous other forms of creative expression that ultimately had an impact on other arts, such as dance, song, music, cinematic production and literature. This creativity also inspired the political, artistic and social struggle (Jarjoura, background paper for the Report).

Arab women's achievements in the production of knowledge

The social sciences

This section focuses on the distinguished achievements of women as scholars, achievements that brought about a movement of exploration and revolution and a complete break with the past. It highlights, in particular, scholars in the field of "women's studies" to underscore how radical their theses were, notably on the problematic issue of authenticity and contemporaneity. This issue, more than any other, goes to the heart of the question of women's position in Arab societies, constantly

swinging between the modernist, Western model and that of traditional society, which springs from the inherited culture and its religious and moral complexities.

The works of pioneering feminists such as Nawal al-Sa'dawi and Fatima Mernissi, for example, evince a joy in the discovery of unknown "continents" in the history, heritage, beliefs and renaissance of the Arab world. For these scholars, such discoveries served as rafts to which they could cling for help and salvation in their fierce struggle to escape from accustomed limits and sail beyond the zone of the harem, with all the connotations of repression, oppression and exclusion that this word holds. The motivations and experience of these feminists may not have been very different from those of the pioneering women scholars who took refuge in modernism and secularism, creating a final break with the past and religion. The latter's writings have their own importance, dazzling the reader with their sparkling intuition and flashes of daring despite their historical, social and religious context, which was often hostile, even under the most progressive of nationalist regimes during the struggle against colonialism.

Perhaps enmity towards the male academic establishment was at the base of these writings

---

BOX 3-6

An Arab woman joins France's "Club of Immortals"

On 16 June 2005, the Algerian woman Asia Jabbar was elected to the French Academy (also known as the "Club of Immortals"). Jabbar won the Neustadt International Prize for Literature in 1996 in recognition of her capacity to transcend the boundaries of culture, language and history in her poetry and prose. Before that, she had won the Gabriel Garcia Marquez prize. Jabbar is also a film director and took the critics' prize at the Venice Biennale in 1979. She writes in French and her works have been translated into many other languages.

Luminary: Nawal Saadawi

Nawal Saadawi is a militant activist for women's rights. She has written on society, ideas, heritage, politics and freedom and is one of Egypt's best known writers internationally, her writings having been translated into more than twelve languages. She attended Cairo University, where she obtained a doctorate in psychiatry in 1955. After first working in her field of specialisation and practising general medicine, she became an official at the Ministry of Health. She has written much on Arab women, addressing their deteriorating situation and calling for their liberation from social constraints and

participation in political and economic life. She has not, however, limited herself to writing. She is a union and NGO activist, editing field studies on women in various parts of Egypt and participating in seminars and lectures locally, in the Arab region and internationally. Her many writings on her religious and political positions have put her life at risk under threats from extremists. As a result, she received police protection at her home in Guiza until she left Egypt to work as a lecturer at universities in North America.

Source: Fouad, background paper for the Report.

that were liberated from the rules of strict methodology, especially since they were biased towards the logic of binary opposition, which is based on the male-female dichotomy. In all cases, the second generation has overcome this issue and its writings will be more scientifically grounded and balanced without compromising the feminist outlook (Fouad, background paper for the Report).

A notable recent development in the production and dissemination of knowledge from the feminist perspective is the appearance of women's focus groups established by Arab women scholars, sometimes with the help of male peers. These groups study, discuss and publish new thinking on women's issues in order to aid the women's movement in the region.

The natural and exact sciences

It is not surprising that some Arab women have distinguished themselves in the fields of literary and artistic creativity or in those branches of knowledge such as the humanities and social sciences that are conventionally considered "appropriate" for women.

However, a galaxy of Arab women has made stellar contributions to the natural and exact sciences as well. The truth is that when Arab women scientists and technicians have

---

Luminary: Fatima Mernissi

A Moroccan researcher and writer, Fatima Mernissi studied in France and America and holds a research professorship at the Institute of Scientific Research of Mohammed V University in Rabat. She is also a member of the Advisory Board of the United Nations University.

Mernissi writes in English and French and all her works have been translated into Arabic. She supervises a number of research groups and publication series concerned with the fields of women and sociology. She has published numerous works, including: Sex, Ideology, and Islam (1983); The Political Harem (The Prophet and Women) (1983); Forgotten Queens of Islam" (1994); Scheherazade Goes West: Different Cultures, Different Harems (1987); and Dreams of Trespass: Tales of a Harem Girlhood (in English, 1994).

Fatima Mernissi is considered one of the leading researchers in feminist sociology. In a brief overview of her work, her book, The Political Harem: The Prophet and the Women, stands out as particularly important. In it, Mernissi tackles a sensitive topic, one that has been passed over in silence in the traditional Islamic canon: the question of human sexuality.

This subject remains the source of confusion and questioning among many of us, both male and female, albeit we may not admit it or have decided to ignore it. Through an intelligent and thought-provoking reading, she reaches striking conclusions concerning the familiar and the conventional.

Forgotten Queens of Islam is considered to be Mernissi's second most important and daring work. Here she discusses the issue of governance in Islam, making an important distinction between the political, earthly ruler on the one hand, and the caliph, God's shadow on earth, spiritual leader of the Muslims, entrusted with the application of shari'a, or divine law, on the other. Later, Mernissi presents us with her own special and striking reading of the biographies of some women who actually ruled in various parts of the Islamic world. These are figures whom history has consigned to oblivion or whom male-centred historians have marginalised or written off, portraying their achievements, at best, as moments of national collapse and decadence.

Source: Fouad, background paper for the Report.

---

been given an opportunity to use their abilities at the international level, they have achieved extraordinary results.

> When Arab women scientists and technicians have been given an opportunity to use their abilities at the international level, they have achieved extraordinary results.

Luminary: Zaha' Hadid – A Diva of World Architecture

The Iraqi architect Zaha' Hadid rose to the pinnacle of her profession internationally, a profession combining art, science and technology. She obtained a first degree in mathematics from the American University in Beirut and studied architecture at the Architectural Association School of Architecture in London. In 1982, when a teaching assistant at the School, she outstripped 538 other architects with her winning design for the Peak Building in Hong Kong. Subsequently, she won a series of international competitions, including for the design of a "habitual bridge" in the middle of London containing theatres, cinemas, hotels and restaurants in 1966.

With the turn of the twenty-first century, Zaha' Hadid had opportunities to design and execute several major architectural projects, such as the Rosenthal Center for Contemporary Art in Cincinnati, a BMW plant in Leipzig and the Bergisel Ski Jump in Innsbruck. In winning the contract to construct a bridge linking Abu Dhabi, the island on which the capital of the United Arab Emirates is situated, to the mainland of the United Arab Emirates, she scored a historic precedent. This is the first bridge ever not only to have been built by a woman but to

have been seen through from design to completion by an architect. In 2005, the Iraqi architect became the first woman to be awarded the Pritzker Prize, architecture's equivalent to the Nobel Prize.

Now in her fifties, Zaha' Hadid, continues to compete not only against other internationally renowned architects but also against herself. In her recent design for the Odrupgaard Museum in Copenhagen, she abandoned her trademark stark, straight-edged contours, which are said to have been inspired by Kufic script, and instead opted for natural, gentle and, if we may say so, "feminine" curves and sloping walls. Hadid says that in designing the museum, she tried "to fuse the architectural space with the natural scenery of the park in which it is enclosed". The "amazing transition from closed to open sites" is what most fascinates her in Arab architecture, which, in her opinion, achieves the fundamental function of architectural structure: "the joyous aesthetic sensation of moving from an enclosed space, such as the prayer area in the Zeitouniya Mosque in Tunisia, to the mosque's courtyard – open to the sun, the air and nature".

Source: 'Aref, background paper for the Report.

The astronomical sciences

The astronomical sciences have attracted a group of the most brilliant Arab women scientists. Could this be due to nostalgia for a glorious past, which saw the birth of the astronomical sciences in the countries between Mesopotamia and the Nile and stupendous advancements in these sciences during the Arab-Islamic scientific renaissance in the Middle Ages? Or is it because astronomy, in the words of the French scientist, Pierre-Simon Laplace, "is the handsomest monument to the human spirit, the most distinguished decoration of its intellectual achievement? "

Astronomy and the space sciences have sparked the interest of women scientists from the Arab East to the Arab West and from such diverse disciplines as physics, mathematics, geology and geography. Four of these women have ascended the arduous path of astrophysics, a branch of science that emerged from the fusion of astronomy and physics. Like most prominent Arab women in the sciences, three of these luminaries graduated from Arab universities before obtaining advanced degrees and conducting research in internationally reputed universities abroad.

Arab women astronomers have put paid to the view that women are biologically unsuited

Arab women astronomers have put paid to the view that women are biologically unsuited for science.

Luminaries in Astronomical Sciences:

Maha Ashour-Abdalla
Professor of astrophysics and director of the Center for Digital Simulation of the University of California-Los Angeles, Maha Ashour-Abdalla obtained her Bachelor of Science degree in physics from the University of Alexandria, Egypt, and her Ph.D. in astrophysics and space plasma from the Imperial College, London.

The Egyptian scientist, who has more than 300 published studies to her name, is regarded as one of the world's foremost specialists in the polar aurora, that entrancing atmospheric phenomenon resulting from the permeation of the earth's magnetic field by solar winds and manifested as luminous waves that stretch for thousands of kilometres over the north and south poles.

Shadia Rifai Habbal
The lengthy academic career of Shadia Rifai Habbal took her from Damascus University, where she obtained her Bachelor of Science degree in physics and mathematics, to the American University in Beirut, where she completed her Master of Arts degree in physics, and from there to the University of Cincinnati, where she obtained her Ph.D. in physics.

The activities of Habbal, a mother of two, have ranged from teaching university classes to taking scientific teams to observe solar eclipses around the world. She has contributed to the development of the first spaceship to be sent to the closest possible point

near the sun in 2007, and spearheaded an academic movement for women scientists called "Adventurous Women".

The studies on solar winds conducted by this Arab scientist and her colleagues were like "bombs going off". At least this was how they were described in America's Science magazine, which cited reactions to Rifai and her colleagues' discoveries as diverse as "heretical", "a gigantic step forward", "controversial" and "revolutionary".

Leila Abdel Haqq Belkoura
A young Moroccan astrophysicist, Leila Belkoura is also a science writer who achieved worldwide fame with her first book, Minding the Heavens. The book relates the discovery, told through the lives of seven astronomers, of the Milky Way, which contains our planet, Earth, our solar system and billions of other stars.

Like an enthusiastic astronomy teacher, Leila Belkoura takes us in her book on a journey beneath the open night sky to what she calls "the inner lining of the celestial dome": "If you lie down on your back, in a dark and quiet space, and look up towards the stars, you may feel that you can sense the slow revolution of the dome as it moves, with all the stars stretched out before you, from the east to the west, and tosses them beneath you to the other side of the globe".

for science. Nevertheless, Harvard University President Laurence Summers fell into this error in a speech he delivered last year, in which he attributed the paucity of women's contributions to the sciences to their preoccupation with the family and "intrinsic aptitude". His remarks drew a widespread outcry both within and outside of American academic circles, forcing Summers as well as the university to offer an apology.

That Leila Belkoura and her colleagues began their scientific journey in physics brings to mind the remark of the celebrated physicist, Ernest Rutherford: "All science is either physics or stamp collecting".

Belkoura obtained her Bachelor of Science degree in physics from Cornell University and her Ph.D. in astrophysics from the University of Colorado. The Year of Physics, 2005, demonstrated that this science remains caught in the tug-of-war between relativity and quantum theories and that the only inroads made so far have been in astrophysics. As Belkoura forged her way through this difficult discipline, she gratefully acknowledged "the enormous influence" her father, Abdel Haqq Belkoura, had upon her intellectual life. In a personal letter, she wrote, "Although I did not follow in his footsteps – he is an economist – he trained me to think in a particular way and to express what I believe. He taught me to try to see the 'bigger picture' or the 'totality' of things".

Perhaps the most beautifully phrased appraisal of Arab women scientists appears in the introduction of the Arabic edition of *Minding the Heavens*. It is written by the young Syrian astronomer Rim Turkmani, who relates: "I, who could not write this short introduction until after I put my baby to bed and made sure he was asleep, was astounded to learn that Leila had begun writing this book while pregnant and completed it after becoming a mother". The introduction concludes: "Leila offers a superb model for Arab women, because of her ability to perform, simultaneously, the role that life had chosen for her and the role that she chose in life. Both are creative roles, so why should they not support one another?" ('Aref, background paper for the Report).

Athletics

In spite of the marginal part that sports plays in forming the traditional conception of the role of women, a small number of women from Arab countries have risen to the highest levels of accomplishment in this field at the international level, becoming gold, silver and bronze Olympic medal winners.

In the last six Olympic Games (1984-2004), six women in the Arab world, five from the Maghreb[11] and one from the Syrian Arab Republic, won one of three high prizes in track and field events. Two thirds of them were gold-medal winners, certainly a relatively high figure when compared to the fact that only a quarter of male Arab Olympic medal winners were gold medallists.

A small number of women from Arab countries have risen to the highest levels of accomplishment in the field of athletics at the international level.

TABLE 3-1

Women in the Arab world who won medals in the last six Olympic Games (1984-2004)

Name	Year	Nation
El Moutawakal, Nawal	1984	Morocco
Boulmerka, Hassiba	1992	Algeria
Shouaa, Ghada	1996	Syrian Arab Republic
Merah-Benida, Nouria	2000	Algeria
Bidouane, Nouzha	2000	Morocco
Benhassi, Hasna	2004	Morocco

[11] Comprising Algeria, Morocco and Tunisia. These are countries where women enjoy a greater respect for their rights and a relatively higher status than in other Arab countries, which suggests a strong correlation between respect for the rights of women and their ability to perform better in various fields of activity.

Arab women entrepreneurs: a growing economic force in Arab countries

Even before the advent of Islam, women played a role in business in Arab countries that did not go unrecognised. One of the legacies of Islam for women's rights is that it conferred upon women autonomous financial rights, which helped to sustain the presence of women in commercial affairs, whether directly or as partners of male relatives or other men. Today, the move towards free market economies, together with growing advocacy for the empowerment of women in Arab countries, has worked to increase the contributions of women entrepreneurs in Arab economies. It has augmented their influence in private-sector business organisations and, indeed, has given rise to their own organisations, even in those Arab countries that are the most conservative with respect to women's issues.

For the purposes of this Report, entrepreneurs are defined as people who organise or manage business ventures, generating income for themselves and others. The success stories of women in business have become so commonplace that they no longer cause the sensation that they did only two decades ago.

Despite the paucity of data on the number of women entrepreneurs, there are indications that their numbers are steadily on the rise. In Bahrain, for example, the number of women employers rose from 193 in 1991 to 815 in 2001 – a 322 per cent increase (Chamlou and Yared, 2003). In Saudi Arabia, estimates of the number of women-owned businesses range between 20,000 and 40,000 (Esim, 2005), and in Tunisia, the number of women-owned businesses increased from 2,000 in 1998 to 5,000 in 2005. Many of these are family concerns, as is generally the case with economic ventures in Arab countries.

Businesses owned by women tend to focus on the service sector, as is the case with 77 per cent of such ventures in Yemen, 59 per cent in Egypt and 37 per cent in Morocco (GEM, 2005). Another survey, conducted in Morocco in 2004, found that the majority of female entrepreneurs were university graduates and three fourths of them managed the companies in which they invested (AFEM, www.afem.ma).

As the share of women in business and wealth increased, so, too, did the number of female directors of bank branches and financial institutions providing services for women. The first bank branch for women was opened by the Kuwaiti Finance House in Bahrain. The branch, which offers Islamic banking services, is managed by a Bahraini woman who also acts as the auditing coordinator on behalf of the banking group.

It was also only natural that, with the growing numbers of women entrepreneurs, there would be a commensurate rise in businesswomen's associations working to overcome the constraints on women in business, such as limited access to markets, information and experience. Egypt, today, has 22 businesswomen's associations in contrast to only one in 1995. In Morocco, Saloua Belkeziz, owner of an information technology firm, established the Association of Moroccan Women Entrepreneurs (AFEM) for Moroccan Business Women, with a membership that rose from 70 in 2000 to 184 in 2004. In Yemen in 2001, Gabool Al-Mutawakkel and her sister founded the Girls World Communication Centre to support women between the ages of 18 and 35 seeking to participate in the labour market and civil society. The Centre also offers training in human rights awareness and advocacy skills to directors of women's NGOs. In Mauritania, the Association of Women Traders has a membership of 270.

This organisational activity extends to chambers of commerce. In the Gulf States, specifically, the Chambers of Commerce and Industry (CCI) have been instrumental in the empowerment of women. Over 400 women participated in the first Gulf Cooperation Council Businesswomen's Forum hosted by Oman and organised by its CCI in cooperation with the Federation of GCC Chambers of Commerce. In November 2005, the Jeddah Trade and Industry Chamber of Commerce and Industry set a milestone by opening nominations to its 18-member board of directors to women. Two women were elected in spite of the great disparity in the numbers of women and men voters (100 versus 4,000). (Hijab, background paper for the Report).

Even before the advent of Islam, women played a role in business in Arab countries that did not go unrecognised.

In Saudi Arabia, estimates of the number of women-owned businesses range between 20,000 and 40,000.

Egypt, today, has 22 businesswomen's associations in contrast to only one in 1995.

Leading Women Entrepreneurs

• Asila al-Harthi, Oman
Initially, Asilah al-Harthi had difficulty in persuading her father to allow her to study abroad and, after graduating from Harvard Business School, to let her take part in managing the family business, the Al-Harthi Group, which began in real estate and moved into information technology-related services. Asila Al-Harthi became the first female member of the Oman Chamber of Commerce and Industry and the first female chief executive of the Oman Oil Company.

• Azza Fahmy, Egypt
Azza Fahmy has made her distinctive mark in international jewellery design and her work has been displayed in more than 200 exhibits around the world, including several museums. After graduating from the College of Fine Arts, she became an apprentice to gold and silversmiths in Cairo's fabled Khan El Khalili bazaar, the first woman to do so. She was chosen by the International Gold Council as one of its permanent members and judges.

• Khalida Ahmad al-Qatami, Kuwait
One of eight daughters, Khalida was chosen by her father to co-manage the Al-Khunaini Al-Qatami General Trading Company and then became chairman of the company in 1995. After her father died, she continued to direct the company but eventually sold her shares and founded a real estate company. She also owns and runs her own pharmacy, which has been in operation for 20 years.

• Layla Khayyat, Tunisia
CEO of Plastiss, an industrial manufacturing firm with 125 employees, Layla Khayyat took over the business after her husband's death. Until then, Khayyat had been a professor of French literature, but she took night courses in management and soon doubled the company's number of employees and output. Khayyat is president of the International Women Entrepreneurs' Union and served for seven years as the president of the World Association of Women Entrepreneurs.

• Lubna Olayan, Saudi Arabia
CEO of Olayan Financing Company, Olayan ranked among Fortune's 50 most powerful women outside the United States.

• Maria Hibri and Hoda Baroudi, Lebanon
Maria Hibri and Hoda Baroudi have achieved regional and international recognition with their textile and design firm, Bokja, which has held ten exhibitions worldwide during the past five years.

• Mona Bahari, Egypt
Mona Bahari founded the Mobaco sports wear company, which grew from three sewing machines, three operators and an output of 30 pieces a day in 1974 to an LE 70 million operation with 700 employees. Many members of her family, including her father, husband, sons and daughters, and their spouses, now work in the firm, whose products are tailored both for the Egyptian market and for export. Mona attributes much of her success to a supportive father, husband and grandmother.

• Nadia Dajani, Jordan
Although she originally studied architecture, Nadia Dajani is now a rising star in the world of jewellery design. The jewellery firm she founded in 2003 is the first such company to be registered with the Ministry of Industry and Trade. Her designs are sold, and imitated, throughout the region.

• Raghda Kurdi, Jordan
Raghda Kurdi founded a pharmaceutical company, currently staffed with 101 employees and the first in Jordan to be fully computerised. She also collaborated with her mother in launching a clothes boutique and co-founded the Jordanian branch of the International Women's Forum.

• Reem Acra, Lebanon
After several years of practical experience as an embroidery artist, Reem Acra established her own fashion house in 1995, which gained international recognition as one of the world's renowned bridal salons. She sells to more than 200 of the most prominent retailers in Europe and the United States where her designs have become a favourite of luxury stores as well as red carpet regulars.

• Sabra al-Riyami, Oman
After working as a journalist with Omani television, she co-founded an events management firm with her husband, the first such company in Oman. Founded in 1995, the company grosses around $1 million a year.

• Suad Amiry, occupied Palestinian territory
An architect, Suad Amiry co-founded the Riwaq cultural organisation in Israeli-occupied Ramallah, with the aim of documenting architectural heritage. After 1996, when it became possible to restore and conserve this heritage, Riwaq became a source of employment for a large number of Palestinians. The organisation renovated 30 buildings, primarily in rural areas in the West Bank, and transformed them into centres that have themselves created more job opportunities.

• Thuraya Yaqoub, Yemen
Thuraya Yaqoub entered business while still in university, starting with a children's clothing project. She then used her inheritance to establish a communications centre, after which she opened an Internet café. She now plans to found a natural medicine centre. Her younger sister hopes to follow in her footsteps and join her in the business.

Source: Hijab, background paper for the Report.

SUMMARY

Arab women have amply demonstrated their capacity to participate in areas of human activity outside the family. However, as illustrated in this chapter, women in Arab countries are still denied opportunities to use their capabilities in traditional economic areas and political institutions, where men tend to remain dominant.

It should nevertheless be recognised that women in the Arab world have made increasingly significant inroads in their fields. Indeed, some have achieved critical acclaim in domains which were, until recently, restricted to men.

CHAPTER FOUR

LEVELS OF HUMAN WELL-BEING

Introduction

Previous chapters have compared the respective positions of women and men in the Arab countries in terms of the acquisition and utilisation of essential capacities since these are two primary dimensions of human well-being from the standpoint of human development. This chapter focuses on other aspects of human well-being as they relate to Arab women.

TOPOGRAPHY OF POVERTY AND GENDER

Despite the limitations of data and taking into account a study undertaken on five Arab States (Egypt, Jordan, Morocco, Tunisia and Yemen), there is no evidence of the "feminisation of poverty", i.e., no clear evidence that women suffer from higher levels of poverty than men, as indicated by income and expenditure, the traditional measures of poverty (Abdel Gadir Ali, background paper for the Report). A better measure within the framework of human development is the extent to which women are deprived of opportunities to acquire capacities and use them to secure the elements of human welfare. These yardsticks indicate that women suffer from higher levels of such "human poverty", which measures deprivation by taking into account the three indices of human development: health, knowledge and income.

Chapter 2 illustrated the great relative deprivation of women in this respect in terms of gaining knowledge through education and of enjoying health in its positive and comprehensive sense.

When it comes to the utilisation of people's capacities in economic activity, women are affected by higher rates of unemployment just as they are at greater risk of losing their jobs in a recession, especially in the large-scale private sector. Likewise, they do not benefit to the same degree as men from the creation of new jobs during an economic revival.

Working women generally receive lower wages than their male peers. The disparity increases in the private sector in that government and public-sector employers more closely adhere to laws concerning equality of wages.

POVERTY AND THE GENDER OF HEADS OF HOUSEHOLD

Accurate investigation requires analysis of the relationship between the gender of heads of household and poverty, distinguishing between two types of female household headship: (a) that which is imposed by widowhood, marital separation or abandonment; and (b) that which is voluntary and results from the husband's migration for the sake of work. In the latter case, legally speaking, a male remains the head of household.

Study reveals that households headed by females are not necessarily the poorest of the poor. Indeed, some families headed by women are better off according to some indicators of social welfare, including, in certain cases, income and wealth, especially if the women's situation is voluntary. Nevertheless, the great majority of households that are headed by women through no choice of their own appear to be poorer than the minority of households headed by unmarried men.

THE SPREAD OF POVERTY AND THE DISEMPOWERMENT OF WOMEN

Inasmuch as empirical evidence does not exist to confirm the feminisation of poverty, the present Report examines how the spread of

Women suffer from higher levels of "human poverty".

Women are affected by higher rates of unemployment just as they are at greater risk of losing their jobs in a recession.

poverty contributes to the disempowerment of women, using cumulative indicators of poverty to represent its spread.

To this end, a regression analysis was conducted to determine the relationship between the "gender empowerment measure" (GEM) as a dependent variable and the head count index (level of poverty) and human poverty indicators as independent variables. The data were drawn from the Human Development Report 2004 (Abdel Gadir Ali, background paper for the Report). It is worth noting that a value for the indicator "gender empowerment" was available for only four Arab States out of 79 countries in the world for which data were available: Bahrain (where the indicator value was 0.395), Egypt (0.266), Saudi Arabia (0.207) and Yemen (0.123). The value for the indicator was the highest in Norway (0.908) and the lowest in Yemen. The results of the analysis show that the spread of income poverty on average leads to the disempowerment of women (as expressed by the indicator 'social gender empowerment'-GEM) as compared to men. Income poverty also leads to the disenfranchisement of women in the areas of parliamentary participation, professional and technical employment, and control of economic resources.

As far as human poverty is concerned, the results of the analysis on average confirm that it results in the disempowerment of women (again, as expressed by the indicator "social gender empowerment-GEM") and the exclusion of women in upper-level legislative,

administrative and organisational jobs as well as in the professional and technical arenas. The results did not reveal a statistically significant effect of the spread of human poverty in developing countries on the political empowerment of women, as reflected in the number of parliamentary seats occupied by women.

THE IMPAIRMENT OF PERSONAL LIBERTY

Women's right to enjoy personal liberty and security is still thwarted on many fronts. Simply making a connection between women and freedom excites controversy in some quarters and conflicts with custom and tradition. Some parties believe in restricting women's freedom of movement in the name of protecting them or their "reputation". In many cases, the law plays its part by legitimising such restrictions, claiming to be acting in defence of obedience or "honour".

The forms and degrees of violence inflicted on Arab women confirm that Arab legislators, governments and social movements need to redouble their efforts to achieve security and development in its comprehensive sense. To discuss violence[1] against women in the Arab countries is not to imply its absence in the rest of the world. It is a world problem, the fight against which has been part of the global programme for human rights. Its extent was recognised at the World Conference on Human Rights through the adoption of the global Declaration on the Elimination of Violence against Women in December 1993. The preamble to the latter asserts that violence against women is linked to the definition of the asymmetrical status of men and women and, consequently, to all types of discrimination against women. Such violence represents an obstacle to equality, peace and development and a violation of human rights and freedoms. The Declaration also established 25 November as the International Day for the Elimination of Violence against Women.

It remains difficult to speak of violence

BOX 4-1

Kemal Derviş*: On the Occasion of the International Day for the Elimination of Violence against Women (25 November 2005)

Violence against women not only devastates lives and fractures communities, but also impedes development. While its extent is hard to estimate given it is so widely under-reported, the World Health Organisation estimates that 25 per cent of women worldwide will be raped, beaten, coerced into sex or otherwise abused in their lifetime. No country or society can claim to be free of domestic violence; it cuts across boundaries of culture, class, education, income, ethnicity and age.

Today, violence against women is still a universally tolerated and often unpunished crime. Women are attacked on the street, in the workplace, in the home, while in state custody, and in conflict situations.

*Administrator, United Nations Development Programme

---

[1] The United Nations Declaration on the Elimination of Violence against Women, Article 1, defines violence against women as "any act of gender-based violence that results in, or is likely to result in physical, sexual or psychological harm or suffering to women, including threats of such acts, coercion or arbitrary deprivation of liberty, whether occurring in public or in private life." (A/RES/48/104)

against women in the Arab world from a statistical point of view[2] because merely talking about it in some Arab countries arouses resistance. Studies investigating violence across Arab societies are in their infancy. Sources of data available to date are reports by the media, presentations made at Arab and international seminars, reports from human rights organisations and women's shelters for victims of violence, and the testimonies of affected women. Though not strictly quantifiable, such accounts indicate that the most important step to oppose violence against women in the Arab world is to fight against its concealment, to remove the cloak of silence surrounding it and to expose it wherever it occurs whether in public or in private. Continued silence on the subject incurs a heavy cost for individuals, society and even the State. It is equally important to place forms of violence that many affected women have come to accept as natural in the category of unacceptable behaviour.

It should be noted that, according to the Report survey, the Arab public overwhelmingly condemns all forms of abuse of women – physical or mental (Box 4-2).

The most important step to oppose violence against women in the Arab world is to fight against its concealment.

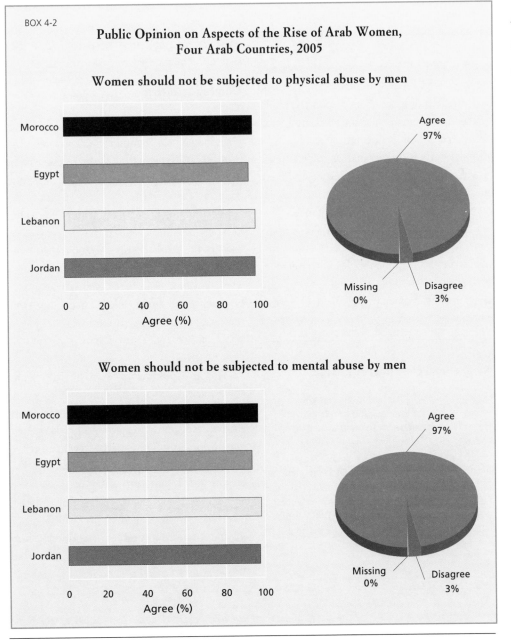

BOX 4-2

Public Opinion on Aspects of the Rise of Arab Women, Four Arab Countries, 2005

Women should not be subjected to physical abuse by men

Morocco
Egypt
Lebanon
Jordan

0 20 40 60 80 100
Agree (%)

Agree 97%
Missing 0%
Disagree 3%

Women should not be subjected to mental abuse by men

Morocco
Egypt
Lebanon
Jordan

0 20 40 60 80 100
Agree (%)

Agree 97%
Missing 0%
Disagree 3%

The Arab public overwhelmingly condemns all forms of abuse of women.

[2] Article 4 of the Declaration on the Elimination of Violence against Women states that it is incumbent upon States to condemn violence against women". States also should "promote research, collect data and compile statistics, especially concerning domestic violence, relating to the prevalence of different forms of violence against women". (Ibid.)

FORMS OF VIOLENCE AGAINST WOMEN IN THE ARAB WORLD

Laws in many Arab countries still protect the killer and allow him to enter a plea of extenuating circumstances.

The family in many parts of the Arab world has been transformed from a place of safety and security into a place where any type of violence against women may be practised.

Honour crimes

The killing of women in defence of honour is an old tribal custom still practised in many local Arab societies, including those of Egypt, Iraq, Jordan, Lebanon and the occupied Palestinian territory. These are premeditated murders carried out by a father, brother, husband or son. The woman is killed under the pretence of protecting her family's honour. Many are killed because "they have been exposed to the disgrace of rape" (The Lebanese Organisation to Combat Violence against Women, in Arabic, 2001, 17). In some Arab societies, the murderers are still treated as heroes who have erased a disgrace visited upon the family by the slain woman. Moreover, many female suicide cases are connected with the issue of honour where the woman is forced to kill herself to spare the family the responsibility for murdering her.

Statistics indicate, for instance, that between May 2004 and March 2005, there were 20 honour killings and 15 attempted killings in the occupied Palestinian territory on the basis of honour. Official statistics also show that 20 women were killed in Jordan annually on the same pretext. Sometimes the

motive is male greed in obtaining a larger portion of an inheritance at the expense of women (UNIFEM, in Arabic, 2005, 17) or the concealment of sexual assault by relatives in the same family. Also, the organisation "Rawan" recorded honour crimes that were inflicted on Kurdish women in northern Iraq (UNIFEM, in Arabic, 2004, 140).

Despite the success of civil society organisations in introducing changes to some criminal laws (in Algeria, Jordan, Lebanon and Morocco) in order to have honour crimes treated as criminal acts, laws in many Arab countries still protect the killer and allow him to enter a plea of extenuating circumstances. Many judges use their discretionary powers to impose light sentences upon murderers (see Chapter 8).

Domestic violence

Domestic violence is not a purely Arab phenomenon; it is found and condemned in many areas of the world. Nevertheless, what is disturbing is the persistent denial in some Arab countries that it exists.[3]

Testimonies heard in discussion groups and in mock trials indicate that the family in many parts of the Arab world has been transformed from a place of safety and security into a place where any type of violence against women may be practised. Family violence may range from the beating and sexual assault of wives to the sexual abuse and rape of immature girls by male relatives.

As a spokeswoman for the family counselling office of the Bahraini NGO, Girls' Renaissance Society, says, "We receive every kind of case of physical and emotional violence, mostly domestic. The violence to which women are subjected is unnatural and degrading. The greatest fear is that a girl will grow accustomed to it and become unable to resist or to break down the barrier of silence"[4].

In a recent report[5] entitled *Gulf Cooperation Council (GCC) countries: Women deserve dignity and respect*, Amnesty

---

BOX 4-3
WHO: Women Find No Shelter from Violence at Home

A study conducted by the World Health Organisation (WHO) in 10 countries found that between 15 per cent (Japan) and 71 per cent (Ethiopia) of the women interviewed had been subjected to physical or sexual violence by an intimate male partner during their lifetime.

...The violence of those in the "ever abused" group was severe enough to result in physical injury including fractures and eye damage.

"Women are more at risk from violence involving the people they know at home than from strangers in the street" (Lee Jong Wook, WHO Director General).

"It has devastating consequences for the women who experience it, and a traumatic effect on those who witness it, particularly children" (Yakin Erturk – United Nations Special Rapporteur on Violence against Women).

Source: Agence France-Presse, 24 Novembre 2005.

---

[3] In answer to a report by Amnesty International about violence against women in the Gulf States, the president of the Supreme Council for Women affirmed, after female journalists publicly concurred with the report, that it is widespread. "Cases of violence are individual and are not referred to the courts because it has become a social phenomenon,... everyone in Bahrain knows that cases of violence against women are not recorded at police stations or in hospitals" (Mona 'Abbas Fadl, Bahraini writer).

[4] Mona Fadl. "Women Gateway." (2005). http://www.womengateway.com/arwg/Qadhya+Almaraa/violence/atameez.htm (Accessed 10 April, 2006).

[5] Document number MDE 04/004/2005, 11 May 2005.

International concentrates on the many forms of discrimination facing women in the Gulf States, and especially domestic violence: "Women suffering gender-based domestic violence often have no practical option but to remain in the home and risk further violence. Economic and social pressures arising from discriminatory attitudes and treatment contribute to women's experience of violence" (Miadi, background paper for the Report).

Other forms of violence against women are practised within full view of the State, such as that inflicted by the *motawa* (volunteer religious advocates) in Saudi Arabia or by religious groups that set themselves up as guardians of the propriety of women's clothing and conduct. Women also suffer from numerous forms of violence in the work place both in the form of sexual harassment or blackmail in return for a pitiful wage and the arbitrary severance that follows in case of refusal. The lack of data indicates the difficulty of estimating the extent of violence of this sort.

Female circumcision

The high incidence of female circumcision[6] in some Arab countries (Table 4-1) leads to serious health complications for women. The operation itself can lead to death from bleeding, and the severe pain that it causes can lead to a nervous breakdown. There are long-term complications such as inflammation of the incision from unsterilised operating tools, blood poisoning, fatal tetanus, hepatitis and AIDS. These afflictions can, in turn, lead to serious disturbance of the urinary system, reduced fertility or even sterility and can create difficulties in childbirth since the incisions often lead to mutilation.

Similarly, sensations of pain or the absence of pleasurable feelings can lead to failure to enjoy a normal sex life. Even when the operation is carried out in the least damaging way, its psychological effects can only be negative, resulting in feelings of sexual inferiority. The wide extent to which this phenomenon is

TABLE 4-1		
Female circumcision rates (up to the year 2000) (%)		
Country	**Year**	**Rate**
Djibouti		98
Somalia		98
Egypt	2000	97
Sudan	1990	89
Yemen	1997	23

Source: WHO (http://www.emro.who.int/rhrn/part5.htm), (5 April 2006).

culturally accepted in some quarters contributes to the difficulty of combating it. An opinion poll carried out in Egypt in 2000 showed that 80 per cent of women with daughters confessed that circumcision had been, or would be, performed on their children. This represented a slight improvement over 1995, when 87 per cent of women had resolved to have their daughters circumcised. Studies in Egypt have shown that among the factors facilitating the spread of circumcision are low levels of education, residence in a rural area and, most of all, personal beliefs. They revealed that eight out of ten women in rural areas believed that men preferred a circumcised wife; in the city, not more than four in ten did. The cultural character of the issue becomes clear when it is noted that circumcision occurs among Egyptian Copts as well as Muslims, though to a lesser degree (El-Zanaty and Way, 2001).

In a positive development affecting the rights of women and children, the Council of State, Egypt's highest administrative court, on 28 December 1997 supported a Ministry of Health decision prohibiting female circumcision after a lower court had declared the decision null a year earlier except under medical supervision. The Council ruled that female circumcision was not an individual right in shari'a (Islamic law) since there was nothing in the Qur'an or Sunna (practices approved by the Prophet Muhammad) sanctioning it. It decided that carrying out a circumcision

The high incidence of female circumcision in some Arab countries leads to serious health complications for women.

Other forms of violence against women are practised within full view of the State.

---

[6] Mutilation of the reproductive organs takes different forms in different countries. These include the partial or complete removal of the clitoris (clitorectomy), the removal of the entire clitoris and the cutting of the labia minora (excision) or, in the most extreme form, the removal of all external genitalia and the stitching together of the two sides of the vulva, leaving a tiny hole for the flow of urine and blood. The operation is generally performed without anaesthesia, with the likelihood of health complications that include severe pain during urination, menstruation and the sexual act. Bleeding or inflammation stemming from the cutting of sexual organs is in some cases fatal (Equality Now, Women's Situations, 1, 20 June 2001).

operation was illegal even if the girl or her parents agreed to it. The Sudanese Ministry of Health also moved towards taking steps to prohibit the practice.

Violence against women under occupation

Women in Arab lands under occupation have been subject to forms of violence inflicted upon them by the occupying powers.

In Iraq, towns and neighbourhoods have experienced the forced displacement of thousands of families. Women are afraid to leave their houses because of the prevailing conditions of insecurity, and they often miss work. Women prisoners in Abu Ghraib prison have been subjected to various violations and abuses including rape and sexual degradation, driving some of those released to commit suicide; others have been killed by relatives to wipe out the "dishonour". Similarly, women have been taken hostage to force their male family members to give themselves up or make confessions regarding the resistance in occupied Iraq (Haifa Zangana, in Arabic, Al-Quds al-Arabi, 30 October 2005).

WOMEN IN MARGINALISED GROUPS

NOMADIC AND REMOTE RURAL WOMEN

The situation of Arab women in rural and desert areas is linked for historical reasons to that of other weak and marginalised social groups, communities and districts. Their situation is the most poverty-stricken, wretched and oppressed and the least fortunate in terms of opportunities for development. Everything about Arab Bedouin life, with its myriad challenges stemming from exceptional societal circumstances,[7] a harsh desert environment and the exhausting search for the rudiments of life and social contact – conditions not much different from those Ibn Khaldun described in the fifteenth century[8] – speaks of an unfavourable situation for women (Al-Rawi, in Arabic, 1972, 223).

The Arab desert and countryside, with their wild expanses and limited contact with modern civilisation, are still ruled by family and tribal solidarity, kinship ties, loyalty to tribal authority and a traditional economy tied to the land, livestock, the weather and simple industries. All of these are conducive to male dominance, permitting no participation for women except in certain activities, such as childbearing, service to the husband and family, and pastoral and agricultural activities that are related to sheer survival (Hijab, in Arabic, 1988, 192).

> Women in Arab lands under occupation have been subject to forms of violence inflicted upon them by the occupying powers.

BOX 4-4

Discrimination against Women under Occupation in the Occupied Palestinian Territory

"Occupation and the separation wall unevenly violate women's rights. Palestinian women are routinely harassed, intimidated and abused by Israeli soldiers at checkpoints and gates. They are humiliated in front of their families and subjected to sexual violence by both soldiers and settlers. There are approximately 120 Palestinian women prisoners of whom 11 are in administrative detention – that is, held without charge or trial. Women prisoners are subjected to gender-based violence while subject to investigation and in detention. Moreover, prison conditions raise concerns for their health and well-being.

Restriction of movement owing to the occupation severely impedes Palestinian women's access to education and health. Restrictions on movement limit opportunities for independence and decrease the number of women seeking formal education or employment ... Women's health has suffered as a result of their inability to reach health centres. Pregnant women are vulnerable to long waits at checkpoints. A number of unsafe deliveries in which both mothers and infants have died have occurred at checkpoints. From the beginning of the second intifada to March 2004, 55 Palestinian women have given birth at checkpoints and 33 newborns were stillborn under these conditions, owing to delays or denial of permission to reach medical facilities.

Unemployment and poverty resulting from the occupation have been shown to produce divorce and domestic violence. The Israeli Nationality and Entry into Israel Law of 2003 aims to stop family unification when one spouse is a resident of the Occupied Palestinian Territory. The result of this law is that thousands of affected family members live separately from one another with no legal means available to unify the family. The only way to maintain the unity of the family is to reside illegally in Israel, in permanent fear of investigation and expulsion. This places an immense burden on the psychological state of Palestinian women. The law, which does not apply to Israeli settlers living in the Occupied Palestinian Territory or to Israeli Jews marrying aliens, institutes a discriminatory system based on national origin and is directed exclusively against Palestinians".

Source: Dugard, 2005.

---

[7] Among the signs of this exceptional status is the scarcity of statistics and qualitative or quantitative information about rural and Bedouin societies or gender-based information and academic studies on the marginal categories. (see UN and ESCWA, in Arabic, 2005, 22, 71).

[8] Pastoralism in Arab societies has attracted little historical and sociological research. Hence, the work of Ibn Khaldun retains its place as a reference for rural, tribal and Bedouin life (see Ibn Khaldun, in Arabic, n.d.; Sabir and Malika, in Arabic, 1986; Al-Marzuqi, in Arabic, 1980).

The challenges and difficulties facing women in the desert and countryside are numerous and vary according to age and place within a complex society (Ghamiri, in Arabic, 1989, 1). They pertain to the basic right to life and to necessities such as food, shelter, clothing, education and health care. From childhood on, women encounter difficulty in obtaining the smallest portion of food. In some countries, such as Iraq, Mauritania, the Sudan and Yemen, especially in socially deprived areas, women lack nutrition as well as basic social supports and are subjected to various forms of violence (Centre for Arab Women Training and Research, in Arabic, 1998).

The lives of women in these areas are threatened as a result of obvious shortfalls in their communities' ability to provide a decent living and human care. In the best of circumstances, women may receive some basic services from the mobile medical units that exist, mainly in some Gulf countries and the Maghreb (Western Arab countries). These units specialise primarily in family practice, free prenuptial examinations and reproductive health (UN and ESCWA, in Arabic, 2005, 27). They do not provide the full range of health care required to assure complete good health. Despite providing some urgent assistance at times, the units operate as gifts from the ruling regimes rather than as an established right of human beings.

In such situations girls are denied the most basic rights, especially the rights to education and knowledge —the very things that could help them escape from the situation imposed upon them. While their urban compatriots enjoy opportunities, afforded by various institutions and organisations, that help to mitigate or transform their situations, by contrast, girls from remote areas are buffeted by deprivation, lack the simplest facilities and services and remain ignorant of their rights. This undermines rural women's physical, mental, and psychological health, reduces life expectancies at birth and affects their prospects for a healthy life, which

are much lower than those of Arab women in general (Centre for Arab Women Training and Research, in Arabic, 2001, 30).

In some Arab countries girls are taken from the countryside and forced to serve as household servants in a form of neo-slavery. This is a black mark on the human development of all the Arab countries.[9] Marginalised Bedouin and rural girls have not benefited from the quantitative expansion of education in Arab countries, while anything resembling a quality education is well beyond their horizon. They are unable to read or write and thus express themselves – and have never heard of their human rights. This erodes their very human status, perpetuates the wrongs done against them and is completely inconsistent with what humanity today regards as the minimum in terms of the broad spread of education, knowledge, and political and social liberty.

Threatening the marginalised Bedouin and rural women with yet more poverty, need and devastation is the lack of will, policies and strategic plans for addressing their position from the ground up. Government agencies could instead take advantage of the obvious difficulties these people face to insist that States adopt contingency solutions and provide special assistance. Such assistance would include basic housing, roads and potable water, using the funds available under various endowments and programmes[10] even if these services do not rise to the level of legally guaranteed rights. Programmes of this kind are usually exploited for their political propaganda value and are controlled by government agencies. Continuing deprivation in turn raises the rate at which girls leave school early to rush into marriage, herding and agricultural work, confirming their imprisonment within the circle of male exploitation (Tlili, background paper for the Report).

Girls from remote areas are buffeted by deprivation, lack the simplest facilities and services and remain ignorant of their rights.

In some Arab countries girls are taken from the countryside and forced to serve as household servants in a form of neo-slavery.

---

[9] See the relationship between gender and poverty, especially the feminisation of poverty, and the importance of studying the structural reasons for poverty, marginalisation and deprivation and of rescuing women from their trap (Droy, in French, 1990, 40-41).

[10] Such as Tunisia's programme for the elimination of underprivileged areas with the support of Solidarity Funds, e.g, the Tunisian National Solidarity Fund, better known as the 26-26 Fund.

WOMEN IN SQUATTER SETTLEMENTS

There is no reliable database on squatter settlements in the Arab States in general and on the status of Arab women in them in particular. However, field research in a number of such areas shows that the residents are of low social status with poor levels of education and weak technical skills, leading to very few job options. This has an impact on their lives as a whole. Residents cannot find jobs and they cannot obtain suitable housing. Families in informal areas are characterised by a high proportion of women providers. While the number of women heading households amounts to 21 per cent in Egypt overall, they range between 25 and 33 per cent of all families in these areas (El Samalouti, background paper for the Report). The high number of female-headed households reflects the high rate of divorce, separation and widowhood in informal housing settlements. Female heads of household rely on assistance and transfers of money to a larger extent than do male heads (El-Samalouti).

Women in squatter settlements are burdened with numerous problems caused by their difficult economic and environmental conditions, which affect their relations with their families and make it difficult for them to raise their children properly. What is more, women in such areas are unaware of their rights and of the services available to them. Often, they do not possess the papers, such as birth certificates, that would permit them to receive such services.

Finally, many women in these settings suffer the effects of violence and most, as in Egypt for instance, still practise the circumcision of their daughters. Around 8.13 per cent of all women in the 15- to 49-year-old age group were married before the age of sixteen and nearly one third of married women have been exposed to physical abuse by their husbands at least once in their married lives.

Such informal settlements generally lack services such as health care. Even so, many women decline to use those services that are available, preferring folk medicine. This behaviour stems from the prevailing culture, which in most cases is that of the rural migrant.

FEMALE MIGRANT WORKERS

While the situations of female migrant workers, both Arab and non-Arab, are similar, this section will focus on non-Arab migrants. Attention to women migrant workers has recently increased in step with the complaints of individuals, international human rights organisations and some labour-exporting States. The cause of these complaints is the constant abuse of the rights of women workers in receiving Arab countries. A particular focus of attention is Asian women in the domestic labour sector.

Among the Arab States, the general characteristics of female migrant workers in different countries vary. Those in the Gulf States come from a wide range of professional, national and ethnic backgrounds while those in other labour-exporting and -importing Arab countries, such as Jordan and Lebanon, share similar skills and origins.

The Gulf States take in women workers from both the West and developing countries, i.e., from Asia, other Arab countries and Africa. These women undertake the different kinds of work that are on offer to them in the Gulf States and thus may be found working in professions both high and low on the occupational scale, in jobs that are socially acceptable and others that are not.

The distribution of female migrant workers by nationality also varies. Generally speaking, women workers from South and South-East Asia are concentrated in the service sector, especially in domestic work. At the same time, there is, in the United Arab Emirates for example, a concentration of European women workers in the banking sector. Arab female migrant workers are to be found in all sectors but are especially numerous in education and health.

The number of foreign women in the Arab Gulf region was estimated at 7.3 million in 2002, of whom around one million were estimated to be workers (Table 4-2). Though the statistics available do not indicate either the nature of their work or the nationality of these women, it is possible to say that the largest number of them (around 30 per cent) work in the service sector, specifically in domestic service (Alnajjar, background paper

Women in squatter settlements are unaware of their rights and of the services available to them.

Attention to women migrant workers has recently increased in step with the complaints of individuals, international human rights organisations and some labour-exporting States.

for the Report). Others work in the health and education services sector and in banks, hotels, restaurants, certain food and pharmaceutical industries and certain recreation sectors. The sex trade has come to absorb increasing numbers of short-term female workers, who come for a few months or even weeks in search of quick material returns. Every now and then, local newspapers report raids by the security forces on dens of prostitution or the capture of gangs of white slave traders. The men involved in this trade are generally from certain Arab countries, the countries of the former Soviet Union, and certain East Asian and East African countries.

Outside the Arab Gulf, Jordan and Lebanon are the countries that import the most female workers. The few studies available, along with first-hand accounts, indicate that in both countries, the domestic service sector represents the principal employer, especially for women from the Philippines and Sri Lanka. In Jordan, hotels, restaurants and places of entertainment have, however, started to absorb increasing numbers of female migrant workers.

Conditions of women workers in the domestic service sector

The domestic service sector constitutes the largest employer of female migrant workers not only in the countries of the Gulf Cooperation Council but also in the less affluent Arab countries, among them Jordan and Lebanon particularly. Conditions in this labour sector in the Arab region are characterised generally by:

- Low wage levels. The average monthly wage in this sector may not exceed $150 and may go as low as $100. Wage scales are linked to nationality, going as low as $95 a month in some cases among Ethiopians and Sri Lankans and as high as $250 and $300 in the case of some Philippine women.
- Non-inclusion within the labour laws. Arab labour laws do not cover female or male domestic workers and wages are not subject to yearly increases. Contracts do not give these workers either weekly or annual paid leave.
- Unspecified working hours. Work for a maid may begin at five or six in the morning

TABLE 4-2

Expatriate working women in Arab countries, 2002

Country	Number (in thousands)	% of female labour force in the country
Saudi Arabia	426	6.8
United Arab Emirates	261	4.8
Kuwait	241	71.5
Oman	145	79.2
Bahrain	36	1.4
Qatar	38	71.6

Source: Alnajjar, background paper for the Report

and continue until late at night. In general, domestic workers are on permanent call.

- No freedom of movement. Workers are not allowed to visit friends or relatives or to create a network of relationships with their peers outside the orbit of the family that employs them. They are permitted to leave the country only under the most pressing circumstances, such as the death of a relative in their home country. Their sponsor usually retains their passports and returns them only on the day of travel.
- Incidents of physical and mental injury inflicted upon them by their employer, male or female. Physical harm may on occasion result in permanent injury or death. The local press has carried stories of workers suffering burns and other wounds inflicted by their employers. Exploitation and bodily injury may lead servants to retaliate, sometimes by murdering their employer or harming young children or damaging the family's possessions and furniture.
- Sexual assaults. Female workers are exposed to sexual assaults by the master of the house, who is generally elderly, or by one of his sons. At other times, one of the young men working in the house, such as the driver or the cook or the gardener, carries out the assault. Others, such as a neighbour or a worker in a neighbourhood shop, have also been reported in attacks on female workers.

The harsh and degrading treatment meted out to foreign female domestic workers is a mark of shame on the brow of those societies

The harsh and degrading treatment meted out to foreign female domestic workers is a mark of shame on the brow of societies that ignore it.

Asian Female Domestic "Servants" Subjected to Physical Abuse

A Jordanian court sentenced a Jordanian national to five years in prison for raping his Sri Lankan servant and attempting to murder her (Al-Ayyam newspaper, occupied Palestinian territory, 8/12/2005).

Kosoma is subjected to physical abuse

Kosoma, a maid, tells the story of her life in an Arab country: "When, after working for three months, I asked the mistress of the house for my wages, she fell on me with blows and kicks, using a metal bar and wooden sticks". She goes on: "Sometimes she would take a piece of hot metal and burn me with it or heat a knife and place it against my body". Kosoma is still trying to understand why her mistress treated her this cruelly when she had done nothing to deserve such treatment. She relates that her employers tired of her and told her they were going to the police station and that she would be arrested. In the end, however, her mistress put her on board a plane to Sri Lanka, knowing full well that she would never be held to account by the courts for torturing the woman.

It didn't make any difference to them that Kosoma was forty-one years old. She remembers the repeated rapes to which the eighteen-year-old son of the house subjected her. She says: "When I tried to resist, he threatened to kill me".Kosoma goes on: "I complained to his mother but she just replied: 'I'll give you contraceptive pills.' Then she beat me".

Source: BBC web site: 23 February 2005 (Marzouki, background paper for the Report).

The restoration of dignity and self-respect to domestic workers may well prove to be inseparable from the recovery of dignity and self-respect by Arab citizens.

that ignore it; it also reveals a deep flaw in those societies' values. The restoration of dignity and self-respect to domestic workers may well prove to be inseparable from the recovery of dignity and self-respect by Arab citizens who seek to be rid of the dishonour that accrues to those who use violence against weaker parties.

Abuse of the rights of women workers from Sri Lanka, Thailand and other Asian countries and Africa can no longer be easily concealed; indeed, it is starting to take on a political dimension, evident in discussion of the issue at the international level. Yet more dangerously, and quite aside from the demeaning impact on the affected women, it reflects a crisis of values within those Arab societies that treat some foreign women as inferiors in whom all the marks of lowly status – femininity, poverty and foreignness—had combined.[11]

ENDNOTE

This chapter concludes the section of the Report that assesses the status of women in the Arab world. The next section examines the societal framework in Arab countries, which partly accounts for women's status at the present time. The analysis to this point has demonstrated that, in terms of human well-being, women in these countries are altogether more deprived than men, a situation sharply incompatible with creating a human renaissance in the region.

[11] A positive development in this regard is the project, "The Protection of the Rights of the Immigrant Women Workers in Jordan", implemented by UNIFEM in collaboration with Jordan's Ministry of Labour, which created a unified work contract for non-Jordanian domestic workers. The significance of this contract lies in the articles that stipulate a day of rest, medical care, life insurance and severance pay. This contract is now a basic requirement for residence and work permits and provides an important basis for the protection of the rights of foreign women workers. It also provides for support from the guest country, as represented by its ministries and security apparatuses, as well as from the embassies concerned.

CHAPTER FIVE

THE ARAB WOMEN'S MOVEMENT: STRUGGLES AND EXPERIENCES

Introduction

The last three chapters surveyed the situation of Arab women within the framework of human development from three angles: acquiring human capabilities, utilising them and levels of human welfare. They indicated that, in spite of significant gains, the rise of women remains a distant goal. This chapter traces how women's movements in the Arab countries were instrumental in securing these initial achievements and presents an analysis of the challenges that they faced as early proponents of women's development. The experiences of these movements today, as social forces seeking to improve women's standing in society, are also examined. To this end, the most important historical milestones that have distinguished the rise of women in Arab countries are reviewed.

The women's movements that Arab societies have come to know arose and developed in a specific environment and within social and economic contexts – local, regional and international – that governed their trajectory. At all times, these groups were sharply tested. Sadly, even today whenever the situation of Arab women is raised as an issue, the ensuing debate tends to be heated, defensive and attended by a volley of questions. Is the Arab women's liberation movement at odds with the demands and needs of society as a whole? Is it anti-male? Do Arab women activists have an authentic agenda drawn from the reality of Arab societies? Are Arab feminists merely imitating women's liberation movements in the West? How is one to interpret Western interest in the situation of women in the East? Do women's liberation movements work against the interests of the Arab family? Is there a hidden agenda to destroy the Arab family? Do demands for women's rights seek to undermine religion?

Finally, is there such a thing as an Arab women's movement committed to bringing about wide-scale social change? (Elsadda, background paper for the Report).

To respond to these questions, it is necessary to answer a number of others that sum up the situation of Arab women's movements. The most important of these questions concern the factors that have intervened to prevent changes in the condition of Arab women and to preserve the gender status quo despite the spread of women's organisations. Indeed, a retreat is beginning to be observed in the number of legal regulations formulated to serve women's interests, which requires an explanation. How is this retreat compatible with the fact that Arab countries have entered the twenty-first century still dragging behind them the dead weight of such issues as a woman's right to education, work and political activity, matters long resolved elsewhere? Is it imaginable that some Arab societies still debate whether a woman has the right to travel without her husband's permission or to drive a car?

This examination and evaluation of the history of the women's movement covers three closely linked, complementary phases. Each phase is important for an understanding of the women's cause as a movement that seeks to enable women to claim their full and uncompromised right to integration within society. The first period is tied to the trauma of imperialism and its impact on women, families and extended families. The second concerns the building of the post-independence nation-state, the tensions arising from the concept and nature of this process, and the parties involved in it. The third relates to the emergence of a new women's consciousness whose strength is an extension of the female body itself and which derives its support from the international

Arab countries have entered the twenty-first century still dragging behind them the dead weight of such issues as a woman's right to education, work and political activity, matters long resolved elsewhere.

discourse on women's liberation, empowerment and integration (Malki, background paper for the Report). Each of these historical phases played a role in establishing women's awareness of their status in their societies, on the one hand, and in shaping the character of the reformist discourse that was maturing, under varied and multiple influences, on the other.

The most influential factor in the history of the Arab women's movement may have been its involvement in the struggle for liberation from imperialism before it embarked on the struggle for women's liberation within Arab societies. The history is therefore divided into two stages: the first examines the movement's involvement in national liberation, the second, its role in establishing women's awareness of their own issues during the period following independence.

THE WOMEN'S MOVEMENT AND ITS ROLE IN THE PROCESS OF LIBERATION

Credit for the growth of the women's movement must go to its pioneers, the women who first came to see their inferior status in society and to understand that such inferiority was not a divinely ordained fate that they were obliged to accept. The emergence of these early women's movements coincided with that of the reformist movement, whose first stirrings arose at the end of the nineteenth century.

What those pioneering women achieved was neither negligible nor easily accepted at that historical juncture. This was a time of sharply competing visions, divided between those dazzled by the discovery of the civilisation of the Other and those who completely rejected that civilisation, demanding instead a stubborn fidelity to the ways of their righteous forbears.

Several observations can be made about this period:

It is clear that the first generation of women's associations was focused on charitable work. They emerged amid the wealthy classes and their standard was carried by aristocratic women or women from ruling families. This observation does not diminish the value of charitable work per se; however, when such work becomes the unique goal of the women's movement, it becomes an isolating wall that restricts the discourse on the rise of women. Charitable work is a job for society as a whole; it should never become the sole domain of women or men alone (Al-Shatti and Rabw, in Arabic, 2001, 26).

Historically, Egypt was distinguished from the other Arab countries by its large number of women's associations. Indeed, the first "women's educational society" was founded there in 1881 with raising public awareness of women's rights as a key objective.

These associations were distinctive in raising issues relating to women's inferior status, the most significant of which was their call to re-examine the personal status laws. The Mohammad Ali Charity Association was founded on this basis in 1908, as was the Instructive Women's Union in 1910.

Women's movements did not attain a degree of maturity until the 1940s, a period marked by the resistance of Arab societies under imperialism. Most of the claims around this time were focused on issues such as polygamy and women's right to education. It is noteworthy that these associations were present in nearly all Arab countries: Egypt gave rise to the Egyptian Women's Party in 1942 and the Daughters of the Nile association in

---

Luminary: Huda Sha'rawi (June, 1879 – December, 1947)

Huda Sha'rawi founded The Society for the Care of Children in 1907, and in 1908, she persuaded the Egyptian University to set a hall aside for women's lectures. The notable political work of her husband, 'Ali al-Sha'rawi, during the 1919 revolution had a major effect on her own activities, and she led several women's demonstrations that year. She also founded and supervised the Wafd party's Central Committee for Women.

In 1921, during the reception for Sa'd Zaghlul on his return to Egypt, Sha'rawi called for the minimum age for marriage to be raised to sixteen for girls and to eighteen for boys while striving to put restrictions on men's powers of divorce. She worked for women's education to enhance their professional and political roles and against polygamy. She also called for the removal of the veil and she herself went unveiled.

Sha'rawi founded the Egyptian Feminist Union in 1923, occupying the post of president until 1947. She was a founding member of the Arab Women's Union and supported the establishment of the Union's bulletin, "The Arab Woman". In 1925, she established the magazine L'Egyptienne and, in 1937, al-Misriyya ("The Egyptian Woman").

In 1938, Sha'rawi organized a women's conference for the defence of Palestine and called on women to organise the collection of foodstuffs and clothes, and to volunteer for nursing and first aid.

Works

'Asr al-Harim ("The Age of the Harem") recounts the memories of Egyptian women in the period from 1880 to 1924; it was translated into English by the British journalist, Margot Badran.

Source: "Sunshine for Women." (2001). http://www.pinn.net/~sunshine/whm2001/huda2.html (Accessed 18 April, 2006).

1948. In Tunis, the Union of Tunisian Women emerged in 1944, while in Morocco the Union of Moroccan Women was founded in 1944, the Association of the Sisters of Purity in 1946, and the Association of Moroccan Women in 1947. In Lebanon, the Lebanese Women's Council came into being in 1943, the Association of Lebanese Women in 1947, and the Committee of Lebanese Women's Rights in 1947. Iraq witnessed the establishment of the Iraqi Women's Union in 1945, while in the Sudan, the Cultural Girl's Syndicate was set up in 1945 as was the Association of Women's Enhancement. 1945 was also the year in which the Society of the Jordanian Women's Union was founded (ESCWA, in Arabic, 2006a, forthcoming).

Women more than men suffered from the effects of a deep split resulting from different factors. Women in colonised countries found themselves thrust into fields that had formerly been the sole preserve of men whether through their participation in the struggle for independence or as wage earners in units of production introduced during the spread and indigenisation of colonialism.

Limited scope and modest intake notwithstanding, women's schooling opened their eyes to the importance of education for a woman's fulfilment and to the resources available for her self-emancipation. Although compared to the Mashreq (eastern Arab countries) the Maghreb (western Arab countries) were relatively late in calling for women's liberation and in founding associations to support it,[1] their elites closely followed the calls of Arab renaissance intellectuals for the education of girls and their release from the worn-out traditions that shackled their potential.[2] The Association of the Sisters of Purity, for example, was founded in the Moroccan city of Tetuan – a Spanish colony during the 1940s. In 1944, the Independence Party also created the first women's cells. On the heels of the Palestinian Nakba of 1948, the Association held its second conference, announcing a package of demands. These included the abolition of polygamy except in cases of extreme necessity,

the judicial management of divorce in order to preserve the equilibrium of the family, and the prohibition of marriage before the age of sixteen (Daoud, in French, 1993, 248).

At this time, the women's movement in Egypt evinced greater political awareness of women's issues and of the need to prioritise them. In 1948, Duriya Shafiq founded the Daughters of the Nile association. In her Arab-revivalist discourse, Shafiq was careful to demand full equality of political rights between men and women. In spite of being criticised for being elitist, this movement dared to confront the opponents of the rise of women. In so far as the movement succeeded, this was because it linked women's liberation to liberation from colonialism.

The lesson of the colonial period lies in realising the dislocation in the structure of Islamic society brought about by occupation. Colonial occupation had shaken traditional Arab economic, social, cultural and moral frameworks to the ground. In all affected countries, it thus became necessary to marshal national sentiment and consciousness in order to conduct national struggles of liberation as the overriding priority. As a result, social development, and the rise of women as a part of it, remained hostage to the drive for national independence, falling much lower on the list of priorities.

The 1940s and 1950s were also notable for moulding women's discourse. Political parties started to form women's associations under their own banners, bringing men into the women's movement. Undoubtedly, the move partly reflected men's wish to monopolise the women's discourse, hold it within limits, rally it to their flag and act as ventriloquist. This politicisation of the women's quest may have been, historically, the first trap into which the movement fell.

Following the end of the Second World War, women's associations of a particular character sprang up throughout the Arab world. The communist parties created a number of these, including the Union of Tunisian Women

Imperialism, and the struggles against it, set back the liberation of women by dislocating national priorities.

Social development, and the rise of women as a part of it, remained hostage to the drive for national independence.

---

[1] Muhammad Ali founded a school for midwives and organised opportunities for training young women in factories producing yarn, textiles, tarbushes and garments to equip the army with its clothing requirements. His grandson, Khedive Isma'il, did the same when, in his turn, he founded The Exalted School, the first for girls, in 1873. Other schools were opened in Iraq, Lebanon, Syria and other Arab countries.

[2] One thinks mainly of the writings of Al-Hajawi, Morocco's Minister of Cultural Affairs at the time. See his work, *The Education of Girls*.

(1944), the Union of Moroccan Women (1944), the Algerian Women's Union (1945), and the Association of Lebanese Women (1947). Others were the offspring of the conservative parties, such as the Association of the Sisters of Purity (1946) in Morocco, which was supported by the Al-Shura Party, and the Muslim Sisters Association in Iraq (1951), supported by the Conservative Party of that time. Among these associations, too, were those that sprang from the womb of the socialist parties, such as the Union of Tunisian Women (1955), supported by the Tunisian Socialist Party.

Under the heavy sway of the general political consciousness of the day among men as among women, the women's movements came close to forgetting, in those difficult circumstances, their founding objectives. All women's movements in the Arab world were affected by this consciousness, which embraced most women, regardless of class. It was reflected in their discourse, which argued that society's consideration of women's issues should be subordinated to national liberation and that solutions to these issues might well be a natural outcome of it. Indeed, how could this not happen when women in their struggle for liberation were standing side by side with men and had tasted real equality?

WOMEN'S CONSCIOUSNESS OF GENDER ISSUES TAKES ROOT AFTER INDEPENDENCE

It is a delicate matter to talk of "the rise of women" at this period in the history of the Arab States because of the mass of historical forces that governed the process. One of the most important of these was the Arab States' recovery of their sovereignty, which took place at different periods. To this should be added the fact that government in these countries took two forms: constitutional monarchy and popular nationalism. Each had its impact on how women's status was envisioned and on the scope of change permissible. Nevertheless, whatever the form of governance, the genuine determination behind the movement was unmistakeable.

It was a resolve conditioned by a host of factors and shaped by the tactics of officialdom against the movement during this period.

Governments tried to amalgamate many of the women's associations, which they then named "unions". The regime in Tunisia resorted to dissolving the two women's organisations, The Muslim Women's Association and The Tunisian Women's Union, and compelled the women affiliated with the Government's Destour Party to form a new Tunisian women's union. From that time, women's activism became subservient to the principles of loyalty to the ruling authority and obedience to its directives on choices and priorities.

These changes took place in an atmosphere abounding in hopes and radiating confidence that the original aspirations of the women's movements were about to come alive. It was believed that the ruling regime, which after all had won the nation its independence, would be able to make light of all difficulties, and why should women's liberation not be among these since women had contributed to independence?

The Arab women's movement went through a host of sweeping changes during this period as a result of social transformations. These include the spread of education among females; the entry of many women into the higher professions (as doctors, university faculty, engineers, lawyers and other professionals); the accession by some women to leadership positions in political parties and governments; the development of a well-rooted consciousness of the situation in which Arab women were living; and an increase in society's sympathy for women's issues. In addition, specialised international organisations emerged and started to have an impact on local movements. These factors played an essential role in impelling women's movements to take women's issues single-handedly upon themselves and to commit themselves to their defence (Guessous, background paper for the Report).

The movement also faced a host of difficulties, however, and was forced to do battle on numerous fronts, which can be termed the political, the social and the goal-driven.

THE POLITICAL FRONT

As noted earlier, governments attempted to bring many women's associations together into amalgamated bodies called "unions".

Governments tried to amalgamate many of the women's associations.

From that time, women's activism became subservient to the principles of loyalty to the ruling authority and obedience to its directives.

This is illustrative of a phenomenon common to the Arab States, namely, their confinement of women within a framework monitored and directed by the male power structure. Women who wanted to participate in public life were prohibited from doing so except within the framework of the official women's organisations subject to the regime. This turned their discourse into that of the men in power, who themselves maintained silence on the problems faced by women.

The prevailing vision of women's issues was tied to social problems, the most important of which were:

- Widespread illiteracy, especially among women, in all Arab countries. This made education of major importance on the agendas of all social movements (parties, trade unions, civil and women's associations).
- Entrenched traditional conceptions of the role of women and their place in society, and the restriction of women to their reproductive role, i.e., that of mother, child raiser and housewife.
- The conception of women's work as merely a temporary material requirement resulting from need and not as something intrinsic to their existence or life choices.

The discourse of the ruling parties started from these basic assumptions, deleting certain old formulations and introducing new and more restrictive ones. Some scholars describe this as the feminisation of the ruling discourse.

The modernisation project that reform-minded Arab countries launched took upon itself the task of conditioning the citizen to a particular concept of society. While the politicisation of motherhood in the nationalist movement was a step forward for women, it had a high price: women could not be acknowledged as individuals. The same was true with respect to the women's movements that had been split up into numerous charitable associations. In spite of their important work in bringing women, and especially middle-class women, out into public, the charitable work of these associations, by its very nature, entrenched the prevailing view of the woman as a mother and child carer. A woman's role in the family was thus extended to the whole of society as her defining function.

In this way, charitable work provided a socially acceptable means for linking women's private and public spheres without threatening the prevailing social construct based on male-female stratification (Guessous, background paper for the Report).

THE SOCIAL FRONT

At this time, Arab societies witnessed a proliferation of civil associations in general and of women's associations in particular, all springing up to champion women's causes. This period also saw efforts to monopolise the discourse of Arab renaissance for the ends of these associations.

This phenomenon coincided during the last three decades with another significant development: the rise of Islamic movements and the spreading influence of proselytizers urging a return to the Islam of the "venerable forebears" (*Salafism*). This movement-based discourse rose on fertile ground, amid traditions and customs that continued to appeal to societies that failed to distinguish between the sacred and the cultural. These were the customs that rallied women's movements in the first place. Most social groups found it easy to respond to the messages of the Islamic movements because they did not require any change in the social status quo. The alarming spread of illiteracy among women reinforced this since it prevented them from networking.

Islamic movements concentrated on holding women responsible for the difficulties that society was undergoing. They based their attacks on the idea that equality in public life would, by its nature, reduce men's opportunities in the job market and that the man was the master of the family and the woman was his dependant. Thus, the only natural place for a woman was the home. They urged that the role of women should be limited to caring for husbands and children and called on women to abandon unrealistic aspirations.

Here it is important to draw attention to a difference that distinguishes the Salafite currents from the school of the Muslim Brotherhood in terms of their proclaimed positions vis-à-vis women. The position of the Salafite movements is clear: a woman's place

Most social groups found it easy to respond to the Islamic message because it did not demand any change in the social situation.

is in the home and her role is to care for the family as opposed to leading an active civic life. This is an espousal of a basic vision of the division of labour where women are limited to childbearing, motherhood and nurturing and are warned against mixing in society, and where the most that they could aspire to would be a public life dedicated to charitable social services. The Muslim Brotherhood, on the other hand, adopts a principled position in support of women's political rights and endorses their inclusion in electoral life. The Muslim Brotherhood has not, however, dealt with ongoing reforms in the area of personal status, such as polygamy, the woman's right to control over her own body and children, and divorce.

Preoccupied with their own struggle, women's associations did not realise the extent of the danger posed by the Salafites and how seriously they meant to attack the rise of women as a movement and social priority. Society itself did not find the Salafite's Islamic view of women's role surprising at the time. The situation of the women's movement at this time partly reflects the severe economic crises that the Arab countries were undergoing. Women thus found themselves offered up as sacrifices again: asked to yield their rights once more as they were forced to do during the resistance to colonisation. The situation became more serious as conservative currents gained strength in the Arab political arena and as most nationalist, Arabist, liberal and socialist currents shrank.

Starting with the 1975 First United Nations World Conference on Women in Mexico and under the influence of international mechanisms working for the rise of women, new instances of the so-called "feminisation of the State" began to emerge. Countries committed themselves to develop their legislation in accordance with international conventions calling for the abolition of all forms of discrimination against women. A host of centres, foundations and organisations concerned with women's affairs grew up in the region.

A new trend emerged at this stage that saw first ladies adopt the cause of women's advancement. Jihan Al-Sadat, for example, considered herself the embodiment of Egyptian

women and their spokesperson. Al-Sadat's position enabled her to realise gains for Egyptian women through high-level manoeuvres and without involving women's organisations. In return for concessions granted from on high, the State placed obstacles before the popular independent women's movements, the very groups that could have consolidated and defended such progress. Thus it was an easy matter for regimes to annul these achievements later, as in Egypt and Iraq.

A number of Arab regimes saw in the Islamic groups a means to weaken leftist and labour forces. Their encouragement fed the growth of the Islamic revivalist movement, whose concerns extended to all spheres of public and private life and whose discourse attracted broad segments of youth, especially young women. In the Sudan, for example, revivalists forced in discriminatory personal status regulations based on concepts of gender inequality garbed in religious authority. They also came close to achieving success in Algeria and their influence became deeply embedded in the sentiments of the middle class and the poor in most countries – Lebanon, Morocco, Tunisia and the Gulf States. The situation became yet more dire in Egypt, where Islamic associations founded schools, hospitals and banks and the country experienced the beginning of a re-envisioning of the domain of Islam – a vision that argues for the structuring of Islamic societies along the lines of traditional Islamic jurisprudence.

The Islamist discourse resonated with traditionalists in Arab society and gained ground with the middle class, whose hopes of reaping dividends from the various post-independence projects had been disappointed and who had lost faith in change. Many sought refuge in introversion, abasing themselves for sins committed against "this nation" of Islam. Women's associations such as The New Woman in Egypt and The Tunisian Association of Democratic Women declared that it had become necessary to restrict Islam to the realm of personal belief and spiritual values. They vehemently rejected the Islamists' contention that secularism was an anomalous condition connected to the European experience. Other associations in Jordan, Morocco, the

The position of the Salafite movement is clear: a woman's place is in the home.

The Muslim Brotherhood, on the other hand, adopts a principled position in support of women's political rights and endorses their inclusion in electoral life.

BOX 5-1

Women's Rights: Political Struggle versus the Constitution

In the 1970s, Egypt witnessed three initiatives to change its personal status laws in favour of women.

In Law 44 of 1979, the State adopted certain proposals to provide women with a modicum of protection and security. The new law stipulated that the husband must give notice of the names of any wife or wives to whom he was married before contracting a new marriage and required the marriage registrar to notify any existing wives of the name of the new wife by registered mail. In the case of the husband taking another wife, the law gave the first wife the right of divorce as an injured party without requiring proof of injury provided she filed for divorce within one year after learning of her husband's second marriage. In addition, the law gave the divorced wife the right to independence within the matrimonial home for the duration of her oversight of any small children in her care unless the husband who had divorced her provided her with an alternative dwelling.

In 1985, a court determined that Law 44 of 1979 was unconstitutional and referred it to the Supreme Constitutional Court which abrogated it in May 1985 on formal grounds relating to the procedures of its publication, preceding which it had not been subjected to material review. Law 44 of 1979 had been issued by presidential decree while the People's Assembly was on vacation and it had not been subjected to review for approval following the reconvention of the Lower House, as required by the Constitution. At the same time, the law did not treat of a matter of emergency that would have justified the use by the President of the Republic of his exceptional powers. Furthermore, the law was linked to the name of the President's wife, Madam Jihan al-Sadat, with the result that the debate over its legality became entangled with opposition to the regime. In other words, the law suffered from its links to State-sponsored feminism.

When news of a possible judgment of unconstitutionality against the 1979 law leaked out, various women's activist groups started a broad campaign to oppose its cancellation and retain the gains for women that it offered. The Committee for the Defence of the Rights of the Woman and the Family was formed and held its first meeting at the Huda Sha'rawi Society, chosen because of the historical and moral values that it represented. The Committee attempted to rally the largest possible number of women, posting notices of its meetings in the newspapers, while participants wrote press and magazine articles.

The Committee encountered fierce opposition from conservative elements in society, its members were defamed and harassed, and it was not always able to find a public space for its meetings. It thus often convened in the houses of members, who made strong team efforts to keep the campaign to save the law coordinated. The Committee succeeded in bringing the issue of women's rights to the court of public opinion, presenting the government with suggestions and demands for the defence of the gains of women. It also benefited from international developments and the imminence of the 1985 World Conference on Women in Nairobi, which helped speed up the review by the People's Assembly of the new law replacing the one that had been cancelled. Law 100 of 1985 was issued, with clauses similar to those contained in the 1979 law. The new law, however, contained concessions designed to pacify conservatives, one of the most important of these being the cancellation of a woman's right to divorce without proof of injury if her husband took another wife. Instead, the new law stipulated that she must prove material or moral injury that would make the continuation of her life with him impossible.

Source: Elsadda, background paper for the Report.

---

occupied Palestinian territory and the Gulf States, however, adopted a modified position. They demanded that the door to independent religious thinking (*ijtihad*) be opened on questions connected with women in the belief that enlightened readings of the regulatory Qur'anic verses would establish a new discourse on women nourished by the heritage.

THE GOAL-DRIVEN FRONT

The political and social contexts directly influenced the quality of the demands put forward by the women's movement, which, by their nature, reflect a tension between social circumstances and the movement's priorities at a given time.

It became necessary for the movement to adopt programmes that responded to the conditions described earlier. The second half of the 1970s witnessed the first steps towards the founding of women's organisations independent of official political organisations.

In 1978 in Tunisia, a women's club known as the Al-Tahir Al-Haddad Club was established. Its founders, a group of female students with a leftist orientation, conceived it as a reaction to the one-sided treatment of women's issues, their monopolisation by the State and their exploitation in party political discourse. It was also clearly a reaction to a spreading Salafite discourse that confiscated the freedoms and gains that women had only recently won. Debate centred on the inadequacy of, and loopholes in, the Personal Status Code in terms of gender equality in spite of its pioneering nature in comparison with family legislation in most other Arab countries. The arguments also concentrated on forms of violence inflicted upon women and on how this violence was reflected in their status in society.

The women's movement saw a qualitative upswing in the 1980s in the establishment and extension of associations. In Morocco, in addition to the official associations (e.g., the National Union of Moroccan Women,

Some associations demanded that the door to independent religious thinking (ijtihad) be opened on questions connected with women.

The 1980s were a crucial period in the transformation of the women's movements, especially in the Maghreb countries.

1969) and the many associations of an institutional character that had been active since independence, there now appeared associations with a political agenda, connected to the parties. At the same time, however, these associations strove to make their respective causes a strategic priority in party programmes. In 1985, the Democratic Association of Moroccan Women was founded, connected with the Party of Progress and Socialism. In 1987, the Women's Labour Party was created,

in alliance with the Popular Democratic Labour Association. In 1988, the Independent Women's Organization came into being, connected with the Independence Party. They were followed by the Democratic League for Women's Rights, with allegiance to the Vanguard Party and by the Democratic Women's Forum, linked to the Socialist Union of Popular Forces.

The 1980s were also a crucial period in the transformation of the women's movements, especially in the Maghreb countries. Their independent-mindedness and courage distinguished these movements as they trod a path strewn with obstacles and thorns, under siege from, and beset by, the ruling regimes. For example, a group of female academicians created the Tunisian Women's Association for Research on Development in 1987, with the sole objective of supporting and encouraging women's research. In 1989, the Association of Democratic Women was founded with the basic intention of abolishing all types of discrimination against women. The Association was so named to stress its independence, neutrality and departure from allegiance to the ruling party as well as its defiance of Islamic discourse. It was also based on an unambiguous call for the firm establishment of secular discourse and the separation of State and religion. This Association believed that women's citizenship would remain deficient as long as the reformist goals were not accomplished and as long as all reservations against the Copenhagen Declaration on Social Development by Arab States remained in place.

Not by coincidence, the names of the new women's associations included words such as "democratic", "progressive" and "rights". In Algeria, women belonging to parties of the left founded a number of independent women's associations.[3] These included the Association for Equality between Men and Women before the Law, the Association for Women's Liberation, the Association for Equality and Citizenship, and the Association for the Advancement and Defence of Women's Rights.

These associations came into being conscious of the limited room for manoeuvre permitted to them in advancing and defending

---

Luminaries: The Women and Memory Forum, Cairo

The scholarly members of the Women and Memory Forum seek to read Arab history from a perspective that takes into account the cultural and social formation of gender. This forum brings together women researchers with diverse and widely differing specialisations from a variety of institutions and hence with diverse approaches, visions and objectives. Huda al-Sadda, professor of English literature at Cairo University and one of the major participating scholars, asks and answers the question, "Why does this group exist?" Her response gives us the following important, stimulating and significant insight: "We are trying hard to adopt a collective style since collective work is not often found in our immediate cultural context. Indeed, we are united in a genuine and insistent desire to surmount the isolation imposed on many women interested in scientific research. We are thus determined to work together and to establish our presence in a positive atmosphere that grows out of the effective sharing and exchange of experience at many levels".

Researchers of the Women and Memory Forum attempt to reread Arab history, taking into consideration the cultural and social formation of gender for primarily political ends. These efforts are not restricted to epistemological or academic goals that take knowledge as an end in itself. Rather, they consider academic enquiry to be an expression of life and are interested in participating positively in cultural and social reality, with the goal of bringing about change or development towards a more equitable and balanced cultural and social life for all members of society.

Accordingly, the Forum's members engage in reinterpreting Arab history from the perspective of gender. They start from the fact that women form a major part of society and that they have been important actors in making and moulding Arab history. They are mindful that women have been excluded from the official historical record for reasons connected with the dominance of a multilayered and masculine conceptual and moral construct. The group believes that the marginalisation of women and the limited public space open for their contributions have led to the misrepresentation of history and of the collective memory. The latter is of major and special importance in the formation of identity and in defining the elements of adherence and connectedness among the members of any given society. It is what gives the historical dimension its special importance.

The various activities of the Women and Memory Forum range from seminars and conferences to the issuing of innovative books and other publications. For example, the Forum has published an important collection of research papers entitled *Zaman al-Nisa' wal-Dhakira al-Badila* (1996), which constitutes the output of a conference convened by the group under the name of "Reading History from the Woman's Point of View: Women's Time and the Alternative Memory". Contributing to the rich and lively research perspectives at this conference were women scholars from Lebanon, Morocco and Palestine, Egyptians resident in the United States and male scholars concerned with the issue.

Source: Fouad, background paper for the Report.

---

[3] These associations could have been founded only in the favourable conditions that resulted from the passing of a special law in 1989 on the organisation of associations.

their causes. How small that space was will become clear by reviewing just one aspect of the pressures confronting them, namely, that exerted by the ruling party, which deemed these associations hybrid movements tantamount to opposition parties. As a result, society's view of these associations became damagingly warped: the various groups ceased to be seen as movements founded to call attention to the declining status of women and came instead to be identified with their position vis-à-vis the regime. The haste with which such associations rushed to express their sympathy with some of the progressive opposition parties and, above all, with rights organisations contributed to the prevailing view of them.

The new generation of women's associations is distinguished by its qualitative closeness to women's issues. In spite of their affiliation with democratic parties, these associations clearly emphasise that women's issues are no longer a minor detail among party preoccupations and concerns. On the contrary, the constitutions of these new associations, the resolutions passed at their conferences and their writings in the press all underline that these issues have become, perforce, no less central than those of democracy, development or human rights.

The international dimension has been no less important for the way in which this new feminist consciousness has evolved. The global discourse on women has been a significant influence on the Arab women's movement and a driving force in the latter's reformulation of its goals and perseverance in its struggle. It has helped in Arab women's efforts to bring laws and national legislative initiatives into line with universal objectives. It has also provided support and backing through networking, which has influenced the organisational structure of women's movements in the Arab countries as elsewhere in the world.

If, as previously noted, women's organisations with a political agenda emerged in the region during the latter half of the 1980s, their new consciousness was reinforced at international conferences, chiefly those convened under the auspices of the United Nations. These include the Conference on Environment and Development of 1992 in Rio de Janeiro, the World Conference on Human

Rights of 1993 in Vienna, the International Conference on Population and Development of 1994 in Cairo, the 1995 World Summit for Social Development in Copenhagen, and the Women's World Conference in Beijing in 1995. All of these shared the same approach, which, in essence, holds that democracy, development, human rights and peace are inseparable and that there can be no democracy and no development without the effective participation of women (Malki, background paper for the Report).

Such was the goal-driven front that the women's associations active in the 1980s took upon themselves to mount and defend. The new approach aimed to dislodge traditional views that still clung to the women's question. Thus, personal status laws were the most important targets among these goals, followed by the enactment of legislation guaranteeing the equality of women and men in political and economic life. Women's associations were also active in urging Arab governments to implement the international agreements that they had approved, especially the Convention on the Elimination of All Forms of Discrimination against Women (CEDAW).

The 1990s are considered to have been difficult years for Arab society, filled with contradictions, tribulations and successive, bitter disappointments. A new sense of realism materialised as many Arabs came to see that their progress as a civilisation had

---

Luminaries: The Lebanese Women Researchers Group

The Lebanese Women Researchers Group is a diverse group that is active across many fields of specialization, focusing on the conditions of women in contemporary Arab societies. Scholars publish research in specific areas on a regular basis. Topics of particular interest to which they have turned their attention include: "Women and the Authorities", "Women and Writing", "Humanities Research and Researchers in the Arab World", "The Position of Women in Politics in Lebanon and the Arab World", "Media and Communication in Our Societies" and "Universities in the Arab World".

These titles reveal the nature of the areas that the group is concerned about analysing or whose explicit and implicit interconnections they seek to uncover. Male participation is noticeably broader than in the case of the Women and Memory Forum, for example, a fact that may be attributable to the production demands of their periodic publications, in which a number of male writers participate.

In 2001, in collaboration with the Women and Memory Forum and the Centre for Arab and Middle East Studies, Beirut, the Lebanese Women Researchers Group convened an important and successful conference on "Arab Women in the Twenties: Presence and Identity".

Source: Fouad, background paper for the Report.

The new generation of women's associations is distinguished by its qualitative closeness to women's issues.

The international dimension has been important for the way in which this new feminist consciousness has evolved.

been marginalised compared to that of other world regions. Many segments of society were abandoned to their own fate, and the gap between the ruling regimes and their societies widened.[4]

The result was a perceptible proliferation of licensed activist associations. In 2000, the number of independent associations in Egypt and Lebanon rose to between 200 and 250 (Ben Nefissa, in French, 2000) and the number increased to 225,000 for the entire Arab world in 2003 and 2004 (UNIFEM, in Arabic, 2004). The phenomenon differed, however, from country to country. This explosion gave the impression that Arab societies were on the move or seeking to improve their conditions, but the question must be asked as to how effective these associations proved to be. How can the discrepancy between the proliferation of these associations and the absence of women in administrative and decision-making positions be explained? Their proportion of representation may have reached 45 per cent in Lebanon and 42 per cent in the occupied Palestinian territory but it is only 18 per cent in Egypt.

Despite there being 87 women's associations in Yemen, the proportion of women in decision-making positions does not exceed 6 per cent (ESCWA, in Arabic, 2006a, forthcoming).

Indeed, women are absent even from associations for the defence of civil rights: out of a total of 25 members of the steering committee of the Tunisian League for the Defence of Human Rights only three are women. The same is true of Egypt and Morocco.

In spite of the explosion in the number of civil associations, the presence of women had no impact at this critical stage. This paradox can be explained only by attributing it to the pressure exerted by international organisations. Women's representation arose as a concession on the part of many Arab countries. The latter accepted the formal incorporation of women into their cultural projects on condition that they remain a mute, motionless presence.

The establishment of the Arab Women's Organisation falls into the same category. The organisation was launched in 2002 by the signing of a founding agreement. At the regional level, efforts have since concentrated on institutionalising the entity and designing its 2004-2007 plan of action, which was approved at the Organisation's second summit meeting, which was held in Bahrain on 12 June 2005. As of that date, 15 Arab States had become members. They agreed to study a programme that would include the totality of Arab States. While the Organisation is a joint institution of the governments included in its founding charter, since its inception, it has striven to cooperate with NGOs on the same basis as international organisations working in this field.

The founding of the Arab Women's Organisation reflects the special attention that Arab governments are now giving to women's issues. Nevertheless, the entity faces many challenges, among the most serious of which are resource mobilisation, opening up to civil society in the different Arab States and avoiding the stifling bureaucracy that has left its stamp on other regional bodies. One is anxious to discover whether this organisation is indeed capable of moving the situation of women in a positive direction (Kiwan, background paper for the Report).

It lies beyond the power and resources of the women's movement to influence this entangled socio-political situation by itself, which only confirms that the fight for women's freedom is the fight of Arab societies as a whole. This explains the modest returns to date on the exhausting efforts expended, yet none of this has discouraged the movement from taking advantage of all means available to it to influence the life of society. These means are the major axes that underlie the struggle and evolving discourse of the women's movement as it endeavours to improve women's conditions in the Arab countries.

EVALUATING ACHIEVEMENTS FOR WOMEN

Without doubt, the participation of women in these national movements helped women and conferred legitimacy on their demands in society's eyes. In Egypt, for example, the period between 1920 and the 1950s, when women's movements were numerous and diverse, is

---

[4] See AHDR 2004.

considered to have been one of the most active and rich. In 1923, Huda Sha'rawi founded the Egyptian Feminist Union, which played an important social and political role in raising awareness of women's issues and in demanding their rights. The Union used the collection of signatures to mobilise public opinion and exert pressure on the political authorities to respond to women's demands. It entered into a political conflict with the Wafd Government (despite its early links to it) when the members of the Union adopted a radical position with regard to issues of national liberation, democracy and Arab solidarity, a conflict that reached its climax when the Union opposed the Treaty of 1936. In Tunisia, a strong liberal reformist movement arose around Al-Tahir al-Haddad, connecting the rise of women to the modernisation of the homeland and also giving priority to the national liberation agenda. In Algeria in 1958, when France called on women to burn their veils in one of the main squares of Algiers while shouting "Algeria is French!" (Nasiri, in Arabic, 2003), women started wearing the veil to show their national allegiance and agreed to postpone their political and social demands in favour of working for independence.

Regrettably, and notwithstanding some palpable gains by women as a result of social transformations in the national liberation movements, this proved to be a poor bargain as far as affirmations of women's capability and effectiveness or the legitimacy given to their demands are concerned. One consequence of the movement's sacrifice was that after independence – and here Algeria is a sad but clear example – the new nationalist governments pretended to forget or simply ignored some or most of these demands, especially those relating to the personal status codes, important differences among the Arab countries notwithstanding. In general, and with the exception of the modifications made to the personal status laws in Tunisia, unequal relations of power within the family survived. Women thus entered into a new phase of contradictions at the heart of the social structures and concepts.

Generally speaking, the number of women's associations and organisations in the Arab world can be counted as a positive phenomenon, indicating a healthy multiplicity at the level of discourse and activities. These associations or groupings work in a wide variety of fields. Some are rights organisations concentrating on changing legislation. Others are research organisations active in changing cultural concepts hostile to women's rights. Diversity also flourishes at the level of discourse. Some organisations take a religious stance to defend women's rights from within a religious framework, whether Islamic or Christian. Others adopt a secular approach, and still others seek to mould a new discourse that transcends the modernist view, which presupposes a contradiction between authenticity and contemporaneity or between the secular and the religious.

All women's groups are united in affirming that women's rights are national rights; indeed, in Iraq and the occupied Palestinian territory especially, the issue is of the highest priority (Elsadda, background paper for the Report).

Everyday reality remains the best witness to Arab women's status at the present time and the best marker of the point that they have reached to date. Nonetheless, it remains true that, since women initially resolved to change their circumstances, they have travelled further and faster on the road that they have paved than many believed possible.

It can be said that the objectives for which the women's movement was founded since the latter part of the nineteenth century have not been fully achieved yet and, indeed, that most women's groups are subject to a new reformist vision. This is hardly surprising since the challenges faced by the women's movement are complex and are primarily a function of political and economic circumstances. This is how it is possible to explain the impasse in the feminist discourse and its tendency to become mired in the same issues over time.

The impact of the women's movement has varied from one Arab country to another. It may be argued that its principal achievement has been increased awareness among women of their inferior status and of the need to work to change it. This awareness has reached Arab women of every creed, class or cultural affiliation, arising from an ethos that has been growing among them for more than a century.

Everyday reality remains the best witness to Arab women's status.

The objectives for which the women's movement was founded have not been fully achieved.

By concentrating its scrutiny on personal status laws, the movement has impelled a number of Arab States to take tangible steps to improve family law and legislation on marriage and divorce in general. Two country examples of these achievements are described in the following section.

THE TUNISIAN EXPERIENCE

The Tunisian experience remains a model among the Arab States. Half a century has passed since the issuing of the Personal Status Code, through which Tunisian law gave legal effect to the principle of women's equality with men. The Code has been further developed during the intervening period through the application of original legal thinking to keep it in step with changing issues in Tunisian society. It can thus be said that the changes to family law instituted by former President Habib Bourguiba sprang from a reformist movement that encouraged the rise of women on the social, economic and political levels.

The Tunisian experience remains a model among the Arab States.

Likewise, it cannot go unremarked that the laws of the Personal Status Code sprang from an initiative by two schools of Islamic jurisprudence: the Maliki and the Hanafi. In 1948, during the reign of Muhammad Amin Bay (1962), a twenty-two member committee, was formed under the chairmanship of the then Minister of Justice to look into the provisions of the Shari'a Code. Muhammad al-'Aziz Ju'ayt the Maliki Shaykh al-Islam for the Tunisian territories (1970), played a fundamental role in the work of this committee, taking part in the drafting, study and discussion of the elements, chapters and sections of the code. The committee came up with the Code of Shari'a Law, which was divided into two parts, one for personal status and the other for fixed property. The Code was approved by the leading religious scholars of the time, among them Shaykh Muhammad 'Abbas, the shaykh of the Hanafi rite; Shaykh 'Ali bin al-Khuja, the Hanafi mufti; the Learned Shaykh Fadil bin 'Ashur; and the Learned Shaykh 'Abd al-Rahman bin Yusuf. (Decree on the Shari'a Code, 1952, issued by the Ministry of Justice in Tunis, 3 July 1952, archives of the Ministry of Justice).

Though prepared in line with due governmental procedures, the Code had not been promulgated by the time that Tunisia achieved full independence. The Government of Tunisia decided to revive the project and commissioned experts in the law, Islamic jurisprudence and the judiciary to work on it. The latter prepared a new code in the form of a contemporary law and in step with the principles of the age without contravening the spirit of Islam (Majallat al-Qada' wal-Tashri', in Arabic, 1975, 145). It is evident that the issuing of the Shari'a Code was, in essence, a response to social demand. It may also be noted that this demand was felt by Tunisian society even while it struggled for liberation, because its view of freedom was comprehensive, one in which the political was complemented by the social.

Many accomplishments in health and in the economy as well as in professional fields followed the issuance of the Personal Status Code. Since these laws are interrelated, for the sake of brevity, those relating to the family are listed in the following table, which sets out the various laws and their revisions in the course of half a century as an indication of how legislation and society changed over time.

These are examples of achievements that prepared the way for the rise of Tunisian women. It must be pointed out that other regulations are also in force and are permitted by the Personal Status Code. For example, family law does not stipulate the religion of the spouse. Thus a Tunisian woman (or man) may wed a partner from another faith. It follows that

TABLE 5-1

Family laws in order of promulgation

Laws	Section	Date	Content of Law
Prohibition of polygamy	18	1956	Imprisonment for violator.
Divorce a prerogative of the courts	30	===	
Legal age for marriage	5	1956	17 years for girls, 20 years for boys.
Request for divorce an equal prerogative of both husband and wife	31	===	
Marital obligations	23	1956	The wife must comply with her husband as the head of the family and obey his orders.
		1993	Deletion of the expression "obey": the husband, as head of the family, must provide for the wife and children according to his means and their needs. The wife must contribute if she has money.
Custody of the children	154	1956	If the child does not have a father or legal guardian, the judge must appoint a legal guardian.
	67	1981	The minor's guardian is the father or, if the father has died, the mother.
		1993	If the mother has been made responsible for the child's upbringing, she shall have jurisdiction over matters pertaining to the child's travel, study and financial dispositions.
Creation of a fund to guarantee the payment of support and alimony.	65	1993	

a Tunisian woman married to a foreigner can pass on her nationality to any children she has by him, whether they were born in Tunisia or abroad, subject only to the father's agreement.

Important as these accomplishments are, in order for their benefits to be fully realised, they still require all the other reforms that the independent women's movements have taken it upon themselves to demand. Even though the Personal Status Code contains some modifications to the regulations concerning inheritance, it still maintains the male's share at twice that of the female. This has created a predicament for broad sectors of society and in particular for those fathers who, over the last fifty years, have been equally supportive of their daughters.

To the present day, equal inheritance remains difficult to achieve, and many are impelled to resort to loopholes in Islamic law to guarantee the principle of equality. For example, a father may make a pro forma sale of a portion of his assets to his daughter, or he may divide up his wealth among his children while he is still alive. A father who has not been blessed with male children may convert to Shiism, which is more flexible in these matters.

It is also noticeable that these positive revisions to family laws have coincided with restrictions on the freedom of action of activist women and with State monopolisation and monitoring of the movement's discourse, leaving only limited scope for women's initiatives and demands. The tendency to transform the rise of women into a political tool for enhancing of the State abroad, even at the expense of women, has become all too clear.

The regime in Tunisia, for example, has tried to exploit the conflict between the Association of Democratic Women and the Islamist current. Faced with the former's determined independence, it has imposed various restrictions on it, such as starving the Association of funds while lavishing large amounts on government-sponsored women's groups. The headquarters of the Association is under constant security surveillance in order to scare off its members. Those steadfast women who still frequent it have been physically and verbally abused and have had their activities disrupted. In addition, there has been a complete media blackout on news about the group.

It is noticeable, too, that these official reforms in favour of the family have been accompanied by a tendency to marginalise independent-minded women who refuse to

The tendency to transform the rise of women into a political tool for enhancing the image of the State abroad has become all too clear.

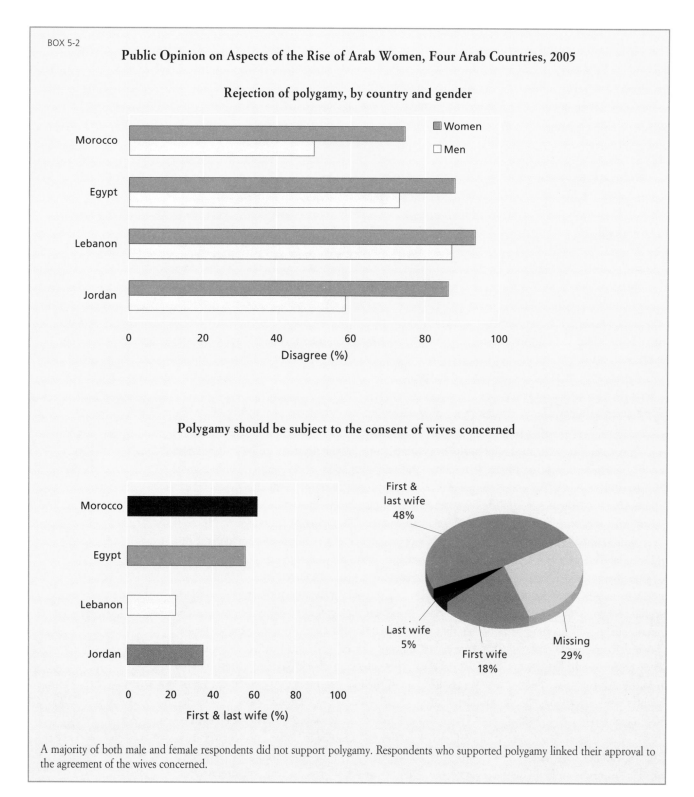

BOX 5-2

Public Opinion on Aspects of the Rise of Arab Women, Four Arab Countries, 2005

Rejection of polygamy, by country and gender

Disagree (%)

Polygamy should be subject to the consent of wives concerned

First & last wife (%)

First & last wife 48%

Last wife 5%

First wife 18%

Missing 29%

A majority of both male and female respondents did not support polygamy. Respondents who supported polygamy linked their approval to the agreement of the wives concerned.

allow their academic and social successes to be exploited to improve the regime's political image. Attempts to bring forward women loyal to the ruling party in their stead, even at the expense of efficiency, are quite common. In fact, this phenomenon is a feature in all the Arab countries, a political peculiarity that springs from the nature of the official ruling regimes. Mentioning it here, in the context of the revolutionary accomplishments of women in Tunisia, does, however, pose a question. Can any model of the rise of women that is kissed by Arab political authorities truly contribute to changing the political culture of States and to propelling them towards a comprehensive renaissance?

THE MOROCCAN EXPERIENCE

The new consciousness of the Moroccan women's movement arises from its conviction that amending the Personal Status Code is the key to women's ownership of their own issues. On 8 March 1991, the Women's Labour Union launched a campaign to collect one million signatures on a radical petition. The document demanded that: the law should view parity between the spouses as the basis of the family; the principle of equality between women and men should be established, implying that a woman would be eligible to engage in legal transactions at the age of legal maturity; divorce should become a prerogative of the courts; polygamy should be conditionally prohibited; and women should be granted guardianship of their children.

The document was heavily criticised; indeed, its signatories were considered to be "participating in the crime of apostasy". In short, conditions were not yet ripe for the amendment of the legal code, and the weight of resistance to change continues to press heavily on the Moroccan body politic. Just as King Muhammad V defined the authoritative judicial framework for promulgating the legal code in 1957, so, too, he moved to cut off discussion of any modification to it. His intention was to prevent the issue from escaping from his jurisdiction and becoming hostage to political tussles and party one-upmanship.[5]

The amendments incorporated into the Personal Status Law in 1993 may be read in two ways. The first turns on the idea of evolution. It assumes that if the amendments do not go far enough in achieving the objectives of the women's movement, they do at least provide a potential for change worthy of investment. The second interpretation sees the amendments as merely marking time and that conservatism and traditionalism remain triumphant, leaving the discriminatory structure of the legal code untouched. One clear objection to the amendments of 1993 is their failure to adopt international standards pertaining to women and children. As a matter of fact, at that time,

Morocco had not yet completed its accession to the agreements and treaties in question and had registered reservations with respect to articles of CEDAW, citing their inappropriateness to Morocco's religious, moral and social particularities. Morocco also registered a reservation with regard to Article 16, which relates to arbitration when a dispute arises between two or more countries regarding the interpretation or application of the agreement (Malki, background paper for the Report).

Significant developments took place in Morocco between the issuing of the amendments to the Personal Status Code (1993) and the end of the twentieth century. On the one hand, the accords that brought together the royal establishment and political parties descended from the nationalist movement were crowned by the appointment of a government headed by the nationalist elite, which had been excluded from power for more than 35 years. At the same time, after the transfer of power, royal speeches in more than one venue emphasised the importance that the women's issue had assumed. If internal developments played a major role in spurring the diverse actors in the Moroccan women's movement to intensify their struggle, international dynamics also contributed to honing women's consciousness and expanding their horizons.

The draft revision of the legal code, which began during 2003, focused on four priority axes: the involvement of women in education, the improvement of reproductive health, women's integration into economic development, and women's self-empowerment. The amendments recommended for incorporation into the legal code were progressive. They included: raising the legal age for marriage to eighteen years to conform with the International Convention on the Rights of the Child; relegation to secondary status of the "guardianship" or "custody" (*walaya*) of one spouse by the other; facilitation of divorce by granting both husband and wife the right of resort to the courts following the irretrievable breakdown of the marriage; prohibition of polygamy except by licence from a judge; and affirmation that individuals

The new consciousness of the Moroccan women's movement arises from its conviction that amending the Personal Status Code is the key to women's ownership of their own issues.

---

[5] King Hasan II, in a speech on 29 September 1992, emphasised that "women's issues were his first priority, and that he would take over the role of defending women's interests himself." He also asked women's associations to present him with their demands, which revolved around custody, alimony, child raising, the seeking and granting of divorce, and polygamy.

of both sexes shall be considered minors until the age of fifteen years. The amendments also covered other areas concerning the marriage of divorced mothers, alimony, the distribution of spousal assets following divorce, the creation of family courts, and the recognition of the right of women judges' to carry out documentation procedures relating to matters of personal status.

A draft of this nature could not go far without arousing opposition and conflict. This time, however, consequences were not limited merely to clashes among points of view but reached a point of real social tension verging on civil strife.

The Family Code that entered into force on 3 February 2004 did not come out of the blue nor was it bestowed as a favour or gift. Rather, it was a major turning point along a long road of struggle by Moroccan women, a journey marked by stumbles and triumphs. This struggle was, however, not limited to women; men also shared in it, and both internal and international democratic forces lent their support to it.

Despite this, much remains to be done and what has been accomplished needs to be carefully defended, nurtured and deepened. Further progress will depend on the extent of women's own capacity to continue to take charge of their own cause freely and responsibly. The distant goal of women's liberation, empowerment and advancement entails transforming the social imagination of the individual Moroccan by linking the rise of women to the twin values of democracy and modernism (Malki, background paper for the Report).

OTHER ARAB EXPERIENCES

While the previous section focused on only two Arab countries that have made substantial efforts to promote the rise of women, this is not to slight the many determined efforts in other States to revise some articles of their legal codes. Examples of such efforts are described below.

Egypt

Egyptian women won their political rights in 1956 after a struggle lasting more than 50

years. The government of the Revolution adopted many of the demands of the existing women's organisations, especially those relating to political rights, education and work. Fortunately, the demands of the women's movement coincided with the need of the State for additional labour while the prevailing socialist ideology was in harmony with the broadening of popular participation in parliamentary life. As a result, the Constitution of 1956 was modified to realise some of the aspirations of the active women's movement of the time. Legislative gains followed, and the Constitution of 1971 confirmed the gains found in that of 1956. Article 14 stipulated that occupation of public posts was the right of all citizens, women and men; articles 10 and 11 stipulated the duty of the State to protect mothers and children and that the State was charged with reconciling the duties of the woman towards the family and her work in the public sphere. Further legislation was issued that guaranteed equal rights to education and work and provided social and insurance guarantees to working women. As a result of these legislative changes, women entered political life. No laws, however, were issued to regulate women's position within the family and the personal status laws of 1925 and 1929 were left as they were despite the efforts of many women to have them changed. At the present time, Egyptian women have only managed to win the right, granted in 2000, to initiate divorce proceedings (khul') after waiving certain financial rights entailed in other forms of divorce. They have also won the right to travel without their husbands' permission and to obtain Egyptian nationality for their children by a foreign husband.

Jordan

Jordan has raised the legal age for marriage to 18 years for both spouses and granted women the right to obtain a passport without their husbands' permission.

Lebanon

An assembly of a number of NGOs has prepared a draft civil status law that will repeal 18 laws governing civil status according to the laws of the various religious and doctrinal sects.

The Family Code that entered into force on 3 February 2004 ... was a major turning point along a long road of struggle by Moroccan women.

Egyptian women won their political rights in 1956 after a struggle lasting more than 50 years.

Algeria

Family law still groans under the weight of the shackles that hamper women, among them the persistence of polygamy. Legislators have, however, worked hard to circumscribe the latter by making it conditional upon the consent of the first wife. A further burden is the law's view that the husband's guardianship or custody of the wife is a condition for the validity of the marriage. Nevertheless, there are certain positive landmarks between the laws of 1984 and the revisions issued in 2005. Thus, for example, Article 31 of the 1984 law regarding mixed marriage stipulates that "a Muslim woman may not marry a non-Muslim man". This was abrogated in 2005 in favour of the principle of equality between women and men with regard to marriage to foreigners of other religions (Majallat al-Risala al-Qanuniyya, in Arabic, 2005). Article 72, revised in 2005, establishes the husband's duty to assure a dwelling for his children from his divorced wife if she has taken on their care (Majallat al-Risala al-Qanuniyya, in Arabic, 2005).

These are achievements, modest as most of them may be. It is hoped that they may be an indication that the march of change is under way in the Mashreq (Egypt, Jordan and Lebanon) and in the Maghrib (Algeria and Morocco) even if it appears to be slower in the Arab Gulf States.

SUMMARY

An optimistic assessment would acknowledge the wide-ranging movement and activities in the area of women's rights. A forward-looking perspective would require that there be consensus regarding the general social, political, economic and cultural conditions that necessarily impact women's empowerment. At the same time, however, there is an obvious knowledge deficit when it comes to assessing the achievements of the women's movement. There is an urgent need for a gendered research lens in Arab countries that would cover all areas and formulate new questions and, by implication, a new discourse to override the current paradigms. Re-evaluating the position of women as a *sine qua non* for a stronger civil society demands a conviction that can overrule the pretext for inaction that rejects all forms of development in this area as part of the culture of "the Other".

THE SOCIETAL CONTEXT OF
THE STATE OF WOMEN

CHAPTER SIX

CULTURE

Introduction

This chapter considers social patterns that contribute to shaping the position of women in Arab societies today. It focuses on the impact of two central sources of influence: cultural and especially religious heritage and Arab intellectual production.

Culture plays a pervasive role in composing the social context of women's position in the Arab world, and religious interpretations provide a field for conflict over the position of women in public perception and general behavioural patterns. Religious heritage, above all, is a key determinant of the cultural norms underpinning the position of women in the Arab world.

Arab intellectual production, as it arose during the Arab Renaissance, also contributed to creating the prevailing social consciousness in relation to women in Arab societies.

The examination of cultural structures that follows also includes how popular culture, the arts and the media, themselves drawing on religious heritage and intellectual production, have altered consciousness and behaviour relating to women.

THE TRADITIONAL RELIGIOUS HERITAGE PROMOTES AND REINFORCES THE EXISTING GENDER HIERARCHY

TEXT AND INTERPRETATION

This section considers how human beings and society are perceived from an Islamic religious point of reference and how these perceptions bear on the image of women and gender relations. However, some caveats first:

it is important to recall that, in Islamic history, religious culture is not built on sacred texts of indisputable authority but, rather, on differing interpretations of the content, substance, forms and views of multiple writings and sayings in the collective memory of society. It is also based on customs and traditions that have been consolidated to preserve a specific order for the family and society. Furthermore, religious culture reflects the different schools of thought that have emerged at various stages of history (Arkoun, in French, 1984, 12; Jid'an, in Arabic, 1985, 442).

If the message of Islam comprises a number of major rules concerning the order of the universe and of society, it follows that there is more than one facet to these general rules since the recipient's interpretations are subject to the historical evolution of society and to developments in methods of reading and understanding the texts.

Because knowledge systems and interpretations do evolve and change, the meaning given to a specific text may not be entirely in keeping with the spirit of its substance: it can be transformed, in the intellectual process of extracting significance, into another aspect of theoretical practice. It thus becomes an interpretation, i.e., an effort to understand that should not be put on the same level as that of the text itself. Also, because interpretation is, in fact, a process of thought that takes place in history and within a given society using the means of knowledge at hand, it becomes part of the system of ideas within society. It is thus subject to the same transformations and corruptions as the symbolic systems of history.

Religious culture is not built on sacred texts of indisputable authority but, rather, on differing interpretations of the content, substance, forms and views of multiple writings and sayings in the collective memory of society.

Interpretation... is subject to the same transformations and corruptions as the symbolic systems of history.

Fahmi Howeidy: Equality Is at the Heart of Islam

There are three considerations the scholar must bear in mind if he wants to preserve his impartiality and objectivity in the course of an examination of the position of women from the Islamic perspective.

First, the question of women in Islam cannot be approached independently of the fundamental principles and tenets of the Islamic message, which confers an inviolable sanctity upon all creatures and holds that every creature must receive a measure of respect. All of God's creatures, as the Qur'an states, "form part of communities like you" (Al-An'am, 38). This embraces all beasts and birds, on land, in the sea or in the air, all of which worship God Almighty. Among all these creatures, mankind is God's chosen creature and His agent for developing the earth. Every human being, male or female, enjoys this special status, as the Qur'an establishes the right of every human being to dignity, regardless of gender, ethnic origin or religious affiliation.

Second, traditional practices have defeated scriptural teachings, in the Arab experience in particular. The early Islamic period – the period of the first four caliphs, to be precise – gave rise to a major transformation in the status of women. It liberated them from the oppression of the pre-Islamic era, during which they were held in such contempt that it was perfectly acceptable to bury female children to spare oneself the shame of their existence. However, the subsequent period brought numerous reversals in this, as well as in many other areas of life, and the gains which women had won under the first four caliphs gradually eroded until, speaking figuratively, the idea of "female burial" resurfaced, albeit symbolically rather than materially. Societies in the period of decline resuscitated the traditions emanating from the shame attached to the existence of women and to anything that betokened that existence, whether in social and public life or in prayer assemblies and mosques.

Third, the root principle in Islamic statutes is equality between men and women, apart from those areas in which the texts explicitly assign a prerogative or a distinction to one of the genders, for reasons pertaining not so much to gender as to social responsibility and legal status. Of particular relevance here is the significance of the Qur'anic verse that speaks of the creation of the two sexes from a single soul: "O mankind! Reverence your Guardian-Lord, who created you from a single person, created, of like nature, his mate, and from them twain scattered (like seeds) countless men and women" (Al-Nisa', 1). Al-Razi cited Abu Muslim who held that "created, of like nature, his mate" means that the mate was created of the same genus as the soul and was thus identical (Rida, in Arabic, 1973, 330).

Thus, we are presented with the crucial fact, clarified in the above-mentioned Qur'anic verse, that human beings originate from two mates both created of a single genus or from a single substance. It is as though this verse, in the foregoing interpretation, was designed specifically to underscore the concept of similarity and equality between the genders and to forestall the notion of discrimination and preference between the two halves of humanity (Al-Ghannushi, in Arabic, 2000, 9).

If men and women are created equal, then they are inherently equal in their rights to life and to dignity, which are fundamental rights of all human beings in Islam. It follows, too, that they are equal in their responsibilities: "The Believers, men and women, are protectors of one another: they enjoin what is just, and forbid what is evil" (Al-Tawba, 71).

Similarly, they are equal in religious duties and in the rewards in the hereafter: "And their Lord hath accepted of them, and answered them: 'Never will I suffer to be lost the work of any of you, male or female: ye are members, one of another'. (Al 'Imran, 195); Allah hath promised to Believers, men and women, "gardens under which rivers flow, to dwell therein, and beautiful mansions in gardens of everlasting bliss," etc. (Al-Tawba, 72); and "It is not fitting for a Believer, man or woman, when a matter has been decided by Allah and His Messenger to have any option about their decision ...", etc. (Al-Ahzab, 36)

They are equal, too, in the punishments meted out to sinners, as can be seen in the divine statutes regarding male and female thieves (Al-Ma'ida, 38) and the adulterer and adulteress (Al-Nur, 2).

Furthermore, they are equal in their eligibility to engage in commercial transactions and contracts. Anyone who is rational, adult and otherwise legally competent has the right to dispose of his or her property freely, through sale, or as a gift, bequest or loan or as collateral, to empower others to act on his or her behalf, and to purchase goods and other such transactions. The verse in which this form of equality is grounded is: "To men is allotted what they earn, and to women what they earn" (Al-Nisa', 32). Nor does the marital contract in Islamic law confer upon the husband any right to interfere in the financial affairs of his wife, even on the grounds of his right to be her keeper, for this is an interpersonal rather than a financial right.

UNIVERSALITY AND DERIVATIVES: PROBLEMS OF INTERPRETATION

In the text of the Qur'an, there is a collection of verses that represent a complete vision of human beings, of society, of nature and of history. Undoubtedly, this vision was formed at a major turning point in the history of Arab society. It criticised and did away with many customs and traditions that were inconsistent with the humanity of human beings and provided alternatives appropriate to the level of knowledge and society in both Arab and world history at that time.

The broad outlines of this vision can be perceived in the following verses:

"Mankind! We created you from a single (pair) of a male and a female, and made you into Nations and tribes, that Ye may know each other (Not that Ye may despise each other). Verily the most honoured of you in the sight of God is (he who is) the most Righteous. And God has full knowledge and is well acquainted (with all things)" (Al-Hujurat, 13).

"O mankind! Reverence your Guardian-Lord, who created you from a single person, created, of like nature, his mate, and from them twain scattered (like seeds) countless men and women" (Al-Nisa', 1).

"We did indeed offer the Trust to the Heavens and the Earth and the Mountains, but they refused to undertake it, being afraid thereof. But man undertook it; he was indeed unjust and foolish" (Al-Ahzab 72).

These verses indicate the general nature of the Qur'anic provisions regarding the origin and nature of human beings and equality in gender relations, all of which affirm the loftiness of the Qur'an's perception of human beings. The principle of the equality of all creatures and the principle of their participation in life on the basis of solidarity (Al-Hujurat) is evident. They also affirm that mankind is subject to testing by the Creator and acknowledge the courage of human beings, both male and female, as reflected in their acceptance of uncertainty in the face of their destiny (Al-Ahzab).

The general principles embodied in these verses, as well as others, enable one to infer the broad outlines of a social system that responds to the objectives accepted by the Islamic community in order to live a life of interdependence and consensus, while recognising the equality of all human beings, males and females. Nevertheless, several jurists set the examples given in these Qur'anic verses on a lower level than other suras devoted to the legislation of minute details concerning the relationship between men and women. Instead of bringing the subsidiary verses closer to the spirit of those dealing with the fundamental and general, the suras indicating equality were used to justify its opposite, i.e., to justify and legitimise the existing hierarchy.

JURISPRUDENCE LEGISLATES IN FAVOUR OF THE HIGHER STATUS OF MEN

Codification in Islamic jurisprudence with respect to the situation of women occupies a strategic cultural position, one that shapes the order of the relationship between men and women. The legislative efforts of jurisprudence gave the social system a form of legality in keeping with the spirit of the message of Islam. The legitimacy of laws thus derived was accepted because of the authority and official rank enjoyed by Islamic jurists, who were consulted not only in matters of personal status but also on a range of issues concerning society and life (Silini, background paper for the Report).

It may be said here that the male viewpoint in the history of Islamic societies has violated the divine principle of equality bestowed upon human beings as a whole; it has construed everything that supports discrimination and differentiation as though it were an absolute rule. This is how an eternal curse was attached to women. Scores of Hadith or sayings were tossed about in a whirlpool of interpretations with the purpose of demonizing women and transforming them into creatures of absolute evil.

In making laws, Islamic jurisprudence referred to the substance of the Qur'an and the Sunna. Beforehand and afterwards, however, it also considered the requirements of a 'balanced society" oriented towards the legislation of personal status. The provisions of Islamic jurisprudence concerning women were established in relation to the situation and conditions of Islamic society at the time when such provisions were crystallised. They were put in place largely in order to preserve the morality of the prevailing social hierarchy and the rules of discrimination between men and women.

Juristic interpretations, formulated in the schools of Islamic jurisprudence, contributed to the establishment of norms sanctioning the principle of discrimination between the sexes. The contents of the *suras* asserting that man is the protector and provider and that a daughter is entitled to half a share of the inheritance were transformed into fundamental and general tenets, though they are not so and deal, in substance, only with subsidiary issues. They were broadened to include the relationship between men and women in different situations and in general in order to bolster discrimination between the two sexes. The authority of such subsidiary *suras* was reinforced by invoking the prophet's Sunna, a long list of unconfirmed sayings of the Prophet that was used to diminish women's humanity. As a result, the positive image of the equality and dignity conferred upon all human beings in the Qur'an was transformed into contradictory provisions. These generalised statements discriminate between what is perfect and what is imperfect, between the original and the branch, between the adult and the minor, between the straight and the crooked (Howeidy, background paper for the Report, 3-4; Bu Talib, in Arabic, 2005, 59-65).

Juristic interpretations... contributed to the establishment of norms sanctioning the principle of discrimination between the sexes.

As a result, the positive image of the equality and dignity conferred upon all human beings in the Qur'an was transformed into contradictory provisions.

The strategy of interpretation that led to laws affirming the inferiority of women centred on two principles: first, a disregard of the fundamental Qur'anic verses that recognise equality and honour human beings; and second, the use of subsidiary verses and other arguments for a hierarchy of the sexes, to justify inequality. The nobility of spirit that characterises Qur'anic texts was thus neglected.

The strictness of legislation in Islamic jurisprudence conceals other matters that originate in Arab Islamic society itself, particularly since jurists deliberately read the canonical provisions through the lens of custom. They believed that any other kind of readings would disrupt the continuity of the social order in its reinforcement of social cohesion, which, in their view, was congruent with "the order of nature".

Men have always been given priority and preference in jurisprudential studies relating to women. This is a predisposition that entrenched itself as a result of reading the Qur'an with a bias in men's favour. The assumptions of books on matrimony reveal a web of concepts, views and arguments whose function is to support men in a position higher than women in society, since the man is always the father, the husband, the son or some other male among the woman's agnates. The jurists, in general, remained loyal to such a view, which served as the foundation for numerous further rules in different areas of society, thus multiplying the complications involved in establishing a system that would allow for equity in the relations between men and women (Silini, background paper for the Report). Nonetheless, enlightened legal interpretations did exist (Box 6-2).

Historically, the dominant masculine view in interpreting the Qur'an did have its critics, even in the middle ages, who expressed dissenting views and tried to change the prevailing bias. These writings and positions convey an altogether more humane approach to organising a system of relations between men and women in Islamic Arab society. In fact, there is in Arab tradition and in some of the phases of Islamic cultural development a collection of intuitive positions that go far in undermining the dominance of men in the Islamic culture of the time. Abul Hasan Al-Basri criticised polygamy and the Isma'ilis refused the principle thereof. Ibn Arabi (560-638 A.H.) in some of his writings considered women far superior to the demeaning images of his day (Al-Rasikhi, in Arabic, 2004, 161; Hamadi, in Arabic, 2003, 63-80).

To speak of texts opposed to the dominant masculine view of women's inferiority is simply to acknowledge the currents and counter-currents that remained a feature of Islamic culture. The existence of such texts does, however, show that is possible to transcend dominant perceptions and admit that differences of opinion are legitimate. The independent reasoning (ijtihad) of enlightened jurists and scholars, who are sensitive to the laws of change and development in society, stands behind several endeavours today to crystallise a noble view of the Qur'an's perception of different social phenomena and historical changes (Al-Dayalimi, in Arabic, 2000, 79-83).

Jurisprudential writings suppressed the verses clearly referring to equality and honouring women in the Qur'anic text. They concentrated on legislation favouring the clan as the point of departure for the legislator. Thus the woman becomes, first and foremost, the custodian of the clan's progeny.

As a general rule, most jurisprudential endeavours do not go beyond a mass of contingent assumptions relating to two matters: a general discourse outlining all of the fundamental principles, and an interpretation considered by them to be the closest to the spirit of a given text and social reality. This feature underscores the relativity and specificity of the jurisprudential product as well as of the possibility of transcending it by referring to

---

BOX 6-2

Muhammad 'Abdu: On Polygamy

"It is undoubtedly possible to abolish this habit, polygamy. First, because the condition for polygamy is the establishment of justice and this condition is not there. Second, the mistreatment of women by their husbands and the denial of their right to maintenance and comfort are common. It is permitted, therefore, to the ruler or judge to prohibit polygamy in order to avoid mischief, which is rampant.

Third, it has been demonstrated that the origin of strife and animosity between children is that they were born of different mothers. Each is brought up hating the other and by the time they become of age, they are deadly enemies of one another (...). Therefore, the ruler or the religious judge may prohibit polygamy and the ownership of bondmaids in order to protect households from strife.

Source: 'Abdu, in Arabic, 1980, 94-95.

---

the fundamental principles set out in the non-interpreted text, the interests of humanity and their ultimate purposes (Al-Shatibi, in Arabic, n.d., 67-68). The examples derived from rules relating to women may in fact reflect the loyalty of the jurists to the customs that governed societies and seek a harmony that would guarantee a balance amidst their changing social dynamics.

Because, however, the dynamics of transformation in contemporary Arab societies are different from those in Arab societies at the time when the schools of jurisprudence were established, earlier endeavours are no longer appropriate to either the nature or pace of current social transformations. Rather, it is a right to try to open the gates of interpretation anew and to seek further understanding of the spirit of the Qur'anic text in order to produce jurisprudential texts based on values of equality. Such texts will seek to embody a jurisprudence of women that goes beyond the linguistic and historical equation of what is feminine with what is natural (pregnancy, childbirth, breast feeding, upbringing and cooking). They will contribute to the promotion of feminine cultural values and transform them into a general attitude (Al-Dayalimi, in Arabic, 2000, 51-57).

The Qur'an has granted human beings (women and men) an elevated position on earth. If Islamic jurists of old were loyal to the needs of their customs and the requirements of their society, those customs and requirements no longer satisfy the needs of our age and society. Thus, turning to international laws that eliminate all forms of discrimination between men and women in no way contradicts religious belief, since these laws are closer to the spirit of the religious texts while also being closer to the changes taking place in contemporary Arab societies.

THE ARAB WOMAN IN POPULAR PROVERBS

IN SUPPORT OF DISCRIMINATION

Arab popular culture projects contradictory images of women, girls and wives at different stages of their lives. Proverbs dealing with

women are repeated in most Arab social classes and generally provide clear examples of the perception of women as inferior, indicating that popular awareness is isolated from the fundamental transformations taking place in Arab societies. The proverbs create several myths about the conditions and state of women, which are often at odds with women's actual circumstances.

Different generations in the history of Arab society have exchanged and reproduced many proverbs purveying the inferiority of women. Arab women are thus demeaned not only by conservative and traditional jurisprudential interpretations but also by sayings, myths and proverbs that confine them to a particular place in society.

Proverbs and colloquial sayings, descended from times immemorial, keep alive old texts, myths and sayings springing from an obscure web of ancient sources that speak of circumstances rather different from those of today. Yet because of the way in which proverbs are widely exchanged across society, and have their own catchy language and cadence, they have been transformed into a collective product and memory serving to perpetuate and entrench particular values within it (Al-Sa'ati, in Arabic, 2003, 75-84).

Anyone reviewing samples of Arab proverbs about women and their situation will note that they contain a number of contradictory images, particularly those about mothers, wives, married women and single women. Such contradictions, however, do not change the general image of women that they purvey, a biased image that reflects male superiority and attitudes and one that a male-dominated society readily circulates through society by various means.

The forms, degrees and characteristics of inferiority attributed to women in current proverbs betray a social conflict, translated into

Turning to international laws that eliminate all forms of discrimination against women in no way contradicts religious belief.

Popular proverbs create several myths about the conditions and state of women.

words and sentences, that stems from efforts to establish and justify women's "inferiority" and, indeed, to turn it into a quality impossible to change. As noted, proverbs are archives of a heritage embodying the experiences of human beings down the years. They variously express the ideas of lunatics, saints and sheikhs. Most have their own special catch phrases, rhythm and suggestiveness and use puns, anecdotes, erudite expressions and rhetoric to good effect. They therefore lodge in the popular mind and attain an emotive status that gives them a privileged position and time-tested credibility. Thus they are preserved and repeated and have wide resonance, particularly in societies where women and girls are mostly illiterate.

ATTITUDES IN PROVERBS PROMOTING DISCRIMINATION AGAINST WOMEN

Different values coexist in today's Arab society, intertwined with various social and cultural attitudes in a complex network. If most proverbs repeated in parts of Arab society are biased in favour of masculine values and portray women as "lacking" and "evil", there are also new manifestations of popular wisdom emerging from social changes since the second half of the last century. The latter expose many traditional sayings as quite alien to today's reality and younger generations, where women have made themselves felt at the very heart of the dynamics of social transformation (Afarfar, in Arabic, 1996, 60-63).

Hundreds of popular proverbs imply that women should be segregated. These are common in more than one Arab country (Arab Mashreq countries, Egypt and the Arab Maghreb). They project an attitude akin to that which led to the burying of girls alive. In order to justify their retrograde spirit, these proverbs use moral and other arguments expressed in the language of tales and myths. Some also rely on psychology. In their various forms, these proverbs serve to underline the inferior social and moral position of women in society. Some go even further, considering a woman to have only half a mind, half a creed and half an inheritance and to be worth only half a male. Their general drift is to limit women's biological and domestic life,

denigrate their worth and independence and shore up men's alleged superiority.

The two following proverbs contain most of the elements mentioned above:
• "Better the voice of a she-devil than that of a girl".
• "If your wife gives birth to girls you shall suffer until the day you die".

Many proverbs put forward the image of a woman as a fiend who bears a permanent grudge and who is cunning, unfaithful and a slave to her sexual desires. This woman is, indeed, synonymous with devilish and reckless behaviour. Ironically, such proverbs project an image of women that unwittingly contradicts the ostensible justification for exclusion from society by showing women to possess a formidable power capable of breaking anyone who stands in their way. It is likely that such sayings originate in efforts to make men wary of women in general. This in turn produces counter-sayings among women that are expressed in tales told by grandmothers to their granddaughters (Mernissi, in Arabic, 1983, 40-59).

In proverbial wisdom, it is only through a man that a woman may reach a haven of security, since a woman cannot do without a man. Women are thus invited to accept the hierarchy established by the biased and conservative religious interpretations that such proverbs reinforce. The social bias against women is quite evident in most of these sayings. Some of them consider that "a maiden is a calamity" but that "marriage is a protection". Others claiming to speak on behalf of women define their life choices as "The hell of my husband rather than the paradise of my father" while a more sinister proverb says: "A girl belongs to her husband or to the grave". Such sayings clearly stem from a system of values and institutions that discriminates between the sexes from a patriarchal point of view and where man remains the husband and the father who guarantees the continuity of the hierarchical system (Sabbar, in Arabic, 1998, 49-67).

POSITIVE PERCEPTIONS OF WOMEN

Nevertheless, there are proverbs that contradict those mentioned above. Several popular traditions and texts present another image of woman, a woman who is intelligent, articulate and, indeed, something of an enchantress but in the positive sense of the word. In popular literature, Scheherazade, for example, exercises a thrilling power and influence through her tales. Proverbs about women as mothers and their position in the family and in society can also project an altogether different image of women. Such contradictory images of women in popular culture may be understood as expressing a range of emotional and psychological states rather than an established theoretical attitude. In the main, however, proverbs, as noted before, tend to inculcate the notion of the inferiority of women (Shams al-Din, in Arabic, 2002).

Below are some examples of the numerous proverbs that elevate women in their role as mothers and as daughters where the mother is considered more important than the father and as the true source of love, care and protection:

- "The mother builds a nest while the father runs away".
- "He who has his mother need have no worry".
- "To the man who loses his mother heaven says, 'You have lost the one person on earth who loves you, poor creature'".
- "Paradise lies at the feet of mothers". (Hadith - Saying by the Profit).

There is also a popular proverb that equates daughters with life itself: "He who has fathered no girls has not really lived".

As such, popular proverbs contain the positive and the negative, clearly underlining the contradiction in the transitory and evolving nature of perceptions of women and their position in Arab societies.

WOMEN IN CONTEMPORARY ARAB THOUGHT

TOWARDS THE EMERGENCE OF NEW SOURCES OF AUTHORITY

Before turning to the image of women in contemporary Arab thought and the intellectual reference points behind that image, it is necessary to emphasise that how

contemporary Arab thought views women and the theories supporting those views are closely tied to the Arab Renaissance movement and its struggles against all forms of inherited traditional authority. For this reason, the intellectual effort related to the "question of women" is characterised by efforts to shrug off the heavy burden of traditional references in their various forms. Since this is a broad subject, the review will focus on the main stages in the development of women's issues in contemporary Arab thought. In the present Report, these stages are termed "the realisation of difference", "the awareness of transformation" and "institutionalisation". The chapter concludes with an overview of the transformation of Arab awareness and its inherent contradictions (Abdellatif, in Arabic, 2003, 9-13).

The realisation of difference: the other woman in the mirror of the self

The "realisation of difference" refers to that moment in Arab thought when scholars identified the beginnings of the transformations that led to the Arab Renaissance. This was the period when reform-minded political and intellectual elites recognised that European societies had specific features that accounted for their strength and progress. They also understood that overcoming the slow development of Arab

Several popular traditions and texts present another image of woman, a woman who is intelligent, articulate and, indeed, something of an enchantress but in the positive sense of the word.

Reform-minded political and intellectual elites recognised that European societies had specific features that accounted for their strength and progress.

societies required making use of the foundations that had created, and continued to create, the attributes of renaissance and power in Europe and the advanced world.

An excellent representation of this particular moment is the reform project of Shaykh Rifa'a Rafi' al-Tahtawi (1801-1873). This section refers to some of his texts in order to illustrate aspects of this particular moment in Arab thought, quoting from two influential books: *The Trusty Guide for the Education of Girls and Boys* and Refining *Gold in Summarizing Paris* (Al-Tahtawi, in Arabic, 1834 and 1870).

The writings of Al-Tahtawi were polemical in nature and were written in defence of his reformist project. When discussing women, he listed a number of prevailing views that prevented any improvement in their condition, such as the refusal to teach them how to read and write. He also challenged misogynist views that portray women as the embodiment of cunning or as creatures of inferior intellect, views that consider that a woman's role is, to quote Al-Tahtawi, no more than that of "a container that preserves offspring".

When confronting traditional discourse on women, Al-Tahtawi insists on the importance of education in life. He not only lists the advantages of education in the life of women, but he also goes much further, to open up

prospects of development for Arab women and to speak of changes quite advanced for the cultural and social system of his time. He links education and knowledge to the issue of work. In his opinion, "women, when necessary, can undertake the same kinds of jobs and work undertaken by men ... This work can preserve women from doing what is inappropriate and if unemployment is a shame for men, it is also a great shame for women" (Al-Tahtawi, in Arabic, 1973, 210).

Al-Tahtawi treated girls' education seriously and his texts took on the vexed questions of the mingling of the sexes and of the veil. When defending women's right to education and work, he resorted to history and to some aspects of Islamic law, attempting to reconcile history and tradition with modern gains in knowledge and social life. In the same way, he set out to establish justifications for co-education, provided that it did not offend modesty. He was very careful to reject all that contributed to the exclusion of women from the real world merely because men feared that work would require women to leave their homes. In his opinion, this was a matter of trust based on good upbringing and education. The new education created the possibility of raising girls in such a way as to enable them to assimilate the values of the age and to adapt themselves to their requirements ('Abdellatif, background paper for the Report).

The awareness of transformation: first attempts to restrict gender-biased jurisprudence

The writings of the reformers and the pioneers of the Arab Renaissance reflected a deep understanding of alternative and more positive images of women, taking modern European history as their guide. Their insights were brought to the fore in the works of Al-Tahtawi, but they show in other cases as well.

For instance, neither Qasim Amin (1863–1908) nor Al-Tahir Al-Haddad (1899-1935) hesitated to defend the idea that advantages could be gained from the experiences of European history and society. They both disputed that any contradictions existed between the latter, or the values of the lifestyle emerging in contemporary Arab society, and

---

BOX 6-5

Freedom Is a Woman

In the dark ages of Europe and elsewhere, the Woman was discarded and despised. She was considered a mere chattel. A man would sometimes sell his wife at a public auction. Writers and poets vied with one another in attacking and criticising her. Theologians had long discussions over "whether the woman had a soul". They claimed that she was "the gate to Hell" and the "factory of the devil's weapons". Her voice was likened to the hissing of snakes"; she was "the devil's arrows", "as poisonous as a cobra" and "as malicious as a dragon".

With the dawn of modern civilisation and as science and knowledge were transformed from theory and tradition into experimentation and analysis, the woman was among the subjects that

interested people. They realised (...) that success would hang on her education and self-development, for she was the mainstay of the family, the one who raised the children and man's partner in his life and livelihood. They advanced the woman, taught her and raised her status. She then started demanding her rights. There was disagreement among writers over the extent of those rights but they agreed in respecting the woman and holding her in high esteem. They even made her a symbol of virtue and pride. If they wanted to personify freedom, they erected a statue for it in the form of a woman. They did the same with unity, eloquence, work and other virtues. They represented them as women.

Source: Zaydan, in Arabic, 2002.

the principles of Islamic law. They also entered into a debate over the reclassification and interpretation of certain Qur'anic verses, with the aim of unmasking biased interpretations. Their efforts also influenced the pioneering work produced by Nazira Zayn al-Din (1908-1976) in Unveiling and Veiling (1998).

The works of Qasim Amin evince the transformation that took place among Arab elites on the nature of women's situation in Arab society and reveal the extent to which traditions and customs were questioned. This transformation appeared in varying degrees in different Arab countries despite the colonial presence that was their most evident reality. Amin was able to diagnose the situation of Arab women in general by considering that of Egyptian women in particular because of the cultural links between Arab countries and their common history and values, however variously expressed.

Amin drew attention to society's subordination of women. In his exposure, the Arab woman is an inferior being confined at home; assigned separate eating arrangements; unable to seek work; under close surveillance by her father, husband, brother and son; easily divorced; regarded as untrustworthy; denied a role in public life and institutions; denied a place in religious beliefs; and seen as lacking in taste and in value to the nation.

His portrayal was both a criticism and a call for reform, and he eloquently exposed the array of social factors entrenching social prejudice against women and the dialectics reproducing that entrenchment. He also sought ways of negating and transcending such entrenched prejudice (Fahmi, in Arabic, 1964, 115-132).

To this end, Amin formulated his reform programme and wrote The Liberation of Women (1899) and The New Woman (1900) under the inspiration of the new, progressive thinkers of the Arab Renaissance and their counterparts in Europe, notably the positivist philosophers. The theoretical background of his reform project was that which appeared with the emergence of industrial society and the transformations that it brought to the social structure and to general perceptions of society and history (Amin, in Arabic, 1899 and 1900).

Amin called for women to be liberated from tradition. He championed the removal of the veil and limits on men's right to divorce.

He also insisted on the equality of women and men in civil rights. His reform programme was a turning point in perceptions of the problems of Arab women, containing a critique that opens new prospects for approaching these problems, notwithstanding the fact that his ambitious ideas could not be implemented in his own time.

Reformers such as Qasim Amin, Nazira

BOX 6-6

Nazira Zayn al-Din: Time, Freedom and Liberation

"Whether we like it or not, we cannot block the path of the modern renaissance and the new ideas it gives us in sociology. Religion has been liberated, science has been liberated, the mind has been liberated, thought has been liberated, art has been liberated, the society has been liberated and every thing in this world has been freed from the grip of slavery and bondage".

Source: Zayn al-Din, in Arabic, 1998, 121.

Zayn al-Din and later al-Tahir al-Haddad and others were acutely aware of the necessity for change in the position of women. Their efforts stand out in Arab cultural history because they succeeded in opening wide a door for women at the centre of the solid wall of Arab society. Amin's call for liberation prompted a lively debate that, in turn, contributed to the forging of new tools and concepts in Arab thought supporting the liberation of women and the development of Arab society ('Abdellatif, background paper for the Report, 15-22).

Institutionalisation: towards a new mindset on Arab women's issues

The foregoing account shows that the battle for the liberation of women in Arab thought and everyday life needs to be redoubled. In varying degrees, hostility towards women remains a scarring feature of ideas, attitudes and feelings among individuals and communities in most Arab countries. Nonetheless the transformation in approaches to the problematic situation of Arab women that took place during the last decades of the twentieth century continues to strengthen resistance to the various perceptions of women as inferior beings.

Certainly, it is possible to point to a slow, gradual process through which some of the needs of women in some Arab countries are being met, particularly in terms of family laws and political participation. To date, however, this budding process has not proved equal to the counter-pressures exerted in many areas of society.

The battle for the liberation of women in Arab thought and everyday life needs to be redoubled.

The participation of women in civil society organisations devoted to legal and political action helped to re-educate society.

The most significant aspect of women's activism in the Arab world today is its transcendence of traditional expectations; it is now a comprehensive position in step with other major changes in Arab societies involving questions of renaissance.

Arab women have made the project of political and economic reform...part of their direct objectives.

It eventually became clear that the theoretical discourse of the reformist movement that characterised Arab social and political thought through the first half of the twentieth century was not able to overturn conservative traditions and thinking regarding women or to change women's position in Arab society in any fundamental way. Thus, starting in the 1970s and in response to these challenges, several Arab governments sought to introduce women as a variable into their development plans and programmes as part of a new vision of development. This vision was not limited to economic growth but sought rather to find in economic growth the key to human development in general.

The direction taken by feminist issues on the international level in the last 30 years should be placed in this context. It marks when awareness of the importance of institutionalisation arose. Regional and international conferences were convened with the aim of putting an end to the inferior situation of women globally and in an attempt to produce a demand-based discourse appropriate to this situation while keeping in mind the disparities in women's conditions around the world. This period saw a profound shift away from trying to address the social problems of one particular gender and towards dealing with human development as a whole.

ASPECTS OF THE NEW AWARENESS: INDICATORS AND PARADOXES

Any observer of women's issues in contemporary Arab thought will note the appearance of new indicators reflecting a transformation in these issues with their institutionalisation. The participation of women in civil society organisations devoted to legal and political action helped to re-educate society and foster acceptance of an active female presence. It replaced old and limiting feminine stereotypes with an image of women engaged in a broad range of activities, affording them much greater space for action, production and creativity.

New developments in economic theory and the social sciences, in psychology and psychoanalysis and in general awareness of matters relating to sexual life all contributed to enriching perceptions and attitudes regarding women's issues and position in society. They constituted a new source of authority resting on modern epistemological gains, scientific and analytical thinking and innovative methodologies. Fresh intellectual perspectives helped to restrict the scope of conservative thinking, traditional knowledge and regressive attitudes in this field.

The concepts, analyses and definitions engendered by the rise of human sciences gave birth to new ideas for improving the conditions of women globally. These developments, which took root thanks to the efforts of women's movements, promoted the idea that history and culture play an important role in constructing social hierarchies. A number of influential concepts came to be applied to illuminate the reality of Arab women – concepts such as equality, justice, participation, empowerment, gender and human development. Together, they ushered in new perceptions relating to social, political and developmental affairs.

This intellectual and methodological revolution, together with the critique of Arab-Islamic thought, brought a new critical approach to bear on traditional customs and on the development of thinking about society in the Arab world (Al-Jabiri, in Arabic, 1984, 1986, 1990, and 2000; Arkoun, in French, 1984). Perceptions of, and attitudes towards, women's issues and how they could be approached and overcome evolved, resulting in new data and concepts and a more progressive discourse that enabled Arab thought to contain yet more powerfully the influence of tradition both in culture and in the popular heritage.

The most significant aspect of women's activism in the Arab world today is its transcendence of traditional expectations; it is now a comprehensive position in step with other major changes in Arab societies involving questions of renaissance, development and progress. Arab women have made the project of political and economic reform and of the establishment of a positive interaction with the human rights system part of their direct objectives; this is reflected in the increasing presence of women in the organisations of civil and political society. This trend augurs well for the more profound interaction of women with the question of change and for their participation in constructing such change, thereby taking public affairs into their own hands. Its importance should not be underestimated in a struggle that encompasses all areas of activity within society without exception ('Abdellatif, background paper for the Report, 22-35).

A key tenet of the project of social transformation to which the Arab women's movement has linked itself is the role of social intermediaries in realising social objectives. The movement now has access to new means and methods of expanding and enhancing public awareness of women's issues and of communicating with its global counterparts.

Contemporary media forms such as the Internet, chat rooms, satellite television channels and their specialised programmes are based on the power of open public dialogue, quick communication and accessible communities of thought and practice. For women, they open up a new avenue of liberation that allows them to occupy spaces that they could not have entered through the conventional print media. The latter in any case are retreating little by little before these new communication technologies that are helping to shake the foundations of the conservative elements of our heritage, particularly of those traditions and ideas that condone hierarchy and look upon it as "natural". These new media help to promote a gender awareness oriented towards social cohesion, equality and the principle of equity as the appropriate alternatives to discrimination between the sexes (Mernissi, in French, 1984, 13-35; 'Abdellatif, background paper for the Report, 15-22).

Yet this qualitative change in Arab thinking should not lead one to neglect the major contradiction easily apparent to any observer of the history of ideas: the large-scale reappearance of traditional perceptions and conservative views about the role of women in society. The latter are as obvious in discourse as they are in clothes and in daily rituals. All aim to confront the transformation achieved by the institutionalisation that raised feminist issues from the local to the universal level and gave them greater depth by linking them to the problems of human development as a whole.

The globalisation of networks for the promulgation of religious edicts (fatwas), for example, has provided conservatives and traditionalists with new platforms from which to attack all discourses that favour liberation, development and the participation of women in production and creative work.

Unfortunately, the continued sway of such throwbacks and restrictions, which attempt to mobilise tradition to resolve the problems of Arab society by excluding women and isolating them at home, represents an obvious paradox. It may be seen as a mark of social failure, of the inability of educational institutions and civil society organisations, despite their increasing numbers, to promote the values of modern knowledge and political reform across society. These are the values conducive to expanding the scope of freedom, the rotation of power and the spirit of citizenship. They are essential in overcoming a conservatism that remains blind to historical change and its role in the development of people's perceptions of themselves and their societies ('Abdellatif, 1997, 67-80).

WOMEN IN THE ARAB NOVEL

IN SEARCH OF A NEW IMAGE OF ARAB WOMEN

This section offers specific examples of the role played by the novel in the process of inculcating, or weakening and critiquing, conservative social values related to the situation of women.

The Arab novel has played a salutary role in destroying the stereotypes of women in our society. The sensitivity of Arab novels to social issues and their presentation of those issues in their true diversity and richness have helped to overcome prevailing stereotypes. The latter have now been replaced in the world of fiction by scores of examples and images that reflect a wide range of women in the reality of Arab society.

In attempting to build new perceptions of women in fiction, the Arab novel has not only attacked female stereotypes; it has also shed light on aspects of women's oppression and their role as accessories in perpetuating male

The women's movement now has access to new digital means and methods of enhancing public awareness of women's issues.

Unfortunately, the globalisation of networks for the promulgation of religious edicts (fatwas) has provided conservatives and traditionalists with new platforms.

The Arab novel has played a salutary role in destroying the stereotypes of women in our society.

dominance. The confusion and contradictions that many Arabic novels reveal point to conditions of cultural refraction that may be interpreted in the context of the global environment and the transitional historical stage through which Arab societies are passing, both of which frame the world of fiction.

IMAGES OF WOMEN REFRACTED IN THE ARAB NOVEL

In order to discover the worlds of women in the Arab novel, one relies on the concept of the "image" and uses it in order to understand the role of the novel in constructing and reconstructing women's situations in society. Although "images" are too restrictive to represent the full diversity of daily life and are a feature specific to fictional narration, they enable one to establish models that, to a great extent, reflect and express the struggles and changes taking place in reality.

The concern here is with how these images interact with one another, for the Arabic novel presents a dossier of givens that reflect different degrees of awareness among Arab female and male authors of the challenges in Arab society in all their complexity, instability and flux.

The worlds constructed by major Arabic novelists (such as Najib Mahfuz, 'Abd al-Rahman Munif, Hanna Mina and others) in their narrative innovation sharply observe the transformations and contradictions of the Arab social situation in all its aspects, especially male-female relationships.

Najib Mahfuz's fictional world, for instance, which is the most prominent world establishing narrative spaces in contemporary Arabic writing, observes, records and builds in the imagination a vast array of images and situations relating to women in the Egyptian society and the Arab society. His trilogy, *Bayn al-Qasrayn* (Between the Two Palaces), *Qasr al-Shawq* (The Palace of Longing) and *al-Sukkariyya* (Sugar Street, a neighbourhood in Cairo), published in the 1960s (Mahfuz, in Arabic, 1957 A,B,C), produces a panorama of women in Arab society across half a century. The varied pictures of women and their suffering, captured with a large degree of accuracy, reflect scenes, situations and events

and various aspects of death, life, sadness, happiness, violence, pleasure, marriage and divorce. All this produces a fictional world that sometimes outdoes the real one in its complications and richness.

It is possible to speak of a network of values connected to a certain vision of women threaded through the succession of events and the multiplicity of women in the trilogy. "Ahmad 'Abd al-Jawad's" dominance in the books, as a representative of masculine patriarchal despotism, contrasts with the submissiveness of his wife, "Amina", in all her psychological and social constriction. Trying to picture the worlds of Amina, who is fortified by her submission, enables people to understand through the novel what they sometimes fail to see accurately and clearly in life. However, following the couple's progeny through its large social world provides evidence of a qualitative change in how society views women. This is what makes the Report team speak of the trilogy as a history of despotism and the manners of submission, as women have lived it and continue to live through it. It is, at the same time, also a history of the splits and contradictions created by domination and submission – one that prompts stirrings of rebellion against a reality that no longer fits in with the new values of contemporary society.

This does not mean that the contrast is constructed simply. The personalities of other men – "Abd al-Jawad's" sons – and other personalities – "Amina's" daughters and grand daughters – do reflect other aspects of the two major personalities whether dormant or exposed. It is possible to read in "Fahmi's" romanticism, "Kamal's" hesitation and "Yasin's" recklessness (Yasin is Kamal's first son by his first wife) something that explains the relationship between Amina and her daughters, "Khadija and 'A'isha".

The same thing applies to grandchildren. In *al-Sukkariyyah*, which is the last part of the trilogy, the age of Marxist revolutionary women is reached and the readers find themselves face to face with indications of the birth of a new society, a world that combines many contradictions and in which one finds contradictory kinds of values. At this specific point, the development of the novel matches

The confusions and contradictions that many Arabic novels reveal point to conditions of cultural refraction.

All this produces a fictional world that sometimes outdoes the real one in its complications and richness.

the complexities of the real situation through which Arab societies actually lived, wherein relationships between men and women are fraught with contradictions such that the values of inferiority and liberation coexist amid images of imitation, collusion and role reversals. Thus a situational novel mirroring reality can become a lamp that helps to shed light on the real world.

NOVELS WRITTEN BY WOMEN: THE BEGINNINGS OF INDIVIDUAL CONSCIOUSNESS AND FIRST CONFRONTATIONS WITH THE CULTURE OF INFERIORITY

The images of women created by female Arab novelists provide readers with a vocabulary for approaching assumptions about women's inferiority and ways to overcome such thinking. These writings seek to open up new creative space in the Arab novel in support of new, alternative values. The trend starts with the appearance of the novel *Ana Ahya* (I Live) (Ba'labakki, 1958), the published works of Colette Khoury such as *Ayyam ma'ah* (Days with Him) and *Layla Wahida* (A Single Night) (Khoury, 1959 and 1961), the novels of Ghada al-Samman, and those written by the generation of Ahlam Mustaghanimi, Huda Barakat, Radwa 'Ashur, Laila Al Atrash, Sahar Khalifa and Layla al-'Uthman. In these works, the reader is faced with an explanation of certain elements of female fragmentation. A number of elements and givens exist that approximate, in the imaginary world of fiction, the actual circumstances of the Arab woman, which testifies to the intersections and interventions between fiction and the reality of women in society.

In her textual study of novels by Arab women, Bothayna Sha'ban analyses their general characteristics as well as their success in portraying the various manifestations of woman's inferiority and exclusion and the attempts made to overcome this state as embodied in the novels' characters (Sha'ban, in Arabic, 1999). In another study of Arab women novelists, Fowziyah Abu-Khalid constructs a four-part template that allows her to transcend prevailing stereotypes of the woman (the woman as riddle, as seductress, as

symbol of cunning and as symbol of honour). This enables her to construct an approach that transforms the numerous events and images of these novels into patterns that can be analysed and that help to identify models of women as refracted by the worlds of the novel (Abu-Khalid, background paper for the Report).

According to Sha'ban, there are four main images of women to be found in women's novels: the woman deprived of her rights, the militant woman, the rebellious woman and the multiple woman. Each of these represents the different course of women's lives under common conditions in reality.

The image of the woman deprived of her rights, for example, is to be found very clearly in the novels *Misk Al-Ghazal* (The Musk of the Gazelle) (Al-Shaykh, 1988) and *Khadija wa-Sawsan* (Khadija and Sawsan) ('Ashur, 1989). The many facets of the image of the woman deprived of her rights that can be found in Arab creative writings must be acknowledged. These writings switch between capturing the deprivation of rights as represented in the unequal relations between men and women, and oppression at the hands of authority figures in social structures, as embodied in customs and traditions and tribal, sectarian, class or patriarchal systems. An example is the case of "Wasmiyya", who emerges from the sea in an early work of Layla Al-'Uthman. These writings present the reader with a further code reflecting the intertwining of two images: that of the woman deprived of her rights and reality (al-'Uthman, 2000). Another example is to be found in the novel by the Saudi writer Qumasha al-'Alyan (2000), *Untha Al-'Ankabut* (The Female Spider), in which she faithfully adheres to the literal meaning of the Saudi proverb that says "Break a girl's rib and ten more will grow" (Abu-Khalid, background paper for the Report).

The image of the woman as activist is cast in terms of the women's struggle in several novels from various Arab countries. They include *Al-Watan fi Al-'Aynayn* (The Cherished Motherland) (Na'na', 1979) and *Al-Ghulama* (The Tomboy) (Mamduh, 2000) as well as Sahar Khalifa's two works, *Al-Sabbar* (The Cactus) (1976) and *'Abbad Al-Shams* (The Sunflowers) (1984), which contain examples

Four images found in women's novels are those of the woman deprived of her rights, the militant, the rebellious and the multiple woman.

The images of women created by female Arab novelists provide readers with a vocabulary for approaching assumptions about women's inferiority and ways to overcome such thinking.

of Arab women active in the resistance in the occupied Palestinian territory. The Lebanese novelist Hanan Al-Shaykh, in her novel *Hikayat Zahra* (The Story of Zahra) (Al-Shaykh, 1980) describes the life and sufferings of a woman of the people in southern Lebanon during the civil war and the forms of resistance that express the capacities of human beings to face their destiny (Sha'ban, in Arabic, 1999, 168).

The image of the rebellious woman shatters the conventional portrait of the contented and unassuming female or of the beautiful and cunning she-devil. It transforms the woman into a positive actor in society's struggle to overcome the hierarchy condoned by the values of prevailing Arab culture. Images of rebellious women are instructive: they show that a woman's rebellion is not a negative value since the energy of revolt is directed towards building new values within society. While rebellion is usually read as a reaction to a specific reality, these images help one to fathom its inner dimensions and to understand the mental and emotional states through which blind imitation and stifling traditions within social relations may be confronted.

Novels of female rebellion represent a cry of protest in which the writers proclaim, through their protagonists, the need to end the age of tyranny in all its apparent and hidden forms. Consequently, the subject of freedom becomes a central starting point from which the female writer directs criticism at male domination and violence and gives voice to the woman as a human being in search of equality, freedom and citizenship.

The fourth and last model, referred to as the "multiple woman", provides an image that encompasses and transcends the other models. The term "multiple" here indicates splitting and fragmentation, and refers to multiple identities within one being, contradiction, collusion and hesitation. The model consists of a complex web of images of multiplicity, which no sooner complete themselves then they start anew and continue, expressing the birth pangs of Arab societies during their present transitional stage.

The multiplicity of this model not only expresses the woman's own self; it also touches upon the self of the group and of society, man and woman, woman and woman. According to

Abu-Khalid, it also deals with "the relationship between the emotional and the cerebral, the private and the public, the actual and the desired". In all these varied cases, one witness the situation of Arab women expressed through a diversity of lives (Abu-Khalid, background paper for the Report).

In Sahar Khalifa's "Memoirs of an Unrealistic Woman", the process by which the female stereotype is shaken is quite apparent in the writing. The process embodies a very careful narration of small details in that the text opens a window onto a woman who is both realistic and unrealistic, revealing the multiple in the one. In the beginning of the novel, she says, "I am the daughter of the inspector. I remained so until I got married and became the wife of a merchant. Sometimes I am both at the same time. When my husband wants to be ironic, he calls me 'the inspector's daughter' and when my father is angry he calls me 'the merchant's wife'". The contradiction exists between the internal, central self within and the social self accepted by others; the gap between what the protagonist considers to be the right understanding and balance and what others consider to be so is enormous. "For these reasons I found it convenient to appear stupid, so I kept my questions, my impressions and my tongue to myself" (Khalifa, 1986, 5).

In Ahlam Mustaghanimi's trilogy, *Dhakirat Al-Jasad* (The Memory of the Body), *Fawda Al-Hawass* (The Chaos of the Senses) and *'Abir Sabil* (Passerby), complex feminist worlds counter the male prejudice that places women in one single mould (Mustaghanimi, 1993, 1998, 2004).

The fourth image of women in Arab feminist novels can be found in the works of Huda Barakat and 'Ulwiya Subh, which depict a number of aspects of the civil war in Lebanon. It can also be found in Batul Al-Khudari's novels *Kam Badat Al-Sama' Qariba* (How Close Seemed the Sky) (2000) and *Ghayib* (Absent) (2004), which reflect the reality of Iraqi women under sanctions and then under the American occupation, and the problems of multisectarianism (Abu-Khalid, background paper for the Report).

Most of these novels illustrate the multiplicity of image of Arab women in the space once occupied by single, closed and paltry stereotypes whose inadequacy appears only the greater amid the social transformations that these works portend. The anxieties, fears and aspirations that they portray are not just those of characters in novels. Rather, they can be viewed as those of individuals facing their destiny in society with energy and determination, a spirit whose warmth and energy the Arab novel captures in its pursuit of a society of equality between the sexes.

THE IMAGE OF ARAB WOMEN IN FILMS

PATTERNS OF STEREOTYPING

The most representative model of women in the Arab cinema is that found in Egyptian films during Egyptian cinema's 70 years of output. These are films that reflect society's perception of itself and of the relationships among its members in the light of both prevailing and emerging social values.

Studies of the image of women in Arab films variously describe and define the aspects of this image. The first studies went hand in hand with the achievements of the Egyptian cinema themselves and revealed that female characters in the films produced between 1962 and 1972 (410 films) showed the following diversity, by percentage:

43.4%	no given profession
20.0%	housewives, wives, divorcees, widows, spinsters
20.5%	working women
10.5%	students
9.5%	artists
5.4%	delinquents

Farid, background paper for the Report.

The most significant, and by far the highest, percentage is that of women without any profession, i.e., women who are simply females. In fact, the woman as just a female accounts for more than 80 per cent of women's roles in commercial Arab films, and this portrayal has had the greatest influence on the public. In such films, the woman is a cunning devil who seeks nothing but pleasure, marital or extra-marital. All she wants is to catch a man, any man, since this is every woman's highest goal (Ramzi, 2004, 177).

Another study of the main characteristics of the cinema in the 1990s lists 31 films produced between 1990 and 2000 and records the following criticisms:

- Shortcomings in the presentation and embodiment of the image of women, and the confinement of the latter to a number of similar models, with the purpose of titillating the public;
- An exaggerated representation of the violence perpetrated by, and against, women;
- The political roles featured in the sample turn out to be largely superficial and unconvincing and have little to do with women's actual roles in life;
- During the 1990s, the films neglected the problems facing peasant and working women, concentrating only on modern urban women without, however, reflecting the various dimensions of their personality as human beings;
- The films offered no portrayals of an exemplary woman who could be counted on to remain steadfast in the face of problems;
- Women's social, political and cultural roles were conspicuously absent from the films, indicating that Arab cinema shows no concern for the evolution of women's position in Arab societies (Farid, background paper for the Report).

Notwithstanding such criticism, it can be said that Arab cinema has, at times, played an important role by raising public awareness of women's issues and the injustice that has beset them as a result of traditions or unfair laws. Here it is worth mentioning Fatin 'Abd Al-Wahhab's movie, "al-Ustahda Fatima" ("Mrs. Fatima") (1952 – starring Fatin Hamama and Kamal Al-Shinnawi), which depicts the story of a female lawyer confronting her fiancé's resistance to her working by challenging him and proving her professional competence. The actress Fatin Hamama played many roles depicting women who struggle through poverty, crime, oppression and submission.

The woman as just a female accounts for over 80 per cent of women's roles in commercial Arab films.

The Arab cinema, at times, has played an important role by raising public awareness of women's issues and the injustice that has beset them as a result of traditions or unfair laws.

In Henry Barakat's *"Du'a al-Karawan"* ("The Call of the Curlew", 1959, starring Fatin Hamama, Ahmed Mazhar, Amina Rizq and Zahra al-'Ula), a woman experiences the pain of rape, poverty and psychological and spiritual torture before she finds love. This proves to be the path of her deliverance from this earthly hell, in the person of a man distinguished from others by his humanity. In another Barakat movie, *"Afwah wa-Aranib"* ("Mouths and Rabbits", 1977, Fatin Hamama, Mahmud Yasin, and Farid Shawqi), a woman lives the reality of poverty and misery and faces her man-made destiny (forgery of a marriage contract in exchange for money) before the truth is revealed in the last moments. Another Fatin Hamama movie sheds light on the trials of women through divorce. Sa'id Marzuq's *"Uridu Hallan"* ("I Need a Solution", 1975, starring Fatin Hamama, Rushdi Abaza and Amina Rizq) tells the story of a woman who finds it impossible to live with her husband, asks for divorce and undergoes an agonising ordeal before she finally receives it.

LOVE, FREEDOM AND VIOLENCE

In the second half of 2004, a storm broke upon Egyptian film-making and the Arab world after the Egyptian film, *"Bahibb is-Sima"* ("I Love the Cinema"), directed by Usama Fawzi, caused a public outcry. The film presents the character of a Coptic woman who suffers from sexual deprivation because of her husband's religious extremism and enters into a sexual relationship with another man. The censors first refused to let the film be released, then allowed it after cutting some scenes, and then reduced some of the cuts. Nevertheless, private individuals and institutions took the film to court and asked for it to be banned. More significantly, both Al-Azhar and the Coptic Church made common cause against the film.

A second major outcry occurred in 2005 and concerned the Egyptian film, *"Al-Bahithat 'an Al-Hurriyya"* ("Women Searching for Freedom"), directed by Inas Al-Dighaydi. The film deals with the problems of three women from Egypt, Lebanon and Morocco living in Paris and searching for the freedom that they had lost in their own countries. Scores of

articles were written against the film, which was dubbed "Women in Search of Sex". Posters were vandalised and there was a general call for people not to see the film. The director was subjected to numerous false accusations and received several death threats.

In Syria, Muhammad Malas directed the film "Bab Al-Maqam" about a true incident that took place in Aleppo at the beginning of the new millennium when a young Syrian killed his sister because she loved to sing the songs of Umm Kulthum at home. According to her father, if she loved those songs, she must have been in love, and if she was in love, "she had committed a shameful act". Though made over a year ago, the film has yet to be shown to the public.

In the same context, the films made in Algeria, Morocco and Tunisia have been increasingly concerned with matters considered taboo, such as problems of sexual violence, the unfairness of laws, and problems of marginalisation and exclusion. This new type of film-making targets and rejects the perception of women as inferior, thus giving greater depth to the role of the new cinema as a force opposed to male dominance.

The most important contribution of Arab cinema to challenging society's sexual hierarchy is its graphic exposure of the broken spirit of submissive women. Such films openly confront inherited values of submission legitimised by obsolete traditions.

Arab cinema plays a dual role stemming from its commercial nature. On the one hand, using the power of moving images to purvey stereotypes, it generalises values of sexual discrimination. At the same time, particularly with the new cinema emerging in more than one Arab country, it sends progressive messages that reflect the wishes of new generations of women seeking freedom and self-assertion in order to realise their full human potential without being diminished or demeaned.

The films made in Algeria, Morocco and Tunisia have been increasingly concerned with matters considered taboo.

The new cinema emerging in more than one Arab country, sends progressive messages that reflect the wishes of new generations of women seeking freedom and self-assertion in order to realise their full human potential without being diminished or demeaned.

WOMEN IN THE CULTURE OF INFORMATION

THE BATTLE FOR THE IMAGE OF WOMEN IN ARAB SOCIETY'S TRANSITIONAL PHASE

The information revolution has swept through societies, creating new cultural institutions capable of influencing and guiding public opinion. Images broadcast instantaneously around the world dominate the news and thrust themselves into people's lives. The psychological and social results of this revolution have yet to be really understood since it is a new experience not only in the Arab region but globally, albeit in varying degrees.

Television and, most dramatically, the Internet underwent a major expansion at the end of the last century and the beginning of the third millennium. Similarly, as noted earlier, modern media have come to assume an important cultural role in connection with women's issues and in popularising images of women in the Arab mind and social ethos, transforming them into actors in the larger changes in society.

In this context, television serials are especially influential in challenging or entrenching the traditional image of women, as are the television advertisements that portray women through different images and settings. This is true not only of Arab television channels but of that vast network of channels that enter Arab homes and present Arab families with images and attitudes that contain more disparities than similarities. The Arab living room has become a veritable battleground in the war of information. Like the wars over the interpretation of Islamic jurisprudence, the clash of popular proverbs and the struggles of Arab civil society to promote the values of freedom and equality, it is a conflict that confronts citizens with different and confusing choices (Ramzi, 2004, 19).

Portrayals of women in the media reflect the contradictions of the transitional period that Arab societies are going through, where a variety of images coexist with varying degrees of tolerance and where the dynamics of social reality support some images and challenge others. Contradiction is the outstanding characteristic of images of Arab women in the media as in society itself.

Women's presence on Arab television raises several questions but here the Report focuses on television's role in spreading and consolidating the idea of women's inferiority through programmes devoted to delivering religious edicts or fatwas. Other programmes will also be mentioned in order to underline some of the positive aspects that reflect the culture of development and change in Arab society.

"FATWAS" AND THE LIMITATIONS OF TRADITIONAL JURISPRUDENCE

Most Arab satellite channels produce religious programmes aimed at spreading an Islamic culture in response to changes taking place in the world. These programmes bear revealing titles such as "Religion and Society", "Shari'a and Life" and "Problems of a Contemporary Muslim". The language of the fatwa is very much in evidence in these programmes, which have turned certain sheikhs into celebrities and the public who ask questions into actors. This makes for lively debate, and it also produces effective propaganda.

In the programme "Shari'a and Life" shown by Al Jazeera, for example, the viewer finds several topics relating to family problems and gender relations. However, despite the moderate tone that characterises some of the episodes of this programme, most of its attitudes ultimately buttress a perception of women as inferior, taking their cue from a restrictive interpretation of texts and customs in Arab society (Touaiti, background paper for the Report).

If the changes presently taking place in Arab society require new efforts of interpretation by specialised jurists and scholars in order to produce laws appropriate to today, the fatwa channels, catapulted into public prominence by information technology, endorse values that are no longer suited to social transformation in Arab countries today (Touaiti, background paper for the Report).

As such, the fatwas broadcast in the media

Contradiction is the outstanding characteristic of images of Arab women in the media.

The fatwa channels, catapulted into public prominence by information technology, endorse values that are no longer suited to social transformation in our countries today.

An increasing number
of conservative
channels are
consolidating the
image of women on
the lower rungs of the
gender hierarchy.

An equally large and
increasing number of
channels that claim
modernity in fact
project a negative
portrayal of women,
seen as physical
bodies and mere
commodities.

have not broached the subject of independent reasoning in religious jurisprudence (ijtihad). They remain limited to efforts aimed at strengthening the existing gender hierarchy regardless of the changes that have taken place in society and through history. The jurists entrusted with the task of issuing fatwas are apparently out of touch with their world, insist on maintaining the prevalent patriarchal system of Arab societies and evidently see no need to modernise or develop Islamic jurisprudence in the light of new social realities.

OTHER MEDIA MESSAGES UNHELPFUL TO THE RISE OF WOMEN

Media events and activities in the Arab region are characterised by great and increasing diversity and a trend towards polarisation. This results in numerous negative outcomes for the rise of women in the Arab world.

On the one hand, an increasing number of conservative channels are consolidating the image of women on the lower rungs of the gender hierarchy. On the other hand, an equally large and increasing number of channels that claim modernity in fact project a negative portrayal of women, seen primarily as physical bodies and mere commodities, whether in advertisements or in video clips (song and dance routines) that tend towards indecency.

Despite the diversity of media messages, a large number of them carry values that celebrate the rise of the individual at the expense of the community and glamourise instant gratification, easy and quick profits, and flashy stardom. In other words, these messages do the work of modern advertising, which markets consumerism and pleasure. Such an industry downplays or excludes a culture of long-term effort, cooperation, solidarity and service to others. Some researchers consider that successful films are not just cinema productions; they have become vehicles for selling food, music, clothes and toys (Barber, in

French, 1999, 70-74). Of concern here is that these orientations often devalue women and cheapen their human dignity.

The Arab media often adopt strategies and criteria for work, recruitment and relations with other media and the public that come from operating within a larger global media system guided by a paternalistic business ideology (David, 1996).[1] Moreover, these Arab media operate in societies governed by strong central powers where the worlds of money, authority and the media intermingle in the shadow of fierce competition with Arab and Western satellite channels for a constrained advertising market. This makes most media channels run after a large Arab public with significant purchasing power, especially in the Gulf States.

The industry has preconceived ideas about this public, drawn primarily from Western media, and shows little sign of understanding the realities, changes and paradoxes that are operating within it. This is why some of these channels, in their early period of growth, turned to men for politics and to women for entertainment while encouraging the latter to believe that appearance on television by itself is a form of accomplishment. Such encouragement prompted many women to emphasise an attractive appearance, thereby creating a media trend that ended in reducing capable media women to their looks alone. However, this trend quickly receded thanks to fierce competition and other developments where superficial criteria of appearance alone were no longer sufficient and the requirement for success extended more to education, professionalism, mastery of languages and wide general knowledge (Kadiri, background paper for the Report).

---

[1] Studies conducted by the Global Media Monitoring Project on women's participation in the news in 70 countries have shown that women constitute 43 per cent of journalists but only 17 per cent of these conduct interviews and 29 per cent of women who are interviewed are victims of various accidents.

SUMMARY

This chapter has presented aspects and examples of the role played by certain cultural constructs in entrenching or challenging the inferior status of women in Arab societies. Diverse currents from the cultural heritage have been reviewed, some of whose formulations reflect a conservative stance that hinders society's evolutionary dynamic. Other elements aim at containing and indigenising the source texts of modernism within the culture and the society of the Arab countries.

It follows that the living dialectics that reflect prevailing cultural patterns in Arab societies must not be ignored. The birth pangs and tensions that attend women's changing situation in Arab society reflect the vitality of this process and indicate a movement in societal consciousness that should not be underestimated. The persistence of male dominance and its resistance to confrontation illustrate the difficulties facing the ongoing transformation. Breakthroughs achieved thus far by pioneering actors show that it is possible to transcend dominant conservative attitudes in this culture.

It is certain that this transformation will require a significant expansion of the practice of political, legal and theological interpretations that are conducive to the spread of values of enlightenment and the principles of human development that reinforce the larger liberation project in society.

CHAPTER SEVEN

SOCIAL STRUCTURES

Introduction

The previous chapter discussed the relation between a number of cultural constructs and the present situation of women in Arab countries. This chapter focuses on other components of the social context: embedded societal structures that have contributed to shaping the status of women.

As previous Reports have shown, through the focus on knowledge and freedom, the rise of women is a trend that straddles the moral and material dimensions of human development. It is important to take a holistic view of this subject as these dimensions have a direct impact on cultural constructs on one hand and human procreation on the other.

With both dimensions in mind, the Report now considers the contributions of traditional and present-day social institutions to the moral and material situation of women in the Arab countries.

TRADITIONAL STRUCTURES: THE ENSHRINING OF MALE DOMINANCE AND WOMEN'S FIRST STEPS TO ESCAPE

What is the nature of the relationship between the patriarchal order and Arab societal structures? What effects do the "Arab marriage",[1] kinship relationships and the different social arrangements for human reproduction have on the relationship between the sexes? Do traditional societal structures protect patriarchy? Is it still the case that "tribal, clan or familial loyalties are among the most entrenched and influential of traditional loyalties in contemporary Arab life?" Do societal structures determine cultural forms or are the two reciprocally related and thus intertwined? What are the features of continuity and rupture, of the constant and the variable, in Arab social structures, and how were they influenced by economic, cultural and political factors?

This chapter tries to deconstruct the elements of Arab social structures and their various components to identify their influence and roles in people's lives. It also explores continuities and discontinuities between social and other institutions that together make up the arsenal defending the patriarchal order.

IN THE BEGINNING WAS THE AGNATE

Historically, kinship relations in Arab society were founded on the agnate (al-'asaba) or relative on the father's side. In the Arabic language and in Arab custom, the agnate is the principle of cohesion within the tribe. The agnate, according to the Bedouin and to Ibn Manzur's Lisan al-'Arab, is based on *al-taraf* (paternity, filiation) and *al-janib* (fraternity, relationship to the paternal uncle). To resort to a mathematical expression, these are the horizontal and vertical axes closest to the supporting base (the man), the closest of his paternal male kin who are capable of fighting, providing reinforcement, conquering and defending (Ibn Manzur, in Arabic, 1982). A man is surrounded and protected by (and also responsible towards) a preceding generation (the father), a succeeding generation (the sons) and a coexisting generation (brothers and paternal male cousins).

There is no doubt that this community, with

The rise of women straddles the moral and material dimensions of human development.

Historically, kinship relations in Arab society were founded on the agnate or relative on the father's side.

---

[1] Marriage that gives precedence to endogamy, and especially marriage to the paternal uncle's son, within the tribe, clan and extended family.

its collective nature, was a result of arduous living conditions owing to the scarcity of natural resources and the competition for them as tribal populations grew. However, it provided the groundwork for what anthropologists refer to as the "Arab marriage", or, in other words, the keeping of assets within the clan in terms of human reproduction and means of subsistence. The salient features of this marriage persisted in urban conditions and were consolidated in one way or another by the emergence of a socio-political order that was to play an important role in the infrastructure of states and old forms of political power. While the agnate divests a man of his individual identity and obliges him to act in solidarity with blood loyalties, it also ensures that he obtains, in return, privileges within the same group. In the patriarchal order, women pay the highest price for this trade off by becoming the main instrument of reproduction in the tribe, with whatever special status this position may at times entail.

Arab tribal society was deeply aware of women's structural and functional importance to it. The tribe considered honour, respect and protection as a unity linking each of its members with the whole and thus also the women with the whole. This made any denigration of the tribe's women a matter touching the very heart of their kinfolk's security and standing. Hence the exercise of power over women within the tribe was, in practice, a nuanced matter, flexible enough to allow women some room for manoeuvre within its otherwise rigid social structure. This limited space permitted women to participate in tribal life and explore their potential, on the one hand, and it also enabled society to redefine gender roles with each forward movement that it took.

It is important to point out here that many of the features of the "Arab marriage" in its traditional anthropological sense are today the subjects of social criticism. Nor is this criticism exclusively civil and political; multiple forms of objection to the traditional concepts of blood money and honour crimes are now quite common. Furthermore, the survey shows that the Arab public today is inclined to prohibit the marriage of first-degree relatives, especially in Lebanon and Jordan (Box 7-1).

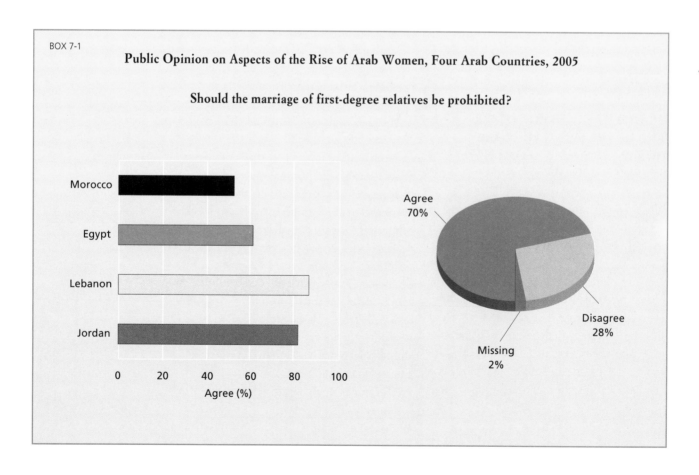

BOX 7-1

Public Opinion on Aspects of the Rise of Arab Women, Four Arab Countries, 2005

Should the marriage of first-degree relatives be prohibited?

THE ARAB TRIBE AND ISLAM

Islam brought with it the concept of the umma (the Islamic community) as an expression of collective identity to replace that of the tribe. However, the Arab tribes, primarily the Bedouin but also the urban-rural tribes, preserved their authoritarian structures unchanged. This is evident in the manner in which the tribes came to meet the Prophet Muhammad and in their pledge of allegiance to him, in their later apostasy and in their subsequent return to Islam.

As the Arab armies sallied forth beyond the Arabian Peninsula, the tribes that went to war advanced on other countries together with their women and children, there to set up their camps and residences according to their tribal divisions. In the army administration, their contribution and their combat were organised according to lineage. The chief of the tribe acted as the intermediary of the Caliphate with his tribe, as the guardian in charge of matters pertaining to his people who was responsible for their actions. In most of the armies of the early conquests, the banners of different tribes accompanied the banner of the army leadership, which comprised a general commander and local commanders representing each of the kinship groups involved in the fighting (al-Duri, in Arabic, 1978, 18-21). Hence, the army appeared to be a quasi-tribal, quasi-regional alliance with one single leadership appointed by the Caliphate and several group leaders determined by the balance of power among those groups.

Although Islam established the notion of individual responsibility for both men and women, as well as emphasising respect for both sexes and their rights, the socio-cultural and economic-political formation of the conquests imposed limits on these broad vistas that the new religion had opened for women.

Mudawi al-Rashid considers that the rights that Islam had granted women, such as the right to inherit, were a threat to the economic unity of tribal society in both desert-nomadic and urban settings. Consequently, the Arab tribes, and especially the pastoral Bedouin or those that settled after Islam, adopted two measures to ensure the sustained economic vitality of the group. These tribes in practice forbade their women from inheriting, despite their legal right to do so, and they continued to apply their law forcing a woman to marry her paternal uncle's son (her first cousin on that side of the family) or relative. Thus, the tribe guaranteed that there would be no dispersal of its economy or its resources such as land and herds (Al-Rasheed, background paper for the Report). In addition, the successive wars on which the Arab-Islamic empire and its civilisation were built led to the system of segregating the sexes as well as polygamy, including with women slaves.

Arguably, only during two periods in history was this structure ever radically shaken in such a way as to change its constituents and functions and the nature of human relationships.

The first occurred along with enhancement of the state's capital towards the end of the Umayyad Caliphate and throughout the Abbasid Caliphate (eighth century C.E. onwards). This was when Arab urban societies evolved, bustling with civic activities and marked by the rise of loyalties based on profession, class and region. This period saw the spread of exogamy and the political economy of women slaves at the expense of the family and the tribe. However, the fall of Baghdad in 10 February 1258 and the decline of Arab-Islamic civilisation curbed these changes, which had yielded an Arab urban society whose backbone, according to the Sufis, was "the perfect man" (in today's parlance, a society based on civic concord that guarantees basic human rights).

The second time was with the penetration of Western capitalism, starting from the beginning of the nineteenth century. Along with this came the stifling of pre-capitalist socio-economic order and the emergence of new institutions and social forces. The latter dealt several blows to tribal units based on patriarchal family labour, as did the consequent adoption by women of new professions – in education, journalism, factories, government administration and free enterprise – side by side with men.

The rights that Islam had granted women, such as the right to inherit, were a threat to the economic unity of tribal society.

Although Islam established the notion of individual responsibility for both men and women, as well as emphasising respect for both sexes and their rights, the socio-cultural and economic-political formation of the conquests imposed limits on these broad vistas that the new religion had opened for women.

AUTHORITARIANISM AND TRIBAL SOLIDARITY

The emergence of the modern authoritarian system played a large role in curtailing the growth of civil institutions. Though European capitalism brought with it new values relating to the state, politics and society, these did not originate in local conditions. Hence the cycle through which the foundations of a law-based state and an independent civil society resistant to oppression might have been established was never completed. Thus, the nation-state faced little difficulty in compromising the foundations of citizenship and civil relations, especially in the name of overcoming its economic dependency and catching up with developed countries. The blow dealt to basic freedoms left its mark on the nascent civil society, which found no public space for itself. In the absence of a viable civil society that could protect citizens' interests, exposed individuals turned their backs on the institutions of civil society and sought the rude shelter of the tribal and clan system, with its feudal and organic bonds. Tribal and clan systems continue to command the devoted allegiance of individuals in such groups through just and unjust causes alike because they are a last recourse for identity, solidarity, security and self-defence. They represent the sole viable definition of an "us".

As Hisham Sharabi puts it, "Tribal loyalty is not an expression of creed; rather, it arises from essential needs. The survival of clannish bonds or denominational loyalties in neo-patriarchal society points to the firm association between modern patriarchy and primitive forms. Neither the city, the society nor the state succeeded in developing social formations capable of producing authentic alternative structures" (Sharabi, in Arabic, 1993, 48). The relevance of this point today can better be appreciated when one sees the stubborn impediments to the launching of a real civil society capable of filling the vacuum in the role of the state in protecting the rights of people and in guaranteeing public participation. This leads to two hypotheses. The first maintains that the structure of the Arab city, with its marked rural complexion, cannot support the type of civil society that grew up and thrived

in the embrace of European cities (Al-Falih, in Arabic, 2002, 34). The second hypothesis is that the ruling authorities' expropriation of civic initiatives is chiefly responsible for the persistence of tribal and clan relationships in modern city life. In other words, tribal systems, values and customs have been perpetuated under the auspices of the non-democratic state that annulled alternative forms of mediation between the individual and the state (Haytham Manna', in Arabic, 1986, 12ff).

The systematic elimination of nascent civil society – which had begun to take root in the Arab world at the beginning of the twentieth century – by restricting its freedom to organise, mobilise, marshal solidarity and support, and express a selfhood independent of political authority led individuals and groups to revert to pre-urban, tribal solidarities. The return to organic ties was evident in the continuing strength of the patriarchal clan and, in certain cases, of the sect (as a form that combines a social structure and a confessional-political formation). In both cases, the security of the organic group (clan, tribe and sect) took precedence over the individual's rights. It remains noticeable how the Arab family still clusters around the pivotal authority of the paterfamilias as the source of security in a system that deprives individuals of their basic rights and impedes the process of individualisation necessary for the articulation of the rights of persons per se.

There is no doubt that, initially, the all-encompassing Arab state contributed to a greater participation by women in the public sphere, professional fields and social services as well as to the relative protection of motherhood and childhood. In the end, however, bureaucratic rigidity, the expropriation of different social and civic initiatives and the sponsoring of the system of the local dignitary (a man, of course) as the sole intermediary between authority and society held women's rights hostage to the nature and vicissitudes of power. The mutually supportive relationship between state authority and patriarchy saw to it that these early achievements soon became opportunities for personal (male) gain, and the position of women continued to deteriorate in the absence of defenders in civil society, which remained hobbled.

Tribal and clan systems...are a last recourse for identity, solidarity, security and self-defence.

The systematic elimination of nascent civil society – which had begun to take root in the Arab world at the beginning of the twentieth century – by restricting its freedom to organise, mobilise, marshal solidarity and support, and express a selfhood independent of political authority led individuals and groups to revert to pre-urban, tribal solidarities.

It follows that confrontation between authority and the nuclei of civil society, in which the former suppressed the latter, prompted a greater regression towards kinship structures, which took on new forms as the arrangements for human reproduction intermingled with those for producing a new material and cultural basis of life. As Halim Barakat puts it, "The solidarity of the extended family arises from the necessities of cooperation" (Barakat, in Arabic, 1985, 82).

THE AGNATE AND WOMEN IN CONTEMPORARY SOCIETIES

The Arab agnate and the Arab marriage are not a given, nor do they remain in the pristine Bedouin condition that delineated their historical features. Nor is clannism limited to Arabs, either in the racial or the national sense, as some of its features can be seen in the Amazight and Kurdish societies. Nevertheless, the clan and the tribe as essential refuges in political authoritarian structures, both historical and contemporary, continue to make their presence felt in relationships between the sexes. They also continue to place women in a complex construct that combines the social, religious and legal and that determines women's role and fate. Their features are conspicuous in the Arabian Peninsula, in the countryside in Iraq, Egypt, Syria, Jordan, in North Africa, Somalia and Mauritania.

The kinship group that those living in the Arab world coexist with to this day is a human group whose patriarchal authority enshrines the hereditary nature of the economic structure and positions of leadership and sovereignty at the expense of women, who are marginalised, surviving in forms adapted to contemporary capitalism. The relationships of human reproduction in Arab societies enshrine, for women, endogamous marriage and marriage to the paternal uncle's son from the tribe while retaining for males the freedom to choose either endogamous or exogamous marriage. Kinship groups established this mode of marriage in the first place as a man's right and a form of compulsion for woman in order to ensure the cohesiveness of agnates through blood relations. As noted earlier, this absolute "right" of the paternal uncle's son is associated

> BOX 7-2
> ### Su'ad Joseph: Patriarchy and Development in the Arab world
>
> Most writers in the Arab world agree that the ties and values of kinship are the cornerstone of Arab societies. They preserve and strengthen the individual's sense of self and identity and shape his social situation. They are also the primary source of economic security. Kinship determines political membership and weaves a web of essential political resources. It also determines religious identities. The centrality of kinship has an impact on patriarchy: kinship transfers patriarchy to all social aspects of life.
>
> Source: Joseph, in Arabic, 2005.

with a system of values and relationships that seek to exercise full control over the reproductive capacity of the tribe's women in order to preserve inherited economic assets and social power. It consequently confines a woman and deprives her of her right to choose her partner.

In some academic circles, this social mode is considered an important factor in, and an inseparable part of, the social heritage that contributes to male domination and woman's deprivation of her most basic rights. This heritage, moreover, is an important factor in the social oppression of women whereby the process of domination and punishment becomes a collective one exercised by the kin, as a "group," against the individual, the "woman". Nor is this confined to marriage choices; it also extends to blood money, honour crimes and the absence of a clear dividing line between the personal and the familial.

A number of Arab sociologists consider that, despite the fact that the tribe is nowadays a thing of the past, its values and concepts remain in place in the Arab consciousness as does its approach to women's issues, even in the absence of a pastoral economy and Bedouinism. Others, by contrast, register changes in kinship relationships as socio-economic units following the expansion in the system of services, state control over the facilities of life and the widening of the scope of bureaucratic employment (Barakat, in Arabic, 1985, 178).

It is no secret that Arab women remain subject to domination, both spiritual and material, directly and indirectly. The degree and strength of this domination vary from one environment to the other depending on the stage of life through which the woman is passing. Hence, any analysis of domination must take

The clan and the tribe as essential refuges in political authoritarian structures...continue to make their presence felt in relationships between the sexes.

Patriarchal authority enshrines the hereditary nature of the economic structure and positions of leadership and sovereignty at the expense of women.

into account what is referred to as a woman's life cycle. The young girl may suffer from more domination than her married or elderly sister. Likewise, a woman who is both married and a mother may be exposed to forms of domination that differ from those to which an elderly woman, divorcee, spinster or widow is exposed. Thus, domination is not an absolute condition suffered by all women to the same degree and in the same strength and form. Rather, it is a condition that varies depending on age, social status, economic circumstances, the political standing of the family and the prevailing socio-political system, among other factors that affect a woman's experience in society.

Relations within the family have continued to be governed by the father's authority over his children and the husband's over his wife, under the sway of the patriarchal order. Those changes to which the framework of the family has been subjected, including the reaffirmation of the nuclear at the expense of the extended family and the decline in the percentage of marriage to kin, cannot be considered far-reaching. Nor can it be claimed that they have affected the functional nature of the relationship between the sexes in any profound way. While they have mitigated some forms of discrimination between men and women, they have not effected a qualitative change in the nature of the relationships between them except in limited circles.

In many of its aspects, progress in relationships between the sexes has been to the benefit of men, for whom new possibilities opened and who obtained personal freedoms not granted to women, which in turn entrenched male control at the economic, social, cultural, legal and political levels. Simultaneously, women did not have access to the education and professional employment necessary to alter the balance of power in a manner that would make for more compatibility. Even when a woman, driven by economic necessity, succeeds in obtaining a wage-paying job, she, in many cases, receives no real, substantial assistance from the man with housework. Nor does her employment allow her to fulfil herself in that it is meant only to help raise the family's standard of living. This is much less true, however, of the economically empowered female cadre, where there has been a

marked spread of domestic service in households. Unlike the situation in developed countries, wage labour in the poor socio-economic sectors does not allow for the individualisation of women or vulnerable groups. This is owing to the weakness of individualisation in general and its complete absence when it comes to the weakest element of society, meaning women, who do not enjoy rights as individuals per se. Indeed, only in the dominant value system can a woman enjoy any rights – through her role in the group and/or the home.

An economic crisis in the region occurred as a result of the collapse of production patterns that were unable to adapt to global conditions without alternative infrastructures. The crisis was exacerbated by the generalisation of wage labour at the expense of traditional social arrangements that guaranteed a certain social and economic protection and the economic ascendance of the global centre over local or regional networks of exchange. This crisis was manifested in the export of "industrial garbage" in environmental, social and economic terms to the countries of the South. New financial elites were created many of which were characterised by corruption and tyranny within a global system that harvested the greater part of countries' assets. This has resulted in the escalating impoverishment of the middle classes and the marginalisation of the intermediary sectors that provide temporary occupations in many Arab countries. The situation poses a real dilemma for male graduates, especially those with higher and specialised qualifications, who are forced to compete with women for whatever jobs exist in the crisis-ridden employment market of many Arab countries.

FROM THE HOME TO SOCIETY

Quite a few Arab women are no longer prisoners of the house. Educational and professional opportunities have afforded them greater participation in public life although some parents still view these opportunities as a means to improve a woman's chances of making a good marriage and enhancing her ability to take care of her husband and children. In addition, some still believe it necessary to control a woman's freedoms to protect family honour, justifying segregation of the sexes in schools and society and insisting that women should wear the hijab (veil).

The public opinion survey, however, places the wearing of the hijab squarely in the "respect for individual freedoms" bracket (Box 7-3). Moreover, it supports the mingling of the sexes at work and indeed in society as a whole even though co-education at all stages is widely unfavoured, especially in Jordan and Egypt (Box 7-4).

The belief in the subordination of women remains, of course, subject to variation across different countries, social classes, standards of living and general consciousness. It manifests itself particularly in the poorer social strata whose social role and status are marginal and hence who enjoy less legal and social protection and are more influenced by the dominant patriarchal culture. The Arab desert and rural areas continue to be subject to family clan practices, kinship, loyalty to tribal authority and the dominance of customs, traditions and rituals that reflect a semi-self-sufficient economy resting on land, cattle, climate and simple craft industries (Al-Rasheed, background paper for the Report). The absence of free time and multiplication of the tasks assigned to women also play a role. In these contexts, women live under patriarchal relationships that prohibit their participation in most public activities and that confine their roles to reproduction, domestic chores and pastoral and agricultural work for survival.

Studies of the Arab world point out that Arab women are largely absent from the political domain, only thinly present in the social welfare sector, shadowy in the civil and cultural spheres, insignificant in the economic domain, and almost completely missing from the official religious domain. Authoritarian structures have not, however, excluded women from journalism, the legal profession, pharmacology, engineering, medicine, modern technology and the institutions of the communications revolution.

Whatever such social progress meant to preceding generations, today Arab societies face a situation of social conflict. This is the clash between a large segment that entered the labour market and public life when these constituted a continuation of the traditional social order and another segment whose entry into the free-enterprise labour market indicates its embarkation on a new vision of personal

The belief in the subordination of women remains, of course, subject to variation across different countries, social classes, standards of living and general consciousness.

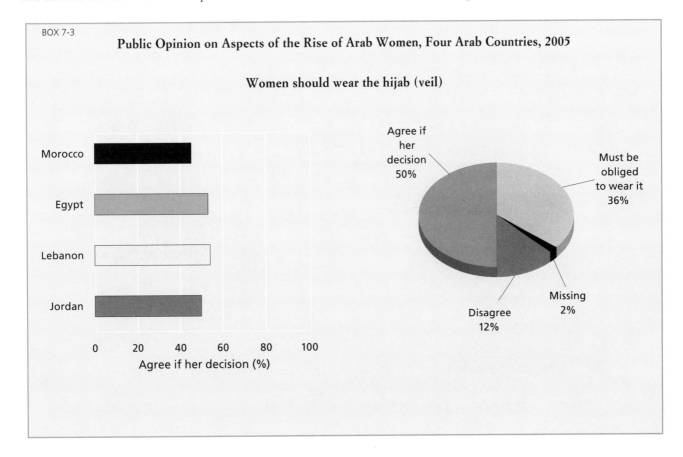

BOX 7-3

Public Opinion on Aspects of the Rise of Arab Women, Four Arab Countries, 2005

Women should wear the hijab (veil)

BOX 7-4

Public Opinion on Aspects of the Rise of Arab Women, Four Arab Countries, 2005

Co-education at all stages is good

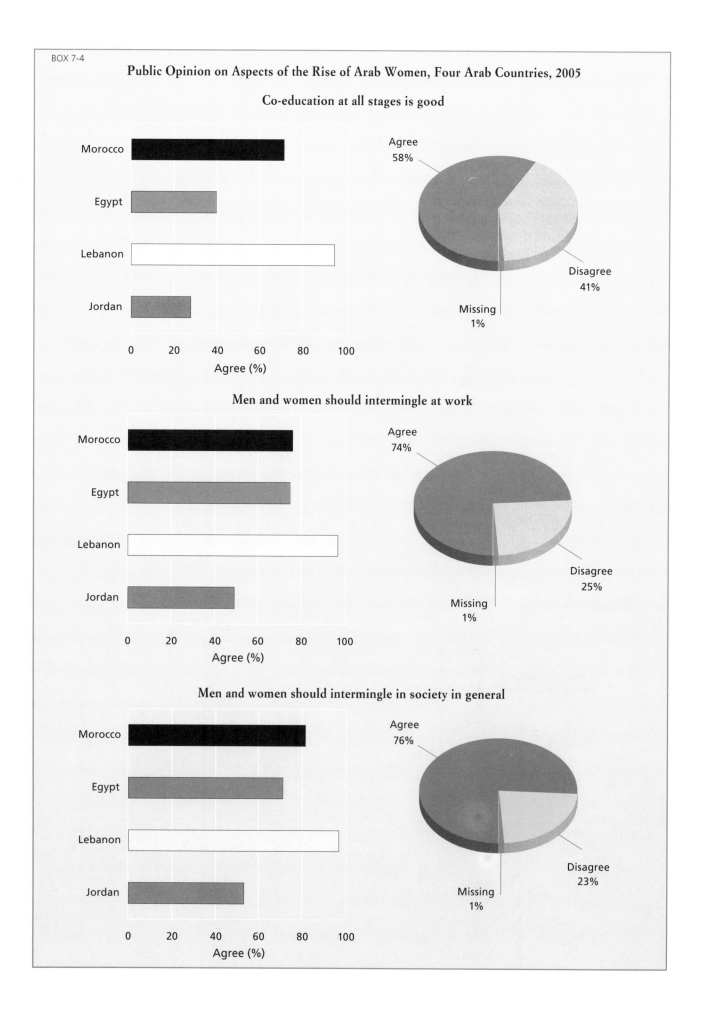

Men and women should intermingle at work

Men and women should intermingle in society in general

BOX 7-5

The Self-reliance of Bedouin Women

'Amasha al-Husayn, from Badiyat al-Shamiyya, is in her fifties. She herds and milks cattle, collects firewood, kneads and bakes on bread tins and washes clothes by hand. Her husband is disabled, and although she lives in a woollen tent at a distance from the other tents, she has no time to feel lonely because she is always busy spinning wool on her hand spindle. She does not hide her smile as she shakes her head and says, "Our life is tough. It's all about seasons. And if we don't do things for ourselves, no one will do them for us. Those who offer us favours ask for much more in return, and some demand that we provide them with ghee and cheese for free – we get nothing from them but trouble".

Source: 'Abd al-Hamid, in Arabic, 1990.

relations. This latter segment espouses the nuclear family, individualisation and financial independence and finds roles different from those ordained by horizontal social relations. Women, however, pay a high price under the rules of the new market, which provide them with insecure temporary work contracts and humiliating work conditions in free economic zones. Such conditions often represent no real gain for women despite the fact that these very changes (flexible working hours; opportunities to work from home) could, in principle, facilitate a reconciliation of wage labour with family-building. The absence of social policies that protect women and the limited services that the government provides play a role in making women victims rather than beneficiaries of flexible work opportunities.

REBELLION PRODUCES INTERMEDIATE FORMS OF FREEDOM

The very strength of social structures based on traditional tribal values should not conceal the strong and violent reactions expressing rebellion and revolution. Rebellion against restrictive and undemocratic family relations does not, however, lay the foundations of a culture based on equal rights and obligations. Individual revolt does not produce a culture with a human rights structure that considers woman's rights an indivisible part of its identity and content.

It is important to note that submission to, or rebellion against, kinship bonds does not necessarily flow from religious considerations, given that, on both sides, one can find veiled women or women who participate in public work through educational or charitable religious institutions. Likewise, because of the restrictions placed on the freedom to congregate and organise in most Arab countries, one cannot construe the many social gatherings, diwaniyyas (literary salons, in the Gulf States), cliques, zajal evenings, holiday and Ramadan celebrations and get-togethers by religious communities as simply a return to traditional lifestyles. Many of these can be ascribed to the natural human need to congregate and communicate that authoritarian laws have frustrated, which in turn has produced intermediate customs that represent a grey zone between kinship and civic forms of free assembly.

In the absence of political freedoms, women often use social conditions and traditional practices to defend their rights by establishing charitable, medical or literary women's or family organisations or they form delegations to demand their rights, benefiting from the social space that is allowed in some countries that nevertheless restrict their ideological space. In certain countries, such as Saudi Arabia and the Gulf States, tribal structures internalised by the state nevertheless permit women a margin of protection and participation. Some resourceful women have taken advantage of this narrow latitude to establish civil society groups for women's rights. Ironically, the latter represent agents of social change born from the very structures and practices that have given the authoritarian state its restraining presence.

At the same time, the negative dimensions of such organic relations intensify whenever the margin of freedom to congregate or to conduct public activity independent of the state is narrowed. Rebellion against clan structures or tribalism is not confined to the non-religious milieu just as it is not restricted to a specific social class. However, traditional organic forms of solidarity are more pronounced in rural areas, shantytowns and urban migrants' quarters, i.e.,

Women pay a high price under the rules of the new market, which provides them with insecure temporary work contracts and humiliating work conditions.

The very strength of social structures based on traditional tribal values should not conceal the strong expressions of rebellion and revolution.

the poorer sectors, where many residents feel the need for the protection against misery offered by traditional, patriarchal bonds of loyalty.

The interaction of the political with the economic, and the national with the international, exerts an influence on the forms of relationships between women and men. The reduction of the economic rights of the majority, the erosion of state sovereignty under new forms of interference in the Arab region and the resulting increase in popular discontent have made it easier for conservative ideologues to penetrate the social discourse. Some have succeeded in persuading the public to link the defence of social identity to national sovereignty and to a limited definition of identity that confines the role of women and considers their rise to be a patent foreign product.

Nevertheless, in some societies, the qualitative accumulation of small victories by woman has caused patriarchal hegemony to retreat to varying degrees. Notwithstanding the enormous burden of heritage and custom and the difficult hurdles that they present to women, today's woman is different from her mother or her grandmother. Thanks to her awareness, her education, her entry into work, the cultural achievements of twentieth-century liberationist thought and victories in the field of human rights, the modern Arab woman has far more options. In addition, women often rise to the challenge of coping with harsh changes and have proven to be the protectors of social existence in exceptionally tough situations as is the case with women under siege and sanctions in Iraq, and under the multifaceted violence afflicting Iraq, Lebanon, the occupied Palestinian territory and the Sudan. In this sense, social structures have not prevented women from becoming active players, in different degrees and forms, in the transition that some Arab countries are undergoing.

In another context, while the growing closeness between the sexes has not put an end to discrimination, it has led to less conflicted relationships in many places and has caused the parental relationship to steer a course closer to democracy than to authoritarianism. Children therefore have developed more confidence in themselves and in those whom they uphold as role models for the building of character and achievement of success, especially given that the mother's image and their status in her eyes are an essential element in the formation of their positive self-image.

Evidently, Arab society must find a new equilibrium for men and women based on nominal equality. To achieve this will require making provisions for basic freedoms and constructing a civil society in the broader sense of the term. This would constitute a capacious network of forms of congregation that lie between the individual and the state; it would occupy the public space that government cannot fill since the latter cannot represent all people on all issues. A political and civic programme of this kind would have to be tied to a guarantee of (one would like to say, a right to) the minimum economic and social necessities for a humanly acceptable life. Otherwise, a confrontation between the state and tribal-based structures will simply entail relocating the latter's victims from a miserable hut to a state of homelessness. Such a civic covenant between society and the state to guarantee the rights of individuals, both men and women, would meet three pressing needs. It would constitute the foundation of citizens' basic security in self and body, provide a public assurance that both sexes have roles to play in the home and in society, and acknowledge all citizens' right to education and medical treatment.

The natural right to build free and independent associations is a key element in the transition from the individual to the citizen-individual. The more self-evident the importance of civic groups becomes to people, the more feasible it becomes to move from focusing on the private condition of some women to addressing the general condition of all women through new forms of cooperation, mutual assistance and civic participation. With the principle of equality established by overwhelming societal demand and in law, civic culture could challenge the culture of discrimination from a position of strength, armed with the material resources to replace those offered by clan ties and not solely with an intellectual critique of their shortcomings. In order to face the submission and subordination that the spirit of tribal solidarity imposes, it is necessary to instil the human and legal

THE FAMILY AND THE STATUS OF WOMEN

The family continues to be the first institution that reproduces patriarchal relationships and values through gender discrimination. The family carries out the processes of socialisation and instilling obedience in an atmosphere charged with contradictions and with stifling structural problems and as part of mechanisms of censorship and coercion. The woman thus becomes the creature rather than the creator of her destiny or, in other words, as just noted, a participant in reproducing the system that governs her.

In spite of woman's entry into education and professional life, the question of sex, good repute and honour has barely been affected by the major structural transformations that took place in the past century. In patriarchal societies where men hold sway over all aspects of life, whether social, cultural, political or economic, a woman's right to personal and bodily safety is still the object of an abuse accepted under prevailing values. This is because the denial of the individual in a woman brings with it the denial of her individual private rights in conflict with the definition of private life and the foundations of personhood as described in the Universal Declaration of Human Rights. At the same time, this abuse itself confronts society with an important contradiction wherever organic and civil relationships coexist: even if weak individualisation has prevented women's access to certain rights whose defence the community (tribe, clan, extended family) has failed to assure, that same community has been the source and intermediary for other guarantees and rights. This implies the need to search in certain Arab societies for new forms and means for the rise of women that do not exclude the mediation of the organic community.

Pressures on women increase in violence at times of crisis when a woman becomes subject to surveillance. The man's right of disposal over her body, his watch over it, his use of it,

his concealment, denial and punishment of it all become more blatant. This violence in turn comes into play to intensify the feminisation of human poverty, political misery, dependency, domination and alienation.

To the present day, personal status laws constitute the most symbolic and profound embodiment of this problem. Matrimony is the first and foremost form of the relationship between women and men whether in the conscious or unconscious mind, in religion or society, in terms of the permissible or prohibited and the sacred or the desecrated. These laws may well represent the most pronounced embodiment of the relationship between Arab patriarchy and the forbidden and the taboo. The most important laws that relate to gender discrimination find refuge in it, allowing family laws to become the lair protecting culture, traditions and customs, whether religious or popular. Observing the debates and events in the course of drafting and promulgating personal status laws in Algeria, Lebanon, Morocco and Syria, it is impossible not to conclude that nationalising or privatising half a country's economy may be easier than issuing one civil, elective personal status law in an Islamic country.

A woman's body, as Lama Abu 'Awda says, moves within a social sphere the boundaries of which are clearly defined and demarcated. Each of these boundaries is guarded by a collection of regulatory laws and restraining prohibitions that women are supposed not to breach, which explains provisions in Arab laws that absolve or reduce punishment for those who commit honour crimes. Hence the importance of introducing human rights legislation to punish the latter crimes. In a questionnaire put to a number of girls who took refuge in shelters in Switzerland, the sentence repeated by most of them was, "Murdering me costs the murderer nothing". The sentiments expressed in the statement "Stop Killing Women", signed by tens of thousands of people inside and outside Syria, give an idea of the size and significance of this social and legal cancer: "Always, and in different forms and under different pretexts, provision 548 of the criminal code, and provisions 239 and 242 of that same law, arrive to free the killer from his punishment,

A woman's right to personal and bodily safety is still the object of an abuse accepted under prevailing values.

A woman's body moves within a social sphere, the boundaries of which are clearly defined and demarcated.

usually in a matter of months not more than the number of fingers of one hand.

Once it is honour, another a bolt of anger or religious sensitivity! Nonetheless it is the blood of female youth that is being squandered by murderers who deserve no less than the fate of their likes". (18/9/2005).

Elements of modernity intertwined in Arab traditional culture, within and across countries, cannot be generalised. Nevertheless, large social sectors still remain closer to tradition than to innovation. A girl pays a heavy price for asserting her independence in milieus where individualisation in both the human rights and economic senses is weak. Therefore, from an early age, marriage becomes her persistent goal so that she may fulfil her needs without a sense of sin, guilt or self-loathing and also in order to gain acceptance and respect from her mother, family and society as a married woman. It is likely that the first man she meets will be the one to whom she will become committed, especially in conservative societies. Of course, that is true only if her parents do not make the decision for her, without her having prior or sufficient acquaintance with the man. Early marriage is not simply a social custom; it has been transformed into a social problem with many causes and dimensions.

A study undertaken in the United Arab Emirates reveals that the strong social pressures on girls and their loss of love and understanding from their families through quarrels often bring out in them violent patterns of behaviour. There are three times as many incidents of suicide among girls are there are among young men[2] (Daguerre, background paper for the Report).

THE EQUIVOCAL RELATIONSHIP BETWEEN MEN AND WOMEN IN ARAB SOCIETIES: SYNERGY AND CONFLICT

Some feminist literature places women and men in diametrically opposed positions. This portrayal, notwithstanding the widespread discrimination against women in Arab countries, is a simplification that contradicts the nature of this basic relationship within Arab societies.

One can refer, for example, to the first supporters of women's rights – men such as Butrus Al-Bustani, who wrote about the importance of educating girls; Qasim Amin, who called for the liberation of women; Al-Tahir al-Haddad, Abdul Rahman al-Kawakibi and so on. These men considered women's issues to be an integral part of a wider issue, namely, the modernisation and progress of society. In the same way, there are among the ranks of those who support the rise of women today a large number of male human rights activists, who base their position on the conviction that the liberation of women is central to the cause of human rights.

Alternative images of fatherhood

Generalising the figure of the father as a tyrant and a symbol of oppression results in the submission of family members to his will and their surrender to his oppression. It is a trend that lays the foundation for the rejection of change within society and excludes the formation of the questioning, critical and independent individual while popularising images of fixity, stagnation and surrender to prevailing ideas. These images do not exactly reflect the reality of Arab societies, and if one thinks about daily life, one can identify differing forms of fatherhood in its interaction with women, whether wives or daughters.

Consider, for example, the participation of Arab women in all forms of resistance, especially in the occupied Palestinian territory. Here, one sees other faces of fatherhood, the kind that encouraged women to express their political views and take action accordingly even though the representation of women was not commensurate, which is a separate issue.

Compare three consecutive generations of women in any Arab country and one can trace the sequence of development between generations as well as real qualitative advances by women in specialised academic knowledge, in employment and its various spheres and in participation in public affairs. To these may be added women's management of reproduction, their development of psychological maturity and self-confidence,

Early marriage is not simply a social custom: it has been transformed into a social problem with many causes and dimensions.

There are among the ranks of those who support the rise of women today a large number of male human rights activists.

---

[2] The study covered 82 cases of attempted suicide (by girls) whose ages ranged from 15 to 24 years. Most were unmarried, and this was not the first attempt for about one quarter of the cases.

and the use of modern technology, which has helped even women of limited education to interact with global cultures.

These fleeting images reveal positive changes in the Arab family, which have led to limited improvements in some forms of conduct among youth and to a change in the system of prohibitions. It should be remembered that the difference in the liberalism of fathers and how they use their authority depends on their educational and economic levels and social environment. In addition, the fact must not be overlooked that these changes are taking place at a social, a national and a global level and are linked to political and economic stages of development.

Fathers, particularly the educated, support the education of their daughters and wives, encourage them to advance in their professions and provide them with the means to do so. The evidence is apparent in the increased number of women at universities, the prominence of females in some faculties and professions, and females' high levels of achievement as students. Some fathers even defend their daughters' right to choose how they dress, against the dictates of hard-line religious movements.

There are numerous aspects of a man's relationship with his wife and children, and these are too complex to characterise as repressive, harsh and tyrannical. How is one to deal with love and solidarity between father and daughter, with the individual female whose self-confidence is due to her father's support (and here it should be noted that women who are successful in their family and professional lives have strong relationships with their fathers) and with the protection and support that the father may provide?

The Arab family is too complex a unit to be summed up in one generalised, absolute characterisation nor is it possible to be content with a negative stereotype of fatherhood.[3] Such one-sided images will lead to surrender to authority figures and give credence to the notion that rebelling against authoritarianism or changing the status quo is impossible. Additionally, to think that all women are simply repressed diminishes the value of their lives, implying that these are wasted. Under the shadow of any harsh environment, a woman can yet take possession of her freedom by taking decisions that will give her unexpected happiness. This freedom is the source of the inspiration for change (Bayoumi, background paper for the Report).

It is not possible to be content with a negative stereotype of fatherhood.

BOX 7-6

A Father Supportive of His Daughter

I do not know how, during the sixties of the last century, my father Rafiq, who had not attended university and had never travelled, conceived an enthusiasm for the idea of sending me, when I was still in my twenties, to complete my studies in Paris.

Neither my mother's misgivings nor the warnings of my relatives and the family's fear for their daughter in "Paris, the City of Sin" reduced his determination, which, I confess, surpassed my own courage. I knew Paris only from picture postcards of the Eiffel Tower and the names of some French authors, the Sorbonne, and the Latin Quarter.

I grew up in a large family. Nine children filled the chairs, windows and beds of the house, six girls and three boys who competed equally at school and university while transforming the home into a large study which our father supplied with more books than he did loaves of bread.

My father would be filled with joy during the successive exam periods, when the home was transformed into books, pens and revision lessons, while he mocked the neighbours who wondered "why he bothered with educating the girls" (especially when they were going to be not his in the end but their husbands'). He maintained his pioneering stance at a time and in a village where a girl's attendance at school (close to home, of course) was effectively a matter of sitting in a waiting room passing the time till the groom should come.

We were six girls and people used to say of Rafiq that he loved his girls so much that God had rewarded him by granting his prayers in abundance. But to my father, who had read a lot and was influenced by the authors of the Arab Renaissance and their calls for liberation, each one of us was a creative project. Through us, he could revive the example of my educated, cultured and daring mother, distinguished amongst the women of her generation, by betting on his faith in the importance of women through the education of his daughters.

When the whole village went to Beirut Airport on my departure for Paris to bid me farewell with tears, yearning and counsel, my father did not burden my happiness with any traditional advice. He did, however, weave an invisible conspiracy between us and bestow upon me the burden and sweetness of being a pioneer. I felt like the heroines of the plays we acted at school: I would either stumble and be struck down by the gods or succeed and blaze a trail for all the girls of my generation.

A deep obsession came over me with the idea that I should be perfect, as repayment for my father's generosity, without letting my eye be destroyed by all the new things that I would see, or my heart, eager as it was to meet every desire and joy.

But my father, who waited for my letters so that he could read the exciting parts out loud to neighbours and visitors, was my constant ally during my periods of calm and of excitement, of faltering and of radiance. He asked for no reward other than that I should succeed, and experience the feeling of natural equality and savour every brilliant flash of this life that had been given to me. This was the secret pact which linked his daring to my responsiveness, feeding his ambition that he relived through me and my ancient desire to explore the magic of the unknown to the limit.

Instead of the father rewarding his daughter, I became the daughter trying through her success to reward her father.

When I look at myself today, after storing up all those human and intellectual experiences which my father granted me through my adventurous journey—albeit in a bag that contained nothing but yearning, amazement and challenge—and I look at the girls in my village, exactly half a century after all that, I find that every girl refers, even today, to my father's example and the course of my life. They do so to convince their fathers that educating girls and allowing them to travel in order to study are the recipe for success, the model and the path for the future of the women of this century.

Ilham Kallab, Beirut. 19/July/2005.

---

[3] See (Bayoumi, in Arabic, 1998, 260). The field study underlines the father's positive role in encouraging his daughters to become aware of public affairs and practice political criticism. This contributes to strengthening their personalities and to their confidence and boldness. It confirms the importance to women of having a positive paternal authority since this is reflected in their marriage and their choice of a partner who holds similar political views regardless of his class or sectarian affiliation. It subsequently influences the upbringing of their children in terms of forming their personalities and providing opportunities for them to make their own choices (272).

SOCIALISATION AND EDUCATION (CURRICULA AND METHODS OF PEDAGOGY AND EVALUATION)

A transition from conformity to creativity in socialisation and education requires "a spiritual and cultural maturity in the family" that does not distinguish between female and male.

Socialisation and education are subjects that bring people face to face with the complex, multi-faceted character of the relationship between the sexes in the Arab world that makes it difficult to borrow models or copy solutions or even benefit fully from generalised experience-sharing. In its broad lines, the issues of socialisation and education are like two walls that sometimes face each other and sometimes intersect.

The first wall is that of traditional upbringing. This may be, at least apparently, the more solid and profound of the two in that it is the product of a long historical process and in so far as modern advances have not found another wall to replace it. This wall is built out of the historical, religious and popular elements of culture. In some places, the "structure" Islamises customs and traditions; in others, it imposes on religion more than it can take. On the whole, however, conservative forces have rarely had reason to complain about its overall reinforcement of tradition, including gender roles.

BOX 7-7:

Mohamad Mahdi Al-Jawahiri: Teach Her!

Teach her! Disgrace enough it is for you and for her that you should consider knowledge a shame And backwardness enough it is for us that we have not taken care of small matters. Teach her! Provide her with enough refinement to make her spirit great. To improve the management of a people, prove that you can manage a house. By your contempt for women today you have made men more contemptible.

In school curricula, the gap between women's progress and stereotyped images of women remains enormous.

The second wall is the West, as the most imposing source of ideas of liberation and equality, including gender equality, in our times. In this sense, Western culture and the Western lifestyle represented the main source of inspiration for most advocates of woman's liberation and equality between the sexes for over a century. In most cases, the "Western exemplar" was seen as a new Mecca. In other words, it was approached in a spirit of imitation and discipleship. The Report team concurs with the Egyptian poet, Georges Henein, when he says that such was the extent of intellectual mimicry among some people that it arrogated in advance the authority to manipulate and

assimilate minds and dispositions. To refer to Ahmed Chabchoub, one can speak of an "imposed modernity" and then a "desired modernity" (Chabchoub, in French, 2000:64) before moving to innovative modernity. It was only the latter stage that saw a transition from conformity (to history and to the West) to creativity in the field of socialisation and education. This transition, however, requires what Munir Bashshur calls "a spiritual and cultural maturity in the family that no longer distinguishes between female and male in education or anything else, just as it requires that the other various institutions of the society, including the school, be in tune with, strengthen and support this maturity. But from where will this maturity come, if not from the educational institutions, including the school, which thus become both the means to, and the object of reform?" (Bashshur, background paper for the Report).

If educational institutions are to become effective tools for attaining the required spiritual and social level, their components and elements and what they do must be examined as well as how they work and the dynamics that govern them in order to make some modifications.

Schools and public institutions that oversee child pedagogy – where these exist – complement the role of the family in shaping the mindset and values of the child. The school, which is a product of its time and place, can be no better than the society around it; and, in the Arab world, the influence of societies lacking institutions of just rule and civic relations is quite clear. The school comes in, after the parents, with a pedagogy that reproduces and instils the dominant social model of obedience, obscurantism and violence. School systems under authoritarian rule rarely give sufficient encouragement to initiative, discovery or the development of creative and critical faculties or personal aptitudes.

Despite the inroads that Arab women have made in political, social and economic fields, in school curricula the gap between such progress and stereotyped images of women remains enormous. These images invariably confine a woman to the roles of mother, homemaker and housekeeper. Most set texts in Arab schools delimit women to a specific context, usually domestic. The illustrations used in school curricula reveal this bias graphically. Rarely do the textbooks of the Ministry of Pedagogy and Education show a female reading a book or sitting in a library; the only place where she needs to be, in these books, is in the kitchen or the fields.

A study conducted by the Sociology Department of Damascus University discovered that public opinion favoured assigning women new roles but that educational curricula continue to consolidate the traditional view that a woman's place is at home. The study analysed pictures in a fourth-grade reading book and showed that educational curricula perpetuated the stereotypical view of the Arab woman as a figure behind, and not beside, the man. Seventy-five per cent of the pictures gave men a social advantage over women, who were usually dumped in the kitchen. There were no pictures of women in the workplace, the monopoly of men.

In a study entitled "The Upbringing of Female Children in Egypt", the researcher, Zaynab Shahin, writes: "a clear sexual bias against girls exists in all Egyptian publications". She points to the complete absence of girls' names from the covers of children's magazines, all of which bear male names such as "Micky", "Samir", "'Ala' al-Din" and "Bulbul". Her analysis of the content of these magazines shows that they attribute most of the positive characteristics and roles to males, girls being cast in roles characterised by weakness and lack of independent opinions or decision-making ability. These distortions become ingrained in the minds of young people from the first stages of education.

Palestinian schools are little different in this respect. The curriculum in schools in the West Bank and Gaza reinforces the traditional perception of women as inferior and simply ignores the changes in their situation since the 1920s. Women's image in school textbooks through all grades is "the mother who cooks while the father works; the mother who irons while daughter, Rabab, helps her in the kitchen; the father who reads the newspaper while son, Basim, plays in the yard". In a study by Aliya Al-'Asali on the portrayal of women in civics

textbooks from first to sixth grades, it emerges that women were not represented in any well-defined, methodical or fair way. When it came to professions, women were presented in a few confined occupations; they were not, as was the case with men, seen in a variety of professional roles. They were not represented as decision-makers, as men often were, or as mayors, judges, lawyers, association presidents, union presidents, school heads or directors of refugee camps, among the many imagined occupations that were entirely reserved for men. To date, Tunisia alone departs from this pattern and has made important changes to educational curricula.

Sociologists emphasise the crucial role of illustrations and pictures at the elementary school stage and the formative impressions that they leave on young minds, which are hard to alter later. A conspicuous feature of many Arab textbooks is their neglect of women's real capabilities, achievements and changing social horizons. The child is presented instead with images of a passive, marginalised creature without a will of her own, someone incapable of participating with a man in taking important decisions about her family or the course of her life. Appalled by these trivialising images, sociologists have demanded that some curricula be modified or withdrawn and that new guidelines and concepts be formulated for more substantial and truthful content reflecting Arab women's achievements by attaining high positions and succeeding in domains monopolised by men.

Pedagogy specialists have recommended injecting into school curricula the social, political and legal rights of the girl as well as her right to work, express her opinion and make choices. They have also called on Arab women to participate in drawing up educational policies, a task from which they have been almost completely excluded. Female participation in the setting of school syllabi was estimated at less than 8 per cent in a random sample of Arab educational curricula (Arab Commission for Human Rights, in Arabic, 2002).

Some Arab countries have moved to begin changing school curricula to make them compatible with recent social developments,

Seventy-five per cent of (4th-grade reading book) pictures gave men a social advantage over women, who were usually dumped in the kitchen.

A conspicuous feature of many Arab textbooks is their neglect of women's real capabilities, achievements and changing social horizons.

but it will take time for this new awareness to translate, through the pedagogical process, into sound patterns of behaviour. It is also imperative that the new cultural output and related practical measures seek to endow the pupil and the teacher with a new, more critical approach to values and principles, one stressing interpretation and deduction rather than simply inculcating the new as an alternative ideology.

It is not possible to talk of a "one-size-fits-all" educational model or recipe. The limited experience of people in the Arab world and elsewhere in the countries of the South has taught human society that it must avoid resorting to ideological discourse. Even when the teaching of human and women's rights is introduced into the academic repertoire, it must remain under the critical eye of the defenders of those rights. Raising the level of spiritual and cultural maturity goes beyond figures and percentages, just as it also transcends reorganisation or redistribution according to educational level and sex. It is a question of the spiritual and cultural sustenance available in the various circles of society, including the school. It is, in short, a more profound and difficult question and one that requires a stricter commitment, larger effort, and steadfast follow-through.

Education will be effective when it is permanent and comprehensive. It must embrace the school and the university. The family certainly has an important role to play, as do the audio-visual and written means of communication. The battle for the rise of Arab women will be won only if the creative potential of society, in the form of artists, writers, poets, journalists and union members, is set to work on its behalf.

SUMMARY

This chapter has tried to illuminate the complex and multisided nature of sexual discrimination in Arab societies. It shows the difficulty of treating the issue of women, starting with preconceptions and abstract data. Like all international treaties, the Convention on the Elimination of All Forms of Discrimination against Women and the Universal Declaration of Human Rights uphold broad human principles agreed to be universally true. Such normative texts, by their nature, cannot represent the particularity of local struggles on the ground or all civic demands on the international front. However idealistic and positive these conventions may be, unless their principles can be adapted and internalised, they will remain an assortment of texts imposed from on high on very different individuals and groups in highly diverse cultures, social conditions, living situations and life styles. It is indeed difficult, if not impossible, to incorporate these broad principles in any automatic or compulsory way into local value systems or to impose them wholesale on social groups, rural or urban, authoritarian or democratic, secular or religious.

It follows that the fundamental challenge for the supporters of the rise of women, whether male or female, is to discover the most successful means for the adoption of the concept of complete equality between the sexes by a highly heterogeneous public. How can meaning be given to texts that contradict local customs, using the cultural, social or political values specific to the rise of women? It is not easy to confront traditional beliefs or the prevailing socio-political system with an abbreviated reading of an external text extracted from the experiences of others. It is also not easy to forge a humane awareness of women's rights that would galvanise both the victims and their milieu without being able to interact directly with the personal beliefs and awareness of the parties to the relationship. The foregoing discussion has raised many of these questions, which chapter 10 attempts to address in detail.

CHAPTER EIGHT

LEGAL STRUCTURES

Introduction

Social and cultural structures affect women's issues by influencing values and establishing individual and institutional norms. Yet the state, through its enactment of laws, plays a direct role in organising social relations in a way that reflects on women's positions in any society. Thus, what is the impact of the law on women in the Arab world? That is to say, where does the Arab legislator stand on women's issues? Does this position conform to the Convention on the Elimination of All Forms of Discrimination against Women (CEDAW) and other international agreements? Are there legally sanctioned forms of discrimination on the basis of gender? How do practitioners of law – judges, legislators, interpreters of the law, law enforcement officials – regard the principle of equality between men and women?

The law is an explicit expression of the orientation and governing values of the state as well as its most practical and effective instrument for managing social relations, particularly in societies in which the state is prominent in regulating society. Consequently, women's status under law not only reveals how far the official establishment is committed to women's issues and the principle of equality, but it also indicates how popular culture views gender equality since the law is, to some extent, a reflection of this culture.

This chapter, therefore, begins by exploring the position of the Arab States on the ratification of the Convention. It considers, in particular, the reservations entered by Arab signatory parties to some of the articles of this Convention, reservations that have tended to void their ratification of substance. This is followed by an analysis of the provisions of Arab civil law relevant to

the principle of gender equality and finally by an assessment of the attitudes of Arab practitioners of law towards this principle.

ATTITUDES TOWARDS THE CONVENTION ON THE ELIMINATION OF ALL FORMS OF DISCRIMINATION AGAINST WOMEN

Most Arab States have signed and ratified the Convention on the Elimination of All Forms of Discrimination against Women (CEDAW) and are thus bound by its provisions, reservations excepted. There is also an optional protocol annexed to the Convention with regard to which no reservations may be entered and which grants individuals and groups the right to lodge grievances with the United Nations Committee on the Elimination of Discrimination against Women. The only Arab State to have signed this protocol is Libya.

Under Article 19 of the Vienna Convention on the Law of Treaties, a state may formulate reservations when ratifying or acceding to a treaty. The Vienna Convention defines a reservation as "a unilateral statement, however phrased or named, made by a State, when signing, ratifying, accepting, approving or acceding to a treaty, whereby it purports to exclude or to modify the legal effect of certain provisions of the treaty in their application to that State" (Article 2, Paragraph 1 (d)).

Article 28 of CEDAW, too, provides that States may enter reservations at the time of signature or ratification or accession to the treaty, but on the condition, as stated in Paragraph 2 of this article, that the reservations are not "incompatible with the object and purpose of the present Convention". Almost all Arab States Parties have exercised the right to enter reservations.

The reservations entered by Arab signatory parties to some of the articles of (CEDAW) have tended to void their ratification of substance.

Particularly worrying are reservations with regard to Article 2, which establishes the principle of equality of men and women.

CEDAW is one of the weakest links in the chain of international human rights law since it has weak implementing mechanisms and is encumbered with reservations.[1] Those entered by Arab States (and they are many) give cause for concern; they put in doubt the will to abide by the provisions of CEDAW. Particularly worrying are their reservations with regard to Article 2, which establishes the principle of equality of men and women, for reservations to this crucial article effectively render the ratifications meaningless.

The declarations and reservations entered by Arab States were confined to the following articles:

- Article 2, which stipulates equality before the law and prohibits discrimination against women in national constitutions and legislation (Egypt, Iraq, Libya, Morocco, Algeria, Bahrain, Syria, and UAE);
- Article 9, pertaining to nationality rights (Egypt, Tunisia, Iraq, Jordan, Morocco, Kuwait, Algeria, Lebanon, Saudi Arabia, Bahrain, Syria, UAE, and Oman);

TABLE 8-1

Ratification by Arab countries of CEDAW and declarations and reservations to it, as of 3 July 2006 (in ascending order, by date of ratification)

Country	Date of signature	Date of receipt of the instrument of ratification, accession or succession	Articles on which declarations and reservations are made						Notes
			2	7	9	15	16	29	
Egypt	16 July 1980	18 September 1981	*						All that contradicts shari'a
Yemen	30 May 1984	30 May 1984							-
Tunisia	24 July 1980	20 September 1985							
Iraq	13 August 1986	13 August 1986					*		All that requires Iraqi-Israeli relationships
Libya	16 May 1989	16 May 1989	*				*		
Jordan	3 December 1980	1 July 1992							
Morocco	21 June 1993	21 June 1993	*				*		
Kuwait	2 September 1994	2 September 1994					*		
Comoros	31 October 1994	31 October 1994							
Algeria	22 May 1996	22 May 1996							
Lebanon	21 April 1997	21 April 1997							
Djibouti	2 December 1998	2 December 1998							
Saudi Arabia	7 September 2000	7 September 2000							All that contradicts shari'a
Mauritania	10 May 2001	10 May 2001							All that contradicts shari'a
Bahrain	18 June 2002	18 June 2002							
Syria	28 March 2003	28 March 2003					*		All that requires Syrian-Israeli relationships
UAE	6 October 2004	6 October 2004							
Oman		7 February 2006							And all that contradicts shari'a
Qatar									
Sudan									
Somalia									

* All that contradicts shari'a

Source: www.un.org\womenwatch\daw\cedaw

[1] The total number of countries that ratified CEDAW reached 180 by March 2005, i.e., more than 90 per cent of the United Nations Member States. In spite of the fact that more than 20 countries have withdrawn their reservations – whether partially or totally – since the Fourth World Conference on Women in 1995, including countries such as France, Ireland, Lesotho and Mauritius, 54 countries still have reservations on important Articles of the Convention.

- Article 15, regarding women's equality with men in their legal capacity in civil matters (Tunisia, Jordan, Morocco, Algeria, Bahrain, Syria, UAE, and Oman);
- Article 16, relating to marriage and family relations (Egypt, Tunisia, Iraq, Libyan Arab Jamahiriya, Jordan, Morocco, Kuwait, Algeria, Lebanon, Bahrain, Syria, UAE, and Oman); and
- Article 29, pertaining to arbitration between States Parties and the referral of disputes over the interpretation or application of the Convention to the International Court of Justice (Egypt, Yemen, Tunisia, Iraq, Morocco, Kuwait, Algeria, Lebanon, Saudi Arabia, Bahrain, Syria, UAE, and Oman).

Arab States based their reservations to the provisions of the Convention on one of two grounds: that the articles concerned contradicted national legislation or that they conflicted with the provisions of shari'a (Islamic law). For the most part, the latter justification was applied specifically to individual provisions of the Convention that the signatory State deemed to conflict with shari'a (Egypt, Saudi Arabia, Mauritania and Oman). There were also cases in which the reservation was intended generally so as to absolve the State of its commitment to any provision of the Convention it deemed conflicted with shari'a (the reservation of Libya and Morocco to Article 2).

This was the case, for example, with the reservations entered by the Libya to this article which refer to the rules of inheritance in the shari'a as between women and men. Morocco had reservations on the same Article after noting the constitutional regulations affecting the inheritance of the throne which bar women from succession and adding the Personal Status Laws while arguing that women's rights differ from those of men, as derived from the shari'a, which, in turn, seeks to maintain equilibrium between them.

In this context, too, come the reservations made by Iraq, Libya, Morocco, Kuwait and Syria to Article 16, which refers to eliminating discrimination within marital and family relations, the reservation referring to contradictions between the article and the provisions of shari'a. (Amnesty International report on the reservations by countries of the Middle East and North Africa to the Convention on the Elimination of All Forms of Discrimination against Women, AI Index: IOR 51/009/2004).

Occasionally, States entered reservations without providing specific reasons, whether incompatibility with national legislation, conflict with shari'a or any other justification. This applies, for example, to the reservations made by Egypt and Kuwait to Article 9, Paragraph 2, regarding women's equality with men with respect to the nationality of their children.

Another type of reservation was entered only by Iraq and Syria, both of which insisted that their accession to the Convention should in no way entail dealings with Israel.

There are numerous examples of reservations entered on the grounds that the article concerned contradicted national legislation. They include: Algeria's reservations to Articles 9 (Paragraph 2), 15 (Paragraph 4) and 16; Kuwait's reservations to Article 9 (Paragraph 2); Morocco's reservations to Articles 2, 9 (Paragraph 2) and 15 (Paragraph 4); and Tunisia's reservations to Articles 9 (Paragraph 2), 15 (Paragraph 4) and 16. None of these States, moreover, restricted the duration of their reservation until national legislation could be reviewed and made consistent with CEDAW. Many provisions of the national legislation of these States are discriminatory. Instead of correcting these provisions to eliminate discrimination and to protect women, States that have entered reservations on such grounds are effectively enshrining discriminatory provisions in their national legislation.

In the case of reservations made by Arab countries citing incompatibility with shari'a, there is no consistent approach among the States that have entered reservations on this basis. It further appears that there is no consistent interpretation or definitive concept acceptable to all the Arab States for applying shari'a in reference to the provisions of the Convention.

It clearly is important for Arab States to take the initiative in reconsidering their reservations. Reference is made, in this regard, to the Beijing Declaration and Platform for Action of 1995, which stresses that, in order to protect the human rights of women, resort to reservations

Arab States based their reservations to convention on one of two grounds: that the articles concerned contradicted national legislation or that they conflicted with the provisions of shari'a .

States that have entered reservations on such grounds are effectively enshrining discriminatory provisions in their national legislation.

must be avoided as far as possible. The Declaration's Platform for Action recommends that states "limit the extent of any reservations to the Convention on the Elimination of All Forms of Discrimination against Women; formulate any such reservations as precisely and as narrowly as possible; ensure that no reservations are incompatible with the object and purpose of the Convention or otherwise incompatible with international treaty law, and regularly review them with a view to withdrawing them; and withdraw reservations that are contrary to the object and purpose of the Convention or which are otherwise incompatible with international treaty law".

In a number of Arab States and at the urging of civil society and some national institutions, legislative reviews are under way to reconsider the State's stand on reservations. This positive move deserves to be encouraged.

It is important that this move coincide with an intensification of efforts by the state and civil society institutions to raise awareness of the Convention among the public and in legislative circles and law enforcement agencies. The public survey indicated that only a small minority of the Arab public is familiar with CEDAW (Box 8-1). Similar efforts need to be undertaken to bring attention to the violations that take place both in the legislative context as well as in practice.

CONSTITUTIONAL CONDITIONS

The constitutions of most of the Arab States contain provisions affirming the principle of equality in general and the principle of equality between men and women in particular.[2] Some of these constitutions contain specific provisions for equality of men and women in, for example, employment in public office,[3]

political rights,[4] and rights and duties.[5] Some also contain provisions stipulating the right to equal opportunity;[6] affirming the state's obligation to preserve the family, to protect motherhood and children, and to guarantee a proper balance between women's duties towards their families and their work in society;[7] and prohibiting the employment of women in certain types of industries or at specified times of day.[8]

Much to their credit, Arab legislators, and constitutional lawmakers in particular, have respected the principle of gender differences and have made provision for regulating the effects of these differences legislatively. Unfortunately, in many areas of law, legislators have leaned so heavily towards the principle of gender differences that they have codified gender discrimination, thereby violating the principle of equality, which is sanctified in religious canons and rendered an international obligation under international treaties. Clearly, respect for gender differences in law is commendable only insofar as it does not give rise to discriminatory legislation incompatible with the values and spirit of the age.

WOMEN'S POLITICAL AND PUBLIC RIGHTS

National legislation in many Arab States contains provisions guaranteeing women's political rights and stipulating the principle of equality of men and women in the exercise of the right to participate in electoral processes and to stand for public office. Kuwait has recently joined those States whose legislations stipulate the enjoyment by women of their political rights on the same footing as men, following the legislative amendment passed in May 2005. In some countries, reference to

---

[2] Article 40 of the Egyptian constitution, Article 52 of the Jordanian constitution, Article 7 of the Lebanese constitution, Article 6 of the Tunisian constitution, Article 29 of the Algerian constitution, Article 5 of the Moroccan constitution and Article 18 of the Bahraini constitution.

[3] Article 14 of the Egyptian constitution, Article 22 of the Jordanian constitution and Article 12 of the Lebanese constitution.

[4] Article 21 of the Lebanese constitution and Article 8 of the Moroccan constitution.

[5] Article 6 of the Tunisian constitution and Article 31 of the Algerian constitution.

[6] For example, Article 8 of the Egyptian constitution.

[7] Articles 10 and 11 of the Egyptian constitution, for example.

[8] Article 69 of the Jordanian constitution.

BOX 8-1

Public Opinion on Aspects of the Rise of Arab Women, Four Arab Countries, 2005

Are you aware of CEDAW?

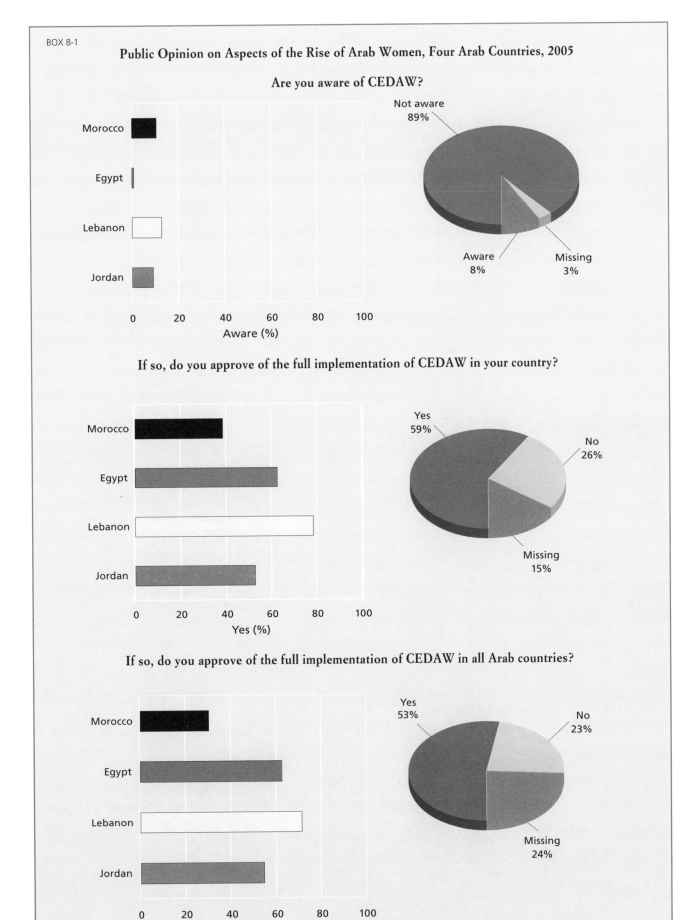

If so, do you approve of the full implementation of CEDAW in your country?

If so, do you approve of the full implementation of CEDAW in all Arab countries?

women's enjoyment of political rights appears in the text of the constitution itself.[9]

Nevertheless, despite these constitutional and legislative guarantees of women's right to political participation, the actual extent of this participation is still miniscule. The paltry representation of women in parliament in the Arab Mashreq (eastern Arab world) should compel States of this region to seriously consider emulating the example of the Arab Maghreb (North Africa), where most States have adopted quota systems to ensure a significant representation of women in their parliaments. Although Egypt had at one point adopted a form of quota system, this was later revoked on grounds of possible unconstitutionality even though the Supreme Constitutional Court had not issued a ruling to this effect.

PARLIAMENTARY QUOTA SYSTEMS FOR WOMEN

Contrary to what some imagine, parliamentary quota systems for women do not conflict with the principle of equality under law. Arab women have historically suffered enormous injustice from their political exclusion, and Arab laws have been traditionally formulated so as to perpetuate this exclusion. Indeed, laws have been entered on the books explicitly depriving women of the right to political participation. However, even when Arab legislators have taken steps to establish gender equality in political participation under law, such formal equality has been of little aid to women in a cultural and social environment inimical to women's acquisition and free exercise of their political rights. It follows, therefore, that affirmative legislative intervention to allocate a quota of parliamentary seats for women aims to help society make amends for its historical injustice against women and to make up for lost time in giving effect to the principle of equal opportunity enshrined in many Arab constitutions.

In this regard, Article 4 of CEDAW allowed temporary affirmative action, stating:

"Adoption by States Parties of temporary special measures aimed at accelerating de facto equality between men and women shall not be considered discrimination as defined in the present Convention, but shall in no way entail as a consequence the maintenance of unequal or separate standards; these measures shall be discontinued when the objectives of equality of opportunity and treatment have been achieved". Naturally, the affirmative measures referred to in this paragraph and that CEDAW regards as legitimate also include legislative measures. The stipulation that such measures are temporary is also understandable since the presumption is that these measures are intended to help overcome an historically entrenched condition, namely, the de facto inequality of women. However, that the Convention uses the term "temporary" in conjunction with the term "special measures" does not imply that the actual legislation effecting these measures must stipulate that they are time-bound.

The Beijing Declaration and Platform for Action urge governments to review the impact of their electoral systems on the political representation of women in elected bodies. It is precisely because of this impact that the Fifth Recommendation of the Committee on the Elimination of Discrimination against Women urged States Parties to make more use of temporary special measures such as positive action, preferential treatment or quota systems in representative bodies. Similar recommendations of the Inter-Parliamentary Union and the United Nations Commission on the Status of Women state that 30 per cent representation should be a minimum threshold for the quota of women in decision-making positions at the national level in both the legislative and executive domains (Farahat, in Arabic, 2003).

Experiences around the world in applying legislative instruments to enhance the parliamentary profile of women have varied. Some governments have applied quota stipulations to political party electoral lists (Finland, France, Norway and Sweden); others,

Parliamentary quota systems for women do not conflict with the principle of equality under law.

Laws have been entered on the books explicitly depriving women of the right to political participation.

Article 4 of CEDAW allowed temporary affirmative action, stating:

"Adoption by States Parties of temporary special measures aimed at accelerating de facto equality between men and women shall not be considered discrimination.

---

[9] See, for example, Article 21 of the Lebanese constitution, Article 8 of the Moroccan constitution, Articles 34, 35 and 42 of the Qatari constitution, Article 1 of the Egyptian Law for the Exercise of Political Rights, Article 2 of the Jordanian Chamber of Deputies Law, Article 2 of the Tunisian Electoral Code, and Article 1 of the Bahraini Law for the Exercise of Political Rights.

where there is a proportional parliamentary electoral system in which candidates run as individuals, reserve a set number of seats for women (Germany). Among the African countries to apply quota systems and realise a significant increase in the ratio of women to men in parliament are Eritrea, Ghana, Morocco and Senegal ('Abd al-Mun'im, in Arabic, 2002, 26).

These successes from other countries are examples for those Arab States that have not yet adopted affirmative action measures. The latter should overcome their hesitation and establish quota systems guaranteeing women a minimum level of representation in their parliaments whether elections to these bodies are held on the basis of individual candidatures or electoral lists.

LABOUR RELATIONS

Labour legislation in many Arab States contains provisions establishing legal protection for working women. Indeed, such protection is explicitly stipulated in some national constitutions, as is the case in the Jordanian and Egyptian constitutions (Article 69 and Article 11, respectively), and the labour laws of some States contain provisions explicitly prohibiting gender discrimination in the work place.[10]

Moreover, many States have laws guaranteeing women the right to maternity leave,[11] prohibiting the dismissal or termination of service of working women during maternity leave[12] or pregnancy,[13] and guaranteeing them the right to child care leave[14] and to a period for nursing infants.[15] In addition to the foregoing provisions, Jordanian labour law provides a male or female worker the right to take extended leave in order to accompany his or her spouse if the spouse has moved to a new work place located in another province or abroad (Article 68).

In spite of the equality in the right to work granted to women in most Arab corpuses of law, these same corpuses contain scattered restrictions on this right. The family laws in many Arab countries, for example, penalise wives who leave their matrimonial home for work without their husbands' consent. This occurs in spite of the fact that public opinion in countries such as Lebanon and Morocco tends to agree that a wife should be free to travel on her own (Box 8-2).

Libyan labour law prohibits the employment of women in work that does not suit "their nature".

Saudi Arabia has severe restrictions on women's right to work. A royal decree of 1985 prohibits women from employment in all fields of work apart from female education and nursing. It also prohibits women from associating with men in the workplace (Hijab and El-Solh, 2003).

As previously mentioned, many labour laws contain provisions prohibiting women from working at certain times (i.e., at night)[16] and in certain types of work even if there are stipulations for exceptions. Regardless of whether these provisions are ostensibly intended to protect women, they constitute an unwarranted restriction on women's right to work, as will be explained below.

To illustrate, Egypt's Labour Law prohibits the employment of women at night except under those conditions and circumstances stated by decree of the Minister of Manpower and Emigration. It further prohibits the employment of women in occupations harmful to their health or moral well-being, in physically

Arab States should overcome their hesitation and establish quota systems guaranteeing women a minimum level of representation in their parliaments.

The family laws in many Arab countries penalise wives who leave their matrimonial home for work without their husbands' consent.

---

[10] Article 5 of the Tunisian Labour Law.

[11] Article 91 of the Egyptian Labour Law, Article 61 of the Bahraini Labour Law, Article 25 of the Kuwaiti Labour Law, Article 37 of the Moroccan Labour Law and Article 64 of the Tunisian Labour Law.

[12] Article 92 of the Egyptian Labour Law and similar articles in other Arab legislation.

[13] Article 27 of the Jordanian Labour Law and similar articles in other Arab legislation.

[14] Article 94 of the Egyptian Law of the Child and Article 67 of the Jordanian Labour Law.

[15] Article 71 of the Egyptian Law of the Child and Article 70 of the Jordanian Labour law.

[16] See, for example, Articles 89 and 90 of the Egyptian Labour Law; Articles 67, 68, 77 and 78 of the Tunisian Labour Code; Articles 23 and 24 of the Kuwaiti Civil Sector Labour Law; and Articles 59 and 60 of the Bahraini Labour Law.

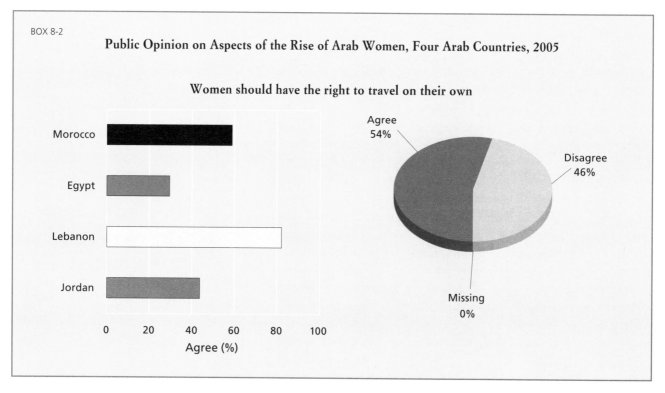

BOX 8-2

Public Opinion on Aspects of the Rise of Arab Women, Four Arab Countries, 2005

Women should have the right to travel on their own

Morocco

Egypt

Lebanon

Jordan

0   20   40   60   80   100

Agree (%)

Agree 54%

Disagree 46%

Missing 0%

The argument that prohibitions against the employment of women in certain occupations or at certain times of day are intended to protect women morally simply does not hold.

strenuous jobs and other types of employment designated by ministerial decree. The Minister of Manpower and Emigration has decreed that women may work at night in certain fields of work, such as the hotel industry and other institutions supervised by the Ministry of Tourism; theatres, cinemas and other such establishments that offer theatrical or musical entertainment; commercial establishments in ports that remain open at night; and hospitals, clinics, pharmacies and other health care establishments. Another ministerial decree prohibits the employment of women in such commercial activities as bars and gambling establishments; domestic service in furnished flats and boarding houses that do not fall under the supervision of the Ministry of Tourism; and dancing establishments unless the women are professional dancers or performers of legal age. It further prohibits women from working in the manufacture of alcoholic beverages, below ground in mines and quarries, in smelting furnaces, in the manufacture of explosives and in other industries that are hazardous to health.

Similar provisions exist in other Arab labour laws, albeit with variations in the types of employment permitted or prohibited to women. Article 27 of the UAE Labour Law

states, "Women may not be employed at night, by which term is meant a period of no less than 11 successive hours that includes the period between 10:00 p.m. and 7:00 a.m." Article 59 of the Bahraini Law for Employment in the Civil Sector states, "Women may not be employed at night between 8:00 p.m. and 7:00 a.m., exception being made for health care establishments and other facilities designated by a decree from the Ministry of Labour and Social Affairs".

In Lebanon, the women's rights movement was instrumental in repealing the prohibition of the employment of women at night.

The argument that prohibitions against the employment of women in certain occupations or at certain times of day are intended to protect women morally simply does not hold. In some of these countries, women are permitted to work in tourist facilities, bars, discotheques and other entertainment establishments licensed by the tourist authorities to operate around the clock. Nor does the argument that these laws aim to safeguard women's physical well-being by sparing them employment in strenuous activities stand up to scrutiny, for women in these countries engage in strenuous labour, in the home and in agriculture, for example, with no legal protection whatsoever. Indeed, the researcher is hard put to identify a standard criterion for such prohibitions; ultimately, they are governed by ad hoc and varying impressions as to what types of employment are or are not suitable for women. One is thus forced to conclude that Arab legislators have accorded themselves a mandate over women entitling them to expropriate their right to work.

One also observes that many Arab laws governing women's employment at night have so narrowed the scope for women's night employment as to render prohibition the rule and permission the exception. This contravenes the International Labour Organisation (ILO) Convention concerning Night Work of Women Employed in Industry (Revised 1948), which solely prohibits the employment of women at night in industrial undertakings as specifically defined by the Convention. Furthermore, the Arab legislator has gone to such extremes in restricting women's work as to prohibit their employment in entire fields of activity, in contravention of the principle of equal opportunity of men and women to work.

Many Arab States have signed the ILO Equal Remuneration Convention: Algeria, Djibouti, Egypt, Iraq, Jordan, Lebanon, Libya, Morocco, Saudi Arabia, Syria, Tunisia, the UAE and Yemen. Again, however, national legislation in this regard varies considerably. Some States explicitly provide for equality in remuneration in the same job (as is the case with Iraq, Kuwait, Libya and Syria, for example), others have no legal provision for this at all (Bahrain), and yet others only stipulate equality in remuneration in the civil service sector (Qatar and Saudi Arabia).

In spite of the many guarantees for the protection of women in the work place in Arab legislation, various forms of discrimination still persist either because the law explicitly sanctions them or because it fails to intervene to remove them. A significant segment of the female working population is employed under temporary contracts, in which capacity they are unprotected by national labour laws. Another large segment, which is engaged in seasonal work, agricultural activities or domestic service, has no legal protection whatsoever. Many women in a number of Arab States suffer from the lack of a binding law to enable the unification of families in the event that the spouses work in separate or geographically remote areas. In addition to the foregoing, women are barred from many positions of responsibility even though no legal prohibitions exist to this effect. Leaving aside the positions of president and prime minister, women in many Arab countries are excluded from becoming governors, mayors, university deans and the like. In many countries, too (such as Egypt and the Gulf States), women are still not appointed as judges. Although one female judge has been appointed to the Supreme Constitutional Court in Egypt, the positions at the lower, middle and most of the higher echelons of the judiciary remain out of reach for women.

Arab women are sometimes subjected to various forms of sexual harassment in the workplace from their bosses. The term "sexual harassment" is understood internationally as the abuse of authority by persons in positions of power with the purpose of coercing persons under their authority into granting sexual favours.

In general, Arab penal codes contain no concrete definition of the crime of sexual harassment. There are laws punishing sex crimes such as rape, sexual assault, sexual abuse and extorting sexual favours. However, while these laws provide for harsher penalties against offenders in a position of power over their victims, the crime of sexual harassment, as defined internationally, is not punishable by law unless it overlaps in some manner with the sex crimes designated in Arab penal codes. Arab legislators should, therefore, take steps to define sexual harassment as a crime in its own right even if it is not as grave as the crimes of rape, sexual assault and sexual abuse that are already addressed in existing legislation.

In spite of the many guarantees for the protection of women in the work place in Arab legislation, various forms of discrimination and harassment still persist.

Arab penal codes contain no concrete definition of the crime of sexual harassment.

BOX 8-3

Al-Tahir al-Haddad: Women in the Judiciary

There is nothing in the Qur'anic texts to prevent women from assuming any post in the state or society, however exalted. This indicates that such matters have nothing to do with the essence of Islam, for otherwise the Qur'an would not have omitted to address them with the required clarity.

Source: Al-Haddad, in Arabic, 1929, 17-18.

INCRIMINATION AND PUNISHMENT

In general, Arab penal codes and criminal procedures deal with women either as a symbol of honour and virtue, as an object that needs to be protected for its childbearing functions, or as a component of a family unit that needs to be safeguarded against desertion and neglect. The statutes orbiting around these three conceptual loci in Arab penal policies towards women abound. There are numerous provisions penalising the crime of adultery[17] whether committed by the husband or wife; others penalising the crimes of sexual assault, rape[18] and the kidnapping of women; and another set penalising the crimes of prostitution and sexual debauchery (*fujur*). There are laws against abortion, laws for ascertaining the validity of marriages and laws to protect family cohesion.

Arab legislation offers several instances of laws aiming to protect the family. Article 279 of the Jordanian penal code calls for the imprisonment of anyone found guilty of contracting a marriage in violation of the Family Rights Law or any other law, or anyone who marries or conducts the marriage rites for a female minor. Article 281 of the Jordanian penal code stipulates a prison term for anyone who divorces his wife without applying to a judge, or a person deputising for a judge, within 15 days to have the divorce officially registered. Under Article 483 of the Lebanese penal code, a cleric who officiates at the marriage of a minor (below the age of 18) without registering in the marriage contract the approval of the minor's guardian is subject to payment of a fine. Articles 479 to 482 of the Moroccan criminal code detail several punishable offences against the family.

Some articles in the criminal procedure codes of these countries also observe gender-specific considerations. These include special provisions regarding the conduct of physical searches on women, the execution of physical punishments (death penalties may not be carried out on women who are pregnant or nursing children) and the implementation of punishments that deprive individuals of their freedom (special conditions apply to female prisoners).

This said, discrimination against women is firmly ingrained in the penal codes of some Arab States. In Egypt, this appears most blatantly in the differentiation between men and women in the crime of adultery. This applies both to the definition of what constitutes the crime and to the stipulations of punishment. In terms of crime, men are guilty of adultery only if the act takes place in the marital home, whereas women are guilty of adultery regardless of where the act takes place. In terms of punishment, male adulterers are subject to imprisonment for a period not to exceed six months, whereas women are subject to a maximum penalty of two years.[19] It should be noted that this discrimination has no basis in shari'a; rather, it is inherited from foreign law. The Egyptian penal code is also discriminatory in the material status it accords to murder committed by a husband or wife upon discovering his or her spouse in flagrante delicto with a third party. Whereas a husband found guilty of this crime is only subject to the penal provisions for non-felonious crimes (Article 237 of the criminal code), a wife similarly provoked is subject to those governing felonies.

As in Egyptian law, Article 562 of the Lebanese penal code provides for a lighter sentence for a husband who kills his adulterous wife and her partner when caught in the act than that for a wife found guilty of murder under the same circumstances. In Lebanese penal code, Articles 487, 488 and 489, pertaining to adultery, are also heavily biased against women in terms of the conditions that establish the crime, the punishment of the perpetrators and the burden of proof. Under Lebanese law, an adulterous woman is one guilty of extramarital intercourse regardless of where this takes place whereas a man is regarded as adulterous only

Discrimination against women appears most blatantly in the differentiation between men and women in the crime of adultery.

---

[17] For example, Articles 282-286 of the Jordanian penal code, Articles 487-491 of the Lebanese penal code and Articles 274-277 of the Egyptian penal code.

[18] Articles 292-299 of the Jordanian penal code, Articles 505-510 of the Lebanese penal code, Articles 267-269 of the Egyptian penal code and Articles 486-487 of the Moroccan criminal code.

[19] Articles 274 and 277 of the Egyptian penal code.

if guilty of extramarital intercourse in the conjugal home (as in Egyptian law) or if he openly takes a mistress. Whereas an adulterous man is liable to a prison sentence of one month to a year, an adulterous woman faces three months to two years in prison. An adulterous woman's partner is subject to the same sentence as the woman only if he is married, while the adulterous man's partner is subject to the same penalty as the man regardless of her marital status. Proving the crime of adultery is also discriminatory as it is much easier to incriminate wives than it is husbands.

On the other hand, some Arab penal codes are free of gender bias as pertains to the crime of adultery (see, for example, Articles 491 the Moroccan criminal and 316 of Bahraini penal codes).

Efforts are in progress to eliminate the current bias in penal code law. In Egypt, Article 291 – now repealed – once read: "If a kidnapper legally marries the woman he kidnapped, he will be exempted from punishment". The ostensible purpose of this provision was to provide a way to cover up the crime so as to spare the victim and her family from its social and psychological fallout and to allow for the stability and continuity of the family unit emerging from this marriage. In practice, this provision was extremely detrimental to women. Instead of acting as a deterrent, the law rendered abduction more attractive to potential offenders, offering an avenue for evading punishment for kidnapping and even rape. In light of this consideration and others, Article 291 was abolished so as to reinstate the full deterrent power of the law against the kidnapping of women by closing off all avenues for escaping punishment.

In spite of this and other inroads made by Arab legislators towards eliminating gender bias in Arab penal codes, the approach remains ad hoc and piecemeal. Attention must be given to developing a more intensive and comprehensive approach.

PERSONAL STATUS LAWS

If legally sanctioned discrimination means disparity in the rule of law in spite of the presumed equality in legal status of citizens, then Arab personal status laws, with regard to Muslims and non-Muslims alike, are witness to legally sanctioned gender bias. This stems from the fact that personal status statutes are primarily derived from theological interpretations and judgements. The latter originate in the remote past when gender discrimination permeated society and they have acquired a sanctity and absoluteness in that confused area where the immutable tenets of religious creed interact with social history.

Fortunately, evidence from the Report's public opinion survey indicates that the Arab public is moving towards a more liberal perspective on personal status issues, such as asserting women's right to choose a spouse (Box 8-4).

THE LACK OF CODIFICATION IN SOME ARAB STATES:

Arab personal status laws remain conservative and resistant to change because a number of Arab States are reluctant to develop a national personal status code. Instead, they favour leaving matters entirely to the judiciary, which is heavily influenced by the conservative nature of classical Islamic jurisprudence (*fiqh*).

Some Arab States, such as Bahrain, Egypt, Lebanon and Qatar, lack any unified personal status code whereas others have unified personal status codes for Muslims.

In Egypt, for example, there exist several personal status laws for Muslims, some dating back to 1920 and 1929. However, where a textual provision is not available in law, recourse is made to the prevailing views of the Hanafi school of jurisprudence. Deferring to classical Islamic jurisprudence can produce rulings repulsive to the spirit of the age and to a human rights culture. A notable instance is to be found in the ruling, upheld by the Court of Cassation, ordering the divorce of an Egyptian intellectual from his wife on the grounds of his alleged apostasy in certain books that he had published. The ruling was founded upon the Hanafi opinion that an apostate must be divorced from his spouse. Clearly, then, it is essential to have clear, precise codification of personal status regulations; the legislative clarity to which this will contribute is a precondition for combating discrimination.

Arab personal status laws, with regard to Muslims and non-Muslims alike, are witness to legally sanctioned gender bias.

Arab personal status laws remain conservative and resistant to change because a number of Arab States are reluctant to develop a national personal status code.

Clear, precise codification of personal status regulations... is a precondition for combating discrimination.

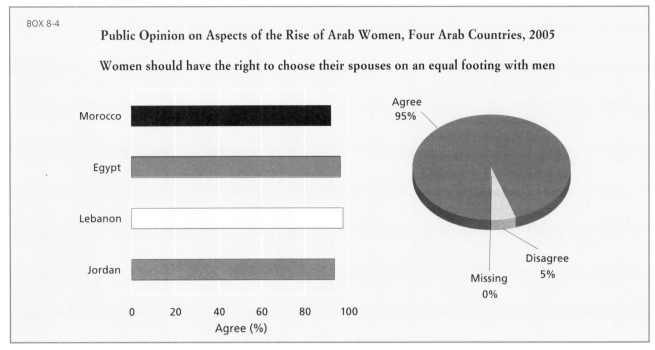

BOX 8-4

Public Opinion on Aspects of the Rise of Arab Women, Four Arab Countries, 2005

Women should have the right to choose their spouses on an equal footing with men

Morocco

Egypt

Lebanon

Jordan

0   20   40   60   80   100

Agree (%)

Agree
95%

Disagree
5%

Missing
0%

Over twenty years ago, the secretariat of the Council of Arab Ministers of Justice drafted a model Unified Personal Status Code. The project adopted the personal status regulations that prevailed in Arab States at the time and that continue today in many of them, bearing the stamp of classical Islamic jurisprudence.

Non-Muslims in Egypt are subject to their denominational canons in personal status matters. However, in the event of a dispute between spouses of different denominations, sects or faiths, shari'a, as the principle source of state law, is brought to bear. Some Coptic clerics regard this as another form of discrimination.

Lebanon, too, does not have a unified personal status code. Rather, family matters are subject to the strictures of the religious community, whether Muslim or Christian. Lebanon recognises 18 religious denominations, each of which has its own religious canon. Perhaps this is why Lebanon entered a reservation to Article 16 of CEDAW, which establishes the principle of equality in family relations.

Bahrain, Qatar and Saudi Arabia also have no unified personal status code. Rather, it is the religious judges in these countries who rule on family matters in accordance with the provisions of Islamic jurisprudence. Recently, however, the King of Bahrain formed a committee to prepare a family law bill. Although the committee has completed its work, the bill has yet to be passed into law.

In some States, the situation is far better in terms of the instrument of legal regulation. In Jordan, for example, the Law of Personal Status for Muslims No. 61 of 1976 has codified the provisions of Islamic jurisprudence as they

pertain to family relations, from engagement through marriage dissolution. Non-Muslims in Jordan remain subject to their own assorted religious laws on these matters. Algeria, Kuwait, Morocco and Tunisia also fare much better in their regulation of personal status affairs, as is described in detail below. In fact, the Tunisian Personal Status Law is applied to all Tunisians regardless of their religious affiliation.

UNIFIED CODIFICATION OF PERSONAL STATUS AFFAIRS IN ARAB STATES

Over twenty years ago, the secretariat of the Council of Arab Ministers of Justice drafted a model Unified Personal Status Code. The project adopted the personal status regulations that prevailed in Arab States at the time and that continue today in many of them, bearing the stamp of classical Islamic jurisprudence. It featured no notable attempts to weed out gender bias in Arab personal status laws. Rather, it adopted a juristic approach in an effort to reconcile modern needs and requirements with the higher aims of shari'a. Article 31 of the draft code permits a man to take up to four wives unless there is doubt over his ability to treat them equitably. The article failed to clarify a procedural mechanism for invalidating a polygamous marriage in the event of demonstrable inequity. Article 52 places the burden of economic support on the husband alone even if his wife is well off. Article 83 defines the dissolution of a marriage initiated by the husband as divorce (*talaq*) and the dissolution of a marriage by mutual consent as repudiation (*mukhala'a*). In the latter case, it is the wife who must pay the husband compensation. Article 96 contrasts with more progressive legislation subsequently adopted by some Arab States restricting such compensation (*khul'*) to marital annulment initiated by the wife.

Nevertheless, the draft code did contain some positive points intended to alleviate gender bias in Arab personal status laws. For example, Article 6 permits the stipulation of conditions in marriage contracts and provides that, in order for a divorce to be valid, the husband must deposit a declaration with a judge who, in turn, must attempt to reconcile the spouses before accepting the declaration.

In all events, given that the draft Unified Personal Status Code is decades old and has long since been surpassed in many areas by subsequent legislation in Arab States, the Arab League should take upon itself two tasks. The first is to revise the draft code so as to bring it into conformity with the demands and spirit of the times and with the international obligations of Arab States. The second is to work to make this legislation a reality through a treaty adopted by the Arab League Council, followed by efforts to enter its provisions into the national legislation of member States.

THE GENERAL CHARACTERISTICS OF ARAB FAMILY LAW

Before turning to the specifics of how family laws in individual Arab States fare in terms of gender equality, the Report will focus on certain characteristics common to family law in all Arab States from the same perspective. Most Arab legislation is characterised by a marked deficit in gender equality in family law. The notion that men are women's keepers and have a degree of command over them is sustained in Islamic scriptures. In legal practice, this has translated into laws requiring husbands to support their wives financially, laws ordaining wifely obedience, laws granting men alone the right to dictate divorce and laws granting men the right to the compulsory return of their wives in the event of a revocable divorce (*talaq raj'i*).

A husband's custodial authority over his wife is evidenced in other provisions. In many Arab States, the right of women to work and to freedom of movement is restricted by the need to obtain the approval of their husbands. Trusteeship over the money and property of minors is held by the father and then passes to the paternal grandfather. In spite of the amendments that have been introduced to the nationality laws of some Arab States, the nationality of the father remains the primary criterion for granting nationality to the spouse and children; however, the reverse might not be true.

Arab legislators generally rest their justification of men's superiority over women in marital relations on the premise that men are in an economically stronger position than women and are therefore obliged to support their wives and children. It was this premise that led some Arab States to enter reservations to Article 16 of CEDAW, which provides for equality of men and women in all matters relating to marriage and family relations. The fact is, however, that the economic justification for perpetuating inequality in marital relations no longer holds water in the face of the reality of many contemporary Arab societies. That wives in these societies are compelled to work alongside their husbands in order to provide for their families applies as much to average-income families as it does to those of limited income.

For the most part, Arab attempts to modernise family laws with an eye to alleviating gender discrimination have focused on halting the more pernicious practices while preserving the original principles intact. For example, Arab legislators have prohibited use of force in the enforcement of rulings ordering wives to return to their marital homes. Husbands must now officially inform their first wives if they intend to take a second wife and men's right to polygamy is restricted by the need to provide acceptable grounds for taking an additional wife and by demonstrable ability to treat the wives equitably. Legislators have also

Most Arab legislation is characterised by a marked deficit in gender equality in family law.

Arab attempts to modernise family laws with an eye to alleviating gender discrimination have focused on halting the more pernicious practices while preserving the original principles intact.

established the right of the wife to demand a divorce on the grounds of personal injury if her husband takes a second wife and her right to *khul*, thereby balancing the spouses' rights to terminate the matrimonial relationship. A husband is now required to inform his wife of his intent to divorce her and register her acknowledgement of having been so informed, and he is required to notarise the divorce and officially notify his former wife of this. Women now have the right to stipulate certain conditions in the marriage contract as long as those conditions do not conflict with shari'a. Finally, legislators have established the right of a wife to retain custody of her children beyond the age at which custody normally passes to the father, if that is deemed in the interests of the children, and to retain the marital home as the custodial dwelling.

It is important to note that Arab public opinion tends to take a more progressive stance than current legislation when it comes to women's rights to seek divorce and custody of children (Box 8-5).

Personal status regulations for non-Muslims are derived from the canons of their respective religious sects or denominations. For the most part, these regulations sharply curtail the right of both spouses to divorce and, in some cases, prohibit it altogether. Adherents of Orthodox Christian denominations may, on various grounds, appeal for a judicial ruling

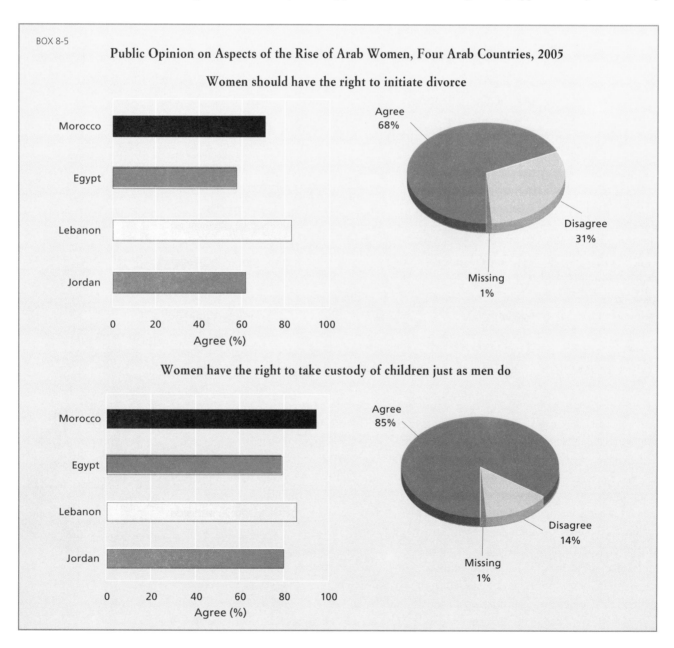

BOX 8-5

Public Opinion on Aspects of the Rise of Arab Women, Four Arab Countries, 2005

Women should have the right to initiate divorce

Women have the right to take custody of children just as men do

granting a divorce, whereas Catholics may only sue for physical separation, in spite of allowing for the possibility of annulment of the marriage contract or declaring it invalid owing to flaws inherent from its initiation. On the whole, the notion of male superiority appears to have governed the formulation of such provisions pertaining to matrimonial relations.

A COMPARATIVE VIEW

One cannot help but observe that personal status law in the Maghreb (North Africa) is more progressive and less discriminatory than that in the Mashreq (the Arab East). Most of the Maghreb states (Algeria, Morocco and Tunisia) have made significant inroads, albeit in varying degrees, towards alleviating the injustices against women in personal status matters without infringing upon the principles of shari'a.

Tunisia is the most progressive country in respect to legislation that approaches the stipulation of the principle of equality in family relations, followed by Morocco and then Algeria, as illustrated below. Taken together, many legislative texts from the Maghreb prove it is possible for Arab legislators to preserve the principles of shari'a by applying interpretations favourable to the equality of men and women and to alleviating the historical bias against women in family relations.

It is instructive to compare the most important provisions of the Kuwaiti Personal Status Law with their counterparts in Maghrebi personal status laws, which will illustrate the progressive nature of the latter. The family law in Kuwait will be the basis for this comparison as it reflects, both in its general and in many of its specific characteristics, family law and judicial practice throughout the Mashreq. The Report will focus here on those areas of family law that are generally the most vulnerable to discriminatory legislation: eligibility for marriage and contracting marriages, the effects of the contractual arrangement and the dissolution of the marital contract.

The Kuwait Unified Personal Status Code for Muslims contains means of protecting women even where there are numerous instances of gender discrimination. Marriages between Muslims in Kuwait are concluded with the assent of the guardian of the fiancée and the acceptance of the fiancé or of a person acting on his behalf (Article 9). Polygamy is unrestricted for men apart from the provision (stated in Article 23) that "[A] man may not marry a fifth wife until he dissolves his marriage with one of his four wives and the divorced wife's 'idda (stipulated waiting period until she can remarry) has elapsed". The article also states that "[A] marriage contract may not be notarised or otherwise authenticated unless the girl has reached the age of 15 and the boy 17 at the time of authentication". Article 31 gives a deflowered woman (*thayyib*) or a woman 25 years or older the right to voice an opinion regarding her marriage, but the contract itself must be concluded by her guardian. If a guardian unjustifiably opposes a woman's wish to marry, she may seek recourse to a judge who may or may not rule in her favour. The same applies in the event that a woman has more than one guardian of equal status with respect to her and who collectively obstruct her wish or disagree with one another over the matter (Article 34). One of the conditions for a Kuwaiti marriage contract to be binding is that the man be competent (kuf') for marriage at the time the contract is concluded. A wife and her guardian have the right to annul the contract in the event that the husband no longer meets this condition (Article 35). The law defines competence (kafa'a) in terms of religious strictures (Article 36). It defines divorce as the dissolution of a legitimate marriage contract at the behest of the husband or a person acting on his behalf through the utterance of a specific formula (Article 85).

Among the provisions of the personal status code intended to protect women is Article 88, which stipulates that a husband may not bring a second wife to live in the home of his first wife without the latter's consent. The code also prohibits the use of force in the implementation of a court ruling ordering a wife to return to her marital home.

Tunisia's Personal Status Code stands alone in the Arab world as a model for promoting the principle of equality in marital relations in law by avoiding archaic interpretations of shari'a prejudicial to the rights of women.

Personal status law in the Maghreb (North Africa) is more progressive and less discriminatory than that in the Mashreq (the Arab East).

Tunisia's Personal Status Code stands alone in the Arab world as a model for promoting the principle of equality in marital relations in law.

Tunisia's personal status law is also the only Arab personal status code that applies to all the country's citizens regardless of religious affiliation. The value that Tunisia accords to equality is evinced in numerous provisions in its family law. Article 18 of its Personal Status Code prohibits polygamy and penalises violators. A woman has the right to act on her own behalf when entering into marriage even if still a virgin.

Tunisia's divorce provisions, too, are founded upon the principle of complete equality of women and men. Divorce, according to Article 30 of the Personal Status Code, can be obtained only "through the courts". Article 31.2 states that either spouse has the right to compensation for any material or moral harm resulting from a divorce, whether filed on the grounds of injury or with no stated cause. The Code is equally impartial with regard to the rights of parents. Article 57 states that "The custody of children is a right shared by both parents as long as their marital life lasts". In the event of divorce, according to Article 67, custody is transferred to the parent whose custodianship a judge determines is in the best interests of the child.

The family laws of Algeria and Morocco reflect a trend in these countries to restrict polygamy through the provision of more stringent conditions and closer judicial supervision. Article 8 of the Algerian family law permits men to take several wives up to the limit stipulated under shari'a. However, they must demonstrate cause and the ability to sustain multiple wives equitably. In addition, a husband must officially notify his current spouse or spouses of his intent to take another wife and any of his current spouses, be they one or more, has the right to demand a divorce if she does not consent to the marriage. In addition to the approval of his current wife or wives, a husband must obtain a permit for an additional marriage from the competent court. Article 40 of the Moroccan Personal Status Code contains a similar provision.

Article 13 of the Algerian family law prohibits coercion into marriage, stating that a guardian may not force a woman under his custody to marry and he may not contract her into a marriage without her consent. In Morocco, women of legal age have full right to act on their own behalf. Article 24 of the Civil Status Code states that "Self-guardianship is a woman's right, to be exercised by an adult woman freely and independently". Article 25 states that "An adult woman may act on her own behalf in entering into a marriage contract, or she may authorise her father or another relative to act on her behalf".

In Algeria, under no circumstances can a divorce be granted or considered valid without a judicial ruling to this effect. Moreover, before such a ruling can be issued, there must be an attempt at reconciliation. In addition, a woman has the right to file for khul' divorce (Article 54), which, if granted, obliges her to pay compensation to her husband. In Morocco, divorce is a prerogative of both a husband and a wife, in accordance with legal provisions for each party, and is exercised under judicial supervision. A husband who wants a divorce must request permission from a court, substantiating his case with the testimony of two witnesses of good standing (Article 79). Before a divorce is granted, there must be an attempt at reconciliation and two attempts in the event the couple have children. Article 83 states that, if reconciliation fails, the court will designate a sum of money to be paid in order to meet the requirements of the wife and children. The husband must deposit this sum with the court within 30 days. If, according to Article 86, the husband does not do so within the stated time, the court will take this as indicating that he has reversed his decision about the divorce. If, on the other hand, he does deposit the required sum, the court will issue him permission, as stated in Article 87, to certify the divorce in the presence of two witnesses of good standing residing within the area of jurisdiction of the court.

Also under the Moroccan civil code, a wife has the right to divorce her husband if he has granted her this right in the marriage contract. Otherwise, a woman has the right to demand a divorce on the grounds of personal injury, abandonment or violation of the conditions of the marriage contract. In addition, in Morocco, a couple may resort to a khul' dissolution of the marriage contract by mutual consent, contrary to the situation in Egypt where *khul'* is only the wife's prerogative.

The family laws of Algeria and Morocco reflect a trend in these countries to restrict polygamy.

From this brief reading of personal status provisions in the Mashreq and the Maghreb, one can only reach the following conclusions. First, there is an urgent need for unified personal status codes in those Arab States that still lack them, such that there is no space for judges to evaluate interpretations and jurisprudential opinions. Second, such new codes must strive to regulate family relations on the basis of the principle of gender equality. Finally, family laws in the Maghreb show that it is possible for shari'a to coexist harmoniously with the principle of equality between husbands and wives. Thus, gender inequality in Arab legal systems is more the product of history, customs and conventions than of authentic religious precepts. Such considerations make it all the more imperative to revise Arab family law in order to end discrimination against women.

AWAY FROM OFFICIAL LAW

The social environment is frequently a crucial factor in discrimination against women regardless of what the law may say. Because of what is commonly considered appropriate or inappropriate behaviour for a dutiful, decent and virtuous wife, recourse by a woman to the courts to demand her rights or those of her children is widely frowned upon as a form of public indecency. As a result, many women refrain from pursuing their family rights through official legal processes. Instead, matrimonial disputes in many Arab societies are resolved either within the family or through the unofficial channels of tribal arbitration. As these mechanisms, as a whole, evolved in the context of a male-dominated culture and male-oriented values, their biased outcomes are often a foregone conclusion.

Even when women do attempt to obtain their legally stipulated rights through family courts, however, they confront a maze of stubbornly slow, needlessly complex and tortuously intimidating procedures that fail to take into account the material, social and psychological properties and needs of the family. From this perspective, the family courts that have been introduced in Egypt merit praise for the practical social considerations that were taken into account in their structural, procedural and functional design. This innovative experience deserves both encouragement and further study as a model for the Arab world even if work needs to be done to filter out whatever negative aspects may have come to light through practical application. It is important that these courts be improved in such a way that judges are provided the necessary time and expertise as well as the required human and financial resources to effectively undertake their job.

Another problem inimical to women's rights resides in the different types of conjugal arrangements available in Arab societies. Some of them look like conventional marriages in that they fulfil the religious formalities for marriage with regard to consent and acceptance, public notarisation and dowry. Yet in substance, they are incompatible with the rationale of the institution of marriage as a domestic bond characterised by mutual affection and compassion and intended to serve as the foundation for the creation of a sound, healthy family. In these marriages of convenience, which go by various names in Arab societies (*misyar* in Saudi Arabia and *siyahi* in Yemen, for example), a wife is contracted to a man in exchange for his payment of a dowry but without his commitment to house or support her permanently. This phenomenon has spread in poorer Arab environments where families are more vulnerable to the temptation of the money offered by wealthy Arabs (generally older men) in exchange for a misyar marriage to their daughters (often under age). In effect, the arrangement is a form of legitimised female enslavement that results in many human tragedies, which is why some Arab legislators have been fighting to contain it (as in Egypt).

A related phenomenon is the common law ('*urfi*) marriage (i.e., marriage that is not documented by a public official). Effectively a form of secret, uncertified marriage, it has become the increasingly widespread recourse of young Arab men unable to afford the financial responsibilities of marriage. Some husbands also find it useful as a way to escape the rights granted to the wife in a legally documented marriage since, as a general principle, the courts refuse to consider the claims of wives in such marriages if the husband denies the marriage relationship.

Family laws in the Maghreb show that it is possible for shari'a to coexist harmoniously with the principle of equality between husbands and wives.

Because of what is commonly considered appropriate...many women refrain from pursuing their family rights through official legal processes.

These circumventions of official law, justified on the grounds that they do not conflict with religious formalities regardless of how they may conflict with the spirit and rationale of marriage, are detrimental to the rights of women as stipulated under law.

NATIONALITY

In general, in Arab legislation, native nationality is determined by paternal descent. If a father is a citizen of a particular Arab country, his children acquire his nationality automatically. The children of a female national only acquire their mother's nationality if the father's identity is unknown or if he is stateless (see Article 6 of the Tunisian Nationality Code. It should be noted, however, that under Tunisian law the child of a Tunisian mother and foreign father may acquire Tunisian nationality with the approval of the father. See also, Paragraphs 3 and 4 of Article 2 of the Jordanian Nationality Law, which grant Jordanian nationality to children of a Jordanian father or children born in Jordan to a Jordanian mother if the father is unknown or stateless. The nationality laws of Bahrain and Morocco –Articles 4 and 6 respectively – contain similarly worded provisions).

Clearly, these nationality laws are biased against women and contravene Article 9 of

CEDAW, which explains why so many Arab States have entered reservations to this article.

Recently Arab lawmakers have been working to counter the inhumane consequences of Arab States' long-held refusal to grant nationality to the children of female citizens married to foreigners. For example, Egypt recently passed Law 154/2004, which grants children of an Egyptian mother and a foreign father the right to nationality. This law consequently addresses the problems of thousands of people with an Egyptian mother and a foreign father who had previously been unable to obtain the Egyptian nationality.

From the Report's public opinion survey, it is clear that Arab society is prepared to accept a woman's equal right to pass on her citizenship to her children (Box 8-6).

The new Algerian nationality law, issued in 2005, states in Article 6 that a child born of an Algerian father and/or mother is deemed Algerian. Under Morocco's nationality law of 1958, a child is only entitled to Moroccan nationality if the father is Moroccan. The law has since been amended so that children of Moroccan mothers may also obtain Moroccan nationality.

Lebanon reveals another facet of discrimination in nationality law. Lebanese law takes paternal descent as the basis for granting native nationality, as is the case with all Arab

Nationality laws are biased against women and contravene Article 9 of CEDAW, which explains why so many Arab States have entered reservations to this article.

BOX 8-6

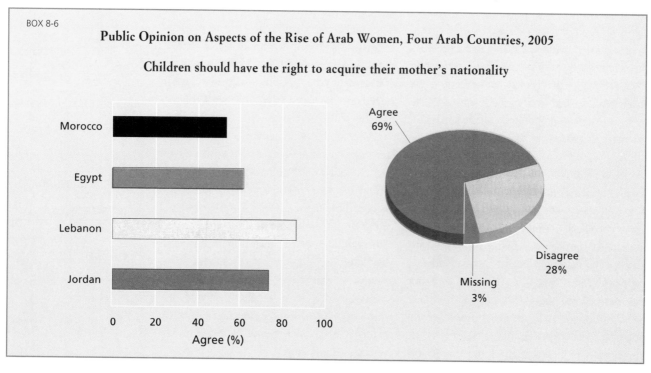

Public Opinion on Aspects of the Rise of Arab Women, Four Arab Countries, 2005

Children should have the right to acquire their mother's nationality

countries. With regard to the circumstances under which a Lebanese woman may confer her nationality upon her children, Lebanese law has added a refinement: a foreign mother who has acquired Lebanese nationality may confer this nationality upon her children if they are minors, and if she outlives her foreign husband, whereas a native-born Lebanese woman (married to a foreigner) does not have this right. Civil society organisations in Lebanon have been pressing for the elimination of this discrimination and for an amendment to the nationality law to provide for equality between the parents with respect to the nationality of their children. They have also called for Lebanon to withdraw its reservation to Article 9, Paragraph 2 of CEDAW. It is noteworthy that Lebanese civil society organisations are acclaimed in this regard as they played a critical role in repealing the law that dropped citizenship from Lebanese women who married foreigners.

AWARENESS OF GENDER EQUALITY AMONG ARAB LEGAL PRACTITIONERS

For equality between men and women to exist, it is not enough to incorporate the principle into law, especially with a legal culture or awareness that is overtly or tacitly opposed to equality between the sexes. Legal awareness here refers to the set legal values that govern and guide practitioners of law in the course of drafting and applying legislation. Practitioners of law refer to all those involved in the practice of law in the Arab world. This ranges from legislators who write the laws and judges who use their discretionary authority in applying them to lawyers who help judges to understand and apply the law and other interpreters of law in the judiciaries, universities or elsewhere. Awareness of the principle of equality of men and women by all these people is a prerequisite for its practical application.

Although there appears to be no field research that has attempted to measure the level of Arab legal practitioners' awareness of gender equality, the available information suggests that pro-male gender bias is widespread in these professions. It requires little scrutiny of

history to realise that Arab tribal culture, which sanctions discrimination against women, has strongly influenced the discriminatory juristic interpretations that establish the inferiority of women to men. Otherwise put, the male-dominated culture has been a crucial factor in shaping juristic judgments and endowing them with religious sanctity.

The positions of some Arab legislators evince hostility towards gender equality, despite the provisions of their national constitutions and the international conventions to which their States are party. Two examples illustrate this bias. The first is the opposition of most representatives in the Kuwaiti National Assembly to granting Kuwaiti women their political rights (Al-'Awadhi, background paper for this Report). The second is the opposition of many members of the Egyptian People's Assembly to establishing a woman's right to terminate her marriage voluntarily in accordance with the Islamic khul' system. In both instances, male opponents to the bills in question grounded their position in Salafi fundamentalist jurisprudence asserting men's superiority to, and custody of, women. Indeed, a member of the Egyptian People's Assembly cited the behaviour of chickens in their coops as proof that females, among birds, animals and above all human beings, are subordinate to males by nature (his remarks were struck from the minutes of that session).

Frequently, the application of the principle of gender equality founders on the reservations of Arab judiciaries, a resistance fuelled by the growth of fundamentalist trends and their increasing impact on the legal consciousness of Arab judges. The depth of male chauvinism among members of the judiciary in some Arab States can be seen in their opposition to the appointment of female judges. The arguments against such appointments have varied from the assertion that women are unsuitable by nature for these demanding positions to the claim that such appointments would go against the grain of society's culture and traditions. Obviously, few have reflected upon the fact that the ancient Egyptian goddess of justice, Maat, was a female deity. In the middle of the last century, 'Abd al-Razzaq al-Sanhuri, perhaps the most famous Egyptian jurist and, at the time in question,

The male-dominated culture has been a crucial factor in shaping juristic judgments and endowing them with religious sanctity.

The depth of male chauvinism among members of the judiciary in some Arab States can be seen in their opposition to the appointment of female judges.

chairman of the Council of State (the judicial body that rules in administrative disputes), ruled against the eligibility of women to serve as judges. Although he acknowledged a woman's constitutional right to serve in this capacity, he held that appointment of women to the judiciary would not be appropriate to Egyptian society. Considerations of social propriety still obstruct women's access to positions at all levels of the judiciary in Egypt. In an attempt to exonerate themselves on this issue, Egyptian authorities appointed a woman counsellor to the Supreme Constitutional Court, but this was not followed by a decision to accept women at all levels of the Egyptian judiciary.

Discrimination by the legal community against women is also evident in the way judges in criminal courts use their discretionary authority to deliver lighter or harsher sentences in cases where a woman is one of the litigants. One notes that in crimes of honour, judges tend to deliver lighter sentences for male offenders against women than for female offenders against men. In murder cases, courts tend to hand down death sentences against women found guilty of murdering their husbands regardless of the woman's motives or circumstances whereas the same does not apply if the genders of the assailant and victim are reversed. There is a hypothesis, supported by casual observation and, therefore, requiring empirical proof, that male judges think of honour crimes as acts perpetrated against males, for which reason they lighten penalties in crimes of honour against women. This prejudice may account for the harshness with which legislators in some Arab countries deal with women. Under many Arab penal codes, female adulterers face far harsher penalties than male adulterers. While as a general principle attempted crime is punishable by law, the attempt to cause a woman to miscarry is not. A woman who kills her adulterous husband upon discovering him *in flagrante delicto* will not receive a reduced sentence, whereas, in the reverse situation, a man will. Clearly, the bias of the judiciary against women has its twin in Arab legislation.

Many interpreters of legislation echo this discriminatory tendency when faced with the principle of equality before the law. The Report team will not emphasise here the commentaries of some modern scholars of shari'a, who still recite the views of classical Islamic jurists regarding men's custodianship over women. In sharp contrast to such views, there exists a body of enlightened Islamic jurisprudence that interprets such texts in their context and inclines, to a considerable extent, to the espousal of the principle of gender equality. However, the first – conservative – school of thought still finds a sympathetic ear in practice and still appeals to the man on the street because of the support it receives from conservative clerics. Merely to illustrate this, there was not a single woman candidate in Egypt's recent presidential elections. Some women did submit candidacy applications; however, they were rejected on the grounds of not meeting the qualifications stipulated under the controversial amendment to Article 76 of the Egyptian Constitution. Odder yet, the former Mufti of Egypt issued a fatwa, published in *Al-Ahram* of 28 February 2005, to the effect that women should not be permitted to run for the presidency. He based his ruling on the opinion of Islamist jurists that held that women should not assume "political leadership" (*wilaya 'amma*), which he took by extension to mean the presidency of the republic.

Of greater concern, however, is the conservative position on gender matters of civil law experts. Most, for example, reject the notion of quotas for women in parliament on the grounds that it violates the principle of equality before the law (Al-Sharqawi and Nasif, in Arabic, 1984, 350). This argument flies in the face of humanitarian rights jurisprudence, which, as noted earlier, sanctions positive discrimination in favour of women in order to eradicate the historically entrenched injustice against them, a principle upheld by CEDAW (see, for example, Ja'far, in Arabic, n.d., 127).

The resistance of a large segment of contemporary Arab legal practitioners to the full principle of gender equality helps explain why all major legislative changes in favour of women have come about under the auspices of Arab presidential offices. (Sceptics may say that this reflects Arab rulers' hopes of acquitting themselves of human rights violations by establishing a positive record on women's rights). The recent legislative amendment in

In crimes of honour, judges tend to deliver lighter sentences for male offenders against women than for female offenders against men.

The bias of the judiciary against women has its twin in Arab legislation.

BOX 8-7

Social Propriety Prevents the Appointment of Women Judges

"Higher constitutional principles dictate equality of women with men in rights and duties. The application of this equality to public positions and activities necessitates that women must not be barred absolutely from assuming these positions and activities, for to do so conflicts with the principle of equality and constitutes a breach of this essential higher constitutional principle. This entails that it must be left to the discretional authority of the administration to determine, with respect to a particular position or occupation, whether women have attained that degree of development that would render them suitable for that position or that occupation. If the administration deems that women have indeed attained that degree of development and met the criteria of suitability, it may, indeed must, open the door to women as it has to men, without infringement of the equality between them.

Egyptian women in our current age have demonstrated their suitability for many positions and fields of activity, such as medicine, nursing and education, many occupations in the Ministry of Social Affairs and the Ministry of Religious Endowments and positions in the Probate Office of the Public Prosecution and the Office of the Notary Public. Indeed, due to the particular qualities with which they are endowed, women may be preferable to men in some of these occupations. Therefore, the preference of women over men in these domains does not constitute a breach of the principle of equality between men and women. Diverging from the foregoing, the administration may also assess, without arbitrariness, whether, for certain social considerations, the time has not yet come for women to assume certain public positions and occupations. On this basis, the administration may take the liberty to exercise its discretionary authority to weigh the societal impact of these occupations, taking guidance in so doing from the conditions of the environment and the limits and conditions imposed by traditions..." – excerpt from the ruling of the Egyptian Administrative Court of 22 December 1953 on Case 243 for Judicial Year 6.

Public Opinion on Aspects of the Rise of Arab Women, Four Arab Countries, 2005
Women should have the right to become judges

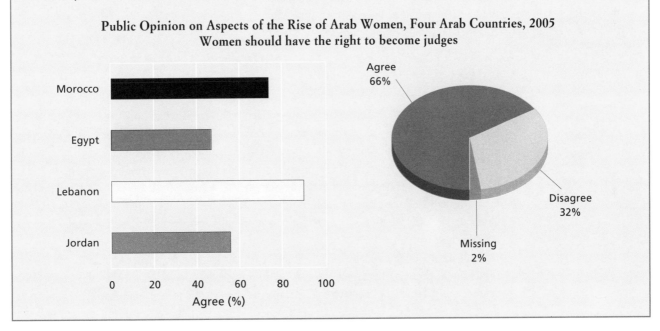

Kuwait permitting the participation of women in politics would not have passed the hurdle of fundamentalist opposition had it not been for the direct and active support that it had received from the government. The personal status measures making it possible for Egyptian women to sue for *khul'* divorce would not have been passed into law had it not been for the open support that they received from the president's office. Similarly, in Morocco, the King put all his personal and religious influence behind the new family code, which alleviated many forms of injustice against women. It would thus appear that Arab ruling establishments are trying to compensate for the underdeveloped awareness of the Arab legal establishment, but only on issues of women's rights.

This, in turn, raises the question as to what would compel traditional legal structures

Lest Women Take All the Seats in Parliament

"… The provisions that discriminate between women and men by reserving specified parliamentary seats for them in addition to keeping open to them the possibility of obtaining other seats are unconstitutional and illogical. They are unconstitutional because they conflict with Article 40 of the Constitution which states that all citizens are equal before the law . . . They are illogical because they allocate to women a certain compulsory number of seats while at the same time women have the right to field themselves in all electoral constituencies and the electorate has the right to elect women in all these constituencies. It follows, then, that this legislation opens the way to the possibility – albeit a remote possibility, but a possibility nevertheless – for a legislative authority consisting entirely of women, whereas the reverse does not hold".

Source: Ja'far, in Arabic, n.d., 127.

Reforms in the law will require the creation and development of a domestic movement for change.

to shed their discriminatory stance against women at a time when the prevailing legal culture forms an obstacle to this. To date, as just noted, change has come from the direction of Arab ruling elites, which may have acted in part under overt or covert foreign pressures. However, sustainable and wide reforms in the law will require the creation and development of a domestic movement for change centred on civil society. It will also require changes in public awareness so as to generate a grass-roots culture favourable to gender equality.

SUMMARY

The foregoing pages have covered the most salient characteristics of how the Arab legal system regulates legal relations to which women are a party. In sum, although women have now been granted their political rights under most Arab constitutions, they remain deprived of the opportunity to fully exercise these rights for reasons outside the framework of the law. The labour laws, penal codes and nationality laws in these countries, on the other hand, still harbour many forms of gender discrimination although tangible legislative steps have been taken to eliminate such discrimination, particularly as it relates to nationality rights and some personal status issues.

This having been said, the most visible discrimination against women in Arab legal systems resides in the domain of personal status law. Although legislators in several Mashreq nations have acted to amend such laws in order to end the crueller consequences of legitimised discrimination, these attempts remain far behind the progressive stance that characterises the current personal status codes in Tunisia, Morocco and Algeria.

Gender awareness within the legal community itself is marred by a distinct bias against women as a general principle. Testimony to this is to be found in equal measure in the legislative process, in the application of the law by the judiciary and in legal exegesis. Such testimony supports the contention that the business of writing the law, applying the law and interpreting the law in the Arab world is governed above all by a male-oriented culture. By no means does this deny the existence of trends in favour of gender equality and affirmative action for women; however, such trends remain insufficiently influential.

CHAPTER NINE

POLITICAL ECONOMY

Introduction

This chapter seeks to shed light on the effect that the political economy structures of Arab countries have on the condition of Arab women, taking into consideration the fact that the economy and politics overlap and intertwine. Emphasis will be placed on the role that political structures play in disempowering women in the Arab countries.

THE PREVAILING MODE OF PRODUCTION, THE LEVEL OF ECONOMIC PERFORMANCE AND THEIR IMPACT

AHDRs 2003 and 2004 concluded that the mode of production in the Arab countries is dominated by rentier economies and levels of economic performance marked by weak economic growth.

The combination of these two characteristics results in weak production structures in the Arab economies and a paucity of means of expansion, creating conditions for the spread of unemployment and poverty. Furthermore, rentier economies and the weak performance of institutional structures needed for the proper management of enterprises and society as a whole are linked to a culture of short-term profit-taking and worsening corruption. The overall result is a pattern of economic activity with disastrous consequences for individual economic empowerment. Other societal conditions magnify the impact of this pattern on women owing to their vulnerable economic position.

These unhealthy effects include high and rising rates of unemployment in the Arab countries, particularly among graduates of education, and the inevitable and consequent increase in poverty and misdistribution of income and wealth since the labour market is the most important economic resource for most people in developing economies. This mix of factors results in a narrow labour market throughout the Arab world, and low rates of its expansion through the creation of new job opportunities. The weak efficiency of the regional labour market exacerbates its impact on unemployment rates. This in turn leads to reliance on foreign labour in those Arab countries that bring in guest workers. Naturally, the weakest social groups, including women, suffer the most.

Given "economic reform" and "structural adjustment" programmes or, as some prefer, "capitalist restructuring", this pattern of production and slow economic growth has reached alarming proportions since the mid-1970s. This occurs in certain Arab unregulated free-market economies in the context of economic globalisation, without the institutional structures necessary for an efficient economy and equitable distribution – prerequisites for an efficient capitalist economic system capable of supporting human development (Fergany, in Arabic, 1998, 47-82).

A tight job market, slow job creation and the spread of women's education along with society's irrational preference that men should take what jobs there are have combined to increase the unemployment of women, especially educated women, even in Arab countries that import non-Arab workers (chapter 3). The state also has withdrawn from economic and service activity and limited government employment, which had previously represented the preferred form of employment for women and a bastion of their rights. As a result, Arab countries are witness to an unfortunate phenomenon: an abundance of qualified female human capital suffering from above average rates of unemployment.

Arab countries are witness to an unfortunate phenomenon: an abundance of qualified female human capital suffering from above average rates of unemployment.

Arab women have undoubtedly secured some gains in political participation during the last three years.

Appointing a woman to a ministerial position has been a general rule in most Arab governments since at least the 1990s.

Another factor that has helped to disempower women economically is the bias in labour practices against women when they do work, particularly in the private sector, which has reduced women's relative earnings. These earnings constitute one of the most important sources of income for most people in developing countries, meaning that women are at greater risk than men from poverty and disempowerment resulting from scarce job opportunities and weak earnings.

The oil boom temporarily helped to expand economic activity and public services, creating a good demand for Arab labour, including that of women, in the Arab oil countries, especially in education, health and government. However, this demand shrank in the mid-1980s when the real value of oil declined and economic growth slowed throughout the Arab region. The effect of the oil boom was similar to that of the Arab countries' engagement in wars (Iraq's with the Islamic Republic of Iran, for example). The absence of men, who were away on the battlefield, contributed to expanding the female labour force, particularly in public services and in the government. However, these were the very same spheres that structural adjustment policies sought to rein in. When the oil boom and the war ended, attempts were made to restrict women's employment in order to limit unemployment among men.

In an international cross-sectional analysis of the relationship between the tempo of economic growth and economic structure on one hand and the GEM[1] index on the other hand, covering a sample of 80 countries, including four Arab countries (Bahrain, Egypt, Saudi Arabia, and Yemen), it was concluded that:

- the level of development is significantly and positively associated with women's empowerment. This relationship explains about 64 per cent of between-country variability in the GEM;
- the relationship has weak predictive power, however, as the coefficient of determination is rather small;[2] and

- transformation in the economic structure during the process of development is likely to improve the empowerment of women with the rising share of the services sector in GDP as this variable is positively and significantly associated with the GEM.

These results should spur Arab countries to pursue institutional reforms aiming at the empowerment of women, as the likelihood of attaining this objective based on economic reforms leading to higher growth alone could require long periods, as the example of Yemen shows (Abdel Gadir Ali, background paper for the Report)

POLITICAL STRUCTURES

GOVERNMENT INSTITUTIONS AND THE LIBERATION OR MARGINALISATION OF ARAB WOMEN

Arab women have undoubtedly secured some gains in political participation during the last three years, with legal recognition of their rights to vote and to stand for local councils and parliament. Their presence is also on the rise at the highest levels of executive authority in most cabinets in the Arab States.

Appointing a woman to a ministerial position has been a general rule in most Arab governments since at least the 1990s, and the practice has grown steadily since then. However, the nature of women's participation in government has generally been:
- symbolic (one or two female ministers in most cases);
- limited to smaller portfolios (usually ministries of social affairs or ministries relating to women); and
- conditional (the number of female ministers fluctuates with numerous changes of government).

This is not to deny that women have achieved representation in Arab government bodies

---

[1] Gender empowerment measure.

[2] For example, Yemen would be expected, according to this relationship, to increase its GEM of 0.123 to 0.163 if it manages to raise its per capita real GDP from $889 (in purchasing power parity (PPP) terms) in 1995 to the real income level of Egypt of $3,950 in 2003, the year of comparison. Based on the experience of income growth in Yemen during the period 1990-2000, with a relatively large average growth rate of 2.4 per cent, Yemen would be expected to attain this result in approximately 63 years.

whether as a result of internal or external pressure or both (Guessous, background paper for the Report). Nonetheless, such progress remains limited, as can be seen from three drawbacks in the trend.

First, women in decision-making institutions, whether executive or legislative, tend to be sidelined since the position of prime minister[3] and the essential ministries that allocate resources, define foreign policy and safeguard internal and external security remain in the hands of men. Furthermore, the positions of speaker of parliament and chair of the overwhelming majority of committees are reserved for men. In those countries that allow political parties, the vast majority of party leaders are also men.

Second, at a time when women's membership in parliament has taken off, they do not enjoy personal safety. In fact, they may have lost other rights, as in Iraq.

Third, the limited extent of Arab women's empowerment becomes apparent when compared with the status of women in other parts of the world (Al-Sayyid, background paper for the Report).

Arab political systems may differ in the democratic margin that they offer, the rights that they grant women, the level of political participation that they encourage and the extent to which their decision-making mechanisms are constitutional and representative. In all cases, however, real decisions in the Arab world are, at all levels, in the hands of men. Decision- and policy-making commonly reflect the patriarchal view of the dominant male elite (Al-Baz, in Arabic, 2002).

Moreover, while equality of the sexes appears as one of the general principles of Arab constitutions, some States fail to apply the principle to their election laws. This is the case with Saudi Arabia, which excluded women from its first municipal elections in February 2005, and with Kuwait, whose election law of 1962 – before its amendment in May 2005 – restricted the right to vote and stand for office to men.

One paradox is that, at first glance, statistics on political participation show advances in the political participation of women in countries under oppressive dictatorial systems or traditional tribal-hereditary regimes. This indicates the weak relationship between increasing the number of women in authority and the progress towards democracy.

Female appointments have grown as some Arab States have learned how to work around pressures from the United Nations agencies for the empowerment of women and the linking of external aid to improvements in the condition of women. The result has been a token representation of women, while citizens in general and women in particular remain on the margins of public affairs (Fayyad, in Arabic, 2004).

The number of seats held by women does not necessarily mean that women are democratically represented; it may, in fact, reflect concessions to a group of women supported by the State against other women on the fringes of dominant political forces. In such cases, the presence of women's groups in power does not express a broad social movement but instead an elite balance of power, economic interest, and internal and external political considerations. This is betrayed by the composition of the dominant women's elite and its failure to represent other more diverse sectors and trends (Ezzat, background paper for the Report).

Arab rule takes different forms – from monarchy to ruling families to pluralistic democracies to governments under the shadow of occupation. These various forms shape - and limit - the means of political and civil participation available to women and men alike, which are usually very limited. The result is that women are doubly-wronged: the dominance of the modern nation-state impedes their full enjoyment of civil and political rights, while the law binds them to the guardianship and protection of their male relatives in all areas of their individual human rights. In a similar vein, national legislation defines women as minors in need of the guardianship and protection of their male relatives in matters relating to their rights of marriage, divorce, child care, employment, travel, or even the entitlement of children to their mother's citizenship. Thus, the social contract applied to Arab women remains mired in patriarchy and nowhere approaches that of "the fraternity of men". Dominated by men (fathers, brothers and husbands), and thus

The essential ministries that allocate resources, define foreign policy and safeguard internal and external security remain in the hands of men.

The number of seats held by women does not necessarily mean that women are democratically represented.

---

[3] Jordan was the first Arab country to appoint a woman as deputy prime minister.

viewed by the State as incomplete individuals, women are denied a direct relationship with society. This relationship is instead mediated by the kinship with men who are viewed as "individuals" and citizens in the light of their sponsorship and leadership of their families. (Jad, background paper for the Report).

POLITICAL PARTIES AND THE ISSUE OF WOMEN

Arab political parties have come to espouse the general cause of women in their programmes, but from that initial point, they diverge on:

- the space given to the subject on their platforms; and
- the ideological context in which their concepts and positions on women are situated.

Political parties tend to assign women's issues to economic, social and cultural categories. They have not viewed the position of women as a gender issue to be differentiated in the general policy discourse. Rather, they see it as part of the general social question. Parties thus promote slogans stressing women's rights to education, employment, health care and welfare and ask for guarantees of their rights under personal status law and in political life by endorsing women's rights to vote and stand for election. The political and ideological conditions under which these parties were founded and their subsequent experiences, positive and negative, have influenced the kind of attention that they give to women's issues. Most of them began life under Western colonialism. Their agendas focused on nationalism, independence and resistance to colonialism. Social issues, including the issue of women, were postponed until after independence.

After independence, the parties began to crystallise general programmes around the desired reforms, with political, social and cultural dimensions all intersecting. The issue of women, as half of society, took on a new dimension. Adopted functional reform slogans acknowledged that reforming the whole (the society) required reforming the part (the family), and reforming the latter entailed an objective re-examination of the status of women, who are fundamental to the family. Attention was therefore paid to personal status laws not in order to guarantee equal human and social rights for women, which would enable them to guide their families better and, in that way, influence society. Rather these reforms were meant to regulate marital relations and guarantee some of the women's rights within the traditional family structure. The education of women was held to be a public good, not because it was considered a basic right, but due to its positive effect on children's upbringing and because it would provide men with educated spouses and companions such as those available to European men. Parties drew their authority from different sources, turning to the new Salafite ideology, nationalism, liberalism or socialism according to their ideological leanings. Their reformist appeals concerning women were influenced by thinkers such as Rifa'a al-Tahtawi, Muhammad 'Abdu, Qasim Amin, Farah Antoine, al-Tahir al-Haddad, Salama Musa, Muhammad Ibn al-Hasan al-Hajawi, 'Alal al-Fasi and others.

Luminary: Djamila Bouhired

Name: Djamila Bouhired
Cell number: 90
Military Prison: Ouran
Age: 22 years
Eyes like the two candles of a "temple"
Black Arab hair
Like the summer
Like the waterfall of sorrows.

With these lines, the poet Nizar al-Qabbani immortalised the Algerian woman militant.

One of the most outstanding of the women militants who fought on behalf of the Algerian national liberation revolution against French colonialism, Bouhired joined the underground resistance movement in 1956 when she was not yet 20 years old. She was captured in a raid by the French Special Forces. Brought before the court in July 1957, she was sentenced to death. Massive pressure from international public opinion however forced the French to delay execution of the sentence and she was transferred in 1958 to the prison at Rheims, in France. Following the progress of Algerian-French negotiations, the signing of the Evian Agreement and the announcement of Algerian independence in May 1962, Algerian prisoners were gradually released, Bouhired among them. After independence, Bouhired assumed the presidency of the Algerian Women's Union, until her resignation.

Of the day she was sentenced to be executed Djamila Bouhired says, "It was the most beautiful day of my life because I was confident that I would be dying for the sake of the most wonderful story in the world . . . I still remember that on returning from the courtroom to the prison, when our brother prisoners shouted to us to ask what our sentence was, we replied with the hymn that those condemned to death would sing and that begins 'God is Most Great . . . Our sacrifice is for the motherland.' I was with Djamila Bou 'Azza and it was a moving moment. Thousands and thousands of voices repeated the hymn with us, to give us courage".

She remembers, too, the day when she, along with her female comrades, were released from prison. She says that she roamed the streets of Paris for 48 hours aimlessly and without resting and that Paris impressed her so much that she asked herself naively, "If their country is so beautiful, how come they want to take ours?"

Farida Allaghi

The political failures that have befallen the Arab world's various projects for reform or change have led to fierce controversies, resulting in sharp political divisions, the balkanisation of the party-political map in Arab countries, and the fragmentation of party positions on women. Fragmentation did not, however, prevent parties from making women's issues an essential cornerstone of their discourse and activities, which led to:

- formation of women's wings within parties;
- formation of ostensibly independent women societies and unions, which in reality were dependent on parties in their structure and political line;
- participation by women in leadership bodies although in small numbers varying from party to party;
- the coordination of party demands with those of civil society, including women's organisations; and
- the inclusion of women's issues in party agendas under both general demands affecting men and women (education, health, employment and social development) as well as specific women's campaigns targeting personal status laws, political rights (to vote and run for local and parliamentary elections; equality in gaining leadership positions in various institutional and administration bodies) and advocating for women's quotas in political parties.

Despite their fragmentation and competition and the common restrictions placed on them by ruling regimes, political parties have helped to push the issue of women to the forefront through:

- party groupings and blocs;
- coordination with organisations in civil society that shared their ideas;
- coordination with women's movements to reinforce their positions and demands; and
- coordination with official agencies and ruling or governing parties when called for by political alliances.

Through these efforts, they helped achieve victories for women in Arab countries (Guessous, background paper for the Report).

Yet for all this, in women's matters, the common legacy of political parties, both those in opposition and those in power, has been the complete restriction of female political activity. No party has corrected the almost total absence of women from executive positions in government and society or the modest level of their presence in lower structures, and no party allows women a decisive voice in its internal affairs.

QUOTAS FOR WOMEN IN POLITICAL INSTITUTIONS

It is understood that quotas should be applied as part of a comprehensive developmental process if they are not to serve as a purely symbolic gesture whose effect will disappear once they are removed.

In Jordan, with its recent experience with democracy, quotas have enabled some women to enter parliament and have helped to break down some of the barriers to women's political participation while also nudging tribal groupings to nominate women for office. There is consensus, however, that quotas are only an interim step towards a society willing to apply full equality.

Growing demands by Arab women's groups and the increasing response from governments for quotas as a way for women to reach decision-making positions have led to certain positive changes. In Morocco, the percentage of women in parliament went from 1 per cent in 1995 to 11 per cent in 2003. In Jordan, the percentage of women in parliament rose from 2.5 per cent in 1995 to 5.5 per cent in 2003. The same is true in Tunisia, where the percentage went from 6.8 in 1995 to 11.5 in 2003 (UNIFEM, in Arabic, 2004, 270), and in Iraq, where it reached 25 per cent with the 2005 elections. UNIFEM states that the experiences of Jordan, Morocco and Tunisia prove that the quota system is a good mechanism for increasing representation of women in various legislative bodies.

Quotas have also helped women to enter local government councils, where, however, resistance to their presence is growing. Women first entered these councils in the occupied Palestinian territory when the Ministry of Local Government promulgated a law, under strong pressure from the Palestinian women's movement, mandating that one woman be

In women's matters, the common legacy of political parties... has been the complete restriction of female political activity.

Some activist and nongovernmental organisations have succeeded in organising national campaigns to change certain laws that discriminate against women.

The Palestinian legislative elections of 2006 provide a unique case permitting the examination of the effect of quotas on the volume of women's parliamentary participation.

Many Arab laws specify that private social and women's associations are forbidden to involve themselves in policy or political matters.

appointed to each of certain local councils. As noted in part one of this Report, in the first elections to these councils under the Palestinian Authority in December 2004, 139 women were nominated and 59 were elected compared to 852 men nominated and 254 elected. In other words, women gained 17 per cent of the total number of seats (306) in the 26 locations where elections were held. Thirty-five of these women won against men – which was considered a victory for the Palestinian women's movement – while 24 won by quota (Al-Ayyam newspaper, 2004, 9).

The Palestinian legislative elections of 2006 provide a unique case permitting the examination of the effect of quotas on the volume of women's parliamentary participation. The elections were held under a mixed system that allowed for the election of half the members of the assembly from party lists and the other half by direct vote in the constituencies. Quotas for women were also fixed for the party lists. The number of women candidates for local constituencies was 15 out of a total of 414 candidates, and not one won. The number of women candidates on the party lists was 70 out of a total of 314 candidates, of whom 17, or 24 per cent, won. Thus the percentage of women in the Legislative Assembly elected in 2006 was 12.9 per cent (17 out of 132 members), while the percentage of women in the previous Assembly had been 5.6 per cent. This difference may be explained by the fact that there had been no quotas for women in the Palestinian legislative elections of 1996 while in 2006, quotas were allocated on the party lists (three per list) and that no quotas were allocated for the constituencies.[4]

A genuine democracy enhances the political participation of women. This, in turn, anchors democracy in Arab countries.

ARAB CIVIL SOCIETY AND THE ISSUE OF WOMEN

Since the early 1990s, there has been a significant spread of activist and nongovernmental organisations in the Arab world. A large number of these organisations deal with issues of empowering women politically, economically, legally and socially. Some have succeeded in organising national campaigns to change certain laws that discriminate against women (such as the Jordanian penal code relating to "honour crimes"). They have also helped to secure women's quotas (in Algeria, Jordan, Morocco, the occupied Palestinian territory and other countries) and to pressure governments into action to curb violence against women.

Many Arab laws specify that private social and women's associations are forbidden to involve themselves in policy or in political matters. This is a legal obstacle to the free expression of opinion, which implies that politics is removed from the activities of civil society and from private charitable and social work (Hatab, in Arabic, 2004, 157-169).

Despite the importance of these organisations and groups in providing services that segments of the female population need, doubts exist about their ability to change the prevailing gender-biased power relationship in Arab societies. Many studies have indicated that these organisations are to be found mostly in urban centres, away from the poor, marginalised regions (Ben Nefissa, 2001; Hanafi and Tabar, 2002; Jad, 2004b; al-Shalabi, in Arabic, 2001; ESCWA, in Arabic, 2006b, forthcoming). This means that the most deprived and needy women are beyond their operational reach. Furthermore, representation of women in such groups is usually restricted to the educated middle class. The spread of this type of social organisation would not necessarily mean greater political or social representation for all segments of the female population. It also appears that many of them do not basically seek to organise women to defend their rights and interests; rather, rights are defended in general since achieving these rights is in the interest of all women. Experience indicates that political forces with greater popular support and representation, find this type of discourse easy to oppose and refute even if they are perceived to be acting against women's interests as in the socially conservative political movements.

---

[4] "Programme on Governance in the Arab Region." (2006). http://www.pogar.org/countries/elections.asp?cid=14 (Accessed 26 April, 2006).

The role of the media

The media usually play an important role in spurring political participation and in changing stereotypes of social gender roles; they are, however, a double-edged sword. They are an arena for the forces of change in social gender relations but also a weapon in the hand of forces hostile to change. Thus, inconsistencies are common in media discourse when episodes of violence against women are reported or when sensitive issues such as so-called "honour crimes", female circumcision or changes in personal status laws crop up.

In the Arab world, broadcast media, notably satellite channels, and print media are expanding, employing more women in some countries as statistics indicate. Other countries, such as Yemen, are actually experiencing a decrease in women's participation in mass communication media (audio, visual and print), although the number of women is gradually increasing in this domain. Society and the family still consider working in these media to be shameful and unacceptable. Noticeably, Arab women's interest in the media is limited mostly to their traditional concerns, such as cooking, housekeeping and cosmetics. At a time when women in Lebanon and the occupied Palestinian territory, for example, are expressing increased interest in the media as a profession, there is no indication that more women are becoming reporters.

With a few exceptions, the ownership of political and hard news media remains a male bastion. Women's ownership of companies that produce social publications is far more common than their ownership of companies publishing political journals. In any event, women play no role in planning media policy or making media decisions. In Lebanon, a small percentage of news agencies – a mere 11.68 per cent of the total – are owned by women. In the occupied Palestinian territory, there are no women on the editorial boards of any of the three newspapers though there is one female chief editor of a newspaper in Iraq.

The question remains to what extent the increasing number of Arab women working in the media would influence the general direction of programming positively and help to counter the stereotyped female images purveyed by commercial media. These are images that imply that women's freedom of choice goes no further than the selection of a specific washing powder or electric appliance and where equality means only women's equality as consumers, with the freedom to purchase goods pushed by an advertising market that distorts society's consciousness and women's consciousness of themselves. The entrance of women to policy-making levels in the media, especially women who are fully aware of social gender relations, would instead help the industry to decide what the true image of women should be.

The emphasis on certain patterns of consumption of cleaning supplies and products reinforces the stereotype of women in these areas. A new wave of commercial media concentrates on the female body as a locus of desire and temptation for men to promote, perfume, clothing and beauty products. This new commercialism, evident in many Arab media, not only strengthens old stereotypes of men's and women's roles but also encourages forces resistant to any change in these roles. Overcoming this new trend requires that the State and civil society take a serious stand to ensure that the media become gender-aware agents of change able to challenge stereotypes and prevailing gender relations.

DIFFERENT POLITICAL POSITIONS ON ARAB WOMEN

Political forces on the Arab scene do not oppose the rise of Arab women or their political and social participation; all accept the legal and political equality of women. The problem lies in these forces' implementation of their principles in party and political life. In all cases, participation by women is weak, though perhaps greater among dominant ruling parties that rely on mass mobilisation, especially among regimes that do not embrace pluralism, such as Syria and Tunisia. The one exception to this stance on the rise of women is the Salafite movement, now in decline in many countries but clearly influential in the Arabian Peninsula in general, with differences among the different countries.

Political currents and forces are not fixed, revolving around ideology alone; rather, as political forces, they move in a

With a few exceptions, the ownership of political and hard news media remains a male bastion.

general sphere governed by a political and social culture. Therefore, it is important to measure party discourse favouring women's political empowerment against performance and understand the controversial, complex relationship between the two. The ruling party in an Arab State such as Egypt may support the participation of women, but at the time of the elections, narrow political calculations take priority over original pledges. Thus, in the recent parliamentary elections, the party nominated only six women out of 444 candidates even though it had originally promised to field 25 (Reuters). A leftist party in Morocco may be ideologically progressive where women are concerned, but women may hold only a few seats on its central committees, etc. There are differences in the various movements in the area. The Maghreb (western Arab countries) left does not necessarily take the same positions as the Mashreq (eastern Arab countries) left on the state, religion and women. The Muslim Brotherhood in Morocco does not have the same political strategies and practices as the Muslim Brotherhood in Egypt and Syria. For this reason, the positions of the political forces may better be described as a complex matrix. The latter cannot be simply divided vertically into major political forces but must be examined horizontally to understand differences on the geographical, regional and even national levels (Ezzat, background paper for the Report).

ISLAMIST POSITIONS ON WOMEN

The position of the Salafite currents was always clear, namely, that a woman's place is in the home and that her role is to care for the family. While Salafites may have accepted women's right to vote by analogy with allegiance to the ruler, they adamantly rejected their right to seek and hold public office "to avoid pitfalls" (saddan al-dhara'i'). The Salafites were opposed to women being active in civil society, adopting, as a principle, a division of social labour that limits women's role to that of reproduction, motherhood and child raising and warning against the mixing of the sexes. The most that could be expected from the Salafites was an acceptance of independent feminist activity in private charities.

The targeting of the Salafite movement, in both its non-violent and violent forms, as a source of terrorism following the events of 11 September 2001 brought about a state of disarray not only in its organisational structures but also in its traditional assumptions. Thus, despite the movement's historical rejection of issues such as the mixing of the sexes and the political participation of women, major differences, or perhaps even struggles, arose within the movement over the role of women. One tendency gave precedence to the concept of male superiority (qiwama) over those of sovereignty (wilaya) and participation, while others acknowledged the participation of Salafi women through military operations in which they shared (as in Iraq) or accepted political rights for women, excepting only the lesser and greater imamates (as in Kuwait). However, the great majority in Yemen and Saudi Arabia rejected the latter tendency. But all accepted the idea of women's independent social activity in the field of private charitable work.

On the other side of the arena, the Muslim Brotherhood adopts a principled position in support of women's political rights, accepting in this regard the independent interpretations of contemporary scholars, from within the movement or those ideologically close to it, such as al-Ghazali and al-Qaradawi, which are based on jurisprudence. In March 1994, before the Population Conference in Cairo, the Brotherhood in Egypt issued a paper on "Muslim Women in Muslim Society" that reflected a moderate position accepting women's political participation (except in the greater imamate). In the reform initiative led by the Muslim Brotherhood in Egypt in 2004, there was also a moderate position on women's issues. The movement's organisations in Algeria, Iraq, Lebanon, Syria and Tunisia hold positions that take as their starting point the rallying cry of the civil state that gives women their political rights. There is also a broad Shiite political current in Bahrain and Iraq that shares the Muslim Brotherhood's point of view on this, while at the same time the conservative Shiite tendency favours basic restrictions on the role of women in public and political life.

Women's activities in the political sphere vary among the different trends that have

---

It is important to measure party discourse favouring women's political empowerment against performance.

The position of the Salafite currents was always clear, namely, that a woman's place is in the home and that her role is to care for the family.

The Muslim Brotherhood adopts a principled position in support of women's political rights.

adopted the Muslim Brotherhood's intellectual vision. Women have a conspicuous presence, and a number of outstanding figures, in Morocco's Justice and Development Party, and these have made their voice heard for several years in the debate over the Personal Status Code. Women came to the forefront in the Moroccan elections of 2002 when 15 women were elected to parliament from the Party's list. As a result of the Party's proportional division of its seats, six of these actually entered parliament along with 35 other women as part of the boom in the number of women in parliament that followed from the national understanding that women would be given quotas on party lists. On the other side of the Arab world, women have a noticeable presence in the Islamic Union of Kurdistan, with five in the Political Bureau out of a total of 35 members and three seats in the Kurdish parliament. Three women from the Union also sit in the Iraqi parliament.

The strength of the Salafite movements in some countries, especially in the Arabian Peninsula, has driven the Brotherhood, despite its intellectually liberal position, to take hard-line stands against women's political rights in, for example, Kuwait and Saudi Arabia, while in Egypt and Syria, their main concern has been related to security. There are three main reasons for this: first, the relative size of the movements and the power relationships between them; second, the relative sizes of the societies themselves, their civilisational backgrounds, and the cultural context in which they operate, in view of the obvious differences between the Gulf States and Egypt, Morocco and Syria; and third, the nature of the political regime and its degree of openness. There is, however, no one model. Thus, while the Islamists in Kuwait are allowed wide political space, they tend to take hard-line positions, and while the Brotherhood is allowed only a narrow margin by the restrictions placed on its legal status, its intellectual and individual positions on rights and women's political participation have become more open. In Morocco, things fluctuate, and in the Sudan, things are better in both theory and in reality because of the weak impact of the Salafite movement there compared to the strength of Brotherhood thinking and the Sufi orders.

BOX 9-1

Shaykh Muhammad Mahdi Shams al-Din: No Objection to Women's Holding High Office

"On the question of the eligibility of women for high state office, an examination of the evidence makes it clear to me – though God, Great and Glorious, knows best as to His commands – that the consensus of the jurisprudents as to the illegality of their undertaking and assuming authority is a claim that has no significant basis".

Source: Shams al-Din, in Arabic, 2001, 5.

BOX 9-2

'Abd al-Halim Abu Shaqqa: Women's Right to Vote and to Stand for Election

Islamic Law Approves Women's Right to Vote

The fundamental rule says, "Things are originally permitted". Since there is nothing in Islamic law that denies women the right to vote, we consider that this right is legitimate ab initio. In practical application, however, we choose from among legitimate things what suits our circumstances and serves our interests.

We would like to present here an opinion by Dr. Mustafa al-Siba'i, may God bless his soul. Dr. al-Siba'i was professor of shari'a (Islamic law) and Dean of the Faculty of Shari'a (Islamic Studies and Jurisprudence) of Damascus University. The opinion of his that we quote is that of a group of shari'a specialists, expressed at a dialogue on the extent to which shari'a approves women's right to vote and to stand for election. Dr. al-Siba'i said, "Following discussion and deliberation on various views, we have determined that Islam does not prohibit giving this right to women. Election is an exercise through which the Nation selects agents to represent it in legislation and monitoring the Government. The election process is one of appointing agents, through which a person casts his vote for those whom he selects to be his deputies in parliament, to speak on his behalf and defend his rights. A woman is not prohibited by Islam from giving a power of attorney to someone to defend her rights and express her will as a citizen".

A Woman's Right To Stand for Election to Legislative Bodies

The discussion here will centre on two themes: first, shari'a's approval of a woman's right to run for office and second, the introduction of special conditions for a woman to exercise this right.

First: Shari'a's Approval of a Woman's Right to Stand for Election

We reiterate that the fundamental rule is that "things are originally permitted". Since there is nothing in Islamic law that denies women the right to vote, we consider that this right is legitimate ab initio. In practical application, however, we choose – from among legitimate things – what suits our circumstances and serves our interests. We quote here an opinion of Dr. Mustafa al-Siba'i, may Allah bless his soul, in which he said: "… If the principles of Islam do not prohibit a woman from being a voter, do they prohibit her from being a deputy? Before we answer this question, we must know the nature of a 'deputy of the nation'. It perforce covers two major functions:

1. Legislation: the enactment of laws and regulations.
2. Monitoring: scrutiny of the acts and work of the Executive Authority.

With regard to legislation, there is nothing in Islam that prohibits a woman from being a legislator, because legislation requires, first and foremost, that a legislator should have knowledge of the basic and indispensable needs and necessities of the society. Islam gives both men and women the right to learn. Our history tells us of women who were scholars of Hadith, jurisprudence and literature, etc".

Second: The Introduction of Special Conditions for a Woman to Exercise this Right

With regard to monitoring the Executive Authority, this falls into the category of enjoining what is right and forbidding what is wrong. In the sight of Islam, men and women are equal in this regard. Allah, glorious and sublime, said in the Qur'an: 'The believers, men and women, are protectors, one of another: they enjoin what is just and forbid what is evil' (Qur'an, At Taubah, verse 71). Therefore, there is nothing in Islamic texts that takes away from a woman her eligibility to participate in parliament's work of legislation and the monitoring of executive authority".

Source: Abu Shaqqa, in Arabic, 1999, 446-448.

Despite the fact that the position of the Muslim Brotherhood is in principle in favour of women's political rights, there are no women on the Brotherhood's Consultative Council in Egypt, Lebanon, the occupied Palestinian territory or the Syrian Arab Republic – the homes of the strongest Brotherhood movements. In Egypt, for example, the movement did not nominate a woman to the people's Assembly until 2000, in Alexandria, a unique case. There are no politically recognisable women's faces in the movement, only "sisters" – actors who are well known within the circles of the Islamist movement but who are not prominent public women. The Muslim Sisterhood wing of the movement was not created by Hasan al-Banna, its spiritual leader, but crystallised under the leadership of Zaynab al-Ghazali, who was from the Muslim Women's Association. She declared allegiance to Hasan al-Banna, joined his group, and led the Muslim Sisterhood within the Brotherhood; historically speaking, however, it was not the Brotherhood that established the women's wing. The expectations of Zaynab al-Ghazali's movement remained higher than Hasan al-Banna's vision. The latter concentrated in his "Letters" on women's social role in the family and the call to join the movement.

In Syria, the Brotherhood recently published "A Political Plan for the Syria of the Future: the Vision of the Muslim Brotherhood in Syria". In this document, it stressed the human symmetry between men and women as well as their asymmetry in certain roles related to motherhood and femininity, the two being reconciled within society. It stated that three injustices threaten the Muslim nation: westernisation, slavish adherence to tradition and extremist thinking. Later, however, the Brotherhood retreated and affirmed that the home is the basic arena for women, that participation in public life should be by merit and that society has an excess of women's efforts. This swing is often evident in the writings of the Brotherhood since Hasan al-Banna became its spiritual leader. It reflects an ideological conviction of human equality on the one hand and concern about the breakdown of the family on the other as if the entry of women into public life was not a support for the family. There is, in the Brotherhood's thinking, a sharp division between the private and the public, between the family and the political, and this division of roles is deeply rooted in its mentality despite

---

Luminary: Zaynab al-Ghazali

Zaynab Al-Ghazali was greatly influenced by the religious education imparted to her by her father, who was an Azhari scholar and who used to call her Nasiba, in happy reference to Nasiba bint Ka'b al-Maziniyya al-Ansariyya, a celebrated Companion of the Prophet. After her father's death, she moved with her mother to Cairo to live with her brothers, who were studying and working there. As her older brother would not agree to her acquiring an education, she went to a girls' school on her own and asked its headmaster to accept her. Al-Ghazali studied in State schools but this was not enough for her. She started taking classes in the religious sciences from sheikhs from al-Azhar in order to combine modern academic sciences with their traditional counterparts that depended on direct transmission from a sheikh.

After obtaining her secondary certificate, al-Ghazali met Huda Sha'rawi and joined the Women's Union. It was planned that she should go on a scholarship to France but she did not do so despite her having been selected, along with two other young women from the Union. Al-Ghazali continued to repeat Sh'arawi's slogans and to adopt her projects for the development of women and their preparation to take on her cultural and social role even as she prayed, fasted, read the Qur'an and wore a European-style hat.

Subsequently, a certain incident constituted a turning point in her life and led to her rebirth as a woman who wore "modest dress", resigning from the Women's Union in the process yet never for a moment losing her faith in Huda Sha'rawi or her friendship for her despite the secular orientation of Sha'rawi's movement and her opposition to "the veil".

Al-Ghazali represented an early response to the calls for an Islamic vision of the liberation of women and an irrefutable retort to all those who sought to link women's backwardness to Islam. She founded the Society of Muslim Ladies in 1937 as a personal initiative unrelated to any political or male organisation and obtained a permit from the Ministry of Religious Endowments when still only eighteen years of age. She held regular weekly meetings for activism and proselytising. Following her success, she initiated a relationship with the Muslim Brotherhood that led to her society amalgamating with the latter.

The activities of the society were not limited to good works and it also turned to political action as something inseparable from social action. In al-Ghazali's view, politics impacted on cultural and social charitable work. Given the society's objective of defending Islam, demanding implementation of the shari'a, and calling Muslims to the Book of God, it naturally collided with all political parties and the authorities. This clash reached its apogee with her house arrest on 20 August 1964 as part of a campaign against the Muslim Brothers that peaked with a sentence of life imprisonment against al-Ghazali, who was released in 1971. Al-Ghazali speaks of this painful ordeal in her famous work, Ayyam min Hayati (Days from My Life) (Dar El Shorouk, 1995), which is regarded as a historical documentation of an important era – from 1964 to 1971 – in the life of the contemporary Islamic movement.

Zaynab al-Ghazali held an optimistic and positive view of the role of Muslim women. Despite her repeated references to "The kingdom of women, on whose throne she would sit and which made of her a queen in her home", she believed that the route to the development and modernisation of the Islamic world was via women and that the advancement of society began and ended with her. She visited most of the countries of the Islamic world as a proselytizer and supporter of the Islamic movements during the second half of the twentieth century. She wrote a number of works, some of which have yet to be published. Her published works are *Nazarat fi Kitab Allah* (Views of the Book of God), *Nahw Ba'th Jadid* (Towards a New Renaissance), *Ila Ibnati* (To My Daughter) and *Mushkilat al-Shabab wal-Banat fi Marhalat al-Murahaqa* (The Problems of Young Men and Women during Adolescence).

Haytham Manna'

its belief in individual rulings that support women's political role. Such vacillation may reflect indecision in the Brotherhood's position as much as concern about the exposure of women to the same risks of imprisonment and torture as men. Certainly, it is clear that every time the group mentions political rights, it feels it necessary to stress the role of the family even in short political statements.

Women's true difficulty with the Islamists is not linked only to their discourse and position on women. It stems from the Islamists' broader ideological system regarding politics. Paradoxically, this system does not reflect the original Islamic vision, which conceived of a society and state based on participation at all levels and on political presence, not just political representation – the type of system, in short, within which it would be easy to find a place for women (Ezzat, background paper for the Report).

The challenge before the Islamist's vision of women is how to develop an Islamic alternative that can coexist with differing or opposing trends and advance women's position forcefully in discourse and practice not as a result of, but as one of the conditions for, building the Islamic society that they desire. In this way, women's participation in the shaping of the model would become part of the empowerment of the model, not simply their own empowerment, and "the woman's voice" would take part in creating, developing and renewing the model as one of the pillars of its "Islamicity". When this happens, the social discord created by backwardness, poverty, the digital divide and the educational decline in the Arab world will be more of a problem for the religion than the supposed problem of women. Moreover, "avoiding pitfalls" will be a guide to help women to enter the public sphere, not to isolate them from it, and will serve to defend their participation, not to justify their exclusion from it. No corruption matches that of oppression. A nation that does not possess its freedom and does not apply standards of justice is a worthless nation even if every woman were to drape her body to the ground and put a thousand veils over her head (Ezzat, background paper for the Report).

Any rereading of the history of the

Islamic movements must use this approach not to understand the past and present but to formulate a better future. If a call like that of the Brotherhood were to bring women into the public, civil and political sphere under a system that believes in democratic action, the face of the Arab nation as it is today would change. Its nationalist currents would be closer to, and more capable of a discussion of the real issues of absolutism, social violence, economic decline and the consumerism that devours people's future while playing with their dreams. What would have happened, for example, if the Brotherhood had put their female leaders onto their election lists from the time that they began participating in parliamentary elections in Egypt in the mid-1980s, or what would have happened if the "re-considerations" by al-Jihad and al-Jama'a al-Islamiyya had begun at the beginning, and not the end, of the 1990s and included their position on women and not just their position on violence?

The connection between the reawakening of religious consciousness on the one hand and the future of democracy and of the Arab woman on the other needs to be made absolutely clear. Escape from the constraints of the "Islamic–secular" dichotomy is the key not just to beginning the process of liberating women from inside the Islamist vision. It is also a way for Islamists to escape from the narrow theoretical and applied constructs of the savage beast of secularism and to deal with their fears of westernisation. It would enable them to

The challenge before the Islamist's vision of women is how to develop an Islamic alternative that can... advance women's position forcefully in discourse and practice not as a result of, but as one of the conditions for, building the Islamic society that they desire.

transcend their embattled and split vision of society and see that the opposite of their core concept of the Islamic state (ruled by men with or without the participation of women) is not necessarily a heretical, secular state out to put an end to Islam. In adopting this view, the Islamists take shelter behind a traditional and largely local cultural legacy without renewing it out of fear of the annihilation of their culture and civilisation. In reality, the alternatives are much broader than that.

Attention should focus on this critical historical moment in the transformation of the concept of the state and the reality of its power. Its influence on conceptions of authority must be studied. So, too, should the political space in terms of content, form, contexts and concepts. The intellectual and jurisprudential system must be reorganised in such a way that sovereignty (*wilaya*) means quite simply citizenship and that women are no longer a "problem" but partners in the formulation and manufacture of the entire "thesis".

THE INTERNATIONAL CONTEXT OF THE SITUATIONS OF ARAB WOMEN

EXTERNAL PRESSURE FOR THE EMPOWERMENT OF WOMEN IN ARAB COUNTRIES

The international agenda has witnessed fundamental changes since the beginning of the 1990s, with the increased importance of issues such as human rights, women's and minority rights, and democratic change. These issues received even greater attention, especially in the Arab world, after the events of 11 September 2001, when a perceptible concentration of interest in women appeared.

One of the consequences of 9-11 was that the Arab world came to be viewed as an incubator of fundamentalism and a seedbed of terrorism owing to uncontainable tensions in its conservative traditional social structure. The focus shifted to the cultural factor, with the goal of envisioning different societies that would embrace alternative values and new ideologies. At the heart of these values lay such issues as

minority rights, democracy, expanding the base of political participation and the involvement of women in the development process. It was in this context that what are now known as "reform issues" began to take shape.

For many Arab countries, the issue of women's political rights became a type of democratic façade. Women offered an easily manipulated symbol for countries that wanted to escape political criticism of their undemocratic conditions at a time when human rights reports and reports on women's affairs were pressing for change.

Western pressure on the Arab States with respect to women does not come out of a vacuum but is a part of the prevalent culture of the country exerting the pressure. As a result, it is laden with many preconceptions about the condition of Arab women. Such pressure is not grounded in past struggles of Arab women. It is often ignorant of their achievements, whether in the framework of civic activities that preceded NGOs or those of national and pan-Arab movements.

If Western criticism of the condition of the Arab woman from the academic, feminist and even political standpoints is sometimes based on fact, it does not occur in a pure form but is often mixed with concepts and ideas circulating in the West about women's liberation. These in turn are linked to developed market economies and the fragmentation of society. They can also include Orientalist concepts characterised by the demonisation of Arab men and an almost theatrical crusade to free women, in body and spirit, from their domination.

The new wave of Western interest in advancing the position of women has led donors to support projects solely because a visible women's or feminist institution puts them forward or to support any projects to strengthen the status of women that seem topical. No proper studies carried out to measure the effect of these projects on the status of Arab women in their society, in the family or in relation to the State. Nonetheless, the Western trend in general is to provide support to women in the public arena who speak on behalf of women's issues demanding appointments in the administration and membership in parliament.

For many Arab countries, the issue of women's political rights became a type of democratic façade

Western pressure on the Arab States with respect to women does not come out of a vacuum but is a part of the prevalent culture of the country exerting the pressure.

Women's empowerment projects sponsored by Western organisations and support funds do not threaten any political system. They convert a major issue into a group of small projects with which any non-democratic system can live. In the most extreme cases, they create a type of tension between the Islamist and conservative movements and the dominant system. The system welcomes this tension, if it is contained, because it helps its image internationally and at the same time results in a compromise domestic solution that does not threaten it.

Western pressure and the ready accommodation of it in some Arab countries are particularly clear with respect to the representation of women in the political framework, such as parliament and the cabinet. Of course, the representation of women in parliament (or men, for that matter) falls short if there is no truly democratic representation of citizens as whole.

While the general trend in the Arab world towards empowering women through new legislation is to be welcomed, the crucial factor is not the issuing of laws but their enforcement on the ground.

It is clear that in this era, it is no longer possible or necessary to pass through all the stages of social transformation; the granting of voting rights to women cannot wait until local conditions are ripe. However, the opposite course should be resisted, i.e., to believe that democracy is merely universal suffrage and that women's equality with men means granting positions to women or simply having them in office. These are necessary but not sufficient conditions for the pursuit of equality. Indeed, they are not nearly enough; on the contrary, they become separated from equality and democracy if undertaken as well-intentioned initiatives to appease a foreign power through the appointment of women from the existing social elite as window dressing for the regime, (Bishara, background paper for the Report).

THE ROLE OF THE INTERNATIONAL AND REGIONAL ORGANISATIONS

International organisations operate on many levels in many spheres at the same time. Though each has its own field of specialisation, each tries to approach the subject of empowering women from a holistic angle, i.e., through the concept of sustainable development and, subsequently, through a concentration on good governance.

The representation of women in parliament (or men, for that matter) falls short if there is no truly democratic representation of citizens.

The granting of voting rights to women cannot wait till local conditions are ripe.

Luminary: Dr. Hala Salaam Maksoud

Hala Maksoud was celebrated as one of the most important leaders of the Arab-American diaspora in the United States from the mid-1970s until her death in 2002.

In 1980, Maksoud, in collaboration with former senator James Abu Rezk, founded the American-Arab Anti-Discrimination Committee, which she headed from 1996 until her resignation for reasons of ill health in 2001.

During her tenure, she was able to expand the activities of this important institution, founding 80 branches and seeing membership rise to 20,000. She also created strong networks with a number of American civil society organisations, thus strengthening the role of the Committee, which came to the fore on the American and international stage as one of the largest and most important Arab-American non-governmental organisations in the United States.

In 1982, Maksoud led a sit-in in front of the White House in protest at the Israeli invasion of Lebanon, mobilising American public opinion and confirming her role in American public affairs.

Hala Maksoud possessed a talent for communicating with different types and groups of people and a capacity for persuasion and for the building of outstanding personal relationships. She devoted most of her time to working for Arab causes in the American arena through her lectures and articles and by participating in conferences and seminars on television and radio, whereby she focused on eliminating negative stereotypes of Arab women.

In addition to these activities, Hala Maksoud was permanent secretary of the American Committee on Jerusalem, treasurer of the Committee for the Preservation of Palestine Heritage, president of the Association of Arab-American University Graduates, and founder and president of the Arab Women's Council.

In 2002, she was awarded the Achievement Prize of the American Immigration Law Foundation in recognition for her overall achievement.

Lebanese by birth, Maksoud obtained American nationality and married the Lebanese Arab thinker, Clovis Maksoud. She had a doctorate in political theory from Georgetown University. Some months before her death, she was preparing to publish a book on "The Islamic Content of Arab Nationalist Thought".

Leila Sharaf

BOX 9-4

The Role of United Nations Agencies and Regional Organisations in Supporting the Empowerment of Women

A brief overview of the work of some of these organisations is highlighted below:

The United Nations Development Programme (UNDP) represents the UN's global development network, which seeks to assist countries in achieving the Millennium Development Goals and in meeting the challenges of democratic governance, poverty reduction, crisis prevention and recovery, energy and environment and HIV/AIDS. UNDP works to ensure that the empowerment of women and human rights are mainstreamed into all of the organisation's programmes; the Economic and Social Commission for Western Asia (ESCWA), seeks to promote economic and social development among its 13 member states and has played an extensive coordinating role since the Beijing and Beijing + 10 conferences; the United Nations Development Fund for Women (UNIFEM), is dedicated to advancing women's empowerment and gender equality to meet challenges that include feminised poverty, the spread of HIV/AIDS among women and violence against women while supporting a number of Arab countries in the translation of the Beijing programmes, strategies and plans; the United Nations Children's Fund (UNICEF), advocates children's rights particularly those related to health, education, equality and protection and is committed to "levelling the playing field for girls"; the Office of the High Commissioner for Human Rights, which has concentrated its strategy on a human rights-based approach to development also aims to promote gender equality in the enjoyment of these human rights; the Food and Agriculture Organisation of the United Nations (FAO), which has given priority to gender mainstreaming and the importance of improving conditions of rural women and to promoting opportunities for rural economic growth, given that women constitute a high proportion of the agricultural labour force,

especially in the informal sector; the United Nations Population Fund (UNFPA), which has concentrated its efforts and its resources on improving women's reproductive health and making motherhood safer through the promotion of gender equality and legal and policy reforms; the United Nations Educational, Scientific and Cultural Organisation (UNESCO), which has given priority to assuring the quality and effectiveness of education for young women and mainstreaming gender issues in the areas of education, the sciences, communication and culture; and the United Nations Environment Programme (UNEP), which has concentrated on increasing women's participation in environmental protection.

Some Arab funds and funding institutions are also active in the area of women's empowerment. These include the Arab Fund for Economic and Social Development (AFESD) that supports the economic and social development of Arab countries through financing development projects, encouraging private and public investment in Arab projects and providing technical assistance services; the Arab Gulf Programme for United Nations Development Organisations (AGFUND), whose initiative to fund projects aimed at the advancement of Arab mothers in the areas of health and education was launched in the 1980s and which collaborated with UNDP and the Government of Tunisia in the establishment of the Centre of Arab Women for Training and Research (CAWTAR) in Tunis in 1993. CAWTAR aims to help forge a new perspective on the Arab woman and to change traditional views of the roles of the sexes in social development through raising the level of awareness among policy-makers, planners, interested and involved groups, and ordinary people about the current situation of Arab women and their actual and potential contribution to comprehensive and sustainable development.

The Fourth World Conference on Women held in Beijing in 1995 constituted a critical turning point by giving international, Arab and local action a significant impetus towards the improvement of the conditions of women in Arab countries. Subsequent international financial contributions were channelled within the framework of the follow-up on the implementation of the Beijing Programme for Action. In this same context, the 2000 and 2005 New York conferences (Beijing + 5 and Beijing + 10) were convened to monitor results and renew momentum. Emphasis was also placed on following up on the implementation of the

Convention on the Elimination of All Forms of Discrimination against Women (CEDAW) (UNIFEM, in Arabic, 2005).

Inter-Arab action and an initiative on the part of ESCWA, UNIFEM, the Arab League and CAWTAR to draw up an Arab Plan of Action for the Advancement of Women to 2005 accompanied the preparations for the Beijing Conference.

This plan outlined nine strategic objectives for Arab women derived from critical areas of concern: safeguarding the right of Arab women to participate in power structures and decision-making mechanisms; poverty alleviation for

Arab women; assuring equal access to all levels of education; assuring equal access to health services; promoting Arab women's economic self-reliance and capacity to enter the labour market; overcoming the effects of war, occupation and armed conflict on Arab women; elimination of violence against women; participation of women in managing natural resources and safeguarding the environment; and the effective use of communications media to bring about changes in roles in society and promote equality between men and women. In order to implement the Arab Plan of Action for the Advancement of Women to the Year 2005, governments and regional and international organisations as well as financial institutions and funds agreed to join together to make the necessary financial arrangements. Budgetary resources were allocated and priority was accorded to supporting NGOs working in the field of the rise of Arab women.

The Arab Plan of Action accorded special attention to the institutional aspect. It urged that programmes and activities organised by the Commission on the Status of Women of the United Nations, the Department of Women's Affairs in the General Secretariat of Arab States and the other relevant international and regional organisations and institutions should be coordinated. It also stated that an official mechanism concerned with women's issues should be established and directly linked to the highest executive authority, with its own budget sufficient for the implementation of the programmes and projects for the advancement of women contained in the national plans and strategies of each Arab country. In 1996, the Arab plans of action were translated into a Unified Arab Programme for Action that focused on three priorities, namely, poverty, the family and women's political participation.

ESCWA and the Arab League directly monitored the phases of implementation of the Arab Plan of Action and the Unified Arab Work Programme as well as the Beijing Programme for Action by continuing contact with all the Arab countries at both the official government and private and research levels. UNDP, UNFPA and UNIFEM took part directly in these efforts along with the League of Arab States and CAWTAR.

In July 2004, the Arab States approved the Arab Women's Beirut Declaration, which establishes a framework and outline for the empowerment of women in the coming decade (2005-2015), i.e., following the ten-year review of the Beijing Conference.

KEY ACCOMPLISHMENTS

1- ESTABLISHMENT OF MECHANISMS TO EMPOWER WOMEN

Support, including technical and educational support, has been provided to establish national mechanisms for women's affairs in several Arab States. In Algeria, a ministry was created to deal with the family and women's issues. In Bahrain, the Supreme Council for Women was established (2001). A ministry for women's issues and advancement was created in the Comoros and a commission for women's advancement in Djibouti (1999). The National Women's Assembly was established in Egypt (2000). Women were empowered in the Ministry of Social Affairs in Jordan and, it may be pointed out, Jordan was the first Arab State to establish a National Commission for Women (1992). The National Committee for Lebanese Women's Affairs was formed (1998) and a ministry for women and to safeguard the family was established in Morocco (2002). A general directorate for women and several government training centres for women, in addition to gender units in the relevant ministries, were established in Oman. The Ministry of Women's Affairs was established in the occupied Palestinian territory (2003). The Supreme Council for Family Affairs was established in Qatar and deals with women's affairs through its Women's Committee (1998). The National Council for Women was created in Syria (1995) and Yemen's Women National Committee, which was created in 2003.

The era following the Beijing Conference has been distinguished by increased international efforts in the Arab region for the advancement of women.

2- APPEARANCE OF ARAB INSTITUTIONS AND MECHANISMS FOR THE ADVANCEMENT OF WOMEN

The era following the Beijing Conference has been distinguished by increased international efforts in the Arab region for the advancement of women. International and regional organisations have played a major role in coordinating and providing links between Arab countries on the official, private and civic levels through workshops, numerous Arab regional conferences, joint research and studies and in preparing strategies for the rise of Arab women.

3- INTERVENTION, NETWORKING AND COORDINATION

Working with Arab governments poses special challenges because of the sensitivity of some women's issues.

As noted, international organisations favour a holistic approach to women's issues, irrespective of their individual specialisation in line with the overarching concepts of sustainable development and good governance. Working with Arab governments poses special challenges because of the sensitivity of some women's issues and the lack of coordination between public departments on the one hand and poor cooperation between governments and NGOs on the other. Arab government departments, for the most part, also lack up-to-date management and communication tools and technology.

4- COOPERATION WITH GOVERNMENTS AND NON-GOVERNMENTAL ORGANISATIONS

In their dealings with Arab countries, the international organisations took an established policy approach based on cooperation with both governments, NGOs and all civil society organisations. Most programmes and activities were based on three-way participation. The general goal was to induce governments and NGOs to work together. Many difficulties that had traditionally hindered such cooperation were addressed and sometimes surmounted by working to reduce fears on both sides. These partnerships in turn allowed for the accumulation of significant efforts and the attempts to harness them towards the advancement of women. International organisations relied on a dual mechanism: to ask the governments and, on a separate track, the NGOs to prepare progress reports on a specific specialisation or a subject connected to an upcoming international conference. The governments prepared a national report while the CSOs prepared a shadow report. This dual approach allowed the international organisations to maintain a critical sense in writing reports on conditions and achievements, permitting an objective appraisal of actual progress, and of obstacles and gaps (Kiwan, background paper for the Report).

TOWARDS THE RISE OF WOMEN
IN THE ARAB WORLD

CHAPTER TEN

A STRATEGIC VISION: TWO WINGS FOR THE RISE OF WOMEN

Introduction

An Arab renaissance cannot be accomplished without the rise of women in Arab countries. This calls for more than the establishment of rights and justice for women in the face of the historic wrongs that they have suffered. The latter is both a duty and a demand, but supporting the advance of Arab women transcends righting wrongs. Directly and indirectly, it concerns the well-being of the entire Arab world.

Undeniably, Arab countries have realised substantial achievements, to which the progress made by women to date bears witness. Nevertheless, there is still far to go to attain the desired goals envisioned.

Indeed, the tide of society's support for the rise of women has ebbed noticeably over the last five decades compared to the end of the nineteenth and early twentieth centuries. Low levels of human development and a lack of essential freedoms in the region arising from a social environment in which conservative and inflexible political forces have gained sway have caused institutional backing for the rise of women to recede (AHDR 2004).

The preceding chapters have shown that substantial tasks remain to be addressed if Arab women are to advance through the acquisition and use of their capabilities and the full enjoyment of rights. The analysis has also demonstrated that a complex web of cultural, social, economic and political factors, some ambiguous in nature, keeps Arab women in thrall. Cultural hangovers perpetuate a strong bias against women while societal structures, especially those that influence child-raising, education, the media and family relations, affect attitudes towards women in society as a whole. Along with numerous legal obstacles,

these factors variously prevent women from acquiring and using capabilities that would help them and society to progress. Moreover, women are also denied the enjoyment of human rights on an equal footing with men, which further blocks their advance.

The present Report places great emphasis on female education. However, it stresses that the importance of educating girls in Arab countries goes well beyond enabling society to deploy their capabilities. It is apparent that the failure to educate girls in the region is due essentially to cultural prejudices against women or to economic constraints of the family or the society. Girls have proven themselves to be excellent students, yet inequality of educational opportunities remains a serious obstacle to the advancement of women, reflected in the fact that illiteracy in Arab countries is more widespread among women than men.

The relatively weak employment of Arab women's capabilities in the economic sector and in the political sphere is also attributable to overall social, cultural and economic conditions and to the state of governance.

Hence social reform for the advancement of women needs to be undertaken as part of a comprehensive human renaissance project in the Arab world, which is one of the two wings supporting the rise of women in the strategic vision presented in this chapter.

Notwithstanding such general constraints, some Arab women have been able to realise outstanding achievements in different fields. Such achievements, however, remain limited to those women who have had the opportunity to acquire skills and to participate in various human endeavours. Their successes illustrate the importance of taking affirmative action to enable women to enter all fields of human activity. This will, in turn, inspire more women

Supporting the advance of Arab women transcends righting wrongs. Directly and indirectly, it concerns the well-being of the entire Arab world.

Substantial tasks remain to be addressed if Arab women are to advance through the acquisition and use of their capabilities and the full enjoyment of rights.

Notwithstanding constraints, some Arab women have been able to realise outstanding achievements in different fields.

to seek higher levels of participation, which will serve both the advancement of women and the goals of human development.

The way forward to successful human development in Arab countries lies in completing the substantial tasks already undertaken to promote the rise of women rather than in lauding earlier achievements. A good omen in this regard is that public opinion, as reflected in the survey, offers strong moral support for the rise of women as part of a comprehensive human renaissance in the Arab world (Box 10-1).

FIRST: KEY FEATURES OF THE STRATEGIC VISION

The rise of Arab women must go beyond a merely symbolic makeover that permits a few distinguished Arab women to ascend to positions of leadership in State institutions, notwithstanding the value and importance of this. Rather, it must extend to the empowerment of the broad masses of Arab women in their entirety.

From the perspective of human development as a process of societal change, the rise of Arab women requires, first, that all Arab women be granted full and genuine opportunities to acquire essential capabilities; this is so especially in the area of health, in its positive and comprehensive sense. As a first requirement, all Arab girls and women must also acquire knowledge on an equal footing with boys and men.

Second, it is a requirement that full opportunities be given to Arab women for effective participation in all types of human activity outside the family and on an equal footing with their male counterparts, and that this effective participation be the consequence of their own freely taken decisions.

It is also essential that the appropriate social value be given to women's role in the family as an indispensable contribution to the establishment of a sound social structure capable of supporting a project for the renaissance of the Arab world. The Arab Human Development Reports, especially those concerned with the two axes of knowledge and freedom, have underlined the importance of social upbringing. They have stressed the primary importance of the family in providing youth with knowledge and critical faculties and thence the capacity to innovate and create and in endowing children with positive values, such as initiative and a sense of belonging to society, all of which make the progress of society possible. Thus, enabling women to build their capabilities is the crucial foundation that prepares them to play a positive, creative role as women in raising children, strengthening family bonds of affection and cohesion, and empowering all family members to participate effectively in the project for Arab renaissance.

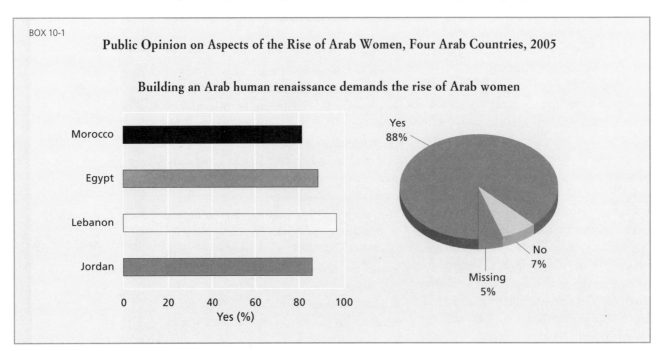

BOX 10-1

Public Opinion on Aspects of the Rise of Arab Women, Four Arab Countries, 2005

Building an Arab human renaissance demands the rise of Arab women

This positive, creative role is, however, beyond the capacity of women who are subjugated and denied their rights, hence the value of a process for the implementation in Arab countries of the Convention on the Elimination of All Forms of Discrimination against Women (CEDAW) and of the Convention on the Rights of the Child, especially those clauses that decree equal treatment between the sexes and guarantee the rights of girls.

Thus, it is of paramount importance to reform Arab education in such a way as to ensure that all girls are guaranteed opportunities to acquire knowledge and to use it within and outside the family.

The next strategic priority is freedom. Focusing on this subject, AHDR 2004 called for the rise of Arab women, and in particular:

- total respect for the rights of citizenship of all Arab women on the grounds that they are a basic axis of the Arab societal structure;

- the protection of women's rights in the area of personal affairs and family relations; and

- guarantees of total respect for women's personal rights and freedoms and, in particular, the protection of women, in all stages of their lives, from physical and mental abuse.

The achievement of these rights requires extensive and profound legal and institutional reform aimed at attaining conformity with international human rights standards and laws relating to the protection of women's rights as reflected in CEDAW. Almost all Arab countries have acceded to this Convention though a number of them have registered reservations to certain articles. Other sections of this Report show that these reservations can be overcome without violating the tolerant essence of shari'a (Islamic law). They also underline the critical need to adopt independent interpretative reasoning in jurisprudence to achieve this objective.

This Report also calls for the temporary adoption of the principle of affirmative action or positive discrimination in expanding the participation of women to all fields of human activity in every Arab society according to the particular circumstances of each. This will allow the dismantling of the centuries-old structures of discrimination against women. Such discrimination has made it difficult, if not impossible, for women to assume, without assistance, their rightful place in Arab societies, which are in the early stages of a shift towards a society that does not defraud women or deprive them of their human rights.

The definitive elimination of all forms of discrimination against women is a struggle against a massive historical injustice, one that will involve thwarting those responsible for it long into the future. This demands the adoption of temporary preferential support, or the principle of affirmative action in favour of women, at least in the initial stages of action, to correct historic injustices. This must be done judiciously and by methods that do not themselves inadvertently weaken those who need to be strong and bold. Affirmative action should enable women to become effective in the face of strengthened competition rather than providing them an absolute protection that might weaken their role. This is not a simple equation, but it is essential.

It is thus important that affirmative action in favour of women does not entice them and the men who support them to waver in the essential struggle to claim their rights on the basis of merit. For example, it might be appropriate to allocate quotas for women in legislative elections at the local and central levels, and even better to see them named on the lists of competing parties. At the same time, however, it would be preferable to maintain the principle of competition between women within the allocations such that this positive discrimination leads to the emergence of the best female candidates.

The Report team sees no validity in the argument that holds that quotas are unconstitutional and undermine equality between citizens. Quotas for women are especially necessary in countries where discriminatory clauses are embedded in their legal structures (AHDR 2004, chapter 4). This also applies to specific countries that already use the quota system for other purposes, such as Egypt, which constitutionally allocates half of its parliamentary seats to "farmers and labourers".

It should be noted at this point that the package of reforms outlined here is consistent

Affirmative action should enable women to become effective in the face of strengthened competition rather than providing them an absolute protection that might weaken their role.

Quotas for women are especially necessary in countries where discriminatory clauses are embedded in their legal structures.

What is required is a historic struggle whose domain is the current power structure and whose objective is the just redistribution of power among people in general.

The rise of Arab women cannot take place in isolation from the rise of their societies.

The rise of Arab women requires a complex, comprehensive review of frameworks of thought and behaviour at all levels.

with the strategic visions presented in earlier editions of the Arab Human Development Report, namely, those for the establishment of a knowledge-based society and for a shift towards freedom in the Arab world.

Societal reforms are envisioned that will enable women to ascend and that will guarantee their rights in line with CEDAW as one wing of a bird on whose back Arab women will soar.

A bird, however, needs two wings to fly. The second wing is the emergence of a broad and effective movement of struggle in Arab civil society. This movement will embrace Arab women and their male supporters in activities of increasing breadth and depth. It will seek to improve their participation in carefully targeted societal reform on the one hand and, on the other, empower all Arab women to enjoy the fruits of changes that serve the rise of both women and the region as a whole.

The completion of the opening act of the izdihar scenario set out in AHDR 2004, which is based on total respect for the key freedoms of opinion, expression and particularly, organisation, will assist in the birth and growth of this movement and set the stage for the rise of Arab women. It is this scenario that will usher in a dynamic civil society able to act as the vanguard of the struggle for human renaissance in the Arab world.

The great majority of Arab women are marginalised, at a higher than average rate, through no fault of their own and in thrall to the current power structure, the most significant of whose evils is the exclusion of various groups.

The Report does not assume that the marginalised will be transformed spontaneously into ascending forces within the power structure in Arab countries. One might dwell on "what ought to be," but nothing will be accomplished without struggle. The social movement is about precisely that. What is required is a historic struggle whose domain is the current power structure and whose objective is the just redistribution of power among people in general. Stated more clearly, what is required is that power be transferred, through effort, debate and struggle, from those who have monopolised it to its true owners, the Arab people, and especially the women among them.

SECOND: THE FIRST WING: SOCIETAL REFORM FOR THE RISE OF ARAB WOMEN

The rise of Arab women cannot take place in isolation from the rise of their societies. Likewise, in this perhaps more than in any other area of human rights, the passing of laws and regulations that aim to eliminate all aspects of discrimination is not sufficient. In addition to laws, women's awareness of their rights and of how these are affected by society and society's awareness of women's issues both need to be strengthened. The weakest obstacle to the realisation of human rights is the lack of awareness by individuals of their rights, and the worst types of violations are those that society accepts. Both constitute a major obstacle in the path to the rise of women.

The rise of Arab women requires a complex, comprehensive review of frameworks of thought and behaviour at all levels. In line with this, new strategies will be proposed that include the various institutions of Arab societies.

ELIMINATING THE ROOTS OF DISCRIMINATION AGAINST WOMEN IN CULTURAL CONSTRUCTS

1. The encouragement of independent scholarship (ijtihad) in religious matters to overcome cultural obstacles to the rise of women

At the level of culture, the fundamental obstacle to the rise of women remains how to deal with certain conflicts between international standards on the one hand and religious and cultural beliefs on the other. The issue is sometimes referred to as "the conflict of authorities". "Religious beliefs" here does not refer to the Islamic religion alone, though that is always the focus, but also includes Christian beliefs since the stance of both divinely revealed religions towards issues such as abortion and a number of reproductive health issues is similar.

Responses to this conflict take one of two forms. One approach, prominent in international efforts and adopted by many supporters of women's rights in the region, is inclined to favour international standards. The other seeks to bridge the gulf between international standards and religious principles through initiatives in interpretation.

Undoubtedly, forcing the public to choose between international standards and their own religious beliefs and cultural traditions will create an insurmountable obstacle to the rise of women. Thus, in the view of the Report team, there is no alternative to supporting the second approach, which tries to use independent interpretation to establish congruence between international standards and religious cultural principles evolving, in the case of Islam, from a holistic understanding of the Islamic shari'a. Since "there is no priesthood in Islam", it follows that such initiatives in jurisprudence must be released from the grip of religious institutions and personages. Rather, independent interpretation must become the right and duty of every qualified Muslim, woman or man, who has the capacity to engage in the study of her or his religion.

2. Upbringing, education and the media; resisting stereotypes of women in order to spread a culture of equality

The lack of clarity in cultural and social concepts at the level of roles, functions and rights constitutes an obstacle to the rise of women. The clarity of the image of women in society is related to the clarity of these concepts; education and the media have a pivotal role in creating authentic images rather than stereotypes. They thus have an obligation to work to change misleading images through a societal programme for the rise of women.

Family upbringing discriminates between the male and female in matters of freedoms, responsibilities and rights. Therefore, discrimination must be investigated, brought to a halt and punished.

Female upbringing in Arab societies is subject to various forms of discrimination deriving from a male system of values about child-raising and a legal philosophy based on perpetuating male authority. This environment shakes women's self-confidence and undermines their self-image. Likewise, male cultural content determines women's fate and

dominates the way in which they think. Thus, even if the law were to allow the participation of women in national decision-making, the culture of society would not easily do so.

In education, efforts to promote equal treatment between the sexes would benefit from the introduction of modern technologies as aids in revamping curricula and teaching and assessment methods.

In the media, the problem is not only that programmes intended to strengthen the status of women and build respect for their role in society are sometimes deficient. It is also that many soap operas and shows as well as vulgar advertisements often erode serious efforts to promote the rise of women. The problem is compounded by the spread of illiteracy, which has made the broadcast media a primary source of popular culture. Hence, the strengthening of methods for monitoring and analysing women's image in the Arab media is an important priority.

The media should also play an active role in educating the public about the Convention for the Elimination of all forms of Discrimination against Women (CEDAW). The Report's field survey revealed a very low level of public awareness of this convention across the Arab countries.

Correcting women's self-image: Women's self-image decides the roles and occupations for which a woman believes that she is fit. A distorted self-image perpetuates this marginalisation, which serves the interests of the paternalistic authoritarian regime and which makes it even more difficult to bring women into the higher levels of institutions. Parents and educators can work to implant positive images of girls and women, starting with the very young and their early childhood experiences and moving up through the education system, supported by an enlightened media.

This wholesome vision of gender relations must be popularised in order to improve personal and social interactions and introduce democracy into the web of institutional relationships. This is a major task for schools, universities and the media, involving values and role models. New and dependable media channels should be opened to support this vision along with major efforts in the family and

Forcing the public to choose between international standards and their own religious beliefs and cultural traditions will create insurmountable obstacles to the rise of women.

Rooting out ingrained biases against women requires educating society to bring about attitudinal shifts.

society to create a mutually supportive culture of equals.

In particular, the purification of the social structure from the roots of discrimination requires a greater role of men in the rise of women.

Women have taken up the cause of their development and rise within a cultural, social and political framework that assumes respect for freedoms, rights and responsibilities. Unless men take up the same cause of their own accord, there can be no hope of changing the relationships between the sexes in the direction of a coherent life governed by love and happiness, and no hope of changing laws. If men do not make this issue their own before it becomes an objective public issue, their perplexed and confused position towards women's pursuit of their own cause will make their own position even more untenable. This entails pain, sorrow and great loss.

POLITICAL REFORM

In the general sections on the rise of women in the Arab world, the Report postulated the critical role played by a struggling civil movement rooted in a lively and active civil society and undertaking the difficult tasks of the development of women. It referred to the fact that such a movement would require a political reform that begins with the opening scenario from the izdihar act in AHDR 2004 (Chapter 9), based on the total respect for key freedoms: opinion, expression and organisation. The latter, being the basis of political and civic organisation, is perhaps the most important in this context. There is therefore a strong correlation between the movement towards a society of freedom and good governance according to the vision of the third AHDR and the institutional requirements necessary for the formation of a social movement for the rise of women in the Arab world.

There is yet another correlation, however. The move towards a society of freedom and good governance requires wide legislative reforms. It is important that these reforms include guarantees for women's development.

There is a strong correlation between the movement towards a society of freedom and good governance...and the formation of a social movement for the rise of women.

Legislative reform

The analysis of trends in Arab legislation in relation to equality between men and women (chapter 8) shows that a review of the Arab legislative structure is essential to eliminate all forms of legal discrimination against women. This overhaul should be accomplished in concrete terms through the following measures:

1. Arab States should review the reservations that they have registered with regard to CEDAW in order to:
   - Remove all reservations against Article 2 of the Convention, which prescribes the principle of equality, because these reservations are incompatible with the objectives of the Convention, contrary to Article 4 of the Convention and incompatible with international treaty law.
   - Remove reservations that use the pretext that the provision in the Convention is contrary to national law because countries are obliged to amend their national law to bring it into conformity with the provisions in the Convention.
   - Undertake a detailed study of the relationship between the provisions of the Convention and the absolute and fixed rules of shari'a (Islamic law) so that incompatibilities, if any, can be identified and specified and reservations clearly defined. General reservations that the provisions of the Convention are in conflict with the rules of shari'a should not be entered without stating the evidence for this. It is also important to adopt enlightened interpretations that bring the ultimate goals of shari'a into conformity with international human rights law.
   - Ratification of the Optional Protocol remains the touchstone of the seriousness of a country's accession to the Convention.
2. Arab countries should review legislation regulating political rights in order to guarantee women the exercise of these rights on an equal footing with men as well as their observance by all public officials

in their functions. This applies particularly to the judiciary at all levels as well as to political, administrative, local government and academic leaders.

3. In this context, it is appropriate that Arab legislators adopt a system of quotas for women, who have historically been denied the right to participation, in the various legislative and representative assemblies.

4. Arab countries should be called upon to ratify conventions of the International Labour Organisation that relate to women's employment, equal pay and working conditions and the provision of protection for working women.

5. Arab countries should review their labour legislation to provide additional protection for working women and to eliminate all forms of discrimination against them, in particular against poor and marginalised women who perform work in sectors that are not protected by labour law, such as domestic service and the rural sector. It is also essential that congruity be attained between Arab legislation and the conventions of the International Labour Organisation, especially the Discrimination (Employment and Occupation) Convention, 1958 (No. 111) and the Equal Remuneration Convention, 1951 (No. 100).

6. A review of criminal legislation and criminal procedures should be undertaken to eliminate all legal texts that contain discrimination against women. This should cover texts that discriminate in punishment for the crime of adultery; those that discriminate in reducing the punishment for crimes of honour committed by a husband rather than a wife; and those that absolve the perpetrator of a crime of rape from punishment if he marries the victim of the rape. Other prescribed legal provisions or procedures that involve discrimination on grounds of sex should also be removed.

7. A review of the legal system relating to personal status in Arab countries should be undertaken to eliminate discrimination against women. In this regard, it is essential that Arab countries lacking unified personal status legislation adopt such legislation. Moreover, Arab legislators must act to adopt

the most enlightened efforts in shari'a and other religious laws for achieving conformity with the principle of equal treatment for men and women, one that accords with the overall intentions of Islamic and non-Muslim religious law.

8. A request should be made to the Arab League through the Secretariat of the Arab Council of Ministers of Justice to modernise the draft unified model of Arab personal status legislation. The goal will be to bring the model in line with modern life and the international obligations of Arab countries, especially those that relate to the elimination of all forms of discrimination against women. Such modernisation should also include solutions adopted in a number of modern Arab personal status laws and be based on responsive and open-minded jurisprudential interpretations.

9. A review of nationality laws in Arab countries should be undertaken to achieve equal treatment for men and women in the granting of nationality to their children.

10. A culture of equal treatment and respect for human rights should be encouraged among men in the judiciary and all those responsible for enforcing the rule of law. The involvement of women on an equal footing with men in all judicial and other functions relating to law enforcement should be a parallel priority.

COMBATING POVERTY IN SUPPORT OF THE RISE OF WOMEN

The most important area of intervention lies in reducing the spread of income poverty which entails supporting economic growth and achieving greater justice in income distribution. While addressing income poverty, it is equally important to reverse the spread of human poverty, by which is meant the denial to people of opportunities to acquire and use essential human capabilities.

Income growth requires in its turn increased investment and institution-building, meaning the laws, rules, regulations and customs that regulate the social interaction between individuals, in addition to strengthening the foundations of good governance. Likewise,

While addressing income poverty, it is equally important to reverse the spread of human poverty.

equity in income distribution is not only a value in and of itself; it also operates in the long run to support growth, especially in developing countries.

Among the most important mechanisms for attaining social justice and combating human poverty are increases in expenditure on education, particularly for girls, and on health and social safety nets. These areas constitute an investment in humanity and lead in the end to an expansion of people's options.

Reducing human poverty also requires significantly more investment in public health, including investment in the health of infants, the health of children below the age of five and the reproductive health of women. It also calls for increased investment in environmental health.

CONFRONTING REDUCTIONS IN WOMEN'S PERSONAL FREEDOMS

Violence against women is abhorrent in itself and also because it constitutes a complete negation of their human rights and freedoms on an equal basis with men as guaranteed under international treaties. Arab countries that seek to achieve human development must necessarily protect women from violence on the grounds that protection from violence is the responsibility of States, as provided for in Article 4 of the United Nations Declaration on the Elimination of Violence against Women.

In order to guarantee the freedom and human dignity of all women in the Arab world, it is absolutely necessary that the protection of personal freedom be extended to female guest workers in the Arab countries, no matter where on the scale their occupations fall. The protection of the rights of the vulnerable guests is a fundamental yardstick for measuring the extent to which personal rights and freedoms are respected in any society.

The protection of women from all forms of violence in the Arab countries demands important changes at the level of collective awareness. It calls for a strategy derived from an understanding that violence against women in all forms is a degradation of their humanity, a violation of their human rights, and a threat to the psychological and physical harmony of the family and children. The strategy should

also recognise that discrimination on the basis of sex is the principal starting point for the use of violence. Foremost in this area are efforts to forbid and criminalise the circumcision of females.

Arab officials need to be aware and convinced that the prevailing perception of the status of women and their role in society must change. This presupposes the spread and strengthening of a culture of human rights, equality of treatment between the sexes and the right of both to full citizenship. These goals can be realised through social education at the levels of the family, schools, mosques and the media.

It is crucial that laws criminalise violence against women and that States as well as civil society organisations provide safe sanctuaries for women victims of violence, as needed.

THIRD: THE SECOND WING: A SOCIETAL MOVEMENT FIT TO BRING ABOUT THE RISE OF WOMEN IN THE ARAB WORLD

There will be no rise of women in the Arab world without a strong and continuously growing societal movement by which Arab women may empower themselves and their male supporters to eliminate the legacy of backwardness by eliminating "all forms of discrimination against women in Arab society" in the context of building a human renaissance on Arab soil. The use here of language from the text of CEDAW is not accidental. Rather, it serves as a reminder that this national objective is, at the same time, an international objective that humanity as a whole seeks to achieve. It is also an Arab commitment towards the international community, which makes it a fundamental component of the legal structure of Arab countries.

There is no doubt that this movement will create, through the struggle, its own particular means and instruments that will lead to the historic goal of the rise of women in the Arab world.

Nevertheless, this historic task requires effort and sacrifice, especially by vanguard social institutions and intellectuals. Are these ready and able to undertake such efforts?

The protection of women from all forms of violence in the Arab countries demands important changes at the level of collective awareness.

There will be no rise of women in the Arab world without a strong and continuously growing societal movement...to eliminate the legacy of backwardness.

Finally, those who desire to build a human renaissance must strive, with a commitment that goes beyond mere aspiration, to build the tools for this struggle. In other words, a strong societal movement geared towards the rise of women is needed in order to overcome the current power structure.

As envisaged in this Report, this movement has two levels. The first is national and will involve all levels of society in every Arab country. The second is regional: it will be founded on trans-border networks for the coordination and support of regional efforts to achieve a comprehensive Arab movement for the rise of Arab women, benefiting as far as possible from modern information and communication technology.

Optimally, the national and regional components of such a movement would form strong ties based on a partnership of equals with United Nations and international organisations, both governmental and non-governmental, that are working for the rise of women and their emancipation in all parts of the world.

The success of Arab countries in achieving results appropriate for Arabs and the position to which they aspire among world nations, is based on the capacity of a women's societal movement to plan, coordinate, monitor, evaluate and create the empowering environment for the rise of Arab women. Guaranteeing a favourable climate in each Arab country (including among the executive, legislative and judicial authorities) is a sine qua non of this enabling social environment. It will permit the growth of the legal and procedural structure for eliminating all forms of discrimination against women. Such a climate will allow organisations defending women's rights to flourish, to champion the most crucial of these rights and to monitor their implementation once established. Paramount among such rights will be equality with respect for gender differences and guaranteed rights of citizenship.

Crucially, such an environment will facilitate the genesis of effective civil society organisations for the rise of women through collective struggle.[1] It will not only encourage the growth of such organisations; it will also support and guarantee their impact as transparent, democratic and sustainable entities and as contributors to society as a whole. This includes strengthening the accountability of such organisations before the majority of women to protect the latter's interests.

In particular, civil society organisations working for the advancement of women must be converted into self-reliant, sustainable institutions in order to be effective. Such organisations need to be truly popular with women and their male supporters, be ready to act as driving forces, and be willing to establish internal democracy, including transparency and accountability before the generality of women and Arab citizens.

The sum of such organisations, if they are interlinked and mutually supportive, can create the framework of a movement for the advancement of Arab women that could serve as an engine of progress for the entire Arab world.

In addition, laws governing civil society must contain provisions that specifically empower citizens, in particular women, to freely establish associations working for the rise of women and to play an effective role in their competent government and management. This area is undoubtedly one requiring the sustained attention of existing agencies, such as the Arab Women's Organisation.

The Report has pointed in several places to the universal nature of the struggle for women's rights and of the women's liberation movement itself. International solidarity opens wide perspectives for women in the Arab world. Such solidarity will have the greatest impact if it takes the form of effective cooperation through equal partnerships between like-minded international civil society organisations, international agencies and Arab women's groups without the political and cultural biases that often vitiate external reform initiatives.

Civil society organisations working for the advancement of women must be converted into self-reliant, sustainable institutions.

---

[1] The Report does not say "women's organisations," as the Report team sees the rise of women as a collective task in which the efforts of women and their male counterparts are mutually supportive.

FOURTH: PRIORITIES IN THE PROGRAMME FOR THE RISE OF ARAB WOMEN

The general trend to ensure positive health for all, which is one of the components necessary to build human development, extends automatically to the provision of special care for the needs of the weak in general and of women in particular.

Putting an end, once and for all, to the denial to girls and women of their human right to education over a period of, say, ten years is an indispensable requirement.

The Arab Human Development Report customarily includes within its strategic vision broad outlines for overcoming the particular deficit that is the focus of the Report. These outlines are offered so that engaged forces in Arab societies can consider the vision presented, place it within their particular context and adopt the means and methods for achieving its objectives after verifying local needs and resources.

In line with this tradition, those that take up the vision may decide to formulate specific plans for women's development within their particular national context, including the necessary steps, means and methods to achieve these objectives. It is hoped that the strategic vision and broad outline of action offered here will encourage the development and adoption of detailed plans conceived and owned by broad social forces, which will ensure the extension and success of the modest efforts of the Report team.

However, the Report team's broad approach does not preclude suggesting some programmatic priorities that may serve as an additional guide for societal action. Thus, the Report proposes a number of priorities and starting points for women's development in the context of a comprehensive project for human development in the Arab world. They are grouped under two basic goals:

- overcoming obstacles to women's acquisition of essential human capabilities, and
- guaranteeing women's ability to effectively employ their capabilities as they choose.

Women's acquisition of basic human capabilities gradually paves the way for removing the relatively greater obstacles to the employment of their capacities. A woman who is well educated and enjoys good health is keener to employ her skills in a wide range of human activities. Nevertheless, experience indicates that, in the current social context, women with highly developed capabilities do not necessarily find society willing or able to employ their capacities in all spheres of human enterprise. Therefore, special efforts are required to enable women in the Arab region to use the full range of their capacities, especially through temporary affirmative action, such as quota systems, while ensuring the principle of competition within such measures.

FIRST: ELIMINATING WOMEN'S LEGACY OF DEPRIVATION IN HEALTH AND IN KNOWLEDGE ACQUISITION THROUGH EDUCATION

Health care

Guaranteeing good health, in a comprehensive sense, is a matter that lies beyond the capacity of most women in contemporary Arab countries and is most difficult for those who are weakest socially. Women suffer more than men because of the problems of pregnancy and childbirth and because of a general lifestyle that discriminates against them, as revealed in high rates of maternal mortality and a greater loss of years of life to illness relative to men.

Thus, the general trend to ensure positive health for all, which is one of the components necessary to build human development, extends automatically, or so it would seem, to the provision of special care for the needs of the weak in general and of women in particular. Implementation of this Report's previous recommendations for the elimination of poverty, and especially human poverty, are relevant here.

Ending the denial of education to girls and women

Putting an end, once and for all, to the denial to girls and women of their human right to education over a period of, say, ten years is an indispensable requirement. There is a long and discredited discussion relating to plans and programmes to eliminate female illiteracy in Arab countries, a goal that remains far from realisation. Thus, the movement for women's development in the Arab world is called upon to embark on a serious, substantial programme, with official and civic dimensions as well as regional and national ones over the time-bound period of a decade, which would ensure all girls and women of a complete basic education. A specific goal, would be to achieve, by 2015, the eradication of Arab female illiteracy and to ensure the completion of twelve years of basic schooling by every Arab girl. These should become the criteria for assessing and measuring the seriousness and success of the women's movement in the Arab nation.

In the overall ordering of education with all its components, committed efforts are necessary to eliminate any seeds of discrimination between the sexes. The two international conventions (CEDAW and the Convention on the Rights of the Child) which, luckily, most Arab countries joined became inseparable parts of the Arab legislative system and provide a conceptual and legal framework for guaranteeing the rights and protections (especially freedom from discrimination on the basis of sex) that their provisions contain.

There is a powerful dialectic between the power structure and the educational system. One outcome of the present crisis between the people and the government system has been the denial of any form of education enabling the mass of women to progress. There is no disputing, however, that the improvement of education, especially the provision of widespread high-quality education, supports the empowerment of the marginalised and is hence a major priority of the social struggle that can lead to the rise of women. These efforts may be assisted by an educational system that is strong, non-governmental and not for profit as a rival to government education, with strong guarantees from an effective quality-control system. If it were possible to breathe life into private non-profit work through civil society organisations, the latter would find ample opportunities in this field.

Because basic education is the entry point for lifelong learning and the primary path to building an essential human capability, namely, knowledge, the Report team proposes several steps for ensuring basic education for girls.

Strategic measures for ending the denial of basic education to girls

The following measures could be considered as priorities:

- provision of good schools designed to cater to the needs of young girls and located at an accessible distance in all residential areas of the country;
- imposition of basic education free of cost without omissions or excuses;
- removal of financial barriers to the establishment in local communities of schools that are open to girls throughout the educational process;
- confrontation of traditions and social trends that impede girls' education, especially non-registration of girls' births and early marriage (the negative medical and social impacts of which are well known);
- reinforcement of the social return on education by providing specific advantages in terms of public services for educated people, in particular females;
- elimination of any bias against females in the curricula, books, teaching methods and educational management of schools;
- elimination of all forms of mistreatment, by beating or in any other form, in all schools, especially for girls;
- introduction of a sound sexual education for both sexes at a preparatory stage to enable youth to reach sexual maturity safely and to avoid the dangers of sexual ignorance or of obtaining incorrect information from unreliable sources;
- mobilisation, in alliance with the state, the private sector and families, of civil efforts that have proved their seriousness in the field of education for the provision of a high-quality education that is friendly to girls;
- boosting economic returns on education through the inclusion in educational programmes of training that qualifies students for good professions in demand in the labour market and that provides excellent life skills;
- provision of special incentives for girls who have chosen the path of education (good job opportunities, material and intangible incentives, promotion of cases of success in the media) and for their families, at all levels, from the local to the national; and
- incorporation of local and individual features of communities into plans to confront the denial of education to girls.

In the overall ordering of education with all its components, committed efforts are necessary to eliminate any seeds of discrimination between the sexes.

There is a powerful dialectic between the power structure and the educational system.

Basic education is the entry point for lifelong learning.

Improvement of the social context of girls' education

Societies can take steps extending beyond the education system that can help to eliminate the denial of basic education to girls. Among the most important are:

- insisting on the registration of births, especially of females, as previously indicated;
- raising the age of marriage for girls to 18 years and ensuring that this requirement is observed;
- taking measures to counter the unemployment of educated people and to confront discrimination against females in employment and in worker dismissals;
- improving working conditions for educated people (raising the real value of wages); and
- combating poverty, notably through income-generating projects that target families with school-age children. (Families with school-age children, especially girls and in particular those not attending school, could be given preference for project loans, subject to their children's enrolment and continuance in school).

Ending the denial of basic education to girls is only the first step – albeit a defining one – on the road to building women's capabilities. The completion of this initial step will be crowned by the adoption, at all stages and in all types of education, especially those that prepare women for the professions and equality with men in society, of methods similar to those proposed here for providing basic education for girls.

SECOND: BREAKING DOWN STUBBORN OBSTACLES TO WOMEN'S USE OF THEIR CAPABILITIES AS THEY SEE FIT

Although the development of women's basic human capabilities is an essential condition for their advancement, it is clearly insufficient. In previous chapters, it was indicated that women's capacities are held back by a number of cultural and social factors, as evidenced by the unemployment of educated women in some Arab countries.

Opening the economic sphere for women

Opening the economic sphere for women when they themselves choose to go beyond the family thus heads the list of reforms for achieving their economic independence, itself a critical condition for their "empowerment".

when they themselves choose to go beyond the family thus heads the list of reforms for achieving their economic independence, itself a critical condition for their "empowerment". This strategic requirement entails a package of societal reforms, particularly in the economic field, which would broadly include the following:

- accelerating the rate of economic growth to enable the creation of employment opportunities on a large scale. The significant increase in the price of oil over the last few years constitutes a revenue source that may enable Arab economies to develop and diversify their productive infrastructure. This is a critical prospect that Arab countries must not lose. Creating the opportunities for the optimum employment of women's capabilities through economic growth requires attention not only to the level of development but more importantly to the form of this development. This also applies to the type of technology used, which should be labour-intensive while ensuring the enhancement of productivity.

It is important to underline that employing women's capabilities can positively contribute to the improvement of productivity. Acquiring the means of knowledge is one of the most important determinants of productivity. As evidence presented in earlier chapter shows, girls are capable of a higher level of academic achievement than boys. Interestingly enough, the Report's field survey indicated that the majority of the public believes that women do not achieve less than men as employees.

- resisting the cultural obstacles to women's use of their full capacities in all areas of human development as freely chosen by them;
- guaranteeing, through constitutions and legislation and through the institutional mechanisms for their implementation, equality of employment opportunities for all regardless of gender;
- guaranteeing women's enjoyment of working conditions consistent with human dignity and, when necessary, providing forms of positive discrimination, protective of their family roles, without making them pay for this preferential treatment by

decreasing their work privileges vis-à-vis men. This may require that the society/state bear some of the subsequent economic costs while protecting women's rights. This implies, for instance, that the state should bear the costs of day care and maternity leave for women employees. Moreover, private-sector enterprises that use women's capabilities should be given incentives such as tax concessions; and

- building the mechanisms of an efficient, and modern labour market both at the regional and the national level, open equally to both women and men.

CONCLUSION

This fourth volume brings to an end the first cycle of Arab Human Development Reports. This series has put forward a comprehensive conception of how a human renaissance in the Arab world may be achieved through the elimination of the region's three deficits: in freedom, knowledge and the empowerment of women.

The vision offered here, and in the earlier editions, is no more than intellectual grist for the forces of renewal in the Arab countries in their efforts to formulate mutually supportive projects across the Arab world. It is hoped that these projects will come together to form a historic initiative to bring the region out of the twilight in which it currently languishes and allow all its peoples to develop and achieve the full blossoming of their potential and a better future for all.

It is also fervently hoped that this historic transformation will be carried out under the preferred future scenario: by taking the path of a complete and vibrant human renaissance (*izdihar*) (AHDR 2004) based on a peaceful process of negotiation for redistributing power and building a system of good institutional governance. The first act of this scenario should begin with the institutionalisation of respect for the key freedoms of opinion, expression and association, the last being crucial. This should lead to the creation of a dynamic, effective civil society as the vanguard of a peaceful process of negotiation that will avoid the "impending disaster" scenario of which the Report has warned and whose dark clouds, sadly, are gathering in more than one key Arab country at this time.

References

In English and French

Abu Harithiyyeh, Muhamed and Farid Qawwas. 1997. "A Comparative Study of Women Rights in Arab Labor Legislation", Democracy and Workers' Rights Center, Ramallah, occupied Palestinian territory.

AEI-Brookings Joint Center for Regulatory Studies. 2005. The Economic Costs of the War in Iraq, AEI-Brookings Joint Center for Regulatory Studies, Washington, D.C., September 2005.

Agarwal, Bina. 1994. A Field of One's Own: Gender and Land Rights in South Asia, Cambridge University Press, Cambridge.

Arkoun, Mohamad. 1984. Pour une critique de la raison Islamique, Maisonneuve et Larose, Paris.

Barber, Benjamin R. 1999. "Culture McWorld contre démocratie", in: Révolution dans la communication, manière de voir, No.46, juillet-août 1999.

Ben Nefissa, Sarah. 2001. "NGOs, Governance and Development in the Arab World: Management of Social Transformation", MOST, Discussion Paper No. 59, Democratising Global Governance: The Challenges of the World Social Forum, UNESCO, Paris.
_____. 2000. "ONG, gouvernance et développement dans le monde Arabe," in "Gestion des transformations sociales", Most, le Caire.

Brzezinski, Zbigniew. 2004. The Choice: Global Domination or Global Leadership, Basic Books, New York.

Chabchoub, Ahmed. 2000. Ecole et modernité en Tunisie et dans les pays Arabes, L'Harmattan, Paris.

Chamlou, Nadereh, and Reem Kettaneh Yared. 2003. "Women Entrepreneurs in the Middle East and North Africa: Building on Solid Beginnings", paper prepared for the Annual Joint Seminar 2003 of the Arab Fund on "Arab Women and Economic Development".

Dahbi, Omar. 2004. La guerre de succession au Maroc, www.Ocnus.ne, 2-12-2004.

Daoud, Zakya. 1993. Féminisme et politique au Maghreb (1930-1991), ed, eddif, Paris.

David, Rina Jimenez (ed.). 1996. Women's Experiences in Media, Isis International Manila and the World Association for Christian Communication.

Droy, Isabelle. 1990. Femmes et développement rural, E. Karthala, Paris.

Dugard, John. 2005. Report of the Special Rapporteur of the Commission on Human Rights on the situation of human rights in the Palestinian territories occupied by Israel since 1967. In Israeli practices affecting the human rights of the Palestinian people in the occupied Palestinian territory, including East Jerusalem. Official Records of the General Assembly, Sixtieth Session, 18 August 2005 (A/60/271).

El-Zanaty, Fatma and Ann Way. 2001. EDS Egypt 2001, National population council, Cleverton, ORC Marco, Maryland.

Esim, Simel. 2005. "Gender Mainstreaming in Chambers of Commerce and Industry in Arab States: A Comparative Analysis of Saudi Arabia, Syria, and Yemen", draft, April 2005.

Fergany, Nader. 1998. "Dynamics of Employment Creation and Destruction, Egypt", 1990-1995, Research notes 11, Almishkat, Cairo, January 1998.

GEM (Gender Entrepreneurship Markets). 2005. "Regional MENA Brief 2005, International Finance Corporation", World Bank Group, see www.ifc.org/menagem.

Goetz, Anne Marie. 2003. "Women's Political Effectiveness: A Conceptual Framework", in: Anne Marie Goetz and Shireen Haseem, eds., No Shortcuts to Power: African Women in Politics and Policy Making, Zed Books, London and New York.
_____(eds.). 1997. Getting Institutions Rights for Women in Development, Zed Press, London.

Government of the United States, Department of State, Office of Research. 2005. "Opinion Analysis: Iraqis Say Corruption Is Worse Now Than Under Saddam", Washington, D.C., 25 July 2005.

Hanafi, Sari and Linda Tabar. 2002. "NGOs, Elite Formation and the Second Intifada", Between the Lines, October 2002, 2.18, Jerusalem. www.between-lines.org

Harriman, E. 2005. "So, Mr. Bremer, where did all the money go?", The Guardian, 7 July 2005.

Hatem, Mervat. 2000. "Modernisation, the State, and the Family in the Middle East", in: Meriwether M. and Tucker, J. (eds.), Social History of Women and Gender in the Modern Middle East, Westview Press (city), Boulder, Colorado.
_____. 1994a. "The Paradoxes of State Feminism", in: Barbara Nelson and Najma Chaudhury (eds.), Women and Politics World-wide, Yale University Press, New Haven, Connecticut.

_____. 1994b. "Egyptian Discourses on Gender and Political Liberalisation: Do Secularist and Islamist Views Really Differ?", Middle East Journal, 48:4.

Hijab, Nadia and Camillia Fawzi El-Solh. 2003. "Laws, Regulations, and Practices Impeding Women's Economic Participation in the MENA Region", Report submitted to the World Bank, Office of the Chief Economist, Middle East and North Africa, Washington, D.C., August 2003.

Human Rights Watch. 2005. Israel/Occupied Territories: Human Rights Concerns for the 61st Session of the UN Commission on Human Rights, Geneva.

Jad, Islah. 2004a. "Women at the Cross-roads: The Palestinian Women's Movement between Nationalism, Secularism and Islamism", Ph.D. Dissertation, Department of Development Studies, School of Oriental and African Studies (SOAS), University of London.
_____. 2004b. "The 'NGOisation' of the Arab Women's Movement", IDS Bulletin, Institute of Development Studies, Vol. 35, No. 4:34-42, October 2004.

Kabeer, Naila. 2003. Gender Mainstreaming in Poverty Eradication and the Millennium Development Goals, International Development Research Centre, Ottawa.

Kandiyoti, Deniz. 1991. Women, Islam and the State. Macmillan Press Ltd., London.

Karam, Azza. 1998. Women, Islamisms and the State: Contemporary Feminisms in Egypt, Macmillan Press, London, and Study. Martin's Press, New York.

Kawar, Amal. 2001. "Palestinian Women: Political Activism since Oslo" in: Feminizing Politics, Al-Raida, Vol, 18, No. 92, Winter 2001, Institute for Women Studies in the Arab World, LAU, Beirut-London.

Kimmerling, Baruch. 2003. Politicide, Verso, London.

Kristeva, Julia. 2001. Des Chinoises, Pauvert, Paris.

Mernissi, Fatma. 1984. Le Maroc raconté par ses femmes, SMER, Casa.
_____. 1983. Sexe, idéologie et Islam, Editions Tierce, Paris.

Milne, S. 2005. "Managed Elections Are the Latest Device to Prop Up Pro-western Regimes", The Guardian, 10 March 2005.

Moghadam, Valentine. 2005. "The Political Economy of Female Employment in the Arab Region", in: Gender and Development in the Arab World Women's Economic Participation: Patterns and Policies, edited by Nabil F. Khoury and Valentine Moghadam, Zed Books, London and New Jersey.

Molyneux, Maxine. 1991. "The Law, the State and Socialist Policies with Regard to Women; the Case of the People's Democratic Republic of Yemen 1967-1990", in: Deniz Kandyioti, Women, Islam and the State. Macmillan Press, London.

Nadeau, R. L. 1996. S/HE BRAIN, Science, Sexual Politics, and the Myth of Feminism, Praeger, Westport, Connecticut.

Platform et al. 2005. "Crude Designs, the Rip-off of Iraq's Oil Wealth", The Looting of the Iraq Museum, Baghdad.

Radtke, H.L. and Stam, H.J., eds. 1994. "Introduction", in: Power/Gender: Social Relations in Theory and Practice, Sage, London.

Rathegeber, Eva M., 1990. "WID, WAD, GAD: Trends in Research and Practice", The Journal of Developing Areas, Vol. 24, No. 4, July 1990.

Reporters without borders. 2005. Annual Report 2005, Introduction, North Africa and the Middle East.

Robalino, David (et al.). 2005. Pensions in the Middle East and North Africa: Time for Change, the World Bank, Washington, D.C.

Rowlands, Jo. 1998. "A Word of the Times, but What Does It Mean? Discourse and Practice of Development", in: Haleh Afshar, ed., Women and Empowerment, Illustration from the Third World, Macmillan Press, London.

Royaume du Maroc, Premier Ministre, Ministère de la Prévision Economique et du Plan, Direction de la Statistique. 1998. "Condition socio-économique de la femme au Maroc", Enquête nationale sur le budget temps des femmes 1997/98, Rapport de synthèse, Vol. 1, Maroc.

Sabbagh, A. 2004. "Electoral Processes in Selected Countries of the Middle East: A Case Study", UN (OSAGI), EMG/ELEC/2004/EP, 1, 12 January 2004.

Shavit, Ari. 2004. "The Big Freeze", Ha'aretz (www.haaretz.com), 12 October 2004

UNDP. 2005. Human Development Report 2005: International Cooperation at a Crossroads: Aid, Trade and Security in an Unequal World, New York.
_____. 2003. Human Development Report 2003: Millennium Development Goals: A Compact among Nations to End Human Poverty, New York.

UNESCO. 2005. "EFA Global Monitoring Report; Education for All: The Quality Imperative", Paris.

UNESCO Institute for Statistics. 2002. "Arab States Regional Report", Montreal, Canada.

Waterbury, John. 1977. "An Attempt to Put Patrons and Clients in their Place", in: Earnest Gellener and John Waterbury, (eds.), Patrons and Clients in Mediterranean Societies, Duckworth, London.

World Bank. 2004. "MENA Development Report: Gender and Development in the Middle East and North Africa; Women in the Public Sphere", Washington, D.C.

_____. 2003. Increasing Girls' Enrolment in the Arab Republic of Egypt, Human Development Group, Middle East and North Africa Region, World Bank, Washington, D.C.

World Health Organisation. 2005. World Health Report 2005: Make Every Mother and Child Count, WHO Press, Geneva.

_____2004. World Health Report 2004: Changing History, WHO Press, Geneva.

_____2003. "Obesity and Overweight: Global Strategy on Diet, Physical Activity and Health", WHO web site.

Yeatmann, Anna. 1990. Bureaucrats, Technocrats, Femocrats: Essays on the Contemporary Australian State, Allen and Unwin, Sydney.

Zangana, Haifa. 2005. "Iraqi Women and the Discourse of the American Occupation", in: Barriers of Reconciliation, Jacqueline Israel and William Haddad (eds.), Washington University Press, Washington, D.C.

In Arabic

'Abbud, S. and H. Sulayman. 2004. Al-Waraqa al-Suriyya [The Syrian Paper], proceedings of the seminar Al-Ada' al-Barlamani lil-Mar'a al-'Arabiyya: Dirasat Halat Misr wa-Suriyya wa-Tunus [The Parliamentary Performance of Arab Women: A Case Study of Egypt, Syria and Tunis], Institute for Women's Studies in the Arab World, Lebanese American University with The Arab Centre for Research on Development and the Future, Beirut, 24-25 February 2004.

'Abd al-Hamid, Bandar. 1990. "Nisa' al-Sahra'" [Women of the Desert] in Shahrazad al-Jadida magazine, Issue no. 25, Al-Ard lil-Nashr, Limassol, Cyprus, September 1990.

'Abd al-Mun'im, Suhayr Isma'il. 2002. Haqq al-Mar'a fi al-Musharaka al-Siyasiyya bayn al-Nusus al-Tashri'iyya wal-Waqi' al-Ijtima'i [Women's Right to Political Participation: Legislative Texts vs. Social Reality], a study presented to the seminar Al-'Awlama wa-Qadaya al-Mar'a [Globalisation and Women's Issues], Girls' College, Al-Azhar University, Cairo, March 2002.

Abdellatif, Kamal. 2003. As'ilat al-Nahda al-'Arabiyya: al-Tarikh, al-Hadatha, al-Tawasul [Questions of the Arab Renaissance: History, Modernism, Communication], Markaz Dirasat al-Wihda al-'Arabiyya, Beirut.

_____.1997.Al-'Arabwal-Hadatha al-Siyasiyya [The Arabs and Political Modernism], Dar al-Tali'a, Beirut.

'Abdu, Muhammad. 1980. Al-A'mal al-Kamila [The Complete Works], 2 vols., Al-Kitabat al-Ijtima'iyya [The Social Writings], Al-Mu'assassa al-'Arabiyya, lil-Dirasat wal-Nashr, 2nd edition, Beirut.

Abu Asbah, Bilqays. 2004. "Waqi' al-Musharaka al-Siyasiyya lil-Mar'a al-Yamaniyya" [The Reality of Political Participation for Yemeni Women], a paper presented to The First Arab Women's Democratic Forum, Sanaa, December 2004.

Abu 'Awwad, Nida'. 2003. Al-Ta'lim wal-Naw' al-Ijtima'i fi al-Aradi al-Filastiniyya fi Zill al-Sulta al-Filastiniyya 1994-1999 [Education and Gender in the Palestinian Territories under the Palestinian Authority, 1994-1999], Women's Studies Institute, Bir Zeit University and Centre for Women's Studies, occupied Palestinian territory.

Abu Nahleh, Lamis. 1996. Al-Ta'lim wal-Tadrib al-Mihani wal-Taqni fi Filastin min Manzur al-Naw' al-Ijtima'i [Education and Professional and Technical Training in Palestine from the Gender Perspective], Women's Studies' Programme, Bir Zeit University and Center for Women's Studies, occupied Palestinian territory.

Abu Shaqqa, 'Abd al-Halim Muhammad. 1999. Tahrir al-Mar'a fi 'Asr al-Risala [The Emancipation of Women in the Age of the Prophet's Mission], Dar al-Qalam, Kuwait.

Afarfar, 'Ali. 1996. Surat al-Mar'a Bayn al-Manzur al-Dini wal-Sha'bi wal-'Almani [The Image of the Woman: Religious, Popular and Secular Perspectives], Dar al-Tali'a, Beirut.

Al-'Alyan, Qumasha. 2000. Untha al-'Ankabut [The Female Spider], Rashad Press, Beirut.

Al-'Awwa, Muhammad Salim. 2005. "Al-Nadhir al-'Aryan fi Mas'alat Huquq al-Insan" [The Stark Warning concerning the Question of Human Rights] in Al-Kutub—Wijhat Nazar magazine, Cairo, June 2006.

Al-Ayyam newspaper. 2005. 12 December 2005, http://www.al-ayyam.com/znews/site/default.aspx

Al-'Azawi, Qays and Haytham Manna'. 2005. Himayat al-Suhufiyyin [The Protection of Journalists], Dar al-Hilal, Damascus and Paris, 2005.
_____. 2004. "Wizarat Shu'un al-Mar'a Tukarrim al-Murashshahat lil-Marhala al-Ula min al-Intikhabat al-Mahalliyya" [Ministry of Women's Affairs Honours Female Candidates for First Stage of Local Elections], Issue no. 3230, Ramallah, occupied Palestinian territory, December 2004.

Al-Baz, Shahida. 2002. "Al-Mar'a wa-Sina'at al-Qarar: Ru'ya Bahthiyya li-Tamkin al-Mar'a" [Women and Decision-Making: a Research View of Women's Empowerment], unpublished paper presented to Al-Nadwa al-Iqlimiyya hawl "Al-Naw' al-Ijtima'i wal-Tanmiya: 'Ilaqat Sharaka wa-Tashbik'" [Regional Seminar on "Gender and Development: Relationships of Partnership and Networking"], Tunis, 20-22 October 2002.

Al-Dayalimi, 'Abd al-Samad. 2000. Nahw Dimuqratiyya Jinsiyya Islamiyya [Towards an Islamic Sexual Democracy], Matba'at Afo-print, Casablanca.

Al-Duri, 'Abd al-'Aziz. 1978. Muqaddima fi al-Tarikh al-Iqtisadi al-'Arabi [Introduction to Arab Economic History], Dar al-Tali'a, Beirut.

Al-Falih, Matruk. 2002. Al-Mujtama' wal-Dimuqratiyya wal-Dawla fi al-Buldan al-'Arabiyya [Society, Democracy and the State in the Arab Countries], Markaz Dirasat al-Wihda al-'Arabiyya, Beirut.

Al-Ghannushi, Rashid. 2000. Al-Mar'a bayn al-Qur'an wa-Waqi' al-Muslimin [Women: the Qur'an vs. the Reality of Muslim Men], 3rd edition, Al-Markaz al-Magharibi lil-Buhuth wal-Tarjama, London, printed by Al-Mu'assassa al-Islamiyya lil-Tiba'a wal-Sahafa wal-Nashr, Beirut.

Al-Haddad, al-Tahir. 1929. Imra'atuna fi al-Shari'a wal-Mujtama' [Our Women in Law and Society], Dar al-Ma'arif lil-Tiba'a wal-Nashr, Sousse (Tunisia), 10 December, 1929.

'Ali, Jawad. 1380 AH. Al-Mufassal fi Tarikh al-'Arab qabl al-Islam [A Detailed Account of the History of the Arabs before Islam], 1st edition, Vol. 5 (Intisharat al-Sharif al-Radi).

Al-Jabiri, Muhammad 'Abid. 2000. Naqd al-'Aql al-Akhlaqi al-'Arabi [Critique of the Arab Ethical Mind], Markaz Dirasat al-Wihda al-'Arabiyya.
_____. 1990. Naqd al-'Aql al-Siyasi al-'Arabi [Critique of the Arab Political Mind], Markaz Dirasat al-Wihda al-'Arabiyya.
_____. 1986. Bunyat al-'Aql al-'Arabi [The Structure of the Arab Mind], Markaz Dirasat al-Wihda al-'Arabiyya.
_____. 1984. Takwin al-'Aql al-'Arabi [The Formation of the Arab Mind], Dar al-Tali'a, Beirut.

Al-Marnisi, Fatima. 1983. Kayd al-Nisa', Kayd al-Rijal [Women's Trickery, Men's Trickery], Mu'assasat Bushra lil-Tiba'a wal-Nashr, Casablanca.

Al-Marzuqi, Muhammad. 1980. Ma'a al-Badw fi Hallihim wa-Tirhalihim [Camping and Decamping with the Bedouin], Al-Dar al-'Arabiyya lil-Kitab, Libya/Tunisia.

Al-Rasikhi, Faruzan. 2004. Al-Mar'a fi al-'Irfan al-Islami wal-Masihi [Women in Islamic and Christian Gnosis], Dar al-Thaqafa, Casablanca.

Al-Rawi, Abd al-Jabbar. 1972. Al-Badiya [The Desert], Iraq.

Al-Sa'ati, Samiya, 2003. 'Ilm Ijtima' al-Mar'a [The Sociology of Women], Maktabat al-Usra, Cairo.

Al-Samiri, Nashwan Muhammad. 2001. Al-Ta'addudiyya al-Siyasiyya fi al-Yaman, Usus al-Tajriba wa-Hudud al-Mumarasa [Political Pluralism in Yemen, the Bases of the Experiment and the Limits of Practice], Maktabat al-Jil al-Jadid, Sanaa.

Al-Sarraf, Qasim. 2001. "Mashru' al-Mu'ashshirat al-Tarbawiyya" [Pedagogical Indicators Project], in Majallat al-Tufula al-'Arabiyya [Arab Childhood Magazine], Vol. 2, No. 8, September 2001.

Al-Shalabi, Yasir. 2001. Al-Ta'thirat al-Duwaliyya 'ala Tahdid Ruy'at al-Munazzamat ghayr al-Hukumiyya al-Filastiniyya wa-Adwariha [International Impacts on the Vision of Palestinian Non-governmental Organisations and Their Roles], Unpublished M.A. Thesis, Bir Zeit University, occupied Palestinian territory.

Al-Sharqawi, Su'ad and 'Abd Allah Nasif. 1984. Nizam al-Intikhab fi al-'Alam wa-fi Misr [Elections in the World and in Egypt], Dar al-Nahda al-'Arabiyya, Cairo.

Al-Shatibi, Al-Imam. n.d. Al-Muwafaqat fi Ousoul al-Shari'a [Correspondence in the Conditions of Shari'a], ed. Muhammad 'Abd Allah Diraz, Dar al-Ma'rifa lil-Tiba'a wal-Nashr, Beirut.

Al-Shatti, Nur al-Duha, and Anika Rabw. 2001. Tanzim al-Nisa', al-Jama'at al-Nisa'iyya al-Rasmiyya wa-ghayr al-Rasmiyya fi al-Sharq al-Awsat [Organising Women: Official and Unofficial Women's Groups in the Middle East], Dar al-Mada, Damascus.

Al-Shaykh, Hanan. 1989. Khadija wa-Sawsan [Khadija and Sawsan], Dar al-Hilal, Cairo.
_____. 1988. Misk al-Ghazal [The Musk of the Gazelle], 2nd edition, Dar al-Adab, Beirut.
_____. 1980. Hikayat Zahra [The Story of Zahra], Dar al-Adab, Beirut.

Al-Tahtawi, Rifa'a. 1870. "Al-Murshid al-Amin fi Tarbiyat al-Banat wal-Banin" [The Trusty Guide for the Education of Girls and Boys] in Al-A'mal al-Kamila [Complete Works], edited with a study by Muhammad 'Amara, Al-Mu'assasa al-'Arabiyya lil-Dirasat wal-Nashr, Beirut, 1973.
_____. 1834. "Takhlis al-Ibriz fi Talkhis Bariz" [Refining Gold in Summarizing Paris] in Al-A'mal al-Kamila [Complete Works], edited with a study by Muhammad 'Amara, Al-Mu'assasa al-'Arabiyya lil-Dirasat wal-Nashr, Beirut, 1973.

Al-'Uthman, Layla. 2000. Al-Muhakama [The Trial], Dar al-Mada, Damascus.

Amin, Qasim. 1900. "Al-Mar'a al-Jadida" [The New Woman] in Al-A'mal al-Kamila [Complete Works], edited with a study by Muhammad 'Amara, Al-Mu'assasa al-'Arabiyya lil-Dirasat wal-Nashr, Beirut, 1989.
_____. 1899. "Tahrir al-Mar'a" [The Liberation of Woman], Maktabat al-Adab, Cairo, 1316/1899.

Amnesty International. 2005a. Al-Taqrir al-Sanawi 2005 [Annual Report, 2005], London.
_____. 2005b. Al-Jama'at al-Musallaha Tartakib al-Intihakat bi-la Rahma fi al-'Iraq [Armed Groups Commit Merciless Abuses in Iraq], Document 009/2005, MDE 14, London, 25 July 2005.
_____. 2004. Fi Azmat al-Sudan As'ila wal-Ajwiba [On the Sudan Crisis: Questions and Answers], Document AFR 54/084/2004, 16 July 2004.

Arab Commission for Human Rights. 2005. Taqrir al-Lajna al-'Arabiyya li-Huquq al-Insan 2005: Naz' al-Jinsiyya Ta'assufan fi Qatar [Report of the Arab Commission for Human Rights 2005: Arbitrary Denial of Citizenship in Qatar], Paris.

_____. 2002. Al-Mar'a fi al-Manahij al-Ta'limiyya [Women in Educational Curricula], Report on the proceedings of the Seminar on Women in Educational Curricula, Malakoff, June 2002.

Arab Organisation for Human Rights. 2006. Al-Taqrir al-Sanawi 2005 [Annual Report, 2005], Cairo, forthcoming.

_____2005. http://www.apfw.org/indexenglish.asp?fname=press\english2006\03\10019.htm

'Aref, Muhammad. 2005a. "Qanun Nift al-'Iraq lil-'Iraqiyyin al-Ahrar" [The Law of Iraq's Oil for the Free Iraqis] in Al-Ittihad newspaper, United Arab Emirates, 15/18/2005.

_____. 2005b. "Qarnan min Nahb Mahd al-Hadara fi al-'Iraq" [Two Centuries of the Plundering of the Cradle of Civilisation in Iraq] in Al-Ittihad newspaper, United Arab Emirates, 21/7/2005.

'Ashur, Radwa. 1999. Atyaf [Phantoms], Al-Mu'assasa al-'Arabiyya lil-Dirasat wal-Nashr, Beirut.

Bahrain, State of, Ministry of Education, Centre for Pedagogical Research and Development, with Almishkat Centre for Research. 1999. Taqyim Itqan al-Kifayat al-Asasiyya fi al-Lugha al-'Arabiyya wal-Riyadiyyat 'ind Nihayat al-Halqa al-Ula (al-Saff al-Thalith) min al-Ta'lim al-Asasi [Assessment of the Mastery of Basic Competencies in Arab Language and Mathematics at the End of the First Primary Cycle (Form 3)], Analytical Report, December 1999.

Ba'labakki, Layla. 1958. Ana Ahya [I Live], Al-Maktab al-Tijari, Beirut.

Barakat, Halim. 1985. Al-Mujtama' al-'Arabi al-Mu'asir: Bahth Istitla'i Ijtima'i [Contemporary Arab Society: An Exploratory Social Research Study], 2nd edition, Markaz Dirasat al-Wihda al-'Arabiyya, Beirut.

Bayoumi, Nuha. 1998. "Al-Mar'a, al-Madina, al-Siyasa (Sayda Namudhajan)" [Woman, the City and Politics – the Example of Sidon] in Mawqi' al-Mar'a al-Siyasi fi Lubnan wal-'Alam al-'Arabi [The Political Position of Women in Lebanon and the Arab World], Al-Bahithat, no. 4, Beirut, 1997-1998.

Bayoumi, Nuha, and Fadya Hatit and Maryam Ghandur. 1999. Dalil al-Bahithat al-'Arabiyyat [Guide to Arab Women Researchers] by Nuha Bayyumi, Fadya Hutayt and Maryam Ghandur, 1st edition, Lebanese Association of Women Researchers, Al-Markaz al-Thaqafi al-'Arabi, Beirut.

Bir Zeit University—Development Studies Programme. 2005. Taqrir al-Tanmiya al-Bashariyya 2005 [Human Development Report 2005], Ramallah.

_____. 2004. Istitla' al-Ra'y al-'Amm al-Filastini hawl al-Ahwal al-Ma'ishiyya, al-Hukuma al-Filastiniyya, wal-Wad' al-Amni wal-Islah [Palestinian Public Opinion Surveys on Living Conditions, the Palestinian Government, the Security Situation, and Reform], No.19, Ramallah.

_____. 2002. Istitla' al-Ra'y al-'Amm al-Filastini hawl al-Ahwal al-Ma'ishiyya, al-Hukuma al-Filastiniyya, wal-Wad' al-Amni wal-Islah [Palestinian Public Opinion Surveys on Living Conditions, the Palestinian Government, the Security Situation, and Reform], No.9, Ramallah.

Burnham, Gilbert. 2004. "Qatla Al-'Iraq fi al-Harb al-Amrikiyya Dahaya Mansiyyun" [Iraq's Dead in America's War Are Forgotten Victims] in Al-Kutub—Wijhat Nazar magazine [taken from The Lancet], Cairo, December 2004.

Bu Talib, 'Abd al-Hadi. 2005. Huquq al-Usra wa-Tahrir al-Mar'a [Family Rights and Women's Liberation], Dar al-Thaqafa, Casablanca.

Campbell, Robert B. 1996. A'lam al-Adab al-'Arabi al-Mu'asir: Siyar wa-Siyar Dhatiyya [Leading Figures of Contemporary Arabic Literature: Biographies and Autobiographies], Vol. II., al-Saharti – al-Yusuf, 1st edition. Markaz Dirasat al-'Alam al-'Arabi al-Mu'asir, Université de Saint Joseph, Beirut.

Centre for Arab Women Training and Research. 2001. Taqrir Tanmiat al-Mar'a al-'Arabiyya [The Arab Women's Development Report], Tunis. www.cawtar.org.
_____. 1998. Al-Mar'a al-'Arabiyya wal-'Amal; al-Waqi' wal-Afaq, Dirasat Halat al-Sudan [The Arab Woman and Work: The Current Situation and Prospects, a Case Study of Sudan], Tunis. www.cawtar.org.

Chekir, Hafidha. 2004. "Al-Waraqa al-Tunusiyya" [The Tunisian Paper], proceedings of the seminar Al-Ada' al-Barlamani lil-Mar'a al-'Arabiyya: Dirasat Halat Misr wa-Suriya wa-Tunus [The Parliamentary Performance of Arab Women: A Case Study of Egypt, Syria and Tunis], Institute for Women's Studies in the Arab World, Lebanese American University with The Arab Centre for Research on Development and the Future, Beirut, 24-25 February 2004.

Egyptian Centre for Human Rights. 2005. Dawr Mu'assasat al-Mujtama' al-Misri fi Da'm al-Musharaka al-Siyasiyya lil-Mar'a [The Role of Egyptian Social Institutions in Supporting Women's Political Participation], Cairo, www.ecrwegypt.org.

ESCWA. 2006a, forthcoming. Taqrir Awda'a Al-Mar'a al-'Arabiyya: Al-Harakat al-Nisa'iyya fi al-'Alam al-'Arabi [Report on Arab Women Conditions: Women's Movements in the Arab World].
_____. 2006b, forthcoming. Al-Harakat al-Niswiyya al-'Arabiyya [Arab Women's Movements], Background Papers, Beirut.

Fahmi, Mahir Hasan. 1964. Qasim Amin [Qasim Amin], Wizarat al-Tarbiya wal-Ta'lim, Cairo.

Farahat, Mohamed Nour. 2003. "Al-Mar'a wal-Musawah, al-Tamyiz li-Salih al-Nisa'" [Women and Equality, Positive Discrimination in Favour of Women] in Rasa'il al-Nida' al-Jadid [New Call Essays], no. 65, Cairo, November 2003.

Fayad, Mona. 2004. Musharakat al-Mar'a fi al-Hayat al-Siyasiyya, al-'Awamil al-Musa'ida wal-Mu'iqa [Women's Participation in Political Life: Conducive and Obstructive Factors] in Qadaya al-Muwataniyya fi Lubnan, Ab'ad wa-Tahaddiyat [Issues of Citizenship in Lebanon: Dimensions and Challenges], Various authors, Al-Markaz al-'ilmi lil-Dirasat, Beirut.
_____. 1998. "Al-Mashhad al-Siyasi al-Lubnani La Yuqliquhu Ghiyab al-Mar'a" [Lebanese Political Scene Is Unperturbed by the Absence of Women] in Mawqi' al-Mar'a [The Position of Women] in Al-Siyasi, Women Researchers, no. 4, 1997-1998, Beirut.

Fergany, Nader. 2006 "Al Shaquo Al Afdhal" [The Better Half]—Wijhat Nazar, Cairo.
_____. 1998. "Athar I'adat al-Haykala al-Ra'semaliyya 'ala al-Bashar fi al-Buldan al-'Arabiyya" [The Impact of Capitalist Restructuring on Human Development in Arab Countries], Development and Economic Policies Magazine, Vol.1, no. 1, Arab Planning Institute, Kuwait.

Ghamiri, Muhammad Hasan. 1989. Dalil al-Bahth al-Anthurubuluji fi al-Mujtama' al-Badawi [Guide to Anthropological Research on Bedouin Society]. Al-Maktab al-Jami'i al-Hadith, Alexandria.

Hamadi, Idris. 2003. Afaq Tahrir al-Mar'a fi al-Shari'a al-Islamiyya [Prospects for the Liberation of Women in Islamic Law], 3rd edition, Dar al-Hadi, Beirut.

Hatab, Zuhayr. 2004. "Al-'Awamil al-Susiyulujiyya li-Du'f Musharakat al-Mar'a al-Lubnaniyya" [The Sociological Factors behind the Weakness of Lebanese Women's Participation] in Qadaya al-Muwataniyya fi Lubnan, Ab'ad wa-Tahaddiyat [Issues of Citizenship in Lebanon: Dimensions and

Challenges], various authors, Al-Markaz al-'ilmi lil-Dirasat, Beirut.

Hijab, Nadia. 1988. Al-Mar'a al-'Arabiyya: Da'wa ila al-Taghyir [The Arab Woman: A Call for Change], Riyad al-Rayyis lil-Kutub wal-Nashr, London.

Howeidy, Fahmy. 1998. "Fath Bab al-Ijtihad fi Jins al-Mar'a wal-Rajul" [Opening the Gateway to Interpretive Religious Reasoning on Men and Women] in Al-Quds newspaper, Palestine, 17 September 1998.

Human Rights Commission. 2005. Taqrir al-Khabir al-Ma'ni bi-Halat Huquq al-Insan fi al-Sumal [Report of the Independent Expert on the Situation of Human Rights in Somalia] presented to the Human Rights Committee, Session 61, document no. E/CN/ 04/2005/ 117, Geneva.

Ibn Khaldun. n.d. Al-Muqaddima, Bab al-'Imran al-Badawi [The Introduction, Chapter on Bedouin Civilisation], Dar Al-Kitab al-'Arabi, Beirut.

Ibn Manzur. 1982. Lesan Al-'Arab [Arab Tongue], Vol. 1, Dar Ihya' Al-Turath Al-'Arabi, Beirut.

Issa, Nahawand Kadiri. 2001. "Al-Lubnaniyyat wa-Jam'iyyatuhunna fi al-'Ishriniyyat" [Lebanese Women and Their Associations in the Twenties] in Al-Nisa' al-'Arabiyyat fi al-'Ishriniyyat, Huduran and Hawiyyatan [Arab Women in the Twenties: Presence and Identity], Lebanese Association of Women Researchers, Beirut.

Ja'far, Muhammad Anas Qasim. n.d. Al-Huquq al-Siyasiyya lil-Mar'a fi al-Islam wal-Fikr wal-Tashri' al-Mu'asir [Women's Political Rights in Islam, Theory, and Contemporary Legislation], Dar al-Nahda al-'Arabiyya, Cairo.

Jid'an, Fahmi. 1985. Nazariyyat al-Turath wa-Dirasat 'Arabiyya Islamiyya [The Theory of Heritage and Islamic Arabic Studies], Dar al-Sharq, Amman.

Joint United Nations Programme on HIV/AIDS. 2004. Al-Nisa' wal-Aydz: Muwajahat al-Azma [Women and AIDS: Facing the Crisis].

Joseph, Su'ad. 2005. "Al-Abawiyya wal-Tanmiya fi al-'Alam al-'Arabi" [Patriarchy and Development in the Arab World], translated by Wamid Shakir, in Jusur magazine, Year 1, no. 9, November, 2005. First published in English in Gender and Development Journal, 2 June-4 November 1996.

Judges Club. 2005. "Egypt's Conscience", http://www.al-araby.com/articles/966/050703-966-jrn01.htm.

Khalifa, Sahar. 1986. Mudhakkarat Imra'a Ghayr Waqi'iyya [Memoirs of an Unrealistic Woman], Dar al-Adab, Beirut.
_____. 1984. 'Abbad al-Shams [The Sunflowers], Dar al-Jalil, Damascus.
_____. 1976. Al-Sabbar [The Cactus], Matba'at al-Sharq al-Ta'awuniyya, Jerusalem.

Khoury, Colette. 1961. Layla Wahida [A Single Night], Al-Maktab al-Tijari, Beirut.
_____, 1959. Ayyam Ma'ah [Days with Him], Dar al-Kutub, Beirut.

Kuttab, Eileen. 1996. "Al-Haraka al-Siyasiyya fi Filastin" [The Political Movement in Palestine] in Al-Mar'a al-'Arabiyya fi Muwajahat al-'Asr [Arab Women Confront the Age] in Research and Discussions of the Academic Seminars Organised by Nur/Dar al-Mar'a al-'Arabiyya lil-Nashr, Cairo.

Lebanese Organization to Combat Violence against Women. 2001. Wirash 'Amal hawl al-'Unf al-Manzili [Workshops on Domestic Violence], Beirut, January/February 2001.

Machsomwatch. 2004. A Counterview: Checkpoints, 2004.

Mahfuz, Najib. 1957a. Bayn al-Qasrayn [Between the Two Palaces], Cairo, Dar Misr lil-Tiba'a.
_____. 1957b. Qasr al-Shawq [The Palace of

Desire], Cairo, Dar Misr lil-Tiba'a.,
_____. 1957c. Al-Sukariyya [Sukariyya Street],
Dar Misr lil-Tiba'a.

Majallat al-Qada' wal-Tashri'. 1975. Al-'Adad
al-Khass bi-Munasabat al-Sana al-Dawliyya
lil-Mar'a [Special Issue on the Occasion of
the International Year for Women], issued
monthly by the Ministry of Justice, Year 17,
no. 7, Tunis, July 1975.

Majallat al-Risala al-Qanuniyya. 2005. Majallat
al-Risala al-Qanuniyya [The Official Gazette],
Algiers, no. 39, March 2005.

Mamduh, 'Aliya. 2000. Al-Ghulama [The
Tomboy], Dar al-Saqi, Beirut.

Manna', Haytham. 1986. Intaj al-Insan Sharqi
al-Mutawassit, al-'Asaba wal-Qabila wal-Dawla
[The Production of Middle Eastern Man: Clan,
Tribe and State], Dar al-Nidal, Beirut.

Maqdisi, Usama. 2000. "Al-Janusa wal-
Muwataniyya: Tasadum Tayyarat al-Hadatha"
[Sexuality and Citizenship: The Clash of
Currents of Modernism] in Al-Muwataniyya fi
Lubnan bayn al-Rajul wal-Mar'a [Citizenship
in Lebanon: Men vs. Women], Dar al-Jadid,
Beirut.

Mustaghanimi, Ahlam. 2004. 'Abir Sabil
[Passerby], Manshurat Ahlam Mustaghanimi,
Beirut.
_____. 1998. Fawda al-Hawass [The Chaos of
the Senses], Dar al-Adab, Beirut.
_____. 1993. Dhakirat al-Jasad [The Memory
of the Body], Dar al-Adab, Beirut.

Naffa', Emily. 1998. "Al-Mar'a al-'Arabiyya
fi al-Sulta al-Siyasiyya: al-Kuta wa-Imkaniyyat
Tatbiqiha" [The Arab Woman and Political
Authority: Quotas and the Possibilities of
their Application] in Proceedings of the
Conference on The Arab Woman and Political
Authority: Quotas and the Possibilities of their
Application, Beirut, 10-12 July, 1998.

Na'na', Hamida. 1979. Al-Watan fi al-'Aynayn
[The Cherished Nation], Dar al-Adab,
Beirut.

Nasiri, Rabi'a. 2003. "Al-Harakat al-Nisa'iyya
fi al-Maghrib: ma'a al-Tawkid 'ala Tunus, al-
Maghrib wal-Jaza'ir" [Women's Movements
in the Western Arab World, with a Focus on
Tunisia, Morocco, and Algeria], in: Al-Ra'eda,
Vol. 20, no. 100, Winter 2003.

National Centre for Human Rights, Jordan.
2005. Al-Taqrir al-Sanawi al-Awwal 2005
[First Annual Report, 2005], Amman.

National Council on Human Rights, Egypt.
2005. Al-Taqrir al-Sanawi al-Awwal 2004-
2005 [First Annual Report, 2005], Cairo.

Palestinian Central Bureau of Statistics. 2005.
Mash Athar Jidar al-Damm wal-Tawassu'
'ala al-Waqi' al-Ijtima'i wal-Iqtisadi lil-
Tajammu'at al-Filastiniyya allati Yamurr al-
Jidar min Aradiha [Survey of the Impact of
the Annexation and Expansion Wall on the
Social and Economic Reality of Palestinian
Communities through Whose Lands the Wall
Passes], June 2005, www.pcbs.org.

Palestinian Centre for Human Rights. 2005.
Taqrira al-Markaz al-Filastini li-Huquq al-
Insan, Raqam 35 wa-36 [Palestinian Centre
for Human Rights, Report nos. 35 and 36],
September 2005.

Qusayr, Qasim. 2004. "Hizb Allah wa-Tarshih
al-Nisa' lil-Baladiyyat wa-Majlis al-Nuwwab"
[Hizbullah and the Nomination of Women
for Municipal and Parliamentary Elections]
in Al-Mustaqbal al-Lubnani newspaper, 14
April 2004.

Ramzi, Nahid. 2004. Al-Mar'a wal-I'lam fi
'Alam Mutaghayyir [Women and the Media in
a Changing World], Maktabat al-Usra, Cairo.

Rida, Muhammad Rashid. 1973. Tafsir al-
Manar [The Lighthouse Commentary], Vol.
4, Al-Hay'a al-'Amma al-Misriyya lil-Kitab.

Sabbar, Khadija. 1998. Al-Mar'a, al-Mithulujiya
wal-Hadatha [Woman, Mythology and

Modernism], Ifriqiya al-Sharq, Casablanca.

Sabir, Muhy al-Din and Luwis Kamil Malika. 1986. Al-Badw wal-Badawa [The Bedouin and Pastoral Life], Manshurat al-Kutub al-'Asriyya, Sidon/Beirut.

Sha'ban, Buthayna. 1999. 100 'Am min al-Riwaya al-'Arabiyya [100 Years of the Arabic Novel], Dar al-Adab, Beirut.

Shams al-Din, al-Imam al-Shaykh Muhammad Mahdi. 2005. Masa'il Harija fi Fiqh al-Mar'a [Critical Issues in the Jurisprudence of Women], Vol. 2, Ahliyyat al-Mar'a li-Tawalli al-Sulta [The Eligibility of Women to Hold Office], 3rd edition, International Institute for Studies and Publication, Beirut.

Shams al-Din, Ibrahim (ed.). 2002. Nawadir al-Nisa' fi Kitab al-Mustatraf wa-Kutub al-Turath al-'Arabi [Anecdotes about Women in "al-Mustatraf" and the Arabic Literary Canon], Dar al-Kutub al-'Ilmiyya, Beirut.

Sharabi, Hisham. 1993. Al-Nizam al-Abawi wa-Ishkaliyyat Takhalluf al-Mujtama' al-'Arabi [Patriarchy and the Problematic of the Backwardness of Arab Society], 2nd edition, Markaz Dirasat al-Wihda al-'Arabiyya, Beirut.

Sha'ul, Milhim. 1998. "Al-Mar'a wal-Sha'n al-'Amm fi Daw' al-Istitla'at wal-Abhath" [Women and Public Affairs through Investigations and Research] in Al-Siyasi, Women Researchers, no. 4, 1997-1998, Beirut.

Shukhshayr, Khawla 2000. Silsilat Awraq Bahthiyya: "Al-Musawah fi al-Ta'lim al-Lamanhaji lil-Talaba wal-Talibat fi Filastin" [Research Papers Series: "Equality in Non-curricular Education for Male and Female Students in Palestine"], Muwatin—The Palestinian Institute for the Study of Democracy, Ramallah, occupied Palestinian territory.

Supreme Council for Culture and Nur Foundation. 2002. Mawsu'at al-Mar'a al-'Arabiyya [The Arab Women's Encyclopaedia], Cairo.

UN and ESCWA. 2005. Al-Mar'a al-'Arabiyya, Bijin + 10" [Arab Women, Beijing + 10].
_____. 2003. 'Ashar A'wam ba'd Bijin; al-Taqrir al-Iqlimi hawl al-Injazat wal-Tahaddiyat wal-Muqtarahat [Ten Years after Beijing: the Regional Report on Accomplishments, Challenges and Proposals], New York, December 2003.

UNICEF. 2004. Nazra 'Amma 'ala Sihhat al-Shabab al-Jinsiyya wal-Injabiyya wal-Huquq fi al-Buldan al-'Arabiyya wa-Iran [General View of the Sexual and Reproductive Health and Rights of Young People in the Arab Countries and Iran].

UNIFEM. 2005. 10 Sanawat ba'd Bijin—Dawr al-Munazzamat ghayr al-Hukumiyya al-'Arabiyya wa-Musahamatiha [10 Years after Beijing: The Role and Contribution of Arab NGOs], Regional Office, Amman.
_____2004. Taqaddum al-Mar'a al-'Arabiyya 2004 [The Progress of Arab Women, 2004], Regional Office, Amman.

World Bank. 2005. Al-Naw' al-Ijtima'i wal-Tanmiya fi al-Sharq al-Awsat wa-Shamal Ifriqiya: al-Mar'a fi al-Majal al-'Amm [Gender and Development in the Middle East and North Africa: Women in Public Life], Arabic edition, Dar al-Saqi, London and Beirut.

Zangana, Haifa. 2005. Al-Quds al-Arabi, 30 October 2005, www.alquds.co.uk.

Zaydan, Jurji. 2002. Rihlat Urubba 1912 [Journey to Europe 1912].

Zayn al-Din, Nazira. 1998. Al-Sufur wal-Hijab [Veiling and Unveiling], revised and presented by Buthayna Sha'ban, 2nd edition, Dar al-Mada, Damascus, 1998.

ANNEX I. LIST OF BACKGROUND PAPERS (AUTHOR NAME; PAPER TITLE; NUMBER OF PAGES)

IN ARABIC

- ‘Abdellatif, Kamal
  - Qadaya al-Mar’a fi al-Fikr al-‘Arabi al-Mu‘asir: al-Tahqib, al-Marja‘iyya, wa-As’ilat al-Taghyir (Women's Issues in Contemporary Arab Thought: Periodisation, Authority and Questions of Change), 44.
  - Nuhud al-Mar’a al-‘Arabiyya wa-Su’al al-Dakhil wal-Kharij: Nahw Tawsi‘ wa-Ta‘mim Kawniyyat Qiyam al-Taharrur (The Advancement of Arab Women and the Question of Inside and Outside: Toward the Expansion and Generalisation of Universal Values of Emancipation), 33.
- Abu-Duhou, Rula – Al-Mar’a al-‘Arabiyya taht al-Ihtilal – Filastin (Arab Women under Occupation: Palestine), 13.
- Abu-Khalid, Fowziyah
  - Al-Nisa’wal-Ibda‘—Al-Mobdia’Al-Arabiyya Bayna Mukhalafat al-Sura al-Namatiyya lil-Mar’a fi al-Dhakira al-Jama‘iyya wa-bayna Tafkik al-Khitab al-Sa’id (Women and Creativity: The Creative Arab woman: The Varying Stereotypes of Women in the Common Memory vs. the Deconstruction of the Prevalent Discourse), 42.
  - Surat al-Mar’a al-‘Arabiyya fi Mera’t al-Waqe’a (Image of Arab Women in Reality), 6.
- Abu Nahleh, Lamis – Musharakat al-Mar’a al-‘Arabiyya fi al-Nashat al-Iqtisadi wa-‘Awa’idih (The Participation of Arab Women in Economic Activity and Its Benefits), 35.
- Al-‘Awadhi, Badria ‘Abd Allah – Al-Musawah bayn al-Rijal wal-Nisa’ fi Wa‘y Rijal al-Qanun fi al-Khalij al-‘Arabi (Equality between Men and Women in the Awareness of Men in the Legal Professions in the Arabian Gulf), 14.

- Ali, Ali Abdel Gadir
  - Intishar al-Faqr wa-Atharuhu ‘ala Id‘af al-Nisa’ fi al-Duwal al-‘Arabiyya (The Spread of Poverty and Its Effect on the Sapping of Women's Strength in the Arab States), 30.
  - Mozaqqera hawla al-Nomow al-Iqtisadi wa Tamkin al-Mar’a fi al-Dowal al-‘Arabiyya (A Note on Economic Growth and Women's Empowerment in the Arab Countries), 11.
- Alnajjar, Baqer – Al-Mar’a al-‘Amila al-Wafida fi al-Buldan al-‘Arabiyya (Women Guest Workers in Arab Countries), 8.
- Al-Rasheed, Madawi – Takris al-Tasallut ‘ala al-Mar’a min khilal al-Bina al- Mujtama‘iyya (The Consecration of the Subjugation of Women through Societal Structures), 11.
- Al-Sayyid, Mustapha Kamil – Hawl al-Tamkin al-Siyasi lil-Mar’a al-‘Arabiyya (On the Political Empowerment of Arab Women), 15.
- ‘Aref, Mohammed – Nuhud Nisa’ al-‘Ilm fi al-Buldan al-‘Arabiyya (The Rise of Women Scientists in the Arab Countries), 19.
- ‘Awad, Mohsen – Intihakat Huquq al-Insan fi al-Watan al-‘Arabi (Human Rights Violations in the Arab Nation), 10.
- Bashshur, Munir – Al-Mar’a wal-Tanshi’a wal-Ta‘lim: al-Mashriq al-‘Arabi (Women, Child-raising and Education: The Arab Mashreq), 13.
- Bayoumi, Noha – Al-‘Alaqa al-Mushkil ma‘a al-Rijal fi al-Mujatam‘at al- ‘Arabiyya bayn al-Ta‘adud wal-Tanaqus (The Ambiguous Relationship with Men in Arab Societies: Synergy vs. Conflict), 24.
- Benmessaoud, Rachida – Al-Mar’a fi al-Lugha al-‘Arabiyya (The Arabic Language and Women), 9.
- Bishara, Azmi – Al-Daght al-Siyasi al-Khariji wa-Tamkin al-Mar’a al-‘Arabiyya (Foreign Political Pressure and the Empowerment of Arab Women), 8.

- Charfi, Mohamed – Al-Qanun wa-Huquq al-Mar'a fi al-Maghrib al-'Arabi (The Law and Women's Rights in the Arab Maghreb), 12.
- Chekir, Hafidha
  - Al-Musawah 'ind al-Qanuniyyin wal-Qanuniyyat fi Duwal al-Maghrib al-'Arabi (Equality in the View of Men and Women in the Legal Professions in the Countries of the Arab Maghreb), 9.
  - Al-Nisa' wal-Ahzab al-Siyasiyya (Women and Political Parties), 10.
- Cherif, Khadija – Al-Nisa' al-'Arabiyyat wal-Mujtama' al-Madani (Arab Women and Civil Society), 12.
- Cherkaoui, Mouna – Musharakat al-Mar'a al-'Arabiyya fi al-Nashat al-Iqtisadi wa-'Awa'idih (The Participation of Arab Women in Economic Activity and Its Benefits), 43.
- Daguerre, Violette – Tamaththul al-Mar'a lil-Qahr wal-Id'af wa-I'adat Intajih: Qira'a Nafsiyya (Women's Internalisation of Oppression and Enfeeblement and Its Reproduction: A Psychological Reading), 12.
- El-Affendi, Abdelwahab – Al-Mujtama' al-Madani al-'Arabi: Naqla Naw'iyya? (Arab Civil Society: A Qualitative Leap?), 5.
- Elsadda, Hoda – Khitab wa-Nashatat Taharrur al-Mar'a fi al-Buldan al-'Arabiyya: al-Ma'zaq wal-Afaq (Women's Liberation Discourse and Activities in Arab Countries: The Dilemma and the Horizons), 21.
- El Samalouti, Ikbal El Ameer – Al-Mar'a fi al-'Ashwa'iyyat: al-Waqi' wa-Mutatallabat al-Mustaqbal (Women in Squatter Settlements: Reality and the Requirements of the Future), 29.
- Ezzat, Heba Raouf – Hawl Mawaqif al-Quwa al-Siyasiyya, Khassatan al-Harakat al-Islamiyya wal-Harakat al-Diniyya, min Tamkin al-Nisa' fi al-Buldan al- 'Arabiyya (On the Positions of Political Forces, Especially Islamic and Religious Movements, with Regard to the Empowerment of Women in Arab Countries), 26.
- Farahat, Mohamed Nour – Al-Awda' al-Tashri'iyya lil-Mar'a fi Ba'd Duwal al- Mashriq al-'Arabi: Dirasa Mujaza li-Tashri'at Misr wal-Urdunn wa-Lubnan (The Legislative Situation of Women in Selected Eastern Arab Countries: A Brief Study of Legislation in Egypt, Jordan and Lebanon), 8.
- Farid, Samir – Surat al-Mar'a fi al-Masrah wal-Sinima (The Image of Women in the Theatre and the Cinema), 8.
- Fayad, Mona – Al-Mar'a wal-Siyasa (Women and Politics), 18.
- Fouad, Hala – Waraqa Mabda'iyya li-Rasd Ba'dan min al-Injaz al-Nisa'i al- 'Arabi fi al-Majal al-Ma'rifi (A Preliminary Overview of Selected Women's Achievements in the Field of Knowledge), 26.
- Guessous, Abdel Aziz – Dawr Munazzamat al-Mujtama' al-Madani fi Nuhud al-Mar'a fi al-Buldan al-'Arabiyya (The Role of Civil Society Organisations in the Rise of Women in the Arab Countries), 30.
- Hamzaoui, Hassina – Tamthil al-Mar'a fi al-Thaqafa al-Sha'biyya: Muqaraba Nafsiyya li-'Ayyina min al-Hikayat wal-Amthal al-Sha'biyya (The Representation of Women in Popular Culture: A Psychological Approach to a Sample of Tales and Proverbs), 6.
- Howeidy, Fahmi – Al-Islam wa-Huquq al-Mar'a (Islam and Women's Rights), 13.
- Jad, Islah
  - Al-Rajul wal-Mar'a bayn al-Musawah wal-Ikhtilaf (Men and Women: Equality vs. Difference), 13.
  - Tatawwur Mafahim al-Mar'a wal-Tanmiya, Taqyim Naqdi min al-Manzur al-'Arabi (The Evolution of Concepts of Women and Development: A Critical Assessment from the Arab Perspective), 9.
  - Huquq al-Mar'a wa-Mafhum al-Muwatana: Itar Tahlili (Women's Rights and the Concept of Citizenship: An Analytical Framework), 12.
- Jarjoura, Nadim – Surat al-Mar'a fi al-Sinima al-'Arabiyya (The Image of Women in the Arab Cinema), 9.
- Kadiri, Nahawand Issa – Bayn al-Nisa' wal-I'lam: Ayyat 'Alaqa, Ayy Dawr? (Women vs. the Media: What Relationship? What Role?), 11.
- Kallab, Elham – Al-Ibda' al-Fanni wal-Adabi – Sura lil-Mar'a (Creativity in the Sciences and the Arts: A Portrait of Women), 21.
- Karam, 'Azza – Nazra Shamila 'ala al-Nahda

al-Niswiyya wal-Durus al-Mustafada minha fi al-'Alam al-'Arabi (A Comprehensive Look at the Rise of Women and Lessons Learned in the Arab World), 10.

- Kiwan, Fadia – Dawr al-Munazzamat al-Duwaliyya fi Tamkin al-Mar'a fi al- Buldan al-'Arabiyya (The Role of International Organisations in Empowering Women in the Arab Countries), 14.
- Kuttab, Eileen – Al-Nisa' fi Manatiq al-Sira' wa-fi Harakat al-Muqawama (Filastin) (Women in Regions of Conflict and in the Resistance Movement (Palestine)), 16.
- Lahham, Maroun – Mawqif al-Adyan al-Ukhra fi al-Buldan al-'Arabiyya min al-Mar'a (The Position of Other Religions in the Arab Countries with Regard to Women), 7.
- Lakhdar, Latifa – Nushu' 'Adam al-Musawah bayn al-Naw'ayn fi al-Manzur al-Tarikhi al-Muqaran, Bil-Tarkiz 'ala al-Hala al-'Arabiyya (The Emergence of Gender Inequality in a Comparative Historical Perspective, with a Focus on the Arab Situation), 7.
- Malki, Mhammed – Al-Maghrib: Kifah al-Haraka al-Nisa'iyya Yutawwaj bi-Isdar "Mudawwanat al-Usra" (Morocco: The Struggle of the Women's Movement Is Crowned by the Issuing of "The Family Code"), 22.
- Manna', Haytham
- Huquq al-Mar'a fi al-Islam (Women's Rights in Islam), 23.
- Nushu' 'Adam al-Musawah bayn al-Naw'ayn fi al-Manzur al-Tarikhi al-Muqaran (The Emergence of Gender Inequality in a Comparative Historical Perspective), 7.
- Marzouki, Moncef – Al-Wad'a al-Sihhi lil-Nisa' fi al-'Alam al-'Arabi (The Overall Health Situation of Women in the Arab World), 22.
- Miadi, Zineb – Al-Intiqas min al-Hurriyya al-Shakhsiyya (The Impairment of Personal Freedom), 6.
- Nasrallah, Emily – Musharakat al-Mar'a Thaqafiyyan wa-jtima'iyyan (Women's Cultural and Economic Participation), 5.
- Rjiba, Naziha – Tahrir al-Mar'a al-Tunusiyya bayn al-Namudhaj al-'Arabi al- Ra'id wa-Waqi' al-Intikas (The Liberation of Tunisian Women: The Pioneering Arab Model vs. the Reality of Backsliding), 11.
- Said, Nader – Filastin wal-Tanmiya al-Bashariyya (Palestine and Human Development), 5.
- Sidaoui, Rafif – Injaz al-Nisa' al-'Arab (The Achievements of Arab Women), 16.
- Silini, Naila
- Al-Ta'wilat al-Fiqhiyya al-Islamiyya al-Mustaghalla li-Id'af al-Nisa' wa-Tafniduha (Islamic Jurisprudential Interpretations Exploited to Weaken Women and Their Rebuttal), 22.
- Bawadir al-Ijtihad wa-Dawruha fi Taqlis al-Masafa bayn Ittifaqiyyat al-CIDAW wa-Tahaffuzat al-Duwal al-'Arabiyya (Initiatives in Religious Interpretation and Their Role in Narrowing the Distance between CEDAW and the Reservations of the Arab States), 8.
- Touaiti, Mustapha – Surat al-Mar'a al-Mu'asira min Khilal al-Fatawa al-Mu'asira (Contemporary Women as Viewed through Contemporary Fatwas), 17.
- Tlili, Mohsen – Al-Mar'a fi al-Bawadi wal-Rif al-Muhammash (Women in the Desert and the Marginalised Countryside), 6.
- Zalzal, Marie Rose – "Al-Irhab" wal-Harb 'alayh ("Terrorism" and the War on It), 12.

IN ENGLISH

- Al-Azmeh, Aziz – Terrorism, 4.
- Hijab, Nadia – Arab Women Entrepreneurs: A Growing Economic Force, 9.
- Karam, Azza – The Missing Ribs of Development: Women's Empowerment, Freedom and Knowledge, 5.

ANNEX II. OPINION POLL ON THE RISE OF WOMEN IN THE ARAB WORLD

Introduction

The methodology of the AHDR has evolved to include an empirical research component on the theme of the Report in order to gain fresh insights that would not be possible through the standard sources of data and information.

For this volume, the Report team supervised the design and implementation of field surveys intended to explore public opinion on a number of issues relating to the theme of "the Rise of Arab Women" in four Arab countries: Egypt, Jordan, Lebanon and Morocco. These countries represent 36.5 per cent of the Arab population and vary in geographic location in the region and in socio-economic structure in ways likely to be reflected in public opinion on issues concerning the rise of women in Arab countries. Reputable field survey organisations were entrusted with the implementation of the surveys independently of the Report team.

Some of the results of the surveys are presented in boxes throughout the Report under the generic title, "Public Opinion on Aspects of the Rise of Arab Women, Four Arab Countries, 2005".

Perhaps the overriding conclusion of the results of the surveys is that the Arab public, represented by the samples of the four countries in which surveys were conducted, aspires to a much higher level of equality among women and men. Naturally, this aspiration is conditioned by the prevalent societal structures, depending on traditional societal strength and the dimension of equality.

It is not unexpected that the results of the surveys presented in the Report reflect an overwhelming aspiration towards a higher level of equality than is currently present in Arab countries, on the one hand, and than would be implied by the continuation of societal structures impeding the rise of women on the other.

These survey results indicate clear support for the directions of the rise of Arab women underpinning the entire Report and presented unequivocally in the strategic vision in Chapter 10.

The results of the surveys in the boxes on "Public Opinion on Aspects of the Rise of Arab Women, four Arab Countries, 2005" at times represent support for the analysis contained in the Report. More often, however, these results engage the analysis in a dialectic that reaches a climax in the contents of Chapter 10.

SURVEY SAMPLE

The survey was conducted in each participating country on a representative sample of each society comprising around 1,000 people divided equally between men and women over 18 years of age.

SAMPLE DESIGN

Jordan

Sample size: 1,000 observations.
Sampling area: All governorates were covered. The country was divided into strata based on the results of the 2004 census of population and housing. The rural or urban segment of each governorate was taken as a separate stratum.
Sample-unit selection criteria: Multistage stratified cluster sampling: Strata were divided into clusters, each containing about 80 households. Clusters were sampled, proportionate to size, within each stratum. Finally, systematic sampling was adopted to select 10 households from each cluster.

Lebanon

Sample size: 1,000 observations.
Sampling area: Beirut, Mount Lebanon, the north, the south and Beqaa.

Sampling-unit selection criteria: residence (urban/rural), gender (male/female), age (18 years or older) and social, economic and educational status.

Sampling selection criteria: cluster sampling technique.

Weighting procedure: self-weighted.

Morocco

Sample size: 1,023 observations.

Sampling area: Grand Casablanca, Rabat-Sale-Zemmour Zaer, Ghrab Chrarda Beni Hssen, Fes-Boulemane, Meknes-Tafilalet, Marrakech-Tensift-Al Haouz and Chaouia-Ouardigha.

Sampling-unit selection criteria: residence (urban/rural), gender (male/female), age (18 years or older), economic and educational status and respondent's occupation.

Sampling selection criteria: quota sampling method.

Weighting procedure: self-weighted.

Egypt

Sample size: 1,000 observations.

Sampling area: All governorates were covered except for frontier governorates.

The representation of each governorate in the sample is equivalent to the distribution of total population, by governorate, in the same age bracket.

Sampling-unit selection criteria: 67 sampling units divided by residence (urban/rural), gender (male/female) and age (18 years or older).

Sampling selection criteria: A random sampling method was used to select minor sampling units first (shiakha/village) and then 15 households or less from each shiakha/village (using Central Agency for Public Mobilization and Statistics (CAPMAS) lists for shiakha/village/household).

Weighting procedure: self-weighted.

OPINION POLL QUESTIONNAIRE

Public Opinion Poll on the Rise of Arab Women (2005)

Confidential Data

Country of Study		
Jordan	1	|__|
Lebanon	2	
Egypt	3	
Morocco	4	

Questionnaire Number : |__||__||__||__|

Basic Data

1. Governorate: _____ |__||__|
2. District: _____ |__|
3. Sub-District: _____ |__|
4. Township : _____ |__||__||__|
5. Region: _____ |__||__|
6. Neighborhood: _____ |__||__|

7. Block No.: _____ |__||__||__||__|
8. Cluster No: _____ |__||__||__|
9. Bldg. No.: _____ |__||__||__|
10. House No.: _____ |__||__||__|
11. Household Serial No.: _____ |__||__||__|
12. Number of Household Members: _____ |__||__|

Household Visit Result	First Visit	Household Visit Result	First Visit
Residential	1	Interview completed	1
Permanently closed	2	Required person is out	2
Empty	3	No qualified person	3
Non residential	4	Travelling away	4
No longer exists	5	Sick / invalid / elderly	5
Refused interview	6	Refused interview	6
Other (Specify): _____	7	Other (Specify): _____	7

Interview completed { Original 1 / Substitute 2

Work Progress

Interviewer	Supervisor	Coder	Data Entry Operator
Name:	Name:	Name:	Name:
Date: / / 2005	Date: / /2005	Date: / /2005	Date: / / 2005

Introduction: ☞

Good morning/Good evening. I am --------------------, from Middle East Marketing and Research Consultants, an independent organisation specialising in studies carried out by talking to people and obtaining their opinions on specific issues.

The organisation is now conducting a survey on the development of Arab women for the United Nations' Arab Human Development Report, and I would like you to give me some of your time to answer some questions. I assure you that the information will remain confidential and will be used only for professional research purposes.

Please tell me about the family members (males/ females) who are 18 years old and above.

Respondent's Selection Table

Sex:		1 - Male ♂					2 - Female ♀							|_|_|	

Serial Number of the Household

Household member number	Household members 18 years old and above, starting with the eldest	1	2	3	4	5	6	7	8	9	10	11	12	13	14	15
1		1	1	1	1	1	1	1	1	1	1	1	1	1	1	1
2		2	1	2	1	2	1	2	1	2	1	1	1	2	1	2
3		3	2	1	3	2	1	3	2	1	3	2	1	3	2	1
4		4	3	2	1	4	3	2	1	4	3	2	1	4	3	2
5		5	4	3	2	1	5	4	3	2	1	5	4	5	2	1
6		6	5	4	3	2	1	6	5	4	3	2	1	6	5	4

Note to the interviewer: Please circle ○ the corresponding response(s).

100	Are you willing to take part in this poll?

Yes	1	
No	2 → End interview	|_|_|

SECTION ONE

GENDER EQUALITY ⤵

101	To what extent do you think that (gender equality) relates to your total concept of freedom? Does it relate to a large, moderate, small extent, or does it not relate at all to your total concept of freedom?

Relate to a large extent	1	
Relate to a moderate extent	2	
Relate to a small extent	3	|_|_|
Does not relate at all	4	
Not sure/Don't know	7	
No opinion	8	
Refuse to answer	9	

102	To what extent do you think that (gender equality)) is secured in -------------- (state the name of the survey country)? (Read out): ⤵

Secured to a large extent	1	
Secured to a moderate extent	2	
Secured to a small extent	3	|_|_|
Not at all secured	4	
Not sure/Don't know	7	}
No opinion	8	} Don't Read Out
Refuse to answer	9	}

103	Do you think that (gender equality) in ------------- (state the name of the survey country) has improved, has stayed at the same level or has deteriorated over the last five years?

Has improved	1	
Has stayed at the same level	2	
Has deteriorated	3	|_|_|
Not sure/Don't know	7	
No opinion	8	
Refuse to answer	9	

SECTION TWO

ADDITIONAL ITEMS ⮑

I will read to you a number of statements. Please tell me to what extent do you agree or disagree with each of them.

201 - To what extent do you agree that "Girls have the same right to education as boys"?
Interviewer :(ask about all the items stated in the table below):

	Large Extent	Moderate Extent	Small Extent	Don't agree at all	I don't know	No opinion	Refuse to answer	
	I agree to a : ⮑							
1- Girls have the same right to education as boys	1	2	3	4	7	8	9	|__|
2- Girls have the right to all phases of education, including university	1	2	3	4	7	8	9	|__|
3- Women have the right to work equal to men	1	2	3	4	7	8	9	|__|
4- Women have the right to employment benefits (income and other advantages) just as men do	1	2	3	4	7	8	9	|__|
5- Women have the right to the same work conditions (working hours, transport, travel) as men	1	2	3	4	7	8	9	|__|
6- Women have the right to political action just as men do	1	2	3	4	7	8	9	|__|
7- A woman's children have the right to acquire her nationality just the same as that of men	1	2	3	4	7	8	9	|__|
8- A woman has the right to assume the position of Judge	1	2	3	4	7	8	9	|__|
9- A woman has the right to assume the position of Minister	1	2	3	4	7	8	9	|__|
10- A woman has the right to assume the position of Prime Minister	1	2	3	4	7	8	9	|__|
11- A woman has the right to assume the position of Head of State	1	2	3	4	7	8	9	|__|

202 - Do you think that girls have the right to choose the specialisation they want in university education or are there disciplines that they should not consider?

They have the right to choose the specialisation they want	1 → Go to question 204	
There are disciplines that they should not consider	2	
Not sure/Don't know	7 ⎫	
No opinion	8 ⎬ Go to question 204	|__|
Refuse to answer	9 ⎭	

203 - Can you give me the name(s) of the specialisation(s) that girls may not choose in university education?

1- _____ |__|__|__|

2- _____ |__|__|__|

3- _____ |__|__|__|

204 - Do you think that women's performance in leadership roles is (Read out): ⮑

Better than men's performance	1	
Close to men's performance	2	
Worse than men's performance	3	
Not sure/Don't know	7 ⎫	|__|
No opinion	8 ⎬ Don't Read Out	
Refuse to answer	9 ⎭	

Interviewer: (Address questions 205/206/207 to "FEMALE RESPONDENTS ONLY", or else move to question 208)

205 - Have you done any paid or unpaid work during the last seven days?		
Yes	1	
No	2 } Go to question 207	|__|
Refuse to answer	8	

206 - Was your work inside or outside the family setup?		
Yes	1	
No	2 } Go to question 208	|__|
Refuse to answer	8	

207 - Did you seek work outside the family setup during the last seven days but could not find it?		
Yes	1	
No	2 } Go to question 208	|__|
Refuse to answer	8	

INTERVIEWER (ASK ALL).

I will read to you a number of statements. Please tell me to what extent you agree or disagree with each of them.

208 - To what extent do you agree that "Women must not be subjected to physical abuse by men"?
Interviewer : (ask about all the items stated in the table below):

	Large Extent	Moderate Extent	Small Extent	Don't agree at all	I don't know	No opinion	Refuse to answer	
1- Women must not be subjected to physical abuse by men	1	2	3	4	7	8	9	|__|
2- Women must not to be subjected to mental abuse by men	1	2	3	4	7	8	9	|__|
3- Banning girls' circumcision	1	2	3	4	7	8	9	|__|
4- Women owning assets (including land and buildings) just as men do	1	2	3	4	7	8	9	|__|
5- Women owning economic projects just as men do	1	2	3	4	7	8	9	|__|
6- Women managing economic projects just as men do	1	2	3	4	7	8	9	|__|
7- Women marrying spouses of their own choice just as men do	1	2	3	4	7	8	9	|__|
8- Prohibiting marriage to first-degree relatives	1	2	3	4	7	8	9	|__|
9- Disallowing early marriage (of a girl under 18)	1	2	3	4	7	8	9	|__|
10- A woman having a divorce of her own will	1	2	3	4	7	8	9	|__|
11- A woman taking custody of her children just as men do	1	2	3	4	7	8	9	|__|
12- A woman travelling on her own	1	2	3	4	7	8	9	|__|

I agree to a :

209 -   In your opinion, what is the most important problem facing women in ------------- (state the name of the survey country)?

The most important problem facing women: ✍ |_|_|_|
_____

210 -   To what extent do women in ------------(state the name of the survey country) enjoy "Protection from physical abuse". Do they enjoy "Protection from physical abuse" to a large, moderate, small extent or do they not enjoy this protection at all?

211 -   Do you think that "Protection from physical abuse" has improved, has stayed at the same level or has deteriorated over the last five years?
         Interviewer : (ask about all the items stated in the table below):

	They enjoy to a : ✍								Has improved	Has stayed at the same level	Has deteriorated	Not sure/Don't know	No opinion	Refuse to answer	
	Large Extent	Moderate Extent	Small Extent	Don't agree at all	I don't know	No opinion	Refuse to answer								
1- Protection from physical abuse	1	2	3	4	7	8	9	|_|	1	2	3	7	8	9	|_|
2- Protection from metal abuse	1	2	3	4	7	8	9	|_|	1	2	3	7	8	9	|_|
3- Choosing a spouse	1	2	3	4	7	8	9	|_|	1	2	3	7	8	9	|_|
4- Obtaining a divorce of her own will	1	2	3	4	7	8	9	|_|	1	2	3	7	8	9	|_|
5- Banning girls' circumcision	1	2	3	4	7	8	9	|_|	1	2	3	7	8	9	|_|
6- Education	1	2	3	4	7	8	9	|_|	1	2	3	7	8	9	|_|
7- Higher education	1	2	3	4	7	8	9	|_|	1	2	3	7	8	9	|_|
8- Work	1	2	3	4	7	8	9	|_|	1	2	3	7	8	9	|_|
9- Owning assets	1	2	3	4	7	8	9	|_|	1	2	3	7	8	9	|_|
10- Owning projects	1	2	3	4	7	8	9	|_|	1	2	3	7	8	9	|_|
11- Managing projects	1	2	3	4	7	8	9	|_|	1	2	3	7	8	9	|_|
12- Participation in civil society (NGOs, political parties and the media)	1	2	3	4	7	8	9	|_|	1	2	3	7	8	9	|_|
13- Participation in political activity	1	2	3	4	7	8	9	|_|	1	2	3	7	8	9	|_|

SECTION THREE

HIJAB (VEIL)/ INTERMINGLING/ POLYGAMY (THE CONVENTION ON THE ELIMINATION OF ALL FORMS OF DISCRIMINATION AGAINST WOMEN) (CEDAW)

301 -   Which of the following positions reflects your views on the hijab? (Read out): ✍
         Interviewer: (One response only).

I disagree with hijab for a woman   1
I agree with hijab for a woman only if she decides to wear it   2
A woman must be obliged to wear hijab   3
Not sure/Don't know   7 |_|
No opinion   8 } Don't Read Out
Refuse to answer   9

302- Do you agree to the intermingling of men and women "in all stages of education"?
Interviewer: (ask about all the items stated in the table below):

	Yes	No	Not sure/ Don't know	No Opinion	Refuse to answer	
1- In all stages of education	1	2	7	8	9	|__|
2- At work	1	2	7	8	9	|__|
3- In society in general	1	2	7	8	9	|__|

303 - Do you agree to polygamy?

Yes, I agree   1
No, I disagree   2
Not sure/Don't know   7 } Go to question 305   \|__\|
No opinion   8
Refuse to answer   9

304 - Do you think that polygamy should be subject to the consent of? (Read out): ↵

The first wife only   1
The last wife only   2
The first and the last wives together   3
Not sure/Don't know   7   \|__\|
No opinion   8
Refuse to answer   9

305 - Are you aware of the "Convention on the Elimination of All Discrimination against Women"?

Yes   1
No   2
Not sure/Don't know   7 } Go to question 311   \|__\|
No opinion   8
Refuse to answer   9

306 - Generally, do you approve of the contents of this Convention?

Yes   1
No   2
Not sure/Don't know   7   \|__\|
No opinion   8
Refuse to answer   9

307 - Do you have any objection against any of the clauses of this Convention?

Yes   1
No   2
Not sure/Don't know   7   \|__\|
No opinion   8
Refuse to answer   9

308 - What is your objection? Any other objection?

1- _____ |_|_|

2- _____ |_|_|

3- _____ |_|_|

309 - Do you approve of its full implementation in ------------- (state the name of the survey country)?

Yes	1
No	2
Not sure/Don't know	7
No opinion	8
Refuse to answer	9

|_|

310 - Do you approve of its full implementation in all Arab countries?

Yes	1
No	2
Not sure/Don't know	7
No opinion	8
Refuse to answer	9

|_|

311 - In your opinion, what is the most important development that can help women enjoy their full rights?

The most important development that can help women enjoy their full rights: _____ |_|_|

SECTION FOUR

RENAISSANCE IN THE ARAB WORLD

401 - Do you see an urgent need for a human development revival in the Arab world by "building a knowledge society"?
Interviewer: (ask about all the items stated in the table below):

	Yes	No	Don't know	No opinion	Refuse to answer	
1- Building a knowledge society	1	2	8	8	9	|_|
2- Rise of Arab women	1	2	8	8	9	|_|
3- Respect for freedoms (of opinion, expression, association, and forming organisations in both civil and political spheres)	1	2	8	8	9	|_|
4- Establishing a good governance system (that protects freedom and is based on representing all people and that is accountable to them under a law that is executed by a just and completely independent judiciary)	1	2	8	8	9	|_|

402 - In your opinion, what is the most important development that can help renaissance in the Arab world?

The most important development: ➘

|_|_|_|

_____

SECTION FIVE

DEMOGRAPHIC DATA

501 - Sex:

Male	1	
Female	2	|_|
Refuse to answer	3	

502 - Age:

_____	|_|_|_|
Refuse to answer 99	

503 - Educational level (highest level successfully completed):

No education (illiterate/ reads and writes)	1
Primary	2
Preparatory	3
Secondary	4
Intermediary diploma	5
First university degree	6
Higher diploma	7
Masters and above	8
Refuse to answer	9

(|_| next to Intermediary diploma row)

504 - Human Resource Relationships:

Working	1	
Not working ➜ Go to question (506)	2	
Refuse to answer ➜ Go to question (506)	9	|_|

505 - Occupation (Specify):

_____	|_|_|_|
Refuse to answer 99	

506 - Marital status:

Single	1	
Married	2	|_|_|_|
Other (Specify):_____	3	
Refuse to answer	9	

507 - Religion:

Muslim	1	
Christian	2	
Other (Specify): _____	3	|_|
Refuse to answer	9	

🕴 **Interviewer:** 🕴

Thank the respondents and tell them that you might visit them again.

Summary Results of the Opinion Poll on the Rise of Women in the Arab World[1]

Sample Size

Country	Jordan	Lebanon	Egypt	Morocco	Total
# of observations	1,000	1,000	1,000	1,023	4,023

SECTION I. Gender Equality

Q101	Gender equality relates to your total concept of freedom				
Country	Jordan	Lebanon	Egypt	Morocco	Total
Yes	83.79	97.30	85.20	71.27	84.31
No	13.96	1.90	12.20	10.75	9.71
Missing[2]	2.25	0.80	2.60	17.99	5.98
Total	100.00	100.00	100.00	100.01	100.00

Q102	Gender equality is secured				
Country	Jordan	Lebanon	Egypt	Morocco	Total
Yes	87.45	90.20	92.10	76.44	86.49
No	10.26	7.90	6.10	14.17	9.63
Missing	2.29	1.90	1.80	9.38	3.88
Total	100.00	100.00	100.00	99.99	100.00

Q103	Gender equality has improved, stayed at the same level or deteriorated over the last five years				
Country	Jordan	Lebanon	Egypt	Morocco	Total
Improved	67.24	69.70	80.00	65.98	70.70
Same	21.07	19.10	13.00	19.55	18.19
Deteriorated	9.04	9.00	5.10	7.04	7.54
Missing	2.65	2.20	1.90	7.43	3.57
Total	100.00	100.00	100.00	100.00	100.00

SECTION II. Additional Items

	Girls/women have the ...				
Q20101	Same right to education as boys				
Country	Jordan	Lebanon	Egypt	Morocco	Total
Agree	98.25	99.60	98.50	98.92	98.82
Disagree	1.75	0.10	1.40	0.98	1.06
Missing	0.00	0.30	0.10	0.10	0.12
Total	100.00	100.00	100.00	100.00	100.00

---

[1] The total may not add to 100% due to rounding of figures.

[2] Total percentages of "do not know", "no opinion", "refused to answer" and "system missing".

Q20102	Right to all phases of education including university				
Country	Jordan	Lebanon	Egypt	Morocco	Total
Agree	97.48	99.50	96.20	97.56	97.69
Disagree	2.52	0.30	3.60	2.25	2.17
Missing	0.00	0.20	0.20	0.20	0.15
Total	100.00	100.00	100.00	100.01	100.01

Q20103	Right to work equal to men				
Country	Jordan	Lebanon	Egypt	Morocco	Total
Agree	86.08	98.60	84.80	93.16	90.67
Disagree	13.93	1.00	14.50	6.74	9.03
Missing	0.00	0.40	0.70	0.10	0.30
Total	100.01	100.00	100.00	100.00	100.00

Q20104	Right to employment benefits (income and other advantages) just as men do				
Country	Jordan	Lebanon	Egypt	Morocco	Total
Agree	85.35	97.70	82.90	91.49	89.38
Disagree	14.55	1.70	16.10	7.62	9.98
Missing	0.10	0.60	1.00	0.88	0.65
Total	100.00	100.00	100.00	99.99	100.01

Q20105	Right to the same work conditions (working hours, transport, travel) as men				
Country	Jordan	Lebanon	Egypt	Morocco	Total
Agree	71.54	93.60	62.30	86.42	78.52
Disagree	27.93	5.90	36.60	12.41	20.66
Missing	0.52	0.50	1.10	1.17	0.83
Total	99.99	100.00	100.00	100.00	100.01

Q20106	Right to political action just as men do				
Country	Jordan	Lebanon	Egypt	Morocco	Total
Agree	76.82	94.20	61.80	83.19	79.02
Disagree	22.44	4.90	35.80	12.22	18.80
Missing	0.75	0.90	2.40	4.59	2.17
Total	100.01	100.00	100.00	100.00	99.99

Q20107	Right of her children to acquire her nationality just the same as that of men				
Country	Jordan	Lebanon	Egypt	Morocco	Total
Agree	73.93	86.90	62.10	53.57	69.03
Disagree	24.72	12.30	35.60	39.69	28.14
Missing	1.35	0.80	2.30	6.74	2.82
Total	100.00	100.00	100.00	100.00	99.99

Q20108	Right to assume the position of Judge				
Country	Jordan	Lebanon	Egypt	Morocco	Total
Agree	55.34	89.90	46.60	73.60	66.41
Disagree	43.71	8.60	51.50	23.26	31.72
Missing	0.94	1.50	1.90	3.13	1.87
Total	99.99	100.00	100.00	99.99	100.00

Q20109	Right to assume the position of Minister				
Country	Jordan	Lebanon	Egypt	Morocco	Total
Agree	67.32	93.10	66.10	79.76	76.59
Disagree	31.75	6.10	32.60	16.62	21.74
Missing	0.92	0.80	1.30	3.62	1.67
Total	99.99	100.00	100.00	100.00	100.00

Q20110	Right to assume the position of Prime Minister				
Country	Jordan	Lebanon	Egypt	Morocco	Total
Agree	54.70	87.80	45.90	74.00	65.65
Disagree	44.41	11.50	52.40	22.09	32.54
Missing	0.89	0.70	1.70	3.91	1.81
Total	100.00	100.00	100.00	100.00	100.00

Q20111	Right to assume the position of Head of State				
Country	Jordan	Lebanon	Egypt	Morocco	Total
Agree	39.00	81.30	25.70	55.61	50.43
Disagree	59.45	17.50	72.50	39.78	47.27
Missing	1.55	1.20	1.80	4.59	2.30
Total	100.00	100.00	100.00	99.98	100.00

	Girls have the right to choose the specialisation in university education				
Q202	Do you think that girls have the right to choose their area of study at the university level or should girls be prohibted from certain areas?				
Country	Jordan	Lebanon	Egypt	Morocco	Total
Yes*	85.67	90.90	90.20	92.47	89.83
No	12.02	8.10	7.40	1.66	7.26
Missing	2.32	1.00	2.40	5.87	2.91
Total	100.01	100.00	100.00	100.00	100.00

* Go to Q204

	Women's performance in leadership roles				
Q204	Women's performance in leadership roles versus men's				
Country	Jordan	Lebanon	Egypt	Morocco	Total
Better	9.02	14.40	12.00	24.44	15.02
Close	52.18	66.50	46.50	42.23	51.80
Worse	36.59	14.90	38.90	30.89	30.32
Missing	2.21	4.20	2.60	2.44	2.86
Total	100.00	100.00	100.00	100.00	100.00

Q205 — **Worked during the last 7 days (paid/unpaid)**

Country	Jordan	Lebanon	Egypt	Morocco	Total
Yes	12.45	44.42	16.31	35.76	26.88
No*	87.55	50.83	83.69	64.05	71.96
Missing	0.00	4.75	0.00	0.19	1.16
Total	100.00	100.00	100.00	100.00	100.00

* Go to Q207

Q206 — **Worked inside or outside the family setup**

Country	Jordan	Lebanon	Egypt	Morocco	Total
Inside	39.76	57.21	46.15	32.09	44.98
Outside*	60.24	42.79	53.85	67.91	55.02
Total	100.00	100.00	100.00	100.00	100.00

* Go to Q208

Q207 — **Did you seek work outside the family setup**

Country	Jordan	Lebanon	Egypt	Morocco	Total
Yes	18.34	16.58	22.79	9.60	17.27
No	81.37	72.70	76.23	87.37	79.30
Missing	0.29	10.71	0.98	3.03	3.43
Total	100.00	99.99	100.00	100.00	100.00

Do you agree that/on "…………."

Q20801 — **Women must not be subjected to physical abuse by men**

Country	Jordan	Lebanon	Egypt	Morocco	Total
Agree	97.67	97.80	94.50	96.58	96.64
Disagree	2.13	2.00	5.00	3.32	3.11
Missing	0.21	0.20	0.50	0.10	0.25
Total	100.01	100.00	100.00	100.00	100.00

Q20802 — **Women must not be subjected to mental abuse by men**

Country	Jordan	Lebanon	Egypt	Morocco	Total
Agree	97.61	98.30	93.70	96.87	96.62
Disagree	2.13	1.60	5.90	3.03	3.16
Missing	0.26	0.10	0.40	0.10	0.21
Total	100.00	100.00	100.00	100.00	99.99

Q20803 — **Banning girls' circumcision**

Country	Jordan	Lebanon	Egypt	Morocco	Total
Agree	86.29	78.90	47.40	73.22	71.46
Disagree	5.76	4.80	48.80	4.89	16.00
Missing	7.96	16.30	3.80	21.90	12.54
Total	100.01	100.00	100.00	100.01	100.00

Q20804	Women owning assets (including land and buildings) just as men do				
Country	Jordan	Lebanon	Egypt	Morocco	Total
Agree	93.52	97.60	91.40	98.24	95.21
Disagree	6.05	2.00	7.70	1.08	4.19
Missing	0.43	0.40	0.90	0.68	0.60
Total	100.00	100.00	100.00	100.00	100.00

Q20805	Women owning economic projects just as men do				
Country	Jordan	Lebanon	Egypt	Morocco	Total
Agree	91.94	97.40	90.30	97.17	94.21
Disagree	7.40	2.20	9.00	1.17	4.92
Missing	0.66	0.40	0.70	1.66	0.86
Total	100.00	100.00	100.00	100.00	99.99

Q20806	Women managing economic projects just as men do				
Country	Jordan	Lebanon	Egypt	Morocco	Total
Agree	87.77	96.50	85.40	95.11	91.21
Disagree	11.84	2.70	13.70	2.54	7.67
Missing	0.40	0.80	0.90	2.35	1.12
Total	100.01	100.00	100.00	100.00	100.00

Q20807	Women marrying spouses of their own choice just as men do				
Country	Jordan	Lebanon	Egypt	Morocco	Total
Agree	93.54	97.40	96.40	91.98	94.82
Disagree	6.24	2.20	3.20	7.62	4.83
Missing	0.22	0.40	0.40	0.39	0.35
Total	100.00	100.00	100.00	99.99	100.00

Q20808	Prohibiting marriage to first-degree relatives				
Country	Jordan	Lebanon	Egypt	Morocco	Total
Agree	81.40	86.30	60.80	51.80	69.98
Disagree	17.80	11.80	37.60	46.24	28.46
Missing	0.80	1.90	1.60	1.96	1.56
Total	100.00	100.00	100.00	100.00	100.00

Q20809	Disallowing early marriage (of girls under 18 years of age)				
Country	Jordan	Lebanon	Egypt	Morocco	Total
Agree	87.89	84.20	78.80	67.94	79.63
Disagree	12.12	15.20	20.70	30.99	19.82
Missing	0.00	0.60	0.50	1.08	0.55
Total	100.01	100.00	100.00	100.01	100.00

Q20810	A woman obtaining a divorce of her own will				
Country	Jordan	Lebanon	Egypt	Morocco	Total
Agree	61.76	83.20	57.50	70.88	68.35
Disagree	37.58	16.30	41.40	27.47	30.67
Missing	0.66	0.50	1.10	1.66	0.99
Total	100.00	100.00	100.00	100.01	100.01

Q20811	A woman taking custody of her children just as men do				
Country	Jordan	Lebanon	Egypt	Morocco	Total
Agree	79.68	85.70	78.90	94.43	84.73
Disagree	19.78	13.50	20.30	4.11	14.36
Missing	0.54	0.80	0.80	1.47	0.91
Total	100.00	100.00	100.00	100.01	100.00

Q20812	A woman travelling on her own				
Country	Jordan	Lebanon	Egypt	Morocco	Total
Agree	43.58	82.10	29.40	58.74	53.48
Disagree	56.03	17.40	70.20	40.96	46.12
Missing	0.39	0.50	0.40	0.29	0.40
Total	100.00	100.00	100.00	99.99	100.00

In your country, do women enjoy ...

Q21001	Protection from physical abuse				
Country	Jordan	Lebanon	Egypt	Morocco	Total
Enjoy	95.32	94.70	88.90	85.15	90.98
Do not enjoy	3.19	1.90	9.50	12.32	6.76
Missing	1.49	3.40	1.60	2.54	2.26
Total	100.00	100.00	100.00	100.01	100.00

Q21002	Protection from mental abuse				
Country	Jordan	Lebanon	Egypt	Morocco	Total
Enjoy	94.03	93.20	90.60	79.28	89.22
Do not enjoy	4.55	4.40	8.50	17.60	8.81
Missing	1.43	2.40	0.90	3.13	1.97
Total	100.01	100.00	100.00	100.01	100.00

Q21003	Choosing a spouse				
Country	Jordan	Lebanon	Egypt	Morocco	Total
Enjoy	96.23	97.20	97.00	93.75	96.03
Do not enjoy	3.50	1.20	2.50	5.08	3.08
Missing	0.26	1.60	0.50	1.17	0.89
Total	99.99	100.00	100.00	100.00	100.00

Q21004	Obtaining a divorce of her own will				
Country	Jordan	Lebanon	Egypt	Morocco	Total
Enjoy	80.86	77.50	73.70	82.20	78.59
Do not enjoy	17.33	18.50	24.50	14.57	18.70
Missing	1.80	4.00	1.80	3.23	2.71
Total	99.99	100.00	100.00	100.00	100.00

Q21005	Banning girls' circumcision				
Country	Jordan	Lebanon	Egypt	Morocco	Total
Enjoy	80.81	68.50	64.40	71.76	71.37
Do not enjoy	5.96	3.20	32.50	3.32	11.20
Missing	13.23	28.30	3.10	24.93	17.43
Total	100.00	100.00	100.00	100.01	100.00

Q21006	Education				
Country	Jordan	Lebanon	Egypt	Morocco	Total
Enjoy	99.62	98.50	99.30	98.04	98.85
Do not enjoy	0.20	0.50	0.50	1.08	0.57
Missing	0.19	1.00	0.20	0.88	0.57
Total	100.01	100.00	100.00	100.00	99.99

Q21007	Higher education				
Country	Jordan	Lebanon	Egypt	Morocco	Total
Enjoy	99.50	98.40	98.00	95.59	97.87
Do not enjoy	0.49	0.30	1.80	2.54	1.29
Missing	0.00	1.30	0.20	1.86	0.85
Total	99.99	100.00	100.00	99.99	100.01

Q21008	Work				
Country	Jordan	Lebanon	Egypt	Morocco	Total
Enjoy	98.81	98.60	96.00	95.31	97.17
Do not enjoy	1.20	0.30	3.80	4.11	2.36
Missing	0.00	1.10	0.20	0.59	0.47
Total	100.01	100.00	100.00	100.01	100.00

Q21009	Owning assets				
Country	Jordan	Lebanon	Egypt	Morocco	Total
Enjoy	96.97	96.30	95.60	94.82	95.91
Do not enjoy	2.29	1.10	3.00	1.66	2.01
Missing	0.74	2.60	1.40	3.52	2.07
Total	100.00	100.00	100.00	100.00	99.99

Q21010	Owning projects				
Country	Jordan	Lebanon	Egypt	Morocco	Total
Enjoy	96.05	96.30	92.30	91.79	94.10
Do not enjoy	3.26	1.60	6.40	3.03	3.57
Missing	0.69	2.10	1.30	5.18	2.33
Total	100.00	100.00	100.00	100.00	100.00

Q21011	Managing projects				
Country	Jordan	Lebanon	Egypt	Morocco	Total
Enjoy	95.19	96.30	89.70	88.96	92.51
Do not enjoy	4.03	1.40	9.20	4.11	4.68
Missing	0.79	2.30	1.10	6.94	2.81
Total	100.01	100.00	100.00	100.01	100.00

Q21012	Participation in civil society (NGOs, political parties and the media)				
Country	Jordan	Lebanon	Egypt	Morocco	Total
Enjoy	92.63	96.30	86.70	81.62	89.27
Do not enjoy	5.40	0.50	9.50	3.42	4.70
Missing	1.97	3.20	3.80	14.96	6.03
Total	100.00	100.00	100.00	100.00	100.00

Q21013	Participation in political activity				
Country	Jordan	Lebanon	Egypt	Morocco	Total
Enjoy	91.29	96.00	80.30	82.50	87.50
Do not enjoy	6.57	1.30	15.60	4.01	6.85
Missing	2.13	2.70	4.10	13.49	5.65
Total	99.99	100.00	100.00	100.00	100.00

" ...." has improved, stayed at the same level or deteriorated over the last five years					

Q21101	Protection from physical abuse				
Country	Jordan	Lebanon	Egypt	Morocco	Total
Improved	73.29	62.00	79.60	72.92	71.96
Same	19.44	23.60	14.20	20.72	19.50
Deteriorated	4.30	8.60	4.30	3.03	5.05
Missing	2.97	5.80	1.90	3.32	3.50
Total	100.00	100.00	100.00	99.99	100.01

Q21102	Protection from mental abuse				
Country	Jordan	Lebanon	Egypt	Morocco	Total
Improved	70.25	53.50	78.10	67.64	67.38
Same	22.47	28.80	15.60	24.73	22.91
Deteriorated	4.94	12.00	4.80	3.32	6.25
Missing	2.34	5.70	1.50	4.30	3.46
Total	100.00	100.00	100.00	99.99	100.00

Q21103	Choosing a spouse				
Country	Jordan	Lebanon	Egypt	Morocco	Total
Improved	77.39	79.00	88.60	78.69	80.91
Same	19.46	13.00	10.10	17.11	14.93
Deteriorated	1.58	1.90	0.30	1.27	1.26
Missing	1.57	6.10	1.00	2.93	2.90
Total	100.00	100.00	100.00	100.00	100.00

Q21104	Having a divorce of her own will				
Country	Jordan	Lebanon	Egypt	Morocco	Total
Improved	62.82	48.20	65.10	65.30	60.38
Same	26.94	35.40	29.70	26.00	29.49
Deteriorated	5.09	8.00	2.10	4.20	4.84
Missing	5.15	8.40	3.10	4.50	5.28
Total	100.00	100.00	100.00	100.00	99.99

Q21105	Banning girls' circumcision				
Country	Jordan	Lebanon	Egypt	Morocco	Total
Improved	68.14	41.10	53.10	18.96	45.18
Same	13.52	20.50	40.20	54.55	32.32
Deteriorated	1.34	1.30	2.40	2.44	1.87
Missing	17.00	37.10	4.30	24.05	20.63
Total	100.00	100.00	100.00	100.00	100.00

Q21106	Education				
Country	Jordan	Lebanon	Egypt	Morocco	Total
Improved	86.57	84.50	91.90	90.22	88.31
Same	11.12	6.40	7.00	8.60	8.28
Deteriorated	0.78	0.20	0.70	0.20	0.47
Missing	1.54	8.90	0.40	0.98	2.94
Total	100.01	100.00	100.00	100.00	100.00

Q21107	Higher education				
Country	Jordan	Lebanon	Egypt	Morocco	Total
Improved	86.11	86.20	90.30	87.39	87.50
Same	11.81	4.40	8.40	10.17	8.70
Deteriorated	1.07	0.40	0.70	0.49	0.66
Missing	1.01	9.00	0.60	1.96	3.13
Total	100.00	100.00	100.00	100.01	99.99

Q21108	Work				
Country	Jordan	Lebanon	Egypt	Morocco	Total
Improved	82.09	77.80	83.30	84.95	82.05
Same	15.28	7.80	13.50	11.44	12.00
Deteriorated	1.01	4.90	2.70	3.03	2.91
Missing	1.62	9.50	0.50	0.59	3.04
Total	100.00	100.00	100.00	100.01	100.00

Q21109	Owning assets				
Country	Jordan	Lebanon	Egypt	Morocco	Total
Improved	76.41	62.10	72.80	75.46	71.72
Same	19.67	25.20	23.90	17.99	21.67
Deteriorated	1.52	3.20	1.10	0.68	1.62
Missing	2.39	9.50	2.20	5.87	4.99
Total	99.99	100.00	100.00	100.00	100.00

Q21110	Owning projects				
Country	Jordan	Lebanon	Egypt	Morocco	Total
Improved	73.55	57.60	71.30	77.13	69.94
Same	21.65	30.10	25.00	15.44	23.00
Deteriorated	1.73	3.40	1.60	0.68	1.85
Missing	3.07	8.90	2.10	6.74	5.21
Total	100.00	100.00	100.00	99.99	100.00

Q21111	Managing projects				
Country	Jordan	Lebanon	Egypt	Morocco	Total
Improved	64.75	43.40	63.50	75.17	61.78
Same	29.30	35.70	32.10	15.64	28.11
Deteriorated	2.44	2.90	1.90	0.88	2.02
Missing	3.51	18.00	2.50	8.31	8.08
Total	100.00	100.00	100.00	100.00	99.99

Q21112	Participation in civil society				
Country	Jordan	Lebanon	Egypt	Morocco	Total
Improved	72.87	78.20	71.80	73.70	74.14
Same	17.93	10.70	20.30	11.53	15.09
Deteriorated	4.54	1.00	2.30	0.49	2.07
Missing	4.66	10.10	5.60	14.27	8.69
Total	100.00	100.00	100.00	99.99	99.99

Q21113	Participation in political activity				
Country	Jordan	Lebanon	Egypt	Morocco	Total
Improved	72.14	81.40	65.40	73.70	73.17
Same	17.06	9.70	26.10	12.22	16.25
Deteriorated	5.50	1.00	2.60	0.98	2.51
Missing	5.29	7.90	5.90	13.10	8.08
Total	99.99	100.00	100.00	100.00	100.01

SECTION III. Hijab/Intermingling/Polygamy/CEDAW

	Hijab				
Q301	Which position reflects your view on the hijab				
Country	Jordan	Lebanon	Egypt	Morocco	Total
Disagree	2.48	38.10	2.90	3.71	11.75
Agree if her decision	49.86	54.00	53.00	45.26	50.50
Must be obliged to wear it	47.32	2.80	43.00	50.44	35.97
Missing	0.34	5.10	1.10	0.59	1.77
Total	100.00	100.00	100.00	100.00	99.99

Q3021	Intermingling of men and women				
	Do you agree on intermingling of men and women in all stages of education				
Country	Jordan	Lebanon	Egypt	Morocco	Total
Agree	27.69	94.60	39.40	70.87	58.21
Disagree	71.45	5.20	59.90	26.30	40.63
Missing	0.86	0.20	0.70	2.83	1.16
Total	100.00	100.00	100.00	100.00	100.00

Q3022	Do you agree to intermingling of men and women at work?				
Country	Jordan	Lebanon	Egypt	Morocco	Total
Agree	49.06	96.80	74.60	75.76	74.06
Disagree	49.76	2.40	24.70	22.29	24.77
Missing	1.19	0.80	0.70	1.96	1.17
Total	100.01	100.00	100.00	100.01	100.00

Q3023	Do you agree to intermingling of men and women in society in general?				
Country	Jordan	Lebanon	Egypt	Morocco	Total
Agree	53.16	96.60	70.90	81.23	75.51
Disagree	45.49	2.50	28.00	16.72	23.14
Missing	1.35	0.90	1.10	2.05	1.35
Total	100.00	100.00	100.00	100.00	100.00

Q303	Polygamy				
	Agree to polygamy				
Country	Jordan	Lebanon	Egypt	Morocco	Total
Agree	24.52	7.40	17.30	34.80	21,08
Disagree	72.36	90.10	81.20	62.46	76.45
Missing	3.11	2.50	1.50	2.74	2.46
Total	99.99	100.00	100.00	100.00	99.99

Q304	Polygamy should be subject to the consent of ….				
Country	Jordan	Lebanon	Egypt	Morocco	Total
First wife only	18.97	29.73	15.03	15.45	17.63
Last wife only	5.92	5.41	2.89	4.78	4.78
Both wives together	36.02	22.97	56.07	60.11	49.08
Missing	39.09	41.89	26.01	19.66	28.51
Total	100.00	100.00	100.00	100.00	100.00

Q305	The Convention on the Elimination of All Forms of Discrimination against Women (CEDAW)				
	Aware of CEDAW?				
Country	Jordan	Lebanon	Egypt	Morocco	Total
Yes	9.04	12.90	0.80	10.65	8.36
No*	88.56	84.40	95.10	87.19	88.81
Missing	2.40	2.70	4.10	2.15	2.83
Total	100.00	100.00	100.00	99.99	100.00

* Go to Q40101

Q306	Approve the contents of this Convention				
Country	Jordan	Lebanon	Egypt	Morocco	Total
Yes	79.73	89.15	75.00	48.62	73.15
No	8.94	4.65	25.00	39.45	17.56
Missing	11.34	6.20	0.00	11.93	9.29
Total	100.01	100.00	100.00	100.00	100.00

Q307	Any objection against any of its clauses				
Country	Jordan	Lebanon	Egypt	Morocco	Total
Yes	20.59	17.83	25.00	18.35	18.91
No	60.28	68.99	75.00	59.63	63.76
Missing	19.13	13.18	0.00	22.02	17.33
Total	100.00	100.00	100.00	100.00	100.00

Q309	Approve the full implementation of this Convention in your country				
Country	Jordan	Lebanon	Egypt	Morocco	Total
Yes	52.65	78.29	62.50	38.53	58.14
No	33.99	6.98	37.50	42.20	26.38
Missing	13.36	14.73	0.00	19.27	15.48
Total	100.00	100.00	100.00	100.00	100.00

Q310	Approve the full implementation of this Convention in Arab countries				
Country	Jordan	Lebanon	Egypt	Morocco	Total
Yes	54.43	71.32	62.50	30.28	53.27
No	36.04	10.08	37.50	26.61	23.06
Missing	9.53	18.60	0.00	43.12	23.67
Total	100.00	100.00	100.00	100.01	100.00

SECTION IV. Renaissance in the Arab World

There is an urgent need for a human development revival in the Arab world by ...

Q40101	Building a knowledge society				
Country	Jordan	Lebanon	Egypt	Morocco	Total
Yes	91.95	97.20	90.00	95.60	93.70
No	4.58	1.00	3.60	0.49	2.41
Missing	3.48	1.80	6.40	3.91	3.90
Total	100.01	100.00	100.00	100.00	100.01

Q40102	Rise of Arab women				
Country	Jordan	Lebanon	Egypt	Morocco	Total
Yes	86.06	97.20	88.70	81.52	88.33
No	10.31	1.20	6.20	10.36	7.04
Missing	3.63	1.60	5.10	8.11	4.63
Total	100.00	100.00	100.00	99.99	100.00

Q40103	Respect for freedoms (of opinion, expression, association, and forming organisations in both civil and political spheres)				
Country	Jordan	Lebanon	Egypt	Morocco	Total
Yes	91.63	98.30	92.50	90.91	93.32
No	5.30	0.30	1.80	1.86	2.31
Missing	3.07	1.40	5.70	7.23	4.37
Total	100.00	100.00	100.00	100.00	100.00

Q40104	Establishing a good governance system (that protects freedom, is based on representing all people, and is accountable to them under a law that is executed by a just and completely independent judiciary)				
Country	Jordan	Lebanon	Egypt	Morocco	Total
Yes	91.07	93.50	91.60	89.83	91.49
No	4.72	2.30	1.70	1.27	2.49
Missing	4.20	4.20	6.70	8.90	6.02
Total	99.99	100.00	100.00	100.00	100.00

SECTION V. Demographic Data

Q501	Sex				
Country	Jordan	Lebanon	Egypt	Morocco	Total
Male	49.89	51.60	44.20	48.88	48.64
Female	50.11	48.40	55.80	51.12	51.36
Total	100.00	100.00	100.00	100.00	100.00

Q502	Age				
Country	Jordan	Lebanon	Egypt	Morocco	Total
18-24	20.82	14.70	26.90	22.48	21.23
25-34	27.95	24.90	19.00	38.22	27.28
35-49	33.17	37.70	29.60	25.81	31.54
50+	18.06	20.80	24.50	12.71	18.98
Missing	0.00	1.90	0.00	0.78	0.67
Total	100.00	100.00	100.00	100.00	99.70

Q503	Education				
Country	Jordan	Lebanon	Egypt	Morocco	Total
Illiterate/read & write	5.65	2.00	36.70	55.43	25.12
Primary	10.23	8.10	7.90	15.35	10.42
Preparatory	19.10	22.50	5.90	0.98	12.05
Secondary	35.69	30.90	13.90	19.84	25.05
Intermediate diploma	12.80	15.60	20.00	3.03	12.80
First university degree	14.17	8.10	13.20	2.15	9.36
Higher diploma	1.05	9.90	1.70	1.66	3.57
Master's and above	1.31	1.90	0.40	1.56	1.29
Missing	0.00	1.00	0.30	0.00	0.32
Total	100.00	100.00	100.00	100.00	99.98

Q504	Human resources relationship				
Country	Jordan	Lebanon	Egypt	Morocco	Total
Working	39.16	69.60	35.80	47.90	48.11
Not working	60.84	30.40	64.20	52.10	51.89
Total	100.00	100.00	100.00	100.00	100.00

Q506	Marital status				
Country	Jordan	Lebanon	Egypt	Morocco	Total
Single	28.14	31.20	28.00	46.53	33.54
Married	68.83	64.40	64.60	50.24	61.95
Other	3.03	4.40	7.40	3.23	4.51
Total	100.00	100.00	100.00	100.00	100.00

Q507	Religion				
Country	Jordan	Lebanon	Egypt	Morocco	Total
Muslim	97.10	43.30	96.10	99.71	84.14
Christian	2.70	55.30	3.90	0.29	15.46
Other	0.19	1.40	0.00	0.00	0.40
Total	99.99	100.00	100.00	100.00	100.00

Opinion on polygamy by gender					
Country	Jordan	Lebanon	Egypt	Morocco	Total
Men					
Agree	38.90	10.47	26.02	47.60	30.72
Disagree	58.55	87.02	72.85	50.00	67.10
Missing	2.55	2.52	1.13	2.40	2.18
Total	100.00	100.01	100.00	100.00	100.00
Women					
Agree	10.21	4.13	10.39	22.56	11.96
Disagree	86.12	93.39	87.81	74.38	85.31
Missing	3.67	2.48	1.79	3.06	2.73
Total	100.00	100.00	99.99	100.00	100.00
Total					
Agree	24.52	7.40	17.30	34.80	21.08
Disagree	72.36	90.10	81.20	62.46	76.45
Missing	3.11	2.50	1.50	2.74	2.46
Total	99.99	100.00	100.00	100.00	99.99

ANNEX III. DOCUMENTS

CONVENTION ON THE ELIMINATION OF ALL FORMS OF DISCRIMINATION AGAINST WOMEN[1]

United Nations

> "...the full and complete development of a country, the welfare of the world and the cause of peace require the maximum participation of women on equal terms with men in all fields"

Introduction

On 18 December 1979, the Convention on the Elimination of All Forms of Discrimination against Women was adopted by the United Nations General Assembly. It entered into force as an international treaty on 3 September 1981 after the twentieth country had ratified it. By the tenth anniversary of the Convention in 1989, almost one hundred nations had agreed to be bound by its provisions.

The Convention was the culmination of more than thirty years of work by the United Nations Commission on the Status of Women, a body established in 1946 to monitor the situation of women and to promote women's rights. The Commission's work has been instrumental in bringing to light all the areas in which women are denied equality with men. These efforts for the advancement of women have resulted in several declarations and conventions of which the Convention on the Elimination of All Forms of Discrimination against Women is the central and most comprehensive document.

Among the international human rights treaties, the Convention takes an important place in bringing the female half of humanity into the focus of human rights concerns. The spirit of the Convention is rooted in the goals of the United Nations: to reaffirm faith in fundamental human rights, in the dignity and worth of the human person, in the equal rights of men and women. The present document spells out the meaning of equality and how it can be achieved. In so doing, the Convention establishes not only an international bill of rights for women but also an agenda for action by countries to guarantee the enjoyment of those rights.

In its preamble, the Convention explicitly acknowledges that "extensive discrimination against women continues to exist" and emphasises that such discrimination "violates the principles of equality of rights and respect for human dignity". As defined in article 1, discrimination is understood as "any distinction, exclusion or restriction made on the basis of sex...in the political, economic, social, cultural, civil or any other field". The Convention gives positive affirmation to the principle of equality by requiring States Parties to take "all appropriate measures, including legislation, to ensure the full development and advancement of women, for the purpose of guaranteeing them the exercise and enjoyment of human rights and fundamental freedoms on a basis of equality with men"(article 3).

The agenda for equality is specified in fourteen subsequent articles. In its approach, the Convention covers three dimensions of the situation of women. Civil rights and the legal status of women are dealt with in great detail. In addition, and unlike other human rights treaties, the Convention is also concerned with the dimension of human reproduction as

---

[1] Source: "United Nations." (Accessed 10 February 2006).

http://www.un.org/womenwatch/daw/cedaw/text/econvention.htm

well as with the impact of cultural factors on gender relations.

The legal status of women receives the broadest attention. Concern over the basic rights of political participation has not diminished since the adoption of the Convention on the Political Rights of Women in 1952. Its provisions, therefore, are restated in article 7 of the present document, whereby women are guaranteed the rights to vote, to hold public office and to exercise public functions. This includes equal rights for women to represent their countries at the international level (article 8). The Convention on the Nationality of Married Women – adopted in 1957 – is integrated under article 9 providing for the statehood of women, irrespective of their marital status. The Convention thereby draws attention to the fact that often, women's legal status has been linked to marriage, making them dependent on their husband's nationality rather than individuals in their own right. Articles 10, 11 and 13, respectively, affirm women's rights to non-discrimination in education, employment and economic and social activities. These demands are given special emphasis with regard to the situation of rural women, whose particular struggles and vital economic contributions, as noted in article 14, warrant more attention in policy planning. Article 15 asserts the full equality of women in civil and business matters, demanding that all instruments directed at restricting women's legal capacity "shall be deemed null and void". Finally, in article 16, the Convention returns to the issue of marriage and family relations, asserting the equal rights and obligations of women and men with regard to choice of spouse, parenthood, personal rights and command over property.

Aside from civil rights issues, the Convention also devotes major attention to a most vital concern of women, namely, their reproductive rights. The preamble sets the tone by stating that "the role of women in procreation should not be a basis for discrimination". The link between discrimination and women's reproductive role is a matter of recurrent concern in the Convention. For example, it advocates, in article 5, "a proper understanding of maternity as a social function", demanding

fully shared responsibility for child-raising by both sexes. Accordingly, provisions for maternity protection and child care are proclaimed as essential rights and are incorporated into all areas of the Convention whether dealing with employment, family law, health care or education. Society's obligation extends to offering social services, especially child-care facilities, that allow individuals to combine family responsibilities with work and participation in public life. Special measures for maternity protection are recommended and "shall not be considered discriminatory". (article 4). "The Convention also affirms women's right to reproductive choice. Notably, it is the only human rights treaty to mention family planning. States Parties are obliged to include advice on family planning in the education process (article l0 (h)) and to develop family codes that guarantee women's rights "to decide freely and responsibly on the number and spacing of their children and to have access to the information, education and means to enable them to exercise these rights" (article 16(e)).

The third general thrust of the Convention aims at enlarging the understanding of the concept of human rights, as it gives formal recognition to the influence of culture and tradition on restricting women's enjoyment of their fundamental rights. These forces take shape in stereotypes, customs and norms that give rise to the multitude of legal, political and economic constraints on the advancement of women. Noting this interrelationship, the preamble of the Convention stresses "that a change in the traditional role of men as well as the role of women in society and in the family is needed to achieve full equality between men and women". States Parties are therefore obliged to work towards the modification of social and cultural patterns of individual conduct in order to eliminate "prejudices and customary and all other practices which are based on the idea of the inferiority or the superiority of either of the sexes or on stereotyped roles for men and women" (article 5). Also, article 10 (c) mandates the revision of textbooks, school programmes and teaching methods with a view to eliminating stereotyped concepts in the field of education. Finally, cultural patterns which define the public realm as a man's world and the domestic sphere as women's domain are strongly targeted in all of the Convention's provisions that affirm the equal responsibilities of both sexes in family life and their equal rights with regard to education and employment. Altogether, the Convention provides a comprehensive framework for challenging the various forces that have created and sustained discrimination based upon sex.

The implementation of the Convention is monitored by the Committee on the Elimination of Discrimination against Women (CWDAW). The Committee's mandate and the administration of the treaty are defined in articles 17 to 30 of the Convention. The Committee is composed of 23 experts nominated by their Governments and elected by the States Parties as individuals "of high moral standing and competence in the field covered by the Convention" (article 17).

At least every four years, the States Parties are expected to submit a national report to the Committee, indicating the measures that they have adopted to give effect to the provisions of the Convention. During its annual session, the Committee members discuss these reports with the Government representatives and explore with them areas for further action by the specific country. The Committee also makes general recommendations to the States Parties on matters concerning the elimination of discrimination against women.

The full text of the Convention is set out herein

CONVENTION ON THE ELIMINATION OF ALL FORMS OF DISCRIMINATION AGAINST WOMEN

The States Parties to the present Convention,

Noting that the Charter of the United Nations reaffirms faith in fundamental human rights, in the dignity and worth of the human person and in the equal rights of men and women,

Noting that the Universal Declaration of Human Rights affirms the principle of the inadmissibility of discrimination and proclaims that all human beings are born free and equal in dignity and rights and that everyone is entitled to all the rights and freedoms set forth therein, without distinction of any kind, including distinction based on sex,

Noting that the States Parties to the International Covenants on Human Rights have the obligation to ensure the equal rights of men and women to enjoy all economic, social, cultural, civil and political rights,

Considering the international conventions concluded under the auspices of the United Nations and the specialized agencies promoting equality of rights of men and women,

Noting also the resolutions, declarations and recommendations adopted by the United Nations and the specialized agencies promoting equality of rights of men and women,

Concerned, however, that despite these various instruments extensive discrimination against women continues to exist,

Recalling that discrimination against women violates the principles of equality of rights and respect for human dignity, is an obstacle to the participation of women, on equal terms with men, in the political, social, economic and cultural life of their countries, hampers the growth of the prosperity of society and the family and makes more difficult the full development of the potentialities of women in the service of their countries and of humanity,

Concerned that in situations of poverty women have the least access to food, health, education, training and opportunities for employment and other needs,

Convinced that the establishment of the new international economic order based on equity and justice will contribute significantly towards the promotion of equality between men and women,

Emphasizing that the eradication of apartheid, all forms of racism, racial discrimination, colonialism, neo-colonialism, aggression, foreign occupation and domination and interference in the internal affairs of States is essential to the full enjoyment of the rights of men and women,

Affirming that the strengthening of international peace and security, the relaxation of international tension, mutual co-operation among all States irrespective of their social and economic systems, general and complete disarmament, in particular nuclear disarmament under strict and effective international control, the affirmation of the principles of justice, equality and mutual benefit in relations among countries and the realization of the right of peoples under alien and colonial domination and foreign occupation to self-determination and independence, as well as respect for national sovereignty and territorial integrity, will promote social progress and development and as a consequence will contribute to the attainment of full equality between men and women,

Convinced that the full and complete development of a country, the welfare of the world and the cause of peace require the maximum participation of women on equal terms with men in all fields,

Bearing in mind the great contribution of women to the welfare of the family and to the development of society, so far not fully recognized, the social significance of maternity and the role of both parents in the family and in the upbringing of children, and aware that the role of women in procreation should not be a basis for discrimination but that the upbringing of children requires a sharing of responsibility between men and women and society as a whole,

Aware that a change in the traditional role of men as well as the role of women in society and in the family is needed to achieve full equality between men and women,

Determined to implement the principles set forth in the Declaration on the Elimination of Discrimination against Women and, for that purpose, to adopt the measures required for the elimination of such discrimination in all its forms and manifestations,

Have agreed on the following:

PART I

Article I

For the purposes of the present Convention, the term "discrimination against women" shall mean any distinction, exclusion or restriction made on the basis of sex which has the effect or purpose of impairing or nullifying the recognition, enjoyment or exercise by women, irrespective of their marital status, on a basis of equality of men

and women, of human rights and fundamental freedoms in the political, economic, social, cultural, civil or any other field.

Article 2

States Parties condemn discrimination against women in all its forms, agree to pursue by all appropriate means and without delay a policy of eliminating discrimination against women and, to this end, undertake:

(a) To embody the principle of the equality of men and women in their national constitutions or other appropriate legislation if not yet incorporated therein and to ensure, through law and other appropriate means, the practical realization of this principle;

(b) To adopt appropriate legislative and other measures, including sanctions where appropriate, prohibiting all discrimination against women;

(c) To establish legal protection of the rights of women on an equal basis with men and to ensure through competent national tribunals and other public institutions the effective protection of women against any act of discrimination;

(d) To refrain from engaging in any act or practice of discrimination against women and to ensure that public authorities and institutions shall act in conformity with this obligation;

(e) To take all appropriate measures to eliminate discrimination against women by any person, organization or enterprise;

(f) To take all appropriate measures, including legislation, to modify or abolish existing laws, regulations, customs and practices which constitute discrimination against women;

(g) To repeal all national penal provisions which constitute discrimination against women.

Article 3

States Parties shall take in all fields, in particular in the political, social, economic and cultural fields, all appropriate measures, including legislation, to ensure the full development and advancement of women, for the purpose of guaranteeing them the exercise and enjoyment of human rights and fundamental freedoms on a basis of equality with men.

Article 4

1. Adoption by States Parties of temporary special measures aimed at accelerating de facto equality between men and women shall not be considered discrimination as defined in the present Convention, but shall in no way entail as a consequence the maintenance of unequal or separate standards; these measures shall be discontinued when the objectives of equality of opportunity and treatment have been achieved.

2. Adoption by States Parties of special measures, including those measures contained in the present Convention, aimed at protecting maternity shall not be considered discriminatory.

Article 5

States Parties shall take all appropriate measures:

(a) To modify the social and cultural patterns of conduct of men and women, with a view to achieving the elimination of prejudices and customary and all other practices which are based on the idea of the inferiority or the superiority of either of the sexes or on stereotyped roles for men and women;

(b) To ensure that family education includes a proper understanding of maternity as a social function and the recognition of the common responsibility of men and women in the upbringing and development of their children, it being understood that the interest of the children is the primordial consideration in all cases.

Article 6

States Parties shall take all appropriate measures, including legislation, to suppress all forms of traffic in women and exploitation of prostitution of women.

PART II

Article 7

States Parties shall take all appropriate measures to eliminate discrimination against women in the political and public life of the country and, in particular, shall ensure to women, on equal terms with men, the right:

(a) To vote in all elections and public referenda and to be eligible for election to all publicly elected bodies;

(b) To participate in the formulation of government policy and the implementation thereof and to hold public office and perform all public functions at all levels of government;

(c) To participate in non-governmental organizations and associations concerned with the public and political life of the country.

Article 8

States Parties shall take all appropriate measures to ensure to women, on equal terms with men and without any discrimination, the opportunity to represent their Governments at the international level and to participate in the work of international organizations.

Article 9

1. States Parties shall grant women equal rights with men to acquire, change or retain their nationality. They shall ensure in particular that neither marriage to an alien nor change of nationality by the husband during marriage shall automatically change the nationality of the wife, render her stateless or force upon her the nationality of the husband.

2. States Parties shall grant women equal rights with men with respect to the nationality of their children.

PART III

Article 10

States Parties shall take all appropriate measures to eliminate discrimination against women in order to ensure to them equal rights with men in the field of education and in particular to ensure, on a basis of equality of men and women:

(a) The same conditions for career and vocational guidance, for access to studies and for the achievement of diplomas in educational establishments of all categories in rural as well as in urban areas; this equality shall be ensured in pre-school, general, technical, professional and higher technical education, as well as in all types of vocational training;

(b) Access to the same curricula, the same examinations, teaching staff with qualifications of the same standard and school premises and equipment of the same quality;

(c) The elimination of any stereotyped concept of the roles of men and women at all levels and in all forms of education by encouraging coeducation and other types of education which will help to achieve this aim and, in particular, by the revision of textbooks and school programmes and the adaptation of teaching methods;

(d) The same opportunities to benefit from scholarships and other study grants;

(e) The same opportunities for access to programmes of continuing education, including adult and functional literacy programmes, particularly those aimed at reducing, at the earliest possible time, any gap in education existing between men and women;

(f) The reduction of female student drop-out rates and the organization of programmes for girls and women who have left school prematurely;

(g) The same opportunities to participate actively in sports and physical education;

(h) Access to specific educational information to help to ensure the health and well-being of families, including information and advice on family planning.

Article 11

1. States Parties shall take all appropriate measures to eliminate discrimination against women in the field of employment in order to ensure, on a basis of equality of men and women, the same rights, in particular:

(a) The right to work as an inalienable right of all human beings;

(b) The right to the same employment opportunities, including the application of the same criteria for selection in matters of employment;

(c) The right to free choice of profession and employment, the right to promotion, job security and all benefits and conditions of service and the right to receive vocational training and retraining, including apprenticeships, advanced vocational training and recurrent training;

(d) The right to equal remuneration, including benefits, and to equal treatment in respect of work of equal value, as well as equality of treatment in the evaluation of the quality of work;

(e) The right to social security, particularly in cases of retirement, unemployment, sickness, invalidity and old age and other incapacity to work, as well as the right to paid leave;

(f) The right to protection of health and to safety in working conditions, including the safeguarding of the function of reproduction.

2. In order to prevent discrimination against women on the grounds of marriage or maternity and to ensure their effective right to work, States Parties shall take appropriate measures:

(a) To prohibit, subject to the imposition of sanctions, dismissal on the grounds of pregnancy or of maternity leave and discrimination in dismissals on the basis of marital status;

(b) To introduce maternity leave with pay or with comparable social benefits without loss of former employment, seniority or social allowances;

(c) To encourage the provision of the necessary supporting social services to enable parents to combine family obligations with work responsibilities and participation in public life, in particular through promoting the establishment and development of a network of child-care facilities;

(d) To provide special protection to women during pregnancy in types of work proved to be harmful to them.

3. Protective legislation relating to matters covered in this article shall be reviewed periodically in the light of scientific and technological knowledge and shall be revised, repealed or extended as necessary.

Article 12

1. States Parties shall take all appropriate measures to eliminate discrimination against women in the field of health care in order to ensure, on a basis of equality of men and women, access to health care services, including those related to family planning.

2. Notwithstanding the provisions of paragraph I of this article, States Parties shall ensure to women appropriate services in connection with pregnancy, confinement

and the post-natal period, granting free services where necessary, as well as adequate nutrition during pregnancy and lactation.

Article 13

States Parties shall take all appropriate measures to eliminate discrimination against women in other areas of economic and social life in order to ensure, on a basis of equality of men and women, the same rights, in particular:

(a) The right to family benefits;

(b) The right to bank loans, mortgages and other forms of financial credit;

(c) The right to participate in recreational activities, sports and all aspects of cultural life.

Article 14

1. States Parties shall take into account the particular problems faced by rural women and the significant roles which rural women play in the economic survival of their families, including their work in the non-monetized sectors of the economy, and shall take all appropriate measures to ensure the application of the provisions of the present Convention to women in rural areas.

2. States Parties shall take all appropriate measures to eliminate discrimination against women in rural areas in order to ensure, on a basis of equality of men and women, that they participate in and benefit from rural development and, in particular, shall ensure to such women the right:

(a) To participate in the elaboration and implementation of development planning at all levels;

(b) To have access to adequate health care facilities, including information, counselling and services in family planning;

(c) To benefit directly from social security programmes;

(d) To obtain all types of training and education, formal and non-formal, including that relating to functional literacy, as well as, inter alia, the benefit of all community and extension services, in order to increase their technical proficiency;

(e) To organize self-help groups and co-operatives in order to obtain equal access to economic opportunities through employment or self employment;

(f) To participate in all community activities;

(g) To have access to agricultural credit and loans, marketing facilities, appropriate technology and equal treatment in land and agrarian reform as well as in land resettlement schemes;

(h) To enjoy adequate living conditions, particularly in relation to housing, sanitation, electricity and water supply, transport and communications.

PART IV

Article 15

1. States Parties shall accord to women equality with men before the law.

2. States Parties shall accord to women, in civil matters, a legal capacity identical to that of men and the same opportunities to exercise that capacity. In particular, they shall give women equal rights to conclude contracts and to administer property and shall treat them equally in all stages of procedure in courts and tribunals.

3. States Parties agree that all contracts and all other private instruments of any kind with a legal effect which is directed at restricting the legal capacity of women shall be deemed null and void.

4. States Parties shall accord to men and women the same rights with regard to the law relating to the movement of persons and the freedom to choose their residence and domicile.

Article 16

1. States Parties shall take all appropriate measures to eliminate discrimination against women in all matters relating to marriage and family relations and in particular shall ensure, on a basis of equality of men and women:

(a) The same right to enter into marriage;

(b) The same right freely to choose a spouse and to enter into marriage only with their free and full consent;

(c) The same rights and responsibilities during marriage and at its dissolution;

(d) The same rights and responsibilities as

parents, irrespective of their marital status, in matters relating to their children; in all cases the interests of the children shall be paramount;

(e) The same rights to decide freely and responsibly on the number and spacing of their children and to have access to the information, education and means to enable them to exercise these rights;

(f) The same rights and responsibilities with regard to guardianship, wardship, trusteeship and adoption of children, or similar institutions where these concepts exist in national legislation; in all cases the interests of the children shall be paramount;

(g) The same personal rights as husband and wife, including the right to choose a family name, a profession and an occupation;

(h) The same rights for both spouses in respect of the ownership, acquisition, management, administration, enjoyment and disposition of property, whether free of charge or for a valuable consideration.

2. The betrothal and the marriage of a child shall have no legal effect, and all necessary action, including legislation, shall be taken to specify a minimum age for marriage and to make the registration of marriages in an official registry compulsory.

PART V

Article 17

1. For the purpose of considering the progress made in the implementation of the present Convention, there shall be established a Committee on the Elimination of Discrimination against Women (hereinafter referred to as the Committee) consisting, at the time of entry into force of the Convention, of eighteen and, after ratification of or accession to the Convention by the thirty-fifth State Party, of twenty-three experts of high moral standing and competence in the field covered by the Convention. The experts shall be elected by States Parties from among their nationals and shall serve in their personal capacity, consideration being given to equitable geographical distribution and to the representation of the different forms of civilization as well as the principal legal systems.

2. The members of the Committee shall be elected by secret ballot from a list of persons nominated by States Parties. Each State Party may nominate one person from among its own nationals.

3. The initial election shall be held six months after the date of the entry into force of the present Convention. At least three months before the date of each election the Secretary-General of the United Nations shall address a letter to the States Parties inviting them to submit their nominations within two months. The Secretary-General shall prepare a list in alphabetical order of all persons thus nominated, indicating the States Parties which have nominated them, and shall submit it to the States Parties.

4. Elections of the members of the Committee shall be held at a meeting of States Parties convened by the Secretary-General at United Nations Headquarters. At that meeting, for which two thirds of the States Parties shall constitute a quorum, the persons elected to the Committee shall be those nominees who obtain the largest number of votes and an absolute majority of the votes of the representatives of States Parties present and voting.

5. The members of the Committee shall be elected for a term of four years. However, the terms of nine of the members elected at the first election shall expire at the end of two years; immediately after the first election the names of these nine members shall be chosen by lot by the Chairman of the Committee.

6. The election of the five additional members of the Committee shall be held in accordance with the provisions of paragraphs 2, 3 and 4 of this article, following the thirty-fifth ratification or accession. The terms of two of the additional members elected on this occasion shall expire at the end of two years, the names of these two members having been chosen by lot by the Chairman of the Committee.

7. For the filling of casual vacancies, the State

Party whose expert has ceased to function as a member of the Committee shall appoint another expert from among its nationals, subject to the approval of the Committee.

8. The members of the Committee shall, with the approval of the General Assembly, receive emoluments from United Nations resources on such terms and conditions as the Assembly may decide, having regard to the importance of the Committee's responsibilities.

9. The Secretary-General of the United Nations shall provide the necessary staff and facilities for the effective performance of the functions of the Committee under the present Convention.

Article 18

1. States Parties undertake to submit to the Secretary-General of the United Nations, for consideration by the Committee, a report on the legislative, judicial, administrative or other measures which they have adopted to give effect to the provisions of the present Convention and on the progress made in this respect:
   (a) Within one year after the entry into force for the State concerned;
   (b) Thereafter at least every four years and further whenever the Committee so requests.

2. Reports may indicate factors and difficulties affecting the degree of fulfilment of obligations under the present Convention.

Article 19

1. The Committee shall adopt its own rules of procedure.

2. The Committee shall elect its officers for a term of two years.

Article 20

1. The Committee shall normally meet for a period of not more than two weeks annually in order to consider the reports submitted in accordance with article 18 of the present Convention.

2. The meetings of the Committee shall normally be held at United Nations Headquarters or at any other convenient place as determined by the Committee.

Article 21

1. The Committee shall, through the Economic and Social Council, report annually to the General Assembly of the United Nations on its activities and may make suggestions and general recommendations based on the examination of reports and information received from the States Parties. Such suggestions and general recommendations shall be included in the report of the Committee together with comments, if any, from States Parties.

2. The Secretary-General of the United Nations shall transmit the reports of the Committee to the Commission on the Status of Women for its information.

Article 22

The specialized agencies shall be entitled to be represented at the consideration of the implementation of such provisions of the present Convention as fall within the scope of their activities. The Committee may invite the specialized agencies to submit reports on the implementation of the Convention in areas falling within the scope of their activities.

PART VI

Article 23

Nothing in the present Convention shall affect any provisions that are more conducive to the achievement of equality between men and women which may be contained:
(a) In the legislation of a State Party; or
(b) In any other international convention, treaty or agreement in force for that State.

Article 24

States Parties undertake to adopt all necessary measures at the national level aimed at achieving the full realization of the rights recognized in the present Convention.

Article 25

1. The present Convention shall be open for signature by all States.

2. The Secretary-General of the United Nations is designated as the depositary of the present Convention.

3. The present Convention is subject to ratification. Instruments of ratification shall be deposited with the Secretary-General of the United Nations.

4. The present Convention shall be open to accession by all States. Accession shall be effected by the deposit of an instrument of accession with the Secretary-General of the United Nations.

Article 26

1. A request for the revision of the present Convention may be made at any time by any State Party by means of a notification in writing addressed to the Secretary-General of the United Nations.
2. The General Assembly of the United Nations shall decide upon the steps, if any, to be taken in respect of such a request.

Article 27

1. The present Convention shall enter into force on the thirtieth day after the date of deposit with the Secretary-General of the United Nations of the twentieth instrument of ratification or accession.
2. For each State ratifying the present Convention or acceding to it after the deposit of the twentieth instrument of ratification or accession, the Convention shall enter into force on the thirtieth day after the date of the deposit of its own instrument of ratification or accession.

Article 28

1. The Secretary-General of the United Nations shall receive and circulate to all States the text of reservations made by States at the time of ratification or accession.
2. A reservation incompatible with the object and purpose of the present Convention shall not be permitted.
3. Reservations may be withdrawn at any time by notification to this effect addressed to the Secretary-General of the United Nations, who shall then inform all States thereof. Such notification shall take effect on the date on which it is received.

Article 29

1. Any dispute between two or more States Parties concerning the interpretation or application of the present Convention which is not settled by negotiation shall, at the request of one of them, be submitted to arbitration. If within six months from the date of the request for arbitration the parties are unable to agree on the organization of the arbitration, any one of those parties may refer the dispute to the International Court of Justice by request in conformity with the Statute of the Court.
2. Each State Party may at the time of signature or ratification of the present Convention or accession thereto declare that it does not consider itself bound by paragraph 1 of this article. The other States Parties shall not be bound by that paragraph with respect to any State Party which has made such a reservation.
3. Any State Party which has made a reservation in accordance with paragraph 2 of this article may at any time withdraw that reservation by notification to the Secretary-General of the United Nations.

Article 30

The present Convention, the Arabic, Chinese, English, French, Russian and Spanish texts of which are equally authentic, shall be deposited with the Secretary-General of the United Nations.

IN WITNESS WHEREOF the undersigned, duly authorized, have signed the present Convention.

UNITED NATIONS SECURITY COUNCIL RESOLUTION 1325 ON WOMEN, PEACE AND SECURITY[2]

United Nations S/RES/1325 (2000)
Security Council
Distr.: General
31 October 2000
00-72018 (E)

Resolution 1325 (2000)
Adopted by the Security Council at its 4213th meeting, on 31 October 2000

The Security Council,

Recalling its resolutions 1261 (1999) of 25 August 1999, 1265 (1999) of 17 September

---

2 Source: "United Nations." (Accessed 10 February 2006).

http://www.un.org/events/res_1325e.pdf#search=%22resolution%201325%22

1999, 1296 (2000) of 19 April 2000 and 1314 (2000) of 11 August 2000, as well as relevant statements of its President, and recalling also the statement of its President to the press on the occasion of the United Nations Day for Women's Rights and International Peace (International Women's Day) of 8 March 2000 (SC/6816),

Recalling also the commitments of the Beijing Declaration and Platform for Action (A/52/231) as well as those contained in the outcome document of the twenty-third Special Session of the United Nations General Assembly entitled "Women 2000: Gender Equality, Development and Peace for the Twenty-First Century" (A/S-23/10/Rev.1), in particular those concerning women and armed conflict,

Bearing in mind the purposes and principles of the Charter of the United Nations and the primary responsibility of the Security Council under the Charter for the maintenance of international peace and security,

Expressing concern that civilians, particularly women and children, account for the vast majority of those adversely affected by armed conflict, including as refugees and internally displaced persons, and increasingly are targeted by combatants and armed elements, and recognizing the consequent impact this has on durable peace and reconciliation,

Reaffirming the important role of women in the prevention and resolution of conflicts and in peace-building, and stressing the importance of their equal participation and full involvement in all efforts for the maintenance and promotion of peace and security, and the need to increase their role in decision-making with regard to conflict prevention and resolution,

Reaffirming also the need to implement fully international humanitarian and human rights law that protects the rights of women and girls during and after conflicts,

Emphasizing the need for all parties to ensure that mine clearance and mine awareness programmes take into account the special needs of women and girls,

Recognizing the urgent need to mainstream a gender perspective into peacekeeping operations, and in this regard noting the Windhoek Declaration and the Namibia Plan of Action on Mainstreaming a Gender Perspective in Multidimensional Peace Support Operations (S/2000/693),

Recognizing also the importance of the recommendation contained in the statement of its President to the press of 8 March 2000 for specialized training for all peacekeeping personnel on the protection, special needs and human rights of women and children in conflict situations,

Recognizing that an understanding of the impact of armed conflict on women and girls, effective institutional arrangements to guarantee their protection and full participation in the peace process can significantly contribute to the maintenance and promotion of international peace and security,

Noting the need to consolidate data on the impact of armed conflict on women and girls,

1. Urges Member States to ensure increased representation of women at all decision-making levels in national, regional and international institutions and mechanisms for the prevention, management, and resolution of conflict;

2. Encourages the Secretary-General to implement his strategic plan of action (A/49/587) calling for an increase in the participation of women at decision-making levels in conflict resolution and peace processes;

3. Urges the Secretary-General to appoint more women as special representatives and envoys to pursue good offices on his behalf, and in this regard calls on Member States to provide candidates to the Secretary-General, for inclusion in a regularly updated centralized roster;

4. Further urges the Secretary-General to seek to expand the role and contribution of women in United Nations field-based operations, and especially among military observers, civilian police, human rights and humanitarian personnel;

5. Expresses its willingness to incorporate a gender perspective into peacekeeping operations, and urges the Secretary-General to ensure that, where appropriate, field operations include a gender component;

6. Requests the Secretary-General to provide to Member States training guidelines and

materials on the protection, rights and the particular needs of women, as well as on the importance of involving women in all peacekeeping and peacebuilding measures, invites Member States to incorporate these elements as well as HIV/AIDS awareness training into their national training programmes for military and civilian police personnel in preparation for deployment, and further requests the Secretary-General to ensure that civilian personnel of peace-keeping operations receive similar training;

7. Urges Member States to increase their voluntary financial, technical and logistical support for gender-sensitive training efforts, including those undertaken by relevant funds and programmes, inter alia, the United Nations Fund for Women and United Nations Children's Fund, and by the Office of the United Nations High Commissioner for Refugees and other relevant bodies;

8. Calls on all actors involved, when negotiating and implementing peace agreements, to adopt a gender perspective, including, inter alia:

   (a) The special needs of women and girls during repatriation and resettlement and for rehabilitation, reintegration and post-conflict reconstruction;

   (b) Measures that support local women's peace initiatives and indigenous processes for conflict resolution, and that involve women in all of the implementation mechanisms of the peace agreements;

   (c) Measures that ensure the protection of and respect for human rights of women and girls, particularly as they relate to the constitution, the electoral system, the police and the judiciary;

9. Calls upon all parties to armed conflict to respect fully international law applicable to the rights and protection of women and girls, especially as civilians, in particular the obligations applicable to them under the Geneva Conventions of 1949 and the Additional Protocols thereto of 1977, the Refugee Convention of 1951 and the Protocol thereto of 1967, the Convention on the Elimination of All Forms of Discrimi-

nation against Women of 1979 and the Optional Protocol thereto of 1999 and the United Nations Convention on the Rights of the Child of 1989 and the two Optional Protocols thereto of 25 May 2000, and to bear in mind the relevant provisions of the Rome Statute of the International Criminal Court;

10. Calls on all parties to armed conflict to take special measures to protect women and girls from gender-based violence, particularly rape and other forms of sexual abuse, and all other forms of violence in situations of armed conflict;

11. Emphasizes the responsibility of all States to put an end to impunity and to prosecute those responsible for genocide, crimes against humanity, and war crimes including those relating to sexual and other violence against women and girls, and in this regard stresses the need to exclude these crimes, where feasible from amnesty provisions;

12. Calls upon all parties to armed conflict to respect the civilian and humanitarian character of refugee camps and settlements, and to take into account the particular needs of women and girls, including in their design, and recalls its resolutions 1208 (1998) of 19 November 1998 and 1296 (2000) of 19 April 2000;

13. Encourages all those involved in the planning for disarmament, demobilization and reintegration to consider the different needs of female and male ex-combatants and to take into account the needs of their dependants;

14. Reaffirms its readiness, whenever measures are adopted under Article 41 of the Charter of the United Nations, to give consideration to their potential impact on the civilian population, bearing in mind the special needs of women and girls, in order to consider appropriate humanitarian exemptions;

15. Expresses its willingness to ensure that Security Council missions take into account gender considerations and the rights of women, including through consultation with local and international women's groups;

16. Invites the Secretary-General to carry out

a study on the impact of armed conflict on women and girls, the role of women in peace-building and the gender dimensions of peace processes and conflict resolution, and further invites him to submit a report to the Security Council on the results of this study and to make this available to all Member States of the United Nations;

17. Requests the Secretary-General, where appropriate, to include in his reporting to the Security Council progress on gender mainstreaming throughout peacekeeping missions and all other aspects relating to women and girls;

18. Decides to remain actively seized of the matter.

Annex IV. Statistical Tables on Human Development in the Arab States

Symbols used in the tables
..   Data not available.
(.)   Less than half the unit shown.
<   Less than half the unit shown.
---   Not applicable.
T   Total

Table A4 -1

HUMAN DEVELOPMENT INDEX

HDI Rank	Human development index (HDI) value 2003	Life expectancy at birth (years) (HDI) 2003	Adult literacy rate (% ages 15 and above) (HDI) 2003	Combined gross enrol-ment rate for primary, secondary and tertiary schools (%) 2002/03	GDP per capita (PPP US$) (HDI) 2003	Life expect-ancy index	Education index	GDP index	GDP per capita (PPP US$) rank minus HDI rank
High Human Development									
40 Qatar	0.849	72.8	89.2	82	19,844	0.80	0.87	0.88	-13
41 United Arab Emirates	0.849	78.0	77.3	74	22,420	0.88	0.76	0.90	-18
43 Bahrain	0.846	74.3	87.7	81	17,479	0.82	0.86	0.86	-7
44 Kuwait	0.844	76.9	82.9	74	18,047	0.87	0.80	0.87	-11
Medium Human Development									
58 Libyan Arab Jamahiriya	0.799	73.6	81.7	96	..	0.81	0.86	0.72	9
71 Oman	0.781	74.1	74.4	63	13,584	0.82	0.71	0.82	-30
77 Saudi Arabia	0.772	71.8	79.4	57	13,226	0.78	0.72	0.82	-33
81 Lebanon	0.759	72.0	86.5	79	5,074	0.78	0.84	0.66	14
89 Tunisia	0.753	73.3	74.3	74	7,161	0.80	0.74	0.71	-20
90 Jordan	0.753	71.3	89.9	78	4,320	0.77	0.86	0.63	14
102 Occupied Palestinian Territories	0.729	72.5	91.9	80	..	0.79	0.88	0.52	26
103 Algeria	0.722	71.1	69.8	74	6,107	0.77	0.71	0.69	-20
106 Syrian Arab Republic	0.721	73.3	82.9	62	3,576	0.81	0.76	0.60	8
119 Egypt	0.659	69.8	55.6	74	3,950	0.75	0.62	0.61	-10
124 Morocco	0.631	69.7	50.7	58	4,004	0.75	0.53	0.62	-16
141 Sudan	0.512	56.4	59.0	38	1,910	0.52	0.52	0.49	-6
Low Human Development									
150 Djibouti	0.495	52.8	65.5	24	2,086	0.46	0.52	0.51	-18
151 Yemen	0.489	60.6	49.0	55	889	0.59	0.51	0.36	15
Without HDI Rank									
Iraq	..	58.9	39.7	63	..	..	..	..	..
Somalia	..	46.5	..	..	..	..	..	..	..
All developing countries	0.694	65.0	76.5	63	4,359	0.67	0.72	0.70	..
Least developed countries	0.518	52.2	53.6	45	1,328	0.45	0.50	0.60	..
Arab States	0.679	67.0	64.1	62	5,685	0.70	0.61	0.72	..
East Asia and the Pacific	0.768	70.5	90.4	69	5,100	0.76	0.83	0.71	..
Latin America and the Caribbean	0.797	71.9	89.6	81	7,404	0.78	0.87	0.74	..
South Asia	0.628	63.4	58.9	56	2,897	0.64	0.58	0.67	..
Sub-Saharan Africa	0.515	46.1	60.5	50	1,856	0.35	0.56	0.63	..
Central and Eastern Europe and the CIS	0.802	68.1	99.2	83	7,939	0.72	0.94	0.75	..
OECD	0.892	77.7	..	89	25,915	0.88	0.95	0.85	..
High-income OECD	0.911	78.9	..	95	30,181	0.90	0.98	0.86	..
High human development	0.895	78.0	..	91	25,665	0.88	0.96	0.85	..
Medium human development	0.718	67.2	79.4	66	4,474	0.70	0.75	0.70	..
Low human development	0.486	46.0	56.6	46	1,046	0.35	0.53	0.58	..
High income	0.910	78.8	..	94	29,898	0.90	0.97	0.86	..
Middle income	0.774	70.3	89.6	73	6,104	0.75	0.84	0.73	..
Low income	0.593	58.4	60.6	54	2,168	0.56	0.58	0.64	..
World	0.741	67.1	..	67	8,229	0.70	0.77	0.75	..

Source: UNDP, HDR 2005, Table 1:219-222

HUMAN DEVELOPMENT INDEX TRENDS

				Human development index (trend)			
HDI Rank	1975	1980	1985	1990	1995	2000	2003
High Human Development							
40 Qatar	..	..	..	..	..	..	0.849
41 United Arab Emirates	0.734	0.769	0.787	0.812	0.814	..	0.849
43 Bahrain	..	0.747	0.780	0.809	0.826	0.838	0.846
44 Kuwait	0.763	0.777	0.780	..	0.813	0.837	0.844
Medium Human Development							
58 Libyan Arab Jamahiriya	..	..	..	0.699	0.738	0.769	0.799
71 Oman	0.494	0.547	0.641	0.708	0.741	0.762	0.781
77 Saudi Arabia	0.603	0.659	0.673	..	0.727	0.742	0.772
81 Lebanon	..	..	..	0.677	0.727	0.742	0.759
89 Tunisia	0.514	0.570	0.622	0.657	0.698	0.738	0.753
90 Jordan	..	0.641	0.664	0.683	0.708	0.742	0.753
102 Occupied Palestinian Territories	..	..	..	..	..	..	0.729
103 Algeria	0.506	0.558	0.610	0.649	0.671	..	0.722
106 Syrian Arab Republic	0.540	0.587	0.623	0.646	0.672	0.692	0.721
119 Egypt	0.439	0.487	0.540	0.579	0.611	..	0.659
124 Morocco	0.429	0.478	0.515	0.548	0.579	0.610	0.631
141 Sudan	0.349	0.376	0.396	0.428	0.465	0.500	0.512
Low Human Development							
150 Djibouti	..	..	..	..	0.477	0.487	0.495
151 Yemen	..	..	..	0.393	0.436	0.470	0.489
Without HDI Rank							
Iraq	..	..	..	..	..	..	..
Somalia	..	..	..	..	..	..	..

Source: UNDP, HDR 2005, Table 2:223-226.

HUMAN AND INCOME POVERTY

HDI Rank	Human poverty index (HPI-1) Rank	Human poverty index (HPI-1) Value (%)	Probability at birth of not surviving to age 40 (% of cohort) 2000-05	Adult illiteracy rate (% ages 15 and above) 2003	Population without sustainable access to an improved water source (%) 2002	Children under-weight for age (% under age 5) (HPI..1) 1995-2003	Population living below $1 a day (%) 1990-2003	Population living below $2 a day (%) 1990-2003	Population living below the national poverty line (%) 1990-2002	HPI-1 rank minus income poverty rank
High Human Development										
40 Qatar	10	7.8	4.7	10.8	0	6	..	..	..	..
41 United Arab Emirates	..	..	2.2	22.7	..	14	..	..	..	..
43 Bahrain	..	..	3.8	12.3	..	9	..	..	..	..
44 Kuwait	..	..	2.5	17.1	..	10	..	..	..	..
Medium Human Development										
58 Libyan Arab Jamahiriya	33	15.3	4.2	18.3	28	5	..	..	..	..
71 Oman	46	21.1	3.9	25.6	21	24	..	..	..	..
77 Saudi Arabia	32	14.9	5.8	20.6	5	14	..	..	..	..
81 Lebanon	18	9.6	5.7	13.5	0	3	..	..	..	..
89 Tunisia	43	18.3	4.7	25.7	18	4	<2	6.6	7.6	27
90 Jordan	11	8.1	6.4	10.1	9	4	<2	7.4	11.7	5
102 Occupied Palestinian Territories	7	6.5	5.3	8.1	6	4	..	..	..	..
103 Algeria	48	21.3	7.8	30.2	13	6	<2	15.1	12.2	29
106 Syrian Arab Republic	29	13.8	4.6	17.1	21	7	..	..	..	..
119 Egypt	55	30.9	7.8	44.4	2	9	3.1	43.9	16.7	18
124 Morocco	61	34.5	8.6	49.3	20	9	<2	14.3	19.0	35
141 Sudan	59	32.4	27.0	41.0	31	17	..	..	..	..
Low Human Development										
150 Djibouti	53	29.5	30.6	34.5	20	18	..	..	45.1	..
151 Yemen	77	40.3	18.8	51.0	31	46	15.7	45.2	41.8	19
Without HDI Rank										
Iraq	..	..	20.5	60.3	19	16	..	..	..	..
Somalia	..	..	38.9	..	71	26	..	..	..	..

Source: UNDP, HDR 2005, Table 3:227-229.

Table A4 -4

DEMOGRAPHIC TRENDS

HDI Rank	Total population (millions)			Annual population growth rate (%)		Urban population (% of total)			Population under age 15 (% of total)		Population age 65 and above (% of total)		Total fertility rate (births per woman)	
	1975	2003	2015	1975-2003	2003-2015	1975	2003	2015	2003	2015	2003	2015	1970-1975	2000-2005
High Human Development														
40 Qatar	0.2	0.7	1.0	5.2	2.3	84.8	92.0	93.6	23.1	21.8	0.9	2.0	6.8	3.0
41 United Arab Emirates	0.5	4.0	5.6	7.2	2.7	83.6	85.1	87.2	22.8	19.8	0.8	1.4	6.4	2.5
43 Bahrain	0.3	0.7	0.9	3.4	1.6	85.8	90.0	91.4	27.7	21.7	2.3	4.4	5.9	2.5
44 Kuwait	1.0	2.5	3.4	3.3	2.4	83.8	96.2	96.9	24.8	23.2	1.1	3.1	6.9	2.4
Medium Human Development														
58 Libyan Arab Jamahiriya	2.4	5.6	7.0	3.0	1.8	60.9	86.2	89.0	30.8	28.9	2.9	5.6	7.6	3.0
71 Oman	0.9	2.5	3.2	3.6	1.9	19.6	77.6	82.6	35.2	30.6	1.8	3.4	7.2	3.8
77 Saudi Arabia	7.3	23.3	30.8	4.2	2.3	58.3	87.6	91.1	38.2	32.3	2.1	3.5	7.3	4.1
81 Lebanon	2.7	3.5	4.0	1.0	1.0	67.0	87.5	90.1	29.5	24.4	5.9	7.7	4.8	2.3
89 Tunisia	5.7	9.9	11.1	2.0	1.0	49.9	63.7	68.1	27.5	21.9	5.0	6.8	6.2	2.0
90 Jordan	1.9	5.4	7.0	3.7	2.1	57.8	79.1	81.1	38.0	31.7	2.3	4.0	7.8	3.5
102 Occupied Palestinian Territories	1.3	3.5	5.0	3.6	3.0	59.6	71.1	75.6	46.0	41.6	2.7	3.0	7.7	5.6
103 Algeria	16.0	31.9	38.1	2.5	1.5	40.3	58.8	65.3	31.2	26.7	3.6	5.0	7.4	2.5
106 Syrian Arab Republic	7.5	18.1	23.8	3.1	2.3	45.1	50.2	52.4	38.0	33.2	2.5	3.6	7.5	3.5
119 Egypt	39.3	71.3	88.2	2.1	1.8	43.5	42.2	44.9	34.3	31.4	3.8	5.5	5.7	3.3
124 Morocco	17.3	30.6	36.2	2.0	1.4	37.8	57.4	64.8	31.9	28.4	3.9	5.2	6.9	2.8
141 Sudan	17.1	34.9	44.0	2.6	1.9	18.9	38.9	49.3	39.7	35.6	2.8	4.3	6.7	4.4
Low Human Development														
150 Djibouti	0.2	0.8	0.9	4.4	1.6	61.6	83.6	87.6	42.1	37.3	2.2	3.4	7.2	5.1
151 Yemen	7.0	19.7	28.5	3.7	3.1	14.8	25.7	31.3	47.1	43.4	1.8	2.4	8.5	6.2
Without HDI Rank														
Iraq	12.0	27.3	36.5	2.9	2.4	61.4	67.2	66.8	41.7	36.8	2.2	3.0	7.2	4.8
Somalia	4.1	7.7	11.0	2.2	2.9	25.5	34.9	42.7	44.1	43.0	2.1	2.7	7.3	6.4
All developing countries	2,967.1 T	5,022.4 T	5,885.6 T	1.9	1.3	26.4	42.0	48.6	31.6	28.0	4.3	6.5	5.5	2.9
Least developed countries	355.2 T	723.2 T	950.1 T	2.5	2.3	14.8	26.7	33.5	42.2	39.5	2.6	3.5	6.6	5.0
Arab States	144.6 T	303.9 T	386.0 T	2.7	2.0	41.7	54.7	59.1	36.3	32.5	3.1	4.4	6.7	3.7
East Asia and the Pacific	1,310.4 T	1,928.1 T	2,108.9 T	1.4	0.7	20.4	41.0	51.0	24.9	20.7	5.4	8.7	5.0	1.9
Latin America and the Caribbean	318.4 T	540.7 T	628.3 T	1.9	1.3	61.1	76.7	80.9	30.8	26.5	4.9	7.5	5.1	2.5
South Asia	838.7 T	1,503.4 T	1,801.4 T	2.1	1.5	21.3	29.8	34.2	34.1	29.3	3.8	5.7	5.6	3.2
Sub-Saharan Africa	313.1 T	674.2 T	877.4 T	2.7	2.2	21.0	35.6	42.4	44.0	42.0	2.5	3.3	6.8	5.5
Central and Eastern Europe and the CIS	366.6 T	406.3 T	396.8 T	0.4	-0.2	56.8	62.9	63.8	19.1	17.3	10.6	12.9	2.5	1.5
OECD	925.7 T	1,157.3 T	1,233.6 T	0.8	0.5	67.2	75.9	78.9	19.8	17.8	11.6	16.1	2.6	1.8
High-income OECD	765.9 T	917.4 T	968.5 T	0.6	0.5	69.9	77.5	80.4	17.9	16.4	13.0	18.0	2.2	1.6
High human development	972.2 T	1,211.5 T	1,289.2 T	0.8	0.5	68.7	77.2	80.1	19.6	17.6	11.7	16.2	2.5	1.7
Medium human development	2,678.2 T	4,205.8 T	4,753.6 T	1.6	1.0	27.9	42.2	48.6	29.2	25.3	4.9	7.2	5.0	2.5
Low human development	359.5 T	788.7 T	1,038.5 T	2.8	2.3	18.2	34.0	41.7	44.9	42.6	2.4	3.1	7.0	5.8
High income	781.8 T	948.3 T	1,005.6 T	0.7	0.5	70.1	78.0	80.8	18.0	16.5	12.8	17.7	2.2	1.7
Middle income	1,849.6 T	2,748.6 T	3,028.6 T	1.4	0.8	34.8	52.9	60.7	25.9	22.3	5.8	8.6	4.5	2.1
Low income	1,440.9 T	2,614.5 T	3,182.5 T	2.1	1.6	20.7	30.2	35.7	37.2	33.3	3.4	4.9	6.0	3.9
World	4,073.7 T	6,313.8 T	7,219.4 T	1.6	1.1	37.2	48.3	53.5	28.9	25.9	6.0	8.4	4.5	2.6

Source: UNDP, HDR 2005, Table 5:232-235.

COMMITMENT TO HEALTH: RESOURCES, ACCESS AND SERVICES

HDI Rank	Public health expenditure (% of GDP) 2002	Private health expenditure (% of GDP) 2002	Health expenditure per capita (PPP US$) 2002	One-year-olds fully immunized against tuberculosis (%) 2003	One-year-olds fully immunized against measles (%) 2003	Children with diarrhoea receiving oral rehydration and continued feeding (% under age 5) 1 1994-2003	Contraceptive prevalence rate (%) 1995-2003	Births attended by skilled health personnel (%) 1995-2003	Physicians (per 100,000 people) 1990-2004
High Human Development									
40 Qatar	2.4	0.7	894	99	93	..	43	98	221
41 United Arab Emirates	2.3	0.8	750	98	94	..	28	96	202
43 Bahrain	3.2	1.2	792	..	100	..	62	98	160
44 Kuwait	2.9	0.9	552	..	97	..	50	98	153
Medium Human Development									
58 Libyan Arab Jamahiriya	1.6	1.7	222	99	91	..	45	94	129
71 Oman	2.8	0.6	379	98	98	..	24	95	126
77 Saudi Arabia	3.3	1.0	534	94	96	..	32	91	140
81 Lebanon	3.5	8.0	697	..	96	..	61	89	325
89 Tunisia	2.9	2.9	415	93	90	..	63	90	70
90 Jordan	4.3	5.0	418	67	96	..	56	100	205
102 Occupied Palestinian Territories	..	..	..	99	..	..	..	97	84
103 Algeria	3.2	1.1	182	98	84	..	64	92	85
106 Syrian Arab Republic	2.3	2.8	109	99	98	..	40	76	140
119 Egypt	1.8	3.1	192	98	98	29	60	69	212
124 Morocco	1.5	3.1	186	92	90	..	50	40	48
141 Sudan	1.0	3.9	58	53	57	38	10	86	16
Low Human Development									
150 Djibouti	3.3	3.0	78	63	66	..	..	61	13
151 Yemen	1.0	2.7	58	67	66	23	21	22	22
Without HDI Rank									
Iraq	0.3	1.2	44	93	90	..	14	72	54
Somalia	..	..	..	65	40	..	..	34	4
All developing countries	.. T	.. T	.. T	85	75	.. T	.. T	59	.. T
Least developed countries	.. T	.. T	.. T	79	67	.. T	.. T	34	.. T
Arab States	.. T	.. T	.. T	86	84	.. T	.. T	70	.. T
East Asia and the Pacific	.. T	.. T	.. T	91	82	.. T	.. T	86	.. T
Latin America and the Caribbean	.. T	.. T	.. T	96	93	.. T	.. T	82	.. T
South Asia	.. T	.. T	.. T	83	68	.. T	.. T	38	.. T
Sub-Saharan Africa	.. T	.. T	.. T	75	62	.. T	.. T	41	.. T
Central and Eastern Europe and the CIS	.. T	.. T	.. T	97	97	.. T	.. T	97	.. T
OECD	.. T	.. T	.. T	..	91	.. T	.. T	95	.. T
High-income OECD	.. T	.. T	.. T	..	92	.. T	.. T	99	.. T
High human development	.. T	.. T	.. T	..	93	.. T	.. T	97	.. T
Medium human development	.. T	.. T	.. T	89	79	.. T	.. T	68	.. T
Low human development	.. T	.. T	.. T	75	61	.. T	.. T	35	.. T
High income	.. T	.. T	.. T	..	92	.. T	.. T	99	.. T
Middle income	.. T	.. T	.. T	95	89	.. T	.. T	88	.. T
Low income	.. T	.. T	.. T	79	66	.. T	.. T	42	.. T
World	.. T	.. T	.. T	85	77	.. T	.. T	62	.. T

Source: UNDP, HDR 2005, Table 6:236-239.

HDI Rank	Population with sustainable access to improved sanitation (%)		Population with sustainable access to an improved water source (%)		Population undernourished (% total)		Children under-weight for age (% under age 5)	Children under height for age (% under age 5)	Infants with low birthweight (%)
	1990	2002	1990	2002	1990-1992	2000-2002	1995-2003	1995-2003	1998-2003
High Human Development									
40 Qatar	100	100	100	100	..	..	6	8	10
41 United Arab Emirates	100	100	..	..	4	2	14	17	15
43 Bahrain	..	..	..	..	..	..	9	10	8
44 Kuwait	..	..	..	..	23	5	10	24	7
Medium Human Development									
58 Libyan Arab Jamahiriya	97	97	71	72	1	1	5	15	7
71 Oman	83	89	77	79	..	..	24	23	8
77 Saudi Arabia	..	..	90	..	4	3	14	20	11
81 Lebanon	..	98	100	100	3	3	3	12	6
89 Tunisia	75	80	77	82	1	1	4	12	7
90 Jordan	..	93	98	91	4	7	4	9	10
102 Occupied Palestinian Territories	..	76	..	94	..	..	4	9	9
103 Algeria	88	92	95	87	5	5	6	18	7
106 Syrian Arab Republic	76	77	79	79	5	4	7	18	6
119 Egypt	54	68	94	98	4	3	9	16	12
124 Morocco	57	61	75	80	6	7	9	24	11
141 Sudan	33	34	64	69	32	27	17	..	31
Low Human Development									
150 Djibouti	48	50	78	80	..	..	18	26	..
151 Yemen	21	30	69	69	34	36	46	53	32
Without HDI Rank									
Iraq	81	80	83	81	..	..	16	22	15
Somalia	..	25	..	29	..	..	26	23	..
All developing countries	33	48	70	79	19	16	..	..	..
Least developed countries	23	35	51	61	34	33	..	..	..
Arab States	61	66	83	84	10	9	..	..	..
East Asia and the Pacific	30	49	71	78	..	..	..	..	..
Latin America and the Caribbean	68	75	81	89	13	10	..	..	..
South Asia	20	37	71	86	25	21	..	..	..
Sub-Saharan Africa	32	36	48	58	32	30	..	..	..
Central and Eastern Europe and the CIS	..	82	..	..	..	..	..	..	..
OECD	..	..	96	98	..	..	..	..	..
High-income OECD	..	..	..	100	..	..	..	..	..
High human development	..	..	..	..	..	..	..	..	..
Medium human development	36	51	74	83	19	15	..	..	..
Low human development	27	32	44	55	32	32	..	..	..
High income	..	..	..	..	..	..	..	..	..
Middle income	48	61	77	83	..	..	..	..	..
Low income	20	35	64	77	27	24	..	..	..
World	43	58	75	83	..	..	..	..	..

Source: UNDP, HDR 2005, Table 7:240-243.

HDI Rank		Survey year for inequality data	Births attended by skilled health personnel (%). Bottom quintile	Births attended by skilled health personnel (%). Top quintile	One-year-olds fully immunized (%) Bottom quintile	One-year-olds fully immunized (%) Top quintile	Children under height for age (% under age 5) Bottom quintile	Children under height for age (% under age 5) Top quintile	Infant mortality rate (per 1,000 live births) Bottom quintile	Infant mortality rate (per 1,000 live births) Top quintile	Under-five mortality rate (per 1,000 live births) Bottom quintile	Under-five mortality rate (per 1,000 live births) Top quintile
High Human Development												
40	Qatar	..	..	..	..	..	..	..	..	..	..	..
41	United Arab Emirates	..	..	..	..	..	..	..	..	..	..	..
43	Bahrain	..	..	..	..	..	..	..	..	..	..	..
44	Kuwait	..	..	..	..	..	..	..	..	..	..	..
Medium Human Development												
58	Libyan Arab Jamahiriya	..	..	..	..	..	..	..	..	..	..	..
71	Oman	..	..	..	..	..	..	..	..	..	..	..
77	Saudi Arabia	..	..	..	..	..	..	..	..	..	..	..
81	Lebanon	..	..	..	..	..	..	..	..	..	..	..
89	Tunisia	..	..	..	..	..	..	..	..	..	..	..
90	Jordan	1997	91.2	99.3	21.3	17.1	10.5	4.5	35.4	23.4	42.1	25.2
102	Occupied Palestinian Territories	..	..	..	..	..	..	..	..	..	..	..
103	Algeria	..	..	..	..	..	..	..	..	..	..	..
106	Syrian Arab Republic	..	..	..	..	..	..	..	..	..	..	..
119	Egypt	2000	31.4	94.2	91.2	92	16.4	7.9	75.6	29.6	97.9	33.7
124	Morocco	1992	5.1	77.9	53.7	95.2	23.3	6.6	79.7	35.1	111.6	39.2
141	Sudan	..	..	..	..	..	..	..	..	..	..	..
Low Human Development												
150	Djibouti	..	..	..	..	..	..	..	..	..	..	..
151	Yemen	1997	6.8	49.7	7.8	55.7	26.4	22	108.5	60	163.1	73
Without HDI Rank												
	Iraq	..	..	..	..	..	..	..	..	..	..	..
	Somalia	..	..	..	..	..	..	..	..	..	..	..

Source: UNDP, HDR 2005, Table 8:244-245.

HDI Rank	Life expectancy at birth (years)		Infant mortality rate (per 1,000 live births)		Under-five mortality rate (per 1,000 live births)		Probability at birth of surviving to age 65, female (% of cohort)	Probability at birth of surviving to age 65, male (% of cohort)	Maternal mortality ratio reported (per 100,000 live births)	Maternal mortality ratio adjusted (per 100,000 live births)
	1970-1975	2000-2005	1970	2003	1970	2003	2000-2005	2000-2005	1985-2003	2000
High Human Development										
40 Qatar	62.1	72.7	45	11	65	15	81.2	74.0	10	7
41 United Arab Emirates	62.2	77.9	61	7	83	8	90.2	85.0	3	54
43 Bahrain	63.3	74.2	55	12	75	15	84.6	78.9	46	28
44 Kuwait	67.0	76.8	49	8	59	9	87.9	82.7	5	5
Medium Human Development										
58 Libyan Arab Jamahiriya	52.8	73.4	105	13	160	16	82.5	74.6	77	97
71 Oman	52.1	74.0	126	10	200	12	84.2	78.8	23	87
77 Saudi Arabia	53.9	71.6	118	22	185	26	81.2	73.4	..	23
81 Lebanon	66.4	71.9	45	27	54	31	81.7	73.0	100	150
89 Tunisia	55.6	73.1	135	19	201	24	84.9	75.7	69	120
90 Jordan	56.5	71.2	77	23	107	28	77.7	71.6	41	41
102 Occupied Palestinian Territories	56.6	72.4	..	22	..	24	81.4	75.0	..	100
103 Algeria	54.5	71.0	143	35	234	41	78.4	75.2	140	140
106 Syrian Arab Republic	57.4	73.2	90	16	129	18	83.2	76.3	65	160
119 Egypt	52.1	69.6	157	33	235	39	79.3	69.3	84	84
124 Morocco	52.9	69.5	119	36	184	39	78.9	70.3	230	220
141 Sudan	45.1	56.3	104	63	172	93	55.4	49.6	550	590
Low Human Development										
150 Djibouti	44.4	52.7	160	97	241	138	48.1	42.9	74	730
151 Yemen	39.9	60.3	202	82	303	113	61.0	54.9	350	570
Without HDI Rank										
Iraq	57.0	58.8	90	102	127	125	61.3	53.7	290	250
Somalia	41.0	46.2	..	133	..	225	41.3	36.5	..	1,100
All developing countries	55.6	64.9	109	59	167	88	69.6	62.3	.. T	.. T
Least developed countries	44.5	52.0	151	97	244	156	47.9	43.5	.. T	.. T
Arab States	52.1	66.9	129	48	197	61	73.3	66.3	.. T	.. T
East Asia and the Pacific	60.5	70.4	84	31	122	39	79.2	71.3	.. T	.. T
Latin America and the Caribbean	61.1	71.7	86	27	123	32	79.7	68.2	.. T	.. T
South Asia	50.1	63.2	130	66	206	91	67.1	60.0	.. T	.. T
Sub-Saharan Africa	45.8	46.1	143	104	243	179	37.0	33.8	.. T	.. T
Central and Eastern Europe and the CIS	69.0	68.1	34	20	43	24	78.8	55.4	.. T	.. T
OECD	70.3	77.6	40	11	53	13	88.4	79.6	.. T	.. T
High-income OECD	71.6	78.8	22	5	28	6	89.9	81.8	.. T	.. T
High human development	70.7	77.9	32	9	42	10	88.9	80.0	.. T	.. T
Medium human development	57.6	67.0	102	46	155	61	73.7	64.6	.. T	.. T
Low human development	44.1	46.0	150	106	254	183	37.5	34.6	.. T	.. T
High income	71.6	78.8	22	5	28	6	89.9	81.8	.. T	.. T
Middle income	62.0	70.1	86	29	125	36	79.0	68.7	.. T	.. T
Low income	48.8	58.2	130	80	209	124	58.3	52.4	.. T	.. T
World	59.9	67.0	96	54	147	80	73.1	64.5	.. T	.. T

Source: UNDP, HDR 2005, Table 10:250-253.

Table A4 -9   COMMITMENT TO EDUCATION: PUBLIC SPENDING

HDI Rank		Public expenditure on education (as % of GDP)		Public expenditure on education (as % of total government expenditure)		Public expenditure on education, pre-primary and primary (as % of all levels)		Public expenditure on education, secondary (% of all levels)		Public expenditure on education, tertiary (% of all levels)	
		1990	2000-2002	1990	2000-2002	1990	2000-2002	1990	2000-2002	1990	2000-2002
High Human Development											
40	Qatar	3.5	..	..	..	..	..	..	..	..	..
41	United Arab Emirates	1.8	1.6	14.6	22.5	..	45.6	..	50.4	..	2.4
43	Bahrain	4.1	..	14.6	..	..	..	45.8	..	..	..
44	Kuwait	4.8	..	3.4	..	53.4	..	13.6	..	16.0	..
Medium Human Development											
58	Libyan Arab Jamahiriya	..	..	..	..	..	..	..	..	..	..
71	Oman	3.1	4.6	11.1	..	54.1	35.9	37.0	47.4	7.4	9.2
77	Saudi Arabia	5.8	..	17.8	..	78.8	..	..	..	21.2	..
81	Lebanon	..	2.7	..	12.3	..	..	..	..	..	28.5
89	Tunisia	6.0	6.4	13.5	18.2	39.8	32.9	36.4	44.4	18.5	22.8
90	Jordan	8.1	..	17.1	..	..	..	62.4	..	35.1	..
102	Occupied Palestinian Territories	..	..	..	..	..	..	..	..	..	..
103	Algeria	5.3	..	21.1	..	..	..	..	..	..	..
106	Syrian Arab Republic	4.0	..	17.3	..	38.5	..	28.2	..	21.3	..
119	Egypt	3.9	..	..	..	..	..	..	..	..	..
124	Morocco	5.3	6.5	26.1	26.4	34.8	39.8	48.9	43.5	16.2	16.3
141	Sudan	6.0	..	2.8	..	..	..	..	..	..	..
Low Human Development											
150	Djibouti	3.5	..	10.5	..	58.0	..	21.7	..	11.5	..
151	Yemen	..	9.5	..	32.8	..	..	..	..	..	..
Without HDI Rank											
	Iraq	..	..	..	..	..	..	..	..	..	..
	Somalia	..	..	..	..	..	..	..	..	..	..

Source: UNDP, HDR 2005, Table 11:254-257.

LITERACY AND ENROLMENT

HDI Rank		Adult literacy rate (% ages 15 and above)		Youth literacy rate (% ages 15-24)		Net primary enrolment rate (%)		Net secondary enrolment rate (%)		Children reaching grade 5 (%)		Tertiary students in science, math and engineering (% of all tertiary students)
		1990	2003	1990	2003	1990/91	2002/03	1990/91	2002/03	1990/91	2001/02	1998-2003
High Human Development												
40	Qatar	77.0	89.2	90.3	98.6	89	95	70	82	64	..	16
41	United Arab Emirates	71.0	77.3	84.7	91.4	99	83	58	71	80	93	..
43	Bahrain	82.1	87.7	95.6	99.3	99	90	85	87	89	99	21
44	Kuwait	76.7	82.9	87.5	93.1	49	83	..	77	..	..	..
Medium Human Development												
58	Libyan Arab Jamahiriya	68.1	81.7	91.0	97.0	96	..	..	..	..	..	31
71	Oman	54.7	74.4	85.6	98.5	69	72	..	69	97	98	..
77	Saudi Arabia	66.2	79.4	85.4	95.9	59	54	31	53	83	91	17
81	Lebanon	80.3	..	92.1	..	78	91	..	..	..	92	28
89	Tunisia	59.1	74.3	84.1	94.3	94	97	..	65	87	96	31
90	Jordan	81.5	89.9	96.7	99.1	94	92	..	80	..	97	30
102	Occupied Palestinian Territories	..	91.9	..	98.7	..	91	..	84	..	..	19
103	Algeria	52.9	69.8	77.3	90.1	93	95	54	67	95	97	..
106	Syrian Arab Republic	64.8	82.9	79.9	95.2	92	98	43	43	96	91	..
119	Egypt	47.1	55.6	61.3	73.2	84	91	..	81	..	98	..
124	Morocco	38.7	50.7	55.3	69.5	57	90	..	36	75	81	19
141	Sudan	45.8	59.0	65.0	74.6	43	46	..	..	94	84	..
Low Human Development												
150	Djibouti	..	..	73.2	..	31	36	..	21	87	80	22
151	Yemen	32.7	49.0	50.0	67.9	52	72	..	35	..	76	..
Without HDI Rank												
	Iraq	35.7	..	41.0	..	100	91	..	33	..	66	10
	Somalia	..	..	..	..	8	..	..	..	..	..	..
All developing countries		67.0	76.6	81.1	85.2	..	..	..	..	..	..	..
Least developed countries		44.2	54.2	57.2	64.2	..	..	..	..	..	..	..
Arab States		50.8	64.1	68.4	81.3	..	..	..	..	..	..	..
East Asia and the Pacific		79.7	90.4	95.0	98.0	..	..	..	..	..	..	..
Latin America and the Caribbean		85.1	89.6	92.7	95.9	..	..	..	..	..	..	..
South Asia		47.7	58.9	61.7	72.2	..	..	..	..	..	..	..
Sub-Saharan Africa		51.1	61.3	68.5	73.7	..	..	..	..	..	..	..
Central and Eastern Europe and the CIS		98.7	99.2	99.7	99.5	..	..	..	..	..	..	..
OECD		..	..	..	..	..	..	..	..	..	..	..
High-income OECD		..	..	..	..	..	..	..	..	..	..	..
High human development		..	..	..	..	..	..	..	..	..	..	..
Medium human development		70.6	79.4	83.2	87.5	..	..	..	..	..	..	..
Low human development		45.1	57.5	63.7	70.1	..	..	..	..	..	..	..
High income		..	..	..	..	..	..	..	..	..	..	..
Middle income		81.2	89.6	93.6	96.8	..	..	..	..	..	..	..
Low income		50.2	60.8	64.4	73.0	..	..	..	..	..	..	..
World		..	..	..	..	..	..	..	..	..	..	..

Source: UNDP, HDR 2005, Table 12:258-261.

TECHNOLOGY: DIFFUSION AND CREATION

HDI Rank	Telephone mainlines (per 1,000 people)		Cellular subscribers (per 1,000 people)		Internet users (per 1,000 people)		Patents granted to residents (per million people)	Receipts of royalties and license fees (US$ per person)	Research and development (R&D) expenditures (as % of GDP)	Researchers in R&D (per million people)
	1990	2003	1990	2003	1990	2003	2002	2003	1997-2002	1990-2003
High Human Development										
40 Qatar	220	261	9	533	0	199	..	..	..	..
41 United Arab Emirates	224	281	19	736	0	275	0	..	..	..
43 Bahrain	191	268	10	638	0	216	..	..	..	..
44 Kuwait	188	196	12	572	0	228	..	0	0.2	73
Medium Human Development										
58 Libyan Arab Jamahiriya	48	136	0	23	0	29	..	..	..	361
71 Oman	60	88	2	228	0	..	0	..	..	..
77 Saudi Arabia	77	155	1	321	0	67	(.)	0	..	..
81 Lebanon	155	200	0	234	0	143	..	..	..	..
89 Tunisia	37	118	(.)	197	0	64	0	1.8	0.6	1,013
90 Jordan	72	114	(.)	242	0	81	..	..	..	1,977
102 Occupied Palestinian Territories	..	87	0	133	0	40	..	..	..	..
103 Algeria	32	69	(.)	45	0	..	(.)	..	..	..
106 Syrian Arab Republic	41	..	0	68	0	35	0	..	0.2	29
119 Egypt	30	127	(.)	84	0	44	2	1.8	0.2	..
124 Morocco	16	40	(.)	244	0	33	0	0.9	..	..
141 Sudan	3	27	0	20	0	9	0	..	..	..
Low Human Development										
150 Djibouti	11	15	0	34	0	10	..	..	..	..
151 Yemen	11	..	0	35	0	..	..	..	..	..
Without HDI Rank										
Iraq	39	..	0	3	..	..	..	..	..	..
Somalia	2	7	0	42	..	..	..	..	..	..
All developing countries	29	113	(.)	134	(.)	53	..	0.6	0.9	400
Least developed countries	3	8	0	16	0	4	..	..	..	..
Arab States	79	94	4	118	0	49	..	..	..	..
East Asia and the Pacific	18	172	(.)	212	(.)	80	..	..	1.5	706
Latin America and the Caribbean	89	165	(.)	239	0	..	2	1	0.6	293
South Asia	7	47	(.)	24	0	18	..	..	0.7	135
Sub-Saharan Africa	5	9	(.)	54	0	..	..	..	..	..
Central and Eastern Europe and the CIS	120	232	(.)	287	0	..	48	2	1	2,213
OECD	365	494	7	644	3	403	248	80.6	2.5	3,046
High-income OECD	439	567	9	705	3	480	310	101.3	2.6	3,676
High human development	289	495	6	652	2	414	250	79.2	2.5	3,004
Medium human development	22	123	(.)	138	0	46	7	0.3	0.8	521
Low human development	3	8	0	25	0	..	..	..	..	..
High income	420	562	9	710	3	477	302	100.1	2.5	3,630
Middle income	46	180	(.)	224	0	77	10	0.6	0.7	760
Low income	6	32	(.)	24	0	14	..	..	..	..
World	81	184	1	226	1	120	62	17.9	2.4	1,146

Source: UNDP, HDR 2005, Table 13:262-265.

Monitoring human development: enlarging people's choices to have access to the resources needed for a decent standard of living

Table A4 -12

ECONOMIC PERFORMANCE

HDI Rank	GDP (US$ billions) 2003	GDP (PPP US$ billions) 2003	GDP per capita (US$) 2003	GDP per capita (PPP US$) 2003	GDP per capita annual growth rate (%) 1975-2003	GDP per capita annual growth rate (%) 1990-2003	GDP per capita, highest value (PPP US$) 1975-2003	GDP per capita, year of highest value	Average annual change in consumer price index (%) 1990-2003	Average annual change in consumer price index (%) 2002-03
High Human Development										
40 Qatar	..	..	..	..	..	..	..	..	2.5	2.3
41 United Arab Emirates	..	..	..	..	-3.3	-2.1	49,432	1975	..	..
43 Bahrain	..	12.2	..	17,479	1.1	1.5	17,479	2002	0.7	..
44 Kuwait	41.7	43.2	17,421	18,047	-1.2	-2.3	29,760	1975	1.9	1.0
Medium Human Development										
58 Libyan Arab Jamahiriya	..	..	..	..	..	..	..	..	3.5	..
71 Oman	..	34.5	..	13,584	2.2	0.9	13,965	2001	0.2	-0.4
77 Saudi Arabia	214.7	298.0	9,532	13,226	-2.4	-0.6	24,461	1977	0.5	0.6
81 Lebanon	19.0	22.8	4,224	5,074	3.4	2.9	5,074	2003	..	..
89 Tunisia	25.0	70.9	2,530	7,161	2.1	3.1	7,161	2003	3.9	2.7
90 Jordan	9.9	22.9	1,858	4,320	0.3	0.9	5,195	1987	3.0	2.3
102 Occupied Palestinian Territories	3.5	..	1,026	..	..	-6.0	..	..	..	..
103 Algeria	66.5	194.4	2,090	6,107	-0.1	0.6	6,319	1985	12.7	2.6
106 Syrian Arab Republic	21.5	62.2	1,237	3,576	0.9	1.4	3,696	1998	4.9	..
119 Egypt	82.4	266.9	1,220	3,950	2.7	2.5	3,950	2003	7.0	4.5
124 Morocco	43.7	120.6	1,452	4,004	1.3	1.0	4,004	2003	3.1	1.2
141 Sudan	17.8	64.1	530	1,910	1.1	3.3	1,910	2003	63.6	..
Low Human Development										
150 Djibouti	0.6	1.5	886	2,086	-4.2	-3.3	..	..	..	..
151 Yemen	10.8	17.0	565	889	..	2.4	889	2003	20.8	10.8
Without HDI Rank										
Iraq	..	..	..	..	-9.6	..	..	..	..	..
Somalia	..	..	..	..	-0.5	..	..	..	..	..
All developing countries	6,981.9 T	21,525.4 T	1,414	4,359	2.3	2.9	..	..	..	..
Least developed countries	221.4 T	895.1 T	329	1,328	0.7	2.0	..	..	..	..
Arab States	773.4 T	1,683.6 T	2,611	5,685	0.2	1.0	..	..	..	..
East Asia and the Pacific	2,893.6 T	9,762.2 T	1,512	5,100	6.0	5.6	..	..	..	..
Latin America and the Caribbean	1,745.9 T	3,947.0 T	3,275	7,404	0.6	1.1	..	..	..	..
South Asia	902.2 T	4,235.9 T	617	2,897	2.6	3.5	..	..	..	..
Sub-Saharan Africa	418.5 T	1,227.4 T	633	1,856	-0.7	0.1	..	..	..	..
Central and Eastern Europe and the CIS	1,189.9 T	3,203.5 T	2,949	7,939	..	0.3	..	..	..	..
OECD	29,650.5 T	29,840.6 T	25,750	25,915	2.0	1.8	..	..	..	..
High-income OECD	28,369.5 T	27,601.9 T	31,020	30,181	2.2	1.9	..	..	..	..
High human development	30,341.0 T	30,941.3 T	25,167	25,665	2.2	1.8	..	..	..	..
Medium human development	5,414.8 T	19,581.1 T	1,237	4,474	1.7	2.4	..	..	..	..
Low human development	202.2 T	590.4 T	358	1,046	2.0	2.8	..	..	..	..
High income	29,052.4 T	28,396.0 T	30,589	29,898	2.0	1.8	..	..	..	..
Middle income	6,021.9 T	18,244.6 T	2,015	6,104	2.0	2.5	..	..	..	..
Low income	1,103.0 T	4,948.9 T	483	2,168	-0.8	0.1	..	..	..	..
World	36,058.3 T	51,150.6 T	5,801	8,229	1.4	1.4	..	..	..	..

Source: UNDP, HDR 2005, Table 14:266-269.

INEQUALITY IN INCOME OR CONSUMPTION

HDI Rank	Survey Year	Share of income or consumption (%) - Poorest 10%	Share of income or consumption (%) - Poorest 20%	Share of income or consumption (%) - Richest 20%	Share of income or consumption (%) - Richest 10%	Inequality measures - Ratio of richest 10% to poorest 10%	Inequality measures - Ratio of richest 20% to poorest 20%	Inequality measures - Gini index
High Human Development								
40 Qatar	..	..	..	..	..	..	..	..
41 United Arab Emirates	..	..	..	..	..	..	..	..
43 Bahrain	..	..	..	..	..	..	..	..
44 Kuwait	..	..	..	..	..	..	..	..
Medium Human Development								
58 Libyan Arab Jamahiriya	..	..	..	..	..	..	..	..
71 Oman	..	..	..	..	..	..	..	..
77 Saudi Arabia	..	..	..	..	..	..	..	..
81 Lebanon	..	..	..	..	..	..	..	..
89 Tunisia	2000	2.3	6.0	47.3	31.5	13.4	7.9	39.8
90 Jordan	1997	3.3	7.6	44.4	29.8	9.1	5.9	36.4
102 Occupied Palestinian Territories	..	..	..	..	..	..	..	..
103 Algeria	1995	2.8	7.0	42.6	26.8	9.6	6.1	35.3
106 Syrian Arab Republic	..	..	..	..	..	..	..	..
119 Egypt	1999	3.7	8.6	43.6	29.5	8.0	5.1	34.4
124 Morocco	1998	2.6	6.5	46.6	30.9	11.7	7.2	39.5
141 Sudan	..	..	..	..	..	..	..	..
Low Human Development								
150 Djibouti	..	..	..	..	..	..	..	..
151 Yemen	1998	3.0	7.4	41.2	25.9	8.6	5.6	33.4
Without HDI Rank								
Iraq	..	..	..	..	..	..	..	..
Somalia	..	..	..	..	..	..	..	..

Source: UNDP, HDR 2005, Table 15:270-273.

THE STRUCTURE OF TRADE

HDI Rank	Imports of goods and services (% of GDP)		Exports of goods and services (% of GDP)		Primary exports (% of merchandise exports)		Manufactured exports (% of merchandise exports)		High-technology exports (% of merchandise exports)		Terms of trade (1980=100)
	1990	2003	1990	2003	1990	2003	1990	2003	1990	2003	2002
High Human Development											
40 Qatar	..	..	..	..	84	89	16	10	..	(.)	..
41 United Arab Emirates	40	..	65	..	54	96	46	4	..	2	..
43 Bahrain	95	65	116	81	91	91	9	9	..	(.)	..
44 Kuwait	58	40	45	48	94	93	6	7	3	1	..
Medium Human Development											
58 Libyan Arab Jamahiriya	31	36	40	48	95	..	5	..	..	..	..
71 Oman	31	35	53	57	94	85	5	14	2	2	..
77 Saudi Arabia	32	24	41	47	93	90	7	10	..	(.)	..
81 Lebanon	100	39	18	13	..	31	..	68	..	2	..
89 Tunisia	51	47	44	43	31	19	69	81	2	4	85
90 Jordan	93	70	62	45	..	31	51	69	1	2	129
102 Occupied Palestinian Territories	..	49	..	10	..	..	..	..	..	..	..
103 Algeria	25	24	23	39	97	98	3	2	..	2	31
106 Syrian Arab Republic	28	33	28	40	64	89	36	11	..	1	..
119 Egypt	33	24	20	22	57	63	42	31	..	(.)	53
124 Morocco	32	36	26	32	48	31	52	69	..	11	106
141 Sudan	..	12	..	16	..	97	..	3	..	7	91
Low Human Development											
150 Djibouti	..	..	..	..	44	..	8	..	..	..	..
151 Yemen	20	36	14	31	..	..	..	..	..	..	..
Without HDI Rank											
Iraq	..	..	..	..	..	..	..	..	..	..	..
Somalia	38	..	10	..	..	..	..	..	..	..	..
All developing countries	24	33	25	35	..	29	58	73	..	21	..
Least developed countries	22	30	13	22	..	..	..	..	..	..	..
Arab States	38	30	38	36	81	86	16	20	..	2	..
East Asia and the Pacific	32	48	33	52	..	13	75	86	..	29	..
Latin America and the Caribbean	15	21	17	24	65	44	36	55	7	14	..
South Asia	13	18	11	17	..	43	71	61	..	3	..
Sub-Saharan Africa	26	33	27	33	..	..	..	..	..	..	..
Central and Eastern Europe and the CIS	26	37	27	37	..	36	..	58	..	13	..
OECD	18	22	17	21	20	16	76	79	18	18	..
High-income OECD	18	21	17	21	19	16	78	79	18	18	..
High human development	19	23	18	22	21	18	76	79	18	17	..
Medium human development	20	28	20	31	..	36	51	63	..	21	..
Low human development	29	37	27	34	..	..	..	..	..	..	..
High income	19	22	18	22	20	17	78	80	18	18	..
Middle income	21	30	22	33	..	34	48	65	..	21	..
Low income	17	24	13	21	..	40	..	60	..	4	..
World	19	24	19	24	..	22	72	77	18	18	..

Source: UNDP, HDR 2005, Table 16:274-277.

FLOWS OF AID, PRIVATE CAPITAL AND DEBT

HDI Rank	Official development assistance (ODA) received (net disbursements) Total (US$ millions) 2003	Official development assistance (ODA) received (net disbursements) Per capita (US$) 2003	Official development assistance (ODA) received (net disbursements) (as % of GDP)		Net foreign direct investment inflows (% of GDP)		Other private flows (% of GDP)		Total debt service (As % of GDP)		Total debt service (As % of exports of goods, services and net income from abroad)	
	2003	2003	1990	2003	1990	2003	1990	2003	1990	2003	1990	2003
High Human Development												
40 Qatar	2	3.2	(.)	..	..	..	..	..	..	..	..	..
41 United Arab Emirates	5.2	1.3	(.)	..	..	..	..	..	..	..	..	..
43 Bahrain	37.5	52.7	3.2	..	..	..	..	..	..	..	..	..
44 Kuwait	4.4	1.9	(.)	(.)	0.0	-0.2	..	..	..	..	..	..
Medium Human Development												
58 Libyan Arab Jamahiriya	10	1.8	0.1	..	..	..	..	..	..	..	..	..
71 Oman	44.5	17.1	0.6	..	1.4	..	-3.8	-5.5	7.0	8.6	12.0	5.3
77 Saudi Arabia	21.9	1.0	(.)	(.)	..	..	..	..	..	..	..	..
81 Lebanon	228.3	50.8	8.9	1.2	0.2	1.9	0.2	0.2	3.5	17.1	3.2	81.5
89 Tunisia	305.5	30.9	3.2	1.2	0.6	2.2	-1.6	3.1	11.6	6.4	25.6	13.7
90 Jordan	1,234.30	232.5	22.1	12.5	0.9	3.8	5.3	-5.4	15.6	11.7	22.1	22.6
102 Occupied Palestinian Territories	971.6	288.6	..	28.1	..	..	..	..	..	..	..	..
103 Algeria	232.2	7.3	0.2	0.3	(.)	1.0	-0.7	-0.1	14.2	6.5	63.7	..
106 Syrian Arab Republic	160.3	9.2	5.6	0.7	0.6	0.7	-0.1	(.)	9.7	1.6	20.3	3.0
119 Egypt	893.8	13.2	12.6	1.1	1.7	0.3	-0.2	-0.7	7.1	3.4	..	..
124 Morocco	522.8	17.4	4.1	1.2	0.6	5.2	1.2	0.3	6.9	9.8	27.9	25.7
141 Sudan	621.3	18.5	6.2	3.5	0.0	7.6	0.0	0.0	0.4	0.2	4.8	1.3
Low Human Development												
150 Djibouti	77.8	110.4	46.4	12.5	(.)	1.8	-0.1	0.0	3.6	2.5	..	..
151 Yemen	243.1	12.7	8.4	2.2	-2.7	-0.8	3.3	0.0	3.5	1.6	7.1	4.0
Without HDI Rank												
Iraq	2,265.30	91.7	0.1	..	..	..	..	..	..	..	..	..
Somalia	175.1	18.2	53.8	..	0.6	..	..	..	1.2	..	..	..
All developing countries	65,401.3 T	9.7	2.7	3.0	0.9	2.3	0.4	0.3	3.5	4.7	21.9	17.6
Least developed countries	23,457.4 T	33.4	13.0	18.7	0.1	3.6	0.4	0.2	2.8	2.1	16.2	7.5
Arab States	8,320.3 T	27.5	6.8	1.6	0.5	1.7	-0.1	-0.1	4.1	2.5	..	15.5
East Asia and the Pacific	7,231.9 T	3.4	1.0	0.5	1.7	3.1	0.6	0.1	3.0	3.2	17.9	10.5
Latin America and the Caribbean	6,090.4 T	9.9	1.3	0.8	0.8	2.1	0.5	0.3	4.0	8.6	23.7	30.7
South Asia	6,623.8 T	4.3	1.6	0.7	(.)	0.6	0.3	0.8	2.6	2.9	19.5	13.5
Sub-Saharan Africa	22,691.8 T	32.9	12.0	18.6	0.4	2.2	0.3	0.7	3.8	2.9	..	9.6
Central and Eastern Europe and the CIS	4,885.9 T	24.0	..	..	(.)	2.9	(.)	2.6	0.5	7.7	13.5	17.3
OECD	269.0 T	..	..	..	1.0	1.4	..	..	..	..	..	..
High-income OECD	.. T	..	..	..	1.0	1.4	..	..	..	..	..	..
High human development	646.1 T	..	..	..	1.0	1.5	..	..	..	..	..	..
Medium human development	27,342.9 T	6.5	1.6	0.9	0.5	2.2	0.3	0.6	2.9	5.3	21.3	16.2
Low human development	18,565.3 T	27.9	11.7	18.7	0.5	2.8	0.4	0.1	6.4	3.3	20.6	10.2
High income	37.5 T	..	..	..	1.0	1.5	..	..	..	..	..	..
Middle income	18,969.6 T	8.4	1.2	0.4	0.6	2.4	0.4	0.7	3.1	6.4	20.8	17.9
Low income	32,128.3 T	13.7	4.6	6.1	0.3	1.5	0.4	0.5	3.6	3.1	24.9	13.5
World	69,783.7 T	10.9	..	..	0.9	1.6	..	..	..	..	..	..

Source: UNDP, HDR 2005, Table 19:280-283.

PRIORITIES IN PUBLIC SPENDING

HDI Rank	Public expenditure on education (% of GDP)		Public expenditure on health (% of GDP)	Military expenditure (% of GDP)		Total debt service (% of GDP)	
	1990	2000-2002	2002	1990	2003	1990	2003
High Human Development							
40 Qatar	3.5	..	2.4	..	..	..	..
41 United Arab Emirates	1.8	1.6	2.3	6.2	3.1	..	..
43 Bahrain	4.1	..	3.2	5.1	5.1	..	..
44 Kuwait	4.8	..	2.9	48.5	9.0	..	..
Medium Human Development							
58 Libyan Arab Jamahiriya	..	..	1.6	..	2.0	..	..
71 Oman	3.1	4.6	2.8	16.5	12.2	7.0	0.0
77 Saudi Arabia	5.8	..	3.3	12.8	8.7	..	..
81 Lebanon	..	2.7	3.5	7.6	4.3	3.5	17.1
89 Tunisia	6.0	6.4	2.9	2.0	1.6	11.6	6.4
90 Jordan	8.1	..	4.3	9.9	8.9	15.6	11.7
102 Occupied Palestinian Territories	..	..	..	..	..	..	..
103 Algeria	5.3	..	3.2	1.5	3.3	14.2	6.5
106 Syrian Arab Republic	4.0	..	2.3	6.9	7.1	9.7	1.6
119 Egypt	3.9	..	1.8	3.9	2.6	7.1	3.4
124 Morocco	5.3	6.5	1.5	4.1	4.2	6.9	9.8
141 Sudan	6.0	..	1.0	3.6	2.4	0.4	0.2
Low Human Development							
150 Djibouti	3.5	..	3.3	6.3	..	3.6	2.5
151 Yemen	..	9.5	1.0	7.9	7.1	3.5	1.6
Without HDI Rank							
Iraq	..	..	0.3	..	..	..	..
Somalia	..	..	..	..	..	1.2	0.0

Source: UNDP, HDR 2005, Table 20:284-287.

Table A4 -17 ENERGY AND THE ENVIRONMENT

HDI Rank	Traditional fuel consumption (% of total energy requirements) 2002	Electricity consumption per capita (kilowatt-hours)		GDP per unit of energy use (2000 PPP US$ per kg of oil equivalent)		Carbon dioxide emissions - Per capita (metric tons)		Carbon dioxide emissions - Share of world total (%) 2000	Ratification of environmental treaties - Cartagena Protocol on Biosafety	Ratification of environmental treaties - Framework Convention on Climate Change	Ratification of environmental treaties - Kyoto Protocol to the Framework Convention on Climate Change	Ratification of environmental treaties - Convention on Biological Diversity
		1980	2002	1980	2002	1980	2002					
High Human Development												
40 Qatar	0.0	10,616	17,489	..	..	56.3	53.1	0.2		•	•	•
41 United Arab Emirates	..	6,204	14,215	7.5	..	35.8	25.1	0.3		•	•	•
43 Bahrain	..	4,784	10,830	1.6	1.7	22.6	30.6	0.1		•		•
44 Kuwait	0.0	6,849	16,544	1.8	1.7	19.7	24.6	0.2		•	•	•
Medium Human Development												
58 Libyan Arab Jamahiriya	0.9	1,588	3,915	..	..	8.9	9.1	0.2		•		•
71 Oman	0.0	847	5,219	8.2	3.0	5.0	12.1	0.1	•	•	•	•
77 Saudi Arabia	..	1,969	6,620	6.8	2.1	14.9	15.0	1.6		•	•	•
81 Lebanon	0.5	1,056	2,834	..	3.8	2.3	4.7	0.1		•	•	•
89 Tunisia	7.8	434	1,205	6.9	7.7	1.5	2.3	0.1	•	•	•	•
90 Jordan	1.4	366	1,585	5.5	3.9	2.1	3.2	0.1	•	•	•	•
102 Occupied Palestinian Territories	..	..	..	..	..	..	..	..				
103 Algeria	6.0	381	881	8.5	5.6	3.5	2.9	0.4	•	•	•	•
106 Syrian Arab Republic	0.0	433	1,570	4.5	3.2	2.2	2.8	0.2	•	•		•
119 Egypt	9.2	433	1,287	5.9	4.6	1.0	2.1	0.6	•	•	•	•
124 Morocco	2.2	254	560	11.4	10.1	0.8	1.4	0.2	•	•	•	•
141 Sudan	73.7	47	89	2.5	3.6	0.2	0.3	(.)		•	•	•
Low Human Development												
150 Djibouti	..	416	296	..	..	0.9	0.5	(.)	•	•		•
151 Yemen	2.3	...	159	..	3.8	..	0.7	(.)		•	•	•
Without HDI Rank												
Iraq	..	878	1,542	..	..	3.1	3.0	0.3				
Somalia	100.0	21	33	..	..	0.1	..	..				
All developing countries	24.5	388	1,155	3.7	4.6	1.3	2.0	36.9 T	..	..	..	..
Least developed countries	75.9	83	106	..	4.0	0.1	0.2	0.4 T	..	..	..	..
Arab States	18.0	626	1,946	5.8	3.5	3.1	4.1	4.5 T	..	..	..	..
East Asia and the Pacific	11.0	329	1,439	2.1	4.6	1.4	2.6	17.6 T	..	..	..	..
Latin America and the Caribbean	19.8	1,019	1,927	6.3	6.1	2.4	2.4	5.6 T	..	..	..	..
South Asia	24.5	171	566	3.8	4.8	0.5	1.2	6.3 T	..	..	..	..
Sub-Saharan Africa	70.6	434	536	3.3	2.7	1.0	0.8	1.9 T	..	..	..	..
Central and Eastern Europe and the CIS	4.1	3,284	3,328	..	2.4	10.1	5.9	12.2 T	..	..	..	..
OECD	4.1	5,761	8,615	3.9	5.1	11.0	11.2	51.0 T	..	..	..	..
High-income OECD	3.0	6,698	10,262	3.8	5.2	12.2	13.0	46.2 T	..	..	..	..
High human development	4.5	5,676	8,586	3.8	5.2	10.9	11.2	53.0 T	..	..	..	..
Medium human development	17.0	368	1,121	3.5	4.1	1.2	2.0	39.0 T	..	..	..	..
Low human development	71.1	135	133	3.3	4.1	0.4	0.2	0.5 T	..	..	..	..
High income	2.9	6,616	10,198	3.9	5.1	12.1	13.0	47.8 T	..	..	..	..
Middle income	9.2	623	1,653	3.7	4.1	2.1	2.9	38.9 T	..	..	..	..
Low income	42.2	174	399	2.3	2.0	0.5	0.8	7.3 T	..	..	..	..
World	7.6	1,573	2,465	3.8	4.6	3.4	3.6	100.0 T	..	..	..	..

· Ratification, acceptance, approval, accession or succession.

Source: UNDP, HDR 2005, Table 22:289-292.

Table A4 -18

REFUGEES AND ARMAMENTS

HDI Rank	Internally displaced people (thou-sands)	Refugees by country of asylum (thou-sands)	Refugees by country of origin (thou-sands)	Conventional arms trans-fers (1990 prices) - Imports (US$ mil-lions)	Conventional arms transfers (1990 prices) - Imports (US$ millions)	Conventional arms transfers (1990 prices) - Exports (US$ millions)	Conventional arms transfers (1990 prices) - Exports (share %)	Total armed forces (thou-sands)	Total armed forces index (1985=100)
	2004	2004	2004	1994	2004	2004	2000-2004	2003	2003
High Human Development									
40 Qatar	..	(.)	(.)	10	0	0	(.)	12	207
41 United Arab Emirates	..	(.)	(.)	554	1,246	3	(.)	51	117
43 Bahrain	..	0	(.)	7	10	0	(.)	11	400
44 Kuwait	..	2	1	37	0	0	(.)	16	129
Medium Human Development									
58 Libyan Arab Jamahiriya	..	12	2	0	74	0	(.)	76	104
71 Oman	..	..	(.)	168	123	0	(.)	42	143
77 Saudi Arabia	..	241	(.)	982	838	0	(.)	200	319
81 Lebanon	50-600	3	25	12	0	0	(.)	72	414
89 Tunisia	..	(.)	3	32	0	..	..	35	100
90 Jordan	..	1	1	5	132	72	(.)	101	143
102 Occupied Palestinian Territories	21-50	0	428	5	0	..	..	..	..
103 Algeria	1,000	169	12	156	282	..	..	128	75
106 Syrian Arab Republic	305	4	20	44	0	0	(.)	297	74
119 Egypt	..	89	6	1,944	398	0	(.)	450	101
124 Morocco	..	2	1	131	0	..	..	196	132
141 Sudan	6,000	138	606	0	270	..	..	105	185
Low Human Development									
150 Djibouti	..	27	1	0	0	..	..	10	327
151 Yemen	..	62	2	4	309	..	..	67	104
Without HDI Rank									
Iraq	..	134	368	0	82	0	(.)	..	..
Somalia	370-400	(.)	402	0	0	..	..	..	..
All developing countries	..	6,484 T	..	.. T	.. T	.. T	..	12,670 T	81
Least developed countries	..	2,476 T	..	.. T	.. T	.. T	..	1,933 T	165
Arab States	..	883 T	..	.. T	.. T	.. T	..	1,866 T	69
East Asia and the Pacific	..	444 T	..	.. T	.. T	.. T	..	4,874 T	65
Latin America and the Caribbean	..	38 T	..	.. T	.. T	.. T	..	1,282 T	95
South Asia	..	2,417 T	..	.. T	.. T	.. T	..	2,923 T	115
Sub-Saharan Africa	..	2,698 T	..	.. T	.. T	.. T	..	1,200 T	142
Central and Eastern Europe and the CIS	..	678 T	..	.. T	.. T	.. T	..	2,352 T	36
OECD	..	2,524 T	..	.. T	.. T	.. T	..	5,002 T	69
High-income OECD	..	2,505 T	..	.. T	.. T	.. T	..	4,055 T	69
High human development	..	2,560 T	..	.. T	.. T	.. T	..	5,165 T	69
Medium human development	..	4,353 T	..	.. T	.. T	.. T	..	12,215 T	71
Low human development	..	2,299 T	..	.. T	.. T	.. T	..	1,076 T	154
High income	..	2,516 T	..	.. T	.. T	.. T	..	4,412 T	72
Middle income	..	2,812 T	..	.. T	.. T	.. T	..	10,614 T	65
Low income	..	4,344 T	..	.. T	.. T	.. T	..	4,640 T	92
World	25,300	9,672 T	..	19,501 T	19,162 T	19,156 T	..	18,560 T	67

Source: UNDP, HDR 2005, Table 23:293-296.

Table A4 -19 — GENDER-RELATED DEVELOPMENT INDEX

HDI Rank		Gender-related development index (GDI) rank 2003	Gender-related development index (GDI) value 2003	Life expect-ancy at birth, female (years) 2003	Life expect-ancy at birth, male (years) 2003	Adult literacy rate, female (% ages 15 and above) 2003a	Adult literacy rate, male (% ages 15 and above) 2003a	Combined gross enrolment rate for primary, sec-ondary and tertiary level schools, female (%) 2002/03	Combined gross enrolment rate for primary, sec-ondary and tertiary level schools, male (%) 2002/03	Estimated earned income, female (PPP US$) 2003	Estimated earned income, male (PPP US$) 2003	HDI rank minus GDI rank 2003
High Human Development												
40	Qatar	..	..	76.0	71.2	..	0.0	84	80	..	..	..
41	United Arab Emirates	..	..	80.8	76.4	80.7	75.6	79	69	..	..	..
43	Bahrain	41	0.837	75.9	73.1	83.0	92.5	85	77	7,685	24,909	-2
44	Kuwait	39	0.843	79.5	75.2	81.0	84.7	85	75	8,448	24,204	1
Medium Human Development												
58	Libyan Arab Jamahiriya	..	..	76.2	71.6	70.7	91.8	100	93	..	..	..
71	Oman	60	0.759	75.7	72.8	65.4	82.0	63	63	4,013	21,614	-4
77	Saudi Arabia	65	0.749	73.9	70.1	69.3	87.1	57	58	4,440	20,717	-5
81	Lebanon	68	0.745	74.2	69.8	81.0	92.4	80	77	2,430	7,789	-4
89	Tunisia	69	0.743	75.4	71.2	65.3	83.4	76	73	3,840	10,420	0
90	Jordan	73	0.740	72.9	69.9	84.7	95.1	79	77	2,004	6,491	-3
102	Occupied Palestinian Territories	..	..	74.0	70.9	87.4	96.3	81	78	..	..	..
103	Algeria	82	0.706	72.4	69.8	60.1	79.5	72	76	2,896	9,244	-3
106	Syrian Arab Republic	84	0.702	75.1	71.6	74.2	91.0	60	65	1,584	5,534	-2
119	Egypt	..	..	72.1	67.7	43.6	67.2	..	..	1,614	6,203	..
124	Morocco	97	0.616	71.9	67.5	38.3	63.3	54	62	2,299	5,699	-1
141	Sudan	110	0.495	57.9	54.9	49.9	69.2	35	41	918	2,890	-2
Low Human Development												
150	Djibouti	..	..	54.0	51.6	..	..	23	31	..	..	..
151	Yemen	121	0.448	61.9	59.3	28.5	69.5	41	69	413	1,349	-4
Without HDI Rank												
	Iraq	..	..	60.5	57.4	..	..	55	71	..	..	..
	Somalia	..	..	47.6	45.4	..	..	..	..	..	..	..

Source: UNDP, HDR 2005, Table 25:299-302.

GENDER EMPOWERMENT MEASURE

HDI Rank	Gender empowerment measure (GEM) rank	Gender empowerment measure (GEM) value	Seats in parliament held by women (% of total)	Female legislators, senior officials and managers (% of total)	Female professional and technical workers (% of total)	Ratio of estimated female to male earned income
High Human Development						
40 Qatar	..	..	—	..	..	..
41 United Arab Emirates	..	..	0.0	8	25	..
43 Bahrain	68	0.393	7.5	10	19	0.31
44 Kuwait	..	..	0.0	..	..	0.35
Medium Human Development						
58 Libyan Arab Jamahiriya	..	..	..	..	..	..
71 Oman	..	..	7.8	..	..	0.19
77 Saudi Arabia	78	0.253	0.0	31	6	0.21
81 Lebanon	..	..	2.3	..	..	0.31
89 Tunisia	..	..	22.8	..	..	0.37
90 Jordan	..	..	7.9	..	..	0.31
102 Occupied Palestinian Territories	..	..	..	12	34	..
103 Algeria	..	..	5.3	..	..	0.31
106 Syrian Arab Republic	..	..	12.0	..	..	0.29
119 Egypt	77	0.274	4.3	9	31	0.26
124 Morocco	..	..	6.4	..	..	0.40
141 Sudan	..	..	9.7	..	..	0.32
Low Human Development						
150 Djibouti	..	..	10.8	..	..	..
151 Yemen	80	0.123	0.3	4	15	0.31
Without HDI Rank						
Iraq	..	..	—	..	..	..
Somalia	..	..	—	..	..	..

Source: UNDP, HDR 2005, Table 26:303-306.

GENDER INEQUALITY IN EDUCATION

HDI Rank	Adult literacy rate Female rate (% ages 15 and above) 2003	Adult literacy rate Female rate as % of male rate) 2003	Youth literacy rate Female rate (% ages 15-24) 2003	Youth literacy rate Female rate as % of male rate 2003	Female primary net enrol-ment rate (%) 2002/03	Primary net enrolment rate (female rate as % of male rate) 2002/03	Female second-ary net enrol-ment rate (%) 2002/03	Secondary net enrolment rate (female rate as % of male rate) 2002/03	Female tertiary gross enrol-ment rate (%) 2002/03	Tertiary gross enrolment rate (female rate as % of male rate) 2002/03
High Human Development										
40 Qatar	..	..	..	..	94	1.00	85	1.06	32	2.71
41 United Arab Emirates	80.7	107	95.0	108	82	0.98	72	1.03	53	2.55
43 Bahrain	83	90	99.3	100	91	1.02	90	1.08	44	1.89
44 Kuwait	81	96	93.9	102	84	1.02	79	1.05	32	2.58
Medium Human Development										
58 Libyan Arab Jamahiriya	70.7	77	94.0	94	..	..	..	..	61	1.09
71 Oman	65.4	80	97.3	98	72	1.01	70	1.01	10	1.67
77 Saudi Arabia	69.3	80	93.7	96	54	0.99	52	0.96	30	1.47
81 Lebanon	..	..	..	..	90	0.99	..	..	48	1.19
89 Tunisia	65.3	78	92.2	96	97	1.00	68	1.11	30	1.28
90 Jordan	84.7	89	98.9	100	93	1.02	81	1.03	37	1.10
102 Occupied Palestinian Territories	87.4	91	98.6	100	91	1.00	86	1.05	35	1.04
103 Algeria	60.1	76	86.1	92	94	0.97	69	1.05	..	..
106 Syrian Arab Republic	74.2	82	93.0	96	96	0.96	41	0.93	..	..
119 Egypt	43.6	65	66.9	85	90	0.96	79	0.95	..	..
124 Morocco	38.3	61	61.3	79	87	0.94	33	0.86	10	0.84
141 Sudan	49.9	72	69.2	85	42	0.83	..	..	6	0.92
Low Human Development										
150 Djibouti	..	..	..	..	32	0.80	17	0.69	2	0.81
151 Yemen	28.5	41	50.9	60	59	0.71	21	0.46	5	0.28
Without HDI Rank										
Iraq	..	..	..	..	83	0.85	26	0.66	10	0.54
Somalia	..	..	..	..	..	..	..	..	..	..
All developing countries	69.6	84	81.2	92	..	..	..	..	..	..
Least developed countries	44.6	70	56.8	81	..	..	..	..	..	..
Arab States	53.1	71	75.8	87	..	..	..	..	..	..
East Asia and the Pacific	86.2	91	97.5	99	..	..	..	..	..	..
Latin America and the Caribbean	88.9	98	96.3	101	..	..	..	..	..	..
South Asia	46.6	66	63.3	79	..	..	..	..	..	..
Sub-Saharan Africa	52.6	76	67.9	88	..	..	..	..	..	..
Central and Eastern Europe and the CIS	98.6	99	99.6	100	..	..	..	..	..	..
OECD	..	..	..	..	..	..	..	..	..	..
High-income OECD	..	..	..	..	..	..	..	..	..	..
High human development	..	..	..	..	..	..	..	..	..	..
Medium human development	73.3	86	84.1	93	..	..	..	..	..	..
Low human development	47.9	73	63.6	86	..	..	..	..	..	..
High income	..	..	..	..	..	..	..	..	..	..
Middle income	86.2	93	96.3	99	..	..	..	..	..	..
Low income	49.9	70	65.4	82	..	..	..	..	..	..
World	..	..	..	..	..	..	..	..	..	..

Source: UNDP, HDR 2005, Table 27:307-310.

GENDER INEQUALITY IN ECONOMIC ACTIVITY

HDI Rank	Female economic activity rate (% ages 15 and above) 2003	Female economic activity rate (index, 1990=100, ages 15 and above) 2003	Female economic activity rate (% of male rate ages 15 and above) 2003	Female employment in agriculture (as % of female labour force) 1995-2002	Male employment in agriculture 1995-2002	Female employment in industry (as % of female labour force) 1995-2002	Male employment in industry (%) 1995-2002	Female employment in services (as % of female labour force) 1995-2002	Male employment in services (%) 1995-2002	Women contributing family workers (% of total) 1995-2003	Men contributing family workers (% of total) 1995-2003
High Human Development											
40 Qatar	42.6	129	47	..	..	..	..	..	..	..	..
41 United Arab Emirates	32.1	110	38	(.)	9	14	36	86	55	..	..
43 Bahrain	34.5	121	40	..	..	..	..	..	..	..	..
44 Kuwait	36.2	96	49	..	..	..	..	..	..	..	..
Medium Human Development											
58 Libyan Arab Jamahiriya	25.9	126	35	..	..	..	..	..	..	..	..
71 Oman	20.3	160	27	..	..	..	..	..	..	..	..
77 Saudi Arabia	22.4	150	29	..	..	..	..	..	..	..	..
81 Lebanon	30.7	126	40	..	..	..	..	..	..	..	..
89 Tunisia	37.7	115	48	..	..	..	..	..	..	..	..
90 Jordan	28.1	165	36	..	..	..	..	..	..	..	..
102 Occupied Palestinian Territories	9.6	153	14	26	9	11	32	62	58	46	54
103 Algeria	31.6	165	41	..	..	..	..	..	..	..	..
106 Syrian Arab Republic	29.5	125	38	..	..	..	..	..	..	..	..
119 Egypt	36.0	119	46	39	27	7	25	54	48	33	67
124 Morocco	41.9	108	53	6	6	40	32	54	63	19	81
141 Sudan	35.7	116	42	..	..	..	..	..	..	..	..
Low Human Development											
150 Djibouti	..	..	..	..	..	..	..	..	..	..	..
151 Yemen	30.9	110	37	88	43	3	14	9	43	26	74
Without HDI Rank											
Iraq	19.4	134	26	..	..	..	..	..	..	..	..
Somalia	62.9	99	73	..	..	..	..	..	..	..	..
All developing countries	56.0	102	67	..	..	..	..	..	..	..	..
Least developed countries	64.3	100	74	..	..	..	..	..	..	..	..
Arab States	33.3	119	42	..	..	..	..	..	..	..	..
East Asia and the Pacific	68.9	100	83	..	..	..	..	..	..	..	..
Latin America and the Caribbean	42.7	110	52	..	..	..	..	..	..	..	..
South Asia	44.1	107	52	..	..	..	..	..	..	..	..
Sub-Saharan Africa	62.3	99	73	..	..	..	..	..	..	..	..
Central and Eastern Europe and the CIS	57.5	99	81	..	..	..	..	..	..	..	..
OECD	51.8	107	72	..	..	..	..	..	..	..	..
High-income OECD	52.8	107	75	..	..	..	..	..	..	..	..
High human development	51.1	106	71	..	..	..	..	..	..	..	..
Medium human development	56.4	101	68	..	..	..	..	..	..	..	..
Low human development	61.3	99	71	..	..	..	..	..	..	..	..
High income	52.5	107	74	..	..	..	..	..	..	..	..
Middle income	59.5	102	73	..	..	..	..	..	..	..	..
Low income	51.2	103	61	..	..	..	..	..	..	..	..
World	55.6	103	69	..	..	..	..	..	..	..	..

Source: UNDP, HDR 2005, Table 28:311-314.

HDI Rank	Year women received right to vote	Year women received right to stand for election	Year first woman elected (E) or appointed (A) to parliament	Women in government at ministerial level (as % of total) 2005	Seats in lower house or single house held by women (as % of total) 1990	Seats in lower house or single house held by women (as % of total) 2005	Seats in upper house or senate held by women (as % of total) 2005
High Human Development							
40 Qatar	—	—	—	0.1	..	..	..
41 United Arab Emirates	—	—	—	0.1	0	0.0	..
43 Bahrain	1973	1973	2002 A	0.1		0.0	15.0
44 Kuwait	—	—	—	0.0		0.0	..
Medium Human Development							
58 Libyan Arab Jamahiriya	1964	1964	..	..	..	..	..
71 Oman	1994, 2003	1994, 2003	..	0.1		2.4	15.5
77 Saudi Arabia	—	—	—	0.0		0.0	..
81 Lebanon	1952	1952	1991 A	0.1	0	2.3	..
89 Tunisia	1957, 1959	1957, 1959	1959 E	0.1	4	22.8	..
90 Jordan	1974	1974	1989 A	0.1	0	5.5	12.7
102 Occupied Palestinian Territories	..	..	..	..	..	..	..
103 Algeria	1962	1962	1962 A	0.1	2	6.2	2.8
106 Syrian Arab Republic	1949, 1953	1953	1973 E	0.1	9	12.0	
119 Egypt	1956	1956	1957 E	0.1	4	2.9	6.8
124 Morocco	1963	1963	1993 E	0.1	0	10.8	1.1
141 Sudan	1964	1964	1964 E	(.)		9.7	..
Low Human Development							
150 Djibouti	1946	1986	2003 E	0.1	0	10.8	..
151 Yemen	1967, 1970	1967, 1970	1990 E	(.)	4	0.3	..
Without HDI Rank							
Iraq	..	..	..	0.2	11	31.6	..
Somalia	..	..	..	..	4	..	..

Source: UNDP, HDR 2005, Table 30:316-319.

Human and labour rights instruments

Table A4 -24

STATUS OF MAJOR INTERNATIONAL HUMAN RIGHTS INSTRUMENTS

HDI Rank	International Convention on the Prevention and Punishment of the Crime of Genocide 1948	International Convention on the Elimination of All Forms of Racial Discrimination 1965	International Covenant on Civil and Political Rights 1966	International Covenant on Economic, Social and Cultural Rights 1966	Convention on the Elimination of All Forms of Discrimination against Women 1979	Convention against Torture and Other Cruel, Inhuman or Degrading Treatment or Punishment 1984	Convention on the Rights of the Child 1989
High Human Development							
40 Qatar		•	•			•	•
41 United Arab Emirates		•	•		•		•
43 Bahrain	•	•	•		•	•	•
44 Kuwait	•	•	•	•	•	•	•
Medium Human Development							
58 Libyan Arab Jamahiriya	•	•	•	•	•	•	•
71 Oman		•	•				•
77 Saudi Arabia	•	•	•		•	•	•
81 Lebanon	•	•	•	•	•	•	•
89 Tunisia	•	•	•	•	•	•	•
90 Jordan	•	•	•	•	•	•	•
102 Occupied Palestinian Territories							
103 Algeria	•	•	•	•	•	•	•
106 Syrian Arab Republic	•	•	•	•	•	•	•
119 Egypt	•	•	•	•	•	•	•
124 Morocco	•	•	•	•	•	•	•
141 Sudan	•	•	•	•		•	•
Low Human Development							
150 Djibouti				•	•	•	•
151 Yemen	•	•	•	•	•	•	•
Without HDI Rank							
Iraq	•	•	•	•	•		•
Somalia		•	•	•		•	O

· Ratification, accession or succession.

o Signature not yet followed by ratification

Source: UNDP, HDR 2005, Table 31:320-323.

HDI Rank	Freedom of association and collective bargaining - Convention 87	Freedom of association and collective bargaining - Convention 98	Elimination of forced and compulsory labour - Convention 29	Elimination of forced and compulsory labour - Convention 105	Elimination of discrimination in respect of employment and occupation - Convention 100	Elimination of discrimination in respect of employment and occupation - Convention 111	Abolition of child labour - Convention 138	Abolition of child labour - Convention 182
High Human Development								
40 Qatar			·			·		·
41 United Arab Emirates			·	·	·	·	·	·
43 Bahrain			·	·		·		
44 Kuwait	·		·	·		·	·	·
Medium Human Development								
58 Libyan Arab Jamahiriya	·	·	·	·	·	·	·	·
71 Oman			·					·
77 Saudi Arabia			·	·		·		·
81 Lebanon		·	·	·	·	·	·	·
89 Tunisia	·	·	·	·	·	·	·	·
90 Jordan		·	·	·	·	·	·	·
102 Occupied Palestinian Territories								
103 Algeria	·	·	·	·	·	·	·	·
106 Syrian Arab Republic	·	·	·	·	·	·	·	·
119 Egypt	·	·	·	·	·	·	·	·
124 Morocco		·	·	·	·	·	·	·
141 Sudan		·	·	·	·	·	·	·
Low Human Development								
150 Djibouti	·	·	·	·	·	·		·
151 Yemen	·	·	·	·	·	·	·	·
Without HDI Rank								
Iraq		·	·	·	·	·	·	·
Somalia			·	·		·		

· Convention ratified.

Source: UNDP, HDR 2005, Table 32:324-327.

ANNEX V. PARTICIPANTS IN THE YOUTH CONSULTATION

Cairo, November 2005

- Nader Fergany, Co-Lead Author for the Report
- Farida Allaghi, Coordinator of the Youth Consultation
- Hanan Amer Ahmad, Libya
- Muhammad Aladdin, Egypt
- Mohammed Hamad Al-Ghanim, Kuwait
- Abdulhakim Al-Khazuri, Libya
- Dalya Mustafa Al-Zeiny, Egypt
- Walid Abdel Aziz, Egypt
- Hessa Buhumaid, United Arab Emirates
- Iman Mohamed Eissa, Egypt
- Ameer Elnager, Sudan
- Mona Hasounna, Lebanon
- Noura Ibrahim, Kuwait